John Umbreit, editor
The University of Arizona

Physical Disabilities and Health Impairments: An Introduction

Charles E. Merrill Publishing Company
A Bell & Howell Company
Columbus Toronto London Sydney

Published by Charles E. Merrill Publishing Company
A *Bell & Howell Company*
Columbus, Ohio 43216

Production Editor: Gnomi Schrift Gouldin
Design Consultant: Cynthia Brunk
Cover Photograph: Strix Pix
Cover Design: Tony Faiola
This book was set in Optima

Library of Congress Catalog Card Number: 82–62477
International Standard Book Number: 0–675–20045–8
Printed in the United States of America
    4 5 6 7 8 9 10—90 89

ED'S C

y. 01962

Physical Disabilities
and
Health Impairments

EDITOR

JOHN UMBREIT, Ph.D., is assistant professor in the Department of
Special Education, The University of Arizona, Tucson.

AUTHORS

MARILEE C. ALLEN, M.D., is instructor in the Department of Pediatrics
at the School of Medicine, Johns Hopkins University, Baltimore,
Maryland.

C. WARREN BIERMAN, M.D., is clinical professor in the Department of
Pediatrics and head of the Division of Pediatric Allergy at the
School of Medicine, University of Washington, Seattle.

J. TIMOTHY BRICKER, M.D., is a fellow in Pediatric Cardiology at Texas
Children's Hospital, Houston.

MILO B. BROOKS, M.D., is professor emeritus in the Department of
Pediatrics at the School of Medicine, University of California at
Los Angeles, Los Angeles.

ARNOLD J. CAPUTE, M.D., is deputy director of the John F. Kennedy
Institute for Handicapped Children and associate professor in the
Department of Pediatrics at the School of Medicine, Johns
Hopkins University, Baltimore, Maryland.

CONTRIBUTORS

MICHAEL W. COHEN, M.D., is clinical associate in the Department of
Pediatrics at the College of Medicine, The University of Arizona,
Tucson, and medical director of the Arizona School for the Deaf
and Blind, Tucson.

JAMES J. CORRIGAN, JR., M.D., is professor and chief of the section of
pediatric hematology-oncology in the Department of Pediatrics at
the College of Medicine, The University of Arizona, Tucson.

ALLEN C. CROCKER, M.D., is associate professor in the Department of
Pediatrics at the Harvard Medical School, Boston, and director of
the Developmental Evaluation Clinic at The Children's Hospital
Medical Center, Boston, Massachusetts.

MARY LOU DAMIANO, B.A., R.N., is nurse coordinator of the
Mountain States Regional Hemophilia Center in the Department
of Pediatrics at the College of Medicine, The University of
Arizona, Tucson.

PATTY DAVY, R.P.T., is physical therapist in the Department of Physical Therapy at Rancho Los Amigos Hospital, Downey, California.

MARY KAY DYKES, Ph.D., is professor in the Department of Special Education, University of Florida, Gainesville.

FRAN Z. FARRELL, R.N., M.S.W., is nurse social worker in the section of pediatric hematology-oncology, Department of Pediatrics, at the College of Medicine, The University of Arizona, Tucson.

EARL FIEWELL, M.D., is clinical assistant professor in the Department of Orthopedic Surgery at the School of Medicine, University of Southern California, Los Angeles, and staff orthopedic surgeon and co-director of the Spina Bifida Clinic at Rancho Los Amigos Hospital, Downey, California.

IRENE S. GILGOFF, M.D., is assistant clinical professor in the Department of Pediatrics at the School of Medicine, University of Southern California, Los Angeles, and staff pediatrician in the Department of Pediatrics at Rancho Los Amigos Hospital, Downey, California.

MICHAEL J. GOLDBERG, M.D., is professor of orthopedic surgery at the School of Medicine, Tufts University, Boston, Massachusetts; senior orthopedic surgeon at the New England Medical Center, Boston; and director of orthopedic surgery at Kennedy Memorial Hospital for Children, Brighton, Massachusetts.

VIRGIL HANSON, M.D., is professor in the Department of Pediatrics at the School of Medicine, University of Southern California, Los Angeles, and head of the Division of Rheumatology and Rehabilitation at Children's Hospital of Los Angeles.

JOHN J. HUTTER, JR., M.D., is associate professor in the section of pediatric hematology-oncology, Department of Pediatrics, at the College of Medicine, The University of Arizona, Tucson.

MARGARET H. JONES, M.D., is professor emeritus in the Department of Pediatrics at the School of Medicine, University of California at Los Angeles, Los Angeles.

JAY A. KATZ, M.D., is associate in the Department of Orthopedic Surgery at the College of Medicine, The University of Arizona, Tucson; chief of orthopedic surgery at Tucson Medical Center, Tucson, Arizona; and attending physician at the Arizona Crippled Children's Clinic, Tucson.

MICHAEL J. KRAEMER, M.D., is senior pediatric allergy fellow in the Department of Pediatrics, School of Medicine, University of Washington, Seattle.

RUSSELL R. LYLE, M.D., is consultant to the Department of Pediatrics at the School of Medicine, University of Mississippi, Jackson, and adjunct professor of special education in the Department of Curriculum and Instruction, Mississippi State University, Mississippi State.

JOHN A. MANGOS, M.D., is professor and chairman of the Department of Pediatrics at the University of Texas, Health Science Center, San Antonio.

DAN G. McNAMARA, M.D., is professor of pediatrics and chief of the Lillie Frank Abercrombie section at Baylor College of Medicine and Texas Children's Hospital, Houston.

DIANE C. MITCHELL, M.D., is clinical assistant professor in the Department of Pediatrics at the School of Medicine, University of Southern California, Los Angeles, and staff pediatrician in the Department of Pediatrics and co-director of the Spina Bifida Clinic at Rancho Los Amigos Hospital, Downey, California.

GABRIELLA E. MOLNAR, M.D., is professor in the Departments of Rehabilitation Medicine and Pediatrics and director of the Pediatric Rehabilitation Service in the Children's Evaluation and Rehabilitation Center at Albert Einstein College of Medicine, Bronx, New York.

JAMES G. T. NEALIS, M.D., is clinical assistant professor of neurology at the College of Medicine, University of Florida, Joint Hospital Education Program, Jacksonville, Florida.

S. J. OBRINGER, Ed.D., is professor and coordinator of special education in the Department of Curriculum and Instruction, Mississippi State University, Mississippi State.

FREDERICK B. PALMER, M.D., is assistant professor in the Department of Pediatrics at the School of Medicine, Johns Hopkins University, Baltimore, Maryland.

ERIC H. PROSNITZ, M.D., is associate in the Department of Internal Medicine at the College of Medicine, The University of Arizona, Tucson, and medical director of the Artificial Kidney Center (Central), Dialysis Foundation of Southern Arizona, Tucson.

BASIL A. PRUITT, JR., M.D., Colonel, MC, is commander and director of the U.S. Army Institute of Surgical Research at Brooke Army Medical Center, Fort Sam Houston, Texas.

LEELA RANGASWAMY, M.D., is assistant professor in the Department of Orthopedic Surgery at the Albert Einstein College of Medicine, Bronx, New York; chief of orthopedics at Blythedale Children's Hospital, Valhalla, New York; and adjunct attending orthopedic surgeon at Montefiore Hospital and Medical Center, Bronx, New York.

BRUCE K. SHAPIRO, M.D., is assistant professor in the Department of Pediatrics at the School of Medicine, Johns Hopkins University, Baltimore, Maryland.

JOHN VENN, Ph.D., is assistant professor in the Department of Special Education, University of North Florida, Jacksonville.

RENEE C. WACHTEL, M.D., is assistant professor in the Department of Pediatrics at the School of Medicine, Johns Hopkins University, Baltimore, Maryland.

ROBERT J. WINTER, M.D., is associate professor in the Department of Pediatrics at the Northwestern University Medical School, Chicago, Illinois, and associate in the division of endocrinology at the Children's Memorial Hospital, Chicago.

ROGER W. YURT, M.D., Major, MC, is senior surgeon at the U.S. Army Institute of Surgical Research, Brooke Army Medical Center, Fort Sam Houston, Texas.

If teachers and other school personnel are to facilitate the education of handicapped children, it is imperative that they understand the physical and health problems which affect function and development. John Umbreit, through the well-coordinated interdisciplinary effort of this publication, has produced a substantive text which addresses the expected anatomic and developmental processes of childhood; children's physical disabilities and health problems, and the concerns of teachers and the appropriate action to be taken when a handicapped child is in the classroom. Doubtless, an alert and knowledgeable educator can identify changes in a child's behavior that reflect symptoms of physical disability and then communicate effectively about them with medical and nonmedical team members.

Physical Disabilities will serve both as a college text and as a reference book for anyone responsible for the education of children with handicapping conditions. It should also be helpful in nonspecialized classrooms, since not all children with histories of such hidden conditions as seizures, allergies, or diabetes are labeled as handicapped. The material is presented in such a manner that the teacher can increase his or her objectivity in dealing with a child's problems.

The physicians who prepared chapters dealing with their own fields of specialization have clearly described causes of deviation, symptoms that might be evidenced, and appropriate interventions. The technical information is written for the nonmedical reader. It is designed specifically to share with educators facts about management

FOREWORD

of disabilities so that teachers and other instructional personnel can increase their understanding of the disabilities and the effects of these disabilities on the preschool and school-aged child. With the resultant knowledge and skill, it can be expected that hesitancy, inconsistent management, and anxieties of the child, the parents, and the techer will be reduced.

In special education, as in rehabilitation programs generally, attention and practice has moved from dependence upon the authoritative dicta from one professional group to a transdisciplinary approach. This approach calls for interactive exchange of roles, with support and supervision from the appropriate professional person, the one with preparation and experience in the intervention area. Through this role release-assumption process, the most accessible individual is designated as primary program implementer and is facilitated in the coordination and integration of efficient individualized instruction for children and youth with physical and multiple handicaps. Therefore, texts such as this one, which present content written by one professional group for use by another, seem to set the foundation for establishing a transdisciplinary approach in educational settings.

The final section of the book should be particularly useful to educators because it deals with environmental modifications and descriptions of roles played by the variety of professional specialists available to children and their parents. It emphasizes the need for related services as legislatively mandated for the education of children with physical and multiple handicaps. Consequently, with such information, there should be no reason for a teacher to assume the total responsibility for the development of individualized educational plans (IEPs) for the pupil with a handicapping condition.

For the isolated teacher, or one without immediate access to supportive personnel, the extensive list of agencies and organizations serving children with special physical and health problems should be invaluable. For example, through contacting a national health agency such as the United Cerebral Palsy Association, state and local resources can be identified and additional materials obtained. Many of these organizations have strong parent involvement and support networks available to other parents and program developers.

This publication together with June Bigge's *Teaching Individuals with Physical and Multiple Disabilities* (Charles Merrill, 1982) comprise a comprehensive instructional package for both prospective and in-service teachers and supervisors. These texts provide extensive current content. They are strongly recommended as part of the repetoire of all educators who are charged with assuring that children with handicapping conditions receive the education most appropriate for them.

Frances P. Connor
Teachers College
Columbia University

This book offers accurate, up-to-date medical information on physical disabilities and health impairments in children. It is written by physicians and edited by an educator. The book is divided into five sections. Section One, *Normal Development,* offers an overview of human anatomy, neuroanatomy, and normal motor and reflex development that will make the disorders and deviations from normal more easily understood. Section Two, *Orthopedic and Neurological Disorders,* examines problems involving the bones, muscles, and nervous system. These include cerebral palsy, curvatures of the spine (scoliosis, lordosis, and kyphosis), epilepsy, hip conditions (Legg-Perthes, congenital dislocation of the hip, and slipped capital femoral epiphysis), limb deficiencies, muscular dystrophy, musculoskeletal disorders (arthrogryposis and osteogenesis imperfecta), spina bifida, spinal cord injury, and spinal muscular atrophy. Section Three, *Other Health Conditions,* examines a variety of disorders: asthma, blood diseases (hemophilia, sickle cell anemia, and thalassemia), burns, cancer, diabetes, cystic fibrosis, enuresis and encopresis, heart disorders, inborn errors of metabolism (Hurler syndrome and PKU), juvenile rheumatoid arthritis, and kidney disorders. Section Four, *The Education Environment,* was written by educators to discuss ways of using the information presented in the first three sections: What does medical information imply about a child's daily functioning in the classroom? The *Resources* section presents information about parent and professional organizations that are concerned with the various

PREFACE

disorders discussed in this book. There is also an extensive glossary of terms.

Each chapter is written by a physician, sometimes alone and sometimes in conjunction with educators or other professionals. To produce accurate, clear, and readable chapters, it was necessary to select authors who are not only respected specialists in their fields, but who are also concerned about the educational, social, and other nonmedical aspects of a child's life. This concern is clearly reflected in the emphasis that each author gives to (a) the potentials and abilities of each person, regardless of disability, and (b) his or her right to participate in society as fully, productively, and independently as possible. All of the topical chapters (Chapters 4–24) use a consistent format for presenting information, each disorder is explained in terms of its etiology, characteristics, diagnosis, treatment, prognosis, and educational implications. This creates cohesiveness across chapters and also makes it easy to find information within any particular chapter.

This book covers all of the disorders typically found in other books, as well as chapters on many areas and disorders that concern the educator but which are not found in other texts: the basics of human anatomy and neuroanatomy, and such specific disorders as spinal cord injury, burns, cancer, enuresis and encopresis, inborn errors of metabolism, and kidney disorders. The book includes several tables and approximately 250 figures, both photographs and illustrations, to ensure the clearest possible understanding of the written material. All of these features combine to make this a comprehensive text for the preservice or inservice introductory course in physical disabilities and health impairments.

ACKNOWLEDGEMENTS

Certain people provided special help which significantly influenced the design and content of this book. They also were actively involved in helping to identify the most appropriate authors for each chapter. For this special assistance, I would like to thank Dr. Margaret H. Jones, University of California at Los Angeles; Dr. Mary Kay Dykes, University of Florida; Dr. John Venn, University of North Florida; Dr. Michael W. Cohen, The University of Arizona; and Dr. Howard C. Shane, Children's Hospital Medical Center at Boston.

I would also like to thank several other people who made important contributions to this book: Gnomi Schrift Gouldin, Production Editor at Merrill, whose contributions to this text are incalculable, and whose skill and good taste are evident on every page; Marianne Taflinger, former Special Education Editor at Merrill, who not only supported this project but was largely responsible for its development; Vicki Knight, current Special Education Editor at Merrill, who "inherited" this project as it entered production and turned what could have been a difficult transitional period into a smooth and enjoyable process; Dr. Fred Orelove, who reviewed the entire manuscript and made several helpful and constructive suggestions; Irene Topor, who amassed all of the information that appears in the Resources section; Elaine Prosnitz, who helped construct the glossary; Drs. June Bigge and Barbara Sirvis, who provided much-appreciated support and encouragement throughout this project; Dr. Frances P. Connor, who not only supported this project, but also graciously agreed to write the Foreword; and Beatrice Gumper, Elvera Vega, Barbara Heefner, Alinda Carter, and Louis Pavelka, who did excellent secretarial work during the various stages of developing and producing this book.

Finally, I want to thank M. J. Demetras and Sidney W. Bijou who, at different times and for different reasons, patiently awaited and encouraged the completion of this project.

PART 1: NORMAL DEVELOPMENT   1

1
Human Anatomy   3
James G. T. Nealis

2
Neuroanatomy   16
James G. T. Nealis

3
Normal Motor and Reflex Development   29
Arnold J. Capute, Renee C. Wachtel, Bruce K. Shapiro, Frederick B. Palmer, and Marilee C. Allen

CONTENTS

PART 2: ORTHOPEDIC AND NEUROLOGICAL DISORDERS   39

4
Cerebral Palsy   41
Margaret H. Jones

5
Curvatures of the Spine   59
Leela Rangaswamy

6
Epilepsy   **74**

James G. T. Nealis

7
Hip Conditions   **86**

Jay A. Katz

8
Limb Deficiencies   **93**

Milo B. Brooks

9
Muscular Dystrophy   **100**

Russell R. Lyle and S. J. Obringer

10
Musculoskeletal Disorders   **108**

Gabriella E. Molnar

11
Spina Bifida   **117**

Diane C. Mitchell, Earl Fiewell, and Patty Davy

12
Spinal Cord Injury   **132**

Irene S. Gilgoff

13
Spinal Muscular Atrophy   **147**

Michael J. Goldberg

**PART 3: OTHER HEALTH
            CONDITIONS**   **155**

14
Asthma   **157**

Michael J. Kraemer and C. Warren Bierman

15
Blood Diseases   167
James J. Corrigan, Jr., and Mary Lou Damiano

16
Burns   175
Roger W. Yurt and Basil A. Pruitt, Jr.

17
Cancer in Children   185
John J. Hutter, Jr., and Fran Z. Farrell

18
Childhood Diabetes Mellitus   195
Robert J. Winter

19
Cystic Fibrosis   206
John A. Mangos

20
Enuresis and Encopresis   214
Michael W. Cohen

21
Heart Disorders   222
J. Timothy Bricker and Dan G. McNamara

22
Inborn Errors of Metabolism   233
Allen C. Crocker

23
Juvenile Rheumatoid Arthritis   240
Virgil Hanson

24
Kidney Disorders   250
Eric H. Prosnitz

PART IV: THE EDUCATION ENVIRONMENT   257

25
Using Health, Physical, and Medical Data in the Classroom   259

Mary Kay Dykes and John Venn

Resources   281
Glossary   285
Index   291

Normal Development

PART

1

James G. T. Nealis, M.D., *is clinical assistant professor of pediatric neurology at the College of Medicine, University of Florida, Joint Hospital Education Program, Jacksonville, Florida.*

The original drawings in this chapter are by Nancy Eber.

Terms in boldface type in this and other chapters are defined in the glossary (p. 285).

Because many of the disorders discussed in this book occur when an organ system malfunctions, it is essential to understand both the location of the various organs within the body (anatomy) and how they function when working properly (physiology). Therefore, this chapter presents the basic concepts of anatomy and briefly discusses the fundamental organ systems. Space limits the in-depth analysis of any particular system; however, the reader is referred to the reference texts listed at the end of the chapter for further investigation.

The nervous system (neuroanatomy) is not covered in this chapter because it is addressed in detail

CHAPTER
1

Human Anatomy

in Chapter 2. The specific groups discussed here include:
1. The **musculoskeletal system** (skeletal system and muscular system);
2. The **respiratory system;**
3. The heart and **circulatory system;**
4. The **digestive system;**
5. The **endocrine system;**
6. The **urogenital system;**
7. The skin and **integument;** and
8. The blood system.

The Musculoskeletal System

The bones, or skeleton (Figure 1–1), constitute the basic structural framework of the human body. They

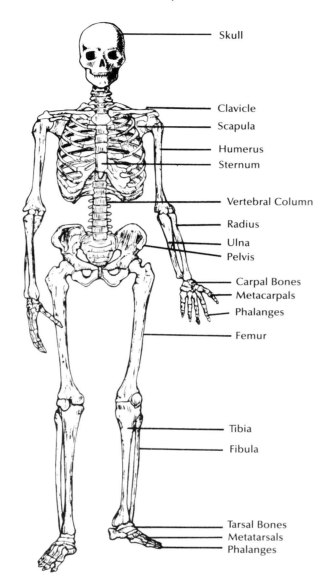

Figure 1—1   The Skeletal System

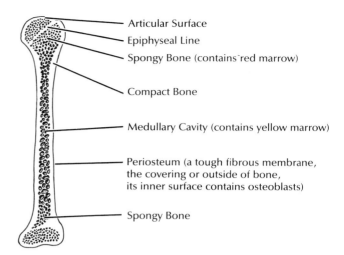

Figure 1—2   Parts of a Long Bone

are among the densest body components. Each bone may be considered as a dense lattice of mineral salts held together in a connective tissue matrix. The skeleton accounts for approximately 14 percent of the total body weight. Individually, bones are classified according to their shape, structure, and function.

Flat bones (membranous bones) are flat, generally curved bones such as those found in the skull. Flat bones protect various organs, such as the brain. Long bone (Figure 1–2) is the term given to a tubular bone that surrounds a cavity, which is filled with the bone marrow. Long bones include the larger, weight-supporting structures of the body such as the femur and tibia of the leg, as well as the small tubular bones of the hands and feet (tarsals, carpals, etc.). At each end of the shaft of a long bone is the articular surface.

The surface is generally made of cartilage, a form of connective tissue, which is smoother and less dense than bone. Cartilage covers the articular surface and is lubricated thoroughly by synovial fluid to form a smooth, freely moving joint. Any interference with the smooth movement of a joint will cause friction and irritation. Continued friction can lead to grinding of the surface and the formation of deposits of calcium and other forms of scar tissue and debris. This produces the painful condition referred to as arthritis.

Each bone is permeated by a series of blood vessels that nourish it. These vessels are important in the bone's development and growth (Figure 1–3). In children, an **epiphysis,** or growth plate, is located at each end of the long bone. The epiphysis has an active metabolic rate and is directly responsible for the growth of that bone. Diffuse metabolic illness, as well as certain vitamin or mineral deficiencies, can affect the growth plate and thus diminish symmetrically the extent of growth. Trauma to the bone in the area of the growth plate can interfere with the proper growth of that particular bone and cause later deformity or asymmetry, stunting one particular side of that bone.

The internal portions of the bones are among the primary areas for forming blood cells. The central cavities of the **sternum** (breastbone, Figure 1–4) and of the **pelvis** (Figure 1–5) are particularly active in blood formation. The central portions of these bones (see Figure 1–2) contain yellow marrow (primarily fat) and red marrow (the active red blood cell forming areas).

The shaft of the bone itself is covered by a membrane known as the **periosteum,** which carries nutrient blood vessels into the bone. Thus it has a key functional role in the maintenance of the bone it supplies.

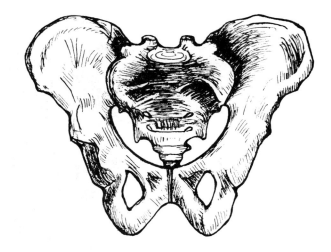

Figure 1—5   A Male Pelvis

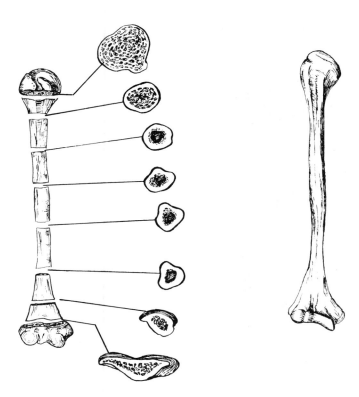

Figure 1—3   The Changing Structure of a Long Bone

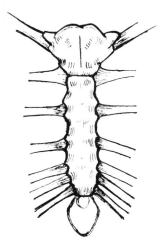

Figure 1—4   The Sternum

The midline bones of the skeletal system are referred to as the **axial skeleton.** These include the bones of the **skull** and the **vertebral column,** as the bones of the spinal cord are known. Moving downward from the neck, the vertebrae are divided into five groups by anatomy, structure, and position. The first seven are the cervical vertebrae; the next twelve are the thoracic vertebrae. They are followed by five lumbar and five sacral vertebrae. In a baby the sacral vertebrae are separate but by adulthood they fuse together into the sacral bone and form the **posterior**

wall of the pelvis. Finally, a varying number of vertebrae (usually three) called the coccygeal bones (coccyx) make up the small rudimentary bones found at the tail end of the vertebral column. The vertebral column serves a key role in maintaining the body in an upright stance and also protects the spinal cord and the nerves that communicate between the spinal cord and the rest of the body. The spinal nerves exit via the intervertebral foramen, and go out to innervate (supply nerve stimulation to) the entire body (Figure 1–6). Intervertebral discs of connective tissue with a gelatinous liquid center separate the spinal vertebrae and allow them to articulate, one with the other. The disc is called the nucleus pulpous and a thickened fibrous rim surrounds it. If the fibrous rim should rupture, the nucleus pulpous will protrude. This is commonly referred to as a slipped disc. Because the discs can pinch on the nerves to or from the spine, they can be extremely painful and cause considerable dysfunction in the peripheral nerves.

All of the vertebrae are present at birth and gradually enlarge as the child matures. In most cases, the bones on both sides of the body grow at the same rate and a symmetrical skeleton is formed. If, however, for one reason or another, growth of the vertebrae is asymmetrical (one side grows faster than the other), or if abnormalities in the structure of the vertebrae are present, curvature can occur. It is important to remember that the vertebral column (as all other bony structures of the body) is an active, growing organ and is constantly subjected to dynamic forces of stress, weight, growth, blood supply, etc. Curvature of the vertebral column to either side, which occurs as the child ages, is known as **scoliosis** (see Chapter 5). Congenital abnormalities in the vertebral column or tumors can cause massive dysfunction and disfigurement of the spinal cord. An abnormal opening at the base of the spine, usually in

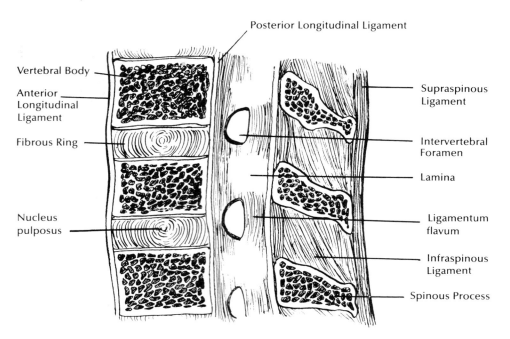

Posterior Longitudinal Ligament

Vertebral Body

Anterior Longitudinal Ligament

Fibrous Ring

Nucleus pulposus

Supraspinous Ligament

Intervertebral Foramen

Lamina

Ligamentum flavum

Infraspinous Ligament

Spinous Process

Figure 1—6   Median Section of Part of the Lumbar Region of the Vertebral Column

the lumbosacral area, from which the membrane of the spinal cord or even the cord itself might protrude, is a congenital condition known as **spina bifida** (see Chapter 11).

The study of muscles is known as myology. The body contains three basic types of muscles: striated muscles (voluntary muscles), smooth muscles (visceral muscles), and cardiac (heart) muscle. Smooth or involuntary muscle fibers make up the contractile elements of the internal organs, gastrointestinal tract, and blood vessels. The cardiac muscle itself is responsible for the contractile elements of the heart, forcing blood through the circulatory system. Skeletal muscle is greatly responsible for the form and posture of the body as well as for movement.

Motor nerves coming from the anterior horn (front) of the spinal cord reach the striated muscle at a **myoneural junction.** The motor nerves then release acetylcholine, a chemical transmitter that triggers a complex series of reactions which ultimately lead to constriction of the muscle fiber. Dysfunction of this chemical transmitter is found in myasthenia gravis, a disease whose cardinal symptom is diffuse muscle weakness.

Some muscles are primarily tonic in function, i.e., they maintain body tone, muscle tone, and posture. Other muscles work as agonists and antagonists. When the biceps contract to flex the elbow, the triceps must relax. Conversely, when the triceps contract to extend the elbow, the biceps must relax. Mus-

cles that work together at the same joint are referred to as muscle groups. Each muscle has an origin and an insertion depending on its function. Muscles can have their insertions on other bones, tendons, or ligaments. Innervation of a given group of muscles is dependent upon the complexity of muscle function. For this reason, the innervation of the muscles of the back might be expected to be somewhat less intricate than the innervation of the eye muscles or the muscles of the hand. Piano playing or typing are examples of tasks that require complex interactions of the neuromusculoskeletal system.

Of particularly intricate design is the muscle system of extraocular movement. Each eye is individually supplied with six separate muscles: the lateral rectus moves the eye to the outside of the face, the medial rectus moves the eye to the inside, the superior rectus moves the eye upward, the inferior rectus moves the eye downward, the inferior oblique rotates the eye and moves it upward, and the superior oblique rotates the eye and makes it move downward. Each of these six muscles in one eye is intricately coordinated with the contralateral six muscles of the other eye to ensure that when one eye moves laterally, the other eye must move **medially** (to ensure binocular vision and prevent double vision).

The fine muscles of the hand, interwoven with a complex group of tendons and ligaments, tend to become more and more complexly ordered as the child matures. Fine-motor dyscoordination of the hand is often seen in central nervous system dysfunctions and may cause dysgraphia (the inability to write properly).

THE RESPIRATORY SYSTEM

The respiratory system (Figure 1–7) is responsible for the exchange of oxygen and carbon dioxide. The respiratory system begins in the mouth and the nose and includes the larynx, trachea (airway), and the bronchial tree and lungs. As air moves downward from the nose and mouth, it passes in front of the esophagus and through the larynx, or voice box. The upper region of the larynx is guarded by a "protective hatch" called the epiglottis. When food or liquid is swallowed, the epiglottis automatically closes and forms a watertight seal to prevent anything from entering the lungs during the swallowing process. When a person breathes in, however, the epiglottis reflexively opens, allowing free access to oxygen. When a person breathes out, it allows carbon dioxide to exit.

In children who are debilitated or who have neuromuscular disease or severe forms of cerebral palsy, the swallowing mechanism may be defective. In this case, liquid and solid foods may enter the trachea instead of the esophagus, which leads to the stomach. For this reason, children with severe neuromuscular dysfunction or debilitation are highly susceptible to frequent episodes of pneumonia, partially induced by foreign materials finding their way down into the trachea. In a very real sense, some children in the terminal stages of neuromuscular dis-

eases (e.g., muscular dystrophy) may be described as choking on their own saliva and other secretions.

The larynx is made up primarily of several cartilaginous elements. These form together to produce a movable slitlike opening lined on either side by the vocal cords (membranous folds). When held widely open, they allow respiration. When juxtaposed, they are extremely important in speech and singing. In general, shorter and thinner vocal cords will be responsible for a higher pitched voice. This will generally explain the higher pitch of children's voices than of men's voices. The particular combinations of overtones and sound that pass up through the larynx or resonator are further modified by the soft palate, nose, tongue, and mouth to produce what we call speech. The lower end of the voice box enters directly into the trachea.

The trachea is about seven inches long in an adult. It is made up of horseshoelike rings of cartilage open along the posterior wall, where it is replaced by a membranous-muscular wall. This wall directly overlies the muscular wall of the esophagus, which is immediately behind the trachea. Not having a hard cartilaginous wall in front of it gives the esophagus the ability to pass larger particles of food downward and makes choking less likely. The diameter of the trachea is slightly less than one inch and is somewhat larger in the male than in the female. It proceeds downward, past the aorta, to divide in the fork or branching, known as the carina, where it becomes the right or the left main bronchus.

The bronchi then branch into each of the lobes of the right and left lungs. There are three lobes to

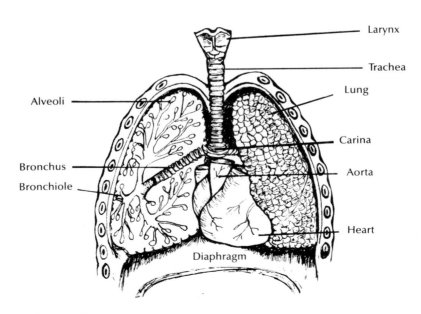

Figure 1–7   The Respiratory System

the right lung—the upper lobe, middle lobe, and lower lobe—and two lobes to the left lung—the upper lobe and lower lobe. A portion of the area on the left side that would otherwise be taken up by lung tissue is occupied by the heart. The division of the bronchi into smaller bronchioles is extremely complex. The air passes through the bronchi into bronchioles, which subdivide further into still smaller terminal bronchioles, and eventually into the alveolar sacs that contain the respiratory tissues of the lung. In the alveolus, the fine membranes of these sacs will exchange the oxygen breathed in for carbon dioxide to be breathed out from the fine blood vessels on the opposite side of the alveolar membane. The whole system is facilitated by the mechanics of respiration.

When a person wishes to breathe in, special impulses are sent from the respiratory centers in the brain stem down through the nervous system to cause the expansion of the rib cage and the chest cavity. At the same time, the diaphragm muscles at the base of the chest cavity also expand and deflect downward. This considerably enlarges the potential space within the chest cavity. When the epiglottis and the airway are opened, a suction type of effect is formed that will force air down into the trachea, the bronchi, bronchioles, and eventually the sacules. In order to breathe out, a person relaxes the muscle strength in the rib cage, allowing the rib cage to close as well as relax and move the diaphragm upward. This diminishes the potential space in the chest cavity and, with the airway and the epiglottis open, air is expelled.

When viruses or bacteria infect the sacules of the lungs, it is called penumonia. When the bronchi are irritated due to inflammation or infection, it is called bronchitis. A chronic and sometimes recurrent disease in which the small muscles of the bronchi are hyperirritable is called asthma (see Chapter 14). During an asthma attack, we find thickened secretions and trapped air in the bronchioles; that is, air can be breathed in, but the bronchioles and bronchi tend to plug up, making it difficult to exhale the air. This causes a wheezing sound as the air passes out. A more serious and often fatal disease of childhood, which has a similar pathology, is called cystic fibrosis (see Chapter 19).

THE HEART AND CIRCULATORY SYSTEM

The heart and the circulatory system (Figure 1–8) function simply as a pump that ensures continuous circulation of the blood, as well as fluid, colloid (a gluelike material), and gaseous and corpuscular elements of the blood system. The heart is the central force or pumping apparatus of the circulatory system. It functions both to pump blood outward into the body or lungs and to suction the returning blood at the end of the circulatory "pipeline." In a sense, it can be looked upon as the beginning and the end of the corpuscular cycle, pushing blood out at the beginning and sucking it back in again at the end.

The heart is a hollow organ, made up mostly of muscular tissue, that contains four separate cavities or chambers. The two chambers located at the base of the heart are called the **atria**; specifically, the left atrium and right atrium. The heart forms a rough, blunted point just below the left fifth rib. Blood from the body normally enters the right atrium. Then, through contraction of the right atrium and dilation of the right ventricle, it is expelled through the tricuspid valve into the right ventricle. The right ventricle then contracts, forcing this quantum of blood outward through the pulmonary artery into the lungs. Oxygenated blood then returns from the lungs through the pulmonary vein and enters in the left atrium. Through contraction of the left atrium, blood is forced through the bicuspid valve into the left ventricle. Upon contraction of the left ventricle, blood is then expelled outward into the aorta or main artery of the chest and abdominal cavity.

The aorta assumes a curve (just over the heart) referred to as the aortic arch. Three major arteries emanate from this arch: the innominate, the left common carotid, and the left subclavian artery. These three blood vessels supply the arms, head, brain, and many of the structures in the neck. The aorta then curves downward and goes through the rear portion of the central chest cavity or thorax. Branches from the aorta supply all of the various portions of the thorax, ribs, muscle tissue, etc. The aorta then pierces the diaphragm and enters the rear of the abdominal cavity, in front of the spinal vertebrae. Major branches are sent to the intestines as well as the other major organs in the abdomen, including the liver, pancreas, and kidneys, and various parts of the urogenital system. The aorta then branches to form the common iliac arteries after sending off a single artery to supply the spinal cord. The aorta branches into the common iliac arteries at approximately the fourth lumbar vertebrae level. This vascular network supplies the urogenital system as well as the lower extremities. Blood returns to the heart through two major venous systems, the inferior vena cava and the superior vena cava. The inferior vena cava is the return system from below the heart. The superior vena cava serves the same function with blood returning from above the heart.

In an adult, the heart is somewhat larger than a clenched fist, weighing between 280 and 320 grams, and is supplied primarily by the coronary arteries. An

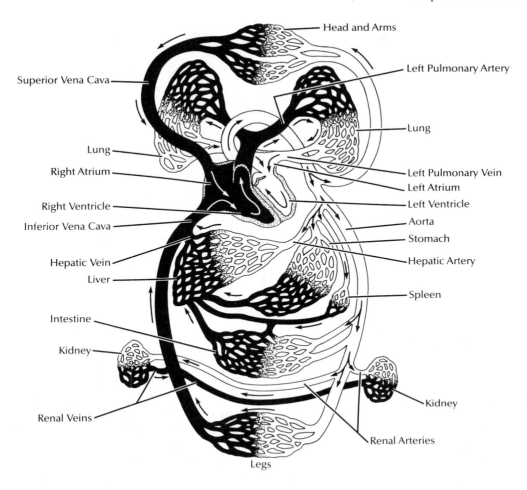

Figure 1–8   The Human Circulatory System

acute obstruction (through **atherosclerosis**) of the right coronary artery or the left coronary artery or its anterior interventricular branch will cause a **myocardial infarction.** This is referred to commonly as a heart attack. The complex interrelationship of constriction and dilation of the atria and the ventricles is maintained by an electrical system within the muscles of the heart from the atrium all the way down to the ventricular cavities. This electrical system is responsible for the rhythmic beating of the heart and is the primary electrical force responsible for the EKG patterns that can be monitored clinically. A weakened heart may dilate in size and fail to pump adequately. This is called congestive heart failure.

The lymphatic system is another group of vessels whose function is to absorb fluid and return it to the heart. The lymphatic system consists of a series of vessels that act in part as filters reabsorbing fluid and, in many cases, sending that fluid through deep lymphatic vessels and nodes, referred to as lymph nodes. Lumph nodes vary in size from 2 to 20 mm. and are very active in the immunization process. They serve as filtering stations, filtering out bacteria and helping

in the immune response to fight infection. The cervical lymph nodes, located in the front sides of the neck, become swollen with certain characteristic infections such as mononucleosis or strep throat. It is for this reason that some children, after even mild viral infections, will have small nodular densities (lumps) in the neck or in the groin area or even in the underarms, i.e., in the locations of lymph nodes. Excessive swelling of these nodes can be seen in certain types of blood cancers such as leukemia and lymphoma (Chapter 17).

THE DIGESTIVE SYSTEM

The digestive system (Figure 1–9) is primarily concerned with the ingestion, transport, and digestion of food, and the elimination of waste materials. It begins in the mouth, where food is initially mixed with the first of the digestive juices emanating from the salivary glands. Once the food's size and density have been reduced, it is then propelled backwards by a complex swallowing mechanism that enables both

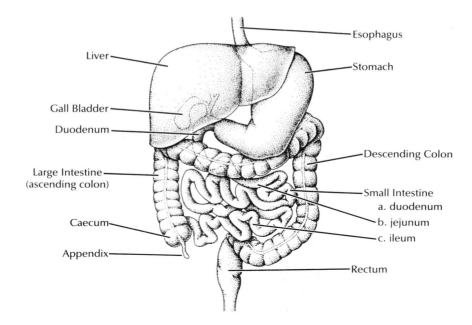

Figure 1—9   The Digestive System

food and liquids to be moved over the airway, placing these materials into the posterior oropharynx and avoiding passage of them into the lungs. From the posterior oropharynx they will pass through the throat and into the esophagus.

The esophagus begins at the posterior region of the pharynx and is approximately 11 to 12 inches long. It ends at the stomach in a junction referred to as the cardiac sphincter (closing valve). This sphincter holds food and gastric acids in the stomach and keeps them from regurgitating upward into the esophagus. A weakness in the sphincter can be called a hiatal hernia. Regurgitation of gastric acid into the esophagus is referred to as gastrointestinal reflux or heartburn.

The esophagus and the stomach both are made of visceral or smooth muscle tissue. Glands that are located in the wall of the stomach secrete digestive juices. By rhythmic constrictions and contractions, the stomach gradually passes the food into the duodenum region of the small intestine. The duodenum passes under the liver, in front of the kidney, and around the pancreas, and then loops back in full circle to empty further into the small intestine. The liver stores its bile in the gallbladder, for secretion directly into the duodenum via the common bile duct. The pancreas also secretes enzymes into the duodenum to aid in digestion.

The areas of the small intestine immediately following the duodenum are referred to as the jejunum and the ileum. These structures form a tubular network, approximately 6 meters in length, which is complexly folded and curled upon itself. They occupy much of the space of the abdominal cavity. The small

intestine eventually enters into the large intestine at the region of the cecum. The large intestine generally varies in length from 1½ to 2 meters. It is called large because it is considerably wider than the digestive areas that have preceeded it. The large intestine has an ascending portion (ascending colon), a portion across the top of the abdominal cavity (transverse colon), and finally a descending portion in the left posterior abdominal region (descending colon). It then enters into the sigmoid colon and the rectum.

An interesting structure that is attached at the very beginning of the first portion of the ascending colon in the region of the cecum (juncture with the small intestine) is the appendix. This so-called vermiform appendix is found only in humans and the higher primates and contains elements of lymphatic tissue. It is of major significance when the small opening of the appendix becomes clogged with intestinal material. When this happens, the intestine can become acutely inflamed and represents a true surgical emergency known as acute appendicitis.

After the digestive contents pass into the cecum, they are moved by the rhythmic contractures of the bowel (peristalsis) upward, then across the transverse colon, and later down to be evacuated by means of the rectum. Inefficient control of the rectal sphincter causes soiling (encopresis) and is often seen in children (see Chapter 20). This may be due to either psychological or physiological dysfunction.

The liver and the pancreas (both glands with ducts) are usually considered as part of the digestive system. The liver is the largest bodily organ and occupies the upper right quadrant of the abdominal cavity. It may weigh over 3 pounds. With its small sac (the gallbladder) on its under surface, the liver serves a key role in digestion, metabolism, and production of bile that is carried into the duodenum by the bile duct. Infection in the liver (hepatitis) causes yellowish discoloration (jaundice) of the skin and may be contagious.

The pancreas, a smaller elongated organ (approximately 7 inches long and 85 grams in weight), is located in the upper posterior abdominal cavity, resting in the "U-turn" of the duodenum. It produces digestive juices and has a key role in the metabolism of carbohydrates; one form of pancreatic dysfunction can be due to diabetes (see Chapter 18).

THE ENDOCRINE SYSTEM

The endocrine system (Figure 1–10) is a system of ductless glands that are responsible for the secretion of hormones. They are found in various locations throughout the body. The hallmark of an endocrine gland is that it is a ductless gland. That is to say, these hormones are secreted directly into the blood stream, not through a duct as in the kidney or liver. These hormones are then sent directly through the blood stream to various organs of the body and have profound consequences on the entire body.

The pituitary gland is usually considered to be the primary endocrine gland and is referred to as the master gland. It is responsible for the functioning of many of the other glands. It is located at the base of the hypothalamus just below the brain and at the point where the optic nerves cross (the optic chiasm). It is quite small, generally measuring 1.3 cm. × .5 cm. and roundish in shape. It is controlled by the nervous cells within the hypothalamus, to which it is attached. It regulates sexual maturation, blood pressure and fluid balance, control of the thyroid and adrenal glands, and metabolism.

The thyroid gland, another important endocrine gland, is in the neck just below the larynx and in front of the trachea. A deficiency of thyroid hormone in an adult can cause obesity, lethargy, and impaired mental functioning, a disorder known as myxedema; impaired thyroid functioning in a child can cause severe mental retardation (cretinism).

The adrenal glands are located just above each of the kidneys. There are actually two functional elements to the adrenal gland. The central part of the adrenal gland is called the adrenal medulla. It secretes adrenalin, which is highly implicated in the fight or flight reflex. When a person perceives a severe threat to his physical well-being, the adrenal medulla excretes adrenalin (epinephrine), which causes the heart to beat faster, the pupils to dilate,

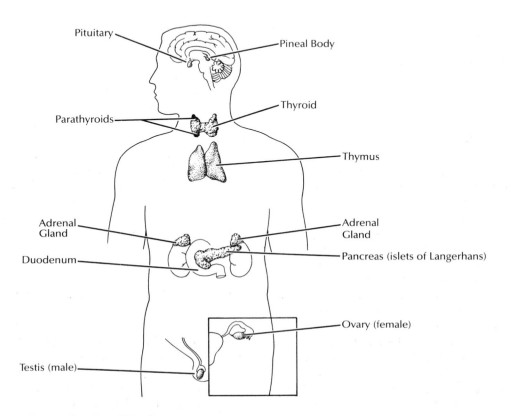

Figure 1–10   The Endocrine Glands

and the blood to circulate better to the muscles of the body so that a person is better able to fight off the threat or to run. The adrenal cortex, on the other hand, secretes a different group of hormones known as the steroid hormones. These have multiple effects both on the metabolism of glucose and electrolytes and on the structural development of the body. There are also steroid hormones that are very active in the development of secondary sexual characteristics.

The parathyroid glands are two pairs of glands usually located behind the thyroid gland. They are approximately 4 mm. in size and are very important for the regulation of calcium and phosphorus.

The thymus, located in the midregion of the chest, usually in front of and immediately between the lungs, has a primary role in the production of white blood cells and in mediating immunity from infection. It is considerably larger in infants and tends to shrink in adulthood.

The Islands of Langerhans (sometimes called the Islets of Langerhans) are small endocrine glands located in small clusters throughout the pancreas. They secrete insulin. Deficiency of the function of these glands produces insufficient levels of insulin, which is the cause of clinical diabetes mellitus (see Chapter 18).

The pineal body is a gland located in the midportion of the posterior brain, just above the midbrain. It is about the size of a small pea. It is believed to have considerable importance in endocrine metabolism of lower animals (specifically birds) and is thought by some to be primarily a vestigial (remnant) organ in humans. There are other data, however, to suggest that it is of far more significance. Further research in this area is currently ongoing.

THE UROGENITAL SYSTEM

The urogenital system (Figure 1–11) is primarily involved with the production and secretion of urine as well as with human reproduction. The primary organ of the urinary system is the kidney. The kidneys function as blood filters. They weigh approximately 100 to 125 grams and are, if you will, bean-shaped in appearance. They are located to the right and to the left of the spine at about the level of the duodenum.

The left kidney is usually positioned somewhat higher than the right. The renal artery transmits blood to the kidney where it is then filtered through a complex system. The filtered blood then returns to the body through the renal vein. During its passage through the kidney, the water, urea, potassium, and other electrolytes are filtered from the blood. The electrolytes and excess fluid are then condensed through a rather complex collecting system and fi-

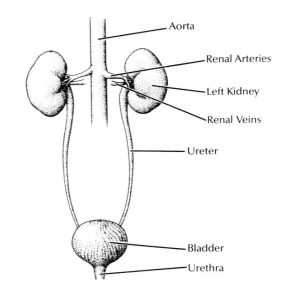

Figure 1–11   The Urogenital System

nally excreted through the ureter (a drainage tube), which emanates from the center of the kidney.

The kidneys are extremely important in maintaining balance among the body's electrolytes as well as the maintenance of blood pressure. As such, kidney disease can be a significant cause of elevated blood pressure. The urine excreted progresses down the ureter until it reaches the urinary bladder, which is positioned in the lowest and front-most portion of the abdominal cavity. The urine is further concentrated in the bladder and is then secreted through the urethra in the act of urination.

In the male, the urethra emanates from the bladder immediately above the prostate gland and is then joined by the ductus deferens and the seminal vesicle coming up from the testicle through which semen is brought to the urethra during the act of copulation. In the female, the urinary bladder is immediately above and in front of the uterus. The urethra drains immediately in front of the vaginal opening. The ovaries and the fallopian tubes are on the side of the bladder. The urethra then exits the body by means of the penis in the male or the anterior vagina in the female.

THE INTEGUMENTARY SYSTEM, THE SKIN

The skin (Figure 1–12) covers the body, which it protects and insulates. Skin is important as a means of temperature control, by retaining body heat in cold climates and expelling body heat in warm climates. The body is further cooled through the evaporation of sweat produced by glands in the skin. The skin contains receptors important in sensing touch, vibra-

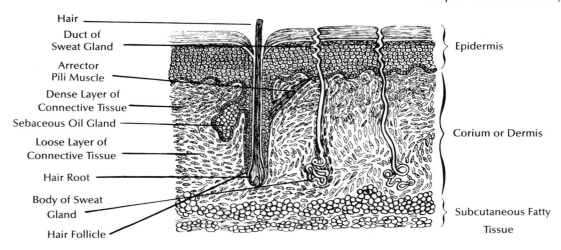

Hair
Duct of Sweat Gland
Arrector Pili Muscle
Dense Layer of Connective Tissue
Sebaceous Oil Gland
Loose Layer of Connective Tissue
Hair Root
Body of Sweat Gland
Hair Follicle

Epidermis
Corium or Dermis
Subcutaneous Fatty Tissue

Figure 1—12   The Skin

tion, heat, cold, and pain. The pigmentation of the skin is due to deposits of a chemical called melanin. Its distribution in varying degrees in human skin, particularly in the layers of the epidermis, is thought to be significant in protecting the skin from sunlight. This melanin system explains the skin's response to the sun (suntan). The sebaceous glands secrete body oils, which serve an excretory function as well as a cleansing function on the skin.

The skin varies in thickness from a millimeter to less than that over various portions of the body. As might be expected, it tends to be thickest in areas of stress and friction (the soles of the feet, palms of the hand, and elbows). The external-most layer is called the epidermis and the layer directly below this is called the dermis. The epidermis is composed of five primary layers: the stratum corneum, the stratum lucidum, the stratum granulosum, the stratum spinosum, and the stratum basale. Below this area, nutrient blood vessels and tactile sensory organs can be found. Loss of a considerable area of epidermis means the loss of the primary line of defense against bacterial infection.

The skin serves a key role in maintaining fluid balance in the body and preventing loss of fluids and electrolytes through seepage. Appendages to the skin include the fingernails, hair and hair follicles, sebaceous glands, and sweat glands. The sebaceous glands are near the hair follicles and in the areas of the underarms and genitalia. They open up directly into the area of the hair follicles. These glands produce body oils and excrete them outward into the skin.

There are also muscle fibers attached to the small individual hairs. These muscle fibers are called the arrector pili muscles. In lower mammals such as dogs, cats, and bears, these muscles have considerable importance in temperature regulation. For example, if a dog is out in the forest in a very cold snow storm, contraction of these muscles will cause the hairs to stand on end and produce a layer of insulation walled by the fur and warm air around it to help maintain body heat. To a lesser extent, this process also occurs in human beings when the arrector pili produce goosebumps when we are cold.

Specialized nerve endings are found in the skin. These are referred to as sensory end organs. They are associated with the various sensations that can be transmitted through the skin. Free nerve endings are associated with pain. Bulbous end organs have been associated with the sensation of pressure. Oval corpuscles are associated with the sense of touch. Lamellated corpuscles are seen to be associated with the sense of pressure and are found in the deeper layers of skin and hands and feet and in tissue near joints. A special spindlelike apparatus is found in muscle fiber sheets and is thought to be associated with the control of muscular contraction.

When the skin is damaged by disease, as in severe eczema, psoriasis, or by massive burns (see Chapter 16), it can be life threatening because of the body's susceptibility to infection, shock, and to fluid and electrolyte imbalance through seepage.

THE BLOOD

The blood is made up of fluid, colloid, and corpuscular elements. The fluid system in the blood contains in solution the various electrolytes—sodium, potassium, chloride, phosphate, etc.—that are of key importance to the metabolism of the body.

The colloid elements of the blood include lipid colloids and are important for the digestive process. Lipid colloid particles called chilomicrons are reabsorbed from the intestines during digestion and enter through the hepatic portal vein into the liver for me-

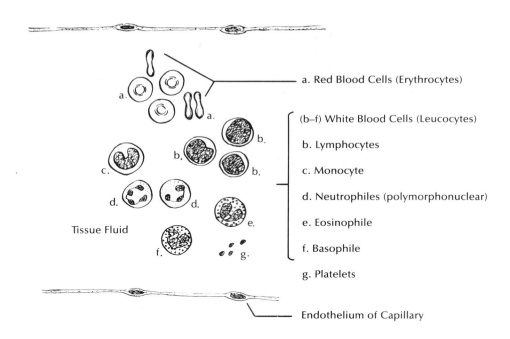

Figure 1–13   The Blood

tabolism. Another important colloid substance in the blood is protein. Proteins are important for various body functions as well as for maintaining fluid balance in the body system. When the blood is low in protein, excess amounts of fluids leak into the perivascular areas (areas surrounding the blood vessels) and into the rest of the body. The colloid and fluid systems of blood are important in the process of carrying nutritive materials to the tissues and carrying waste products away.

The corpuscular elements of blood are of two types: the red blood cells and the white blood cells (Figures 1–13 and 1–14). Red blood cells greatly outnumber white blood cells and are thought to have a life span of approximately 120 days. They are thin, disc-shaped elements without nuclei. They contain hemoglobin, which is the active iron-containing compound that picks up oxygen through the alveolar membrane in the capillaries of the lungs and then carries this oxygen in the red blood cell to the other

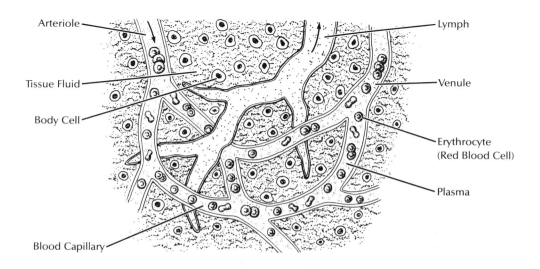

Figure 1–14   Relation of Blood and Lymph Capillaries to Tissue Cells

capillaries of the body where the oxygen is needed. In essence, hemoglobin will pick up oxygen where it is present in high concentrations and release it where the concentrations are low. Deficiency of iron, poor nourishment, or diffuse debilitated states from chronic illness can cause a person to be relatively anemic. The normal serum hemoglobin level should be approximately 13 or 14 grams per ml. The normal red blood cell density of blood when the blood is centrifuged (separated by a machine) should be approximately 45 percent, which is referred to as the hematocrit.

White blood cells are larger in diameter than red blood cells and contain a nucleus. Depending upon their staining characteristics under light **microscopy,** they are referred to as lymphocytes, polymorphonucleocytes, monocytes, etc. The white blood cells function predominantly in fighting disease and in the immune process. They can produce antibodies as well as directly ingest, attack, and eat (phagocytize) elements in the body that are felt to be foreign to the individual. Such elements might include bacteria, viruses, elements of dirt as in deep wounds, etc., or surgical sutures. The white blood cells are also of extreme importance in the reaction to inflammation or infection. The white blood cells are produced in the lymphatic tissue, lymph nodes, spleen, and thymus. White blood cell deficiency states are seen in some viral syndromes, a condition known as leukopenia. Excessive amounts of white cells are seen in some viral and bacterial illnesses like mononucleosis (in

fact, an elevated white blood count is often considered a sign of infection), but are also seen in severe forms of blood cancer such as leukemia (see Chapter 17). The particular tragedy in leukemia is that, although the white blood cells can be enormously increased in their numbers, they are ineffective in fighting infection.

SUMMARY

This chapter has presented a brief overview of a most complex universe—the human body. We have covered the basic anatomy and physiology of several of the body's systems: the musculoskeletal, respiratory, heart and circulatory, digestive, endocrine, urogenital, skin and integument, and blood systems. The reader is encouraged to pursue further study of these systems in the reference books listed below.

SELECTED READINGS

Grant, J. C. B. *Atlas of anatomy.* Baltimore: Williams & Wilkins, 1962.

Pansky, B., & House, E. *Review of gross anatomy: A dynamic approach.* New York: MacMillan, 1967.

Romanes, G. J. (Ed.). *Cunningham textbook of anatomy.* London: Oxford University Press, 1964.

Williams, P. L., & Warnick, R. (Eds.). *Gray's anatomy* (36th British edition). Edinburgh: Churchhill Livingstone, 1980.

James G. T. Nealis, M.D., *is clinical assistant professor of pediatric neurology at the College of Medicine, University of Florida, Joint Hospital Education Program, Jacksonville, Florida.*

The original drawings of Figures 2-1 through 2-12 are by Nancy Eber.

The study of the structure and function of the human nervous system is known as neuroanatomy. Of all the systems in the human body, this system more than any other has achieved remarkable complexity, so much so that it may be used to differentiate humans from all other creatures. The very acts of life, growth, movement, wakefulness and sleep, and even thought itself are properties directly attributable to the nervous system. The communication going on this instant between the author and the reader is a direct communication between two central nervous systems, separated in time and place.

It is not surprising, therefore, that the nervous system has commanded the fascination of great mas-

CHAPTER 2

Neuroanatomy

ters, perhaps since before recorded time. From the description of the optic nerves by Alcmaeon to later observations by Hippocrates and even Aristotle, we find repeated mention of the human nervous system. Plato suggested in his philosophy that the brain is the center for thought and perception. Throughout the great civilizations—Greek, Egyptian, and Roman—there were references to the study of the nervous system. Leonardo da Vinci's fascination with neuroanatomy is well known. In later days, the contributions of great German and English neuroanatomists were to increase in almost logarithmic fashion the understanding of the human brain. It should come as no great surprise that Sigmund Freud, who initially began his writings on the neuroanatomy of the brain, was to later use this knowledge in his detailed and integrated analysis of the behavioral aspects of the nervous system, which forms the basis for psychiatry.

Certain anatomical terms will be used in the following text. To avoid any misunderstanding, their definitions are given here:

Anterior—in front of
Posterior—behind
Lateral—to the side, either right or left
Medial—toward or closest to the midline
Proximal—toward or closest to the starting point or point of origin
Distal—away from or farthest from the starting point, point of origin, or point of reference
Cephalad—toward or closest to the top, above
Caudad—toward or closest to the bottom, below
Afferent—impulses coming toward an area
Efferent—impulses going away from an area

The nervous system is divided into several categories: the central, peripheral, and autonomic nervous systems. The central nervous system generally includes the brain itself, the brain stem, and the spinal cord. Its general function is to serve as the controlling center of the complex neuronal elements that govern our behavior as well as our sensory and motor functions. The peripheral nervous system generally includes the nerves that, after they exit from the spinal cord, progress peripherally to the skin and extremities, transmitting impulses both from the spinal cord to the periphery and transmitting sensation from the periphery back to the spinal cord. The autonomic nervous system is made up of two basic subsystems, the sympathetic and the parasympathetic nervous systems. The autonomic nervous system generally is thought to be responsible for the regulation of a person's internal environment—body temperature, blood pressure, respiratory rate, etc.—as well as the functioning of the internal organs. The sympathetic and parasympathetic nervous systems are differentiated by their positions in the nervous system and the type of synaptic neurotransmitter that each uses. In general, the sympathetic nervous system automatically puts the body into high gear in response to a threat, whereas the parasympathetic nervous system restrains that response to avoid overacceleration.

THE NEURON

The neuron (Figure 2–1) is a functional element of the nervous system, the living cell that is responsible for all activity within this system. As we can see in Figure 2–1, the neuron consists of a soma (cell body) attached on one end to a long appendage known as an axon and, on the other end, to several smaller appendages known as dendrites. The neuron functions by producing brief action potentials ("electric sparks") in the soma and in the dendrites. It transmits these action potentials, or electrical currents, through the axon to its end, where the neuron of the axon branches out, known as the synapse. At the end of the axon is the synaptic cleft, the space between cells. Transmitter chemicals released by the electrical charge traverse across the cleft to communicate with

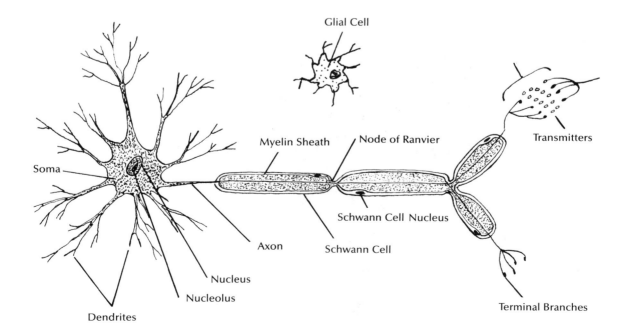

Figure 2–1 Structure of a Motor Neuron

the cell on the opposite side of the cleft. This is known as synaptic transmission. The chemicals that are released across the synaptic cleft are referred to as neurotransmitters. Among the many neurotransmitters that are now recognized as such are acetylcholine, noradrenaline, and dopamine.

In a sense, the function of each neuron is to communicate with other neurons. The axon, because it is in a very real sense a conducting wire carrying electricity, is itself often insulated. The form of insulation is actually a sleeve of myelin. Myelin courses down the axon, insulating it and allowing the more effective transmission of electrical current from point A to point B. When several billion neurons form a functioning element of the nervous system, they are held together by glial cells, named for the Greek word meaning glue. The glial cell supports and nurtures the functioning neurons.

THE BRAIN—CEREBRAL HEMISPHERES

The brain itself (Figure 2–2) is composed of many elements. It is usually divided into two basic parts, the cerebral hemispheres and the brain stem. The cerebral hemispheres are separated by a central cleft called the interhemispheric fissure. Each cerebral hemisphere is almost a mirror image of the other, composed of a layer of gray matter surrounding a portion of white matter. The gray matter is actually a thin band on the external surface of the brain that contains the soma or nerve bodies. The white matter, on the other hand, is largely the axons and other neu-

ronal filaments as well as myelin, their insulation. Myelin is what makes it appear to be white. Inside of the white matter itself is a hollow open space that carries the cerebrospinal fluid, a fluidlike substance which resembles water. The cerebrospinal fluid is in direct communication with the spinal fluid farther down the brain stem and through that with the spinal cord itself, providing a continuous circulation of fluid from the top of the brain all of the way down to the spinal cord. The fluid maintains cleanliness within the area and supplies it with various constituents.

Each cerebral hemisphere is made up of several lobes (Figure 2–3): the frontal lobe, the temporal lobe, the parietal lobe, and the occipital lobe. Various brain functions are assigned classically to different lobes of the brain. The frontal lobe is generally considered to be active in behavior, judgement, and reasoning. Speech and coordination of various motor activities are also believed to emanate from this area of the brain. Motor activity is primarily a function of the frontal lobe, which is conveniently separated from the parietal lobe by the rolandic fissure. Immediately anterior to the rolandic fissure is the motor strip. It is to be remembered that motor functions emanate from the anterior portion of the brain and sensory functions are generally in its posterior portion, i.e., the parietal lobe and behind. Keep in mind that the brain is just like an American automobile—the motor is in the front. Another important concept is that all of the functions of the brain are effectively crossed over (both top-to-bottom and side-to-side) with regard to influence and activity in the body. In other words, movement stimulated in the high *right*

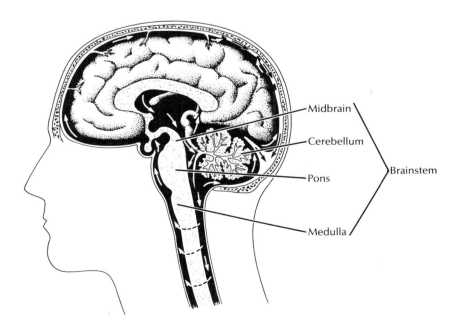

Figure 2–2   The Brain

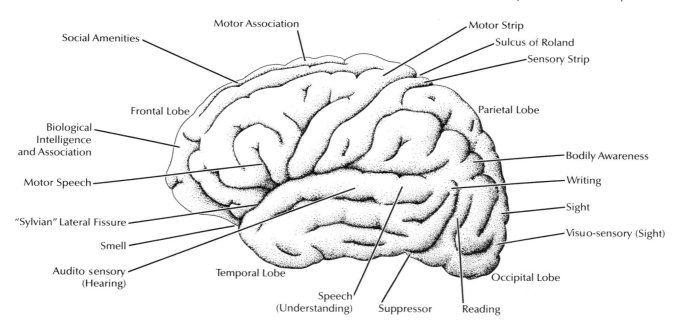

Figure 2—3   The Cerebral Hemisphere

frontal area of the brain would move the *left* leg, etc. Much intellectual association and regulation of behavior are centered in the frontal lobe regions. As a result, bilateral damage to the frontal lobes may result in prominent antisocial behavior or forms of dementia and insanity.

The temporal lobes are located immediately under the sylvian fissure. Temporal lobes are prominent in the area of memory and are closely associated with a complex structure known as the limbic system. The limbic system will be discussed later in this chapter. The temporal lobes are also active in areas apart from memory: likes and dislikes, some emotional behavior, speech, language, music, and the transmission of some visual fibers.

The parietal lobe processes sensory input. A sensory strip closely corresponding to the motor strip is seen posterior to the sulcus of Rolando. A well-organized homunculus of organizational function is seen in the sensory strip (Figure 2–4). (A homunculus is a diagram of an imaginary little man used for instructive purposes.) For this reason, when electrical discharge occurs in the neurons of the lowest portion of the homunculus, one might expect the face and hands to contract or to move. If the stimulation occurs in the sensory area, posterior to the sulcus of Rolando, one might expect the child to have a subjective sensation of some sort in the hand or in the face. This explains why a focal seizure (discussed in Chapter 6) coming from the temporal lobe, which is lowest in the lateral portion of the homunculus, is often associated with twitching movements of the side of the mouth or face. It would explain why an abnormal dis-

charge occurring in the sensory area of the medial portion of the homunculus might be felt in the foot or leg. It further explains why the white matter axons coursing from the gray matter homunculus for the leg would be the first to be damaged should the ventricle become pressurized and expand with cerebrospinal fluid. Increased pressure (**hydrocephalus**) will often cause abnormalities in the legs (**spasticity**).

Many other cortical functions are believed to reside further posteriorly in the parietal lobe. Among

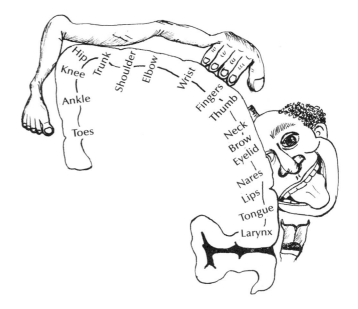

Figure 2—4   Homunculus of the Sensory Strip, or How the Sensory Strip Views the Body

these are the appreciation of right and left, understanding speech (written or spoken), simple calculations, speech organization, understanding complex symbolism, recognizing one's own body parts, and finding one's way around one's environment. A person who has suffered structural damage in this area, whether from a stroke, tumor, or trauma, may find himself getting lost in his own house or may awaken in bed and not recognize his own arm as in fact belonging to him. In the author's experience, patients with structural abnormalities located in the parietal area may complain bitterly that they were unable to get any sleep the night before because someone "kept throwing his arm on top of me" when in fact it was the patient's own arm. Such patients can be severely debilitated intellectually or be unable to find their way back to their room in a hospital or from the bathroom in their own house. They may have considerable difficulty with a simple task such as putting on a shirt and may even forget to put the shirt over one arm while being very careful to put it over the other.

Posterior to the parietal lobe is the occipital lobe (Figure 2–3). The primary function of the occipital lobe is that of vision and various associated functions of vision. The primary cortex in the occipital lobe is called the calcarine fissure. Just anterior to the calcarine fissure are the various visual association areas that accept the information gathered by the primary visual cortex, process it, and refer it to the appropriate area of the brain. The impulses may be sent toward simple recognition areas in the parietal lobe or association areas in the frontal lobe or to memory centers in the temporal lobe or other "emotional" centers in the limbic system.

If we were to look at the brain from the central portion, the epicenter of the brain is referred to as the limbic system (Figure 2–5). The limbic system is made up of areas that deal with the basic functions of the human organism, including the hypothalamus, fornix, medial portions of the temporal lobe, and other areas of the brain. Basic emotional drives as well as some primeval forms of memory are located in the limbic system. The central locus of instincts is in this region, as is a great deal of the activity of the autonomic system (discussed later).

Closely adherent to this limbic system is the pituitary gland or "master gland," which is thought to secrete hormones that regulate other hormonal glands scattered throughout the body. Electrical stimulation or experimental lesions placed in the limbic system can have dramatic effects on the organism. Cutting of the fornix, for example, can result in profound memory loss. Swabbing of one small area with a cotton swab during surgery may produce uncontrollable peals of laughter. Patients undergoing neurosurgery during the wakeful state report that stimulation of certain areas of this portion of the brain can bring back memories of one's childhood. Artificial lesions in this area can produce rage, antisocial behavior, and hypersexuality, as well as alterations in appetite causing excessive overeating or starvation.

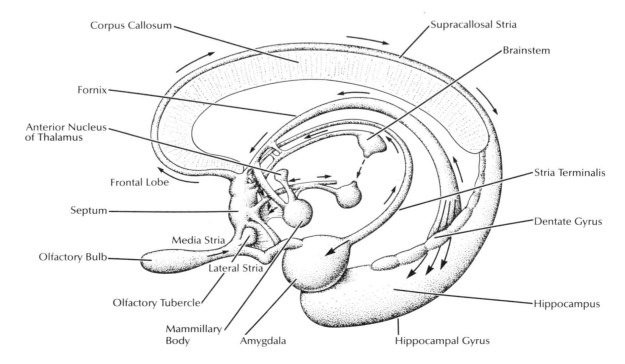

Figure 2–5   The Limbic System

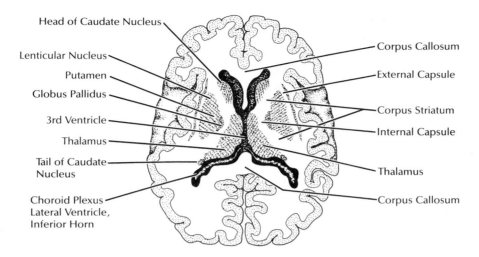

Head of Caudate Nucleus

Lenticular Nucleus

Putamen

Globus Pallidus

3rd Ventricle

Thalamus

Tail of Caudate Nucleus

Choroid Plexus Lateral Ventricle, Inferior Horn

Corpus Callosum

External Capsule

Corpus Striatum

Internal Capsule

Thalamus

Corpus Callosum

Figure 2–6   The Basal Ganglia—Horizontal Section of Brain

The white matter centrum of the cerebral cortex contain the ventricular system (for the circulation of cerebrospinal fluid) as well as other gray matter islands placed in each of the cerebral hemispheres. These islands serve many functions, among which is the regulation of motor activity. These extensive gray matter islands are referred to as the basal ganglia (Figure 2–6). Among the basal ganglia are included the caudate nucleus, the globus pallidus, the putamen, and the thalamus. The basic function of the basal ganglia is to integrate communications between the cerebral cortex and those elements of the nervous system and body below it. The communication can take the form of motor, sensory, or other electrical brain or nerve activity. These basal ganglia, and especially the thalamus, also serve as integrative circuits for electroactivity coming from below the brain (spinal cord) and destined upward toward higher areas of the nervous system. The basal ganglia, therefore, serve as relay centers for afferent impulses up toward the cerebral cortex as well as for efferent impulses downward.

THE BRAIN STEM

The cerebral cortex rests upon the **brain stem.** The brain stem contains four areas of brain: the midbrain, the pons, the **cerebellum,** and the medulla oblongata (see Figure 2–2). The midbrain, pons, and medulla oblongata serve as the primary centers for the majority of the cranial nerves (see Figure 2–12). The brain stem functions as a relay center that connects motor activity emanating from the cerebral hemispheres down to the spinal cord and conducts afferent impulses from the spinal cord back up to the thalamus

and other regions of the cerebral hemisphere. The brain stem achieves considerable prominence in the regulation of eye movement and contains much of the reticular activating system.

The reticular activating system, among other things, is primarily involved in maintaining states of wakefulness and sleep and the waking/sleep cycle in the human. It is also thought to be keenly active in the ability to concentrate. This area of the brain is affected by sedative medication. In fact, it may be the site of action of other medications that are thought to affect, positively or negatively, the state of attentiveness or distractibility in a person. The senses of hearing, balance, and somatic sensation all send their afferents through the brain stem centers. Finally, the coordination of autonomic activity such as regulation of heartbeat, blood pressure, respiratory patterns, and basic life-support systems all are regulated through the brain stem. Directly adherent to the brain stem and forming the roof of the fourth ventricle (another cavity containing spinal fluid) is the cerebellum. Once again, the cerebellum is a most complex organ having considerable influence upon movement, coordination of movement, and muscle tone throughout the body.

The brain stem and the cerebellum assume particular importance in children because most childhood brain tumors occur in this area. Key symptoms of such tumors will often include progressive difficulty in coordination (so-called **ataxia**) as well as visual symptoms, abnormalities of eye movement, and progressively increasing intracranial pressure. Increased intracranial pressure occurs because of the strategic location of these tumors that can occlude (close) the cerebrospinal fluid pathways and prevent spinal fluid from circulating properly and exiting from the cranial cavity. Increased intracranial pressure can also exert pressure directly around the optic nerves, thus causing a situation known as papilledema (swelling of the optic nerves). For this reason, to a physician, a child who complains chiefly of a headache, progressive visual loss, and progressive loss of motor coordination will be considered to have an **intracranial** brain tumor or hydrocephalus ("water on the brain") until proven otherwise.

The brain and brain stem exit from the cranial cavity through a round hole at the base of the skull known as the foramen magnum (Figures 2–7 and 2–8). At this point, the medulla oblongata directly connects to the spinal cord. The spinal cord then progresses downward through the spinal cavity to approximately the lumbar$_1$ to lumbar$_2$ junction, where it ends. A brush of nerves exits downward from the spinal cord, which is referred to as the cauda equina (probably because it bears some resemblance to the hairs on a horse's tail). At each segment of the spinal cord, there are two holes, or foramen, in the boney spine.

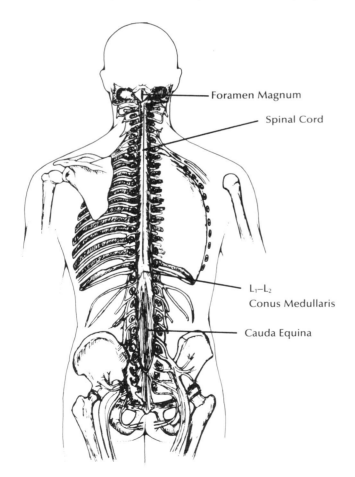

Figure 2–7   The Spinal Cord and Peripheral Nerves

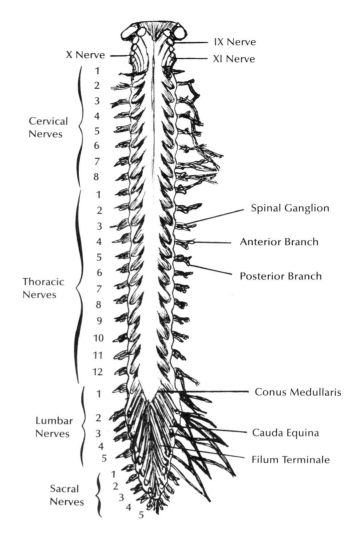

Figure 2—8   The Spinal Nerves

Through these holes, the spinal nerves communicate with the peripheral nervous system (see Figure 2–9, which is a cross section of the spinal cord).

Contrary to the cerebral cortex, the gray matter in the spine itself is on the inside and the white matter is on the outside. Because the gray matter of the spine extends in a somewhat pointed fashion anteriorly and posteriorly, these have been referred to as the anterior horn and the posterior horn of the spinal cord. Gray matter is surrounded by the white matter, which consists of axons and nerves distal to that area. Generally speaking, the anterior portion of the spinal cord deals with motor functions, and the posterior region deals with sensory input (remember the American automobile). The spinal cord governs reflex activity and the conduction of the afferent activity up to the brain and efferent activity down from the brain.

An example of a reflex arc is the classical knee jerk reflex in which the patient's knee is tapped with

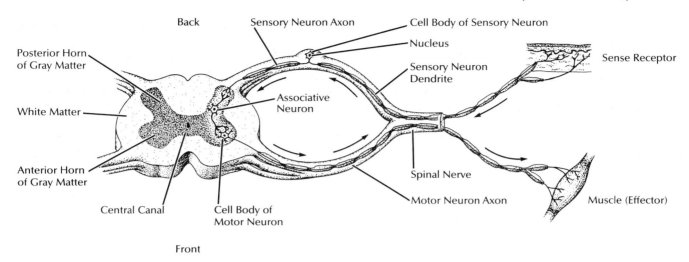

Figure 2—9   Cross Section of the Spinal Cord With a Reflex Arc

a rubber hammer and the leg suddenly jerks forward. What actually happens is that the rubber hammer suddenly puts pressure on the connecting fibers to the muscles in the leg. This pressure is then transmitted through the peripheral sensory nerve as sensory input into the posterior horn of the spinal cord. It is then transmitted to the anterior horn of the spinal cord and causes the anterior horn cells of the spinal cord to send a motor impulse back down to that leg, which is then transmitted as anterior movement of the leg (the knee jerk). This entire circuit involves one synapse (monosynaptic reflex) and takes place in a split second's time. The lower portions of the spinal cord involve some of the so-called autonomic functions of the body, control of the urogenital system, etc.

THE AUTONOMIC NERVOUS SYSTEM

The autonomic nervous system controls the body's internal environment. This system gradually involves clusters of neurons grouped together in small packets outside of the spinal cord itself and located elsewhere in the body. These small clusters are known as ganglions. There are two subdivisions of the autonomic system: the sympathetic and the parasympathetic. In the sympathetic nervous system, ganglions are lines in small chains immediately lateral to the spinal cord. In the parasympathetic nervous system, ganglions are more peripherally located and generally seen in the vicinity of the organ they innervate.

The sympathetic and parasympathetic nervous systems seem to serve contradictory roles. For exam-

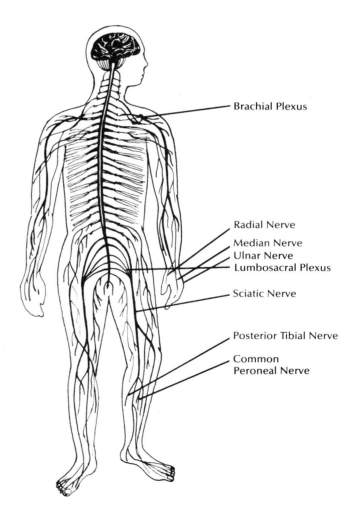

Figure 2—10   Nerves of the Body That Radiate From the Spinal Column

ple, the sympathetic nervous system speeds up the heart rate, whereas the parasympathetic nervous system slows it down. Similarly, one system may act to constrict the bladder, whereas another may act to the contrary. One system may act to tighten bladder sphincter control, whereas the other may act to loosen it and allow urination. A detailed analysis of the autonomic nervous system is beyond the scope of this text. However, the reader should understand that severe alteration of the autonomic nervous system's control of blood pressure, heart rate, and respiratory rate, etc., can be life threatening.

The peripheral nervous system is that system of nerves that exits from the spinal cord and finds its way distally to the outer reaches of the body. Most peripheral nerves can contain either motor or sensory fibers or any combination of the two. They are generally a bundle of small nerve fibers bound closely together in a connective tissue matrix. The nerves consist of axons held together in small groups, each individually surrounded by myelin (particularly if it is a rapidly conducting fiber), surrounded by a membrane called a perineurium. Large numbers of perineuriums are then bound together again in a final large cable which, in fact, is the nerve itself, surrounded by a membrane called the epineurium.

Many large nerve fibers come together in large consolidations of neurofibers that serve together for a coordinated function. These are referred to as a nerve plexus. An example of a nerve plexus is the brachial plexus of the neck, shoulder, and axilla (armpit) (Figure 2–10). Into the brachial plexus come various nerve roots from the cervical spine that will exit from the nerve plexus in the form of the varied peripheral nerves that go to the arm. The most important of these peripheral nerves to the arm are the radius, the ulnar, and the median nerve. A similar lumbosacral plexus in the lower spine innervates the leg (see Figure 2–10).

THE CRANIAL NERVES

Classically, there are twelve recognized cranial nerves (Figure 2–11). The mnemonic device for remembering the cranial nerves used by generations of medical students has always been On Old Olympus' Towering Top, A Finn And German Vaulted A Hop. Corresponding to this mnemonic device, the nerves are:

1. Olfactory nerve—this nerve mediates the sense of smell
2. Optic nerve—this nerve is the afferent nerve of vision

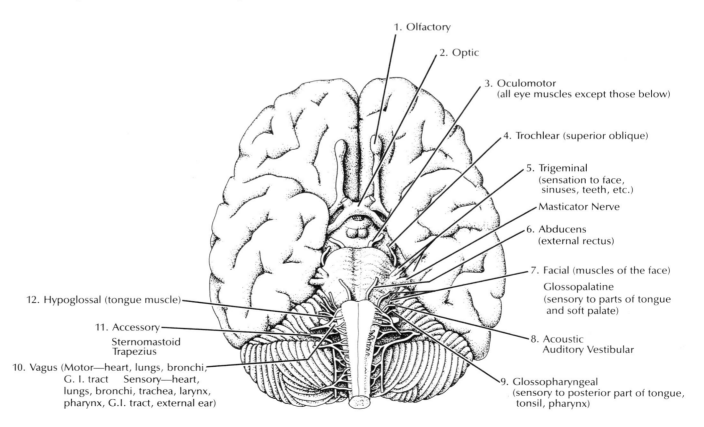

1. Olfactory
2. Optic
3. Oculomotor (all eye muscles except those below)
4. Trochlear (superior oblique)
5. Trigeminal (sensation to face, sinuses, teeth, etc.)
   Masticator Nerve
6. Abducens (external rectus)
7. Facial (muscles of the face)
   Glossopalatine (sensory to parts of tongue and soft palate)
8. Acoustic Auditory Vestibular
9. Glossopharyngeal (sensory to posterior part of tongue, tonsil, pharynx)

12. Hypoglossal (tongue muscle)
11. Accessory
    Sternomastoid
    Trapezius
10. Vagus (Motor—heart, lungs, bronchi, G. I. tract   Sensory—heart, lungs, bronchi, trachea, larynx, pharynx, G.I. tract, external ear)

Figure 2–11   The Cranial Nerves

3. Ocular motor—this is one of the nerves of eye movement
4. Trochlear—this is another nerve of eye movement
5. Trigeminal—this nerve mediates taste and sensation from the face, and movement of the jaw
6. Abducens—this nerve mediates lateral eye movement
7. Facial—this nerve mediates facial movement
8. Acoustic—this is the nerve of hearing
9. Glossopharyngeal—this nerve innervates the structures of the tongue and palate
10. Vagus—this nerve governs the autonomic functions of the heart, lungs, stomach, etc.
11. Accessory—this nerve governs movement in some of the paraspinal muscles in the shoulder and neck
12. Hypoglossal—this nerve moves the tongue outward.

THE VISUAL SYSTEM

The visual system is primary to the learning process. It has been estimated that when one includes all of the nerves involved in visual input as well as all of the nerves involved with other aspects of vision (specifically, movement of the eyes, coordination of the eyes, visual association areas, visual memory areas, etc.), one is speaking of approximately 30 percent of the entire central nervous system. Thus, it is clear that the visual system is of extraordinary importance in the survival of the organism. When this system is significantly impaired, the individual must be taught to compensate in order to function efficiently in society.

The physiology of vision is seen roughly illustrated in Figure 2–12. What we see in Figure 2–12 is that images registered on the retina are conducted backwards through the optic nerves. These fibers are partially crossed over at the region where the two optic nerves meet (the chiasm). The visual images are then conducted backward through the optic tracts and are finally transmitted to the occipital cortex where they are interpreted. It is of particular interest to note that all images seen in the occipital cortex of the brain are upside down and backwards. Transmission must then be sent to the visual association areas and visual memory areas of the brain and several other areas related to higher cortical function so that this information will be deciphered and made meaningful.

THE HEARING SYSTEM

Acoustic stimuli and the various frequencies of sound are funneled into the brain through the pinna or external ear, then conducted in through the external

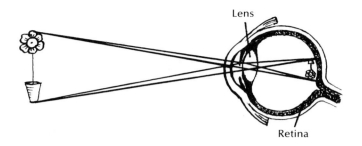

Visual Fields

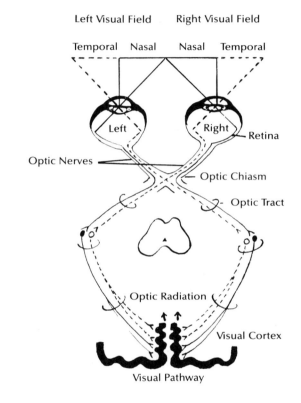

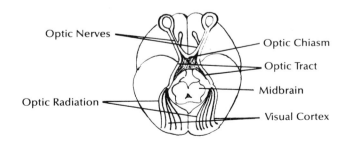

Figure 2–12   The Physiology of Vision

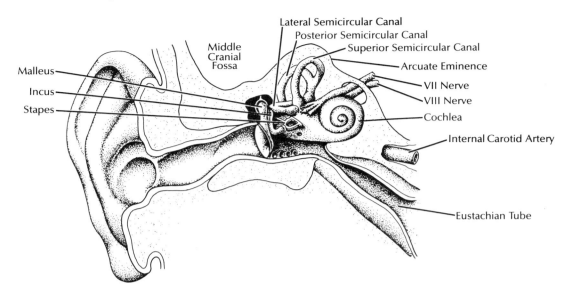

Figure 2—13   The Human Ear

auditory canal. The external auditory canal leads to the tympanic membrane. The tympanic membrane is made up of two layers of epithelium with a layer of fibrous tissue sandwiched in between. The membrane is drawn across the ear canal and acts very much like an animal hide drawn tautly across a drum top, in order to pick up the vibrations. The middle ear is interior to the tympanic membrane. It is an oblong cavity, lined by mucous membrane, and contains the small bones called ossicles. There are three main ossicles: the malleus, the incus, and the stapes. The malleus articulates with the incus, which in turn, articulates with the stapes. Each of these articulations are true bony joints. Muscles are found within the middle ear; specifically, the tensor tympani muscle and the stapedius muscle.

The function of these muscles is to help protect the internal ear by finely adjusting the ossicles in response to noises of various intensity, specifically very loud noises, that tend to threaten the functioning of the system. The eustachian tube is an open canal that empties down into the nasopharynx in the region of the tonsils and the adenoids. Finally, the inner ear is that portion of the ear which consists of the cochlea (the end organ receptor for acoustic stimuli) and the labyrinth (the end organ for balance and for the various other functions involved in spacial orientation and movement). Dysfunction of the labyrinth can produce many unpleasant subjective sensations, the most common of which is dizziness.

Sounds, of either high or low frequency, are transmitted in through the pinna, down the external auditory canal, and then cause small excursions and vibrations of the tympanic membrane. This tympanic membrane motion and vibration cause transmission of the vibration to the malleus, incus, and stapes, thus effectively transmitting sound through the middle ear and into the inner ear. The stapes then communicates directly with the inner ear through a foot plate, into the inner ear itself.

In the inner ear, the cochlea is the end organ for hearing. The specific organ of Corti, located within the cochlea, is excited by the vibrations, and this creates an electrical impulse that is carried along the cochlear nerve or the VIIIth cranial nerve. The electrical sensation comes from the acoustic nerve into the brain stem, in the pons, and then sends its electrical activity to the dorsal or ventral cochlear nuclei. The electrical stimulation then progresses along the brain stem to the cerebral cortex making stops at various other stations on the way. Some acoustically stimulated electrical activity will stop at the superior olive, the nucleus of the lateral lemniscus, and the inferior coliculus in the midbrain and the medial genicular body. All of these brainstem way stations mediate various reflexes that are stimulated by sound. The acoustic electrical impulses streaming through the medial genicular body are then relayed to the supratemporal transverse gyrus, just visible over the lower lip of the sylvian fissure.

When the stimulus is speech, the receptive areas for speech are activated in the dominant hemisphere of the brain; this is called Wernicke's area for speech, which interprets word meaning. This then stimulates a conduction bundle that will transfer electrical activity to the frontal area of the brain, or Broca's area. Broca's area manufactures the speech that will respond to the speech just heard.

NEURODEVELOPMENT OF THE NERVOUS SYSTEM IN THE CHILD

At birth a child already has most of the neurons (gray matter) that he will ever need. With a few minor exceptions, gray matter does not develop as the child ages. Consequently, the neurodevelopment we see as the child matures from an infant to adulthood must involve regions other than the gray matter itself. As the child develops more and more myelin (insulating material) for the nerve fibers, his nervous system matures. Greater amounts of myelin will, at least physiologically, facilitate better conduction of electronic impulses from one nerve to another and from one group of neurons to another. It is also believed that microscopic connections between neurons and tiny branches connecting one dendrite to another (dendritic spines) can also occur as the nervous system matures. Once again, this would entail a better and more efficient means of communicating from one neuron to another. The function of intersynaptic chemical transmitters and their development as the child matures is a subject of active and ongoing research at this time.

The integration and function of the nervous system starts out as a unit. Thus, many of a newborn baby's actions and reflexes are somewhat primitive and not very much advanced above the brain stem level; most movements are reflexive. As the child progressively develops, more and more complicated forms of behavior are observed.

If one makes a loud clapping noise or presents a startling stimulus, the newborn baby will, by reflex, jerk both arms outward and upward and move both legs, then gradually pull the extremities in toward himself and release a cry. This total action is referred to as the Moro reflex (see Chapter 3). If the newborn baby were to move only one side, a physician would be concerned about the possibility of paralysis and would arrange for further evaluation of the child. At about seven months of age, the child is able to reach out with one arm, grab a toy, and then transfer it to the other hand. At around ten years of age, the child is expected to be able to use his right hand and move the muscles in an intricate fashion without necessarily moving the fingers on the contralateral (left hand) side. Should this contralateral finger movement persist to any great extent, it is referred to as synkinesis. This is considered by many to be an indication of central nervous system immaturity.

Hand movement is a simple, basic movement. Talking, speaking, reading, and higher cortical functions are far more complicated. Imagine that a little girl sees a little boy in the schoolyard and says, "Good morning. How are you?" The little boy responds,

"Fine." This seems like a rather basic interchange. However, the neuronal circuitry functioning between the two children is extremely elaborate. The little girl sees the little boy. The retina in her eye transmits an upside-down and backwards image of the little boy to her occipital cortex. This image is then interpreted by the visual association areas, then sent forward to the frontal and temporal lobe centers of memory and intellectual integration. She then selects and formulates the words, "Good morning. How are you?" These words from her frontal speech area in the left hemisphere, most likely, must progress down her brain stem in the form of electrical impulses to move her mouth and tongue so as to pronounce the words properly. The little boy, on the other hand, must have totally intact hearing mechanisms in the ear to pick up the sound waves transmitted by the little girl. The small bones in his ear must then translate the sound waves made by the little girl into electrical impulses that can then be carried by the little boy's acoustic nerve into his brain stem. The brain stem must then conduct these electrical fibers up through the thalamus, as an integrating center, and up to the hearing cortex of the brain in the parietal region. The sounds of the words must then be interpreted in the auditory association areas and in the center for verbal meaning, also known as Wernicke's area. Once the words are interpreted in this center of the brain, they must be sent forward through the conduction bundle to the anterior portion of the child's brain for expressive speech (Broca's area). The little boy must then select and formulate an appropriate reply—"Fine."

This has been only one very basic arc: speech, hearing, and response. What of the far more complex arcs that occur with regard to learning, reading, writing, the basics of handwriting and interpretation, attention, and distractibility? Is it not logical that the child with neuronal deficit or immaturity in certain reflex areas of the central nervous system might also have considerable difficulty in the school situation? The best mental status examination of a small child is his report card. The child who has academic difficulties in school, even if they are due to neuronal dysfunction, might also exhibit behavior problems because of the academic difficulties or the original neuronal dysfunction. This is by no means intended to imply that all school-related problems are in fact neurological, but it is to stress that, without doubt, some of them are.

SUMMARY

This chapter has presented an overview of basic neuroanatomy. The material has included some commonly used terms and their definitions, as well as information about neurons, the cerebral hemispheres of the brain, the brain stem, the autonomic nervous system, the cranial nerves, the visual and hearing systems, and neurodevelopment of the nervous system. The intent has been to provide to the reader a better understanding of neuroanatomy in general and information that will lead to a better understanding of many of the disorders to be discussed in subsequent chapters of this book. For additional study, the reader is referred to the following sources.

SELECTED READINGS

Netter, F. H. *The nervous system* (Vol. 1). New York: CIBA, 1965.

Raner, W. W., & Clark, S. C. *Anatomy of the nervous system*. Philadelphia: W. B. Saunders, 1963.

Truex, R. C., & Carpenter, M. B. *Human neuroanatomy*. Baltimore: Williams & Wilkins, 1964.

Williams, P. L., & Warwick, R. *Functional neuroanatomy of man*. Philadelphia: W. B. Saunders, 1975.

Arnold J. Capute, M.D., *is deputy director of the John F. Kennedy Institute for Handicapped Children and associate professor in the Department of Pediatrics at the School of Medicine, Johns Hopkins University, Baltimore, Maryland.*

Renee C. Wachtel, M.D., *is assistant professor in the Department of Pediatrics at the School of Medicine, Johns Hopkins University, Baltimore, Maryland.*

Bruce K. Shapiro, M.D., *is assistant professor in the Department of Pediatrics at the School of Medicine, Johns Hopkins University, Baltimore, Maryland.*

Frederick B. Palmer, M.D., *is assistant professor in the Department of Pediatrics at the School of Medicine, Johns Hopkins University, Baltimore, Maryland.*

Marilee C. Allen, M.D., *is an instructor in the Department of Pediatrics at the School of Medicine, Johns Hopkins University, Baltimore, Maryland.*

Preparation of this chapter was supported in part by Maternal and Child Health Project 917, Maternal and Child Health Services, Department of Health and Human Services.

CHAPTER 3

Normal Motor and Reflex Development

The development of motor abilities that permit an infant to move in any direction and become an exploring toddler who walks independently has fascinated developmentalists for many years (Illingworth, 1980; Knoblock & Pasamanick, 1974). The neurodevelopmental changes that allow the newborn to progress from a "locked-in" posture (Figure 3–1), determined by a predominance of **flexor** muscle tone and the presence of primitive **reflexes,** to performing voluntary motor acts have been recognized scientifically but have not been analyzed in the normal population. The remarkably consistent sequential changes that are observed as each infant and child develops the prerequisites for the achievement of motor milestones depend on complex neurologic networks that are preestablished, or prewired, to oc-

Figure 3–1   Normal Newborn. The infant is in a flexor pattern; that is, with arms and legs flexed and hands forming fists.

cur during the early years of life. Since education has been mandated to evaluate and initiate programs for the handicapped from ages three through twenty-one years (The Education for All Handicapped Children Act, Public Law 94–142), it is important for teachers and psychologists to become familiar with normal motor development in early infancy and the preschool period.

Although motor development does not predict future intelligence, it should be used as a neurodevelopmental marker. Not only should concerns be raised about outright motor delay, but the quality of motor activity should be highlighted because there is clinical significance to motor manifestations such as clumsiness, **hypotonia, tremor,** and poor coordination in using the upper and lower extremities. Because damage to one area of development is usually accompanied by damage to other areas, deviation from a normal motor pattern should arouse suspicion of neurological dysfunction and suggest further evaluation.

In order to understand a child's final attainment of overt motor skills, one must examine the sequential changes in neurologic substrates (strength, tone, primitive reflexes) and the evolution of postural reactions during the first years of life. Overt motor attainment can be subdivided into the development of posture and locomotion (gross motor) and the development of eye-hand coordination (fine motor). This development proceeds in cephalocaudal progression (head-to-foot). Motor development occurs in a sequential fashion, as do other streams of development (e.g., language, problem-solving, adaptive, and social). Gross motor development which involves mainly lower extremity function should be separated from fine motor development which focuses upon upper extremity function.

NORMAL GROSS MOTOR DEVELOPMENT

The ability to explore the environment is partly determined by an infant's or child's motility (power of

spontaneous movement). Therefore, despite functional sensory systems (vision and hearing), the normal newborn is extremely dependent upon others for sensory stimulation and mobility. The newborn can move its arms, legs, and head, but frequently triggered reflex patterns cause additional nonvoluntary movements and changes in tone. Although the infant can turn its head from side-to-side while lying in a prone position (on the stomach), it cannot lift its head to look around nor can the infant move from one place to another. The newborn's posture of predominant flexion and lack of neck extension causes the head to drop back when the child is pulled to a sitting position.

By one month of age, however, improved control allows the infant to pick its head up while prone for minutes at a time so that, in this turtlelike position, he can visually track a moving person for a brief period. At two months, the infant has sustained head control while lying prone and can even raise his chest from the bed or table, allowing a much larger view of the world. However, as the imbalance in flexor muscle tone diminishes, the infant is able to support itself on extended forearms while in a prone position by four months of age. Because this provides much greater stability and requires much less physical effort, the position can be sustained for long periods of time.

Up to this point, however, the infant must remain wherever placed. The first locomotor pattern to develop occurs by five months of age, when the involuntary flexor tone of the trunk is sufficiently inhibited to allow the infant to roll over from front (prone) to back (supine), and shortly thereafter from back to front. A new world has unfolded! No longer does everything have to come to the infant because he has achieved independent mobility. As a means of exploring the world, however, rolling over has its limits; one can only move laterally, not forward or backward. Moving forward is first accomplished by creeping, in which the seven-month-old infant, while lying on his stomach, reciprocally moves his arms, pulling his body and trunk behind him like a snake (belly crawl). By eight months, the infant develops crawling, wherein the trunk is elevated and supported on extended forearms and knees (up on all fours) that are moved reciprocally, allowing rapid forward and backward movement.

In order to do this, the infant needs to develop sufficient head control and trunk extension along with anterior protective extension, which will be described later. At about six months of age the infant, with sufficient assistance, can support his trunk vertically against gravity in a position called supported or "tripod" sitting (Figure 3–2). The wide base required for sufficient balance when the infant begins to sit

Figure 3–2   Tripod Sitting. The legs form a circle and the infant uses his arms for support.

Figure 3–3   Early Walking. Although walking independently, the infant's hands are held high in mid-air for support (high regard).

alone (without support) is initially maintained by the legs, forming a circle, and the extended arms. By seven months of age, sufficient balance reactions have developed for the infant to sit unsupported. The child can sit independently for long periods of time, playing with toys and not requiring the use of the arms for support. He can bring himself to a sitting position independently (come to sit) by eight months of age.

The development of the ability to stand begins when the infant is about six months of age. The trunk and legs develop sufficient extension to allow them to support the body's weight while standing with assistance, at first briefly and then for lengthening periods of time. By nine months of age, the infant can pull himself up to a standing position while holding on to the bars on the crib. Because the ability to stand with support for a fairly long period of time has already developed at about nine months, the infant can begin to take a few tentative steps along the crib while still holding on for stability (cruising). The child learns to shift body weight from one foot to another, so that one foot at a time can be lifted. With the development of pelvic rotation and sufficient equilibrium reactions (to be discussed below), less support is required and the infant is able to walk, first with one hand held, then alone, at about twelve months. Although clumsy at first, with the hands held high in the air, known as high regard (Figure 3–3), better equilibrium reactions and balance develop over the next few months, which allow the arms to drop to the sides and the walking (ambulation) to be quicker and

surer. By fifteen months of age, the infant has become a toddler, able to walk stably both forward and backward and frequently able to outrun his parents.

Table 3–1 summarizes the gross motor milestones that were determined in a recent study of normal infants by the Clinical Research Unit of the John F. Kennedy Institute. Subsequent gross motor development

Table 3–1   Normal Gross Motor Milestones

Milestone	Mean Age of Attainment
Rolls over prone to supine	4 months
Rolls over supine to prone	5 months
Sits (tripod)	6 months
Sits unsupported	7 months
Creeps	7 months
Comes to sit	8 months
Crawls	8 months
Pulls to stand	9 months
Cruises	9 months
Walks alone	12 months
Walks backward	15 months
Runs	15 months

Source: Primitive Reflex Profile: Early Motor Diagnosis. Maternal and Child Health Services Research Grant MC-R-240392-01-0, U.S. Department of Health, Education, and Welfare, 1981.

has not been given its due recognition because of poor standardization of observable motor milestones after fifteen months of age. Although gross motor milestones are rarely used by professionals to determine more than motor disability, a frequent misconception is that all retarded children have delayed gross motor achievement. Although profoundly retarded children may have totally normal gross motor development, delays in sitting or walking may be indicative of neurologic abnormality (Shapiro, Accardo, & Capute, 1979). It should be recognized that gross motor development is a poor predictor of future intelligence (Accardo & Capute, 1979), and is far inferior to language development as a predictive tool.

FINE MOTOR DEVELOPMENT

The development of posture and locomotion focuses predominantly on the attainment of gross motor

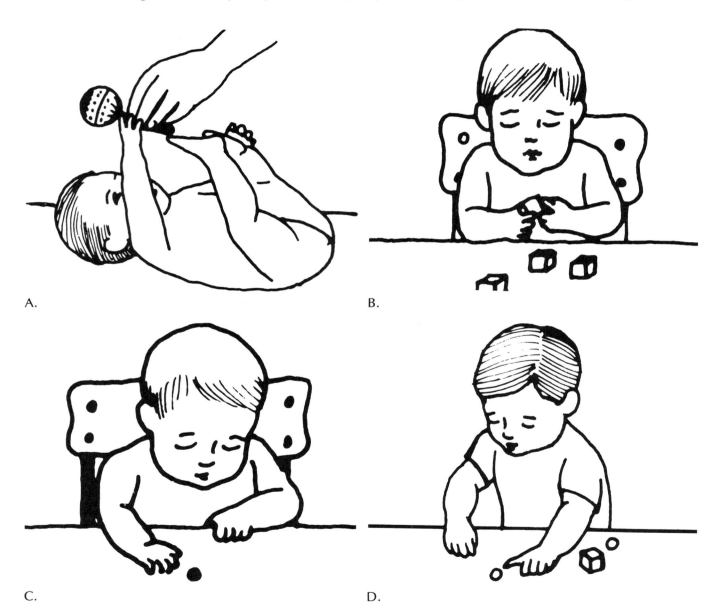

A.

B.

C.

D.

Figure 3—4   Development of a Voluntary Grasp.
A. The infant reaches for a larger object with his whole hand in an imprecise manner.
B. The baby transfers a block from one hand to the other.
C. The toddler reaches for a smaller object with a radial rake.
D. Isolation of the forefinger is part of the development of a pincer grasp.

skills. Gross motor skills, in turn, hinge largely upon the development of head and trunk movement coordinated with movement of the lower extremities. Fine motor development, in contrast, is concerned primarily with the development of upper extremity facility and eye-hand coordination. The ability to locate an object in space, secure it, and manipulate it appropriately is the prelude to such important skills as writing and buttoning. The sequence of this development occurs in an orderly fashion.

The newborn infant's arms are predominantly flexed and the hands are held closed in fists (see Figure 3–1). An object placed in the fisted hand will be retained for some period of time and released involuntarily as reflex activity influences hand tone. This is augmented by a grasp reflex, which causes the newborn to tightly clench an object or finger in his hand. It is not until two to three months of age that the hands are held most of the way open. By four months of age, when some primitive reflex activity is beginning to wane, the infant is able to bring the hands together to the body's midline. At this point, handplay begins. The infant is able to visually, tactually, and orally explore his hands. When a toy is presented in front, the infant will become excited and show a generalized increase in motor activity. He may even make some swipes at it, but is unable to coordinate the spatial localization with appropriate hand-opening and -closing movements. An object presented close to the body (e.g., on the chest), may be grasped, but only after several attempts.

A voluntary grasp starts to develop at about five months of age, when the infant can secure a large object with an imprecise raking motion of the whole hand. The grasp becomes more precise over the next few months (Figure 3–4), as individual parts of the hand are isolated and gain skill. Skill progresses from the ulnar (little finger) side to the radial (thumb) side. By ten months of age, the infant can deftly secure a small object (pea-sized) using only the thumb and forefinger in a pincer grasp. At twelve months of age, the infant develops a voluntary release, enabling the child to put cubes into a cup. Further refinement of upper extremity function together with visual and cognitive development occurs during the next few years, and culminates in the manual dexterity required to write or play a piano.

Fine motor development ceases to have isolated milestones after one year of age, when it is incorporated into problem-solving skills, which are represented by eye-hand coordination. Problem-solving abilities require cognition (going from the concrete to the general using abstraction and conceptualization). Thus, there is a pure motor aspect to hand and arm development in addition to a cognitive aspect, when hand use is coordinated with eye-hand functioning. This combination thus results in problem-solving which, after language, is the second best predictor of future intelligence.

Problem-solving abilities commence during infancy and extend through the preschool, school, and adult years of life. During these periods of life, they are measured by infant developmental scales and intelligence tests to determine cognitive functioning. Unlike gross motor function, eye-hand coordination is closely associated with cognition, and thus, problem-solving is significantly delayed in the retarded child.

MOTOR DEVELOPMENT AS A COMPLEX NEUROLOGICAL PROCESS

Primitive Reflexes

Many neurodevelopmental processes are required for the accomplishment of motor skills. The primitive reflexes represent factors that most inhibit volitional or gross motor development. Basically, the brain is an inhibitory organ; as the cortex develops brainstem activity is inhibited.

During the first six months of life, infant movement is primarily controlled by the brainstem, that is, a good many involuntary or automated motor responses that preclude voluntary motor action are present. As mentioned, the main stumbling block to neuromotor development is the wide array of primitive reflexes that represent the earliest motor activity of infancy. The primitive reflexes develop during gestation (Starrett & Wachtel, 1981) and are exhibited in the movement of a fetus in utero. They are subsequently noted in the newborn and disappear somewhere between three to six months of age.

Primitive reflexes are present at birth and extremely prominent during the first few months of life, but they are inhibited and assimilated into normal voluntary activity until they finally disappear. The sequential changes in each of these reflexes over time, along with the development of postural reactions (see below) and tonal changes, allow for the development of gross and fine motor skills as previously noted. Significant primitive reflexes involved in these changes include the Moro reflex, the asymmetric tonic neck reflex, the tonic labyrinthine reflex, and the positive support reflex. The strength of these reflexes during the first year of life have been objectively quantitated in a Primitive Reflex Profile (Capute, Accardo, Vining, Rubenstein, & Harryman, 1978).

The *Moro reflex* can be elicited by a rapid change in head position; usually, the infant's head is raised

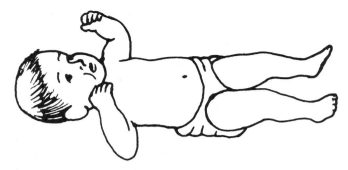

Figure 3–5   The Moro Reflex. The arms are extended and then abducted into an "embrace" with the legs extended.

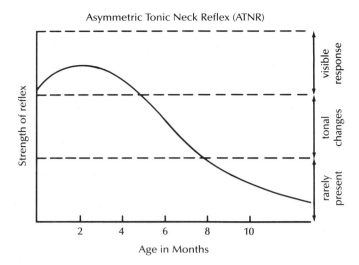

Asymmetric Tonic Neck Reflex (ATNR)

Figure 3–7   Asymmetric Tonic Neck Reflex. At birth the reflex is usually elicited but diminishes markedly between four and six months of age.

slightly, then the support is abruptly withdrawn and the head falls back. The arms are immediately extended and abducted (move away from the midline) (Figure 3–5) and the hands open, after which the arms adduct (move toward the midline) into a position of embrace. The legs may also extend. The Moro reflex is present in virtually every newborn, but its prevalence falls rapidly so that by six months of age, very few normal infants will demonstrate it. This is necessary because a persistently strong Moro reflex will interfere with the development of nearly all motor acts. An absent Moro reflex in a newborn is associated with central nervous system dysfunction.

The *asymmetric tonic neck reflex* (ATNR) is elicited by passively rotating the infant's head and observing the movement of the extremities. The reflex causes the arm and leg on the chin side to extend and the arm and leg on the occiput (back of the head), side to flex, known as the fencer's position (Figure 3–6). This reflex is present in almost all normal newborns and largely disappears by six months of age

(Figure 3–7). This is consistent with the infant's ability to roll over voluntarily and the commencement of hand-to-mouth activity by four months of age, when the ATNR has been greatly diminished. If this reflex is present to an abnormal degree and the child remains in this position for months to years, hip dislocation will take place on the occiput side. In addition, because of the inequality of tone, scoliosis (curvature of the spine) will develop. This reflex, along with the tonic labyrinthine reflex, must be significantly suppressed before normal voluntary motor activity occurs.

The *tonic labyrinthine reflex* (TL) is also present at birth in normal infants and plays a large role in mediating tone during the first six months of life. It can be elicited by passively extending and flexing the neck, while holding the child in a supine position (TLS) or a prone position (TLP). Extension of the neck (Figure 3–8) in the supine position causes the shoulders to retract and the trunk and legs to extend, whereas flexion of the neck (Figure 3–9) causes the upper and lower extremities to flex. This reflex is thought to originate from the labyrinths of the inner ear. The TLS and ATNR show similar developmental patterns: they are both generally present at birth and are most active during the first two to three months of life, then rapidly decrease (Figure 3–10). Presence of a strong TL reflex interferes with an infant's ability to raise himself from a prone position and maintain that posture because his shoulder retracts whenever his neck is extended. Similarly, the TL reflex interferes with sitting because the trunk extends when the head is lifted, causing the infant to fall backward. This re-

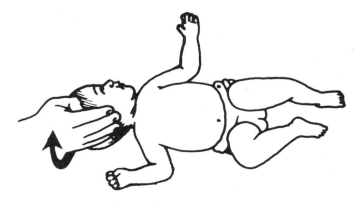

Figure 3–6   Asymmetric Tonic Neck Reflex. The arm and leg on the chin side extend and the arm and leg on the occiput side flex when the head is rotated laterally.

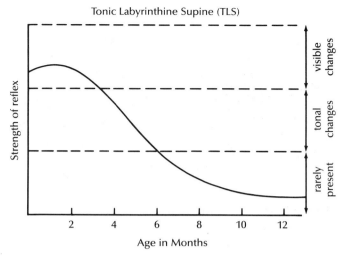

Tonic Labyrinthine Supine (TLS)

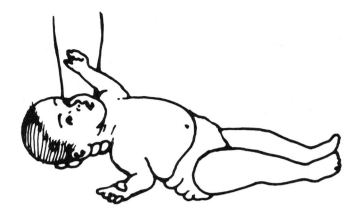

Figure 3—8   Tonic Labyrinthine Reflex. The infant is held in a supine position. When the neck is extended, the shoulders retract and the trunk and legs extend.

Figure 3—10   Tonic Labyrinthine Reflex. Visible changes are seen from birth through four or five months of age, and rarely seen beyond ten months.

flex has great clinical significance as an indicator of a disordered central nervous system when it is evident to an extreme degree or remains past the physiological age. It is probably the most important primitive reflex because it is very difficult to inhibit or "work around" when physical therapy is rendered to a child with cerebral palsy.

The *positive support reflex* (PS) is particularly useful for detecting a problem in the neurological integrity of the lower extremities. It is elicited by holding the infant under the axillae (armpits) and bouncing the balls of the feet on the table top. By two months of age, the infant's lower extremities should extend for an instant and momentarily support the body. By four to six months of age, the infant will fully

support its body weight. Asymmetry or an exaggerated response (toe standing) should be noted.

As discussed above, all primitive reflexes are present at birth and are suppressed by the third to fourth month of life. They are no longer clinically significant after six months of age. If they are present to an unusual degree or remain for a prolonged period of time, cerebral damage may be indicated. In eliciting the above responses, one should note any asymmetry, because this might indicate whether the upper or lower extremities and whether the right or left side are more involved.

The sequential changes in the above primitive reflexes (and others not discussed) and their interaction play a large role in motor activities during the first few months of life. Sequential diminution of primitive reflexes allows postural reactions to emerge and motor development to proceed.

Postural Reactions

As the primitive reflexes become suppressed, **postural reactions** appear, which are mediated through the midbrain. These reactions are highly correlated with the appearance of motor milestones. Postural reactions become clinically evident by six months of age and continue throughout the remaining months of infancy. Physical therapists who work with cerebral palsied children have developed methods of inhibiting primitive reflexes in order to facilitate the appearance of postural reactions. This type of therapy is referred as the inhibitory and facilitory methodology. Postural reactions are responses of righting, equilibrium, and protection that form the substrate for the

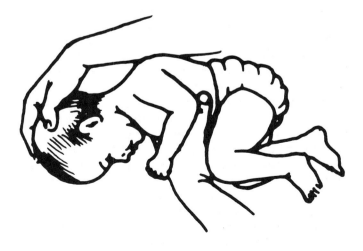

Figure 3—9   Tonic Labyrinthine Reflex. The infant is held in a prone position. When the neck is flexed the arms and legs flex as well.

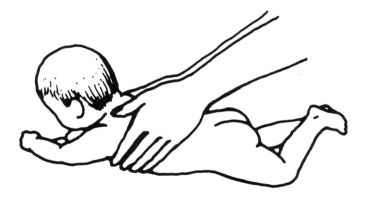

Figure 3–11   Landau Reaction. When suspended in a prone position, the infant's head raising causes the trunk to extend.

development of functional motor acts. They include the ability to right one's body in a prone position (Landau reaction) and upper extremity protective reactions (propping reacting). Their expression requires a certain degree of tonal development and diminution of interfering primitive reflexes. A few examples of postural reactions will be discussed.

The *Landau* reaction is elicited by holding the infant off the table in a prone position while allowing the head and neck to extend (Figure 3–11). This causes the trunk to extend (axial righting). This ability of the infant to right itself against gravity develops between two to four months of age (Capute, Wachtel, Palmer, Shapiro, & Accardo, 1982), and the presence of a very strong TL reflex would interfere with its development. The Landau reaction is referred to as a series of midline postural reactions that denotes truncal stability and is required for rolling over to occur.

The *segmental roll* or *derotative righting* reaction appears at four to five months, following the development of the Landau response. It is elicited by completely turning the infant's head to either side while he is in the supine position (on his back). When the head is completely rotated to one side, the shoulders, body, hips, and legs roll over in a segmental fashion. This is referred to as a series of axial midline postural responses and is required before the infant can roll over voluntarily.

Upper extremity propping reactions or *protective extension* allow the child to maintain equilibrium while sitting and prevent falling over. By six months of age, the infant will extend his arms anteriorly to protect himself when falling forward in the sitting position. This is utilized in an early method of sitting called tripod sitting (see Figure 3–2). Lateral protective extension develops at about eight months of age and allows for stable sitting. Posterior protective extension develops later, at about ten to twelve months

of age, and is related to pivoting while sitting and to walking.

For normal motor development to occur, many other factors such as tone and strength must be considered. If an infant has a significant decrease in tone, he is described as being hypotonic. If too much tone is evident, he is described as being hypertonic. Essentially, the primitive reflexes are manifestations of tone elicited primarily by head movements. If a child is either hypotonic or hypertonic, this will affect not only the head movements but also the development of the primitive reflexes and postural reactions.

ABNORMALITIES OF MOTOR DEVELOPMENT

Although severe disorders of motor development are discussed in other chapters, several aberrations of motor development deserve mention here because they may be useful in focusing upon the quality of motor activity and serve as neurodevelopmental markers for aberrations in nonmotor spheres of development. These aberrations include motor delay, deviance, and dissociation.

While severe delay in the attainment of motor milestones may indicate disorders such as cerebral palsy, milder delays may be associated with mental retardation or learning disabilities. It is not uncommon for learning disabled children to have mild or "soft" signs of motor impairment manifested by early hypotonia or hypertonia and later clumsiness in both gross motor and fine motor skills (Capute, Shapiro, & Palmer, 1981). Although the motor delay in learning disabled children is frequently the focus of much parental concern, its chief importance is as a neurodevelopmental marker of dysfunction in other nonmotor areas. When any of the streams of development are delayed, another stream of development is at very high risk for being involved as well. Thus, if the motor area within the brain is damaged, the infant is at high risk for having accompanying involvement in the language and problem-solving areas as well.

Motor deviancy is another developmental phenomenon that serves to alert the pediatrician to possible neurologic dysfunction. Deviancy is detected by the nonsequential appearance of otherwise normal motor milestones. Some examples of deviant motor behavior include an infant who is able to sit unsupported and pivot (a twelve-month function) but is unable to independently reach that sitting position (an eight-month function); an infant who develops handedness (a two-year skill) before one year of age but demonstrates hemiplegic cerebral palsy in the unused hand; and an infant who rolls over at one to two months but uses an abnormally strong tonic labyrinthine reflex in order to roll over.

Dissociation refers to the presence of different rates of development between two developmental streams. This can frequently be seen in the normally intelligent child with cerebral palsy who may have language and cognitive skills progressing at a faster rate than motor skills. Milder degrees of dissociation are frequently seen in communicatively impaired or learning disabled children. Thus, the learning disabled child may have problem-solving abilities significantly better than his language abilities.

Employing the concepts of motor delay, deviance, and dissociation allows one to select children who are showing aberrations of development and require more careful scrutiny of both their motor and nonmotor skills. Therefore, the concepts serve as neurodevelopmental markers of neurologic dysfunction. No longer are orthopedic surgeons telling parents that Johnny is perfectly normal when Johnny walks at 18–20 months of age. They have learned that motor delay is not uncommonly coupled with some other dysfunction, and are recommending an interdisciplinary evaluation to be certain that the child does not have an associated deficit, such as mental retardation or a communicative disorder. It is most important for teachers to understand that motor delay, dissociation, or deviancy can be markers of other dysfunction, such as mental retardation or even a future language disorder or learning disability.

Similarly, teachers must be aware of motor dysfunction in their learning disabled children. A learning disability in the medical arena is commonly called **minimal cerebral palsy** or **choreiform syndrome** because it is not uncommon for learning disabled children to show very mild signs of motor impairment manifested by the above mentioned deviation, delay, or dissociation. Children with learning disabilities are very commonly found to be hypotonic and awkward or clumsy. In addition to academic underachievement and motor dysfunction, these children demonstrate a specific behavioral profile or cerebral dysfunction called the **Strauss syndrome.** This syndrome is characterized by hyperactivity, attentional aberrations (from short attention span and distractibility to perseverance), emotional lability (variable moods and reactions of varying intensity), and impulsivity. Thus, while recognizing that a learning disability has academic underachievement as its hallmark, the ability of teachers to pick up early motor discrepancies might mean earlier diagnosis and intervention.

THE TEACHER AND MOTOR DYSFUNCTION

In infancy or the preschool years, if children have been identified as being clumsy or as having hypotonia or motor delay or any of the above described motor deviancies, they should be referred for evaluation to determine whether they are at high risk for a later learning disability. During the school years, underachievement is commonly found with the above mentioned motor deviant skills, and teachers should consider the possibility of an organic etiology for the learning disability and not immediately blame the parents or psychological factors. Teachers, as well as orthopedic surgeons, should be aware of the association of poor motor development with later poor school performance.

With the passage of PL 94-142, there has been a proliferation of motor therapies claiming to improve academic performance by improving gross motor or fine motor abilities. This approach has been generally accepted and implemented despite a lack of scientifically demonstrated efficacy. Parents should not be told that improvement in gross motor or fine motor skills will rub off into the cognitive areas. Furthermore, serious consideration should be given to whether the family should be given an additional chore that is both time consuming and expensive.

Until scientific studies have been carried out, it is improper to give parents false hopes by claiming that these various motor therapies will significantly alter the course of the child's academic progress. Because motor deficits are manifestations of cerebral dysfunction, it is essential that methods employed by physical and occupational therapists to enhance these skills be subject to scientific scrutiny to demonstrate efficacy. Even if the primary goal of motor therapy (improving learning) is not accomplished, it should be noted that therapy puts children into group contact and this may enhance the development of social and adaptive skills.

CONCLUSION

Motor development is a sequential progression of changes mediated by changes in tone, reflex activity, and postural reactions. Deviations from the normal pattern may indicate early neurologic dysfunction and, therefore, must be followed carefully during the first year of life. It is hoped that teachers will gain greater familiarity and understanding of the normative data concerning motor milestones and be aware of three developmental phenomena: delay, deviance, and dissociation. These phenomena are useful in the early detection of abnormality and their presence usually means the child is at high risk for a perceptual or cognitive dysfunction. If any of these phenomena is present, the child should be referred for an interdisciplinary evaluation so that the most appropriate programs might be formulated and implemented in a realistic fashion.

REFERENCES

Accardo, P. J., & Capute, A. J. *The pediatrician and the developmentally delayed child.* Baltimore: University Park Press, 1979.

Capute, A. J., Accardo, P. J., Vining, E. P. G., Rubenstein, J. E., & Harryman, S. *Primitive reflex profile.* Baltimore: University Park Press, 1978.

Capute, A. J., Shapiro, B. K., & Palmer, F. P. Spectrum of developmental disabilities. *Orthopedic Clinics of North America,* 1981, *12,* 3–22.

Capute, A. J., Wachtel, R. C., Palmer, F. B., Shapiro, B. K., & Accardo, P. J. A prospective study of three postural reactions. *Developmental Medicine and Child Neurology,* 1982, *24,* 314–320.

Illingworth, R. S. *The development of the infant and young child: Normal and abnormal.* New York: Churchill Livingstone, 1980.

Knobloch, H., & Pasamanick, B. *Gesell and Armatruda's developmental diagnosis.* Hagerstown: Harper & Row, 1974.

Shapiro, B. K., Accardo, P. J., & Capute, A. J. Factors affecting walking in a profoundly retarded population. *Developmental Medicine and Child Neurology,* 1979, *21,* 369–373.

Starrett, A. L., & Wachtel, R. C. Assessment of development of premature infants. *Developmental Medicine and Child Neurology,* 1981, *23,* 117.

PART 2

Orthopedic and Neurological Disorders

Margaret H. Jones, M.D., *is professor emeritus in the Department of Pediatrics at the School of Medicine, University of California at Los Angeles.*

The term cerebral palsy (CP) describes a disorder of movement and posture that is due to a defect or a lesion of the immature brain (Bax, 1964). The term does not designate a disease in the usual medical sense. It is, however, a useful term that covers individuals who are handicapped by motor disorders due to nonprogressive abnormalities of the brain (Crothers & Paine, 1959).

Those who work with CP children should be aware that, in addition to their obvious motor handicaps, the majority also have other, so-called associated problems. These may include: deficits in the oropharyngeal area (i.e., control of the tongue and lips in eating and speaking); eye muscle control (**strabismus** or **nystagmus**); visual deficits; hearing loss (congenital or acquired, sometimes not suspected

CHAPTER 4

Cerebral Palsy

before audiometric testing); visual-perceptual difficulties; loss of tactile discrimination or proprioceptive sensation (i.e., knowledge of location of a body part in space); extreme slowness; lack of concentration; behavioral or learning problems; and seizures. In one recent study of children ages four–sixteen years, 18.6 percent were found to have one associated handicap, 21.3 percent had two, and 42 percent had three or more (Lagergren, 1981). Associated problems may be of major importance in determining the overall outcome for a child.

Estimates of the frequency of CP, as defined above, vary from 0.6 to 5.9 per thousand live births (Cruickshank, 1976). The frequency in school children has been reported to be between 2.0 and 2.5 per thousand (Rutter, Graham, & Yule, 1970). A recent study in Sweden based on children four–sixteen years of age reported that 1.9 per thousand had CP. The same frequency was found among children born between 1963 and 1967 and those born from 1968 to 1972 (Lagergren, 1981).

The purpose of this chapter is to present basic information about the etiology, diagnosis, treatment, and prognosis of children included under the term cerebral palsy. Educational implications will also be stressed.

ETIOLOGY

Etiological factors are classified according to presumed time of onset (prenatal, perinatal, or postnatal), and the cause or possible cause of the condition. **Prenatal** factors include:
1. Hereditary static conditions such as familial athetosis, familial paraplegia, and familial tremor, all of which are rare;
2. Congenital conditions (those acquired in utero) such as those resulting from infection, including **toxoplasmosis,** viral infections, and especially rubella, herpes, and cytomegalic inclusion disease; and
3. Other causes including maternal **hypoxia** or **anoxia** (lack of oxygen), **toxemia,** abnormalities of the umbilical cord, kinking or twisting of the cord, drugs, and dietary factors.

Perinatal factors include:
1. Mechanical anoxia such as that due to respiratory obstruction or atelectasis (i.e., when the lungs do not expand fully);
2. Trauma resulting in **intracranial hemorrhage,** etc.; and
3. Complications occurring during the neonatal period related to prematurity, "small-for-date" babies, infections, etc.

Postnatal factors include:
1. Trauma to the head;
2. Infections such as **meningitis, encephalitis,** or a brain abscess;
3. Vascular accidents that damage the blood vessels of the brain;
4. Toxins such as arsenic or lead;
5. Anoxia such as in monoxide poisoning, strangulation, or drowning; and
6. Neoplasms (tumors) that cause defects of the brain during its development after birth.

In the past, perinatal factors have been considered to be the most frequent cause of CP. However, in a recent study, Holm (1982) looked at the causes of cerebral palsy in light of current knowledge of fetal development and the implications of maternal and neonatal conditions. She concluded that 50 percent of the cases were probably prenatal in origin. The prenatal category in this study included those with a history of definite or possible prenatal factors plus cases without perinatal or postnatal causes. Recent Swedish reports (Hagberg, Hagberg, & Olow, 1975; Lagergren, 1981) have presented similar findings if the category of unknown is added to that of prenatal factors.

It is difficult and often impossible to determine what region or regions of the brain may be involved in a particular child who has CP. It is seldom that only one system (one series of nerve cells that work together) is damaged. Some clinical pathological studies have attempted to link etiology, symptomatology, and pathology. The major areas involved in the different clinical types of CP—the cortex and pyramidal tracts, the basal ganglia (or extrapyramidal regions), and the cerebellum—are identified in Figure 4–1.

The *pyramidal* tracts originate in the cerebral cortex. This is the area for voluntary control of the face, limbs, trunk, and extremities. The fibers from the nerve cells in the cerebral cortex pass through the area of the basal ganglia and into the midbrain and hindbrain, where they cross. Those from the right side of the cortex go to the left to innervate the left side of the body. Those from the left innervate the right side of the body. Damage to the nerve cells or to the fibers arising from them leads to spasticity in the muscles supplied by those nerves. Injury or abnormality of the *basal ganglia* results in a disturbance of movement (dyskinesia) frequently seen as athetosis. The *cerebellum* is involved with coordination of the various muscles and with balance and equilibrium. Damage to this area of the brain can result in ataxia.

Fibers from nerve cells in the brain make various connections with other nerve cells, resulting in a very complex organization. Pure cases of any of the clinical types of CP are probably rare. In an individual child it is difficult, if not impossible, to determine the exact type and amount of damage to the brain during life. The clinical classification, therefore, is based on the predominant type of posture and movement.

CHARACTERISTICS

Clinical types of CP are described on the basis of the posture and movement patterns displayed. These include **spasticity, dyskinesia** (including **athetosis, dystonia, rigidity,** hypotonia, and tremor), **ataxia,** and mixed types. The predominant pattern is usually identified, although "pure" cases are uncommon. The limb involvement and degree of severity are de-

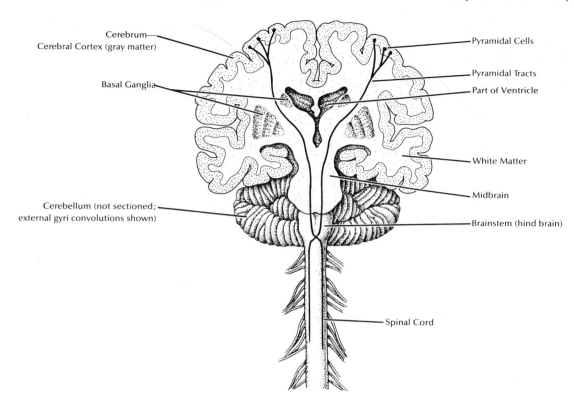

Cerebrum—
Cerebral Cortex (gray matter)

Basal Ganglia

Cerebellum (not sectioned;
external gyri convolutions shown)

Pyramidal Cells

Pyramidal Tracts

Part of Ventricle

White Matter

Midbrain

Brainstem (hind brain)

Spinal Cord

Figure 4—1   The Brain (vertical section of the cerebrum; cerebellum not sectioned)

scribed by the various terms presented in Table 4–1. In this section, the different clinical types of CP will be described. Information about changing physical findings and associated problems will also be presented.

Spasticity

In the child classified as spastic, some muscles show spasticity, others are weak, and still others are normal. Muscles termed spastic show a "clasp knife response," that is, on rapid passive movement of the affected limb, an initial increase in resistance can be felt. This is followed by a sudden release of resistance similar to the sudden release of the spring at a certain point in the openning of a jackknife. Voluntary movements involving spastic muscles tend to be slow.

As the child grows taller, elongation of the bones tends to increase any unequal muscle pull around a joint. For example, a spastic calf muscle will exert a greater upward pull at the heel than the muscle involved in raising the forefoot. Tightening or **contracture** of the heel cord may result.

The four basic types of spastic CP are spastic hemiplegia, spastic paraplegia, spastic diplegia, and spastic quadriplegia.

Table 4—1   Terms Used to Describe Limb Involvement and Degree of Severity

Limb Involvement

Hemiplegia: the leg and arm on the same side are involved, usually the arm more than the leg.

Paraplegia: only the legs are involved

Quadriplegia (or Tetraplegia): all four extremities and often the trunk and face are involved.

Diplegia: there is greater involvement of the lower extremities than the upper.

Double Hemiplegia: this indicates more involvement in the arms than in the legs and often one side more than the other.

Monoplegia: this refers to the involvement of only one extremity. Monoplegia is seldom seen in CP children but frequently follows birth injuries of the arm due to brachial plexus trauma.

Degree of Severity

Mild: very little limitation of activity or incoordination.

Moderate: severe enough to be a handicap in ambulation, self-help, and communication, but not sufficient to disable entirely.

Severe: almost totally incapacitating.

(a)

(b)

(c)

Figure 4–2   A Boy with Spastic Hemiplegia That Affects His Right Side. He is seen here (a) standing, (b) playing, and (c) working.
Source: Photographs by David Luna.

Spastic Hemiplegia   In this type of spastic CP (Figure 4–2), spasticity is limited to the arm and leg on the same side of the body. Usually the arm is more affected than the leg. The posture of these children resembles that of a person who has had a stroke: namely, the arm is flexed at the elbow and wrist, the thumb is adducted (i.e., in the palm), and the child tends to walk up on tiptoes on the affected side. The hemiplegic arm and leg are usually shorter and smaller than those on the other side when the condition has been present from birth.

In comparison with the more extensively involved CP child, the spastic hemiplegic may appear to have only minor problems because one arm and leg are unaffected. However, there are many routine tasks that normally require the use of both hands or both legs. Quite frequently, perhaps due to frustration, these children may develop aggressive behavior.

Socially, the simple act of shaking hands may be embarrassing if the right hand is involved. Sensation in the affected hand may be poor with respect to object identification and kinesthetic sense (knowledge of where the fingers are in space). The child may not be able to attend, visually, to objects approaching from the hemiplegic side until they come to the midline. In spastic hemiplegics, seizures may occur, but sometimes not until the age of puberty. Seizures can usually be controlled by medication. If the hemiplegia starts after birth (after a normal period of growth and development), some other type of abnormal movement will often be seen in addition to the spasticity.

Spastic paraplegia   This type of spastic CP involves only the lower extremities. Spastic paraplegia due to nonprogressive brain disease is quite rare. Occasionally, it is hereditary.

Spastic Diplegia   This term refers to the individual who has spasticity in both the upper and lower extremities but with greater involvement in the lower extremities than in the upper. Spastic diplegia (Figure 4–3) is the most common type of CP following premature delivery. It is difficult to diagnose during the first six to eight months of the child's life. Tightness of the legs, seen when spreading the legs as for diapering, is an early sign. Because of the spasticity, the legs tend to cross. This tendency is demonstrated well when the child is held suspended in an upright position.

The eyes are often crossed, although the child may be bright-eyed and alert. Speech usually develops early. However, visual-perception, reading, and understanding of the meaning of words may present real problems for the child.

Spastic Quadriplegia (or Tetraplegia)   This refers to involvement of all four extremities, with the legs often more affected than the arms. In infancy and early childhood, hypotonia may be the major sign, but deep tendon reflexes (elicited by tapping over the tendons near their insertion) are stronger than normal. Spasticity usually develops and may be severe (Figure 4–4). The muscles most frequently showing

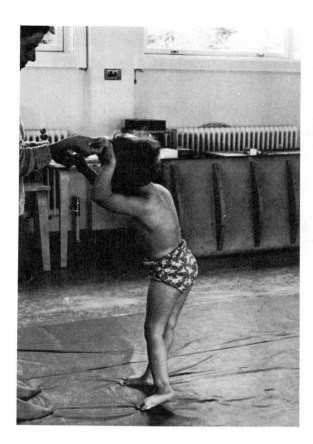

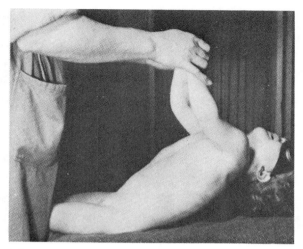

(a)

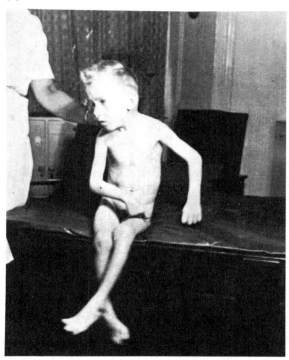

(b)

Figure 4–3 A Boy With Spastic Diplegia Being Helped to Walk. The right heel is down with flexion of the hip, and there is excessive flexion of the trunk and left arm.

Source: Reprinted with permission from B. Bobath and K. Bobath, *Motor development in the different types of cerebral palsy.* London: William Heinemann Medical Books Ltd., 1975, page 35.

Figure 4–4 Children With Spastic Quadriplegia. Note (a) the lack of head control when pulled to a sitting position and (b) the ATNR with extension of the "face" arm and leg.

Source: Reprinted with permission from B. Bobath and K. Bobath, *Motor development in the different types of cerebral palsy.* London: William Heinemann Medical Books Ltd., 1975, pages 85 and 88.

spasticity are the elbow flexors, the pronators of the forearm (which prevent rotation of the forearm to a palm-up position), the wrist flexors, and the finger flexors. In the leg, the muscles concerned are usually the hip flexors and adductors (those muscles that bring the legs together), the knee flexors, and the calf muscles (those that pull the heel up).

Range of motion of the affected joints tends to decrease as the child grows because of unequal muscle pull. Dislocation of the hips may occur prior to adolescence. Figure 4–5 shows a series of X rays of a child's hips from ages two–seventeen years. At two years, the head of the femur (the bone in the upper part of the leg) is slightly out of the socket on both sides. There was not much change by age three, but by age twelve, the left was completely out. By age seventeen, the right also was coming out.

Problems with the back are frequent (Horstmann & Boyer, 1982). Problems found include **kyphosis**

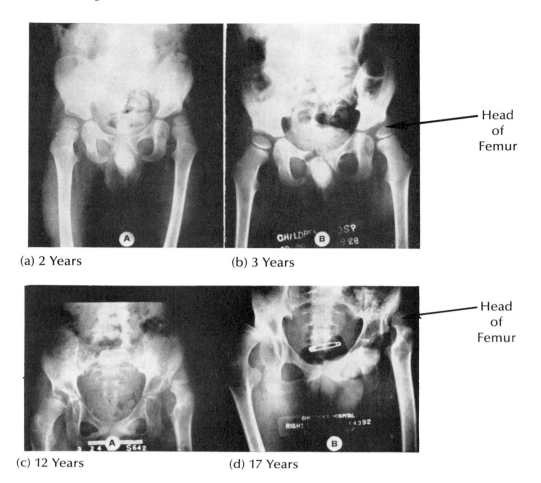

(a) 2 Years   (b) 3 Years

(c) 12 Years   (d) 17 Years

Figure 4–5   Progressive Dislocation of the Hip   Hip derangements seen in cerebal palsied children. *American Journal of Physical Medicine,* August 1953, *32*(4), 220, 221.

Source: S. S. Mathews, M. H. Jones, & S. C. Sperling.

(hunchback, usually in the chest area), **lordosis** (sway-back; anterior-posterior curve, convexity looking anteriorily, usually in the lumbar area), and scoliosis (curvature of the spine in a lateral curve, main curve, or compensatory curve). Twisting of the spine is suspected if one side of the rib cage is more prominent than the other.

Abnormalities of the infantile **automatisms** and primitive reflexes are usually found. Several of these reflexes and their normal time of appearance and duration are described in Figure 4–6. For example, spastic quadriplegic children frequently show a head lag when pulled to a sitting position. The parachute reaction may be absent or poor. The parachute reaction can be tested in three ways: sideways, forward, or backward. In the *sideways* parachute (or buttress), the child is sitting and is pushed sideways at one shoulder. The opposite arm extends to touch the

floor. In the *forward* parachute, the child is held in a vertical position and is quickly tilted forward. The arms extend forward to protect the fall. In the *backward* parachute, the child is sitting and is pushed backwards. The arms extend backward to protect the fall. Spastic quadriplegic children will also show a supporting reaction (with the legs extended and the knees straight) when standing, an asymmetrical tonic neck reflex (ATNR) that should have disappeared by six months of age, and a symmetrical tonic neck reflex that persists beyond one year of age. Also, a Landau response may be absent.

The child's facial expression may be "flat" because of muscle weakness or spasticity. Consequently, the child may appear dull. Muscles involving the lips, tongue, and swallowing are often abnormal, thus leading to problems in biting and chewing as well as in speaking. The more severely involved spas-

SOME NORMAL DEVELOPMENTAL REFLEXES IN THE INFANT AND YOUNG CHILD

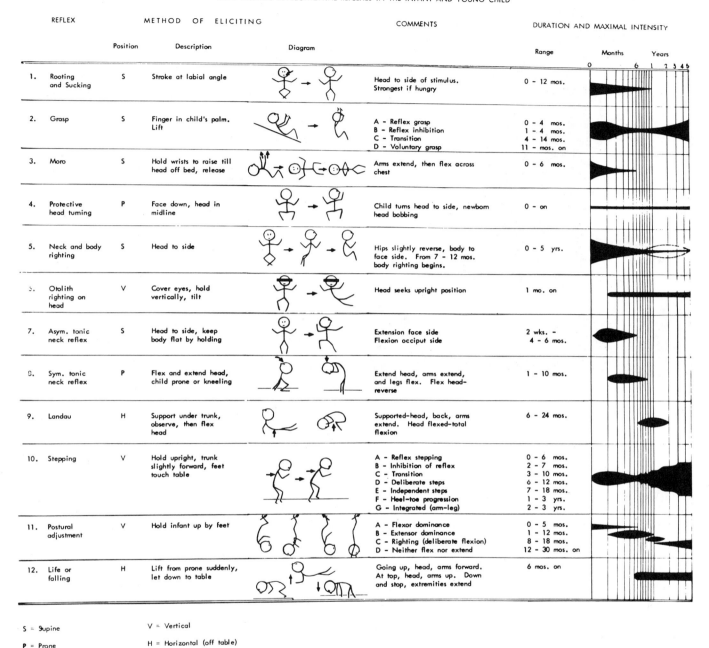

Figure 4—6   Some Normal Developmental Reflexes in the Infant and Young Child

tic quadriplegic child is likely to have seizures and learning problems, although some who have very severe physical deficits may have good intelligence. Therefore, each child needs to be evaluated very carefully.

Dyskinesia

The term dyskinesia is used to indicate various types of uncontrolled and uncoordinated movements.

These movements may be accompanied by varying degrees of tension. As applied to the CP child, the term includes athetosis, the dystonic form of athetosis, rigidity, hypotonia, and tremor.

Athetosis   In athetosis (Figure 4–7), the abnormal motion consists of writhing movements or coarse alternating movements in flexion-extension, pronation-supination, adduction-abduction, and rotation. It is not seen during sleep. Athetosis increases with vol-

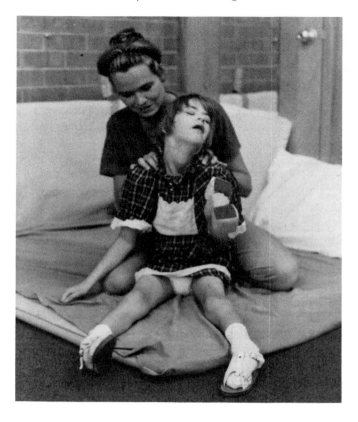

Figure 4—7   A Girl With Severe Athetoid Cerebral Palsy

Source: Photograph by David Luna.

untary movement. Voluntary motions are initially purposeful but, because of the abnormal motion, are difficult to accomplish. For example, in the hand, this may lead to an alternating grasp and then reflexive, involuntary release. This is termed the avoiding reaction. Abnormal postures are assumed intermittently.

Usually, the entire body is involved, although occasionally only one side may be affected. Facial movements are frequently abnormal and can involve the tongue, lips, and breath control. Speech as well as eating is often difficult because of difficulty in control of the tongue, lips, and breathing. Indeed, a history of early feeding problems suggests the possibility of later difficulty in speech development (Jones, 1975a).

Infantile automatisms and primitive reflexes are usually abnormal and persist beyond the normal time, especially the ATNR which may be strong throughout life. This reflex is often responsible for the poor sitting position of the athetoid. A midline position of the head is important because continual sitting or lying with the head turned to the side (due to the ATNR) not only interferes with the develop-

ment of eye-hand coordination but may lead to curvature of the spine or hip dislocation in severe cases. The older child or adult may show evidence of dislocation of the cervical spine (neck).

Hearing loss is frequent in those whose athetosis is due to Rh factor (blood incompatability). Despite their severe motor disorder, many athetoid children have good intelligence. The more tense they become, the more difficult it is for them to control their voluntary movements. If they concentrate on a task rather than on how they perform the movements to do it, they are more successful. Some quite involved athetoids can learn to perform intricate motor tasks such as playing a piano.

The term choreoathetosis is used if the movements are sudden, rapid, and jerky. In comparison with the spastic child, in which the greatest brain damage is often found in the cortex, in the athetoid child, lesions (sometimes called extrapyramidal lesions) are usually seen in the basal ganglia, the central part of the brain.

Dystonic Posturing   The dystonic type of dyskinesia describes those who show slow, rhythmic movements, trunk rotation, and increased tension in the muscles of the trunk and extremities (torsion spasm) in addition to athetoid movements. On passive motion, resistance increases as the limb moves away from the resting point.

Rigidity   The term rigidity is used when there is resistance to passive movement throughout the entire range of motion either constantly (lead-pipe type) or intermittently (cogwheel type). Therefore, rigidity can be contrasted with the clasp-knife type of response referred to in the section on spasticity. Rigidity is frequently found both in patients with spasticity and in those with athetosis, but may occur alone. It may vary from time to time. Patients with spastic quadriplegia and rigidity may show marked opisthotonos (hyperextension of the head, trunk, and legs). Mental retardation is often present if rigidity is severe. Pathologically, such patients have both basal ganglia and cortical lesions (Christensen & Melchior, 1967).

Hypotonia   The term hypotonia refers to poor muscle tone. There is real doubt that hypotonia exists as a so-called type of CP. It may be, and frequently is, the presenting symptom in a child with delayed development (Figure 4—8). It is usually transient and is replaced by spasticity, athetosis, or normal motor development. The hypotonic child's diagnosis is likely to include muscle disease, mental retardation, degenerative conditions, or malnutrition, rather than CP alone.

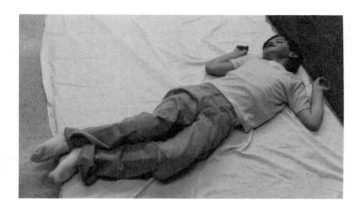

Figure 4—8   A Boy With Hypotonia

Source: Photograph by David Luna.

Paine (1963) suggested that the hypotonic children should be divided into three groups: (a) those with a family history of double joints and delayed walking but no other neurological abnormalities, (b) those with no family history of double joints, no delay in walking, and no neurological abnormalities, and (c) those with definite or borderline neurological abnormalities in the development of the primitive reflexes. He concluded that persistence of the tonic neck reflexes, even as an isolated sign, should make one suspect some central nervous system abnormality.

Tremor   The term tremor refers to rhythmic, regular oscillations of the extremities or trunk. It is rarely seen in a child who has any other manifestations of a nonprogressive condition of the immature brain. Tremor is sometimes seen after head injury, but in this situation it is coarse and likely to be irregular. Most children with fine regular oscillations of the hands have no other neurological problem. Most have a family history of tremor, sometimes beginning in childhood.

Ataxia

In the ataxic child (Figure 4–9), balance and equilibrium are poor. Specific tests to identify ataxia include: the finger-to-nose test (coarse oscillations of the finger are seen, they become more prominent as the finger approaches the nose); Rhomberg (balance in standing with the feet together and the eyes closed is not possible); walking (wide-base stance, the feet raised too high, gait staggering and reeling); and heel-toe walking (placing one foot directly in front of another while walking a straight line is not possible). Nystagmus is often present.

In the very young child or one with severe handicap, it is very difficult to perform some of these tests. Poor balance and equilibrium may also be due to muscle weakness. Pure ataxia is rare among those with CP, but some ataxia may be present together with athetosis or spasticity (see the section on etiology).

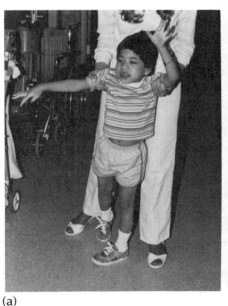  

(a)   (b)   (c)

Figure 4—9   A Girl With Ataxia (a & b). She wears a special weighted jacket (c) for better balance and coordination.

Source: Photographs by David Luna.

Mixed Types

As has been suggested previously, any of the above motor patterns may be, and often are, found in the same individual at the same time. One pattern may be so dominant that it obscures the others; or diagnosis and treatment may focus on the dominant pattern to the neglect of the others. Yet, because pure types are rare and the child is not affected solely by the dominant movement patterns, it is important to observe for signs of the other types of CP. This is especially true in the more severely involved children.

Changing Physical Findings

Regular, periodic examinations are essential in evaluating the motor problems of the CP child. A lack of definite etiology or knowledge of specific pathology in the individual case often makes definite diagnosis difficult. In a young child, for example, hypotonia may predominate but later give way to spasticity as the child grows. Clumsiness in a young child may be difficult to classify. Is it due to ataxia, athetosis, or immaturity? In a study of seven infants with varying but definitely abnormal motor signs on initial evaluation (five had a clear history of cerebral insult at birth), all were considered to have CP (Paine, 1964). However, on follow-up, all seven had lost evidence of motor abnormality; three were mentally retarded and the others were normal. In another study (Hanson, Berenberg, & Byers, 1970), this time with three children, an early acute episode resulted in a diagnosis of CP with rather stable mild motor deficit. Somewhere between the ages of eight–fourteen years, each child rather rapidly developed more severe extrapyramidal motor disability (dyskinesia). Nelson and Ellenberg (1982) made a follow-up study of 229 children diagnosed at age one as having CP; about 50 percent were free of motor handicap by seven years of age. However, approximately 20 percent of the children whose motor signs had resolved were found to be mentally retarded. Nonfebrile seizures, abnormalities in speech articulation and extraocular movements, and certain abnormalities of behavior were more frequent among the children who "outgrew" CP than in the general population.

Associated Medical Problems

Problems commonly associated with CP include ophthalmalogical problems, hearing loss, tactile-kinesthetic loss, abnormalities of the oropharyngeal area, and convulsions.

Ophthalmalogical Problems   These problems are present in 50 percent or more of CP children. Strabismus (crossed eyes) or lack of following with both eyes simultaneously is most frequent. If the child continually uses only one eye, the visual ability in the unused eye may diminish. Use of the eyes alternately may preserve vision in both, but binocular vision will not develop. Nearsightedness or farsightedness may be found, as well as other deficits.

Hearing Loss   Hearing problems are found in approximately 25 to 35 percent of CP children. Loss is usually due to nerve deafness or to ear infections. A hearing loss is often not suspected until audiometric testing is done. A child with repeated ear infections may experience great difficulty in interpersonal relations because of the varying ability to hear. Special hearing tests may be needed for very young children and those with severe CP.

Tactile-Kinesthetic Sensory Loss   This can occur especially in the spastic hemiplegic child's hand, but may also occur in those with spastic quadriplegia. The child's tactile sense is diminished, although not in the sense of pain (as to a pinprick), but in the ability to discriminate. The child may not be able to differentiate two points on the skin if they are close together. He may be unable to identify familiar objects by feeling them. The child's muscle sense (proprioception), which is needed to know where, for example, a finger is in space, may be poor.

Abnormalities of the Oropharyngeal Area
Problems in eating and in speaking are found in about 40 percent of CP children (Lagergren, 1981). This is to be expected because the postural and righting reflexes, which are often abnormal, involve the muscles of the head, neck, mouth, tongue, jaw, and throat. Problems may occur because of the bite, rooting, and gag reflexes. The bite reflex is tested by placing a tongue stick between the teeth. It normally disappears by age five months. The rooting reflex involves touching the lips at the side of the mouth (the head will turn to the side that was touched). This reflex is normally present from birth to three months of age. To elicit the gag reflex, the back of the tongue and the pharynx are touched with a sterile cotton swab.

Several other problems can also occur. The child's lips may have abnormal tone. The child may have difficulty placing the tongue laterally up or down. The position of the child's head, mouth, and tongue in relation to his body position may be abnormal. The child may involuntarily open his mouth when his head and body extend. He may have problems breathing through his nose, and exhalation may be irregular and poorly controlled. The position of the child's head when he swallows may be abnormal.

Convulsions Convulsions (seizures) occur in about 30 percent of those with CP as compared to 0.5 percent of the general population. In a retrospective study of 250 CP adults who participated in a vocational training program, a total of 32 percent had seizures (Jones & Maschmeyer, 1958). However, 17 percent reported seizures only up to six years of age, and 5 percent had seizures that continued from birth until age sixteen. The remaining 10 percent had seizures that continued into adulthood. In the last group, some had very severe physical disability (mainly spasticity, rigidity, or both) and seizure control was most difficult. Others had hemiplegia. Their seizures could usually be well controlled by medication, but they were often dependent upon anticonvulsant medication throughout life. The seizures seen in this group resembled those in the general population, and the medications used to control them were equally effective.

DIAGNOSIS

What does the physician look for in diagnosing CP in a child who has delayed motor development? To the physician, there are six questions to be answered when evaluating a child for suspected CP. Each question represents a major area that guides the diagnostic evaluation.

1. Is there a disorder of motor development? What are the characteristics of the child's spontaneous movements and voluntary movements? What is the status of the child's developmental reflexes, muscle tone, and strength?
2. Is the condition progressive?
3. Is there some abnormality that suggests a specific syndrome or disease?
4. In addition to the problems in motor function, what sensory deficits are present?
5. Does the child have any other medical problems or evidence of mental retardation or behavioral difficulties?
6. Are any environmental factors affecting the child's growth and development?

Each of these questions, in turn, will be discussed in this section. A summary of the information to be gathered in the diagnostic evaluation is presented in Table 4–2.

Table 4–2 Summary of Information Gathered in a Diagnostic Evaluation

Medical	Type, degree, and extent of the cerebral palsy
Associated Handicaps	Vision
	Eye coordination
	Hearing
	Oropharyngeal and speech
	Tactile sensory loss
	Kinesthetic sensory loss
	Seizures (controlled?)
	Learning problems
Measurements	Head
	circumference (% of normal)
	Weight (% of normal)
	Height (% of normal)
Period of Onset	(prenatal, perinatal, postnatal)
Etiological factors	
Abnormalities suggestive of some syndrome	
Medical problems other than those listed above	
Environmental factors of importance in management	

Is There a Disorder of Motor Development?

In the medical evaluation of the infant and young child, knowledge of normal growth and development and use of charts that show primitive and righting reflex development provide tools for identifying deviations from normal growth and development. Charts for head circumference and for weight and height are also needed.

From the pediatric viewpoint, getting acquainted and establishing contact and communication with the child is the first step. This is important because it is difficult and usually unsatisfactory to assess motor problems without the child's cooperation and relaxation. To do this, observation optimally occurs before undressing the child. The pediatrician will observe the child's alertness, interest in persons and things, response to auditory and visual stimuli, evidence of squint, and spontaneous posture and movement. Next, the child's ability to fix and follow objects will be tested. The physician may use a red ball or other object that is held first in the midline, then slowly moved laterally and vertically. Next, the child's hearing will be checked. The physician will present a rattle or small bell lateral to each ear, being careful that the child does not see his motions. The physician will watch for head turning or quieting to the sound.

Following observation, the physician will remove the child's clothes and look for abnormalities in the skin (including palmar creases) and the body (any body structure that seems abnormal). Muscle strength and tone can be evaluated. The physician would then check range of motion in the joints and look for characteristics of the different types of CP. Spasticity can be determined by quick extension of the joint, which elicits a clasp-knife reaction. In the ankle, quick dorsiflexion (i.e., bringing the foot up quickly) may lead to repeated jerky motions (clonus) of the foot. In a muscle with rigidity, resistance will be felt throughout the stretching of the muscle. In a muscle with athetosis and tension, rapid repeated stretching often causes decreased muscle tension. If rigidity is severe, it may mask the presence of spasticity or athethosis.

The deep tendon reflexes (DTR) are tested by tapping the tendon of the muscle near its insertion in the bone. In the spastic muscle, the response is hyperactive. In the other types of CP, the response may be normal or decreased. If rigidity is severe, a DTR response may not be obtained. The **Babinski reflex** is a sign relating to the pyramidal tract. It is elicited by stroking the lateral border of the sole with a blunt object. It is positive if the great toe extends and the other toes flair.

Developmental reflexes (see Figure 4–6) should be checked in relation to the child's chronological age. Some reflexes are not normally present until a certain age, some disappear normally at a certain age, and some normally persist. Therefore, regular, periodic evaluations are needed for the infant and young child. By the end of the first year, all of the primitive reflexes should have appeared and disappeared, and all of the righting, parachute, and equilibrium responses should be present.

Is the Condition Progressive?

It is important to determine whether the motor problem has shown any deterioration other than what might be expected from the basic problem. So-called secondary deformities such as contractures, curvatures of the spine, and dislocation of the hip will add to the child's problems, but they do not indicate a change in the condition of the brain.

Is There a Specific Syndrome or Disease?

Differential diagnosis is important because there are many conditions that include spasticity, rigidity, dys-

kinesia, or other abnormalities of motion, but are based on neurological, metabolic, or other conditions that are usually progressive (unlike CP). Also, various syndromes are known to show motor abnormalities similar to those in CP.

What Sensory Deficits are Present?

Because sensory deficits are common among those with CP, management of the problems greatly depends on early identification and treatment.

Are There Any Other Medical, Learning, or Behavior Problems?

CP children are, of course, subject to other medical conditions as are other children. Some will have learning problems and some will have behavior problems that are indirectly related or totally unrelated to their CP.

Are Environmental Factors Affecting Growth and Development?

Family relations, emotional problems, and community resources need to be known. These factors can greatly influence a child's progress and status. Without adequate information about the role these factors may be playing, suitable plans for management cannot be developed.

TREATMENT

In addition to normal child care, treatment of the child with CP involves (a) techniques for improving motor function, including feeding problems, (b) overcoming contractures and deformities, (c) correcting, if possible, deficits in sensory function, (d) helping develop a means of communication if speech is not satisfactory, (e) using medications as needed for seizure control and behavior, and for improving muscle tone, and (f) assisting parents and teachers in helping the child to develop personality traits that, despite the disability, will permit optimal functioning in society.

Motor Function and Speech

Motor function Improvement of motor functioning is the goal of the therapists. Their role involves not just hands-on treatment, but also teaching the family and school personnel ways of handling the child during daily activities, proper sitting arrangements, opportunities for standing, locomotion, feeding, etc. This is perhaps their most important role.

Many techniques have been proposed to improve motor function. Some of these are outlined briefly below. Many of these techniques are discussed in more detail in Gillette (1969).

Crothers, a pediatrician, counseled the parents to be more relaxed and accepting toward their child with CP, thereby allowing the child to develop unhampered by the restrictive bonds of overprotection. He appreciated the necessity for movement and participation in meaningful activities. However, he denied the efficacy of the specific measures of the physical and occupational therapist.

Phelps, an orthopedist, evolved a treatment system for CP that retained some techniques that were part of the conventional treatment for poliomyelitis, and added training in the patterns and inhibition of movement. He employed both physical and occupational therapists and braces or supportive equipment. In treatment for spasticity, weak muscles were strengthened and spastic muscles were stretched or braced. Surgery was seldom used.

Deaver, a physiatrist, had a philosophy that centered about functional activities and independence. Extensive bracing was used to maintain all segments of the body in normal alignment.

Fay, a neurosurgeon, and *Doman,* a physical therapist, developed a program that follows the successive stages of locomotion adopted by animals as they ascend the evolutionary scale. Motion is elicited by facilitating the abnormal reflex patterns present in the brain-injured child. Therapy is stated to be directed toward the central nervous system and its control mechanisms. The Doman-Delacato system is an outgrowth of this approach. Techniques consist of four, five-minute periods daily of "patterning," which involves about five adults, one turning the child's head and one at each extremity, to carry out specific patterns of movement. The child also goes through the stages of crawling, creeping, and walking. Development of "cerebral dominance" is promoted.

Brunnstrom, a physical therapist, utilized synergistic movement patterns that first develop in fetal life in order to develop purposeful motion. This technique is most appliable to those who have spasticity.

Berta *Bobath,* a physical therapist, and Karel *Bobath,* a physician, developed a system based on the principle of reflex postural adjustment. Their premise was that the CP child's chief obstacle to performance of normal movements is impairment of the postural reflex mechanisms. Their hypothesis was that patterns of normal postural adjustment could be facilitated by specific techniques of handling the child. These techniques involve using righting reflexes and equilibrium reactions to inhibit abnormal movements while simultaneously stimulating and developing normal postural responses. The Bobaths believe that normal movement patterns in developmental sequence can be obtained in the infant or young child who has moderate involvement.

Kabat, a physiatrist and neurophysiologist, developed a therapeutic system directed toward increasing voluntary muscle contraction by increasing excitation (stimulation). Mass movement patterns that are spiral and diagonal in direction (such as those found in the golf swing or backhand tennis stroke) are used. In the young or uncooperative patient, maximal resistance is obtained through functional activities.

Rood, an occupational and physical therapist, places equal emphasis on both sensory and motor aspects of movement. Her goal is to activate muscles through sensory receptors in order to develop a sequence of "developmental patterns." Different stimuli are used over what she terms light work muscles as compared to those considered heavy work muscles. Co-contraction is facilitated for joint stability. Therapy in the infant and young child whose patterning movements have not been established aims to develop an awareness of a normal pattern.

Ayres, an occupational therapist and educational psychologist, developed a sensory integration approach with the goal of using sensory stimulation to strengthen neural integration. The techniques focus on the vestibular systems (systems relating to the inner ear and having to do with balance) and the somato-sensory systems (sensory systems of the body). For adequate balance reactions, purposeful play activities are designed to provide appropriate stimulation to the vestibular apparatus and to the sensory nerves of the muscles and tendons. Swings, rotary equipment, scooters, and other pieces of play equipment are selected. Matching the therapeutic activity to the child's developmental level is essential for appropriate learning and responses.

Rolf, a neurochemist, developed an approach called structural integration. This is concerned with the alignment of the different parts of the body in relation to gravity. The basis of the technique developed is that the fascia (connective tissue that envelops the body beneath the skin and encloses the muscles) is an intricate web. Fascia is elastic. Injury or infection may damage this tissue. The application of pressure is hypothesized to provide energy that results in a change in the physical-chemical properties of the collagen (a chemical compound in the fascia) to increase elasticity in the fascia. Thus, pressure over tendons and muscles that seem "glued together" frees them.

By definition, those classified as having CP have some abnormality present in the brain. This does not change with therapy. However, therapy can help a child learn to live more effectively despite those problems; to "get around them" better.

Feeding   Because the primitive reflexes (especially the total body extension and the ATNR) involve the head and neck, it is important to test these reflexes in order to determine the best position for feeding. Often, special seating is needed to restrain the child's trunk and head in midline position, with the head slightly flexed. If the head is extended, the pharynx is widened in an anterior posterior direction. Then, liquids slide down as through a tube, and little or no muscle action is needed. Although nourishment may be given in this way, the child does not learn to use the lips, tongue, and muscles of the pharynx that are needed for swallowing. The mandible may not move easily from side to side. Therefore, the child may need help in learning how to chew. Also, the ability to breathe through one's nose is needed for normal swallowing. Therefore, it is important to check nasal breathing before trying to teach the child to swallow with his mouth closed. If the lips are weak, then activities such as kissing, lip smacking, pursing the lips, and blowing can be helpful. Placing a tiny bit of peanut butter at the sides of the lips and encouraging the child to try to find it may help the child to develop tongue-tip motion. For further discussion of the treatment of feeding problems, the reader is referred to Mueller (1972).

Contractures and Deformities

The orthopedist evaluates the child's posture, locomotion, and hand function to determine whether contractures or deformities are developing. He looks at the child's movements in various positions—standing, sitting, and lying (supine and prone)—and checks for asymmetries and spinal curvatures as well as functional abilities. He considers the type of motor problem or problems present. Contractures are most likely to be found at the hip (flexion and adduction), the knee (flexion), and ankle (plantar flexion, inversion, or eversion), the shoulder (adduction), the elbow (flexion), the forearm (pronation), and the wrist and fingers (flexion). Contractures occur most often in those who have spasticity, but can occur in those with other types of CP if abnormal positions are maintained over long periods of time. Muscle weakness is often found in the muscles that oppose those having spasticity. For example, the dorsiflexors of the foot, used to bring the foot up, are weak as compared to the spastic calf muscles, which bring the heel up.

Braces are recommended to help keep the body in good alignment. Braces are commonly used to treat curvature of the spine. In the lower leg of a child who walks up on the toes, bracing may be used to keep the foot at the proper angle. In the upper extremities, splints may be used to stretch wrist flexion tightness or to improve hand function.

Walking aids include canes of various types, including some with four "feet" so they can stand alone. Walkers, again of many types, may also be advisable. So-called "ring walkers" that allow the child to sit and to stand provide a means of locomotion, but they do not help the child develop good foot placement on the floor nor the balance needed for independent walking. Special equipment is often helpful. For example, the prone stander (Figure 4–10) permits standing with good foot and body position and gives support to the trunk, thus extending the back which is often curved forward because of prolonged sitting. On the prone stander, good eye-hand coordination may be attained.

The amount of energy required for certain goals and activities, such as independent walking, may limit their practicality (Waters, Hislop, & Perry, 1978). Wheelchairs, manual or electric, may be optimal for everything except standing or transferring from one place to another. Electric go carts or other suitable equipment can often be handled successfully by children three–five years of age or younger, even if they have severe physical problems. The earlier that children can manage such equipment, the more they become independent and interested in and able to explore their environment (as any normal young child).

Surgical procedures are of benefit mainly for spasticity. They include (a) transferring muscle tendons from strong muscles to assist the function of weak muscles, (b) releasing tight muscles that are re-

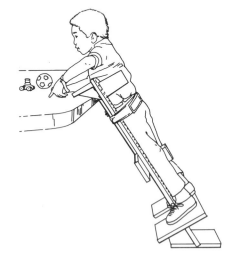

Figure 4–10   A Prone Stander (or Board). A velcro strap should be placed across the buttocks.

Source: Reprinted with permission from J. L. Bigge, *Teaching individuals with physical and multiple disabilities,* 2nd ed. Columbus, Ohio: Charles E. Merrill, 1982, p. 28.

stricting joint movement, and (c) surgery on the bones (for example, on the foot to improve its position in standing or to repair or replace a dislocated hip). Electromyographic (EMG) studies of involved muscles (usually done by placing needle electrodes in the muscles to be tested) are now being carried out in some hospitals in order to study more precisely which are the principal muscles involved (Perry & Hoffer, 1977). EMG studies may also be done after surgery to reevaluate muscle function. Surgical stabilization of the spine is sometimes necessary. Sometimes, steel rods are inserted to maintain the correction.

Neurological surgery has been proposed in order to stimulate certain parts of the brain. This is done by inserting electrodes over the brain or, more recently, over certain areas of the spinal cord. There are reports of success with individual cases, especially those with the severe dystonic type of CP. However, these approaches appear to need considerable further investigation.

Sensory Function

Hearing   Because of the frequency of hearing loss due to repeated ear infections (conductive loss), abnormality of the nerves (sensorineural loss), or congenital malformation, it is important to plan for regular auditory screening (at least annually) with this group of children. If a child has poor communication or is difficult to test, an audiologist who has expertise in testing young children or the handicapped should be consulted.

Repeated attacks of middle ear infection can present real problems during the attacks. Because of intermittent hearing loss, sounds that would not usually be disturbing may prove particularly unpleasant and disturbing to the child. This situation may make it less likely that a child will attempt to communicate.

Vision   Many children with CP lack the ability to fix and follow conjugately (with the eyes together). Although the eyes do not follow as smoothly in the first year, they do follow together normally (Dayton & Jones, 1964). Children with spasticity often show strabismus. If alternate eyes are used for fixing on an object, vision in both is likely to be maintained. However, if one eye is used almost exclusively, visual acuity in the other may diminish. In these cases, surgical treatment may be needed. Particularly in the dyskinetic or other types of CP, although no definite pattern of eye movement is seen, the eyes fail to move together. In this case, it may be fatiguing for the child to fix and follow. By being aware of this, the teacher can present objects in the midline and move them only slowly and for short distances. Also, long periods of visual attention by the child can be avoided.

Communication

Perhaps the most important area for teacher and parent concern is communication. Communication between infant and mother normally begins at birth. If the child with CP does not develop oral communication, first priority should be given to developing an alternate means of communication.

Currently, various types of communication devices are being developed. Some are merely scrapbooks of familiar objects organized so that the child can point to what he wants. Other devices require the child to scan letters or words. Still others use a typed output or, more recently, a voice output. Devices are only useful when they are appropriately selected and adapted to the individual child's level of receptive and expressive language functions and cognitive and physical ability. Also, the desires and needs of the child are most important in programming for the use of the equipment. Motivation is necessary for success in using the device.

Medications

For the CP child, medications are used for three main purposes: control of convulsions, relaxation, and prevention of hyperkinetic behavior. Although medications can be very helpful, they also can have very definite and negative side effects. For control of seizures, the major medications used are *phenobarbitol* and *Dilantin*. The side effects of phenobarbitol include drowsiness and, occasionally, a paradoxic reaction, hyperactivity. The side effects of Dilantin can include hypertrophy of the gums. Medications given for relaxation include *Valium* and *Tegretol* (which is also an anticonvulsant). The side effects of Valium include drowsiness and imbalance. The side effects of Tegretol can involve dizziness, drowsiness, imbalance, unsteadiness, and nausea. Medications used for hyperkinetic behavior include *Dexedrine* and *Benzedrine*, *Ritalin*, and *Thorazine*. The side effects of Dexedrine and Benzedrine include excess crying (a paradoxic effect), loss of appetite, and lethargy. For Ritalin, the side effects include nervousness and insomnia. The side effects of Thorazine include drowsiness and jaundice.

Medications should be given under direct medical supervision. The teacher should report to the parent any unusual behavior by a child who is known to be on medication. The teacher is often in the best position to observe carefully any seizure or suspected seizure activity. A brief record that includes the events preceding the episode, what happened during and following it, the time of day, and the duration of the episode can be very helpful to the physician.

Personality Development

Particular attention should be paid to personality development and to helping the parents assist the child in developing a good self-image. According to Teplin, Howard, and O'Connor (1981), children with CP will begin to regard themselves as being different as early as age four. However, these self-views and their potential negative effects on self-esteem do not appear to crystalize until the children reach elementary school.

PROGNOSIS

Retrospective studies have shown that the long-term outcome for CP children depends to a great extent on other than the physical factors: namely, emotional stability, social adjustment, ability to deal effectively with the handicap, and ability to concentrate (Wortis & Cooper, 1957). A vocational counselor (Curtis, 1968), in summarizing his experiences in job placement for a group of CP adults, concluded that the single most important factor in job placement was the way in which the parents had handled their children during the first five years of life. Long-term follow-up surveys have indicated that, of those children who attended special schools, 44–60 percent were employed or were expected to be employed on completion of vocational training (cf. Jones, 1975b).

Prospectively, a prognosis determined at birth or during the first weeks of life is often unreliable. Even when there is definite clinical central nervous system damage, some young infants will make tremendous spontaneous improvements; with today's medical advances, others may be helped to the extent that they will cope well. Current studies of risk factors in the mother and infant, together with greater emphasis on regular, periodic evaluations, make possible earlier detection of deviations from normal development. Thus, mother-infant training programs can be initiated earlier to help the parents understand their child's problems and ways of coping with them.

In the past, the greatest emphasis was placed on physical training. Today, concern for development of communication skills is also recognized as being of major importance. Use of the eyes for exploration and for communication begins at birth. If a child does not develop vocal communication, it may be possible for that child to learn sign language, even in the first year of life. Mechanical or electrical aids and computer programming can be used beginning at the toddler age.

In children over one year of age, Bleck (1979) has found that the prediction of independent walking is related to several of the infantile automatisms and postural reflexes, namely, the ATNR, neck righting reflex, Moro, symmetrical tonic neck reflex, an absent parachute reaction, foot placement, and a strong extensor thrust on vertical suspension. Studies of the energy cost of walking have revealed that some children who learned to walk with crutches or walkers during their preteen years, later went back to using a wheelchair except for short distances, transferring, or toileting (Waters et al., 1978). The reason was the increased energy cost of walking.

EDUCATIONAL IMPLICATIONS

In providing effective educational programs, the teacher has several concerns. First, it is important to understand the particular motor problems of each individual CP child in the classroom. Why does the child have difficulty in sitting, standing, or walking? Does the child need an aid to improve hand use or communication? Are any sensory problems (particularly hearing or vision) present? Second, the teacher must identify the professional resources available to consult in programming so that each child will have an optimal opportunity for learning. A child's ability to learn may be difficult to assess because of communication problems. Also, the child's previous experience may have been very limited because of the physical handicaps. Third, the teacher must determine whether the child will need special aids or assistance to learn independent toileting and feeding and to participate in recreational and sports activities. If a special aid or assistance is needed, the teacher will need to determine the best way to handle the situation. Fourth, the teacher will need to make plans for helping the parents of both handicapped and non-handicapped children to understand the advantages of integration or mainstreaming if this is planned.

Some children who are included in the CP category may have very mild motor deficits that may seem insignificant in comparison to most of the group. However, what may appear as clumsiness can make it difficult for the child to meet normal standards (e.g., writing quickly and neatly). In such a situation, pushing may make the child more tense and less able to do his best. Difficulty in processing visual, auditory, and tactile-motor information often occurs. Slowness of performance is frequent. Therefore, optimal positioning when seated or standing is essential for the development of good eye-hand coordination. Children who are severely involved often have difficulty in expressing themselves. For this reason, they may not seem to be intelligent even if they are very bright.

Group discussions among the professionals involved (rather than just amassing records for review) is usually the best method for joint planning. Psychologists are now looking not only at the usual "intelligence" tests but also at modes of learning ability. The overall average test result (IQ) may give little information to the teacher who needs to know specific areas of strength and weakness. Teacher observation over time may give more meaningful data than formalized, standardized testing (Pearson, 1969). Educational programming needs to offer reasonable, developmentally appropriate choices and opportunities for the child to make his own decisions (Bigge, 1982). This process is often facilitated by teacher aides or assistants, if available, in the classroom. If teacher assistants are not provided for in the budget, then volunteers can be utilized *if* the teacher is willing to select, train, and supervise them and to assign specific tasks to them.

SUMMARY

The term cerebral palsy describes motor deficits due to various central nervous system abnormalities that occur in the immature brain during the prenatal period, at birth, or in early life. Many, if not most, of the children with CP will also have sensory loss (visual, auditory, tactile, or kinesthetic) that will interfere with exploration and learning. Communication may be difficult or delayed for these children, and frustration may be a common experience.

The clinical types of motor abnormality are identified as spasticity, dyskinesia (athetosis, dystonia, rigidity, hypotonia, and tremor), ataxia, or mixed types. For children with CP, head control may be poor, balance when sitting or standing may be difficult, coordinated movements may be slow, and voluntary movements may be interrupted by involuntary, jerky, nonpurposeful movements. The diagnosis given for a child (e.g., spastic diplegia) indicates the major type of motor abnormality. However, many children with a specific diagnosis will also have some aspects of other types of CP. Pure types of CP are rare. The pathological correlation of clinical types and brain pathology is often poor.

In identifying the CP infant and child, the physician takes into consideration not only neurological abnormalities and syndromes that involve abnormalities of the brain, but also the sequential development of infantile automatisms and primitive reflexes. In the newborn or young infant, reliable prediction of the long-term outcome is difficult. The long-term outcome has been found to depend to a great extent on early care and treatment. Current medical knowledge is improving the outlook during the neonatal period.

Infant training programs offer parents assistance in handling the atypical tiny infant and young child.

There are many educational implications of CP. Teachers who deal with this heterogenous group of children need to have overall awareness of the different characteristics of the children. They also need to be able to work with parents and with the other professionals who are concerned with a child's care. Many different kinds of adaptations of facilities and equipment may be needed. Assistance from volunteers can be a source of help to the teacher if the teacher trains and supervises the volunteers and assigns real responsibilities to them. All of these concerns are essential in developing optimal, total educational programs.

REFERENCES

Bax, M. C. Terminology and classification of cerebral palsy. *Developmental Medicine and Child Neurology,* 1964, 6(3), 295–297.

Bigge, J. L. (Ed.). *Teaching individuals with physical and multiple disabilities,* 2nd ed. Columbus, Ohio: Charles E. Merrill, 1982.

Bleck, E. E. *Orthopedic management of cerebral palsy.* Philadelphia: W. B. Saunders, 1979.

Christensen, E., & Melchior, J. Cerebral palsy: A clinical neuropathological study. *Clinics in Developmental Medicine* (No. 25). London: William Heinemann Medical Books, 1967.

Crothers, B., & Paine, R. *The natural history of cerebral palsy.* Cambridge, Mass.: Harvard University Press, 1959.

Cruickshank, W. M. (Ed.). *Cerebral palsy: A developmental disability,* 3rd ed. Syracuse, N.Y.: Syracuse University Press, 1976.

Curtis, L. W. *Vocational placement of the cerebral palsied.* New York: United Cerebral Palsy Association, 1968,

Dayton, G., & Jones, M. H. Analysis of characteristics of fixation reflex in infants by use of direct current electro-oculography. *Neurology,* 1964, 14, 1152–1156.

Gillette, H. *Systems of therapy in cerebral palsy.* Springfield, Ill: Charles C Thomas, 1969.

Hagberg, B., Hagberg, G., & Olow, I. The changing panorama of cerebral palsy in Sweden. *Acta Paediatrica Scandinavia,* 1975, 64, 187–192.

Hanson, R. A., Berenberg, W., & Byers, R. K. Changing motor patterns in cerebral palsy. *Developmental Medicine and Child Neurology,* 1970, 12, 309–314.

Holm, V. A. The causes of cerebral palsy. *Journal of the American Medical Association,* 1982, 247(10), 1473–1477.

Horstmann, H., & Boyer, B. The incidence of scoliosis in cerebral palsy. *Developmental Medicine and Child Neurology,* 1982, 24(2), 235.

Jones, M. H. Differential diagnosis and natural history of the cerebral palsied child. In R. Samilson (Ed.), *Orthopedic aspects of cerebral palsy.* London: William Heinemann Medical Books, 1975. (a)

Jones, M. H. Habilitative management of communication disorders in young children. In E. L. Eagles (Ed.), *The nervous system (Vol. 3): Human communication and its disorders*. New York: Raven Press, 1975. (b)

Jones, M. H., & Maschmeyer, J. Seizure problems in 250 cerebral palsied adults. *California Medicine*, 1958, *89*(5), 338–342.

Lagergren, J. Children with motor handicaps. *Acta Paediatrica Scandinavia*, (Supplement No. 289; whole issue), 1981.

Mueller, H. A. Feeding and prespeech development. In P. H. Pearson (Ed.), *Physical therapy in the physical disabilities*. Springfield, Ill: Charles C Thomas, 1972.

Nelson, K. B., & Ellenberg, J. H. Children who "outgrew" cerebral palsy. *Pediatrics*, 1982, *69*(5), 529–536.

Paine, R. The future of the floppy infant. *Developmental Medicine and Child Neurology*, 1963, *5*, 115–124.

Paine, R. Evaluation of postural reflexes in normal infants and in the presence of chronic brain syndrome. *Neurology*, 1964, *14*, 1036–1048.

Pearson, D. Object discrimination learning set acquisition in young cerebral palsied children. *Journal of Consulting and Clinical Psychology*, 1969, *33*, 478–484.

Perry, J., & Hoffer, M. M. Preoperative and postoperative dynamic electromyography (EMG) as an aid in planning tendon transfers in children with cerebral palsy. *Journal of Bone and Joint Surgery*, 1977, *59*(4), 531–537.

Rutter, M., Graham, P., & Yule, W. A neuropsychiatric study of childhood. *Clinics in Developmental Medicine* (No. 35/36). London: William Heinemann Medical Books, 1970.

Teplin, S. W., Howard, J., & O'Connor, M. J. Self-concept in young children with cerebral palsy. *Developmental Medicine and Child Neurology*, 1981, *23*, 730–735.

Waters, R. L., Hislop, H. J., & Perry, J. Energetics: Application of the study and management of locomotor disabilities. *Orthopedic Clinics of North America*, 1978, *9*, 351–377.

Wortis, H., & Cooper, W. Life expectancy for persons with cerebral palsy. *American Journal of Physical Medicine*, 1957, *36*, 328–344.

Leela Rangaswamy, M.D., *is assistant professor in the Department of Orthopedic Surgery at the Albert Einstein College of Medicine, Bronx, New York; chief of orthopedics at Blythedale Children's Hospital, Valhalla, New York; and adjunct attending orthopedic surgeon at Montefiore Hospital and Medical Center, Bronx, New York.*

Spinal deformity has been recognized as a vexing medical problem since the time of Hippocrates (Hardy, 1974). During the Middle Ages, deformed individuals were treated with scorn and derision. Their handicaps were considered a form of Divine punishment. Even today, the ramifications of spinal curvature on posture, **cardiopulmonary** function, and self-image present formidable problems for treatment, especially during the normally difficult period of adolescence. Cardiopulmonary impairments are proportional to the severity of the curvature. The emotional problems that accompany spinal deformities vary in nature and intensity and may be altered

CHAPTER 5

Curvatures of the Spine

by the manner in which the problem is addressed by the physician, family, teachers, and peers. Furthermore, the individual's own psychological stage of development strongly influences adjustment to the condition.

There are three types of spinal deformities: scoliosis, lordosis, and kyphosis. Deformities are further classified according to their magnitude, location, direction, and etiology. *Scoliosis* is a lateral curvature of the spine when viewed from the back. *Lordosis* is an anterior curvature of the spine when viewed from the side. *Kyphosis* is a posterior curvature of the spine when viewed from the side.

The treatment of scoliosis has changed dramatically in the past few decades (Moe, Winter, Bradford, & Lonstein, 1978). Emphasis on early detection has reduced the incidence of severe cardiopulmonary compromise and, therefore, also decreased the associated mortality rate which, in untreated cases, was as high as 30–40 percent. The ability to arrest the development of a spinal curvature is now available to everyone and it behooves us to prevent a spinal deformity from becoming worse and affecting physical and mental functions.

Figures 5–1 and 5–2 show the results of untreated idiopathic scoliosis and the earlier devastating results of spinal deformity due to neuromuscular disease. Appreciation of the nature of scoliosis and its management requires an understanding and knowledge of the *terminology* used to describe scoliosis. The normal spine has curves when viewed from the side, but no lateral deviation when viewed from the front or back. When viewed from the side, a normal spine curves forward. In the region of the neck, this is termed *cervical lordosis*. It then curves backward in the region of the chest, corresponding to the normal rounding of the back, and this is termed *thoracic kyphosis*. In the region of the lower back, a normal spine curves forward corresponding to the hollow in the low back region, and this is termed *lumbar lordosis*. These curves have a normal range; exaggera-

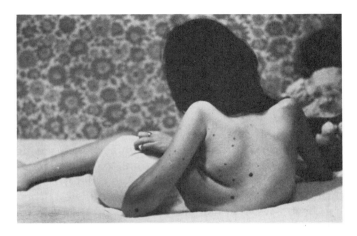

Figure 5–2   A Child With Untreated Spinal Deformity Due to Neuromuscular Disease

tion of these normal curves can themselves be pathological and produce problems.

Scoliosis is a lateral curvature of the spine. The spine needs to be viewed from the front, back, and also tangentially (i.e., with the individual bending down to touch his toes). Scoliosis can alter the level of the shoulders, causing one shoulder blade to appear more prominent, rotating the entire chest so that one side appears larger than the other, altering the waist creases, and tilting the pelvis. Because of these changes, the alignment of the trunk can be altered so that the head, chest, and pelvis are no longer balanced exactly over each other.

ETIOLOGY

The classification of spinal deformities by etiology is quite extensive and gives an idea about the diverse conditions that affect the growth and development of the spine. Deformities can be due to **idiopathic,** congenital, and neuromuscular scoliosis, and they can result from tumors, infections, metabolic disorders, and **osteochondrodystrophies.** Because of their relatively greater frequency, only the idiopathic, congenital, and neuromuscular etiologies will be discussed here.

Idiopathic

Idiopathic curvature of the spine is the type seen most frequently. It is grouped according to the age at which it appears: infantile, juvenile, or adolescent. Today, we know that idiopathic curvatures are found more frequently among girls than boys and that they run in families, but the actual cause of the curvature is not known; hence the designation idiopathic.

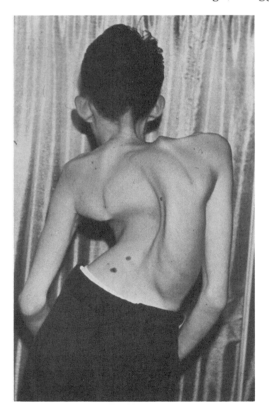

Figure 5–1   A Child With Untreated Scoliosis of the Idiopathic Variety

School screening programs have helped to detect these curves early and to prevent their progression.

Congenital

Congenital spinal deformity may be detected in an infant, or it may not be detected until adolescence. This type is usually due to an **anomaly** of the vertebrae, which leads to a curvature. These types of curves require early treatment by a specialist in the field.

Neuromuscular Scoliosis

An individual with neuromuscular scoliosis usually has associated clinical problems and requires treatment by a team of health care specialists. A large number of those with neuromuscular diseases have special medical, psychological, educational, social, and vocational needs. Although neuromuscular scoliosis constitutes a small portion of the total number of spinal curvatures, the incidence of scoliosis among people with neurological and muscular disorders is high. In the past, poliomyelitis was the major cause of neuromuscular scoliosis. Today, the common neuromuscular disorders that are associated with spinal deformity are spinocerebellar degenerative disease, neural spinal dysraphism, motor unit disorders, muscular dystrophy, poliomyelitis, cerebral palsy, neurofibromatosis, and trauma. It is essential to identify the presence of a neuromuscular disorder because this influences the mode of treatment to be used and its outcome.

Spinocerebellar Degenerative Disease These are degenerative disorders that affect multiple areas of the central nervous system and often affect several members of a family. They simultaneously involve both the central and peripheral nervous systems, and have a high incidence of orthopedic complications. Those with spinocerebellar degenerative disease have high arched feet, clawed toes, an unsteady gait, and scoliosis. Only a thorough neurological evaluation and an awareness of this entity will help one to identify the problem.

Neural Spinal Dysraphism This is a pathological condition due to improper development of the primary neural tube and the vertebral column around it. Open defects include **myelomeningocele** and **meningocele** (see Chapter 11). Closed defects include spina bifida occulta (see Chapter 11), diastometamyelia, intraspinal tumors (lipomas, chordomas), myelodysplasia, and errors in skeletal segmentation.

Motor Unit Disorders The term motor unit signifies the lower motor neuron (i.e., the anterior horn cell, axon, and terminal nerve endings; see Chapter 2 on Neuroanatomy) and all of the muscle fibers innervated by it. Recent studies have shown the motor unit to be a functional and anatomic entity and have identified it as the basic unit of muscle movement. The diseases that affect the motor unit are categorized as *neuronal diseases,* such as spinal muscular atrophy (Werdnig-Hoffmann disease; see Chapter 13) and peripheral neuropathies (Charcot-Marie-Tooth disease), *neuromuscular junction disease* such as myasthenia gravis, and *myopathic disease.*

Muscular Dystrophy In muscular dystrophy, the muscle itself is found to be abnormal. Duchenne's disease (see Chapter 9), also called progressive or pseudohypertrophic muscular dystrophy, is the most common type. Duchenne described lumbar lordosis as the commonest early sign of muscular dystrophy. He also described its progression. Gowers described the severe kyphosis and the collapsed sitting posture, with the ribs resting on the iliac crests, that is typical of these children. The spinal deformity further compromises an already decreased pulmonary function.

Poliomyelitis The residual effect of poliomyelitis is paralysis of muscles, which can produce spinal deformity if the muscles of the spine and hip are involved.

Cerebral Palsy The etiology of this form of scoliosis is unknown, but the curve patterns resemble those of paralytic scoliosis. This is a difficult condition to treat and no two cases are alike. The degree of spasticity or athetosis, status of the hips, and general level of functioning make treating the spinal deformity difficult. The type of treatment selected and its efficient completion are strongly influenced by these factors.

Neurofibromatosis In this disorder tumors form along portions of the central and peripheral nervous systems. Neurofibromatosis may first show up as pigmented skin lesions. Scoliosis and kyphosis both can result from the tumors, usually in the form of severe curves that progress rapidly.

Trauma The paralysis resulting from spinal cord trauma in children (see Chapter 12) causes severe spinal deformity in virtually all cases. The type and severity of deformity depends on the patient's age at injury, the degree of spinal cord paralysis, and the spinal level of the injury.

Every patient must have a thorough clinical evaluation, which should include a complete history and physical examination. The orthopedic surgeon is primarily responsible for making the appropriate diagnosis and outlining a plan of treatment. Members of the health care team taking care of multiply handicapped individuals must have some knowledge and understanding of the nature of spinal deformity and its possible etiologies.

CHARACTERISTICS

Scoliosis

Scoliosis is a lateral curvature of the spine and is always abnormal. In the early stages, the curve is more apparent when the individual bends forward. The ribs and shoulder blade appear unusually prominent when the spine is viewed from the back. In the majority of patients, multiple curves develop. This occurs when the patient attempts to maintain an upright position. The direction of these other curves is usually opposite to the first curve. Initially, the primary curves are flexible and can be corrected, but they gradually become rigid.

If scoliosis is untreated, it usually progresses and can result in a severe deformity. In the thoracic area, progression of the curve distorts the rib cage, causing cardiopulmonary dysfunction leading to an increased risk of illness and death. The curve distorts the facet joints of the lumbar spine, causing severe back pain that can be incapacitating.

Not all curves progress. However, many curves over a certain degree of curvature do progress, become painful, and produce altered clinical states and psychological problems. For this reason, treatment must be individualized. The etiology of the scoliosis will influence the treatment and will also increase the problems caused by the curvature. For example, a child with idiopathic scoliosis who has normal intelligence will understand about the need for a spinal brace. However, a child with neuromuscular scoliosis who has impaired comprehension presents a great problem in management. Therefore, one must first understand the natural course of spinal deformity and what to expect based on the etiology, then assess the problem in relation to the individual child.

Kyphosis

Kyphosis is a curvature of the spine seen in the antero-posterior plane. While the spine normally curves posteriorly (backward) in the thoracic area, in kyphosis this curve is exaggerated, which may be seen when viewed from the side. The curve can be sufficient to decrease pulmonary capacity. At times, it can

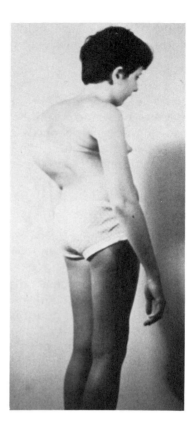

Figure 5–3   A Girl With Severe Kyphosis That Is Producing a Stooped Posture

become very noticeable and produce a deformity with a decrease in stature (Figure 5–3). In the very severe stages, neurological damage can occur with resultant paralysis.

Kyphosis can result from different etiologies. Most commonly, kyphosis is due to poor posture, characterized as round-back. This can be quite pronounced, producing not only a cosmetic problem, but pain and neurological involvement as well. Other etiologies include congenital factors, trauma, postsurgical recovery, postirradiation, infections, tumors, and neuromuscular problems. The condition of greatest concern is myelodysplasia, in which congenital anomalies of the vertebrae, usually in the lumbar area, cause the curvature. This is potentially serious because it is progressive. The skin may break down over the apex of the curve as the child begins to sit and tends to balance on the curve, which increases stability by broadening the sitting base and freeing the hands for other activities. Figures 5–4 and 5–5 show some of the problems that can occur.

Except for a rounded back due to poor posture, kyphosis usually requires surgical intervention. Otherwise, the condition will deteriorate over time due to an imbalance of forces in the front and back of the

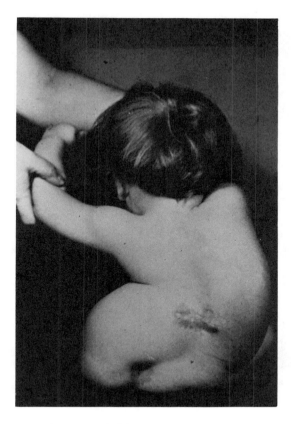

Figure 5—4   A Child With Myelomeningocele and Kyphosis Who Is Unable to Maintain Sitting Balance

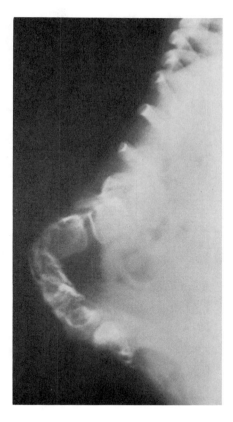

Figure 5—5   The Kyphosis in the Lower Spinal Area Becomes a Natural Extension of the Sitting Area

spine. This is analogous to a child sitting on the limb of a tree. The further the child is from the trunk of the tree, the more the limb bends. In a like manner, as the child leans forward for stability, the kyphosis increases and the atypical angle becomes more acute, resulting in irritation and skin breakdown. This situation increases the difficulty of bracing and makes surgical intervention hazardous and at times impossible.

Lordosis

Lordosis is an exaggeration of the normal anterior (forward) curve of the spine in the lumbar area. In neuromuscular disorders (particularly cerebral palsy, muscular dystrophy, and myelomeningocele), it can be so exaggerated that sitting, lying, and walking are difficult if not impossible (Figure 5–6).

When evaluating spinal deformity, it is essential to remember the entire patient. In multihandicapped individuals, the position of the hips is important in addition to the spinal deformity, because they are primarily sitters. Deformity due to contractures of muscles surrounding the hip can cause the pelvis to become tilted, with or without an associated dislocation of the bones. *Pelvic obliquity* describes the po-

sition of the pelvis when the top is not parallel to the gound (Figure 5–7).

Pelvic obliquity can be the cause or effect of spinal deformity. The problems associated with pelvic obliquity are numerous and can be of grave consequence. Severe obliquity of the pelvis interferes with sitting balance, can produce malalignment of the trunk to one side or the other, and can increase and exaggerate lumbar lordosis. All of these complications lead to greater difficulty in the management of scoliosis (Figure 5–8).

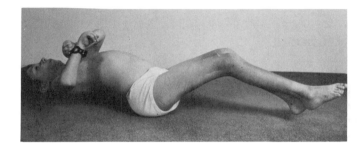

Figure 5—6   An Individual With Severe Lordosis That Interferes With Lying Down

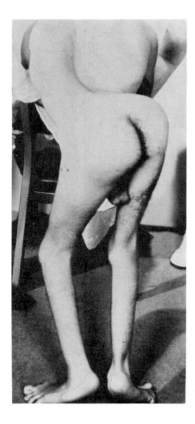

Figure 5–7   A Patient With Pelvic Obliquity That Interferes With Maintaining an Upright Posture

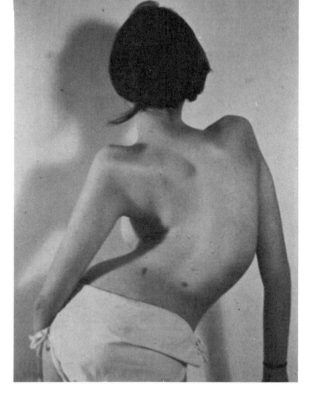

Figure 5–8   A Patient With Pelvic Obliquity, Scoliosis, and Severe Chest Deformity

Combined Forms

Scoliosis can and does occur by itself. It can also occur in association with kyphosis and lordosis in the thoracic or lumbar region, with or without pelvic obliquity. Multiple spinal deformities increase the difficulties of caring for such individuals. Early detection of spinal curvatures helps to decrease the difficulties of living with such problems and maintain good functional ability. Thus, individuals involved in helping multihandicapped children should be aware of the potential seriousness of these deformities as well as the difficulties of treatment.

DIAGNOSIS

A patient with a spine deformity must be seen by an orthopedic surgeon. Accurate evaluation and documentation are imperative, and help in correctly determining the etiology. The presence of complications such as pain, cardiopulmonary insufficiency, and neurologic deficit are also sought and documented. A complete history is essential. This includes information about the patient's general condition, developmental history, family history, intellectual and psychological development, and whether the maturity of the individual is commensurate with the chronological age.

The functional details required are determined by the etiology of the spinal deformity. To a certain degree, the questions asked and the issues considered are different when an idiopathic spinal deformity is suspected than when the spinal deformity is believed to be due to neuromuscular disease. All curvatures can progress; however, in individuals with neuromuscular disease, both the curve and the disease progress. This difference is crucial because the outcome of the disease and the choice of treatment are influenced by the etiology of the spinal deformity. The prognosis is also affected and altered by the characteristics of the spinal deformity.

The evaluation of a patient with a spinal deformity begins with a history and a physical examination. In addition, an X-ray evaluation is an important feature in selecting the appropriate mode of treatment.

In idiopathic spinal deformity, the decision to treat is usually based upon and influenced by:
1. The child's chronological age;
2. The bone age;
3. The degree of curvature;

4. The rate of progression;
5. The X-ray findings;
6. The type of curvature;
7. The patient's cardiopulmonary status;
8. The clinical picture;
9. Any associated problems; and
10. The cooperation of the child and parents.

When the spinal deformity has a neuromuscular etiology, the decision to treat, the timing of the treatment, and the type of treatment considered are based upon:

1. The underlying disease process;
2. The functional level of the individual;
   a. Is he an independent ambulator?
   b. Does he use braces or crutches?
   c. Is he a wheelchair ambulator?
   d. Is he a sitter—independent or dependent upon chair support?
   e. Does he require special bracing to sit?
   f. Does he use his upper extremities to support his trunk?
   g. Are the upper extremities involved—partially or totally?
   h. Are there contractures at the hip?
   i. What is the general condition?
   j. Is there loss of sensation?
   k. What is the cardiopulmonary status?
   l. What is the normal course of this disease?
   m. What is the mental level of functioning?
   n. What are the specific goals of treatment?
   o. What is the functional potential of the individual as assessed by the different specialists?
   p. How cooperative is the individual?
   q. What is the child's level of abstract reasoning and comprehension?
   r. What social, emotional, and economic factors are involved?
3. The specific advantages and need for treating the spinal deformity compared to the risks of treatment, particularly in multihandicapped individuals. The factors mentioned for idiopathic scoliosis are also to be considered.

TREATMENT

This discussion is primarily related to the special issues and implications of spinal deformity in the multihandicapped individual. There is no question that a patient's physical disability must not be allowed to progress to the extent that he is unable to even sit in a chair. Regardless of the child's intellectual and physical level of functioning, whether in the home or an alternative residence, the minimum requirement is that the patient be able to sit in a chair with or without support. This makes it easier for the individual to

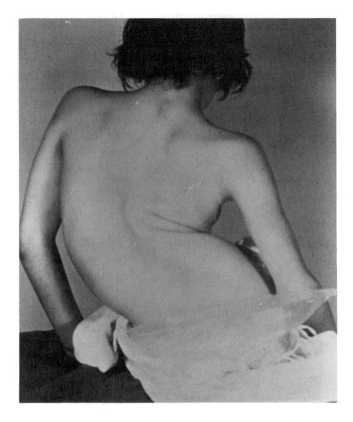

Figure 5—9   A Child With Neuromuscular Scoliosis Who Is Unable to Sit Without Using His Hands for Support; Therefore, He Cannot Participate in Activities

function at his or her maximum potential either with or without assistance (Figures 5–9 and 5–10).

The management goals of spinal deformity are to improve sitting balance, to maintain good cardiopulmonary function, and, most important, to provide to the individual an opportunity to develop his functional potential and attain an improved quality of life. It is essential that an individual be able to sit so that educational, social, and vocational needs can be met (Figures 5–11 and 5–12).

The treatment for spinal curvatures includes observation, orthotics, and surgery. Treatment must be employed with care and understanding because the indications and complications differ among modes of treatment and are different in neuromuscular spinal deformities as compared to idiopathic scoliosis.

Observation

This is the most difficult and important modality. Observation is used in minimal idiopathic scoliosis in younger patients. However, it also has a role in the multiply handicapped individual. Observation gives one the opportunity to know the patient thoroughly,

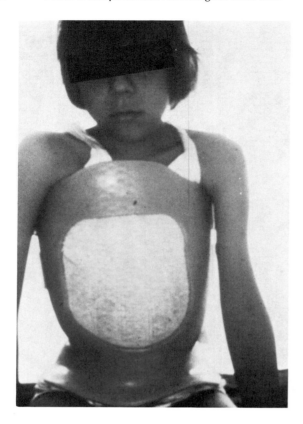

Figure 5–10   The Support Allows This Child to Use His Hands for Other Activities

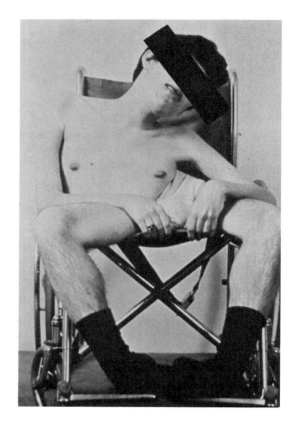

Figure 5–11   A Patient Who Is Unable to Sit in a Wheelchair Because of Neuromuscular Spinal Deformity

to assess the potential function, and to identify the goals for the particular patient. Patients with progressive curves who are still attempting to sit may be observed over a period of time while the functional ability and skills are being improved. This allows assessment of the patient's ability to tolerate a particular treatment modality, and selection of the mode that best meets the patient's total needs. Patients with associated problems and deformities usually require bracing or surgery unless the deformity is minimal and does not progress.

Orthotics

Patients with neuromuscular disease who have progressive spinal deformities often require a brace. However, in multihandicapped patients, this is only a temporary device as surgery is usually required. The patient may have difficulties in withstanding the forces of the brace that is needed to correct the curvature, align the spine, and maintain this position; and physical and psychological problems are associated with wearing a brace.

Providing stability for the patients with an unstable and deformed spine allows the individual to focus

on other problems and develop his functional potential. In a patient who lacks head, eye, and trunk control, stabilizing the spine allows concentration for developing better eye control and arm and head control. This can be achieved by a thoraco-lumbar brace or by moulded seat inserts in a wheelchair (Figure 5–13).

Before providing support to the spine (either by a brace on the patient or inserts in the chair), one must be aware of the problems and the functional activities of the patient. The devices provided must improve the stability of the spine as well as the child's functional capacity and maintain whatever function has been achieved.

Bracing requires compliance and tolerance from the patient. Orthopedic, neurologic, urologic, social, and emotional handicaps create problems in adapting to a brace. At times, it may be possible just to provide a supporting jacket that permits an upright posture, thus enabling the individual to meet social, educational, and vocational obligations. However, this goal might be met only by providing a support built into the chair. Reasons for this could include noncompliance by the patient, or the inability to provide adequate orthosis because of the patient's deformity and

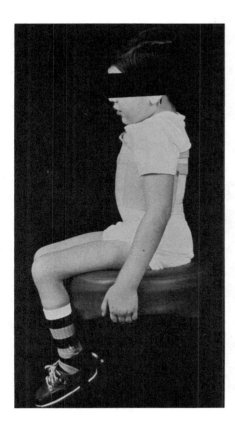

Figure 5–12   This Child Has a Brace for Management of His Spinal Deformity

Figure 5–13   A Spinal Deformity Can Sometimes be Accommodated by Building Inserts Into a Wheelchair, Which Hold the Individual Upright

general physical condition or inability to tolerate a brace.

Orthoses may be difficult to use in treating spinal deformity of neuromuscular origin because of a patient's limited understanding or severe medical and neurological problems associated with this etiology. This patient may be unable to tolerate this modality of treatment. Surgery may be the most suitable alternative for many patients. At times, it is also the most conservative approach.

Surgery

Surgery is performed to stabilize the spine. This aligns the trunk upon the pelvis to provide a stable support for sitting and leaves the upper extremities free for other functions. Whether to perform surgery on a neuromuscular spinal deformity is determined by both the progression of the curve and the extent of its interference with the child's ability to function independently and to maintain adequate cardiopulmonary function. The common indications for surgical correction are:

1. A progressive curve in a patient who cannot tolerate a brace because of a lack of cooperation or skin breakdown;

2. Collapsing curves that require the patient to use his upper extremities to maintain balance while sitting;
3. Compromise and deterioration of cardiopulmonary function;
4. Pelvic obliquity that decreases tolerance for sitting and is associated with skin breakdown;
5. Interference with the patient's ability to function in daily life, independently or with assistance; or
6. Progression of the curve resulting in a decrease in the individual's ability to function in social, educational, and vocational activities.

Some patients may meet all or some of the above criteria but they are severely impaired by medical problems such as cortical blindness, uncontrollable seizures, quadriplegia, and severe mental retardation. It is sometimes doubtful whether these patients would obtain any real benefit from surgery because their lifespan is shortened and their functional potential is extremely limited, and the risks of surgery are enormous. As long as these individuals are not suffering, surgery would be heroic but ill-advised. Surgery must always be considered in terms of actual benefits, i.e., the practicality of performing it must be weighed against the risks of the procedure itself.

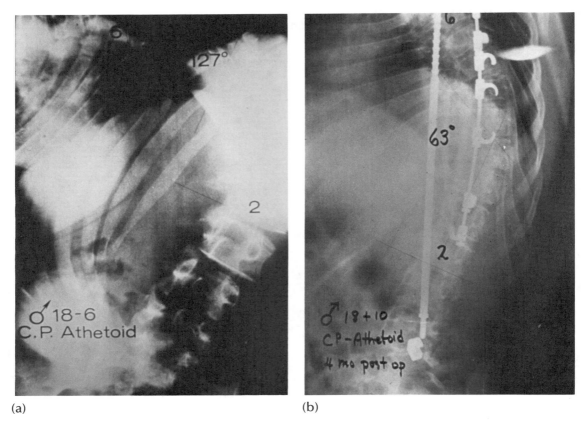

(a)   (b)

Figure 5–14   X Rays Showing a Scoliotic Deformity (a) Prior to Surgery and
(b) After Surgical Correction Using the Harrington Rod Instrumentation

In the multihandicapped, the goals of surgical intervention are to straighten the spine as much as is safely possible, and to achieve a solid fusion of the vertebrae involved in the deformity. The final result must be a vertical trunk over a level pelvis. The type of surgery selected and the postoperative therapy must reduce to a minimum the need for patients' cooperation and interference with the patients' social and educational environment. Therefore, it is best to use sufficient internal fixation so that long-term confinement to bed can be avoided. Internal fixation devices are used to help correct the curvature and maintain correction while the bone is fusing, i.e., while the normal process of bone union takes place. The end result is a solidly fused spine, thus creating a physiologic state that promotes bone formation, maturation, and union.

The most commonly used internal fixation is the Harrington rod instrumentation system used on the posterior of the spine (Figure 5–14). In neuromuscular spinal deformity, it is often necessary to fuse the spine from the front as well as from the back to provide greater stability. The anterior fusion of the curve is usually accomplished by the Dwyer system of an-

terior instrumentation (Figure 5–15). The Harrington rod system is fixed only at each end. The Dwyer instrumentation is fixed only on one side of the spine. Hence, the instrumentations by themselves do not provide stability. A cast is essential to maintain stability when these devices are used. The cast can be difficult to maintain in a severely handicapped patient.

Recently, another internal fixation device has been developed. The latest instrumentation is the use of Luque rods (Figure 5–16). This is a procedure that involves preoperative cast correction. Surgery consists of fusion and the placement of two rods, one on each side of the spinous processes. Wires are passed under each lamina and tightened over the rod. This fixes the rod firmly to each vertebra so that rigid internal fixation is obtained. The tremendous benefit of this procedure is that the spine is rigidly fixed during surgery, in its corrected position, to each involved vertebra, and this makes it unnecessary for the patient to wear a plaster cast after the operation. This has opened up a whole new era in the management of spinal deformities in multihandicapped individuals.

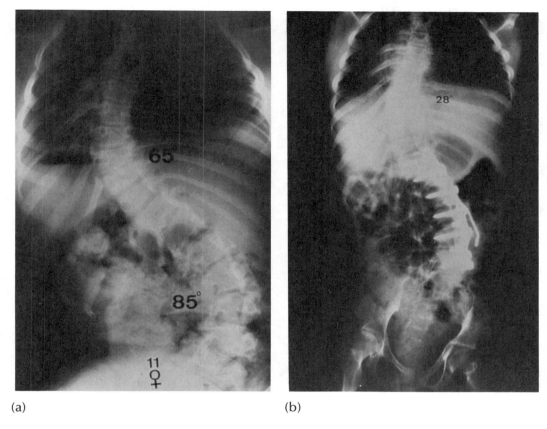

(a)   (b)

Figure 5—15   X Rays of a Curve (a) Before an Anterior Fusion and (b) After Surgical Correction Using the Dwyer Anterior Instrumentation

PROGNOSIS

Spinal deformity, if allowed to progress unchecked, can put the patient in much greater risk of cardiopulmonary failure as well as other illnesses and death. The quality of a person's life is considerably altered by the psychological problems, degenerative arthritis, and spinal cord and nerve root compression associated with spinal deformity. In addition to a shortened life span, social and socioeconomic habits are affected. Different studies show that 40 percent of adults with untreated moderate to severe scoliosis become partially to totally disabled.

In multihandicapped individuals, spinal deformity will not only produce cardiopulmonary disability, but also will impede or prevent effective walking. The severity of the curve and associated deformities in the pelvic region may even make sitting upright difficult. This is a very broad statement but it emphasizes the potentially serious consequences of allowing spinal deformities to progress.

The series of X-ray photographs in Figure 5–17 demonstrate the fact that curvatures do progress. Particularly during the growth phase, the progression is rapid. However, at times, some curves do not progress. The only way to predict the end result of a curve is by observation over time (Figure 5–18). Spinal deformity, if untreated, leads to impairment of function, which is even greater in the multihandicapped individual.

EDUCATIONAL IMPLICATIONS

Spinal deformity in the multihandicapped child can affect and alter the individual's social, educational, and vocational functioning, usually to the individual's disadvantage. Advance in the treatment of idiopathic scoliosis and increased understanding of the course of the disease have lessened the prevalence of deformity among schoolchildren. Therefore, only the problems of those with neuromuscular scoliosis will be addressed here. The dramatic advances made in the efficacy of surgical treatment of spinal deformity have opened a whole new era in the treatment of spinal curvatures, particularly among the multiply handicapped. The surgical techniques are identical for idiopathic and neuromuscular spinal deformity,

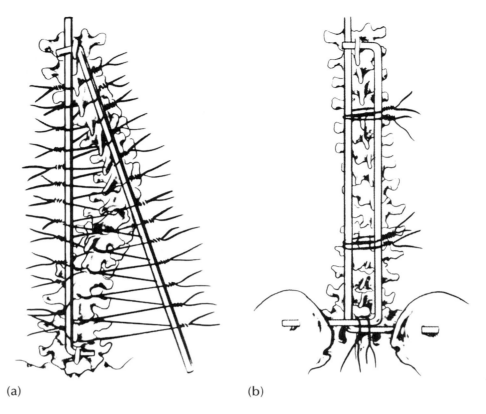

(a)   (b)

Figure 5–16   Illustrations of (a) Use of the Luque Rods and (b) the Corrected Position With the Use of Luque Rods

although the preoperative evaluation, treatment goals and indications, and postoperative problems may be quite different. An important philosophical consideration arises in the treatment of individuals with severe physical and mental deterioration: when to offer treatment and when to withhold it. The goal should not be to produce straight spines, but to prevent progression of the deformity.

The care of multiply handicapped children requires a multidisciplinary approach. Adequate care and treatment of the multiply handicapped depends upon recognizing that their needs far exceed the range of the separate specialties. Each specialist retains freedom to make judgement and determine treatment within that person's specialty. However, the treatment plans of all the members of the group must be integrated. One member of the team should coordinate the treatment for the affected individual. The member of the team who has the greatest rapport with the patient is often the best person to reassure and explain the program to the individual. Once treatment has been decided upon, particularly if surgery or bracing is needed, the patient's compliance and cooperation are required. First, the patient's level of functioning and comprehension must be ascer-

tained so that appropriate, simple, and suitable explanation can be provided.

The nature of the spinal deformity and the problems attendant upon failure to treat it must be clearly understood by all members of a multidisciplinary team. It is also essential that individuals within the multidisciplinary team discuss their philosophies towards these disabilities and develop a consensus of ideology. Failure to understand individual attitudes and failure to communicate the specific medical problems can lead to numerous misunderstandings and interfere with smooth medical management.

Another vital concern is that long-term planning must include not only medical treatment, but education, prevocational and vocational training, and employment. The thrust of all treatment should be to integrate the affected individual into the community and society as much as possible.

The role of teachers and therapists is to help identify problems at an early stage and assist with the treatment program. This involves providing psychological support to the patient and making certain that the treatment program is carried out. Early detection is the key to preventing spinal deformities from progressing.

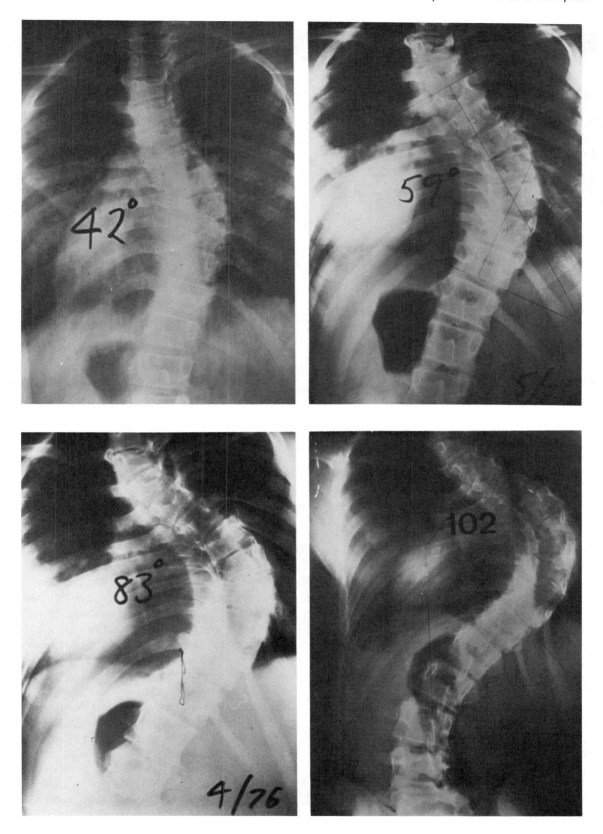

Figure 5—17   Four X Rays Demonstrate the Progressive Increase of Spinal Deformity That Can Occur in a Relatively Short Space of Time

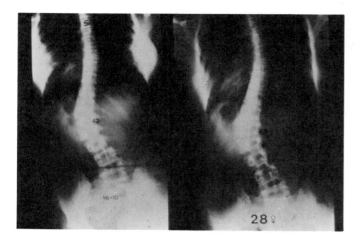

Figure 5–18   X Rays of a Patient With Idiopathic Scoliosis in Which the Curve Remains Unchanged

SUMMARY

Treatment for a patient with neuromuscular disease and spinal curvature requires realistic and concrete goals. The effects of the disease should be separated from the effects of the deformity. This is an important factor to be considered when selecting the treatment program. The ability of the patient to withstand treatment, the general physical condition of the patient, the presence or absence of sensation, the presence or absence of pelvic obliquity and hip deformity, the magnitude of the curvature, and the location of the curve are factors that determine the type of surgery to be performed and the postoperative course. The spinal curvature is only one facet of the problem. Treatment has to be coordinated with the general condition and needs of the patient.

All people have some concept of body image. The change in patients and their families, once a curve is corrected, is at times impressive and may appear to have improved function. However, one must always remember that the ratio of risk to benefit may be prohibitive; improvement of appearance alone should not be the reason for surgical intervention.

The preoperative evaluation is the single most important factor contributing to the success of the overall surgical management. This should include an evaluation by all members of the rehabilitation team. It is surprising how many times a patient's potential may have been underestimated. Appropriate equipment and adaptive changes in the environment may be sufficient to improve the patient's functional mo-

bility and capacity to handle the demands of daily living. Finally, the decision to intervene or withhold surgery will depend on the amount of measurable improvement in the quality of life to be realized. One must remember that, at times, it is better to withhold intervention in the best interests of the patient. The risks of intervention might outweigh the benefits.

The goal of correcting spinal deformity in the multiply handicapped patient should be to minimize interference with the social, intellectual, and general development of the individual. In many of these patients, one can expect little or no cooperation. Thus, the postoperative program should be as simple as possible.

The new tools of internal fixation have made spinal surgery feasible even if a patient is unable to cooperate or has spasticity, seizures, or other medical problems. These techniques have certainly made surgery a more feasible entity for the multihandicapped person, but they also have raised further philosophical, ethical, and even economic questions.

The result to be achieved by surgery is to stabilize the spine, prevent further progression, and center the head and trunk over a stable pelvis, not simply to decrease the degree of curvature. This in turn will (a) enhance the individual's ability to sit with his hands free and ambulate more easily (if he is an ambulator), (b) provide ease of respiration, (c) decrease pain due to the changes in the posterior facet joints of the vertebrae, and (d) pull the chest out of the pelvis and prevent pain due to rubbing of the ribs on the crest.

Early diagnosis is the key to preventing the progression of spinal deformities to the point where the individual's functional capacity is greatly decreased or where his functional potential cannot be fully developed. The family, teachers, nurses, therapists, and physicians must be aware of the crippling effects of progressive spinal deformities. Deformities detected early can be treated by observation or bracing or supports in a chair. Early detection also provides an opportunity to surgically correct a progressively worsening deformity at an earlier stage, when the risks are considerably reduced.

Treatment includes consideration of the nature of the disease producing the spinal deformity and of all the other factors discussed earlier. It is important to obtain rapport with the patient and family within the limits of the individual's level of understanding. The staff must have the flexibility to provide the type of care needed. It may be necessary to be firm and limit this to support and encouragement, which is possible if the staff understands the nature of spinal deformities and the ravages of allowing them to become progressively worse.

The difficulties of correcting spinal deformities and preventing progression of the curve lie not in the surgical technique itself, but in determining the need for intervention. The consideration of surgery and its timing require more than just the presence of a curve. Surgery is done on patients, not on X rays. The goal is not to straighten the spine, but to take care of patients who have spinal deformities. Thus, multiply handicapped patients who have spinal deformities must be cared for by health personnel who are aware of all of their needs.

REFERENCES

Hardy, T. H. (Ed.). *Spinal deformity in neurological and muscular disorders.* St. Louis: C. V. Mosby, 1974.

Moe, T. H., Winter, R. B., Bradford, D. S., & Lonstein, J. E. *Scoliosis and other spinal deformities.* Philadelphia: W. B. Saunders, 1978.

James G. T. Nealis, M.D., is clinical assistant professor of pediatric neurology at the College of Medicine, University of Florida, Joint Hospital Education Program, Jacksonville, Florida.

Epilepsy is a multifaceted disease of great significance to both the educator and the health professional. It is undoubtedly one of the most common disorders of mankind. There are many definitions of the term, none of which is completely satisfactory. For our purposes, we shall define epilepsy as an episodic and recurrent disease of the nervous system evidenced by an electrical dysfunction of neuronal circuitry that, at least temporarily, disrupts the function of the central nervous system.

The key to understanding the disorder is an appreciation of the basic philosophy of thought involving the seizure itself. In the English language, the word seizure suggests capture, entrapment, or possession, even when not used to describe a sudden attack. It has its roots in the age-old association of

CHAPTER 6

Epilepsy

seizure disorder (or epilepsy) with possession by demons. In fact, ancient treatises suggest exorcism as a treatment for the unfortunates suffering from this disease. The history of epilepsy parallels the history of mankind itself. It is believed that primitive man treated this disorder by trephining, cutting holes in the skulls of loved ones suffering from the disease. It can only be surmised that this was an attempt to "let out the evil spirits."

We know that treatments for seizure disorders were described in the Mesopotamian lore and laws were passed in ancient Egypt that forbade the marriage of epileptics to "clean individuals." We know from the Old Testament that individuals who were seized by devils would exile themselves to the desert to fast for 40 days and 40 nights—to cast out the demons. Although the reasons would not be understood until the twentieth century, this treatment did actually reduce seizures. By fasting for such a long period of time, one builds up ketone bodies in the blood, which are in fact antiepileptogenic (that is, they inhibit seizure activity). In 400 BC, Hippocrates described epilepsy in a particular series of writings entitled *On the Sacred Disease*. It is tempting to wonder if the Hippocratic collection was meant to discredit the "divine character" of the disease as a mere shelter for ignorance and fraud. The art of the Middle Ages and later the Renaissance is replete with examples of saints casting demons out of patients who are pictured in the classic posture of a grand mal seizure. Often, the demons are leaving by way of the patients' mouths, either in the form of creatures or as puffs of smoke. Before the twentieth century epileptics were frequently admitted to insane asylums, where they tended to have fewer seizures, according to papers written at the time. At these asylums, they often were routinely starved, although the treatments were based more on frugality than medical theory. As mentioned above, starvation builds up ketone bodies in the blood, which may be antiepileptogenic.

To be sure, the history of such mistreatment may be understood in reference to the ignorance and scientific naivety of the times. However, the injustice and superstition are not without their counterparts today. The prejudices and fears surrounding epilepsy are not terribly different in our society. To this day, epileptics suffer enormous social and professional injustices based not on the medical limitations of their disease but on prejudice. They may be virtually unemployable, unable to buy life insurance, and they may be refused a license to drive a car or fly a plane. It is not unusual to hear of teachers scotch-taping tongue blades to the blackboard above the head of a child who has had a seizure in the past "just in case." In all these situations, the epileptic is handicapped less by the disease than the superstitions surrounding it. Epilepsy can be less inhibiting than diabetes.

Throughout the history of mankind, epilepsy has survived a long fight with those who have equated it with manifestations of possession, superstition, and evil. Although a fairly common disease, epilepsy has the unique quality of combining the physical sphere with the psychic or emotional sphere in its manifestation. In other words, a seizure can either be dramatically physical (grand mal convulsion) or simply involve an alteration of behavior (psychomotor seizure). Perhaps the only valid excuse for the superstition surrounding this disorder is that, even today, certain key factors regarding its etiology remain shrouded in mystery.

ETIOLOGY

The disorder is extraordinarily common—varying between 2 and 18.6 seizure sufferers per 1,000 depending on location, population studied, and author—and generally affects children. In fact, it is said that 5–7 percent of all children will have at least one convulsion before the age of seven. The greatest risk is to children below the age of four. To make these statistics more meaningful, the incidence or prevalence of seizure disorders can be compared with other illnesses. If one were to take all of the people with muscular dystrophy, *plus* all of the people with multiple sclerosis, *plus* all those with tuberculosis, *plus* all those with cerebral palsy, *and* those suffering all the forms of cancer, they would not add up to the number of epileptics. In a very real sense, these numbers are staggering, but they only refer to those children whose seizure disorders have been diagnosed. At this moment, thousands of children sit in classrooms quietly having petit mal spells day after day after day. These children will go unnoticed and may be referred to the school counselor as having behavior problems later on in the year.

Although it is universally believed to be the contrary, the overwhelming majority of seizure disorders *do not run in families*. However, as seizures occur in 5–7 percent of all human beings, anyone whose immediate family contains more than ten people (and this includes aunts, cousins, etc.) is quite likely to have at least one relative who has suffered a seizure. Statistically speaking, one would expect that perhaps one person in that family may in fact have had one or more seizures. This does not mean that one side of the family or the other is "the side that is carrying the epilepsy."

As was discussed in Chapter 2 (on neuroanatomy), the basic function of the neuron (the singular unit of the central nervous system) is to produce electronic discharges. Generally speaking, the neuron will produce a *dipole* of positive and negative electrical discharges. This electrical discharge will be transmitted down the axon, which is insulated by myelin, and transmitted through the synapse to a second neuron. The function of the nervous system, in essence, is for one group of neurons to maintain continuous communication with all other groups of neurons and to exhibit both inhibitory and facility (encouraging) behavior on other neurons. In a functioning nervous system, each group of neurons are continuously communicating with each other group in harmony. The basic form of communication between all neuronal elements begins as an electrical discharge, which later becomes a chemical transmission of substances. Therefore, it is hardly surprising that many nervous system disorders involve aberrant conduction of this electricity or abnormalities of chemical transmitters. This could best be described as "a short circuit." A seizure discharge can be regarded as a short circuit of the nervous system. The clinical manifestations of the seizure may depend on the locus, severity, and type of short circuit coming from a particular portion of brain. Often, the clinical manifestations of the seizure will depend on the area of the brain from which the seizure discharge emanates.

In most cases, the etiology of epilepsy falls into the category referred to as idiopathic. This means, basically, that it is of undetermined causation or origin. However, not all seizures are idiopathic seizures. Certain abnormalities of brain can sometimes cause seizurelike phenomenon: tumors, benign and malignant, as well as focal congenital abnormalities of the brain, vascular abnormalities, arteriovenous malformations, and **aneurysms** are a few causes. Some of the above mentioned abnormalities can be quite serious and, if undiagnosed, can cause serious harm to the brain. A young lady, who was nine years of age, had seizures and was noted to have progressive difficulty in school for about two years. Because she seemed to have progressive difficulties seeing the backboard, she was moved forward in the classroom so that she could be closer to the blackboard. Throughout the year, she had more and more difficulty seeing the blackboard and was eventually sent to eye training experts to train her eye movements so as to enable her to see the board. She finally came to a neurology clinic. She had fluid pressure behind her eyes (papilledema), severe increased intracranial pressure, and a massively incurable brain tumor. What this story indicates is that whenever a school-related problem seems to worsen and is combined with headaches or any other neurological disorder, such as seizures, it should be a warning. Further neurological evaluation is necessary to rule out the possibility of intracranial pressure, tumor, or other disorders.

Every human being can have convulsions and no one is exempt from a seizure disorder. The level of stress beyond which we cannot go without succumbing to a seizure is the seizure threshhold and is different for each and every individual. Therefore, in a very real sense, it is a very human characteristic to be susceptible to seizures. Each and every one of us, when subjected to the proper stress at the proper intensity, will develop at least one and perhaps recurrent seizures. Understanding this concept of seizure threshhold is the key to understanding why some of us are prone to seizures in the first place. Secondly, it explains why the patient who has a lowered seizure threshhold and is more susceptible to seizures tends to run into problems in a given set of circumstances. It also helps us to understand the nature of this disorder itself. The reader should realize that the child who has even the most severe form of seizure disorder is not convulsing most of the time. He is "normal" almost all of the day. At times, however, he does succumb to a seizure. It is important for us to try to determine what it is about that particular time and place that caused that child to convulse.

CHARACTERISTICS

There are as many classifications of seizure disorders as there are physicians treating them. The classification of epilepsy defined by the World Health Organization is currently used in neurological circles. Unfortunately, even this classification has its critics. However, from a practical point of view, certain easily recognized seizure types may be differentiated by clinical and therapeutic criteria. Each of these seizure types would easily fit into John Eulings Jackson's (1890) original definition of epilepsy as an occasional, excessive, and disorderly discharge of nerve tissue. For our purposes, a brief and somewhat stylized classification will suffice. The reader is cautioned that any or all of the following categories may, and often do, overlap. The classification is:

1. Febrile Seizures
2. Grand Mal Seizures
3. Petit Mal Triad
   a. Petit Mal or Absence Attack
   b. Myoclonic Seizures
   c. Akinetic Seizures
4. Psychomotor Seizures
5. Focal Seizures and Jacksonian Seizures
6. Unusual Seizure Types
   a. Gelastic
   b. Cursive
   c. Music Induced
   d. Photic Stimulated
   e. Startle Induced
   f. Aphasic Seizures
   g. Reading Epilepsy
   h. Other
7. Status Epilepticus

These seizure types shall be explained briefly in the text that follows. None of the above categories is mutually exclusive; a given child may have several types of seizures simultaneously.

Febrile Seizures

Without doubt, the most common convulsive disorder of childhood is the benign **febrile** convulsion. It has been estimated, by various authors, to involve between 3–5 percent of all children. The febrile seizure was probably first described by Hippocrates, who stated that "children do convulse with fever especially before the age of seven." There is considerable controversy among neurologists and pediatricians with regard to many of the manifestations of benign febrile convulsions. Most would agree, however, that a simple febrile convulsion is a convulsion that occurs in an otherwise normal child and does not necessarily require anticonvulsant medication. The characteristics of a benign febrile convulsion are as follows:

1. A generalized tonic/clonic seizure,
2. brief in duration,
3. in a child between the ages of six months and five years,
4. in a child with a previously normal neurological history of development,
5. in a child found normal in a neurological examination following the seizure, including
6. a normal EEG ten to fourteen days after the seizure,
7. a temperature above 101° F. at the time of the seizure, and
8. often a family history of single febrile seizures.

A single seizure in a feverish child is quite common and most of these children are perfectly normal. These children do not necessarily need to be treated prophylactically with anticonvulsant medication; however, they should have neurological examinations. Many convulsive disorders and seizure disorders of childhood can begin as simple febrile convulsions and later reveal themselves as true seizure disorders of childhood and later life. For this reason, electroencephalograms (EEGs) may be helpful in differentiating the former from the latter.

The Grand Mal Seizure

Few afflictions are quite as terrifying as the true grand mal seizure. A child may suddenly hurl himself to the ground, arch his back upward, and become extended, stiff, and rigid (tonic phase). Then, the child will begin violently jerking his arms and legs due to rhythmic contractures of the flexor muscles (clonic phase). The two phases together are referred to as a tonic-clonic seizure. The patient may bite his tongue, causing blood and frothy saliva to ooze from his mouth. He may also lose control of urine and feces. Severe injuries (fractured bones, etc.) are not uncommon due to the violence of such attacks. Breathing may be impaired, turning the lips and fingers a bluish color (cyanosis). Vomiting may occur, requiring care by those nearby to prevent the child from aspirating vomitus into the lungs. In a very real sense, grand mal seizures can be life-threatening. Furthermore, when the seizure is concurrent to very high fever, lack of oxygen (suffocation), low blood sugar, or resulting head trauma, brain damage may occur. This is why physicians are usually very aggressive about seizure prevention.

A common question asked by parents is what to do if a child has a grand mal seizure. Usually, the best approach is to quickly move away all furniture (so the child will not hurt himself) and turn the child on his side to allow saliva to exit from the mouth. This also allows the tongue to fall to the side, maintaining a clear airway. Do not worry about a child swallowing his tongue. It is impossible. He cannot. The tongue is attached to the head, just as the nose is. One cannot swallow one's nose and one cannot swallow one's tongue. Pressing the forehead back will cause the neck to extend and open the trachea to aid in breathing. If available, oxygen may be administered.

Do not stick a finger into the child's mouth. It will be bitten. Furthermore, forcing any object into the mouth during a seizure may do more harm than good. Forks, spoons, and other objects may cut the *mucosa* of the mouth or, on occasion, cause teeth to break. A broken tooth may then fall back into the airway of the larynx and cause serious suffocation problems that require immediate tracheostomy (cutting an opening in the throat).

A good thing to remember is that seizures usually stop by themselves. The child will usually be very sleepy after the seizure (postictal depression). He will usually have total amnesia about the incident.

Petit Mal Triad

Three basic types of petit mal seizures make up what is called the petit mal triad: the petit mal or absence attack, the myoclonic seizure, and the akinetic seizure.

Petit Mal or Absence Attack   The most common type of petit mal seizure is the absence attack. More will be said of this type of attack later.

In essence, the child will be sitting in
to his teach

for a
few sec   he "tunes out"
again in midsentence several seconds, or minutes, later. The child
realize this   . Thus, an otherwise
or history becomes
as well as   dull.

The reader has just experienced a series of brief petit mal seizures. The above paragraph will be repeated.

In essence, the child will be sitting in the classroom, listening to his teacher, and suddenly black out, stare into space, and perhaps blink his eyes for a few seconds. It is as if he "tunes out" his teacher in midsentence and tunes in again in midsentence several seconds, or minutes, later. The child does not realize this is happening. Thus, an otherwise dull subject like arithmetic or history becomes incomprehensible as well as (to the child) dull.

It was not until 1630 that Jan Marek, then professor at the University of Prague, pointed out that not every **paroxysmal** disorder of brain causes the patient to fall down, convulse, bite his tongue, and lose consciousness. In a sense, Marek pointed out that seizure disorders can be associated with momentary loss of consciousness, i.e., the first absence seizure. This is the type of seizure in which the patient can stare blankly into space and be momentarily "absent" from his environment. Clinically, an absence-type seizure can involve one of two basic types of paroxysmal events. The first is the classic petit mal seizure. The second is the psychomotor (complex-partial) seizure (to be discussed later). Many ways have been suggested to differentiate between the two, although it is not always easy. The petit mal seizure is an instantaneous lapse of consciousness extending for a few seconds during which the patient is absent. The patient is generally motionless, although blinking spells or minor twitchings of fine muscles can occur. The patient is totally unaware of the seizure and there is no postictal sleepiness. Electroencephalographically, it is classically associated with a classic 3 per second spike and wave abnormality (Figure 6–1). The patient

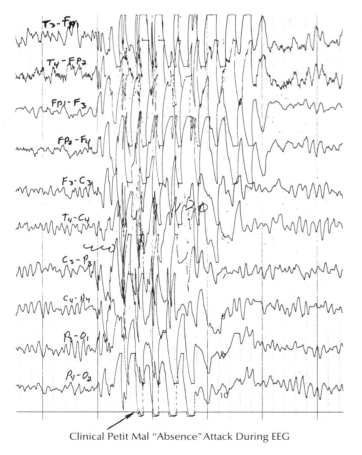

Clinical Petit Mal "Absence" Attack During EEG

Figure 6–1   Classical Petit Mal "Absence" Attack During EEG

most at risk for petit mal seizures is a girl, five to fifteen years old and, in the author's experience, this condition is as often diagnosed by the teacher as it is by a parent. For some reason, this type of behavior is often totally missed by the parent and is first brought to medical attention by an observant and astute teacher.

As we said, a child's seizures can be of either the petit mal variant or the psychomotor seizure type. EEG study will usually help determine which of the two it is, although they can sometimes be differentiated clinically. Petit mal seizures are generally shorter in duration, lasting two to three seconds or perhaps ten to fifteen seconds; psychomotor seizures can persist for five to ten minutes or longer. Petit mal seizures may occur as often as several hundred times per day; psychomotor seizures will generally occur once or twice a day or week. The EEG pattern is quite different in the two disorders: petit mal seizures give a classical 3-per-second spike and wave pattern; psychomotor seizures are more likely to show temporal lobe focal abnormality of either the spike reversal type or focal asymmetrical delta slowing.

It is necessary to distinguish between the two forms of seizures because they are treated with quite different medications. Zarontin, Depakane, Valium, Clonopin, or Dimaox can be very helpful with petit mal seizures. Dilantin, Tegretol, phenobarbital, and Mysoline are more helpful for psychomotor seizures. Furthermore, petit mal seizures can be made worse by hyperventilation. A physician can reproduce the seizure in his office by asking the child to breathe rapidly. On the other hand, a psychomotor seizure is more often precipitated by lack of sleep and other special stimuli. For this reason, many physicians will insist on keeping the child up all night before an EEG, because it is more likely to reproduce either a frank seizure or a positive EEG by lowering the seizure threshold.

A petit mal seizure can also occur in a status epilepticus variant (state of prolonged continuous seizure activity, to be discussed later). Contrary to the grand mal status epilepticus, the petit mal status epilepticus can occur as a confused state in which the child "seems out of it" for long periods of time. Such a child could be brought to the emergency room by his parents with a chief complaint of confusion. The child does not seem to answer questions appropriately, but is walking around and in all other respects appears normal. EEGs in such children can show continuous epileptic discharges. The **pathophysiology** of such disorders can vary.

Infantile Myoclonic Seizures   Infantile myoclonic seizures were perhaps first described by Dr. West in *Lancet Magazine* in 1841. The original article by Dr. West faced one on the opposite page that recommended treating intractible nosebleeds by using roofing putty. This may seem rather humorous until one wonders what some of our current scientific papers will look like a hundred years from now.

The pathos of the story lies in the fact that Dr. West was describing his own child. Since that time, West's syndrome has been described as (a) infantile spasms, (b) **hypsarrhythmia,** and (c) mental retardation. This disorder is of great import to the physician and to the special educator. Generally speaking, infantile spasms (also known as "salaam attacks") occur in the first year of life. Some of these children may be seen in special care nurseries. Many older, profoundly retarded children who suffer severe seizure disorders may have begun in this category.

The key to diagnosis is that an instantaneous neuronal discharge causes muscular activity of a sudden nature, although the activity may take different forms. The most common type is the "flexor spasm" or salaam seizure. A child, who is perhaps eight months of age, will be sitting up, playing happily, then suddenly bend forward and flex all his muscles. The child will literally throw his arms in front of himself, cast his head down, and draw his arms up slowly in a way very much reminiscent of a Moslem at prayer. This salaam action has been described as embracing movements because the muscles of the arms and the trunk flex in a manner that suggests an embrace; the seizure has also been referred to as a flexor or jack-knife spasm. Such seizures can occur several hundred times in a day or simply three or four times. Of key importance is that the child remains conscious throughout the spell. The child at play can suddenly fold to the ground, sit up just as quickly, and return to his play.

Often the family and even the physician will confuse these flexor spasms with abdominal cramps. This may be understandable because the children do, in fact, appear to be grasping their abdomens in pain. This particular type of seizure can also occur in an extensor form in which the muscles that undergo sudden jerking activity are the extensor muscles of the body. The child tends to jerk both arms upwards in what has been termed the Dallas Cowgirl posture, i.e., a posture of jumping upwards with both arms extended.

Akinetic Seizures   A third type of seizure is the so-called akinetic seizure. In this type, we have a total loss of all muscle tone of all the muscles. The child, who is often a toddler in his early walking stages, will suddenly collapse to the ground, having lost all muscle tone throughout the body. Once again, these children do not lose consciousness and the entire episode can be mistaken for clumsiness or tripping. Although this particular type of seizure disorder may be resistant to treatment, many cases respond to ACTH, Depakene, Clonopin, and other forms of medication.

Psychomotor Seizures

A psychomotor seizure can be associated with dysfunction of the behavioral systems of brain. In some people, the seizure is preceded by an aura. Something occurs that warns these children that a seizure is imminent. Children below the age of three are unable to describe the type of aura they are experiencing. A rather introspective nine-year-old once told me that prior to each seizure, he felt "like he was looking at things through a telescope backwards so everything became very, very small." Mothers commonly tell the physician that her toddler will run to her in a state of panic, grab her skirt, and have a seizure while holding onto her dress. Presumably, something alerted this small child that a seizure was forthcoming. This is the so-called "aura" that is a hallmark of psychomotor seizures.

Some children with psychomotor seizures will also have what is called a premonitory phase. What this means is that for a period prior to the seizure the child's behavior changes. Generally, this period is short, lasting a few hours or perhaps a day prior to the spell. It is quite significant that the mothers of children who suffer psychomotor seizures can predict when the child is going to have a seizure. Something about the child's behavior differs enough to signal the mother, who will empirically increase anticonvulsant medication so as to prevent such a spell.

Focal Seizures and Jacksonian Seizures

Clinically speaking, a focal seizure should involve only one limited area of the body. It may be motor or sensory, such as a transient jerking of one hand or one side of the mouth, or feeling numbness in one part of the body. These spells may include brief, poorly formed visual hallucinations. The spells are over quickly and may indicate a focal brain abnormality or diffuse medical disease.

When a focal seizure grows stepwise from one limited area of the body to become a much larger seizure, it is called a Jacksonian seizure. For example, the thumb may begin to twitch, then it is joined by the hand, the arm, and the face; then the entire body may go into a grand mal seizure.

Unusual or Special Seizure Types

There are several unusual or special seizure types: the gelastic, cursive, music-induced, photic-stimulated, startle-induced, asphasic, and reading seizures.

Gelastic Seizures   Seizure forms can be atypical. A patient does not necessarily have to fall down, jerk, twitch, convulse, bite his tongue, lose sphincter control, or even stare blankly into space in order to fit into a classical diagnosis of seizure disorder. During a gelastic seizure, the patient will stare blankly into space, then suddenly laugh. They may have recurrent episodes of peculiar and sometimes very bizarre laughter. In fact, it is a laughing seizure.

Cursive Seizures   During a cursive seizure a child will run straight full-speed ahead and knock down anything that gets in the way. The seizure manifests itself in the compulsion to run. It is a running seizure.

Music-Induced Seizures   A child might only have seizures when exposed to a certain song or a certain tune. Needless to say, an EEG that is performed without playing the song can miss the correct diagnosis. This type of seizure disorder is extraordinarily rare.

Photic-Stimulated Seizures   This is perhaps the most common special seizure syndrome. A blinking light stimulates these children into a seizure. Such children could have a seizure while at the beach. The strobic effect of sunlight bouncing off the ocean can bring on a seizure. Some teenagers only have seizures when they go to a discotheque or parties with blinking strobe lights. In the experience of the author, some of these children only have seizures when watching television, especially when the television sets have poorly adjusted vertical holds, which cause the picture to flip. Other children only have seizures in classrooms with fluorescent lightbulbs that malfunction. Sometimes these seizures can be avoided by using blue or green filters over the light or by wearing sunglasses or by closing one eye.

Startle-Induced Seizures   Once again, certain children only have seizures when startled. The precipitating stimulus must be reproduced while an EEG is being run.

Aphasic Seizure   This is a syndrome of seizure disorder in which an abnormality in the pattern of brainwaves prevents speech. The child, who may have been speaking perfectly normally, has one or two grand mal convulsions, then suddenly is unable to speak. The child might not regain speech until anticonvulsant medication is begun. The author has found this disorder to be relatively common, although according to the literature it is quite rare. It is a treatable cause of speech dysfunction. Aphasic sei-

zure is also referred to as Worster-Landau-Draught-Gascon syndrome.

Reading Epilepsy   Certain children only have seizures when they attempt to read. This particular type of seizure can only be diagnosed if the EEG is performed while the child is reading. The routine EEG is obtained while the child is awake, drowsy, and perhaps asleep, but not reading. Therefore, the diagnosis may be totally missed.

Status Epilepticus

Status epilepticus is the medical term used to refer to a prolonged, uncontrolled single seizure. Such seizure activity may go on without stopping for hours or days. This can occur in any form of seizure but is most frequently seen in grand mal and other generalized seizure types.

DIAGNOSIS

The majority of children with seizures have a disorder termed idiopathic (of unknown cause) epilepsy. In most instances, a physical examination will uncover nothing that is not completely within normal limits. Although almost any physical abnormality of the brain could be associated with epilepsy, the reverse is not true; epilepsy does not indicate a physical abnormality.

The physician will examine the child for white patches or white spots on the skin. Sometimes these white patches can only be seen with the help of a black light in a dark room. This light will cause the white patches to stand out remarkably and indicate tuberous sclerosis, a disorder that can be associated with seizures and, in severe cases, may also progress to mental retardation, brain tumors, and other neurological dysfunctions. It is particularly important to diagnose this disorder because it is one of the rare forms of epilepsy that is transmitted genetically and can run in a family.

Neurological consultation and examination of children in these families is helpful because, in some cases, the physical findings associated with epilepsy can be quite subtle. An abnormal size or shape of the head, asymmetrical reflexes, an asymmetry in the size of the thumbnails (a thumbnail on one side of the body that is smaller than the other thumbnail could indicate atrophy of the brain), one arm that doesn't swing as well as the other when the child walks, or simply a tendency to wear down the heels on one's shoes asymmetrically can all be signs of significant abnormality in the brain. The abnormality can be of a static nature, as in cerebral palsy, or of a progressive nature, as in a brain tumor.

Certain tests should be done on any child who has had a seizure disorder of any kind. These tests, of course, will always be dependent upon the individual and the situation. They might include routine blood tests (such as blood sugar, calcium, and magnesium levels); sometimes a spinal tap or lumbar puncture, to ensure that one is not dealing with an acute case of meningitis, encephalitis, or intracranial hemorrhage; X rays; computerized axial tomography (CAT or CT scan—X ray of the brain); or even a cerebral arteriogram to rule out vascular abnormalities in the brain. Many of these tests will be performed in a hospital.

One of the most common tests performed will be the EEG (brain wave). This test may be done either as an outpatient procedure or along with other tests in the hospital. The EEG is designed to record the differences in electrical potentials emanating from the brain. It is extremely useful in the diagnosis of epilepsy. Metal plated discs are placed on the child's scalp and held there with a greasy paste, then they are connected to the amplifier system of the EEG machine. A graph documents the normal electrical frequencies occurring in the child's brain. These may be classified according to number of waves per second: beta, alpha, theta, and delta. Beta is the fastest (most waves per second) and delta is the slowest. Certain configurations of wave patterns (e.g., spike-wave) correlate highly with epilepsy. There is no risk to a properly run EEG.

A word must be said about the difficulty of diagnosing certain seizure disorders and the possibility of confusion with other neurological abnormalities. A normal EEG in no way rules out a seizure disorder. EEGs are limited in function, stimulus, and duration. First, if the EEG does not test the area of brain considered in a seizure disorder, e.g., if nasopharyngeal (inside the nose) leads are not applied, a seizure disorder can be totally missed. Second, if the child is not sleep-deprived and the EEG does not demonstrate waking, drowsiness, and sleep, one runs about a 33 percent chance of missing the abnormality. Third, if a particular type of stress (e.g., blinking lights, reading, or music) induces the patient's seizures, the disorder will be totally missed if the particular stimulus is not introduced during the EEG recording. Lastly, even if all of the above conditions are adhered to, the brain of the patient may simply not have a paroxysmal disturbance while the EEG machine is running, and the diagnosis will not be documented. Consequently, the longer the EEG, the better. For this reason, the new development of 24-hour EEG monitoring and so-called neuromonitoring, in which the patient carries EEG monitors and a battery pack 24 hours a day, is sometimes absolutely essential to diagnose subtle forms of seizure.

TREATMENT

The treatment of epilepsy almost inevitably requires anticonvulsant medications. Several medications, their uses and most common side effects, and special notes for the teacher are presented in Table 6–1. Certain general principles must be stressed on the use of medication to control seizure disorders:

1. Use the least medication needed to control the seizure. The obvious corollary is that too much medication can be as damaging as too little medication.
2. Every medication has side effects. As the sage once put it: if a medication had no side effects, that would mean it didn't work. Or: no drug is as safe as water, not even water (too much water will make you drown).
3. One should try to stay with the fewest drugs possible in order to control seizures, preferably just one drug of proper dosage.
4. A physician must see the child periodically in order to monitor for side effects of medication.
5. No physician can monitor accurately for side effects without the cooperation of the educator and parent.
6. Because the various aspects of epilepsy can radically change from year to year, a multidisciplinary approach is often needed for the treatment of a given child. The team must include at least the physician, the family, and most importantly the educator. Such groups might also include psychologists, social workers, psychiatrists, nursing personnel, etc.
7. Dosages will generally need to be increased as the child grows and matures.
8. One of the most common causes of poor seizure control is noncompliance (the patient does not take the medication). Nothing a doctor does can make up for what a family or patient will not do. Consequently, it is of paramount importance that the child be given the medication as prescribed. This is not as easy as it sounds. Some teenagers will deliberately pretend to take their medication but not actually do so for many reasons. Some neurologists estimate that the most common cause of poor seizure control in adolescence is the patient's reluctance to take medication for one reason or another. The teacher's cooperation can be extremely helpful in cases like this.
9. A child is constantly changing. Consequently, the treatment may need to be flexible and change to

Table 6–1   Anticonvulsant Medications

Drugs	Uses	Most Common Side Effects	Special Notes: Teachers Should Watch for
Phenobarbital	Grand mal seizures Focal seizures	Hyperactivity/Sedation/ Irritability	Hyperactivity/Behavior problems/ Irritability/School difficulties
Mebaral	Grand mal seizures	Hyperactivity/Sedation	Behavior Problems/Sedation or irritability/ More or less hyperactivity
Dilantin	Grand mal seizures	Overgrowth of the gums in the mouth/Double vision/Rashes/Ataxia	Crooked teeth/Thickening of the gums/Skin rashes/Coordination problems/Mental dullness
Depakene	Absence seizures/ Myoclonic seizures/Some generalized seizures	Liver Disease/Tremor/Nausea/Hair Loss	Liver toxicity/Somnolence & sedation/Gastrointestinal disturbances/Behavior problems/Hair loss
Zarontin	Absence seizures/ Myoclonic seizures/Some generalized seizures	Sedation/School problems	Sedation/Hiccups/Anemia
Tegretol	Psychomotor seizures/Some grand mal seizures	Anemia/Sedation/Blood problems	Anemia/Frequent infections/Sedation/ Vomiting
Valium	Status epilepticus/Grand mal seizures/ Some absence seizures/ Myoclonic seizures	Sedation/Respiratory arrest	Sedation/Generalized seizures may worsen
Mysoline	Temporal lobe seizures/Some grand mal seizures	Sedation/Gastrointestinal upsets/Hiccups	Sedation/Gastrointestinal disturbance
Paraldehyde	Grand mal seizures/Withdrawal seizures/Status epilepticus	Sedation/Odoriferous/ Generally unacceptable treatment of seizures as outpatient	Not applicable
Tridione	Absence seizures/Some grand mal seizures	Severe blood abnormalities	Sedation (seldom used)

Table 6–1   Anticonvulsant Medications (continued)

Drugs	Uses	Most Common Side Effects	Special Notes: Teachers Should Watch for
Clonopin	Myoclonic seizures/Some absence seizures/Some grand mal seizures	Sedation	Sedation/Grand mal may worsen
ACTH	Myoclonic seizures/Salaam seizures	Hypertension/Gastric irritation/Susceptibility to infection/Multisystemic toxicity	Usually given intramuscularly
Ketogenic diet	Myoclonic seizures/Salaam seizures/ Akinetic seizures	Gastrointestinal upsets	May be added to diet as medium chain triglycerides

meet the needs of the growing, maturing, and developing patient. Concomitantly, seizures may change with time. The patient who is seen annually is quite a different child than the child first interviewed. Obviously, this is different than a 40- or 50-year-old patient who is followed for the same problem. In a very real sense, among children, one is never seeing the same patient twice. This is true both physically and psychologically.

10. Children with seizure disorders are entitled to bad days just the same as everyone else. For example, it is extremely difficult sometimes to determine whether a petit mal patient is having an absence attack, or simply daydreaming. This question is extremely important because of the fine balance between medication dosage and seizure control. Too much medication can be worse than too little.

11. Not all manifestations of untoward behavior are related to the seizures. Children with seizure disorders are entitled to behavior problems as other children. However, children with various emotional stresses related to the seizures may be more prone to acting-out forms of behavior than uninvolved children. These behavior problems could emanate from family problems, emotional stresses, overprotection, or a basic feeling of inferiority and alienation due to the seizure disorder, which might also explain some of the attention-getting behavior noted in these students.

Generally speaking, a child who has a seizure disorder should be allowed to partake in all childhood activities (sports or games) with as few exceptions as possible. Obviously, a child who has a blinking-light or photic-induced seizure disorder might be encouraged to avoid discos and parties with blinking lights. Children with trauma-induced seizures should be encouraged to avoid contact sports: karate, boxing, or perhaps even football. When a child is likely to have more seizures when exposed to head trauma, these considerations should be kept in mind. Children who are prone to seizures must have careful supervision when swimming. Older patients who have active seizure disorders may not be allowed to drive cars or motorcycles.

PROGNOSIS

The prognosis of seizure disorders generally depends upon the cause of the seizures. Children with brain tumors and significant brain abnormalities will do less well, statistically, than those with idiopathic seizures. Most children (perhaps as much as 60 percent) will eventually "grow out of" their seizures. Even during the period of active seizures, medication is usually very effective. For the most part, these children can lead perfectly normal lives, but may require special understanding and patient support from time to time. For example, a nine-year-old epileptic boy, when asked to draw a picture of a man, once told the author, "I can't do that, Doc!" When asked why not, he replied, "Because I have brain damage!" When asked what "brain damage" meant, he replied, "Well, I guess my brain must have holes in it. You know, like

Swiss cheese!" To be sure, forming a positive self-image can be a problem for these children.

EDUCATIONAL IMPLICATIONS

Children with epilepsy are not terribly different from other children, apart from having a lowered seizure threshold. Lowered thresholds of tolerance characterize other human ailments, such as migraine headaches, fainting spells (syncope), allergies, asthma attacks, hay fever, and many others. Their disorder does not exempt these children from all the normal behaviors of childhood, bad as well as good. A girl who has petit mal spells daydreams; and a boy who has psychomotor seizures can also have temper tantrums. The key to differentiating between a behavior problem and a seizure is in the individual child's history. Behavior problems, by definition, should not be treated with medication dosage changes. Without doubt, there is certainly room for counseling and psychological and psychiatric intervention.

Input from the teacher is essential to the care of children with epilepsy. Often, the teacher is the first to witness a petit mal seizure. Often, the teacher is in the best position to know whether or not a specific medication or combination of medications truly interferes with the school routine and learning. Without question, certain treatments and medications can impede school performance more than the disease itself. Because a great deal of the child's time is actually spent under the direct observation of the teacher, an astute teacher's observations can be instrumental in making decisions about the best therapy for a given child. Teachers can be the best sources for determining the side effects and efficacy of medication for a particular child. Only teachers can monitor a child's behavior to uncover learning disabilities, hyperactivity, attentional deficits, or various other problems that are often associated with seizure disorders. Only if these problems are found early enough can the child be treated as an entire person, who can be offered an optimal educational plan for the future.

When a child suffers from seizures during the school day, the information and history obtained from the teacher are absolutely indispensable. For example, it is important to know if, in fact, the seizures only occur when the child first enters the classroom and the teacher turns on the light. (Is there a flickering fluorescent light in that classroom?) Do these seizures only occur when the child is reading? (Could it be reading epilepsy?) Do these seizures only occur when the child is riding in the school bus and is it

only in the morning or only in the afternoon? (Photic stimulation can be caused by the sunlight filtering through the leaves of trees?) Do these seizures only occur when the child is struck on the head? (This could indicate trauma-induced epilepsy.) Or, do these seizures only occur at a certain time every day (say, three hours after breakfast, when the child might tend to become somewhat hypoglycemic)? Furthermore, what does the seizure look like? Is it different from past seizures this child has had? Do the eyes turn to one side or the other? (This may suggest a focal brain abnormality.) Or, does the child have chewing movements of the mouth (temporal lobe epilepsy)? What about the child's medication? Does it interfere with schoolwork, make him sleepy, hyperactive, or irritable?

The teacher is often the only person who can provide this information. Therefore, the observations of the teacher are absolutely crucial in the diagnosis and treatment of seizure disorders in childhood. Unfortunately, the lines of communication between teacher and physician are not always optimally utilized. This is unfortunate for the teacher, the physician, and most importantly for the child. With optimal communication between the educator and the physician, not only can and should the seizure disorder be better controlled, but a myriad of other problems can be reduced. For example, to what extent does medication interfere with the child's schoolwork? Is the child actually getting too little or too much medication? Is he lethargic or sleepy during class? Does the child have an associated learning disability, or does the child have difficulties with attention or hyperactivity? Could the hyperactivity be induced by anticonvulsant medication or at least be made worse by it? These are the types of questions that can be answered accurately only when the physician and educator communicate.

SUMMARY

Epilepsy is among the most misunderstood of all disorders. Many popularly held misconceptions about the disorder and its treatment are rooted in superstitions that date back to ancient times. Although there is no universally accepted definition of epilepsy, here we have described an episodic and recurrent disease of the nervous system manifested by an electrical dysfunction of neuronal circuitry that, at least temporarily, disrupts the function of the nervous system. In most cases, its etiology is idiopathic (unknown).

The characteristics of epilepsy vary depending on which of the many different types of epilepsy is affecting a person. Treatment almost inevitably involves the use of anticonvulsant medications, combined with various precautionary and preventive procedures. In most cases, the long-term outlook for control of seizures and for full participation in life's activities is good. The educator, because of a constant contact with the child and concern for the child's educational program, can play a critical role in identification, diagnosis, treatment, and overall care of the child's disorder. The reader who is interested in further study of epilepsy is referred to the following sources.

SELECTED READINGS

Baker, A. B., & Baker, L. H. *Clinical neurology*. New York: Harper & Row, 1977.

Menks, J. H. *Textbook of child neurology* (2nd ed.). Philadelphia: Lea & Febiger, 1980.

Nelson, K., & Ellenberg, J. *Febrile seizures*. New York: Raven Press, 1981.

O'Leary, J. L., & Goldring, S. *Science and epilepsy*. New York: Raven Press, 1976.

Temkin, O. *The falling sickness*. Baltimore: Johns Hopkins Press, 1971.

Wilder, B. J. *Epilepsy*. Philadelphia: F. A. Davis, 1968.

Jay A. Katz, M.D., *is associate in the Department of Orthopedic Surgery at the College of Medicine, The University of Arizona, Tucson; chief of Orthopedic Surgery at Tucson Medical Center, Tucson, Arizona; and attending physician at the Arizona Crippled Children's Clinic, Tucson, Arizona.*

Although many disorders can affect the hips of school-age children, the most frequent by far are Legg-Perthes disease, congenital dislocation of the hip, and slipped capital femoral epiphysis. Therefore, these disorders are the focus of this chapter.

The hip is basically a ball and socket joint (Figure 7–1). The socket is referred to as the **acetabulum** and the ball is referred to as the **femoral head.** All of the conditions described in this chapter affect one or both components of the hip joint.

CHAPTER
7

Hip Conditions

LEGG-PERTHES DISEASE

Legg-Perthes disease, or coxa plana, is a self-limited disease of the hip. In 1910, coxa plana was described independently by Legg of the United States, Calvé of France, and Perthes of Germany, and thus is often referred to as Legg-Perthes or Legg-Calvé-Perthes disease. An interruption in the supply of blood to the femoral head results in the death of the bone of the femoral head.

Etiology

The etiology of Legg-Perthes disease is still speculative. The cause of the temporary disruption in the blood supply to the femoral head is not fully under-

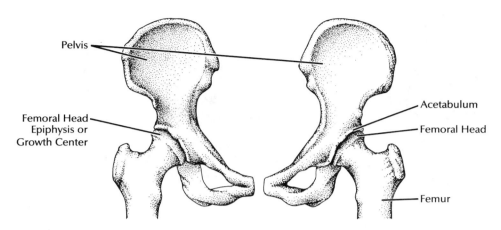

Figure 7–1   Normal Anatomy of the Hip

stood. The death of all or part of the bone results from insufficient blood, its primary source of nutrients (Salter, 1966). Eventually, the dead bone is reabsorbed, as part of the healing process, and replaced by live bone.

One theory is that a viral infection of the hip causes increased fluid in the hip joint (synovitis). This synovitis increases the pressure within the hip joint, which reduces the flow of blood to the femoral head. A substantial amount of experimental data supports this theory.

Characteristics

Legg-Perthes disease is common in children, usually between the ages of three and twelve, and is much more common in boys than in girls. Generally, only one hip is involved, although both hips can be affected.

It is first noticed when a child, who has complained of pain for several months, develops a limp. Frequently, the pain is referred from the hip to the knee region, where the child actually feels it. Physical activity aggravates the pain and rest relieves it.

Diagnosis

The diagnosis is usually made from X rays. The X rays show flattening and fragmentation of the femoral head with areas of increased density and widened joint space (Figure 7–2). Laboratory tests show no abnormal findings due to Legg-Perthes disease.

Treatment

The primary goal of treatment is to contain the femoral head within the acetabulum (socket) until the dead bone is reabsorbed and new bone formed (Petrie & Bitenc, 1967). The acetabulum thus acts as a mold for formation of the new femoral head in order to retain the original round shape. Without the acetabulum to mold it, the new femoral head could turn out flattened and widened.

The child is usually kept in bed until the initial pain and muscle spasms subside. This usually takes

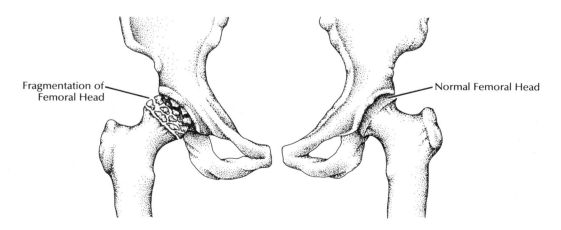

Figure 7–2   Fragmentation of the Femoral Head

Figure 7—3   The Special Brace Worn by Children With Legg-Perthes Disease

seven to ten days, at which time the patient can usually be fitted with a special brace (Figure 7–3) to keep the legs spread widely apart and the femoral head deep within the socket. The brace is worn until X rays show that the hip has healed and new bone has been formed. This will often take 18–24 months. The child usually has to wear the brace constantly and is allowed out of it only to bathe. Occasionally, surgery is necessary because the brace has failed.

Prognosis

Legg-Perthes disease is self-limiting and heals spontaneously as the dead bone is reabsorbed and new bone is formed. The amount of impairment depends on the amount of deformity in the newly formed femoral head. The prognosis is more favorable in younger children.

Educational Implications

While in the brace, the child can participate in those activities that do not require running and jumping. The primary problem facing the child is the psychological handicap that accompanies wearing a brace for several years. No special equipment is required for the classroom. The child is **ambulatory** with the brace and crutches.

CONGENITAL DISLOCATION OF THE HIP

In a congenital **dislocation** of the hip (Figure 7–4) the femoral head is displaced from the acetabular socket. It occurs while the fetus is in the womb or shortly after birth.

Etiology

The primary cause of a congenitally dislocated hip is unknown, although many factors seem to play a role (Smith, Coleman, Olix, & Sloger, 1963). Genetic factors are quite important and 20–30 percent of the babies with this disorder have a family history of the problem. Ligamentous laxity during the first days following birth also appears to be important. The **ligaments** that help hold the femoral head in the socket are affected by the maternal sex hormones, which are secreted by the mother just prior to labor to help relax the birth canal ligaments. Also, a breech presentation of the fetus during birth seems to be important. In the breech position, the hips are flexed and the knees extended. During delivery, the hips are extended and traction is applied to the lower limbs. This could force the femoral head out of the socket.

Characteristics

If is often difficult to recognize congenital dislocation of the hip in early infancy. It takes a very careful physical examination by the pediatrician and a strong suspicion to pick it up early. Timing is crucial because if it is detected in the first days of life, the treatment is simple. If it is not discovered until the child begins to walk or reaches school age, the treatment will be much more complex and the results are usually not as good. In younger children, the displacement causes no pain and impedes leg function very little.

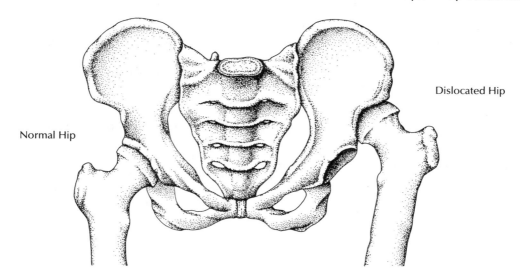

Figure 7–4   Congenital Dislocation of the Hip

However, as children grow older, they may tire easily and have pain with some activities. If both hips are dislocated, the person will walk with a characteristic duck waddle.

Diagnosis

The diagnosis is usually made by careful examination of the child and confirmed by X-ray changes. Right after birth, most children are checked by a pediatrician for the possibility of a dislocated hip. The examiner will actually try to piston the hip to make sure the head is in the socket (Figure 7–5). If a click is felt, it

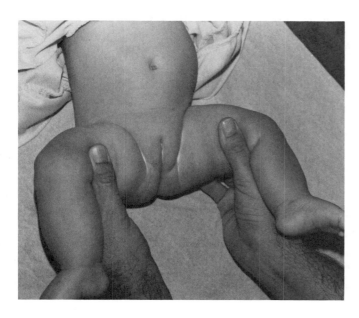

Figure 7–5   A Physician Checks an Infant for Congenital Dislocation of the Hip

means that the hip either is dislocated or can be dislocated. In either case, treatment is instituted immediately to keep the head in the socket so that it cannot be inadvertently dislocated in the first few weeks of life. If the hip is stable during the first few weeks, the ligaments have time to tighten up and future problems are avoided.

Often the affected leg is shorter than the non-affected leg, causing the baby's thigh folds to be asymmetrical. Also, the motion of the hip may be limited.

X rays can then be taken to confirm the diagnosis. Classical radiographic signs of dislocation are an upward and outward displacement of the femoral head and a shallow acetabular socket.

Treatment

The type of treatment depends on the age of the child when the dislocation is discovered. Treatment is begun as soon as the diagnosis is made. The earlier that treatment is instituted, the better are the results.

In the first year of life, the hip can usually be brought back into the socket by gentle manipulation (Weissman & Salama, 1966). The hip is then held in place by either a special brace or a cast for six to twelve weeks. If the child is several months old before the dislocation is discovered, the child may have to be placed in **traction** in the hospital to first stretch out the tight muscles and ligaments around the hip before the hip can be reduced (replaced) into the socket.

If the hip dislocation is not discovered until the child is one to three years of age, surgery is often necessary. By this age, the muscles and ligaments around the hip are often contracted and must be surgically lengthened. Also, soft tissue has had time to grow into the socket and can block the reduction. Therefore, the socket must be surgically cleaned out before the hip can be reduced into the socket. After surgery, the child usually has to wear a body cast for about three months.

After age three, the chances of ending up with a normal hip are slim, even after surgery. Not only do the muscles and ligaments have to be lengthened and the socket cleaned out, but extensive bone surgery must be done as well. Often, the socket is shallow and underdeveloped because of lack of stimulation. The socket must be deepened surgically in order to stabilize the head within it. This is a major operation and requires immobilization in a body cast after. surgery.

Prognosis

The prognosis of a congenitally dislocated hip depends directly on the age of the child when the diagnosis is made and treatment begun. If the diagnosis is made within the first few months of life, the child should recover without any permanent disability. If the diagnosis is made during school age, the child will probably always have limited motion in the hip and may develop **arthritis** in the hip in early adulthood.

Educational Implications

The child who has been diagnosed and treated in infancy should show no sign of the disorder by school age. The school-age child who is currently undergoing treatment will probably miss three to six months of classes due to surgery and the time spent in a body cast. Provisions for homebound education will have to be made. Once the child returns to school, his activities will be modified. He will often be encour-

aged to participate in water sports or less vigorous activities and to avoid running and jumping. The child usually will be ambulatory without the need for any form of external support.

SLIPPED CAPITAL FEMORAL EPIPHYSIS

In a slipped capital femoral epiphysis the femoral head (or ball) slips off the neck of the femur (Figure 7–6). The slip takes place through the growth center (epiphysis) and occurs in children ten–sixteen years of age during a period of rapid growth (Joplin, 1964).

Etiology

The epiphyseal slippage is thought to be due to an **endocrine** abnormality. It is usually seen in adolescent children who are undergoing rapid growth spurts. It seems to be most common in tall, thin children, who may have increased levels of growth hormone, or obese hypogonadal children, who have decreased levels of sex **hormones.** In experiments, both hormonal abnormalities were found to weaken the growth center and predispose it to slipping.

Characteristics

This is a condition of school-age children. It is more common in boys than in girls and can be seen in both hips about 40 percent of the time. It usually occurs in boys ages thirteen–sixteen and in girls ages eleven–fourteen.

The symptoms are usually minimal and often are very gradual in onset. The child may complain of groin or thigh and knee pain and, as time goes on, may limp slightly. When examined, the child may

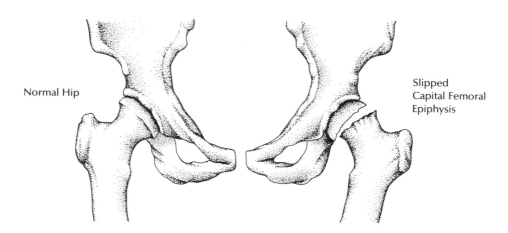

Normal Hip

Slipped Capital Femoral Epiphysis

Figure 7—6   Slipped Capital Femoral Epiphysis

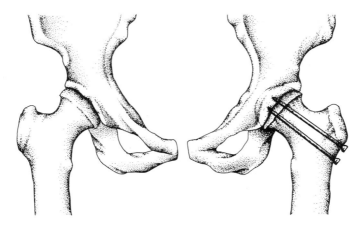

Figure 7—7   Surgically Inserted Pins Used to Hold the Femoral Head in Place

have slightly restricted hip motion. Frequently, there is no **trauma** associated with the slip.

Diagnosis

The diagnosis may be difficult to make. All that may be seen is a slight widening and irregularity of the growth center. As the disease progresses, the diagnosis becomes obvious; there is upward and forward displacement of the femoral neck on the head of the femur (see Figure 7–6). It is important to determine if the slip is recent and whether it occurred all at once, or if the slip has occurred gradually and healing has already begun. This usually can be determined by an X ray and affects the type of treatment and prognosis.

Treatment

The goal of treatment is to correct the displacement, if possible, with a minimal amount of trauma, and to maintain the correction until bone unites with the epiphysis. The type of treatment depends on the amount of slippage that has occurred and its duration.

Usually, if the slip appears to be recent, it can be corrected by a period of traction in the hospital, or by a gentle manipulation of the hip under general anesthesia. Once the slip has been corrected, it will be held in place by pins that are surgically inserted into the femoral head (Figure 7–7) and are left there until the growth center has closed and the femoral head is firmly united to the rest of the femur.

If the slip is severe and cannot be reduced because of early healing, a more complicated surgical procedure is usually necessary. This involves surgically cutting across the upper end of the **femur**, redirecting the femoral head into a more proper alignment, and holding it in place with a special plate or with pins.

Prognosis

If the slip is slight and is diagnosed and treated early, the child should have a normal hip. If the problem is discovered late and the slip is severe, the child may never have a normal hip and may develop arthritis in the hip in early adulthood, despite having limited his activities.

Educational Implications

Once the disorder is diagnosed, the child is usually put into the hospital immediately to prevent any further slipping. The child is likely to be out of school for six to twelve weeks. When first returning to school, the child will often need to use crutches. The child will usually have to be put into an adaptive physical education class for six months to a year, and be encouraged to participate in swimming or more sedentary activities instead of those that require running or jumping.

SUMMARY

This chapter has presented information about three disorders—Legg-Perthes disease, congenital dislocation of the hip, and slipped capital femoral epiphysis—that can affect the hips of school-age children. Legg-Perthes is a self-limited disease of unknown etiology that affects children three–twelve years of age. Congenital dislocation of the hip is also of unknown etiology (although genetic factors may play a role) and is present at birth. Slipped capital femoral epiphysis is thought to result from an endo-crine abnormality and is usually seen in children ten–sixteen years of age, during periods of rapid growth. For all three disorders, early detection and treatment significantly improves the chances for complete recovery.

REFERENCES

Joplin, R. J. Slipped capital femoral epiphysis: The still unsolved adolescent hip lesion. *Journal of the American Medical Association,* 1964, *188,* 379–381.

Petrie, J. G., & Bitenc, I. The abduction weight-bearing treatment and Legg-Calvé-Perthes disease. *Journal of Bone and Joint Surgery,* 1967, 49–A, 1483.

Salter, R. B. Experimental and clinical aspects of Perthes' disease. *Journal of Bone and Joint Surgery,* 1966, *48–B,* 393.

Smith, W. S., Coleman, C. R., Olix, M. L., & Sloger, R. F. Etiology of congenital dislocation of the hip. *Journal of Bone and Joint Surgery,* 1963, *45–A,* 491–500.

Weissman, S. L., & Salama, R. Treatment of congenital dislocation of the hip in the newborn infant. *Journal of Bone and Joint Surgery,* 1966, *48–A,* 1319–1327.

Milo B. Brooks, M.D., *is professor emeritus in the Department of Pediatrics at the School of Medicine, University of California at Los Angeles.*

Congenital limb deficiencies are quite rare, occurring only about once in every 20,000 births (Setoguchi & Rosenfelder, 1982). Acquired amputations are slightly less frequent. Consequently, the appearance of such a child in a classroom can pose problems for the uninformed teacher. This is particularly true because of many misconceptions in the current body of knowledge. A clearer picture of the problems and capabilities of limb-deficient children is needed.

ETIOLOGY

Little is known of the cause of congenital limb deficiencies. Congenital means that the child was "born with" the condition, not that the condition was necessarily hereditary. In fact, only 3–5 percent of con-

CHAPTER

8

Limb Deficiencies

genital deficiencies exhibit a hereditary link. Some type of "growth arrest," probably occurring in the fourth to sixth week of gestation as the limb bud is developing, accounts for most cases. A very small percentage of cases are probably true intrauterine amputations resulting from constricting bands as the fetal limb grows.

The tranquilizer Thalidomide produced many limb deficiencies in children, when it was used in the few years before 1962. Since then, the drug has been effectively banned from use worldwide and no other drug has been conclusively proven to have a similar effect. Some drugs do produce other kinds of anomalies, but very few if any limb deficiencies are presently found to be due to drugs. Although much research has been done and is continuing, the actual mechanisms of growth arrests, constricting bands, Thalidomide action, or even of genetic action remain unknown.

Acquired limb deficiencies can properly be called **amputations.** They are caused by accidents, disease, or surgery. Surgery can be used to remove disease or malignancy or to modify anomalous limbs for better function or to allow use of a prosthesis. The most common causes of accidental amputations are automobile and motorcycle accidents, followed by burns, explosions, and accidents involving trains or farm machinery.

CHARACTERISTICS

Table 8–1 provides some idea of the relative frequency of different types of limb deficiencies. The Table lists the type and etiology of limb deficiencies among the first thousand children treated at the Child Amputee Prosthetics Project at the University of California at Los Angeles. A limb that ends below the elbow and above the wrist is by far the most common deficiency seen in this clinic or in others. The percentage of acquired amputations may be higher in some other clinics, depending on their location and emphasis.

Phocomelia "seal limb" (Figure 8–1) is a condition in which the long bones of a limb are shortened. When the limb is completely absent, the resulting condition is a hand at the shoulder or a foot at the hip. Proximal femoral focal deficiency (PFFD) is a type of phocomelia in which, primarily, the upper portion of the femur (thigh bone) is missing. It occurs frequently enough to deserve a separate listing.

Above all, limb-deficient children are people and delightful ones as well. Because their intelligence is normal and they have had to strive harder to accomplish some tasks, they are often high achievers in the positive sense of the term. Many limb-deficient children have had occupational or physical therapy from early life and have acquired learning and problem-solving skills that are very useful in school.

Children with limb deficiencies usually have become accustomed to the curiosity and stares of others since birth, and generally adapt well to their classmates. At a new school, curiosity about the limb deficiency and **prosthesis** can be handled by allowing the child to show what he can do and by emphasizing his

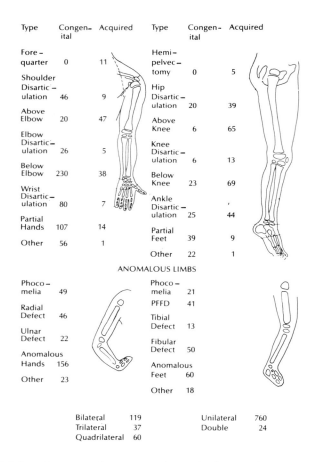

Type	Congenital	Acquired	Type	Congenital	Acquired
Fore-quarter	0	11	Hemi-pelvectomy	0	5
Shoulder Disarticulation	46	9	Hip Disarticulation	20	39
Above Elbow	20	47	Above Knee	6	65
Elbow Disarticulation	26	5	Knee Disarticulation	6	13
Below Elbow	230	38	Below Knee	23	69
Wrist Disarticulation	80	7	Ankle Disarticulation	25	44
Partial Hands	107	14	Partial Feet	39	9
Other	56	1	Other	22	1

ANOMALOUS LIMBS

Type	Congenital		Type	Congenital	
Phocomelia	49		Phocomelia	21	
Radial Defect	46		PFFD	41	
Ulnar Defect	22		Tibial Defect	13	
Anomalous Hands	156		Fibular Defect	50	
Other	23		Anomalous Feet	60	
			Other	18	

Bilateral	119		Unilateral	760
Trilateral	37		Double	24
Quadrilateral	60			

Table 8–1   An Example of the Relative Frequency of Different Types of Limb Deficiencies in Children

Note: 1,582 Deficient limbs in 1,000 children.

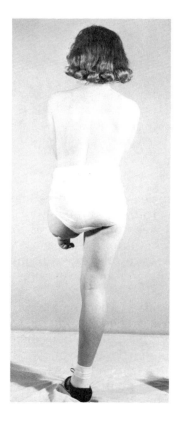

Figure 8–1   A Child With Phocomelia (Seal Limb)

achievements. When new or difficult tasks are encountered, the child can usually figure out ways of doing the tasks on his own if given the chance. When the teacher has questions, the child's parent or a local therapist familiar with prosthetics can be of assistance. The danger that children with prostheses will hurt themselves or others with the artificial limb is highly exaggerated. It is not a weapon but a helper.

The limbs are covered by over half of a normal body's skin surface with its complement of sweat glands. Therefore, the absence of two or more limbs seriously hinders the body's ability for fluid balance and temperature control. Limb-deficient children often have high fevers from minor infections. For example, a child may spike a temperature as high as 105° from a mild cold. In addition, their body fluid balance is upset, thus adding greatly to their symptoms of illness. They perspire freely under normal conditions and always need to be lightly dressed. Because of perspiration, wet underclothing may need to be changed frequently during the day.

DIAGNOSIS

The diagnosis of congenital limb deficiency is easily made at birth by observing that one or more limbs is partly or completely missing. Several nomenclature systems have been devised (see Setoguchi & Rosenfelder, 1982). In order to completely classify each type, it is necessary to use many terms that are not commonly used. These terms are presented in Table 8–1.

TREATMENT

Treatment of limb-deficient children is best handled at a regional center in a densely populated area. Here the staff is likely to treat a sufficient number of children to gain meaningful experience and expertise in this specialized area. In a large treatment center, the staff usually includes physicians who specialize in **orthopedic** surgery, physical medicine, and pediatrics; medical social workers; physical and occupational therapists; and prosthetists (limb makers). Some centers also have orthotists (brace makers), engineers, psychiatrists, geneticists, or other specialists either on the staff or available for consultation.

The goal of treatment is to assist the limb-deficient child to become independent and able to compete successfully and enjoy a satisfying life with his peers and his family, in school and in the community. Where this is not possible, the goal is to maximize the child's independence. A treatment program of this sort involves much more than replacing a miss-

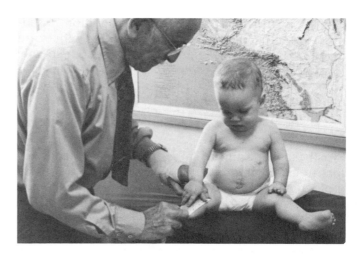

Figure 8–2   A Pediatrician Examines a Young Child

ing limb with an artificial limb or prosthesis. In a number of cases, an artificial limb is not even necessary.

In the clinic, the pediatrician (Figure 8–2) or other physician is interested in assessing the child's general physical condition as well as the health care the child is receiving. The doctor checks whether the child's diet and health habits are adequate and whether immunizations are complete. Although the physician looks for other anomalies, they are seldom found. The mental capacity of limb-deficient children is equal to that of other children in the population: the majority are average, some are gifted, and some are mentally retarded. Because neuromuscular disorders are not associated with limb deficiency, these children follow normal developmental patterns.

The medical social worker (Figure 8–3) can be of great help to the parents following the birth of a limb-deficient child. Often, this is the greatest sadness the family has ever met. Feelings seem overwhelming:

Figure 8–3   A Medical Social Worker Interviews a Girl and Her Mother

alienation, frustration, and anger, in addition to sadness. Some families are overwhelmed but others are made stronger by the experience and need help only for special problems. The medical social workers also help the family find sources of financial help and needed community services.

Prostheses

Prostheses, or artificial limbs, are usually made of nylon stockinet impregnated with a plastic resin and molded over a plaster cast of the residual limb (Figure 8–4). Prostheses are molded to the individual and are held on with straps or a webbing harness. They are never sewn on or attached permanently. When properly fitted, they are not at all painful.

Prosthetists are trained to fabricate and fit the prosthesis. The training requires a college degree followed by one year of intensive prosthetic (limb making) and **orthotic** (brace making) clinical laboratory training. Another year of experience in a certified shop is required before taking the oral and written examination for certification.

Fitting children requires greater skill and patience than fitting adults. The prosthesis must be

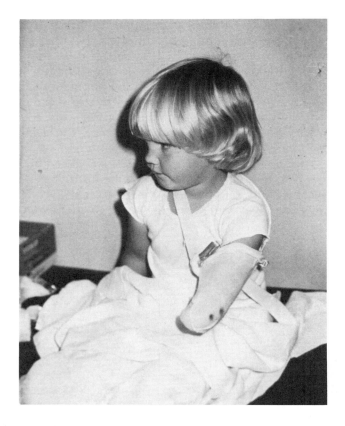

Figure 8–4   Socket Fabrication for a Child Missing Part of an Upper Limb

planned to allow for normal growth and development. Accurate measurements must be taken on rounded, chubby features of a child who never sits still and has a short attention span. In addition, the margin of error is less with a child, and the need for accurate fit and alignment is greater. When properly fitted, a child makes the most natural and efficient use of his prosthesis.

The remaining discussion of prostheses deals first with upper-limb prostheses, and then with lower-limb prostheses.

Upper-Limb Prostheses   Training in the care and use of upper-limb prostheses is usually carried on by Registered Occupational Therapists (OTRs) who have completed a four-year college program, practiced under a registered therapist, and passed a national examination supervised by the American Medical Association.

When a new prosthesis is first fitted, it may seem more of a burden than a useful tool. This will change as the child learns to use it properly. Training may require several daily sessions following the initial fitting of a prosthesis, with periodic sessions later until the child's skills are refined and spontaneous. Patients with upper-limb deficiencies below the elbow and only on one side are usually fitted when the child has attained stable sitting balance, between nine and twelve months of age. Fitting may be deferred for children with more severe deficiencies. Active harness controls are added when the child is between two and three years of age, and able to learn to use the controls. Most children have completed training before formal schooling begins.

The most common terminal device is an aluminum split hook that can be used for grasping (Figure 8–5a). It may be coated with plastic to prevent damage while teething, to prevent scratches on furniture, and

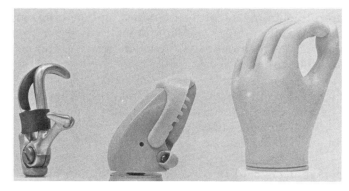

Figure 8–5   Upper-limb Prosthetics for Grasping: (a) a split hook, (b) the CAPP terminal device, and (c) an artificial hand

especially to keep infants from slipping when they lean on the prosthesis. Although the hook looks dangerous, injuries to the child or his playmates are very rare and usually minor. A terminal device that is shaped like a hand (Figure 8–5c) looks more natural but may be less useful and durable for an active child. Another choice is the CAPP terminal device (Figure 8–5b) that resembles neither a hook nor a hand, but is equally useful (Figure 8–6).

(a)

(b)

Figure 8–6   Children Using a CAPP Terminal Device for (a) Drawing and (b) Cooking

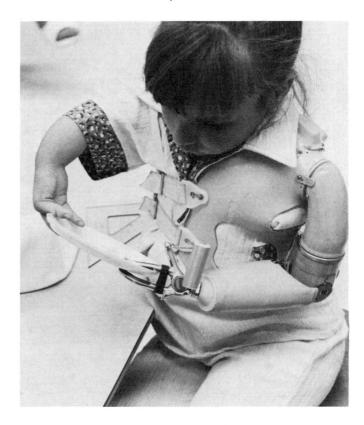

Figure 8–7   A Child with an External Powered Terminal Device and Elbow

External powered terminal devices and elbows (Figure 8–7), which rely on batteries to supply energy, have recently become sufficiently reliable to be useful and practical. They are controlled by myoelectric sources (small muscle contractions on the residual limb) or push-button switches. They are quite expensive, costing several thousand dollars, and repair facilities must be readily available.

It is possible for children who have no arms or hands (absent at the shoulder) to become completely self-sufficient with the free use of their feet for prehension (Figure 8–8). By using their feet, these children may be able to accomplish more than they could by using artificial arms, even electrically powered prostheses. Thus, these children can be free of all encumbrances. If permitted to use their feet, the children will be able to do all the things they must to succeed in school. They learn to overcome the stares and questions of playmates and classmates quickly, and are soon admired for their accomplishments. A child who is armless from birth and is permitted to use his feet will learn all these skills with little or no training. These children may choose to wear a prosthesis for some activities or social occasions where they meet the public.

Figure 8–8 This Child has Figured out a Different Way to Accomplish a Normal Task

Lower-Limb Prostheses Lower-limb prosthetic care and training is usually done by physical therapists, many of whom have graduate degrees. Children missing a lower limb have a natural drive to walk at the same age as other children. If these children are given the opportunity to walk, and if they are provided with a properly fitted and aligned prosthesis at that time, they will seek their own best method of ambulation with little training.

The prosthesis for the lower limb, like that for the upper limb, is made of polyester resin and nylon stockinet and is molded to fit intimately with the residual limb. It terminates in a rubberlike foot that fits into a normal shoe. For below-knee limb deficiencies on only one side, the restoration is most functional and results in a near normal gait with *no* restrictions for play and sports activities. The prosthesis can be removed like a boot, and is usually held on by a strap over the knee (Figure 8–9).

Higher-limb deficiencies (above the knee) result in a more abnormal gait, more energy required for walking, and the inability to perform some activities. This is even truer when both legs are affected.

Unless children are severely disabled, they usually receive their first lower-extremity prosthesis when they pull up and try to stand, at about one year of age. The physical therapist will teach the child how to maintain balance and walk, and how to put on the prosthesis and care for it.

Prostheses, both upper and lower, are usually outgrown and worn out in a year to a year and a half, when they must be replaced. They can cost a few thousand dollars or more. Government agencies, which provide financial assistance for crippled children in each state, help families pay for them, as most families need some help.

PROGNOSIS

Parents and teachers are concerned with the long-term potential of limb-deficient children. The condition will never disappear but it is not life-threatening. Because associated systemic anomalies are not common, a normal, healthy lifetime can be expected.

At the time of the child's birth, the parents have many questions: Will their child be able to sit or stand? Will the child be able to walk? Will the child need crutches or a wheelchair? Will she be able to drive a car? Will he have friends or get married? By the time their child reaches school age, many of these questions have already been answered, and the parents are pleased and surprised at their child's accomplishments.

Stares and teasing are a problem for all children with deficient limbs. Although none of us is perfect, few people have deficiencies as obvious as a missing limb. How the child learns to handle teasing and stares can be greatly helped by parents and teachers.

The great majority of limb-deficient children can handle schoolwork on a basis fully competitive with other children. In the severely involved, a few permissive alterations may be needed to allow full participation. These may include the use of a wheelchair or the free use of the feet for an armless child. Social adjustments may or may not be a problem. To a great extent, this depends on the child's and parents' attitudes and adjustments.

EDUCATIONAL IMPLICATIONS

Limb-deficient children, being so much more normal than abnormal, thrive on being treated just as other children are treated. They are real people, and they make delightful pupils. In contrast with that of some children with other anomalies, the intelligence quotient of limb-deficient children does not differ from that of the normal population.

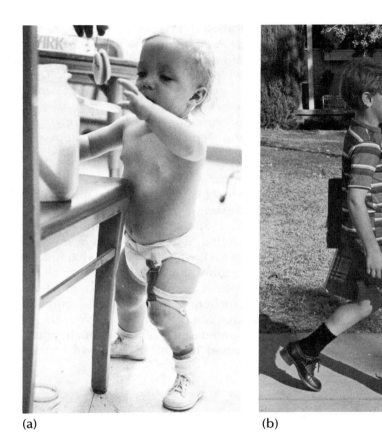

(a)   (b)

Figure 8—9   Below-the-Knee Prosthesis for a Toddler (a) and (b) School-Age Child

Occupational and physical therapy, if given early, can help children to develop learning skills and can make school adjustment easier. Because limb-deficient children have had to do many things the hard way, they often become high academic achievers. The severity of a child's limb deficiency is not related to his or her learning capacity (Clarke & French, 1978). Furthermore, lack of early experience in crawling or other neuromuscular activities, which is sometimes considered necessary for learning, is not a factor in limb deficiency. Being so normal in every other way, limb-deficient children can easily be integrated into a regular classroom.

SUMMARY

This chapter presented basic information about limb deficiencies in children, focusing in particular on the etiology, characteristics, diagnosis, treatment, and prognosis for such children. In the process, we have reviewed a number of different prosthetic devices used by children missing upper or lower limbs. Limb-deficient children are more normal than abnormal and have excellent learning potential. Only a few are so severely disabled as to require special education facilities. All of the others, if adequately fitted with prostheses when needed, can assume normal classroom activities. Limb-deficient children are delightful people who, like the rest of us, need to love and be loved, to know that they are loved, and to know that their lives are worth living.

REFERENCES

Clarke, D., & French, R. Can congenital amputees achieve academically? *American Corrective Therapy Journal,* 1978, *32*(1), 7–11.

Setoguchi, Y., & Rosenfelder, R. *The limb deficient child.* Springfield, Ill.: Charles C Thomas, 1982.

Russell R. Lyle, M.D., *is consultant to the Department of Pediatrics at the School of Medicine, University of Mississippi, Jackson, Mississippi, and adjunct professor of special education in the Department of Curriculum and Instruction, Mississippi State University, Mississippi State, Mississippi.* **S. J. Obringer, Ed.D.,** *is professor and coordinator of special education in the Department of Curriculum and Instruction, Mississippi State University, Mississippi State, Mississippi.*

Muscular dystrophy (MD) is a general weakening, or wasting away, of the body's various muscle groups that affects approximately 200,000 people in the United States. There are a number of classifications of MD, which are somewhat different in their clinical manifestations but share given characteristics. The most common classification of this disorder is the Duchenne form of MD, sometimes referred to as childhood or progressive MD. The disorder was named after Gullaume Duchenne who, in 1868, published the first description of the condition. Other

CHAPTER 9

Muscular Dystrophy

less common forms of MD include **facioscapulohumeral** and **limb-girdle MD,** which are referred to as adolescent or adult MD because their onset generally is in the late teenage years. In Table 9–1 these forms of MD are classified by age, sex, characteristics, and life expectancy. The classroom teacher is most likely to see a student who has the Duchenne form of MD. Therefore, this chapter will emphasize only this form.

Another early contributor to the field was William Gowers, also a physician. In the mid-1800s, Gowers described an upright motion typical of most children with MD. They tend to push up their legs with their hands to reach the standing position. Today, this motion is referred to as Gowers sign and is an important symptom in the diagnosis of MD. With amazing ex-

Table 9—1   Major Categories of Muscular Dystrophy

Type	Sex	Onset	Characteristics	Life Expectancy
Duchenne or Progressive Muscular Dystrophy	90% male	Preschool	Progression upwards from calf muscles—false enlargement of muscles (pseudohypertrophic)	Eighteen years
Limb-Girdle Muscular Dystrophy	Male or female	Late teenage years, approximately	Develops from shoulders to pelvis first, then spreads	Fifty years (variable)
Facioscapulohumeral Muscular Dystrophy	Male or female	Late teenage years, approximately	Develops from face-shoulders-arms, and then spreads	Middle to late age

Figure 9—1   Duchenne's "Harpoon"

Source: E. Ogg. *Milestones in muscle disease research.* New York: Muscular Dystrophy Associations of America, Inc., 1971, page 5. Reprinted with permission.

actness these early pioneers described the disease and the suggested diagnostic procedures. For example, Duchenne developed a surgical instrument (Figure 9–1) to remove sections of muscle tissue for microscopic examination. He then theorized that the basic condition was caused by diseased connective tissue. Because patients had noticeably enlarged calf muscles, Duchenne described the disease as pseudohypertrophic (false enlargement) muscular paralysis. Today, the term pseudohypertrophic MD is also used.

ETIOLOGY

Approximately 90 percent of the time, Duchenne MD can be traced to a sex-linked genetic error. Everyone, male and female, has 23 sets of chromosomes; and the 23rd set controls the reproduction process. In females, the 23rd set is made up of two X chromosomes (XX); in males, the 23rd set is made up of one X and one Y chromosome (XY). Women produce only X chromosomes, men X or Y chromosomes. When an X chromosome from a man joins an X chromosome from a woman, a daughter is produced. When a Y chromosome from a man joins an X chromosome from a woman, a son is produced. In rare cases, a woman has a defective X chromosome that can produce an offspring with MD. When the woman's defective X chromosome joins with the man's Y chromosome, a son with MD is produced. Also, when the woman's defective X chromosome joins with the man's X chromosome, a daughter who is a carrier of MD is produced.

As can be seen in Figure 9–2, the defective X chromosome (D) of the female has no complement in the Y chromosome (B) of the male. Therefore, the woman's defective X chromosome becomes a dominant force. However, when this defective X chromosome of the female is countered with a normal X chromosome (A) of the male, the MD trait is not manifested. In these cases, a female carrier is produced. The sex-linked genetic error in the case of Duchenne MD means that the condition is carried by the mother and is passed on only to sons. In the remaining 10 percent of the cases of Duchenne MD, the cause appears not to be sex-linked but, rather, an autosomal recessive trait. In these cases, both the mother and father must carry the recessive gene. Occasionally, a gene **mutation** in conception can cause Duchenne MD. In both of these cases, MD can afflict both sons and daughters.

The family of a muscular dystrophied child has a responsibility to the female offspring to inform her, before she starts planning to have children, of the genetic error within the family. She then can seek genetic counseling and decide on her future family plans.

With each pregnancy, the carrier mother runs a 25 percent chance of having an MD male, a 25 percent chance of having an MD carrier female, and a 50 percent chance of having a normal male or female. Therefore, genetic counseling is strongly recommended. In genetic counseling, a complete genealogical study is initiated to determine previous carriers

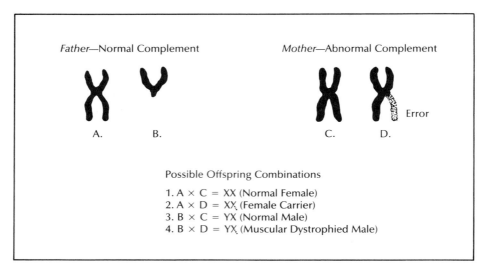

Figure 9-2   Possible Offspring Combinations for Duchenne MD

within the immediate and extended family. Also, her blood is tested for an elevated level of creatine phosphokinase (CPK), an enzyme. The CPK blood test is approximately 70–80 percent effective in identifying female carriers of MD (Brooke, 1977).

CHARACTERISTICS

Since inoculations have brought about a decline in the incidence of polio, MD has become the most frequent and most disabling childhood neuromuscular

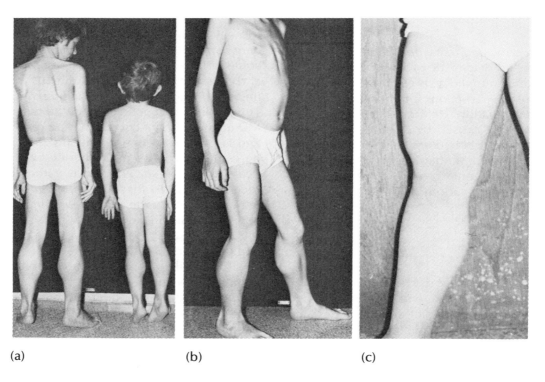

(a)   (b)   (c)

Figure 9–3   Pseudohypertrophy in Two Brothers. Two brothers who had pseudohypertrophy of the calf muscles and stood and walked on their toes (a). The mother felt this was a "habit" since both boys could stand with their heels on the ground when so instructed (b). Pseudohypertrophy is not limited to calf muscles. In this boy (c), the quadriceps were enlarged.
Source: M. H. Brooke. *A clinician's view of neuromuscular diseases.* Baltimore: The Williams & Wilkins Co., 1977, page 96. Reprinted by permission of the publisher and courtesy of M. H. Brooke.

disorder. MD tends to run the following clinical course:

1. Onset of symptoms between three to five years of age;
2. Progressive muscle weakness, wasting, and contractures in the pelvic and shoulder muscles;
3. Calf muscle pseudohypertrophy (false enlargement) in most cases;
4. Loss of independent ambulation by age nine to eleven years;
5. Slow progressive generalized weakness and spinal curvature during the teenage years; and
6. Respiratory failure before the third decade of life.

As stated earlier, MD predominantly affects boys. It is not usually apparent in early infancy, but often the child has a history of delayed walking, frequent falls, and clumsiness. The pseudohypertrophy (Figure 9–3) of certain muscle groups results from the deposition of fat and fibrous tissue in the weakened muscle. It imparts a firmer than normal, ropy consistency to the muscle. The weakness and atrophy (loss of true muscle tissue) progresses steadily, giving way to con-

tractures, deformities, and disability (Figures 9–4 and 9–5). In the advanced stages of the disease, the heart may enlarge and this is often the cause of death.

Studies of intellectual functioning have shown that children with MD operate at lower levels than a variety of control groups, but that they do not exhibit true retardation. The learning problems are usually evident early in life, are nonprogressive, and are not proportional to the severity of the muscle disease. Learning problems tend to limit academic achievement and narrow even further the activities available to the dependent MD child. The often resulting passivity and lack of motivation further curtails the child's efforts toward self-improvement.

DIAGNOSIS

Patients with MD present no diagnostic problem once the symptoms and signs have become well established. Even at five years of age, a boy who has difficulty walking, spinal curvature, a waddling gait

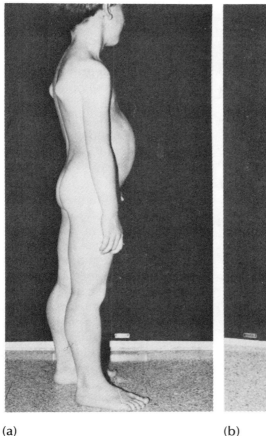 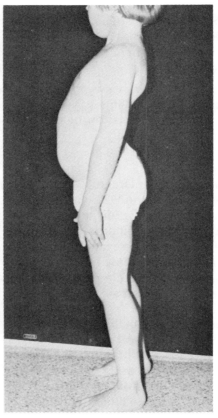

(a)   (b)

Figure 9–4   Lordosis (Swayback) Associated With the Disease

Source: M. H. Brooke. *A clinician's view of neuromuscular diseases.* Baltimore: The Williams & Wilkins Co., 1977, page 97. Reprinted by permission of the publisher and courtesy of M. H. Brooke.

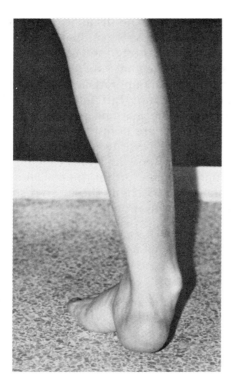

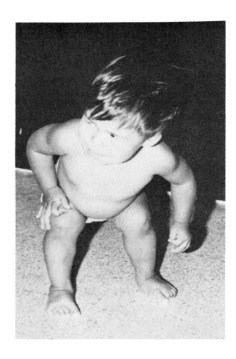

Figure 9—5   Foot Contractures. The foot assumes a position of inversion and plantar flexion. This is associated with tightening of the heel cords, although it is not necessarily caused by that.

Source: M. H. Brooke. *A clinician's view of neuromuscular diseases.* Baltimore: The Williams & Wilkins Co., 1977, page 98. Reprinted by permission of the publisher and courtesy of M. H. Brooke.

Figure 9—6   Mild Hip Weakness. In arising from the floor, this child placed his right hand transiently on his knee but required no other assistance.

Source: M. H. Brooke. *A clinician's view of neuromuscular diseases.* Baltimore: The Williams & Wilkins Co., 1977, page 23. Reprinted by permission of the publisher and courtesy of M. H. Brooke.

(especially when running), enlarged calves, and Gower's sign (Figure 9–6, 9–7, and 9–8) is sufficiently distinctive to warrant the tentative diagnosis of Duchenne MD. Final confirmation emerges from laboratory studies that show marked elevation of CPK in the blood, electromyographic (EMG) evidence of small motor dysfunction, and muscle biopsy finding of marked variation in muscle fiber size, fibrosis, and fatty infiltration.

The CPK enzyme is elevated in the blood of those with MD, and in 70–80 percent of carrier mothers. The highest concentrations (fifty to a hundred times normal) have been found in infants under six months of age, who have no clinical signs of the disease. Elevated CPK levels persist until weakness and muscle atrophy is advanced, at which time the level may decline.

The clinical picture of MD may be mimicked also by other neuromuscular syndromes such as spinal muscular atrophy (see Chapter 13), **dermatomyositis,** and more rare congenital muscle diseases. Because

the prognosis and genetic therapeutic implications vary with each of these disorders, precise identification is mandatory.

TREATMENT

Despite a great deal of research, no specific therapy (including drugs and physical therapy programs) has proven effective for MD. The disease runs a relentlessly progressive course. The most rapid progression occurs in patients with disease of early onset. Most patients are confined to a wheelchair by approximately ten years of age. Therefore, the main goals of therapy and management should be family orientation and acceptance, genetic counseling, maintenance of activity, and emphasis on maintaining the quality of life for as long as possible.

The initial information phase for the family should include a general description of the signs, symptoms, and protracted relentless course of MD. Positive aspects of the anticipated disability should be emphasized. These include the fact that the child will be able to attend public schools and participate in

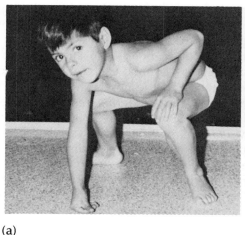
(a)

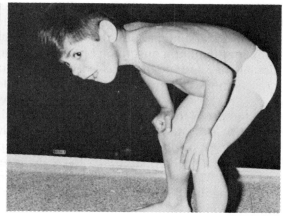
(b)

Figure 9—7   A Boy With MD Stands Up. This patient arises from the floor (a) with unilateral hand support on the floor but then (b) requires bilateral hand support on the thighs in order to attain the upright position.

Source: M. H. Brooke. *A clinician's view of neuromuscular diseases.* Baltimore: The Williams & Wilkins Co., 1977, page 25. Reprinted by permission of the publisher and courtesy of M. H. Brooke.

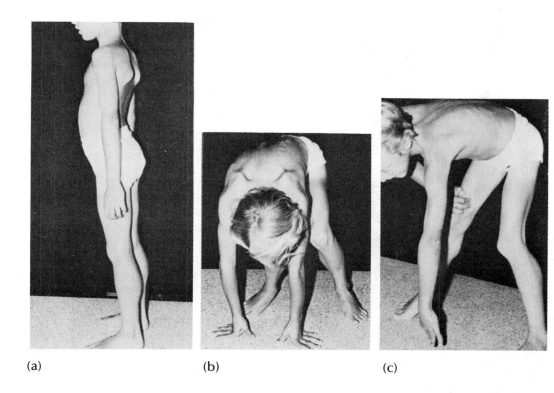
(a)   (b)   (c)

Figure 9—8   Weakness in a Boy With MD. In this child, the degree of weakness is sufficient to produce a moderate degree of lumbar lordosis. The shoulder weakness is also apparent in the way in which the scapulae (shoulder blades) jut backwards (a). When he tries to arise from the floor (b), he needs bilateral hand support on the floor in the "butt first" maneu-

ver. He then transfers his hand to his thigh (c), and stands by using bilateral hand support on the thighs.

Source: M. H. Brooke. *A clinician's view of neuromuscular diseases.* Baltimore: The Williams & Wilkins Co., 1977, page 25. Reprinted by permission of the publisher and courtesy of M. H. Brooke.

most social activities for an extended period of time. Ample time must be allowed to assess parental attitudes, anxiety, and uncertainty about the disease. Family acceptance may be time-consuming but is crucial because denial may lead to medical shopping, which can increase the child's disability and incite family discord.

Although the tempo of the muscle degeneration cannot be reversed or even temporarily retarded by any known pharmacologic or physical agent, the physician can still propose a positive approach to treatment based on three ideas. First, some of the complications that magnify the functional disability are predictable and preventable. Second, an active program of physical therapy and timely application of braces (Figure 9–9) can prolong ambulation and more closely approximate the normal independence of later childhood. Third, if a specific treatment ever becomes available, those who are in optimal physical condition are most likely to benefit.

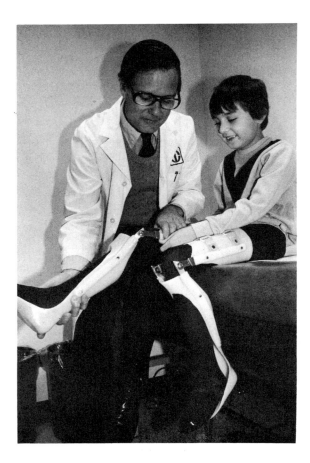

Figure 9–9   A Patient Fitted With Special Braces

Source: I. M. Siegel. *101 questions and answers about muscular dystrophy.* New York: Muscular Dystrophy Association, 1981, page 12. Reprinted with permission.

Active exercise is desirable, although overexertion may lead to falling and must be avoided. Ambulation sufficient to satisfy the child's home, school, and recreation needs can substitute adequately for routine programmed exercise. Prolonged inactivity is detrimental to the child who has MD. Even one or two hours of continuous inactivity, aside from sleep, should be discouraged. Time spent on sedentary activities such as watching television can be better spent on standing or ambulation. A daily goal of at least three hours of ambulation is realistic and probably adequate to maintain strength and minimize contracture if the disability is moderate. The child who regresses to less than three hours per day of ambulation will, within months, lose the ability to walk unassisted.

Use of a wheelchair should be avoided unless one is necessary. Prolonged standing or walking is unduly fatiguing and risky. In busy school corridors, the child who has a slow gait can leave class early to proceed to his destination unimpeded. Activity, as tolerated by the child, should be allowed as long as fatigue is relieved by an average night's rest.

The physical therapist plays a crucial role in supporting, motivating, and training such a patient during the transition to stable, braced ambulation. Success will give several additional years of independent walking, greater self-sufficiency, and substantial postponement of the restrictions imposed by a wheelchair.

PROGNOSIS

As stated earlier, the relentless progression of this disease is not affected by drugs or therapy programs. Ultimately, in the second or third decade of life, the complications of diminished muscle strength, heart involvement, and poor respiration causing pneumonia lead to death from heart failure or infection. Although parents may be given some hope because of current research efforts, they should not be led to think that the disease is currently treatable or that, in light of current information, the child's life can be prolonged in any way beyond the second or third decade. The parents' acceptance of this situation and their ability to help the child deal with it is perhaps the most important aspect of management and prognosis.

EDUCATIONAL IMPLICATIONS

Because MD is usually terminal, the teacher's relationship with the child is often very important. Children with MD may seek out the teacher as a confidant to discuss life goals and possibly even life expectancy. The child needs to be able to express his feelings fully and feel free to ask various questions concerning his unique condition and potential. In all likelihood, an open discussion will occur. Quality of life versus quantity of life should be emphasized. Many MD students feel awkward in approaching their parents or relatives about their condition. The teacher, then, is often the adult close to him with whom the student can share his thoughts.

Academic progress tends to diminish in the teenage years. Constant fatigue and restricted opportunity to interact with the environment cause the student to lag behind the normal curriculum expectations. Periodic breaks or rests may be needed during the school day. Also, if fatigue becomes a major limitation, a shortened or modified school day is suggested. Homework should be of reasonable length so as to allow the student to obtain proper rest. Scores on intelligence tests are generally not applicable in designing academic and social programs for these students. A reliable criterion-referenced test is more useful for identifying appropriate instructional levels and activities for the MD student.

Students with MD usually die from respiratory ailments, such as influenza leading to pneumonia. Any observation of respiratory problems—characterized by coughing, wheezing, or shallow breathing—should be immediately reported to the parents and the school nurse.

Physical education should involve sedentary games such as chess or other table games. If outdoor activities are included, caution should be used against overexertion. If a school has a swimming pool, a modified swimming program may be designed. Swimming is an excellent activity for the MD child if it meets the approval of the parents and family physician.

Because the MD child cannot engage in vigorous physical exercise, many of the children may become obese. Besides the negative social implications, obesity makes it more difficult for the child to support himself in a wheelchair. The child's obesity also makes it difficult for the teacher, parent, or attendant, who has to lift or transport the child many times each day. A well-planned diet prescribed by the pediatrician or family physician is essential and should be strictly observed both at home and at school.

The school psychologist and counselors need to work closely with the classroom teacher to make sure the child has a positive self-concept and healthy emotional state. Also, the administration of formal intelligence and academic tests may need modification. Shorter time periods, frequent rests, and less empha-

sis on manual dexterity (performance items) are suggested.

SUMMARY

MD has been described as a general weakening, or wasting away, of the body's various muscle groups that affects approximately 200,000 people in the United States. The most common type is the Duchenne form, referred to as childhood or progressive MD. This is usually a genetic disease, which is manifest in a sex-linked transference through a defective X chromosome. It is carried by the mother and passed on in manifest form to sons and in carrier form to daughters. Carriers can often be detected by serum enzyme studies. Genetic counseling is strongly recommended for all families with histories of MD.

The disease usually becomes evident when the child is between three and five years of age. It appears as muscle weakness and altered gait. The diagnosis of Duchenne MD can be made with enzyme studies and muscle biopsies. At the present time, the progression and ultimate prognosis of the disease cannot be altered. The therapeutic implications involve emotional stability for the family and patient, and physical rehabilitation to maintain ambulation as long as possible. Death is inevitable in the second or third decade of life, and occurs as a result of cardiac failure or respiratory infection.

The main role of the educator is to assist the child in the classroom to fully and freely express his feelings about his unique condition. Activity should be encouraged. Social interaction with others should be held to as normal a level as possible. Homework should be reasonable in length, to allow the student to obtain the proper rest. Excessive sedentary activity should be discouraged. Any observable indication of respiratory problems, such as coughing, wheezing, or shallow breathing, should be reported to the parents or school nurse immediately. The teacher should work closely with the family, school psychologist, and the child's physician to help the child maintain a positive self-concept and to minimize the child's physical problems as long as possible.

REFERENCES

Brooke, M. H. *A clinician's view of neuromuscular diseases.* Baltimore: Williams & Wilkins, 1977.

Duchenne de Boulogne. *De la paralysie musculaire pseudohypertrophique ou paralysie myosclerosique.* (Extrait des Archives generales de Médecine.) Paris: Asselin, 1868.

Gabriella E. Molnar, M.D., *is professor in the Departments of Rehabilitation Medicine and Pediatrics and director of the Pediatric Rehabilitation Service in the Children's Evaluation and Rehabilitation Center at the Albert Einstein College of Medicine, Bronx, New York.*

Arthrogryposis multiplex congenita and osteogenesis imperfecta are both diseases that manifest themselves in skeletal deformities; otherwise, the two conditions are unrelated. They do not share any similarity of etiology and underlying **pathology,** and have dissimilar course.

ARTHROGRYPOSIS MULTIPLEX CONGENITA

Arthrogryposis is derived from the Greek words arthron, meaning joint, and gryposis, meaning abnormal curvature. The name describes the characteristic signs of the disease: deformities that affect multiple joints and are present at birth (Speck, 1979). The condition was first reported in 1841, but it was nearly a century before the nature of the deformities was clarified.

CHAPTER 10

Musculoskeletal Disorders

Etiology

The actual cause of the disease is not known. For some reason, the muscles surrounding the affected joints fail to develop. The anatomic configuration of the bones that form the joint structure is not distorted. However, the absence of muscle action results in lack of motion, stiffness, and deformity. There are two different mechanisms that can be responsible for this muscular maldevelopment. In some cases, degeneration of the muscle tissue itself is primary; that is, it does not result from a preceding condition. In other instances, pathologic changes in the muscles appear to be secondary to (caused by) an abnormality in their nerve supply, a decreased number of anterior horn cells in the spinal cord, which normally serve to control muscle function (Swaiman, 1975). The former type is designated as the myopathic (muscle disease) and the latter as the neuropathic (nerve disease) form of arthrogryposis, denoting their differences in pathogenesis. (Sharrard, 1971; Tachdjian, 1972).

Although the precipitating cause has not been identified in either type, it is known that the disease runs its course while the fetus is still in the womb. Arthrogryposis, it is speculated, may represent intrauterine fetal **myopathy** or **neuropathy** that is burned out and nonprogressive by the time of birth. Or, another hypothesis suggests, a developmental defect interferes with fetal maturation of muscle tissue. It is thought that the joint stiffness and congenital deformities are the consequence of absent intrauterine movements. Arthorgryposis is not a hereditary condition. However, for reasons discussed later, the diagnosis must be established without a doubt prior to advising the family about the chances of having another child with similar problems.

Characteristics

The infant is born with multiple **contractures,** which are usually symmetrical and can involve any joint in the extremities. The limbs appear wasted and show a spindle-shaped contour. This is because the loss of muscle mass around the affected joints makes the bony articular structures look relatively more prominent. One can feel a fibrous band replacing the usual muscle mass. Sometimes there is a dimple over the deformed joint, and the skin may be loose, wrinkled, or thickened around it.

The deformed joint is often so completely stiff that it cannot be moved at all from a certain position. Some contractures may yield slightly to passive stretching. Nevertheless, the joint's range of motion remains significantly curtailed. At times, the child may be able to move the affected joint actively to a limited extent. However, these movements are restricted in excursion and are also weak, thus reflecting the underlying defective muscle development.

Although contractures can occur in virtually any position, there is some predilection for particular types of deformities at certain joints. The shoulders usually rotate inward. Elbows are fixed in **extension** or partial **flexion** and positioned with the palms facing downward. At the wrist, the hands commonly bend toward the palm and sometimes toward the side of the fifth digit (little finger). Various finger joints may be stiff in a bent or straight position and the thumb may be pulled toward the palm. The hip joints are often drawn up in flexion and turned outward. The knees have either flexion or extension contracture; that is,

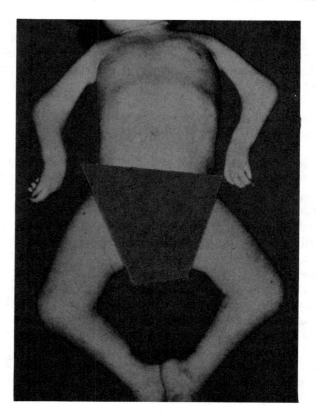

Figure 10–1   Infant With Arthrogryposis Multiplex Congenita. Note the typical deformities, spindle-like appearance of the elbow and knee joints, and lack of muscle mass in the arms and calves.

the legs are constantly bent at the knees or stiff. The latter can be so excessive that the knee is actually bent in the wrong direction. Ankle deformities cause the feet to point downward and turn in. Figure 10–1 shows an infant with these deformities. There are, however, variations from these most commonly observed contractures. Furthermore, not all joints are affected in every case and either the upper or lower extremities can be spared entirely.

At times, arthrogryposis is accompanied by additional abnormalities or malformations. The most frequent are scoliotic curvature of the spine (see Chapter 5) and congenital dislocation of the hip (see Chapter 7). Facial anomalies, congenital heart disease, malformations of the urinary system, premature closure of the cranial bones, thin elongated fingers, and respiratory problems also have been reported. Intellectual ability and development in nonphysical areas are normal.

Diagnosis

Diagnosis is based on the presence of multiple congenital joint deformities without familial history of similar problems. Radiologic (X-ray) examination shows normal bone and joint structure except in those with congenital hip dislocation or scoliosis. If a biopsy is performed, microscopic examination indicates that the muscle has largely been replaced by fat and scar tissue, and that the remaining muscle fibers are smaller than normal. Electromyography, a laboratory test to demonstrate muscle action potential, is usually normal.

An essential part of the examination is to eliminate the possibility of other diseases, most importantly spinal muscular atrophy (see Chapter 13) and congenital muscular dystrophy (see Chapter 9). Occasionally, these diseases can mimic arthrogryposis because they may be manifested by contractures at birth. Muscle biopsy and electromyography show characteristic abnormalities in such cases. Unlike arthrogryposis, these diseases are generally progressive and hereditary. Therefore, a definite diagnostic distinction has significant implications for the child's prognosis and in counseling the family about the potential risk of recurrence in subsequent pregnancies.

Congenital contractures occur in a number of genetic syndromes. Those due to other diseases can be distinguished by the characteristic combinations of other associated anomalies and by the absence of the spindle-shaped joint deformities, typical of arthrogryposis.

Treatment

There is no specific treatment that could influence the underlying abnormality. The principal goals of treatment are to correct those deformities that interfere with function. By ensuring adequate joint mobility and functional **prehension** in the upper extremities, the child can attain some independence in self-care and other activities of daily life. Proper joint alignment in the lower extremities to allow standing and walking is another consideration in rehabilitation.

Methods of treatment include a combination of surgery, casts, braces, and physical therapy to release deformities and to prevent their recurrence. Although corrective casting may be used initially, particularly in infancy, satisfactory correction of contractures usually requires surgery. Postoperative casting and, in some cases, continued bracing is required to maintain joint correction because deformities tend to recur. Physical therapy is an adjunct to utilize function gained from surgery and to prevent subsequent loss in range of motion.

Hip and knee flexion contractures can seriously hinder the ability to stand erect and walk, and foot deformities interfere with a stable supporting base. These deformities need to be corrected, generally through a combination of surgery, casting, and brac-

ing. A unilateral or partially fixed deformity of this type may well be left alone. In addition to their postoperative uses, short- or long-leg braces are used to substitute for weak muscles and to steady unstable joints, particularly the ankles and knees.

Shoulder deformities generally do not necessitate treatment because upper extremity function is not affected significantly by limitations at this joint. At the elbow, fixed extension deformity is the most serious functional impediment because virtually all daily activities require the ability to bend one's elbow. Surgical release is indicated, although restoration of complete range of motion may not be achieved. Wrist flexion contracture interferes with hand function because finger muscles used in grasping and manipulation do not work effectively in this position. When partial joint mobility is preserved, splinting or bracing to hold the wrist in extension may be sufficient. However, surgery may be needed for a marked fixed deformity. It is quite remarkable that, in spite of stiff finger joints, most children develop good hand function, essentially by learning to use various movement substitutions. For this reason, surgical correction is generally not advisable unless the thumb is contracted against the palm, where it gets in the way of grasping.

Adaptive devices and techniques help to enhance function. Some children, who have considerable weakness in their legs, can walk only with crutches or must rely on a wheelchair. Crutch-walking requires reasonable strength and control in the arms and shoulders. The ability to transfer to and from a wheelchair is a necessary skill for all children using this mode of locomotion. In some cases, adapted implements can improve hand and finger facility, grasping, and manipulation. For example, built-up handles make it easier for the child to complete school assignments despite difficulties with fine hand function.

Physical therapy cannot correct deformities. However, after surgery, it can help a child to maximize the increased joint mobility. Once the anticipated goals are attained, no further gain can be expected from continuing exercises. The child and family must be advised that physical activity is the best way to avert recurrent contractures. For school-age children, adaptive physical education is a more appropriate and enjoyable form of maintenance program than formal physical therapy. Although children with arthrogryposis have physical limitations, they should not be excluded from sports selected on the basis of their abilities. For instance, swimming is one of the most suitable sports for virtually any type of handicap and is particularly beneficial to exercise weakened muscles and to maintain joint range, as in arthrogryposis. Children who cannot walk should be encouraged to participate in wheelchair sports.

Prognosis

Arthrogryposis is a nonprogressive disease. The condition does not get worse; its course is stable. However, abnormal joint appearance, stiffness, and limitation of movements remain evident throughout life, even when fixed deformities have been corrected.

The functional outcome depends on the extent of the joint deformities and the active muscle function. The majority of children are able to walk but their gait is abnormal. Nonambulatory youngsters can achieve independence in a wheelchair. Compensatory movements, adaptive techniques, and assistive devices enable most children with upper extremity impairment to become self-sufficient in daily activities. Because intellectual ability is not affected, well-motivated children have a good educational and vocational outlook.

Educational Implications

Educational programs should take full advantage of the fact that these children have normal intelligence and that they do not have a progressive disability. In view of permanent limitations in general mobility and hand dexterity, it is important to stress academic skills, because future employability and ultimate success in life will depend greatly on these achievements.

Surgical treatment and other modes of physical rehabilitation are usually completed by the time the child enters school. Active therapy cannot bring further improvement. Physical status and fitness can be maintained through adapted physical education. Therefore, school placement should be guided primarily by educational needs and priorities instead of the availability of ancillary treatment services. In the event of additional corrective procedures, only short-term subsequent physical rehabilitation will be required.

Certain children may need to use some of the previously mentioned compensatory adaptations so that they can keep up with their peers in schoolwork. Often, teachers are in the best position to recognize such needs and to help find appropriate solutions. In order to provide full benefits of mainstreaming, classrooms and other facilities should be made accessible to children who have gait difficulties or use braces, crutches, or wheelchairs.

Although teachers should consider the child's physical handicap, it is equally important to foster physical independence and emotional growth by avoiding undue restrictions or concessions not justified by the disability. Due to limitations in upper and lower extremity functions, these youngsters will not be able to compete in jobs that require fine motor dexterity or a great deal of walking. Coordinated educational and vocational planning should be initiated early.

OSTEOGENESIS IMPERFECTA

Osteogenesis imperfecta is a generalized systemic disease of the bony skeleton (Speck, 1979). Osteon is a Greek word for bone; therefore, osteogenesis imperfecta means imperfect bone formation. The condition is also known as brittle bone disease, because frequent fractures constitute the most significant clinical problems. The condition is quite rare, but it has been recognized for almost 200 years because of its striking manifestations. The symptoms and course of the disease are so dramatic that several thousand cases have been described, including many well-documented cases in the early medical literature.

Etiology

The exact cause is unknown. The basic pathology consists of a disturbance in the manufacturing of **collagen fibers** (Sharrard, 1971). It is possible that the disease is related to a genetically determined defect or defects in the enzymes that regulate the production and chemical composition of collagen fibers. These connective tissue elements (collagen fibers) are widely distributed in the body as important constituents of diverse anatomic structures, including the protein matrix of bones, the **sclera** (the white of the eye), the ligament bands that support the joints, and connective tissue under the skin. The widespread presence of collagen fibers explains why the abnormality exhibits a wide variety of signs and symptoms, although the most prominent clinical problem is bone fragility.

Normal bone formation takes place in several steps. In the initial stage, a protein matrix that consists mostly of collagen fibers is produced. It is called osteoid or fiberbone. Subsequently, inorganic salts composed mainly of calcium and phosphorous are laid down over this fibrous mesh. It is the inorganic salt content that makes bones hard and provides their strength. In osteogenesis imperfecta, the deposition of inorganic salts is reduced because the osteoid matrix is defective. Essentially, bone formation becomes partially arrested due to the abnormal fiberbone in the first step of the process. As a consequence, the second stage, in which hard mature bone tissue forms, cannot proceed normally. Hence, the bones are brittle, although the mechanism of calcification itself is not defective.

Osteogenesis imperfecta is a hereditary disease. In the severe congenital form the condition is inherited through a recessive gene, but children with this form of the disease generally die young and do not reproduce. In the less severe type, osteogenesis imperfecta shows up in infancy or later, but not at birth. Here the gene is usually dominant. The condition may also appear without previous familial history, most likely due to spontaneous genetic mutation. From then on it will be transmitted through a dominant gene. In osteogenesis imperfecta there is no genetic predilection for any sex, race, or ethnic group.

Characteristics

The cardinal symptoms are bone fragility, a blue discoloration of the sclera, a high incidence of deafness, poorly formed brittle teeth and, in some cases, increased laxity of the joints and skin (Tachdjian, 1972). Because the bones are brittle and unable to resist even normal stresses, repeated fractures occur from minor or unnoticed injuries, which would be harmless to a nonaffected person. Several thousand fractures were reported in one individual, but this was an extreme case. The long bones of the limbs are particularly prone to break. For reasons poorly understood, fractures heal normally; in fact, at times there is exuberant bony callus formation.

Severe bone deformities develop from the recurrent fractures and healing in abnormal positions. The limbs are considerably bowed and may be shortened. The chest is usually barrel shaped. Bones of the spine are flattened (compressed). The back is excessively rounded and the spinal column may develop scoliotic curvature. Instead of growing, the child's stature actually can become shorter because of repeated fractures, increasing deformities, and progressive spinal curvature. In severe cases, there may be dwarfing. The skull is usually misshapen; the child has a protuberant broad forehead and temples, which make the face appear smaller. Compared to the shortened stature, the head seems relatively large.

Blue sclera is a rather frequent sign, because the underlying layer, rich in blood vessels and pigment, shows through. Either the sclera is thinner than normal or the defective collagen fibers cause this discoloration. The color may vary from a slight bluish tinge to robin's-egg blue. Scleral discoloration does not affect the child's vision or cause other problems.

The high incidence of hearing impairment or deafness might be due to abnormalities in the small bones of the middle ear, which participate in transmitting sound vibrations, or to anomalies in the bony inner ear, which plays a role in perceiving sound. Alternatively, the auditory nerve itself could become impaired by compression during its passage in the temporal bone. Hearing loss can develop over the course of years.

Dental defects are very common because essentially the same process is involved in bone and tooth formation. The anomaly, dentinogenesis imperfecta, affects those parts of **deciduous** and permanent **teeth** that are composed of **dentin.** The teeth are usually translucent, discolored, gray or yellowish-brown, and prone to cavities and breakage. Crowns and roots are often poorly developed and abnormally shaped. The outer enamel layer, having a different embryonic origin than bone and dentin, is normal but chips easily because of its defective foundation.

Due to poor quality collagen fibers, some children with osteogenesis imperfecta have remarkably lax joints and hyperelastic skin. The joints can be hyperextended or bent backwards, as if the person were double-jointed. The skin may be loose and easily stretched. At times, the child may tend to bruise easily.

On the basis of age at the onset of symptoms, two forms of osteogenesis imperfecta are distinguished. Osteogenesis imperfecta congenita represents the more severe form. The infant is born with numerous fractures; the limbs are short, severely bowed, or otherwise deformed at birth (Figure 10–2). Bones of the skull feel soft. Some newborns do not survive the trauma of delivery. Others may die in infancy or childhood following a virtually continuous series of fractures despite the most careful physical

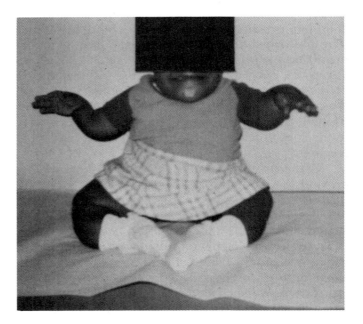

Figure 10–2   Twelve-Year-Old Child With Osteogenesis Imperfecta Congenita. She has severe dwarfing with the height of a four year old, and short, curved extremities.

handling. Apparently, some fractures can result from normal movements by the infant.

In osteogenesis imperfecta tarda, the infant appears normal at birth. Fractures begin to occur during infancy or childhood. Depending on when the symptoms begin, this form of the disease is further classified into infantile and juvenile types. There are also considerable variations in the severity and the resulting disability. In general, however, fractures are fewer and deformities are less severe than in the congenital form (Figure 10–3). The problem of fractures tends to improve once the child has attained full growth after puberty, possibly because of the decreased demand for new bone formation. It is not unusual to see partial signs, such as blue sclera, deafness, or joint laxity in the other family members whose bones are not abnormally fragile.

An interesting observation is that ligamentous laxity and, in particular, blue sclera are usually associated with mild bone disease, whereas children with severe bone fragility often have white sclera. It is possible that the differences in clinical signs reflect some variations in the collagen fiber defects. Indeed, this

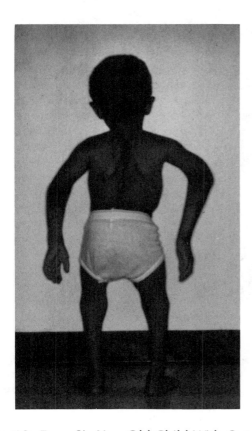

Figure 10–3   Six-Year-Old Child With Osteogenesis Imperfecta Tarda. He has bowing of both legs and the right upper arm, and scoliosis of the spine. His legs appear shorter due to bowing.

was suggested by comparative biochemical analyses of **biopsies** obtained from patients with different types of clinical disease. Differences in the mode of inheritance is another indication that osteogenesis imperfecta probably includes several diseases rather than a single disease despite the general similarities in signs and symptoms.

Diagnosis

Multiple fractures at birth are diagnostic of the congenital form. In osteogenesis imperfecta tarda, the infant or child comes to attention because of repeated fractures. Blue sclera, dental anomalies, joint laxity, and familial history provide supportive evidence. The diagnosis is confirmed by radiologic examination showing old and recent fractures in various stages of healing, and systemic bone disease with characteristic abnormal signs.

A universal feature of osteogenesis imperfecta is decreased bone mass, indicated by marked thinness in the outer, dense bone layer and a paucity of fine markings in the inner, less dense portion of the bone. Additional radiologic signs depend on the clinical form and severity of the disease. The thick bone type of radiologic appearance is generally associated with the congenital form or, less often, with the severe infantile form. The long bones are shortened, broadened, and severely curved. Sometimes there seems to be a complete derangement of bone structure (Figure 10–4). More common is the thin bone type radiologic picture that usually accompanies the late onset, less severe disease. The long bones are slender, except for their end portion, which is relatively large (see Figure 10–4). There is typical bowing that affects the hip and shin bones, in particular, as they bend under the stress of bearing the child's weight. In spite of the generalized bone disease, laboratory blood chemistry findings are normal.

It is most important to differentiate between children with osteogenesis imperfecta and battered children, because both groups show many of the same signs. Battered children suffer repeated and multiple fractures that result from true injuries. Their X rays show numerous fractures but radiologic signs of generalized skeletal disease are absent in these children. In addition, battered children are often bruised and have other symptoms of injury but no signs associated with brittle bone disease. However, it must be considered that a child with osteogenesis imperfecta also could be mistreated either by careless negligence or willful intention.

Deformities seen in osteogenesis imperfecta congenita can be easily distinguished from those in arthrogryposis multiplex congenita by their differ-

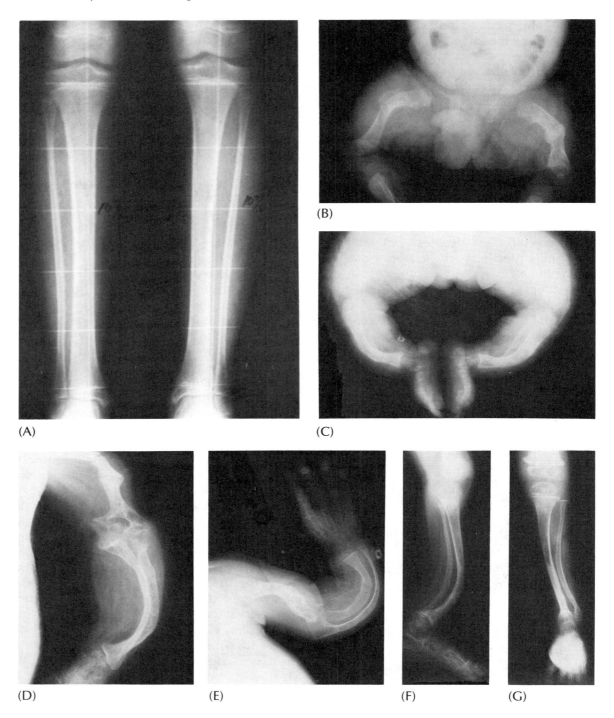

(A)

(B)

(C)

(D)

(E)

(F)

(G)

Figure 10–4   Comparative X Rays of Normal and Abnormal Bone.

A: X ray of normal bone. Note dense, compact outer layer surrounding a more radiolucent but well calcified inside structure. (The square grid is not part of the normal bone.) *B–E:* Serial X rays of the child shown in Figure 10–2. B: Healing fractures at the midportion of both hip bones at two weeks of age. C: Progressive deformities, broadening of hip and shin bones following multiple fractures at twelve months of age. Radiologic picture of the severe thick bone type of abnormality. D: Multiple fractures, exuberant callus formation and deformity of upper arm bone, bowing of forearm bones at three years. E: Severe progressive bowing and shortening of the same extremity at four years. *F–G:* Side and front views of the leg below the knee of the child shown in Figure 10–3. F: Note thinness, decreased bone mass, and bowing. G: Side view shows anterior bowing of shin bone, called saber shin deformity.

ences in appearance. In brittle bone disease, joint motion is not impaired and deformities affect the bones.

Skeletal deformities and a weakened, fracture-prone bone structure also occur in other generalized skeletal disorders, metabolic bone diseases, and some neurologic conditions. Differentiation among these diseases is based on other clinical, radiologic, and laboratory abnormalities.

Achondroplasia is a systemic bone disease unrelated to osteogenesis imperfecta. The clinical signs are dwarfism, a relatively large head, and bowing of the extremities. This appearance may bear a slight resemblance to osteogenesis imperfecta in older children. However, an achondroplastic child is not prone to fractures and X rays of the bones show different signs.

In some hereditary connective tissue diseases joint laxity and hyperelastic skin are the prominent clinical symptoms. Sometimes, the sclera shows a bluish discoloration. These diseases are not accompanied by systemic bone disease and by fractures that represent the most significant abnormality in osteogenesis imperfecta.

Treatment

There is no treatment that can cure or alter the course of this disease. Administration of drugs and chemicals (including fluoride, magnesium oxide, steroids, and sex hormones) has not proven effective. Treatment concentrates on the symptoms instead of the disease, providing support, and preventing further damage when possible.

The treatment of fractures in these children requires special considerations. Immobilization in a cast leads to additional loss of calcium from the bones, which enhances their brittleness. However, it may be impossible to avoid using casts on lower-limb fractures in ambulatory children. Otherwise, malalignment of the bone during healing can aggravate already existing deformities. The period of immobilization may be shortened, and associated bone loss decreased, by using a walking cast or fracture braces, or by allowing the child to stand and move in water, where buoyancy will bear some of the child's weight.

Bowing of the hip and shin bones can be corrected by surgery. During the operation the midportion of the bone is cut into pieces and threaded on a metal rod anchored in both bone ends (Figure 10–5). This procedure is recommended only for ambulatory youngsters whose deformities would jeopardize their ability to walk.

Light-weight braces are sometimes helpful for external support of fragile bones and for stabilization after fracture or surgery. The inflatable pneumatic

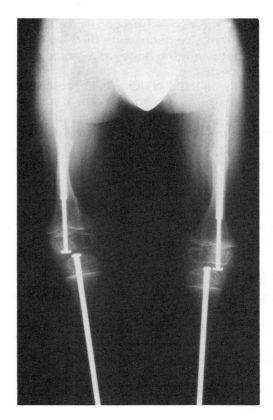

Figure 10–5   X Ray of the Child Shown in Figure 10–3 After Surgical Insertion of Metal Rods to Both Hip and Shin Bones

brace was designed specifically for osteogenesis imperfecta by a person who himself has this disease.

Protection from inadvertent injury under normally innocuous circumstances is a necessity that must be kept in mind when handling these children. Some severely affected infants can even sustain fractures as they are dressed or picked up. Reasonable protection and adaptations in daily life are important. However, youngsters who have a more benign form of the disease and can walk should not be excessively restricted, because physical activity is a physiologic stimulus of bone formation. There are no hard, fast rules as to what should be permitted, but the children learn to adjust to their affliction as they grow older.

In some cases, a wheelchair will be needed either full time or for strenuous activities. Propelling a wheelchair may not be possible with extremely short arms or it may put too much stress on brittle bones. In these instances, a motorized wheelchair could provide independent mobility. Periodic hearing evaluation is part of these children's care.

Prognosis

The course and the extent of the handicap depend on the severity of bone disease. Generally, the congenital form has the poorest prognosis, but varying degrees of progressive deformities develop in all types. On the other hand, the bones may become less fragile after puberty.

Severely affected children will require a wheelchair to get around and their fragile deformed arms may hamper complete independence in daily activities. In the less severely afflicted, ambulation is possible, although braces or other supportive devices may be needed. As a rule, ambulatory youngsters can perform ordinary daily activities but not heavy physical work. A person with brittle bone disease must avoid the stress and strain of vigorous physical activities in all of his life, even if the symptoms are mild or become arrested during adolescence.

Educational Implications

The educational potential of these children is good because they have normal intelligence. The curriculum should emphasize academic achievements to prepare them for an intellectually oriented, sedentary occupation that would best suit the child's aptitudes.

A protected environment is often a necessity, as is an attendant available to help the more severely affected and partially dependent child. However, mainstreaming is desirable and should be encouraged, even though precautions and some physical assistance may be needed. When the child enters regular school, it is usually very helpful to explain the problem to his classmates. Nonhandicapped children, once they understand the nature of the handicap, develop a considerate attitude and healthy peer relationship.

Teachers should be aware that the child's hearing may deteriorate, sometimes insidiously, over the years and should alert the parents and physician responsible for the child's care when a suspicion of this problem arises. Although these children should be encouraged to exert themselves at the maximum level of activity that can be tolerated, they should not participate in physical education or sports. An exception is carefully supervised and monitored nonstressful swimming. Diving is contraindicated. Playing a musical instrument and sedentary social games, such as chess or Monopoly, are good substitutes for recreation involving physical activities and are a source of great satisfaction for these children.

SUMMARY

Both diseases discussed in this chapter interfere with the integrity of the skeletal system and result in physical disability. In arthrogryposis multiplex congenita, defective muscle development leads to limited joint mobility and deformities. The disease is not hereditary and does not progress. In contrast, osteogenesis imperfecta is a hereditary systemic bone disease with progressive deformities resulting from repeated fractures. Defective collagen production is responsible for the bone fragility and other characteristic signs of this disease.

In both conditions, the etiology is unknown, treatment is to relieve symptoms as the diseases are incurable, and intelligence is normal. Children affected by these diseases are permanently handicapped, although the extent of physical limitations can vary considerably. The quality of education received by the children is crucial in preparing them for a suitable occupation that will enable them to become productive adults.

REFERENCES

Sharrard, W. J. W. *Paediatric orthopaedics and fractures.* Oxford: Blackwell Scientific Publications, 1971.

Speck, W. T. Hereditary and developmental lesions of bone and cartilage. In V. C. Vaughn, R. J. McKay, & E. Behrman (Eds.), *Nelson textbook of pediatrics.* Philadelphia: W. B. Saunders, 1979.

Swaiman, K. Anterior horn cell and cranial motor neuron disease. In K. Swaiman & F. S. Wright (Eds.), *The practice of pediatric neurology.* St. Louis: C. V. Mosby, 1975.

Tachdjian, M. O. *Pediatric orthopedics.* Philadelphia: W. B. Saunders, 1972.

Diane C. Mitchell, M. D., *is clinical assistant professor in the Department of Pediatrics at the School of Medicine, University of Southern California, Los Angeles, and staff pediatrician in the Department of Pediatrics and co-director of the Spina Bifida Clinic at Rancho Los Amigos Hospital, Downey, California.* **Earl Fiewell, M.D.,** *is clinical assistant professor in the Department of Orthopedic Surgery at the School of Medicine, University of Southern California, Los Angeles, and staff orthopedic surgeon and co-director of the Spina Bifida Clinic at Rancho Los Amigos Hospital, Downey, California.* **Patty Davy, R. P. T.,** *is physical therapist in the Department of Physical Therapy at Rancho Los Amigos Hospital, Downey, California.*

Until the past few decades, schools and the general public have been unaware of congenital defects of the spinal cord and the vertebral column, variously called myelodysplasia, myelomeningocele, spina bifida, or neural tube defects. These birth defects are

CHAPTER 11

Spina Bifida

very common; yet, until good treatment evolved, they represented a private tragedy to affected families. Now, this chapter can be written in a spirit of optimism.

Initially, the terminology is imposing. A defect in the bony arch of the vertebrae, which protects the spinal cord, is called spina bifida (split in two). *Spina bifida occulta* (Figure 11–1b), refers to the malformation of a few vertebrae, usually in the low spine, which is present in 30 percent of the general population. If the flexible casings or covers of the spinal cord (meninges) escape through the defect in the developing fetus, the infant is born with a protruding *meningocele* (sac), which may or may not be covered by skin (Figure 11–1c). Generally, neither of these malformations causes loss of function to the child.

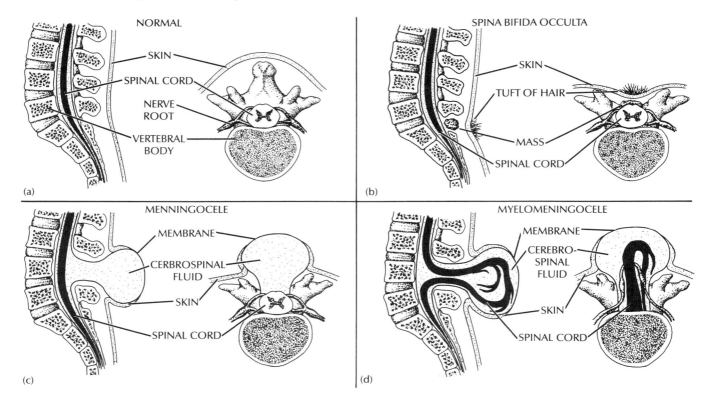

Figure 11–1   Myelodysplasia
A: *Normal spine*—lateral and cross-section views.
B: *Spina bifida occulta*—fatty mass and hair may or may not be present.

C: *Meningocele*—no nerves from the spinal cord are displaced.
D: *Myelomeningocele*—note disrupted, abnormal spinal cord and nerves.

However, when the sac contains a portion of the spinal cord or nerve roots, it is a *myelomeningocele* (or meningomyelocele) and severe neurologic consequences usually occur (Figure 11–1d). *Myelodysplasia* is a term used to encompass myelomeningoceles and other defects of the spine in which nerve loss, and therefore loss of normal function, is manifest. Spina bifida has come into general use as a synonym for the myelomeningocele condition. Although it is not semantically accurate, the ease of spelling and pronunciation have favored the term's acceptance throughout the world. Spina bifida will be used here.

Most infants born with a myelomeningocele have associated developmental abnormalities in the structure of the brain. The base of the brain (the medulla), which contains many of the cranial nerves, may be present in the cervical vertebrae (at the top of the neck) rather than within the skull, as would be normal. This is called the Arnold-Chiari malformation. Furthermore, up to 90 percent of the children with this disorder also have an obstruction in the circulation of cerebrospinal fluid, causing hydrocephalus (water-head).

Although the condition of spina bifida has been recognized for centuries, the defects usually pre-sented insurmountable problems and the children died in infancy. Most of the infants died from a nervous system infection or the effects of the excessive brain pressure.

Modern medical and surgical care opened the door to effective treatment. Neurosurgeons devised techniques to enclose and "tuck in" the myelomeningocele and to cover the exposed portion of the nervous system. Procedures were designed to treat hydrocephalus by shunting the excess fluid from the brain. Antibiotics were discovered to treat infections. There has been a "quiet revolution" in interest, knowledge, quality of care, and realistic hope for persons born with spina bifida.

ETIOLOGY

Although the basic cause of spina bifida still remains an enigma, it appears plausible that genetic factors interact with environmental factors to trigger the malformation in the developing embryo very early in the pregnancy. The four-week-old embryo (only 5 mm. long) has a primitive brain and spinal cord differentiated as parts of the **neural tube.** When the distal neural tube fails to fuse, spina bifida occurs.

The condition is common, annually affecting over 6,000 newborns in the United States. Rates vary from 1 in 500 to 1 in 1,000 births, according to region. The genetic influence is evident: a couple with one affected child has one chance in fifty of a spina bifida child in each subsequent pregnancy. A similar incidence occurs in pregnancies of a parent who has spina bifida.

CHARACTERISTICS

Spina bifida is a complex disorder involving multiple systems of the body, although the affected child may appear to have only orthopedic problems, e.g., difficulties with the bones, joints, and muscles. Most commonly, the leg muscles are paralyzed because of nerve damage associated with the myelomeningocele. The amount of paralysis depends on the location of the lesion in the spinal cord. There is a predictable assignment by nature of nerves to specific muscles. For example, the chest muscles are moved by the thoracic nerves, the leg muscles by the lumbar nerves, and the foot muscles by the sacral nerves.

The muscles controlling bladder and bowel functions are also controlled by the sacral nerves. Spina bifida children, therefore, have serious bowel and bladder problems. Similarly, the nerves from the various parts of the body that control sensation (pain, temperature, etc.) return to the spinal cord at predictable locations en route to the brain, where awareness is perceived.

Motor level and sensory level are terms to describe the location of spinal cord and nerve loss, rather than the level of the vertebral defect. To a degree, these levels predicate the child's disabilities. It is not uncommon, however, to have variations between the motor and sensory levels and even variation between the right and left sides.

The type of paralysis in spina bifida is usually flaccid (floppy) because of malformation of the nerves from the spinal cord to the muscles. If, however, the nerves *below* the motor level are present, but disconnected from communication and direction from the brain through the spinal cord, a spastic (uncontrolled, stiff) paralysis occurs.

Because of hydrocephalus and the Arnold-Chiari malformation, difficulties in breathing and swallowing may be life-threatening complications, especially to an infant. Strabismus (cross-eye) and other eye problems are common. Seizures develop in one out of ten children. Problems in arm movement and strength, eye-hand coordination, and balance give further complications, as do significant learning problems. Other birth defects, particularly skeletal anomalies and heart and kidney malformations, occur frequently.

Because of the extraordinarily complicated nature of spina bifida, we have found it helpful to organize the multiple problems into primary and secondary disabilities. Each child presents a unique set of clinical characteristics. The manifestations of the primary disabilities include muscle paralysis and deformities, loss of sensation, hydrocephalus, urinary and bowel incontinence, sexual problems, mental retardation and other learning problems, visual problems, and other congenital defects. Secondary disabilities are those that result from complications in the primary difficulties. Many can be prevented; these include joint contractures, bone fractures, obesity, kidney disease, pressure sores, constipation, infections, emotional disorders, and educational deprivation.

Six areas will be discussed in some detail: hydrocephalus, orthopedic and motor development problems, sensation impairment, urinary and bowel problems, sexual problems, and learning problems.

Hydrocephalus

The brain and the spinal cord are suspended and protected within the skull and vertebral bones by the cerebrospinal fluid (CSF), which is produced within the cavities (ventricles) of the brain. The CSF has a closed circulation, traveling downward to bathe the base of the brain and the spinal cord and then moving over the surface of the brain where the fluid is reabsorbed, thus allowing space for the influx of more CSF. Under normal conditions, an exquisite balance of CSF production and reabsorption is maintained by this low pressure circulation. If the flow of CSF through the series of ventricles is blocked in any of the narrow, connecting channels, a damming effect occurs. The ventricles behind the block swell to accommodate the extra CSF and the pressure rises, producing hydrocephalus (Figure 11–2). The small infant's skull bones are unfused to allow the normal rapid head enlargement due to brain growth and development. Hydrocephalus due to blocks in CSF circulation occurs in 80–90 percent of infants with spina bifida. Disproportionate head growth is the initial clinical characteristic. If untreated, some children develop huge heads from the excessive ventricular fluid and pressure, and brain structures are distorted and damaged. Although a few untreated patients survive into adulthood, death usually occurs when the pressure is sufficiently high to affect the base of the brain, which controls the respiratory and cardiac centers—the basic "life support system." Thousands of children have survived, however, when the CSF has obtained equilibrium by various compensatory mechanisms of

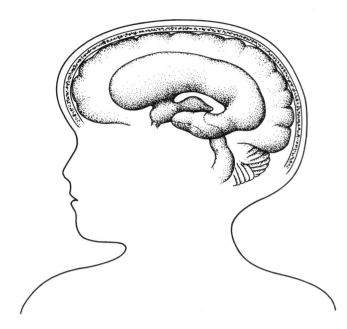

Figure 11–2   Hydrocephalus With Ventricles, Very Dilated

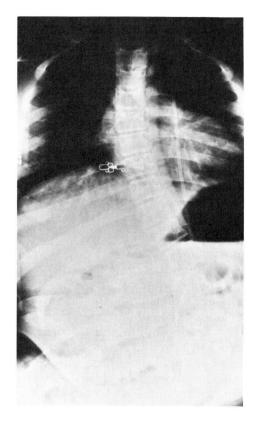

Figure 11–3   Scoliosis of the Spine. The tube to the right of the spine is shunt tubing.

the nervous system. Mild to moderate head enlargement is seen. This is termed compensated or arrested hydrocephalus.

Orthopedic and Motor Development Problems

Orthopedic problems in spina bifida children result from the paralysis due to the motor nerve loss. The problems are always complicated by virtue of muscle imbalance. Contractures develop when joints have normal muscles that move the joint in one direction but lack balancing muscles that move it in an opposite direction. The functioning muscles on one side of a joint tighten without the compensating effect of functioning muscles on the other side of the joint and the joint freezes in a contracture. In some cases, dislocations of the joints occur. Bone deformities (bending and twisting) also occur as a result of imbalanced muscle pull. These deformities may be present at birth and progress in the growing child.

Severe scoliosis (Figure 11–3) can cause marked deformity of the chest, thus decreasing cardiopulmonary function and eventually cause cardiac failure. Scoliosis requires increased energy for walking. It causes the person to be off-balance when sitting, decreasing the ability to perform two-handed tasks such as putting on a shirt over the head. Also the tilted pelvis distributes the person's weight unevenly decreasing the ability to sit comfortably and increasing the risk of pressure sores (Piggott, 1980).

Spine deformities occur most frequently in the higher level lesions, and the incidence decreases pro-

gressively as the level of paralysis begins lower in the spine. However, the clinical picture changes when complications develop. Fractures, which are common in high level lesions, can lead to further deformities. Obese children become less active and their intact muscles become weaker from disuse. Consequently, an obese youngster with a low level lesion who can walk with braces becomes a teenager with the more limited capabilities of a person with a higher level lesion.

Normal motor development in infancy and early childhood is severely compromised in proportion to the motor and sensory deficits. Moreover, developmental progress is dependent upon the interaction among multiple factors including muscle strength, joint range of motion, intelligence, motivation, and perceptual skills. Perceptual skills develop from organization in the brain of the sensory input from movement, touch, sight, and awareness of position in space, with motor experiences. Because a spina bifida child has a congenital lack of many of the nerves that provide this information, perceptual skills lag behind motor abilities, thus compounding the difficulties in mastering developmental tasks. Particular problem areas include spatial judgement, concepts of direction and distance, and motor organizational

Figure 11—4   Self-Portrait by a Spina Bifida Child —Note the Absence of Legs

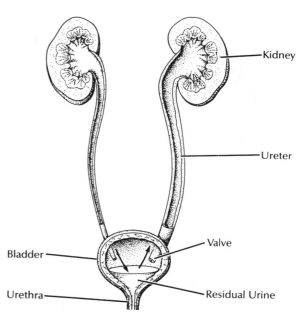

Figure 11—5   Normal and Disabled Kidneys
The right kidney and ureter are normal. However, the left kidney and ureter are swollen due to reflux of urine from the bladder because the valve is not functioning properly.

skills. All of these problems are magnified in any child with congenital nerve loss, compared to the child whose spine is injured later in life. Never having experienced feeling in some body parts, there is failure to incorporate these insensitive areas into the child's body image and awareness (Figure 11–4).

Sensation Impairment

Loss of sensory nerves makes the child unable to perceive pain below the sensory level. The child cannot feel the size, shape, or temperature of objects against the affected skin. He is unprotected by the body's main alarm system: pain. He is unaware of the blister on his foot from shoe or brace pressure or numbness in his buttocks from sitting too long in one position. He is unaware of sunburn on his feet, abrasive sand in his shoes, or stubbed toes. Skin ulcerations, therefore, are a constant threat to the child and adult. Discomfort forces us to move constantly, even in sleep. Pressure sores develop when circulation to a small area of skin and muscle is cut off by pressure, such as the skin between an ankle bone and a tight brace. In about two hours, tissues begin to die. This becomes life-threatening when pressure sores progress to deep tissue death and infection of the entire body.

Urinary and Bowel Problems

The normal bladder acts as an efficient storehouse of urine until it is sufficiently full, then it signals the brain of its full state. The toilet-trained person urinates at a socially acceptable time and place. The bladder is completely emptied of urine by contraction of the bladder muscle and complete relaxation of the sphincter muscles of the urethra (the outlet tube). Special one-way valves prevent urine in the bladder from returning to the kidneys. After voiding, the urethral muscles tighten again to prevent urine leakage while the relaxed bladder refills. This seemingly effortless act is accomplished by the smooth coordination of three sets of nerves. Each set contains sensory and motor nerves. Almost all spina bifida persons have serious bladder problems resulting from the loss of any of these nerves, or the loss of coordination of the nerves in the spinal cord.

Normal toilet training is not possible. This results in incontinence, a severe disability. Moreover, the **neurogenic** bladder frequently does not empty urine completely, thus allowing residual urine in the bladder (Figure 11–5). The result is a bladder infected by the abnormal growth of organisms normal to the urine, just as any pool of stagnated water becomes polluted. If the bladder problems progress, the urine can back up (reflux) to the kidneys. The kidneys then become swollen and damaged by the pressure of the urine (hydronephrosis) (Figure 11–6). Infection of the kidneys (pyelonephritis) compounds the kidney damage. Severe kidney problems can occur without outward signs of illness. If untreated, these kidney problems lead to renal failure and death. (See Chapter 24 for further discussion of kidney disorders.)

Problems in bowel incontinence also hamper the spina bifida child. If the anal sphincter muscles are

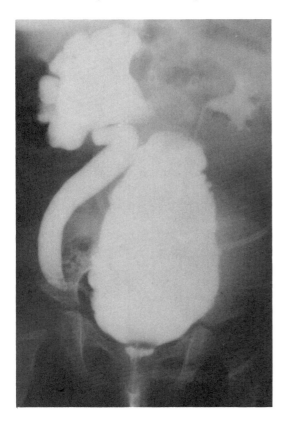

Figure 11—6   X-ray Study of the Kidneys
A normal left kidney and a swollen right kidney (on the left side of the X ray) due to reflux of urine from the bladder because the valve is not functioning properly.

floppy, fecal material is not retained. An overly tight anus prevents passage of stool and leads to constipation. (See Chapter 20 for further discussion of bladder and bowel problems.)

Sexuality

Spina bifida children, teenagers, and adults are *not* asexual beings. Production of sex hormones, secondary sexual characteristics, sexual drives, and a desire for intimacy develop normally. Most women with spina bifida can bear children and some men can father children. Unless there is a severe mental handicap, most adults can have happy marriages.

Learning Problems

Intelligence is not a fixed trait. It is highly dependent upon environmental factors. The child born with spina bifida faces many challenges that can hamper his intellectual development and ability to learn in school. Multiple operations, hospitalizations, dependence, delayed self-care, and poor self-esteem are some of the unfortunate consequences of the

child's early life. Additionally, visual problems, learning disorders, hydrocephalus, and infections impede the learning process; as do sensory deficits and simple lack of mobility.

The incidence of mental retardation has greatly decreased because of early treatment of hydrocephalus and aggressive management of medical problems. However, specific learning disabilities are common and include problems in visual-motor perception, motor planning, visual discrimination, and auditory discrimination. Some youngsters have attention deficits and some have emotional disorders as additional problems that complicate their education.

DIAGNOSIS

The diagnosis of spina bifida is usually apparent at birth if a myelomeningocele is present (Figure 11–7). A careful physical examination is the most important diagnostic tool. This general examination is supplemented by a variety of other examinations. The motor and sensory levels are determined by muscle and sensory testing. The condition and functioning of the kidneys and bladder are studied by special examinations and urine cultures. Early diagnosis of hydrocephalus has been facilitated by the technology of computers applied to x-ray studies. The computerized axial tomogram, understandably given the eponym of CT scan or CAT scan, allows a direct picture of sections of the brain and ventricles in a safe and painless manner.

Prenatal (before birth) diagnosis of myelomeningocele has become possible in recent years with the discovery that a fetus with an open neural tube defect has an elevated alpha feto-protein (AFP) level in the amniotic fluid, which surrounds the fetus in the uterus. Amniocentesis (removal of a small amount of

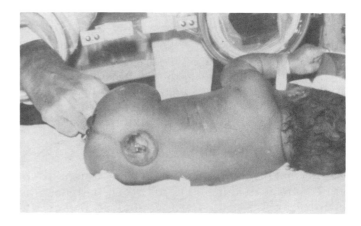

Figure 11—7   A Newborn Infant With Unrepaired Myelomeningocele

fluid for testing) can be done between the 16th and 20th weeks of pregnancy. Other conditions can raise AFP in the amniotic fluid and in the maternal blood. At present, most medical centers offer amniocentesis and other diagnostic studies to pregnant women who are at high risk of having a child with a neural tube defect. Mass screening of all pregnancies is being investigated and is a controversial issue (Milunsky, 1980).

TREATMENT

The myelomeningocele is closed by neurosurgeons soon after birth. However, there is no cure for the nerve loss and its effects, or for the hydrocephalus condition. The goal of treatment is to provide the most effective management of the primary disabilities, while preventing the secondary disabilities. A habilitation team must work cooperatively to meet the needs of the child and the family. Effective management requires the services of not only physicians and nurses, but also of social workers, psychologists, physical and occupational therapists, orthotists, and educators. As treatment of the most prominent disabilities is discussed, the reader must remember that education of the family to become the "experts" for their child is an important part of the treatment process; with growth and development, the child becomes the expert. The disease of spina bifida is not static. Ongoing diagnosis of the status of the disabilities is the cornerstone for treatment.

Hydrocephalus

Hydrocephalus became a treatable condition in the last few decades when neurosurgeons and engineers combined their skills to devise methods to divert (shunt) the blocked CSF, thereby maintaining normal CSF pressure, normal-sized ventricles, and hopefully, normal brain growth and function. Various shunt systems consisting of tubing and valves have been utilized. Earlier shunts diverted the CSF to the heart, but most shunts now end in the peritoneal (abdominal) cavity, where the fluid is easily absorbed (Figure 11–8).

Monumental improvements in the safety and reliability of shunts have occurred in the past few years. Shunt infections do occur, however, and the shunt systems may become clogged or broken, like any plumbing system. All persons who care for a youngster with shunted hydrocephalus should be alert to signs of shunt malfunction or infection. These signs include vomiting, fever, headache, irritability, drowsiness, and sudden appearance of eye muscle weakness. By use of the CT scan (Figure 11–9), malfunctioning shunts can be quickly diagnosed and

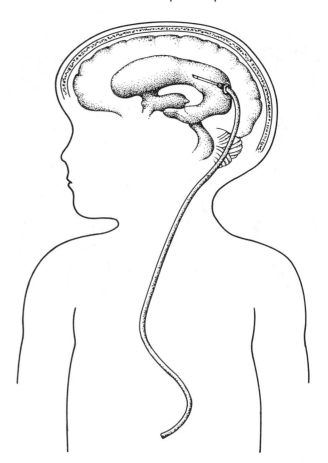

Figure 11–8   A Ventricular-Peritoneal Shunt Ending in the Abdominal Cavity

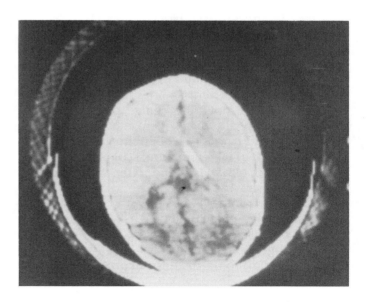

Figure 11–9   A CT Scan With Well-Shunted Hydrocephalus. The white "bar" across the brain tissue is the shunt.

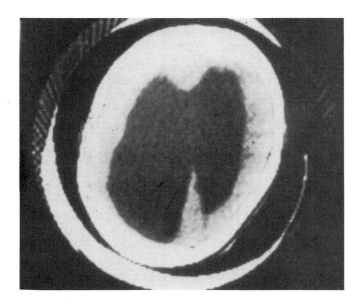

Figure 11–10 A CT Scan Showing Huge Ventricles in Arrested Hydrocephalus. (Black = ventricles; White = compression of the brain, surrounded by the skull bone.)

treated. Most children can now grow up with well-controlled hydrocephalus.

New diagnostic technology has allowed better understanding of the condition of arrested (compensated) hydrocephalus, which occurred in the many persons who survived without a shunt or in persons whose shunts became gradually nonfunctional, prior to the era of CT scans. The CT scans show enlarged ventricles (Figure 11–10). Enlargement of the spinal cord may be present, acting as the "safety valve" for excessive CSF pressure. Although many persons are functioning well, these older children and adults may have unique problems as the price of the central nervous system's adaptation. Recent research suggests that many severe disabilities may be caused by the effects of the not truly benign condition of arrested hydrocephalus (Hall, Lindseth, Campbell, & Kalsbeck, 1976; Hammock, Milhorat, & Baron, 1976). These include mental retardation, scoliosis, spasticity, arm and hand weakness, and poor motivation to achieve.

Placing a shunt in a person with chronically enlarged ventricles entails serious risk. However, the potential benefits may outweigh the risk, especially if signs of progressive neurologic changes occur in the untreated child. Some of these neurologic changes include:

1. Loss of vision;
2. Recurrent headache and back and neck pain, especially if worst in the morning (CSF pressure rises during sleep);
3. Development of spasticity in previously normal muscles;
4. Progressive decline in balance, coordination, and arm strength;
5. Progressive scoliosis (back curvature) above the motor level;
6. Decline in serial IQ testing and school performance; and
7. Personality deterioration, irritability, and a decline in motivation and personal care.

Orthopedic and Motor Development Problems

Orthopedic care for spina bifida children involves two major goals: to provide maximal musculoskeletal function for the neurologic level and to allow a normal sequence of developmental experience despite the child's physical limitations (Kupka, Geddes, & Carroll, 1978). The basic concept (overall long-term goal) is to promote maximal habilitation for adulthood. The motor level is the initial keystone to the prognosis of the child's ultimate physical abilities.

If the motor level is low (i.e., paralysis of the muscles is from the fifth lumbar nerves through the sacral nerves), the leg muscles and most of the muscles of the feet will function. These children will walk and will continue to walk as adults. In most cases, they will be community ambulators, implying independence from the need for a wheelchair. The likelihood of being able to walk deteriorates with each successively higher level of paralysis. Some will walk within the house (household ambulator) but will use the wheelchair for outside travel covering any great distances. Middle to high lumbar level children may be walkers but, as adults, may prefer the mobility offered by wheelchairs. Persons with a thoracic level paralysis, and no motor function below the hips, may always require a wheelchair (see Table 11–1).

It is important that a prognosis about the eventual method of mobility be developed early in childhood so that reasonable treatment may be rendered, thus promoting development of the child into the most functional adult. It is not reasonable to insist that a child walk during the six- to ten-year-old period if he will not walk as an adult, especially if it would require repeated surgery, wearing cumbersome orthoses (braces), multiple trips to medical centers, and hours and hours of ambulation training (Figure 11–11). Rather, the goal would be to promote mobility and allow the child time to attain age-appropriate accomplishments in education, play, self-care, and forming friendships.

There are many innovative devices to assist the child in successfully participating in the normal activities for each period of development. During the first year of life many crucial learning experiences are

Table 11—1   Levels of Paralysis

Anatomic Level	Functional Levels	Major Motor Function	Major Deformities	Childhood Mobility	Adult Mobility
T12	Thoracic	Totally paralyzed lower limb	Scoliosis Pelvic obliquity	Standing brace Wheelchair Exercise Ambulation	Wheelchair
L1 L2 L3	High lumbar	Hip flexion Hip adduction Knee extension	Scoliosis Pelvic obliquity Hip flexion contracture Hip dislocation	Crutches Long braces with hip support(1) Household or community ambulation Wheelchair	Wheelchair in 75% Household, or community ambulation with long braces (2) and crutches
L4 L5 S1	Low lumbar	Knee flexors (medial hamstring) Ankle extensor (anterior tibialis) Lateral hamstrings	Hip subluxation Hip flexion contracture Calcaneus foot deformity Foot ulcers	Short braces (3) Crutches for long distance Community ambulation	Ambulation in 75% Crutches or none Short braces
S1 S2 S3	Sacral level	Ankle flexors inner (posterior tibialis) Outer (peroneal foot muscles) Lack small foot muscles	Foot ulcers Claw foot (toe deformity and high arch foot)	Community ambulation Supports in shoes	Limited distances in 90%

Orthotic Terminology:
1. HKAFO—hip knee ankle foot orthosis (brace).
2. KAFO—knee ankle foot orthosis.
3. AFO—ankle foot orthosis.

dependent upon handling and movement. This year sets the foundations for personality and motor development.

Orthopedic surgery is frequently required to meet the goal of maximum habilitation. Orthopedic treatment is designed to correct deformities by changing the imbalance of the muscles; lengthening them to decrease the fixed positions (contractures) of joints, transferring one end of a muscle so that it pulls in a different direction, or correcting the bones or joints themselves. The purpose is to provide the best positioning for function augmented by bracing and training.

When they anticipate the child will walk as an adult, orthopedic surgeons strive for an extended position. This position provides the greatest stability and requires the least expenditure of energy during walking. There must be a straight spine, a level pelvis, extended hips and knees, and plantargrade (flat) feet distributing the pressure of the body's weight equally over the sole of the foot. In order to sit well (especially important for people who will primarily use a wheelchair for mobility), it is important to have a straight spine, a level pelvis, flexible hips, and bendable knees.

The higher the level of neurologic involvement, the more likely a curvature of the spine will develop. Treatment of spinal curvatures is important for both sitting and standing persons. The spine is closely observed throughout growth of the child. Once a curve is discovered and found to be progressive, a body jacket is used to support the spine and to attempt to

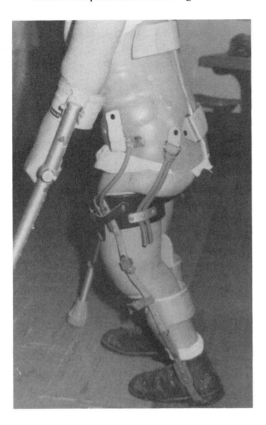

Figure 11–11   A Well-Braced Child. Ambulation was so slow, however, that the patient has stopped using the braces. The child is now doing well as a wheelchair ambulator in a regular junior high school.

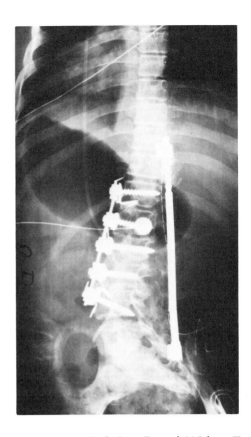

Figure 11–12   A Spine Fused With a Two-Stage Procedure

counteract the progression of the curve. If this fails, surgery is necessary. The surgical procedure involves insertion of metal devices to provide support and enhance bony healing (stability) to each vertebral segment found to be abnormally curving (Figure 11–12). The patient is then placed in a cast or plastic body jacket until the portion of the spine has become fused in a single unit, instead of the segmental spine that was allowing excessive movement and spine curvature.

The muscles that flex the hips and knees can become taut in a contracture. Hip and knee joint contractures are common and prevent the ambulator child from achieving the extended position. Therapy programs are instituted for stretching exercises. Hip stretching is promoted when the child sleeps or rests in a prone position (on the stomach). Knee contractures are treated with progressive stretching and plaster of paris casts. If these conservative measures fail, surgery can release the contractures. Bracing can help maintain position but cannot correct it, nor can bracing overcome marked muscle imbalance.

Hip dislocations are common in lumbar-level patients because of muscle imbalance (Figure 11–13).

Treatment in infancy is directed towards prevention or replacement of dislocations. Older children who have dislocations, however, may be left untreated when it doesn't affect their ambulation or functional status.

Foot deformities are common (Figure 11–14a) and may turn the foot in any direction, depending upon the muscle imbalance created by the level of paralysis. These deformities create problems in fitting shoes and braces. With lack of sensation, pressure sores and ulcers develop. Treatment to obtain a stable, flat foot free of bony prominences on the sole (Figure 11–14b) is essential to allow walking. The wheelchair sitter also must have a sufficiently standard foot position to allow fitting shoes and to protect against injury to the sides and tops of the feet.

Rotational deformities occur as a result of twisted bones from muscle imbalance or joint contractures. These rotational deformities are surgically corrected only if they affect function of the limb, not for cosmetic purposes.

Sensation Impairment

The key to treating those with sensation impairments is prevention of trauma to all insensitive skin. Bare

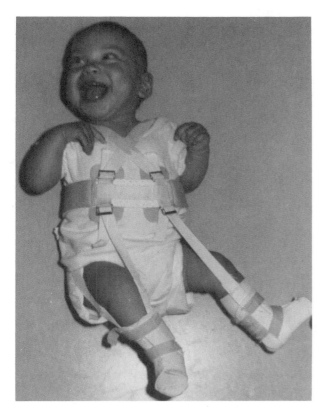

Figure 11–13   A Spina Bifida Infant in a Pavlik Harness for Treatment of Hip Dislocation

feet, sandboxes, and hot water must be avoided. Tolerance for new braces and shoes must be built up gradually. Wrinkled socks must be avoided. Parents must inspect every area of affected skin twice daily for signs of injury. The child must be taught to assume responsibility for inspection at the earliest possible time.

Mirrors are used to check the bony prominences under the buttocks, which are particularly vulnerable to pressure sores. "Raises" or "reliefs" by lifting the torso for fifteen seconds every fifteen minutes (Figure 11–15) should become an unconscious habit. Special weight redistributing cushions are useful. One type is made of high density foam and can easily be "cut out" to relieve the areas prone to pressure sores (Figure 11–16). Treatment of actual ulcerations involves removal of all pressure, medical and surgical procedures, and time—the most difficult and costly of all.

Urinary and Bowel Problems

It is mandatory to monitor the status of the kidneys and bladder throughout childhood and adulthood. Urine infections must be promptly diagnosed and treated. Neurogenic bladders can function fairly efficiently, avoiding infection or reflux, for months or

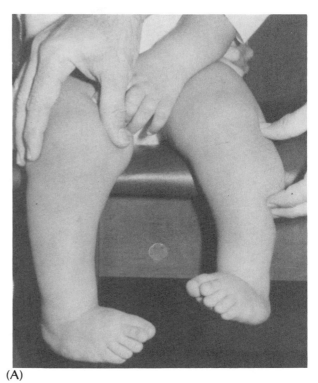

(A)

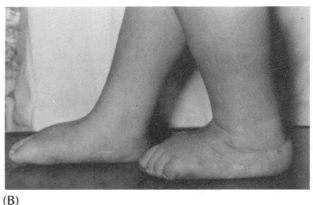

(B)

Figure 11–14   Correction of Foot Deformities
A: Club feet birth deformities.
B: The same child after surgery, with flat (plantargrade) feet, is now able to wear braces and shoes and is able to walk.

years and then unpredictably become "unbalanced" with residual urine and ensuing renal (kidney) disease. Effective treatment hinges on periodic complete emptying of urine from the bladder, avoiding residual urine and high bladder pressure. Earlier methods of treatment consisted of leaving catheters (tubes) within the bladder, or circumventing the neurogenic bladder by surgically relocating the ureters into a segment of bowel. Urine was collected in a bag attached to an opening on the abdominal wall. These solu-

Figure 11–15 An Adult Spina Bifida Man "Raises" to Relieve Pressure on His Buttocks

tions were helpful, and even lifesaving to some persons, but many complications occurred from these treatments.

The use of *intermittent* catheterization has become popular in the last decade (Enrile & Crooks, 1980). Gratifying results have occurred by this relatively simple procedure. Kidney function is being preserved by good bladder drainage. Many children now are able to be out of diapers. Drug therapy can assist

Figure 11–16 Foam Cutout Cushions (with and without Cover)

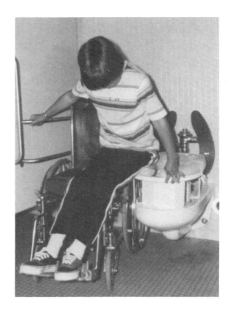

Figure 11–17 A Boy Transfers to the Toilet From His Wheelchair

in achieving continence (dryness) between catheterizations (Applebaum, 1980).

By age seven, most children can learn to insert a catheter into their bladders. Children in wheelchairs are taught to transfer to the toilet for self-catheterization. The success of IC (intermittent catheterization) or CIC (clean intermittent catheterization) is directly related to the enthusiasm and diligence of the medical team, the family, and the school.

Many boys prefer the use of external condom catheters to collect urine, which is then stored in a leg bag hidden under the trousers. This system works well if no leakage occurs. Many girls prefer padding (the term "diaper" should be avoided after infancy). A variety of supplies and acceptable undergarments for incontinence is now available. With good hygiene and frequent changes, offensive odors can be prevented.

Bowel problems are best managed by establishing a regular, daily elimination pattern utilizing aids such as suppositories and mini-enemas to stimulate rectal emptying. Laxatives may be needed and diet is important. The program should be started in infancy. Young children are given potty chairs. Older children should learn to transfer onto toilets (Figure 11–17). An effective bowel and bladder program is crucial to the child's success in obtaining and keeping friends, attending regular schools, and in vocational planning (Henderson & Synhorst, 1977).

Sexual Problems

A satisfactory adjustment in adulthood is possible. Appropriate information on sexuality should be given

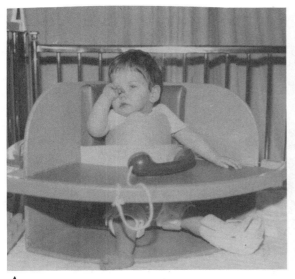

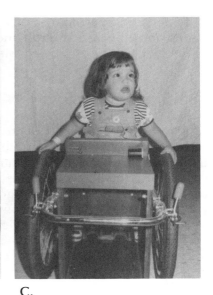

A.   B.   C.

Figure 11–18   Adaptive Devices for Toddlers   B: A castor cart for a preschool child
A: A corner seat for a child who cannot sit unassisted   C: A batmobile for mobility in a standing position

to the growing child and adolescent by parents and the school as it would be for other children. Specialized counseling is now widely available for persons with congenital or acquired spinal cord problems.

Learning Problems

Treatment for learning problems begins in infancy and stresses prevention. It seems clear that positive, loving, nurturing experiences must occur in infancy if a child is to experience satisfactory personality and intellectual development. The maintenance of a happy, loving, and accepting family is the most important factor in educational success.

The challenge to the therapy team in infancy and early childhood is to devise adaptive equipment (Figure 11–18) that allow attainment of appropriate experiences and skills despite the child's physical limitations. Early diagnosis and treatment of perceptual and speech and language problems is possible. Hearing loss, visual problems, and seizures must be looked for and treated promptly.

PROGNOSIS

The prognosis for a child born with spina bifida was grim until the past twenty-five or thirty years. Only 5–10 percent of the babies lived past infancy or early childhood, and many of the survivors were severely disabled mentally and physically. Nevertheless, even with educational deprivation because of their incontinence, many surviving children have become happy,

successful adults, and some have achieved eminence in professional fields. In retrospect, it is a tribute to the tenacity of the human spirit.

The overall prognosis for life and for normal intellectual functioning has always been more optimistic for children with sacral and low lumbar lesions because of their lower incidence of hydrocephalus. In contrast, 95 percent of high lumbar and thoracic level children have hydrocephalus in addition to their other disabilities. Almost all reports show higher rates of mental retardation in this group.

It is easy to get into statistical gamesmanship because reports in the literature from various medical centers have shown variable results. The lack of CT scans in the past makes it impossible to evaluate the meaning of hydrocephalus (controlled versus uncontrolled) in some previous reports. Nevertheless, one major center that offers comprehensive treatment starting in infancy studied a large group of children born in the mid-1960s. They reported that 80 percent lived and that almost half of the children requiring shunts and 90 percent of the nonshunted children had normal intelligence (Ames & Schut, 1972).

With even more aggressive early treatment by prompt closure of the myelomeningocele and vastly improved management of hydrocephalus, neurogenic bladders, and infection control, the prognosis for longevity, health, and better intellectual functioning has improved even more. This year, 90–95 percent of the babies born with spina bifida should live (McLone, 1979). The quality of their lives should be equally improved because of intensive early therapy and stimulation programs, family support, excellent orthopedic management, availability of school programs, incontinence control, and improved attitude of the public towards persons with disabilities.

EDUCATIONAL IMPLICATIONS

Children with spina bifida were excluded from the school systems in many parts of the United States until the recent national legislation mandating education for all children. There is still much to do to obtain optimal educational programs for spina bifida children. Many of our bright youngsters are "caught" in classrooms for the orthopedically handicapped or in other special education classes that offer continuing emphasis on gait training, cooking, community activities, etc. Many high schools emphasize menial vocational programs. Our plea is simple: schools should carefully evaluate a child's intellectual capabilities and place the child in a program suitable for his intellectual and educational needs, not just his physical problems. Although unable to become a bricklayer, the child could become a computer programmer.

The needed medical and surgical care in early childhood often delays a child's acquisition of independence and healthy aggression. The medical team needs the school to push and prod children into the world of competition, academic success, and eventual vocational success. Self-esteem is a byproduct of successful experiences. Protective environments diminish the chances for success.

With careful planning and communication between professionals, practical arrangements can be made (Lauder, Kanthor, Myers, & Resnick, 1979). Private toilet areas are needed. Attendants should be hired to give any needed physical assistance, including catheterization and bracing assistance. Making these adjustments is cheaper than placing the child in a segregated classroom.

Success for the child who is mainstreamed into regular classes requires bowel and bladder continence, which is possible. Occasional accidents may occur and should be treated unemotionally. Teachers should briefly explain the child's problems to the class, or the child can do this. All children have some type of problem. Teasing is part of the give-and-take of children growing, learning, and playing together. Classmates of a physically handicapped child are frequently enriched by greater tolerance and understanding because of the child's placement in the classroom.

Physical education programs can easily be adapted to maximize the child's participation. Walking children who use braces can play soccer and baseball, and can ski, bowl, and dance. Wheelchair-bound

Figure 11–19   Wheelchair Sports

children can ride horses, swim, and do a variety of wheelchair sports including basketball (Figure 11–19), tennis, and bowling. Mentally handicapped children can participate in the Special Olympics activities.

Earlier, we mentioned the importance of recognizing the signs of shunt problems and progressive hydrocephalus. These concerns should not be frightening to teachers. The responsibility for obtaining medical care is the province of the parents. Teachers must be tolerant of their own initial anxieties when accepting a spina bifida child. Parents and physicians have been through the same feelings and they understand that it takes time to acquire knowledge and confidence. The rewards are worth the effort.

SUMMARY

Spina bifida is a serious birth defect caused by faulty development of the embryo early in pregnancy. The manifestations, unique in each child, include loss of feeling and paralysis of the legs, loss of bladder and bowel control, hydrocephalus, and learning problems. Until twenty-five or thirty years ago, most affected infants died. The children who survived had bleak futures. The prognosis has become more optimistic with advances in surgical and medical techniques. Children with spina bifida now have the potential for healthy and happy lives if provided with comprehensive and enthusiastic medical, social, and educational programs, and good interdisciplinary communication and planning.

REFERENCES

Ames, M. D., & Schut, L. Results of treatment of 171 consecutive myelomeningoceles—1963–1968. *Pediatrics,* 1972, *50,* 466–470.

Applebaum, S. M. Pharmacologic agents in micturitional disorders. *Urology,* 1980, *16,* 555–568.

Enrile, B. G., & Crooks, K. K. Clean intermittent catheterization for home management in children with myelomeningocele. *Clinical Pediatrics,* 1980, *19,* 743–745.

Hall, P. V., Lindseth, R. E., Campbell, R. L., & Kalsbeck, J. E. Myelodysplasia and developmental scoliosis: A manifestation of syringomyelia. *Spine,* 1976,*1,* 48–56.

Hammock, M. K., Milhorat, T. H., & Baron, I. S. Normal pressure hydrocephalus in patients with myelomeningocele. *Developmental Medicine and Child Neurology,* 1976, *37,* 55–67.

Henderson, M. D., & Synhorst, D. M. Bladder and bowel management in the child with myelomeningocele. *Pediatric Nursing,* 1977, 24–31.

Kupka, J., Geddes, N., & Carroll, N. C. Comprehensive management in the child with spina bifida. *Orthopedic Clinics of North America,* 1978, *9*(1), 97–133.

Lauder, C. E., Kanthor, H., Myers, G., & Resnick, J. Educational placement of children with spina bifida. *Exceptional Children,* 1979, *45,* 432–437.

McLone, D. G. The results of early treatment of 91 consecutive newborns with myelomeningocele. *Spina Bifida Therapy,* 1979, *2,* 145–150.

Milunsky, A. Prenatal detection of neural tube defects. *Journal of the American Medical Association,* 1980, *244,* 2731–2735.

Piggott, H. The natural history of scoliosis in myelodysplasia. *Journal of Bone and Joint Surgery,* 1980, *62–B,* 54–58.

Irene S. Gilgoff, M.D., *is assistant clinical professor in the Department of Pediatrics at the School of Medicine, University of Southern California, Los Angeles, and staff pediatrician in the Department of Pediatrics at Rancho Los Amigos Hospital, Downey, California.*

The spinal cord is less than ½ inch wide and 18 inches long in the full grown adult male (Elliott, 1969). Yet, through this small structure, the brain communicates with the body below. Voluntary movement of the arms and legs depends on an intact system of many components. First, the idea of movement must occur. Whether the movement contemplated is the perfection of a ballet leap in *Swan Lake* or simply scratching an itch, varying areas of the brain must conceive of the desire to move. This desire is quickly passed on to the precentral gyrus of the frontal lobe, the motor area of the cerebral cortex (Figure 12–1). The precentral gyrus is subdivided into separate sections that control movement of the arms, the legs, or the face. The message to each essential area involved in the

CHAPTER 12

Spinal Cord Injury

movement desired is relayed to the corticospinal tracts located in the ventral horns of the spinal cord. Here, it passes down the cord until it reaches the connection to the desired peripheral nerves, the nerves that individually give force to every muscle in the body. It is relayed from the spinal cord to the peripheral nerve, which carries the message to the final connection, the muscle. The muscle contracts and movement begins. Through separate pathways, the brain is informed of the accomplishment of its desired task.

An injury to the spinal cord interrupts the relay of messages between the brain and the muscle. An interruption at this level does not prevent the brain from formulating a plan or desire for movement. The muscles, still alive and in touch with their energy

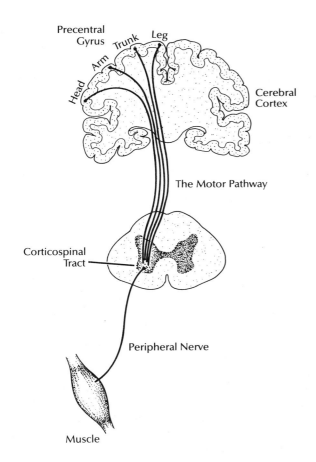

Figure 12–1   The Precentral Gyrus of the Frontal Lobe

force, the peripheral nerves, await instructions that never arrive. Voluntary movement can no longer occur. Depending on the level at which the interruption occurs, movement of the arms may be spared but movement of the legs is lost, or movement of both the legs and the arms may be lost. The signal to the muscles that allows us to control the times we choose to urinate or have a bowel movement may be lost. Lesions high enough in the spinal cord can also affect the major muscles of breathing. In these cases, breathing may cease without the assistance of a respirator.

Movement is only one of the many relay systems that passes through the spinal cord. Like a complex telephone switchboard, many systems are working simultaneously. Relay systems to the skin pass from the brain, through separate areas in the spinal cord, to inform the skin of pain, touch, pressure, heat, or cold. The bowel or bladder is given information that it is either empty or full. Lesions of the spinal cord can interrupt any or all of these circuits.

Unless separate injury has been inflicted, the person with a spinal cord injury has an intact brain in a body that is no longer in control of all that the brain

desires to do. The intellectual desires remain. The intellectual ability to replan and reshape one's own destiny is also intact. Because of this, teachers with the responsibility to educate a child with a spine injury have before them an added challenge and also the potential of immense satisfaction.

ETIOLOGY

It is difficult to determine the local prevalence of a condition such as spinal cord injury. Our society is a mobile one, changing addresses every few years. Added to this is the fact that spinal cord injury initially may be overlooked in the comatose patient who has been in an accident. Even considering these problems, one large study (Kraus, Franti, Riggins, Richards, & Borhani, 1975) attempted to determine the incidence of spinal cord injury in eighteen counties of northern California. They found an annual incidence rate of 53.4 persons per million (this includes people of all ages). Other studies estimate the incidence rate to be lower, closer to 30 cases per million (DeVivo, Fine, Maetz, & Stover, 1980). In the California study, a low incidence of injury was seen for children below fifteen years of age. Although people fifteen years of age and younger or 75 years of age and older had the lowest rate of spinal cord injury, they had the highest rate of fatalities at the time of injury.

Although permanent spinal cord injury can occur at birth, the frequency of injury increases with age. The reason for this is not difficult to understand when one considers that accidents are the major causes of injury. In children, motor vehicle accidents rank first as a cause of spinal cord injury. This includes children as automobile passengers and children as pedestrians struck by automobiles. Falls comprise the second largest cause of injury. Articles differ as to whether gunshot wounds or recreational activities are third on the list of causes; this possibly is due to differences in the population groups studied (Anderson & Schutt, 1980). Many types of recreational activities have been known to cause spinal cord injury: diving accidents, winter sports, bicycle riding, and gymnastics head the list.

The newborn infant also faces the risk of a spinal cord injury. In these infants, the injury results from the birth trauma; 75–80 percent of birth-related spinal cord injuries follow vaginal breech deliveries (Byers, 1975). In a breech delivery the fetus in utero is positioned so that the feet are delivered prior to the head. Breech positioning of the unborn child makes delivery difficult. In order to extract the child's head, traction must be applied. The combination of traction and hyperextension of the neck during the delivery process is thought to account for the spinal cord injury. This correlates with the area of the cord that is most commonly damaged. The most common level of injury is in the low cervical or high thoracic area, located at the base of the neck (Leventhal, 1960). Position of the head and neck in utero is also an important factor in the risk involved in vaginal breech deliveries. The risk of a spinal cord injury in breech deliveries of children with hyperextended heads in utero is felt to be as high as 21 percent. The mortality rate of such an injury is extremely high and severe permanent damage affects the infants that survive.

The mortality rate immediately following a spinal cord injury in children in general is also quite high. Death usually is not specifically related to the spinal cord injury, except in high cervical injuries in which breathing is impaired. Usually, death is due to other organ system damage from the same traumatic incident. Approximately 10 percent of the children die during the acute stage, the first week or two following the onset of the injury (Anderson & Schutt, 1980). Once the patient survives the acute period, the outlook for long-term survival is good (DeVivo et al., 1980).

Level of spinal cord injury resulting from all forms of trauma taken together is fairly evenly divided between injuries affecting all four extremities and those affecting only the legs and feet. Certain types of injuries, however, tend to lead to certain levels of injuries. For example, gunshot wounds are more commonly associated with paraplegia (lower extremities only). Diving injuries are more often associated with quadriplegia (all four extremities).

Interestingly, there is no great sexual predisposition seen in spinal cord injury in children. Until the age of fifteen, boys and girls are affected fairly evenly, at about 1.3 males to 1.0 females (Kraus et al., 1975). This is due to the mode of injury. In automobile accidents or birth injuries, the child is the passive, hapless victim of circumstances at the time. However, at around the age of fifteen, there is a rather drastic increase in the prevalence of spinal cord injuries in young men as opposed to women. Beyond age fifteen, the incidence of injury is about four times higher in men. This is due to the more active role of the patient in precipitation of the injury.

There are rare causes of spinal cord injury not associated with trauma. Tumors can invade the spinal cord and cause permanent paralysis. The blood supply to an area of the spinal cord can be cut off for multiple reasons. A medical syndrome, called acute transverse myelitis for want of a more specific term, has also been discussed frequently in the medical literature (Altrocchi, 1963). Basically, this describes the acute onset of spinal cord damage with no known precipitating traumatic cause. Etiologies suggested

for this syndrome include infection, **vascular lesions,** drug-related injury, and allergic responses, among many others. Over half of these patients will recover completely from this illness; about a third, however, will be left with significant spinal cord damage.

CHARACTERISTICS

The spinal cord is a long, thin tubelike organ composed of nervous tissue extending from the brain to the low back. Within its protective covering, the vertebral column, the spinal cord is submerged in cerebrospinal fluid, which surrounds the cord and flows through its central canal. The vertebral column is composed of 33 bones; seven cervical vertebrae, twelve thoracic vertebrae, and five lumbar, five sacral, and four coccygeal vertebrae (Figure 12–2). The cervical vertebrae are the bones of the neck. The thoracic vertebrae occupy the back of the chest wall, where they join the rib cage. The lumbar vertebrae are the bones of the low back. The sacral and coccygeal vertebrae form the tailbone. In the adult, the five sacral vertebrae fuse to form one bone called the sacrum, and the four coccygeal bones fuse to form the coccyx.

The spinal nerves, the beginnings of the peripheral nervous system, consist of eight cervical nerves and twelve thoracic, five lumbar, five sacral, and one coccygeal nerve exiting from the spinal cord (as shown in Figure 12–2). These peripheral nerves supply the energy force and transfer the message from the brain and spinal cord to the rest of the body.

As can be seen in Figure 12–2, the spinal cord is actually much shorter than the vertebral column. In the adult, the spinal cord is about 25 cm. shorter than the vertebral column. The spinal cord ends around the first or second lumbar vertebra. The spinal nerves of the lumbar and sacral areas travel a long distance within the vertebral column before exiting between their individual vertebrae. These long nerves as a group are called the cauda equina.

The spinal cord is an extremely complex structure. A compact collection of nervous tissue, in cross section it consists of well-organized separate tracts. Each tract carries special signals from the brain to their final destination. Separate areas are concerned with movement, interpretation of pain sensation, knowledge of one's position in space, and sensation such as pressure and vibration, to list just a few. The message that originates in a specific area of the brain is carried through the spinal cord on its separate tract, often crossing to the opposite side of the body somewhere along the way. The spinal cord enlarges in the cervical area and the lumbar area where the nerves supplying directions to the upper and lower extremities, respectively, exit.

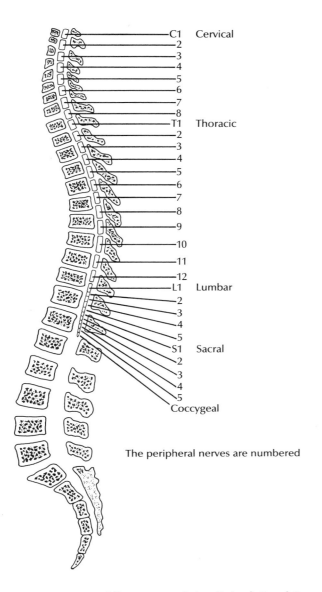

C1 — Cervical
2
3
4
5
6
7
8
T1 — Thoracic
2
3
4
5
6
7
8
9
10
11
12
L1 — Lumbar
2
3
4
5
S1 — Sacral
2
3
4
5
Coccygeal

The peripheral nerves are numbered

Figure 12—2   Alignment of the Spinal Cord Segments, Vertebral Bodies, and Spinous Processes

The characteristics of a spinal cord injury depend on several things: First is the level of the spinal cord at which the injury occurs. Also important is whether the lesion cuts across the entire cord (a complete cord lesion) or only part of the cord (an incomplete lesion). The etiology of the injury is significant as well.

The level at which the spinal cord is injured is of paramount concern. The nerves that supply the muscles of the arms exit from the spinal cord in the low cervical region, approximately C_5 through T_1. A neck injury above the fifth cervical vertebra would cause paralysis of both the arms and the legs (a quadriplegia) because messages would no longer be able to pass from the brain to the spinal cord segments that supply these areas of the body. Lesions between C_5 and T_1 spare some muscles of the lower arm; therefore, some elbow and hand function will remain.

The nerves that supply the muscles of the legs exit from the spinal cord in the lumbar and sacral areas, L_1 through S_2. A complete spine injury that causes permanent damage to the spinal cord between T_2 and the first lumbar vertebra will cause permanent loss of function to the muscles of the legs but spare the arms (referred to as a permanent paraplegia). Injuries that occur below L_1 will damage the nerves of the cauda equina. Varying degrees of paralysis in the muscles of the lower legs will result, depending on which nerves are affected.

An incomplete lesion allows some messages to transverse from the brain to their final destination because the cord is not totally severed. In this way, varying combinations of injury might be seen; for example, one arm and one leg or part of one arm may be left intact.

Therefore, the characteristics of a spinal cord injury are determined by the level and the area of the spinal cord that is affected. In general, a traumatic injury (e.g., a gunshot wound) slices the spinal cord from the outside inward. Rare traumatic lesions can cause what initially seems to be a strange pattern of damage. These are injuries to the cervical spinal cord often from an abnormal hyperextension of the neck. Referred to as a central cord lesion (Figure 12–3), they show a characteristic pattern of involvement (Schneider et al., 1954). This pattern of involvement is best explained as due to an injury to a blood vessel, either from trauma or the effect of an underlying predisposing abnormality. Simply, the center of the spinal cord is nourished by the anterior spinal artery, which is formed from the vertebral arteries. Although there is some cross circulation from branches supplying the posterior spinal cord, any major vascular accident involving the vertebral arteries or the anterior spinal artery would damage the center of the spinal cord. A distinct lesion would occur because of the fiber tracts located most centrally in the cord, a lesion very different from other cord lesions. Characteristics of this lesion include more involvement of the arms than the legs, some loss of control of urination, and variable sensory loss. Therefore, the central cord spinal lesion should be remembered when attempting to explain the rare injury where the legs are relatively spared in comparison to the arms and hands.

Detailed studies of the vascular supply of the spinal cord point out several areas along the cord where the vascular supply is decreased (Schneider & Crosby, 1959). The areas where there is minimal overlap of blood supply are around the upper to middle thoracic area, around T_4, and at the upper lumbar section, L_1. This fact is reflected in the clinical evidence. A large percentage of patients whose spinal

Figure 12–3   A Central Cord Lesion. The upper extremeties are affected more than the lower extremeties.

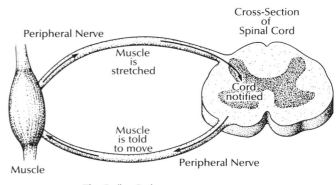

The Reflex Pathway

Figure 12–4   The Reflex Pathway

cord injury resulted from an insufficient blood supply suffer paraplegias in the midthoracic area.

The patient with a spinal cord injury will continue to have some reflex activity. Communication with the brain is not necessary for many types of reflex activity to occur. The maintenance of simple reflexes depends only on the viability of the segment of cord and the peripheral nerves of the cord at the level of the reflex itself. This is why the patient with complete paralysis from a spinal cord injury may be seen to move spontaneously. This movement is due to spasms activated by the reflex motor system (Figure 12–4). The movement is entirely involuntary.

It is important to remember that the spinal cord does not only relay information concerning movement of the body. The sensory modalities of pain, pressure, and touch, for example, are also carried in the spinal cord. Injury to the cord also affects perception of sensation below the level of involvement of the spinal cord. Complete injuries of the spinal cord, therefore, prevent the patient from any awareness of pain or pressure below the level of the injury.

Initially, it might seem that no longer feeling the multiple injections and medical procedures to which these patients are often exposed is advantageous.

However, the feeling of pain is really a very necessary protective device. The patient who has a spinal cord injury is not able to tell when he has been hurt in those areas of his body where sensation is lacking. Hot drinks spilled on him might go unnoticed. Tight shoes or braces may not be removed. The consequence of not being aware of pain can be significant skin sores that can become deep and infected.

The spinal cord also sends nerves to the bowel and bladder. Therefore, a complete injury to the spinal cord will affect voluntary control of urination and defecation. Abnormal control or loss of control of bladder function is referred to as a neurogenic bladder. Varying with the type of injury, a patient may either constantly dribble urine, or have great difficulty in successfully voiding and emptying the bladder. The patient will lose control of when he has a bowel movement. Because of the decrease in physical activity by the patient following paralysis, constipation will also become a problem.

The spinal cord also sends out peripheral nerves to those muscles vital in maintaining normal respiration. Without these connections, breathing is impossible. The diaphragm, the major muscle of breathing, is innervated in the neck by cervical segments C_3, C_4, and C_5. A lesion above C_3 would be fatal if artificial respiration were not initiated immediately. The intercostal muscles, innervated by the thoracic spinal cord segments, aid the diaphragm in its task. A patient with a high thoracic lesion would be able to breathe because his diaphragm would remain intact. However, his breathing would be compromised to 50 percent of normal breathing capacity, because of the loss of the intercostal muscles. Therefore, this patient would be more susceptible to any respiratory infection because of his decreased reserve.

The cough is a very important aspect of normal breathing. When excess secretions, such as phlegm, accumulate in the lungs, a strong cough keeps the airways clear. The muscles responsible for a strong, effective cough are basically some of the abdominal muscles, with some assistance from the thoracic, intercostal muscles. The major nerve supply of these muscles comes from the lower thoracic and upper lumbar areas of the spinal cord. Lesions above this area will eliminate the ability to cough or will decrease its effectiveness. Patients with this problem are prone to respiratory infections and also have increased difficulties in combatting these infections.

In summary, the characteristics of a spinal cord injury vary. Many different body functions are involved. The level of spinal cord injury is the single most important factor in determining the problems that the patient will experience. Although less visible than the paralysis, respiration, skin sensation, and bowel and bladder function are equally important aspects of spinal cord injury.

DIAGNOSIS

The onset of paralysis, especially after an acute injury, should be enough to make one very suspicious of a spinal cord injury. Because the great majority of spinal cord injuries are the result of trauma, the diagnosis is made more difficult in a comatose patient who has suffered other injuries at the time of the acute injury. In these instances, the spinal cord injury might go unnoticed for an extended period of time, perhaps until the patient regains consciousness. In the newborn infant, the diagnosis can also be difficult. Here again, the knowledge of a difficult delivery (especially breech presentation) should make one suspect the possibility of a spinal cord injury.

Other than the history of a preceding trauma, the most important tool in making a diagnosis is a thorough physical examination. Paralysis following injury to the spinal cord can usually be differentiated from paralysis from severe muscle weakness or head injury. This is done through a sensory examination. Loss of sensation is always present in a complete spinal cord injury. By using a simple safety pin, one tests the patient's ability to feel a pinprick. The spine-injured patient whose cord was completely severed will not feel the pin below the level of the injury. Even in a newborn infant, the careful examiner can discern a sensory loss.

In an older patient, the loss of control of bladder and bowel function is also an important indicator of spinal cord injury. The patient above several years of age who has severe weakness from muscle disease will still be aware of when to urinate or defecate. Even if he is unable to get to the bathroom on his own, the muscle-diseased patient can warn caretakers of the need to void. The spine-injured patient will be unable to predict when he must void. The head-injured patient who has severe brain injury also may be unaware of the need to void. In this case, this is due to the brain injury itself that causes a lack of understanding of the voiding process. In the spine-injured patient, the patient will understand and very much want to control these body functions. Unfortunately, the spine-injured patient will no longer feel the sensation of bladder or bowel fullness. More importantly, he will no longer have control of the sphincter muscles that control voluntary opening and closing of the bladder and bowel orifices and allow voiding to occur only when desired.

In high cervical injuries, the immediate loss of respiration is of primary importance. Because the great majority of infants born with spinal cord injuries have lesions high enough to cause respiratory depression, this problem in the newborn should alert the clinician to the possibility of spinal cord injury.

The diagnosis of a spinal cord problem, therefore, is made by a knowledge of the patient's history. Various medical procedures (called **myelograms** or **arteriograms**) may, at times, be useful. They are especially useful for the patient who has a slow onset of spinal cord misfunction and are used in these cases to uncover intrinsic problems of the spinal cord, such as tumors or vascular malformations. However, these medical procedures often add nothing to the diagnosis of traumatic spinal cord injury. Even X rays often supply no additional information about the young child with a spinal cord injury. Studies that have been published about spinal cord injuries in children agree that X-ray findings of fractures of the vertebral column correlate only slightly with the actual occurrence of spinal cord damage. In fact, in about 50 percent of the children with significant spinal cord injuries, no fracture or dislocation of the vertebral column had occurred (Burke, 1974). The correlation between fracture of the vertebral column and underlying spinal cord damage increases with age. In newborns with spinal cord injuries due to birth trauma, a fracture is rarely seen. In fact, over 90 percent of newborns with significant spinal cord injury will have had no dislocation or fracture.

Studies have been done to explain the reason for the lack of positive X-ray findings in newborns and in young children with spinal cord injuries (Leventhal, 1960). These studies have shown that, in the infant, the vertebral bodies of the bones surrounding the spinal cord have not formed into solid bone. Instead, at birth, the vertebral column is made up of elastic cartilage. On the other hand, the spinal cord itself is well anchored in several areas. Above, the cord is fixed by the large cervical roots and the brainstem. At the bottom, it is secured by the large lumbar roots forming the peripheral nerves to the legs. Fetal autopsy specimens have shown that the vertebral column can be stretched 2 inches because of its elasticity, but the spinal cord can only be stretched ¼ inch. Because of this, especially in injuries in which the spine is stretched, the vertebral column offers little protection for the infant and young child. A fracture need not occur before there is permanent damage to the important nerve tissue of the spinal cord.

TREATMENT

Although a great deal of research is being done in this field, at the present time there is no medical method of stimulating injured neural tissue to regrow (Gunby, 1981). Medical treatment given immediately following the injury primarily attempts to prevent further damage. Various medications have been used in attempts to prevent unwanted swelling of the spinal cord after injury and spread of injured tissue. Occasionally, surgery is necessary either to relieve pressure on the spinal cord or to stabilize fractured or dislocated vertebrae. There is no surgical procedure, however, that can reconnect the split neural tissue of the spinal cord itself. The patient with an acute incomplete injury of the spinal cord will often have some return of function during the first few months following the injury. This is due primarily to the decrease in swelling of the acutely injured cord, but also possibly to a small amount of regeneration that occurs from natural body forces. However, the return of any degree of function to the patient with a completely severed spinal cord is rare.

The major thrust of treatment of the spinal cord injured patient is in rehabilitation. Because little can be done to physically restore functions lost to the patient, intensive efforts are aimed at teaching new skills so that the patient can regain as much independence as possible. This is accomplished by preparing patients to return to their preinjury environment with as much ability to cope with that environment as is possible. To accomplish this goal, health care professionals from many different areas must work together as an efficient, coordinated team. Most spinal cord injury centers, therefore, work as a team: five to ten people are involved in each patient's care.

With children, the family is an integral part of the functioning team. Other team members include: a pediatrician, involved in coordination of team efforts and care of the child's health needs; various surgeons, including orthopedists who are skilled in spine care and surgeons who are skilled in tracheostomy care (if necessary); physical therapists; occupational therapists; inhalation therapists for patients who need respiratory therapy; orthotists to make necessary braces; social workers; psychologists; specially trained nurses; dieticians; and recreation therapists.

The rehabilitation process begins with a thorough evaluation of the patient's status. The evaluation is done by each team member in order to assess as fully as possible the physical and emotional state of the patient and his family. Any medical problems that preceded the spine injury are reassessed in light of the new major medical problems. General health requirements, such as immunizations, are kept up to date.

The patient's nutritional status is monitored carefully. Many children, especially those with high cervical lesions, have severe eating difficulties after so catastrophic an injury. The lack of appetite is a normal reaction to severe depression, at least partially due to frightening medical experiences. In young children, it also may be due to their separation from their parents. Therefore, the nutritional care of the patient is a joint concern of the physician, nurse, dietician, and psychologist. The child's appetite usually begins to return when the patient leaves the hospital for home. Until the patient is stable enough for discharge, however, stimulating the child's interest in food remains a major medical challenge.

The physical therapist and occupational therapist evaluate the patient's remaining muscle function at the time of admission. Repeat evaluations are done each month to check the progress of the therapy program and for possible neurological return. The major aim of therapy is to strengthen the functioning muscles to their optimum potential and to teach the patient to use these muscles in as practical a fashion as possible. For the patient who has some remaining musculature in the legs (Figure 12–5), the program will aim for ambulation, usually with the support of braces.

The therapy program also works to prevent contractures, the permanent tightening of a muscle that prevents the joint from moving to its full capacity. These result from the lack of movement and stretching of the muscles in the paralyzed extremities, or from spasticity, the abnormal muscle pull resulting from the spinal cord injury. The basic problem caused by contractures is the loss of potential to accomplish a skill. For example, the patient who might possibly walk would lose that potential if a contracture of the knee makes it impossible to straighten the leg. Severe contractures also create significant hygiene problems. They can make comfortable positioning of the patient in bed or in a chair extremely difficult. Various braces or splinting devices can be used to prevent contractures from occurring. Orthotic devices may be used to help maintain the limb in a straight position while it is not in use. The patient or his attendant are also instructed to move each extremity through its

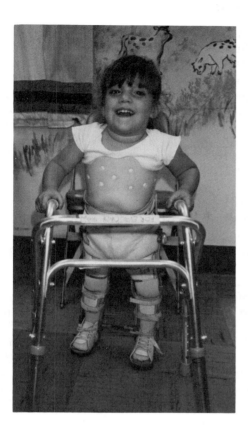

Figure 12—5   An Ambulatory Patient With Braces and a Walker. She is wearing a body jacket to support her back muscles to prevent curvature of the spine.

Figure 12—6   A Quadraplegic Patient Typing With a Mouthstick

entire range of possible movements on a daily basis. If problem contractures do occur, surgery is sometimes necessary to release the frozen joint.

The ingenuity and skills required of the therapist increase with the amount of paralysis, such as for the quadriplegic patient. The patient with no movement of his arms or legs is the ultimate challenge. Skilled therapists and innovative engineers have developed countless devices to give the quadriplegic patient some control over his environment. Training each patient to use these devices is a long process that may require months of intensive therapy. However, with this therapy, even a five-year-old child can learn to type with a sticklike device held in her mouth (Figure 12–6). With these mouthsticks, the child can again draw and paint. She can operate an electric wheelchair by movements of her tongue. Once again, she has the ability to move and explore on her own. Electronic games, playing cards, and turning pages in books are only a few of the various activities again made possible through the use of special devices. A device that allows the patient to operate a telephone without help not only gives her the ability to communicate with friends but privacy for their conversations. The devices available are too numerous to

mention and are increasing daily. The job of the therapist requires constantly searching for new methods of increasing the patient's function and independence.

As mentioned earlier, the patient with a spinal cord injury has no sensation below the level of the cord damage. These patients are unable to feel pressure or pain in affected areas. Therefore, they can sit in one position for hours without feeling discomfort. The person with normal sensation will feel uncomfortable long before skin damage occurs and will fidget or change position. The patient lacking in sensation will unknowingly allow pressure on the skin to continue until tissue death occurs. The skin breakdown that follows tissue death in a pressure injury accounts for most readmissions to hospitals following the acute care admission. Any area that bears the body's weight or where the skin may be pressed between a bony prominence and an outside barrier (e.g., a shoe or brace) is in danger of experiencing significant skin breakdown. For example, the buttocks of a seated patient are at greatest risk for pressure sores. Areas exposed to rubbing, such as ankles where braces may abrade the skin or the buttocks of a patient who scoots along the floor must also be monitored.

Pressure cuts off circulation to small areas of tissue, causing the tissue cells to die. This can happen in as little as 2 hours. Unless the circulation returns quickly, the dead tissue cells begin to fester. By the time the patient's skin breaks down, the necrotic (dead) tissue may be infected. The surface wound is like the tip of an iceberg. A dime-sized wound could indicate a half-dollar-sized wound nearer the bone. These sores create a serious health threat to the patient. Healing takes an extended amount of time and can be very costly. Hospitalization and surgery are often necessary.

The overwhelming point to keep in mind is that pressure sores are preventable. Prevention is accomplished by increasing the patient's and family's awareness of the problem itself. It is not at all difficult to prevent these problems, but it takes constant vigilance. Because the patient is not warned of impending breakdown by pain, the family and patient must inspect the skin daily for any beginning signs of redness or pale patches (Figure 12–7). In this way, visual awareness is used to replace pain awareness. At the first sign of a problem, pressure is relieved in the problem area. For example, in the seated patient with a red area on the buttocks, the patient is kept in bed until the area returns to normal. One day in bed may save a patient a three-month hospitalization.

In order to prevent pressure areas from turning into open sores, patients and families are instructed in techniques to relieve pressure. These techniques include easy methods of raising the patient in the chair, or shifting him from side to side and frequently turning him in bed. Pressure raises are done every hour or two. Each patient also is given a specially fitted wheelchair cushion and a special mattress for his bed. This type of daily care can successfully prevent serious pressure sores.

One of the leading causes of death in spinal cord injured patients is renal (kidney) failure. Although the failure of the kidneys causes a significant medical threat, the kidneys are not the primary site of the actual problem. The kidneys are involved only sec-

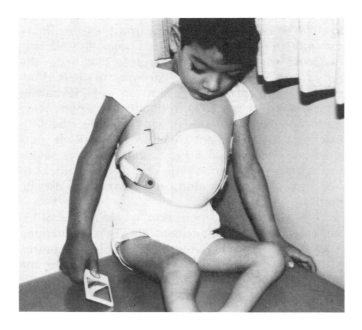

Figure 12–7   A Patient Uses a Mirror to Inspect for Pressure Sores in Body Areas Hidden From View

ondarily. The primary area of concern in the urological system is the urinary bladder. Spinal cord injury patients with sacral involvement, which includes the great majority of these patients, have what is called a neurogenic bladder. As mentioned earlier, this means that the muscles that control urination no longer function normally. The bladder may not empty completely or it may fill too full and cause urine to flow back toward the kidney. Urine retained in the bladder is very prone to infection. Therefore, these patients have recurrent problems with urinary tract infections. Overfilling of the bladder and infections can lead to urine backing up from the bladder into the ureters (the connecting tube to the kidneys) and eventually exposing the kidneys to infection. It is this phenomenon (referred to as reflux) that causes kidney disease in these patients. If not treated adequately and in time, infections can eventually lead to renal failure.

The treatment of bladder problems in spinal cord injured patients may vary from physician to physician. Basically, it requires adequate follow-up and treatment of infections, plus maintenance of a bladder adequately drained of urine. Drainage of the bladder is usually accomplished by use of a catheter, a tube-like instrument. Sometimes a catheter is left in the patient, connecting the bladder to a bag outside the patient where urine may be stored until it is thrown away. More commonly now, a technique referred to as intermittent catheterization is used. With this technique, the patient or his attendant inserts a sterile catheter into the bladder several times a day to drain leftover urine. The catheter is removed once all the urine has been drained. This procedure is (a) easy and takes little time, (b) not at all uncomfortable because the patient with a neurogenic bladder has no sensation in this area, and (c) effective in protecting the kidneys from disease.

Various forms of urine collection bags are used to keep the patient with no bladder control dry. Special underwear with additional padding also is available to allow the patient the assurance of continuing social acceptability. The well-managed patient need not live in fear of embarrassing accidents. Bowel programs that use suppositories with other means of bowel evacuation effectively retrain the bowel for daily emptying at home at night. Therefore, episodes of soiling should not occur.

Patients who have high cervical lesions are subject to autonomic dysreflexia. This syndrome consists of rapid rises in the blood pressure, resulting from an overfull bowel or bladder in a patient who is unable to empty his bowel or bladder effectively. It requires immediate medical attention. Teachers of patients prone to this syndrome should be given additional information about their particular student (Erickson, 1980).

Lack of normal sensation in the sacral area includes the sexual organs as well as the bladder and bowel. A spinal cord injury affects not only the sensation of these organs, but again affects the muscle control (Comarr & Gunderson, 1975). Generally, the male patient loses control of penile erections and ejaculations. Erections will still occur in well over half of the men after spinal cord injury. These erections are in general by reflex action; they are not psychologically stimulated as in the normal sexual responses. Less than 25 percent of the men with spinal cord injuries will have psychologically stimulated erections. However, many patients have been able to find methods for stimulating these reflex erections and have successfully been able to have intercourse. Successful ejaculations, however, are very rare. Therefore, most males with sacral involvement are sterile. Although sensation also is changed for females, they are able to become pregnant. Many spinal cord injured women have successfully delivered and raised normal children.

Respiratory infections also can be a problem in patients who have a high-level spinal cord injury. In patients who have a weak or absent cough, but who have good muscle strength remaining in the major muscles of breathing, quick antibiotic treatment of respiratory infections may be all that is needed to prevent serious illness. In the patient who has a higher lesion, the problem may be more complex.

The patient with a high cervical cord injury requires the use of a respirator to maintain respirations. Without functioning respiratory muscles, the patient can no longer breathe by himself. Therefore, the respirator breathes for the patient. A respirator is no more than a machine that pushes air under pressure into the patient's lungs. How much air, under what amount of pressure, and how rapidly the air is delivered all may be adjustable by dials on the equipment.

In the patient who is permanently on a respirator, air is delivered through a tracheotomy. A tracheotomy consists of surgically opening the neck, and placing a permanent tube directly into the trachea (the upper airway of the patient) (Figure 12–8). Delivery of the air directly into the trachea is more efficient through this opening (called a stoma) than delivery higher up, such as through the mouth or nose. Also, the tracheotomy tube allows the patient to continue to use his upper airway (his mouth, for example) for other important and enjoyable tasks such as eating and talking. Some patients on respirators also learn to use their mouths to capture some air that they guide into their lungs. In some cases, this can allow the patient some time off the respirator. This is a special technique that is taught by skilled therapists who are able to monitor the patient at all times.

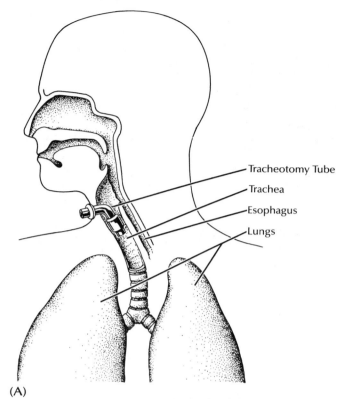

(A)

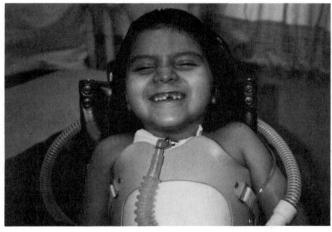

(B)

Figure 12–8   Tracheotomy
A: View of insertion of tracheotomy tube.
B: A patient proudly demonstrates his tracheotomy and his lost tooth.

A tracheotomy tube also aids in clearing excess **phlegm** and mucous from the patient's lungs. Without a cough, the patient can no longer clear his lungs of excess phlegm. A tube attached to a vacuum device can be placed through the tracheotomy tube to accomplish this task. This procedure (called suctioning; Figure 12–9) may look uncomfortable, but actually is not painful to the patient. Patients describe the sen-

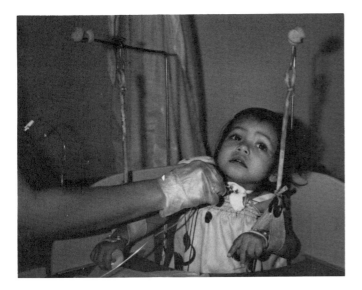

Figure 12–9   A Spine-Injured Patient Being Suctioned

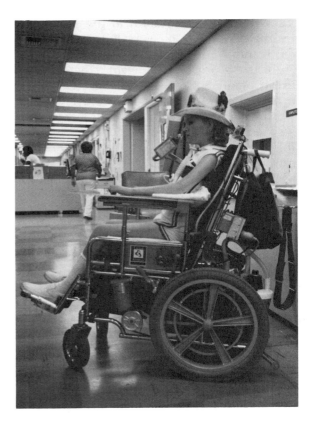

Figure 12–10   A Respirator-Dependent Quadriplegic in Her Electric Wheelchair. Her compact respirator rides on the chair behind her.

sation more as a temporary shortness of breath than pain.

A child on a respirator may initially be frightening to the observer. Once one is familiar with the equipment, the fear disappears. Respirators are now available in compact luggage cases. They attach easily to the back of an electrical wheelchair (Figure 12–10). Patients on respirators may be more prone to develop respiratory infections. However, these problems are often quite easy to manage. Antibiotics and temporary respirator adjustments by a physician may be all that is necessary. The fear of the respirator or the fear of possible infection is often more a threat to the patient than the infection itself. Careful medical management can correct pneumonia, but nothing can correct the isolation faced by patients forced to exist in sterile cages.

The vertebral column in the patient who has a spinal cord injury also is something that requires medical follow-up. After the acute injury, stabilization of the spine either by surgery or bracing may be necessary. Even immediate care of the spine, however, may not prevent significant problems in later life (Campbell & Bonnett, 1975). The spine is not fully grown in a child who is injured at an early age, prior to about twelve years. The injury to the spinal cord does not prevent future growth. Therefore, the bones of the vertebral column will continue to grow after the injury. The problem with this growth lies not in the bone itself, but rather in the muscular support of the vertebral column. In the child who has a high spine lesion (cervical or thoracic), the muscular support to these growing bones is lost. Lacking muscular support, the spine will almost inevitably develop a

curvature. Scoliosis is the curving of the vertebral column (see Chapter 5). To prevent severe curving of the spine, a brace is used, often followed by spine surgery at a later age.

Consideration of the psychological state of the patient and his family is paramount in the treatment

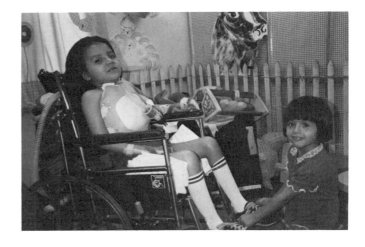

Figure 12–11   Rehabilitation Is a Family Affair. A sibling ties her brother's shoes.

program. A spinal cord injury often requires the patient to reshape all his plans for the future. The patient must adjust to a whole new body image. The patient and the family all experience an individual sense of loss and grief. Multiple emotions—anger, denial, and guilt—intertwine. It takes months before the shattered puzzle of life begins to piece itself together again. Treatment must provide for assistance to the patient, family, and friends (Figure 12–11). It is useless to rehabilitate the body if the spirit is lost in the process.

PROGNOSIS

The chance of long-term survival for a child who has a spinal cord injury is assumed to be very good. Unfortunately, no detailed information specifically concerning children exists at the present time. On the other hand, detailed information does exist from which one can make suppositions. Much of the basic data from which information can be drawn comes from studies at veteran's administration hospitals. Record keeping by these facilities possesses advantages that are lacking in private facilities, such as the potential to follow the patient from one locality to another.

One such study (Mesard, Carmody, Mannarino, & Ruge, 1978) followed a group of patients for ten years. This study found three factors that significantly influenced survival rates: age at time of trauma, level of the lesion, and the degree of paralysis (meaning whether or not the spinal cord was completely severed. The information yields no big surprises. Younger patients had a better chance to pull through and survive for a longer period of time. (The high mortality rate of the newborn with a spinal cord injury was not reflected in this study because the patients were old enough to be veterans.) The greatest chance of long-term survival was for the patient with a sacral or L_3 to L_5 lesion. This was followed by the patient with a T_{12} to L_2 lesion, then the patient with a T_7 to T_{11} lesion, and then the patient with an injury at T_1 to T_6. The cervical lesions from C_5 to C_7 were second highest in mortality rate. Highest, and significantly higher in mortality rate than its nearest competitor, were patients with lesions from C_1 to C_4. (These patients, of course, have the added risk of dependency on a respirator to deliver each life-sustaining breath.) The third, and not surprising, influence on life expectancy was the completeness of the lesion itself. The patient with an incomplete lesion of the cord had a higher life expectancy than the patient with a complete cord transection.

A recent study (DeVivo et al., 1980) looked at spinal cord injuries in the general population. Information from this study basically agrees with the study by Mesard et al. (1978). The patients' ages ranged from nine–eighty-six years. An overall mean life expectancy for spinal cord injury patients was found to be 30.2 years of life following the injury. Again, this paper stressed the importance of age at the time of injury and the completeness of the injury itself. The younger patient with an incomplete lesion had the greatest chance of long-term survival. For example, a normal ten-year-old child with no injury can look forward to an average life span of 69 years. If he suffers an incomplete paraplegia, his life expectancy falls to 67 years (a difference of only two years). With a complete paraplegia, he can expect to live to be 52 years of age. With an incomplete quadriplegia, his life expectancy would be slightly higher (60 years) due to the incomplete nature of the lesion. Suffering as devastating an injury as a complete quadriplegia would lower his life expectancy to 39 years.

In all kinds of spinal cord injuries, the greatest risk of death occurs during the first three months following injury, the acute phase. It is in the area of acute care medicine where the most rapid advances are being made. With this in mind, we can expect that in the future a greater number of patients will survive their acute injury and live for longer periods of time. Even at the underestimated life expectancy figure of 30 more years for the pediatric group, one can expect many years of life ahead for the spinal cord injured child. Depending largely on the involvement of the family and society, these can be years full of stimulating experiences or years of boredom.

EDUCATIONAL IMPLICATIONS

The spinal cord injured child is a child with a bright and inquisitive mind trapped in a nonmobile body. The developmental effects of such a situation are monumental. The quadriplegic child longs to reach out to a toy that is ever out of reach. He wishes to feel the thrill of scribbling, watching blues and reds fill empty papers at his command. The paraplegic child longs to race beside his friends, roller skate, and ride a bike. Instead these children, like so many other handicapped children, are left behind by peers who are too involved in life's activities to stop and share the pain. Adults, afraid or unable to face the injured child's pain, may also be unable to share.

The first step on the road home for each afflicted child is the education of those who meet him at each step on the way. The child's parents must look again into their son's eyes and see again the love that is not lost as a result of injury. The child's teachers must again see past the body that has jailed him, to the spirit of adventure that still wanders freely in his brain. The teacher who stops long enough to look will see the challenge that lies ahead—the challenge to find the keys that, even in the face of so major an injury, will again set him free.

Each child who has a spinal cord injury is an individual. Each child's needs are different. For some, the fear of reentry to the competitive world of able-bodied children is too threatening. A special school, with its protective walls, may be the answer for this child, permanently or just until the need for protection no longer exists. For other children, the same protective walls form a jail, shutting out needed stimulation. For this child, being barred from the regular school environment is a gross injustice. The child who is ready to return to his pre-injury environment is one who has the potential to succeed within that environment if given the opportunity. His handicap makes the long road to success longer, but the job of education to assist him along that road should not fail him.

The younger the child is at the time of his injury, the more disruption occurs in the normal developmental stages. The teacher of young children must be aware of basic normal child development in order to attempt to expose the spine-injured child to as many of the normal stages of development as possible. The quadriplegic child obviously presents more of a challenge for normal developmental stimulation than the paraplegic child. Multiple devices do exist, however, to allow the quadriplegic to interact with his environment. The teacher can work with the occupational therapist to learn to use these devices.

Mouthstick devices allow the quadriplegic child to scribble, the initial art form. With increased practice, some children have emerged as very competent artists (Figure 12–12). Watching children with a catastrophic handicap as they progress along their own

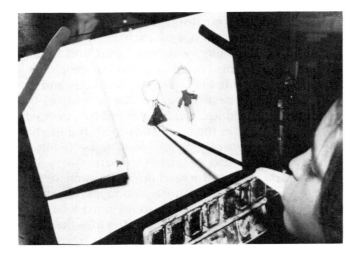

Figure 12–12 A Quadriplegic Patient Rediscovering How to Draw

modified developmental stages constantly reminds one of the powerful drive of the human spirit. The first impression when meeting a quadriplegic child is a deep sense of pain at the immense loss this child has experienced. Getting to know the child allows one to see past the loss to the entire spectrum of life that still remains.

Children explore their world in many ways. They look, listen, and touch. The quadriplegic patient can see and hear, but touch is a sensation that is virtually lost. Sensation for the high cervical cord patient may be present in a normal fashion on the face alone. Some patients may have scattered areas on the body where at least a pressure sensation remains. The loss of sensation is important to remember for several reasons. The most obvious reason is that the quadriplegic child, as much as any child, enjoys physical contact. He needs to feel the warmth of another human being and feel pats of praise. Affection, expressed by holding the quadriplegic child's hand, might go totally unnoticed by the child. A light stroke on the cheek, however, will retain all its meaning.

Another important aspect of the loss of sensation is the vast loss of knowledge gained through touch and knowing how an object physically feels. This area can be compensated for by allowing the child to feel an object against his cheeks. The softness of velvet or the coldness of a glass of ice water are enjoyable sensations to the exploring child. A quadriplegic child need not miss these experiences. When a child is old enough to know not to swallow dangerous objects, the mouth also can serve as a sensory area with a greater potential for exploratory sensations. Even without holding an object in the mouth, the tongue (for a younger child) can serve the same purpose.

Movement is again a multifaceted area of childhood enjoyment. On the one hand, it is used for exploration. For the paralyzed patient, a wheelchair can return to him at least some ability to explore his environment on his own. On the other hand, movement is also enjoyed for the sake of movement itself; dancing at all levels of expertise is proof of this (Figure 12-13). From several months of age, the human spirit wants to move. For the quadriplegic child, techniques for enjoyable movement experiences can be arranged. Coordination between the child's teachers and physical therapists is necessary to accomplish this.

Although children who have spinal cord injuries are unable to participate in the regular physical education program, an alternative program of activity is important. To best assist the child, the program should combine several elements. First, physical activity should be individually designed to stimulate and strengthen the remaining physical abilities of the child. For the paraplegic child, this can include a va-

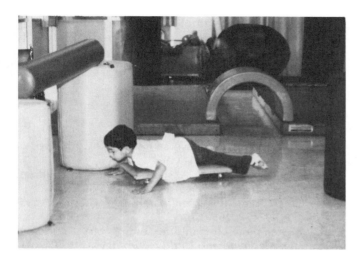

Figure 12–13   An Alternative Means of Moving for a Paraplegic Child

riety of wheelchair sports. Secondly, and equally important, some means should be attempted to involve the spinal cord injured child in the group activities of able-bodied children. Sitting on the sidelines of a baseball game, if only as a team spirit leader, can foster self-confidence and enable the child to become an active group participant. Able-bodied children are wonderfully accepting of handicapped individuals once the fear of the unusual is gone.

Through special groups, the handicapped child's world of physical activities and enjoyments are ever expanding. The school should be a participant in this expansion. It is in school that the child who sees so clearly what he cannot do should be able to learn to see, instead, that much of life is still awaiting his active participation (Figure 12–14).

Children who have been mainstreamed into a regular classroom may still, at times, be made to feel outside the flow. Wheelchair-bound children are sometimes forgotten on the most exciting of school days, the field trip. Unfortunately, the parents of these children are often asked to keep their child at home on field trip days because of lack of transportation for the paralyzed child or because the child on crutches moves too slowly to keep up with the group. For a child already isolated from his peers, the lost opportunity to participate is particularly unfortunate. Not only is the child further alienated, but the thrill of learning on a field trip is curtailed. The school, teachers, and other students also have lost a valuable learning experience.

The physical barriers that face a wheelchair-bound individual are impossible for someone without direct contact to understand. If classrooms of children at early ages see a friend's unjust restrictions, they will see the reasons for change. If, as a group,

Figure 12–14   Paralysis of the Body Doesn't Stop the Spirit

these children can participate in clearing some barriers along the way, they will share in the pleasure.

The most important factor to remember in educating a child with a spinal cord injury is that only the child's body is paralyzed, not the mind. The most significant deterrents to the child's education are lack of understanding of the patient's needs and the fear that surrounds this shortage of information. Even the most severely handicapped of these children, the respirator-dependent child, can survive at a regular school. Successfully mainstreamed students have already set an example for the children who will follow them. The key to success for the child in school is open communication between the child's health care providers and the school. Several visits between the two centers may initially be necessary. With time, only minimal contact between the two will be needed. Often, therapists and other team members are available to go into the school for consultation.

At this time, many spine-injured students have graduated from high school, and even respirator-dependent quadriplegic students are succeeding in college. The future for these children is changing. No longer are the severely handicapped children whose lives are being spared by technological advances in medicine being sentenced to lives of intellectual and social starvation. Instead, schools are actively joining the families and health providers in the total rehabilitation of the injured child. With this support, the child can again look towards the future with goals and plans.

SUMMARY

Because the spinal cord relays multiple messages between the brain and the body below, injury to the cord involves a complex group of problems. A patient with a complete spinal lesion suffers paralysis below the level of the injury. He also loses sensation to the skin over these same paralyzed areas. Control of the muscles of the bladder is lost, and the bladder no longer empties completely, thus exposing the patient to recurrent urinary tract infections. In the patient who has a high cervical lesion, automatic respiration ceases and ventilation by a machine must take over. Care of the patient who has a spinal cord injury requires careful follow-up of all these possible problem areas.

Spinal cord injuries are comparatively rare among children. They can occur from many causes, with motor vehicle accidents by far the most common. Gunshot wounds, diving accidents and other sports-related injuries, falls, and birth injuries also account for a significant number of new patients annually. Although the incidence of new injuries may be relatively small, the number of children in any one area soon grows due to the good long-term survival rate. These children can be expected to survive well into adulthood, with life expectancies exceeding 30 years after the injury.

The child with a spinal cord injury is a significant challenge to the educational system. Injury to the spinal cord alone leaves the patient with an intact brain but a significant physical handicap. The potential for a useful and functional life remains. In order to achieve the greatest benefit for each individual child, the school, with its teachers, nurses, and principals, should be considered a community-based extension of the entire rehabilitation health care team.

Through an open channel of communication among all those involved in his care, even the most severely handicapped child can successfully reenter the mainstream of life.

REFERENCES

Altrocchi, P. H. Acute transverse myelopathy. *Archives of Neurology*, 1963, *9*, 111–119.

Anderson, J. M., & Schutt, A. H. Spinal injury in children. *Mayo Clinic Proceedings*, 1980, *55*, 499–504.

Burke, D. C. Traumatic spinal paralysis in children. *Paraplegia*, 1974, *2*, 268–276.

Byers, R. K. Spinal-cord injuries during birth. *Developmental Medicine and Child Neurology*, 1975, *17*, 103–110.

Campbell, J., & Bonnett, C. Spinal cord injury in children. *Clinical Orthopedics and Related Research*, 1975, *112*, 114–123.

Commar, A. E., & Gunderson, B. B. Sexual function in traumatic paraplegia and quadriplegia. *American Journal of Nursing*, 1975, *75*, 250–255.

DeVivo, M. J., Fine, P. R., Maetz, H. M., & Stover, S. L. Prevalence of spinal cord injury. *Archives of Neurology*, 1980, *37*, 707–708.

Elliot, H. C. *Textbook of neuroanatomy*. Philadelphia: J. B. Lippincott, 1969.

Erickson, R. P. Autonomic hyperreflexia: Pathophysiology and medical management. *Archives of Physical Medicine and Rehabilitation*, 1980, *61*, 431–440.

Gunby, P. From "regeneration" to prostheses: Research on spinal cord injury. *Journal of the American Medical Association*, 1981, *245*(13), 1293–1302.

Kraus, J. F., Franti, C. E., Riggins, R. S., Richards, D., & Borhani, N. O. Incidence of traumatic spinal cord lesions. *Journal of Chronic Diseases*, 1975, *28*, 471–492.

Leventhal, H. R. Birth injuries of the spinal cord. *Journal of Pediatrics*, 1960, *56*(4), 447–453.

Mesard, L., Carmody, A., Mannarino, E., & Ruge, D. Survival after spinal cord trauma. *Archives of Neurology*, 1978, *35*, 78–83.

Schneider, R. C., Cherry, G., & Pantekh, H. The syndrome of acute central cervical spinal cord injury. *Journal of Neurology*, 1954, *11*, 546–577.

Schneider, R. C., & Crosby, E. C. Vascular insufficiency of brain stem and spinal cord in spinal trauma. *Neurology*, 1959, *9*(10), 624–656.

Michael J. Goldberg, M.D., *is professor of orthopedic surgery at the School of Medicine, Tufts University, Boston, Massachusetts; senior orthopedic surgeon at the New England Medical Center, Boston; and director of orthopedic surgery at Kennedy Memorial Hospital for Children, Brighton, Massachusetts.*

Spinal muscular atrophy of childhood is a genetically determined disease that affects the anterior horn cells of the spinal cord and, at times, the motor nuclei of the cranial nerves in the brain stem (Figure 13–1). The disease is characterized by hypotonia (floppiness), symmetrical muscle atrophy, and weakness. The proximal muscles (those nearest to the trunk) are affected more than the distal ones (those farthest from the trunk) and the lower extremities are affected more than the arms. The distal muscles may be involved, as well as the muscles of the trunk. In some instances, the facial muscles also may be affected. Spinal muscular atrophy can show a great variety of

CHAPTER 13

Spinal Muscular Atrophy

clinical symptoms. However, these symptoms do *not* include loss of sensation, long track signs (spasticity), seizures, or mental retardation.

In the past, certain diseases were inappropriately considered spinal muscular atrophies because their symptoms included degeneration of the anterior horn cells and muscle wasting. Arthrogryposis is an example. Likewise, several detailed classifications were made of the typical forms of hereditary spinal muscular atrophy. Although severe infantile spinal muscular atrophy (Werdnig-Hoffmann disease) and mild spinal muscular atrophy (Kugelberg-Welander disease) may be readily recognized, between the two diseases are a large group of patients who demonstrate a wide range of involvement and disability. These cases are difficult to classify and label.

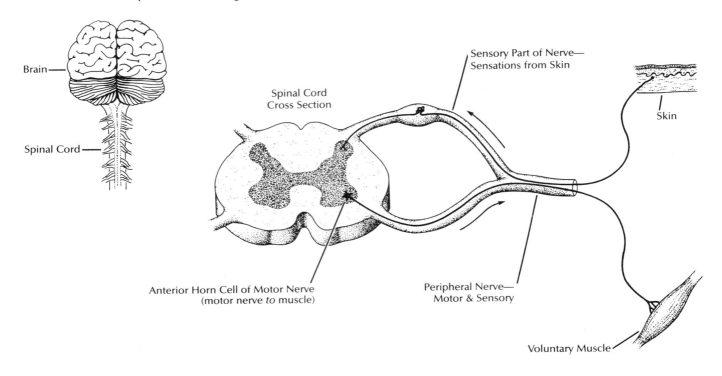

Figure 13—1   Areas Affected by Spinal Muscular Atrophy of Childhood. Disease, destruction, or loss of anterior horn cells of the spinal cord eliminates the motor impulses to the muscles and results in muscle paralysis and atrophy.

Infantile spinal muscular atrophy was first described by Werdnig in 1891 and Hoffmann in 1893. Werdnig-Hoffmann disease became synonymous with the severe form of the condition, which is present at birth or shortly thereafter and inevitably terminates in death, usually before the child's first birthday. Despite the fact that some of the children originally described survived for several years, it was not until

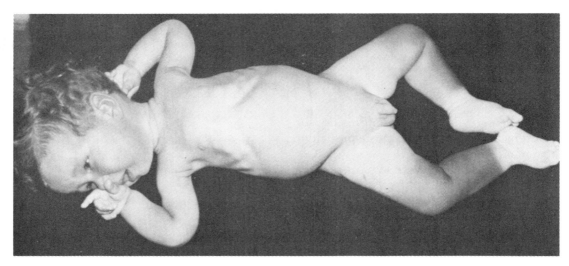

Figure 13—2   Severe Spinal Muscular Atrophy. One-year-old infant with severe spinal muscular atrophy showing intercostal recession and diaphragmatic breathing. Note frog posture of legs, ability to flex elbows and move hands, and normal facial expression.

Source: Reprinted with permission from V. Dubowitz, *Muscle disorders in childhood.* Philadelphia: W. B. Saunders Company, 1978, page 150.

1956 that Kugelberg and Welander reported a far more benign form of the disease, one with an onset during childhood (as the child began to walk independently) and survival into adult life. Then Dubowitz, in 1964, described a spinal muscular atrophy of intermediate severity in which the child was able to sit without support but unable to stand or walk. The onset of the disease usually occurs at 4–24 months. Although spinal muscular atrophy is a disease of motor neurons (the anterior horn cells), it has a variable course that ranges anywhere from chronic, minimally disabling weakness to moderate disability to a rapid downhill course, with complete incapacitation and early death.

Although there may be some merit in classifying subgroups in order to gain a better understanding of the genetics or of the pathophysiology involved, it often only leads to confusion for the patient's family. The family is interested in what the particular disability will be—what to expect for their child—and the prognosis is related only to the actual degree of muscle involvement by the disease.

Thus, the classification of the spinal muscular atrophies by Dubowitz (1978) is the most practical:
1. *Severe*—unable to sit without support (Figure 13–2);
2. *Intermediate*—able to sit unsupported, but unable to stand or walk without aid (Figure 13–3);
3. *Mild*—able to stand and walk (Figure 13–4).

Studies of those with spinal muscular atrophy indicate that about 80 percent of the patients will be able to sit without support. Therefore, the mild and intermediate forms of the disease are far more common than the severe, incapacitating form.

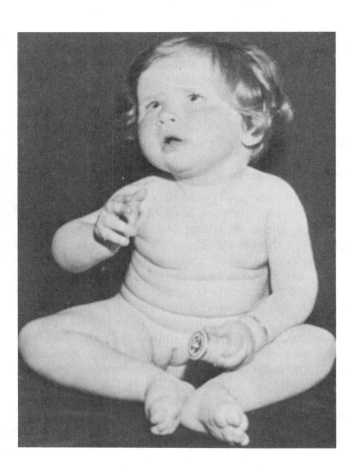

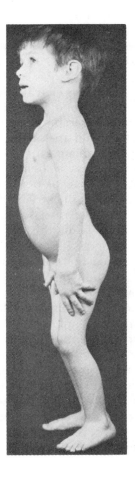

Figure 13–3 Intermediate Spinal Muscular Atrophy. Spinal muscular atrophy of intermediate severity in an eighteen-month-old child with ability to sit unsupported but unable to stand.

Source: Reprinted with permission from V. Dubowitz, *Muscle disorders in childhood.* Philadelphia: W. B. Saunders Company, 1978, page 152.

Figure 13–4 Mild Spinal Muscular Atrophy (Kugelberg-Welander). Four-year-old boy with normal motor milestones and walking at 22 months. Note clinical resemblance to Duchenne dystrophy.

Source: Reprinted with permission from V. Dubowitz, *Muscle disorders in childhood.* Philadelphia: W. B. Saunders Company, 1978, page 155.

ETIOLOGY

All forms of spinal muscular atrophy have a hereditary genetic basis. The basic pathologic changes are in the anterior horn cells of the spinal cord at all levels, and in the motor nuclei of the V to XII cranial nerves of the brain stem (See Figure 13–1). There is degeneration of the anterior horn cells with characteristic histologic (cell) changes, as well as distinctive histologic changes in the muscles innervated by these nerves. Aside from the genetic etiology, the underlying cause of this disease is largely unknown.

This disease often seems to follow a febrile illness, as has been noted in the literature; however, this is not the usual course. Furthermore, it is unclear how, if at all, the fever is related to spinal muscular atrophy.

Spinal muscular atrophy is not a rare disease, although it is uncommon. From a clinical standpoint, it is one of the more common forms of childhood neuromuscular disease. Boys and girls are affected equally, in 4 to 6 cases per 100,000 live births.

The pattern of inheritance is usually autosomal recessive; that is, the disease-carrying genes are recessive and two genes (one from either parent) are required. Therefore the implication is that both parents of the affected child are carriers of the disease. Future offspring from this partnership will have a 25 percent (one in four) risk of being affected, 25 percent (one in four) chance of being normal, and 50 percent (one in two) risk of carrying the disease.

Autosomal recessive diseases exhibit a typical pattern: no previous family history of the disease, multiple siblings affected by the disease, and an increased incidence of consanguinity (marriage between blood relations). This is true for spinal muscular atrophy.

In rare instances, the disease exhibits an autosomal dominant mode of inheritance (requiring only one disease-carrying gene). In such instances, the family history includes both affected siblings and parents. In autosomal dominant disorders, the risk of occurrence in the offspring of either the affected parent or an affected child is 50 percent. For those who are affected by the more common autosomal recessive disease, the risk of recurrence in their children is *not* increased unless the mate is a carrier or is also affected by the disease.

Arguments exist as to whether spinal muscular atrophy represents a single gene that expresses itself in various ways or more than one distinct genetic clinical condition. Until the basic defect has been identified, the distinction remains imprecise. Families have been described in which various members have been affected by different forms of the disease. Whether this represents variable penetrance or different genetic forms of the disease remains unclear. Therefore, care must be used in genetic counseling and prognosticating (Bartoshesky & Singer, 1979).

CHARACTERISTICS

The characteristics of this disorder depend upon the severity of the disease and the number of muscles involved.

Severe Form

The onset is early, occasionally before birth, but usually shortly after birth or within the first three months. The infant may initially appear normal, then develop severe weakness, generalized loss of muscle tone, inability to move the limbs, and a loss of or inability to develop any head control (See Figure 13–2). Typically, the baby appears floppy, one who lies in a characteristic froglike position with legs apart and rotated outwardly. There is paralysis of the limbs and trunk, and the child is never able to roll over. The face is often spared. However, the baby frequently has difficulty in sucking and swallowing, and there is a weak cry. Breathing is mainly abdominal (with the diaphragm). The baby suffers recurrent respiratory infections and usually dies during the first year of life.

Intermediate Form

The child may pass the early motor milestones normally, developing control of his head, trunk, sitting balance, and even sitting unaided (see Figure 13–3). However, the baby's legs are unable to bear his own weight and he never achieves the ability to stand or walk. The muscles of both legs are equally affected though the weakness is greatest toward the hips and body and least toward the toes. The arms are not affected as greatly and frequently are spared. It is unusual to have respiratory difficulties early, but they may develop later. Children with the intermediate form commonly survive into adolescence or young adulthood.

Mild Form

Typically, the baby has passed all the normal milestones during the first or second year of life. The child usually begins walking independently at the normal age or slightly late (see Figure 13–4). The child will then develop weakness with gait abnormalities usually demonstrating a broad-based waddling gait, difficulties in climbing stairs, a decreased tolerance for exercise, and difficulty in keeping up with other children. The weakness is usually in the pelvic girdle and proximal thigh muscles, thus the child may seem to have muscular dystrophy. The upper extremities may occasionally be affected, but usually they are spared. Respiratory problems are rare and the child frequently has a normal life expectancy. The child will usually reach all the motor milestones although with difficulty.

A fine tremor in the hands is present in about half of those affected, especially children with the intermediate or mild form.

Some children with spinal muscular atrophy do not fall firmly into any of these groups or show features of two or more forms. These children are described as borderline, or mixed, cases.

DIAGNOSIS

The diagnosis is based on hypotonia, weakness in the characteristic muscles, and absent deep tendon reflexes. Certain diseases may, on occasion, have been confused with spinal muscular atrophy, due to similarities in symptoms, and should be excluded: muscular dystrophy, Charcot-Marie-Tooth, Guillain-Barré, polio, benign congenital hypotonia, arthrogryposis, and hypotonic cerebral palsy. A careful physical exam usually gives the correct diagnosis.

In laboratory tests the cerebral spinal fluid and muscle enzymes are normal, although the CPK may be mildly elevated in the intermediate form of spinal muscular atrophy. The EMG (**electromyogram**) is also used diagnostically.

Although the diagnosis may be reasonably sure on clinical grounds, and confirmed by the EMG, a surgical muscle biopsy is used to establish the diagnosis with complete certainty. The basic histologic pattern is atrophy of all muscle groups. This pattern is similar in all forms of the disease. The muscle biopsy serves only to establish the diagnosis. It does not help in determining the prognosis. Cardiac involvement is not a feature of spinal muscular atrophy, but an EKG may show an irregular pattern that reflects involuntary contractions of the skeletal muscles.

TREATMENT

Treatment for the severe form of spinal muscular atrophy is mainly supportive. The child will have sucking and feeding problems and respiratory insufficiency. Even the most vigorous supportive program is usually unable to prevent death in the first year.

Patients with the intermediate and mild forms of spinal muscular atrophy frequently have orthopedic complications that require treatment. Muscle imbalance, faulty positioning, and efforts to combat the effects of gravity lead to fixed contractures in the extremities and the trunk.

Attention must be paid to the posture of the wheelchair-bound child. Prolonged sitting leads to flexion and adduction contractures of the hip that in turn cause new problems in sitting and transferring. Inability to fully extend the knee is a common contracture that can interfere with the ability to stand or wear a brace. Contractures of joints of the arms are rare.

Performing daily range-of-motion exercises to the lower extremities helps maintain flexibility of the joints and retards contractures. A muscle strengthening program helps maintain the power in existing muscles. Both are important physical therapy measures. The prevention of deformities is of utmost importance and is often easier to accomplish than the treatment of fixed, established deformities. In addition to physical therapy and attention to sitting positions, resting splints, orthoses, or casts at night or part-time during the day often help maintain position and prevent contractures (Schwentker & Gibson, 1976).

Children with the milder form of the disease who have ambulation potential may benefit from either short-leg or long-leg braces to help stabilize the joints and allow for or improve standing and walking. Braces are usually made of lightweight plastic. They

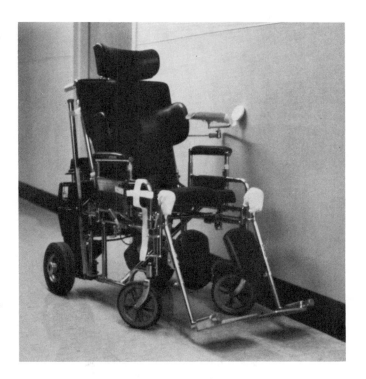

Figure 13–5   A Motorized Wheelchair. A motorized wheelchair with a high back and head rest, lateral spine/trunk supports for scoliosis, and mobile arm support (on left of chair) for shoulder/arm weakness to help in feeding.

tend to be prescribed when the child is three to five years of age, although there are no stringent rules. The use of braces depends on the individual child and the muscles involved.

On occasion, surgery is needed to release tight muscles and tendons around the hip, knee, or ankle. Surgery is indicated (a) when flexion contractures of the hip interfere with transfers or sitting balance, (b) if a deformity is such that it prevents bracing in a child with ambulatory potential, or (c) if it prevents an able patient from standing at a workbench. Functional contractures of the heel cord and of the anterior hip structures (with increased swayback) are commonly seen in patients with weak thigh muscles to enable them to stabilize their knees. Great caution must be taken to ensure that lengthening the muscles would not result in a loss of functional ability (Letts, Fulford, & Hoben, 1976).

Sadly, for many parents, the success of rehabilitation is judged strictly: "Will my child walk?" Early acceptance of the disorder and establishment of realistic goals are very important if the child is to achieve any measure of rehabilitation success. We cannot measure the rehabilitation potential strictly by whether the child will be able to walk, but rather by

methods of providing as much independence in locomotion and the activities of daily living as possible. Very often, this means prescribing a wheelchair for a young child. Care must be taken to provide the child with the right type of wheelchair (Figure 13–5). The back must provide support and spinal control. Adjustable seats may be needed to control the angle of the pelvis. Because these children have normal intelligence, motorized wheelchairs may be used at an early school or preschool age. The severely affected child may require a total support chair or a wheelchair with a thoracic suspension orthosis to control scoliosis.

A major deformity that needs attention early is scoliosis (Hensinger & MacEwen, 1976; also see Chapter 5). The growing spine is particularly sensitive to alterations in spinal muscles. As a result, spinal deformity is common in neurological disease. More than 50 percent of the children affected will develop scoliosis. The onset of scoliosis is early, often before the fourth birthday, and occurs earlier in the nonwalking children. Scoliosis must be looked for at every medical visit. The early detection and prophylatic splinting of even the mildest curve is important. Any progression justifies vigorous treatment.

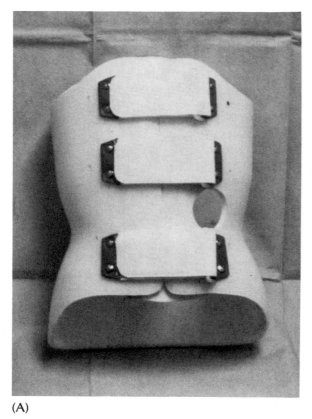

(A)

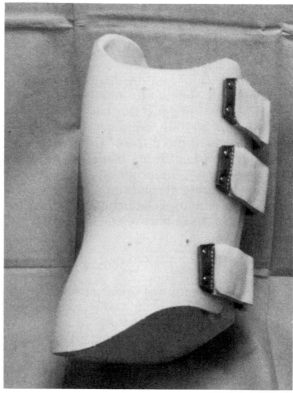

(B)

Figure 13–6   A Lightweight Plastic Body Jacket/ Brace for Control of Scoliosis

A: Front view
B: Side view

For the mild curve, total contact lightweight plastic jackets (Figure 13–6) are helpful, but care must be exerted so that they do not interfere with the child's respiration. Milwaukee braces, or a modified, low-profile brace, may be needed for progressive curves. Curves of more than 60 degrees will rapidly progress. In these cases, surgery typically is required. Long posterior fusion of the entire spine, from the lower neck to the sacrum, is often needed (see Figures 13–7 and 13–8).

At present, an aggressive surgical approach to scoliosis is being recommended. The curves are difficult to control with braces alone and the curves continue to progress even after growth is complete. An increasing spinal curvature may lead to loss of ambulation. The wheelchair-bound patient may lose sitting balance. In all patients, scoliosis further impedes pulmonary and respiratory function. Surgery should be performed before the degree of trunk deformity is so great that the child cannot maintain his balance either sitting or standing. If surgery is not performed, the child becomes forced to use his hands and weakened upper extremities for support and balance, which eliminates normal use of the arms and hands. Surgical fusion of the spine depends on the progression and magnitude of the scoliotic curve and not on the age of the child. Surgical fusion in a young child of eight may be appropriate.

Scoliosis surgery is not to be minimized. It is a major undertaking with significant risks. Furthermore, most patients who undergo spinal fusion and the long postoperative immobilization period lose muscle strength, may lose a particular motor skill, and may suffer a decrease in pulmonary function. However, gains in comfort and benefits of a stabilized spine appear to far outweigh such losses.

Occupational therapy aids are very helpful in assisting the child to achieve independence in the activities of daily living (Figure 13–9). Long-handled brushes and sponges to assist in daily grooming and hygiene, devices to assist in independent toileting, long-handled spoons to assist with eating, and assistive hand/wrist orthoses used to hold a pencil or fork all lead to greater independence for the child who has spinal muscular atrophy. Some severely involved children who have significant trunk and abdominal weakness may sometimes be **incontinent.** In these cases, specific toileting training is appropriate.

For patients who have the intermediate and milder forms of spinal muscular atrophy, life expectancy is often good. Therefore, vigorous treatment of lower respiratory infection is important. Antibiotics,

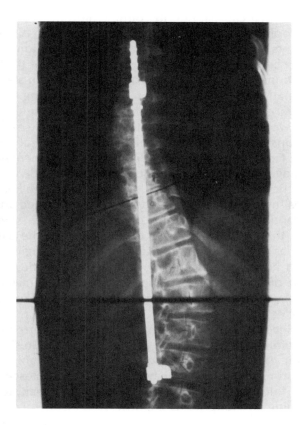

Figure 13—7   Posterior Spinal Fusion Using a Harrington Rod

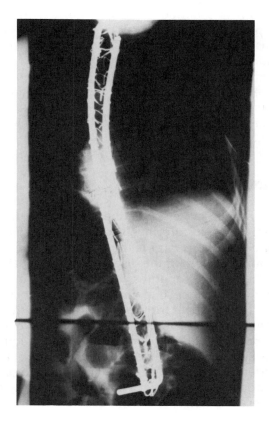

Figure 13—8   Posterior Spinal Fusion Using Luque Rods

Figure 13—9   Assistive Devices for Motor Weakness. A fork with a Velcro wrist attachment, a plate that won't skid and is stable, a spoon with a wrist attachment, and a spoon with a wide handle for easy gripping.

pulmonary therapy, and even mechanical ventilation may be needed at times.

Muscle weakness and a sedentary life result in osteoporosis, a thinning and weakening of the bones. Fractures are a frequent problem. In addition, skeletal growth is retarded. By and large, children who have spinal muscular atrophy tend to be small. However, as with so many people who are sedentary and hypotonic, weight gain is a major problem. The increased weight significantly interferes with fitting orthotic equipment, maintaining range of motion and ambulation potential, and also contributes to spinal collapse. Diet planning and nutrition counseling are important.

PROGNOSIS

In general, the more severe the form of the disease, the more muscles are involved, and the earlier the age of onset, the poorer is the prognosis. The Werdnig-Hoffmann form of the disease, with onset at birth or in the first few months, usually results in death within the first or second year of life. The child who has the intermediate form of the disease, with onset between three and fifteen months of age, typically has survival beyond age four, but death frequently before age ten. The child who has the Kugelberg-Welander form of the disease often is likely to survive childhood and live a normal life span.

These expectations are not absolute, they are averaged from a continuity of cases of spinal muscular atrophy. Grouping is often difficult. Age of onset alone cannot determine the severity because it depends on when parents notice symptoms, the availability of medical care, and the physicians' diagnostic acumen. Furthermore, the intermediate and mild forms may begin early or late and often intermingle in prognosis. Although the earlier the disease has its onset, the more severe it usually is, nonetheless, it is only the actual number of affected muscle groups and the extent to which these muscles are involved that determine the prognosis.

In practice, the single most important factor in determining prognosis is the respiratory function. The more intercostal (chest) musculature involved, the poorer the outlook becomes because of respiratory insufficiency and secondary infection. If weakness is noted in the face, neck, and trunk, then the risk of pulmonary complications and infection increases, and the prognosis worsens.

Tongue fasciculations (involuntary contractions) often indicate that the degree of disability is likely to be severe. The general tendency of the disease is to remain relatively stable. Following diagnosis, there is often a period of about two years during which the muscles become progressively weaker but then the condition stabilizes. A few patients affected with the intermediate and mild form of the disease may show apparent improvement during the early preschool years. This may be due to reinnervation of some muscles, which can happen in young children, or to hypertrophy (overgrowth) of existing muscles. A few patients show definite continued deterioration on each clinical examination. However, in spite of these variations, the great majority of patients remain static and stationary, neither worsening nor improving.

Parents of children with this disorder frequently note worsening even though the clinical muscle exam demonstrates no change. This is due to several factors. First, in young children motor skills increase with age. A child with muscle weakness may be able to achieve early motor skills, then not be able to keep up as the motor skills become more complicated and demanding (e.g., walking, then running, then skipping, then hopping). This is often viewed by the parents as deterioration because the child originally could keep up with the more infantile activities. In point of fact, the child simply is not able to master more complicated skills with stable but weakened muscles.

Second, an adolescent experiences a growth spurt followed by a sudden gain in weight and in size. Often, the weakened muscles are no longer able to perform as well in the heavier body. The adolescent then finds that he is fatiguing easily and that stair climbing and long walks are now burdensome. More energy is needed to perform the same task than earlier. The adolescent who was a community walker may become a household walker or even become wheelchair-bound. Teenagers who were walking independently may need to use crutches, and those with crutches may choose to become sitters.

Third, the development of contractures may impede ambulation and the child will appear to deteriorate. The weakened muscle may be able to move a free joint through a range of motion but not one that is contracted. Thus the muscles may seem to deteriorate despite a static muscle picture, which emphasizes again the importance of maintaining physical therapy.

Even though spinal muscular atrophy is a stable disease, the child frequently appears to become progressively weaker with intercurrent illness (pneumonia, etc.) and following an accident or surgery that requires periods of immobilization.

EDUCATIONAL IMPLICATIONS

In general, children with spinal muscular atrophy have normal intelligence. There have been some reports that, as a group, the children are above average in intelligence. On the other hand, there also have been reports that the incidence of mental retardation is 9 percent, which is greater than the 3 percent commonly found in the general population.

The important issue here is that the child with spinal muscular atrophy has normal intelligence and frequently has a long-term or near normal life expectancy. Therefore, this child will require appropriate educational and vocational planning. All affected individuals have muscle motor weakness. Therefore, career planning must avoid jobs that would require prolonged standing or significant muscular expenditure. Job training must be based mainly on the use of intellectual skills. Although manual dexterity and fine motor skills are often preserved, care must be taken to separate those patients who have normal hand and arm control from those who have involvement in the upper extremities or tremors that may interfere with some fine motor skills. Periodic hand function testing by a trained occupational therapist is an important part of education programming.

Surveys have shown that many children who are mildly involved are educated in regular classrooms. However, some children are segregated in schools for physically or multiply handicapped children. These schools often include a significant number of students who have mild to moderate mental retardation or learning disabilities. Because many children with spinal muscular atrophy have only a physical handicap, they can easily be educationally absorbed into regular schools if the buildings are adapted to the physically handicapped. Those children who are in-tegrated into regular classrooms have increased opportunity for academic education.

Unfortunately, some early educational testing relies on fine and gross motor skills. Children who have muscle weakness may be thought to be less intelligent than they actually are. Care must be taken when educationally testing the young child who has spinal muscular atrophy to avoid using tests that require fine and gross motor skills. Testing should be related, as much as possible, to cognitive function only.

Adaptive physical educational programs are important. The child can participate within his limited capability, and when doing so, has an increased sense of well-being. Great caution must be exercised to avoid placing the child in a competitive situation in which the goals far exceed the child's muscle capabilities.

Even for the mildly involved child, fatigue is common. Greater flexibility must be allowed for finishing assignments, especially those that require prolonged writing or prolonged library research. Manual writing may be fatiguing and often takes longer for the child. Early instruction in typing skills and the use of an electric typewriter should be encouraged and permitted in the school setting. Work assignments submitted by tape recording also may be appropriate.

The child will need adequate time to transfer between classrooms. Managing in schools that have sprawling layouts or multiple levels can often significantly impede participation in the educational process. As already noted, illness or accident may weaken muscles and result in reduced activity levels afterwards. In these cases, adjustments in programming may be required.

A compassionate understanding and sensitivity by the teachers towards the frustrations that children with handicaps experience when mainstreamed is important. Furthermore, adolescents, whether handicapped or not, have the same social, emotional, and sexual problems, and counseling to deal with adolescent identity crises should be available.

SUMMARY

Spinal muscular atrophy of childhood is a genetically determined disease that is characterized by hypotonia, symmetrical muscle atrophy, and weakness. The severe form of the disease (Werdnig-Hoffmann disease) is evident at birth or shortly afterward and usually causes death within the first year or two. The intermediate form of the disease has its onset between three and fifteen months of age, and usually causes death before age ten. The mild form of the disease (Kugelberg-Welander disease) has its onset during early childhood, but often has a good prognosis for living a normal life span. In general, children with spinal muscular atrophy have normal intelligence. Therefore, if school buildings can be adapted to meet these children's physical needs, they should be educated in regular classrooms.

REFERENCES

Bartoshesky, L. E., & Singer, W. Spinal musclar atrophy. In D. Bergsma (Ed.), *Birth defect compendium,* D. (2nd ed.) New York: Alan R. Liss, Inc., 1979.

Dubowitz, V. Infantile muscular atrophy. *Brain,* 1964, *87,* 707–718.

Dubowitz, V. *Muscle disorders in childhood.* Philadelphia: W. B. Saunders, 1978.

Hensinger, R. N., & MacEwen, G. D. Spinal deformity associated with heritable neurological conditions: Spinal muscular atrophy, Friedrich's ataxia, familial dysautonomia, and Charcot-Marie-Tooth disease. *Journal of Bone and Joint Surgery,* 1976, *58-A,* 13–24.

Hoffmann, J. Veber chronische spinal Muskelatrophie im Kindesalter auf familiarer Basis. *Deutsche Zeitschrift für Nervenheilkunde,* 1893, *3,* 427–440.

Kugelberg, E., & Welander, L. Heredo-familial juvenile muscular atrophy simulating muscular dystrophy. *Archives of Neurology and Psychiatry,* 1956, *75,* 500–509.

Letts, R. M., Fulford, R., & Hoben, D. A. Mobility aids for the paraplegic child. *Journal of Bone and Joint Surgery,* 1976, *58-A,* 38–41.

Schwentker, E. P., & Gibson, D. A. The orthopedic aspects of spinal muscular atrophy. *Journal of Bone and Joint Surgery,* 1976, *58-A,* 32–38.

Werdnig, G. Zwei frühinfantile hereditare Fälle von progressiver Muskelatrophie unter dem Bilde der Dystrophie aber auf neurotischer Grundlage. *Archiv für Psychiatrie und Nervenkrankheiten,* 1891, *22,* 437–481.

Other Health Conditions

PART

3

Michael J. Kraemer, M.D., *is senior pediatric allergy fellow in the Department of Pediatrics, School of Medicine, University of Washington, Seattle, Washington.*
C. Warren Bierman, M.D., *is clinical professor in the Department of Pediatrics and head of the Division of Pediatric Allergy at the School of Medicine, University of Washington, Seattle, Washington.*

The word asthma was originally used by the Greeks to describe the panting, wheezing respirations that were characteristic of a person who was suffering from an acute attack of this disease. Francis Adams, a nineteenth century Scottish surgeon, translated Hippocrates. The famous Greek physician made the following observations about asthma in Aphorisms 19 and 22: "All diseases occur at all seasons of the year, but certain of them are more apt to occur and be exacerbated at certain seasons." He then noted that asthma is most apt to occur or get worse in the autumn. Aphorisms 26, 27, and 28 describe asthma as a disease common to children past the age of cutting

Asthma

CHAPTER 14

canine teeth. Aphorism 28 observes "that such asthma in children as remains and does not pass away with puberty, or in females about the commencement of menstruation, usually becomes chronic." Aphorism 46 tragically observes that "such persons as become hump-backed from asthma or cough before puberty, die."

Most of Hippocrates' observations are as true today as they were in classic Greece. Asthma continues to be a disease that can occur at any time of the year, though attacks are especially common in autumn. It remains still the most common **pulmonary** disease of childhood. It frequently begins in early childhood, but some children may not develop symptoms until late childhood or even adolescence. It occurs in at least 3–10 percent of children, and is probably more prevalent. Although asthma frequently lessens in adolescence, some children will develop more severe symptoms with puberty, which persist into adult life. In fact, at least half of the adults who have chronic asthma had asthma as children, and many other former asthmatics continue to have abnormal lung function on sensitive lung function tests or have trouble with exercise. The major difference between Hippocrates' times and ours is in the prognosis for severe asthma. Patients who developed chronic severe asthma died in ancient Greece. Now, with modern knowledge of the disease and modern methods of management, no child need die from asthma, and even those with very severe asthma can lead relatively normal active lives.

Asthma, by definition, is a complex disease in which inflammation of the airways is both the cause and effect of the problem. It causes a substantial proportion of school absenteeism, emergency care, and hospital admissions. It can be provoked by a variety of stimuli including **allergens,** viral infections, irritants, emotions, and exercise. It is complicated further because (a) the relative importance of asthma-producing stimuli may vary in each individual with the disease and (b) the symptoms may range from mild coughing attacks to breathing difficulty of life-threatening proportion. Unlike chronic **bronchitis** and **emphysema,** asthma can be reversed with treatment. The asthmatic child can live a relatively healthy life if he learns to understand and cope with episodes of asthma. He will have an easier time if the adults in his life (parents, teachers, athletic coaches, etc.) also become better educated about the sometimes irritating and occasionally frightening manifestations of asthma.

ETIOLOGY

To appreciate the abnormalities of asthma, a basic understanding of normal lung function is required. The lungs are a complicated system of bellows and airways that deliver fresh oxygen to the bloodstream and remove waste carbon dioxide (Figure 14–1). The airway resembles an inverted tree with a trunk dividing into two main branches. The trachea represents the trunk, the left and right main stem bronchi the first limbs. These divide into progressively smaller branches (bronchi, bronchioles) to which the leaves (alveoli) are attached. With inhalation, air is pulled down through the trachea and bronchi through progressively smaller airways into the terminal clusters of alveoli. Passive diffusion of gases between the alveoli and the adjacent bloodstream results in the appropriate transfer of oxygen and carbon dioxide. In normal breathing, the size of the airways determines the efficiency of air movement in and out of the alveoli.

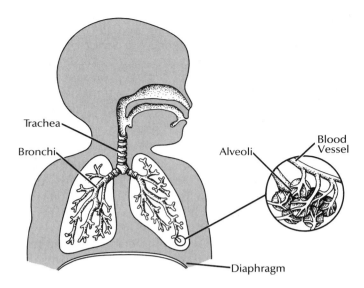

Figure 14–1   Schematic of a Child's Airways and Lungs. Asthma involves inflammation and spasm of the bronchi and smaller airways.

The epithelial cells (Figure 14–2) line the inside of the airways. On the side of the cells exposed to the airway, there are a number of tiny hairlike projections (cilia) that beat rhythmically to sweep **mucus** and debris up and out of the airway gently. Individual cells are joined together by tight intercellular junctions to provide a protective barrier between inhaled irritants and the lung. These epithelial cells are bathed by a thin watery secretion produced by cells that also line the airway.

Asthma is a disease that results from episodic narrowing of these airways. This narrowing increases the resistance to the flow of air in and out of the lungs, which forces the individual to work harder to

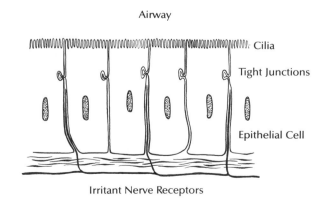

Figure 14–2   Epithelial Cells in a Normal Airway. The epithelial cells line the normal airway to provide a protective barrier. Inhaled irritants do not normally gain access to subepithelial irritant nerve receptors.

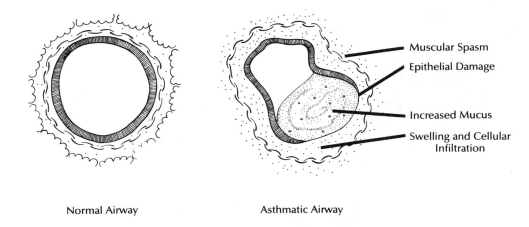

Normal Airway   Asthmatic Airway

Figure 14–3   The Effect of Asthma on an Airway. Microscopic changes in the asthmatic airway are muscular spasm, epithelial damage, increased mucus, and cellular infiltration. These create turbulence in the smooth flow of air to produce the characteristic wheeze.

breathe. The turbulent flow of air in the larger airways create eddy currents, which produce the sound of an asthmatic wheeze. Breathing tests can measure the period of time required to fully exhale and provide a means of measuring the severity of asthma.

If the airways of the asthmatic lung are examined microscopically (Figure 14–3), a number of features are striking. One will note damage to the epithelial lining with loss of surface cilia and destruction of many lining cells, local swelling of the tissues with infiltration of various types of white blood cells, increased sticky mucus within the airways, and muscular spasm. As a result, the cells and irritant nerve receptors, which underlie the damaged epithelium, are no longer protected from irritants. They may be hyperreactive to inhaled smog, cigarette smoke, or even to cold air so that even slight exposure could result in a severe episode of coughing, which may constrict the airway further (Figure 14–4).

In asthma, the mast cell is of key importance. This cell is found beneath the lining of the airway and contains potent chemicals that can cause inflammation. The surface of the mast cell is coated with allergic **antibodies** (known as IgE), which may be specific for allergens such as pollens of trees, grasses, or weeds, or to house dust, animal dander, or molds. When these substances are inhaled, they may combine with the allergic antibody and stimulate the mast cell to release its potent chemicals (Figure 14–5). These chemicals create local inflammation, enlarge blood vessels, cause the tissue to swell, attract white blood cells that increase the inflammation, and cause the smooth muscle of the breathing tubes to go into spasm. The end result is a decrease in the diameter of the airways that we recognize as an acute attack of asthma.

Although muscular spasm can be relieved promptly by appropriate medications, the epithelial damage, local inflammation, and impaired mucus transport may require days or even weeks for complete recovery. These inflammatory changes set the stage for chronic changes in the lungs that require long-term therapy (months to years) for control.

CHARACTERISTICS

Asthma tends to run in certain families, making at least some elements of the disease heritable (Pearlman & Bierman, 1980). It is also more common among

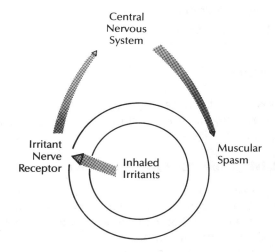

Figure 14–4   How Irritants Trigger a Muscular Spasm. Inhaled irritants that gain access to irritant nerve receptors can trigger a reflex muscular spasm of the airways.

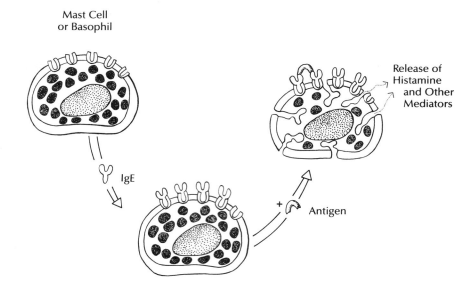

Mast Cell
or Basophil

IgE

Antigen

Release of
Histamine
and Other
Mediators

Figure 14—5   An Asthmatic Attack From an Allergy. The allergic release of mediators from sensitized mast cells creates a potent stimulus for an asthmatic attack.

boys than among girls. Patterns of asthma symptoms vary widely. Some children have very mild symptoms such as recurrent night coughing, which might be misinterpreted as chronic bronchitis because they never have audible wheezing. Children who have chest tightness following exercise may not be aware that this is an abnormal reaction. Such subtle patterns of asthma can be diagnosed by appropriate lung function tests.

The more familiar pattern of asthma symptoms is the sudden onset of wheezing, chest tightness, and rapid breathing. These attacks may occur as isolated events, with normal lung function between episodes. They may also appear as repeated severe attacks superimposed on chronic airflow obstruction.

DIAGNOSIS

Diagnosis of asthma can be made by identifying specific provoking factors, testing lung function, and testing for exercise-induced asthma.

Identifying Specific Provoking Factors

As noted previously, the diagnosis of asthma is very complicated because every child has a different repertoire of factors that can trigger asthma. Each of these factors varies in importance with each individual. Control can be as easy as getting rid of a pet or keeping the animal outside most of the time, or improving housekeeping procedures to minimize the amount of airborne dust. Many factors will be apparent from the details of the patient's history. Others require more extensive laboratory tests or skin tests for diagnosis.

Tests of Lung Function

Many children with asthma will have periods of time when they suffer no symptoms and their physical examination is normal (Souhrada & Buckley, 1980). Measurements of lung function by breathing tests are required to establish the diagnosis of asthma correctly. These tests detect the typical obstruction to airflow and prolonged expiration (Figure 14–6). Be-

Figure 14—6   Pulmonary Function Test. Even young children can have an accurate assessment of airflow obstruction using readily available tests of pulmonary function.

cause the airways remain hyperreactive to a number of factors, standardized provocation tests sometimes have been employed to confirm the suspicion of asthma. A child with asthma will develop a **bronchospasm** on inhaling a drug, such as histamine or methacholine, at a concentration one-fiftieth to one-hundredth of that which would affect a normal child. This reaction will occur even if lung function is normal at rest.

Exercise-Induced Asthma

Exercise is a very common provoking factor for childhood asthma. Most children with clinical asthma symptoms will develop asthma following a short period of strenuous exercise. Some children may have asthma only with exercise. The most effective way to diagnose exercise-induced asthma is by measuring lung function before and after some standardized exercise. The exercise must be strenuous (e.g., running or stair climbing) and of sufficient duration (5–8 minutes). Obvious wheezing may not be present even though lung function tests show substantial decreases. This reaction resolves over time. Many children will recover in 20 minutes (Figure 14–7), but in others, symptoms may persist for periods of 1–2 hours.

TREATMENT

Increasingly more specific and effective therapy becomes available as our understanding of asthma improves. With appropriate care, most children can

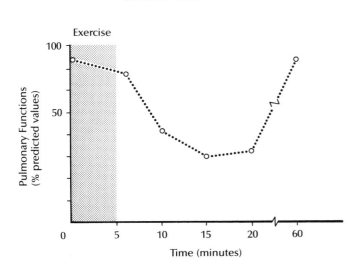

Figure 14—7   Exercise-Induced Asthma. An acute bronchospasm can follow a period of sustained exercise in children with hyperreactive airways.

return to school and recreational activities. Care of a child with asthma should include identification of significant provoking factors, control of significant allergic factors in the environment, and appropriate medications to further prevent and control acute episodes (Bierman & Pearlman, 1983). Some children benefit from immunotherapy (allergy shots), and those with severe disease may need special sports or conditioning programs and family psychological guidance.

Environmental Control

The importance of defining specific provoking factors should not be underestimated. Some of these agents can be easily avoided. For example, a child's problem of allergic sensitivities to pets may be controlled in large part by removing the animals from the home or classroom. Specific foods or medications (such as aspirin) can also be avoided totally if they induce asthma. Unfortunately, most asthma is exacerbated by a combination of allergic factors rather than just one or two. Some factors, such as house dust, molds, and irritants such as cigarette smoke, cannot be totally eliminated. Nevertheless, a concerted effort at home and at school to reduce **ambient** levels of irritants may produce fewer and less severe asthma symptoms. Some environmental factors (e.g., weather changes, smog, seasonal pollens, and viral infections) cannot be controlled. If they are important in inducing or aggravating asthma, medications will be required to minimize the symptoms.

Treatment of Exercise-Induced Asthma

Children with exercise-induced asthma are handicapped in physical exercise and recreational or competitive sports. They often avoid participation in physically demanding activities and may be excluded from sports because of limited stamina. This may result in withdrawal from peer groups, and being characterized as a loner. Psychological problems inherent in having a chronic lung disease will be increased.

Some general principles can be employed to lessen the impact of exercise-asthma. A warm-up period is helpful because short periods of moderate exercise are less likely to induce exercise-asthma. The type of exercise is also important. Swimming, gymnastics, and wrestling provoke less exercise-asthma than comparable physical exertion by running. In track events, asthmatic children perform better in short sprints than in long distance running events. Similarly, exercise is less likely to trigger this reaction when done indoors or in a warm, humid environment than outside in cold, dry air. Finally, antiasthma medications, taken shortly before exercise, can minimize subsequent asthmatic reactions.

With appropriate management, asthmatic children can compete effectively even in sports such as track, soccer, and basketball. If exercise-induced asthma is recognized, specific medications can be prescribed to minimize its effects. The majority of asthmatic children should be able to enjoy the benefits of physical education activities and competitive sports programs. With proper treatment, asthmatic adults compete in such professional sports as major league baseball.

Medications for Childhood Asthma

Most children with asthma require medication to control symptoms. As with every other aspect of this disease, the medication requirements vary with the severity and the types of factors that induce asthma. Effective medications include four broad classes: beta adrenergic agents, theophyllines, cromolyn, and steroids. Each of these will be discussed briefly, with emphasis placed on the actions and side effects one might reasonably expect with their use in children.

Beta Adrenergic Agents Epinephrine (adrenalin) has been used for many years to treat acute asthma. It is usually given by injection to produce prompt relaxation of bronchial muscular spasm. Epinephrine is not a good drug for the chronic case of asthma because it affects organs other than the lung and because it cannot be given orally. In the past thirty years, a number of epinephrinelike drugs have been developed. Those commonly used today are isoproterenol, metaproterenol, terbutaline, and albuterol. These medications cause the constricted muscles of the airways to relax so that the patient with asthma can breathe more easily. They also help to decrease the release of chemical mediators from mast cells. They are all particularly effective in treating acute asthmatic attacks and may help prevent asthma caused by exercise.

Isoproterenol was the first synthetic derivative of adrenalin. Like adrenalin, it is destroyed in the intestinal tract and is effective only by inhalation. Accordingly it is dispensed as a pressurized hand nebulizer or as a vaporized mist (Figure 14–8). The major disadvantages are that it increases the heart rate, has a short duration of action, is easily abused (especially by adolescents), and loses its effectiveness with chronic use. Too much may actually make asthma worse. In addition, it may cause psychological addiction in children who employ it as the sole method of controlling asthma. Other children may dislike using it because they are embarassed when they use it in front of peers. More specific agents, which have a longer duration of action, are now available.

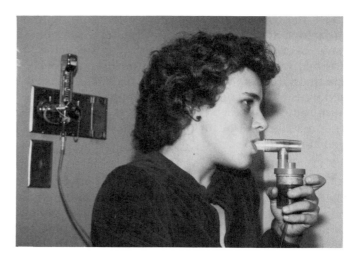

Figure 14—8 An Asthma Attack Treated With a Vaporizer. An acute attack of asthma can be effectively treated with inhaled isoproterenol, which is given as a mist with oxygen.

Metaproterenol has been used in the United States since 1973 and in Germany since the early 1960s. It is active when administered as a tablet or a syrup, as well as by inhalation. It has a longer duration of action than isoproterenol, and is less likely to increase heart rate. When administered orally, it can produce a tremor because it also acts on skeletal muscles. This side effect may be important in school because it adversely affects writing. Teachers unaware of these adverse side effects of the drug may penalize the student for sloppy work.

Terbutaline has been available since 1975 as an oral agent for children older than twelve years of age. It can be particularly effective in those older asthmatic children because it has even less effect on the heart and lasts longer than metaproterenol. Unfortunately, it may also cause significant tremor.

Albuterol, only available in the United States since 1981, has been used quite successfully in other parts of the world since 1971. At this writing, it is available only as a hand-held nebulizer and as a tablet. It is particularly effective in providing sustained relief of acute asthma symptoms but may still have the same potential for abuse or overuse as the other pressurized hand nebulizers.

Theophylline This drug is structurally related to caffeine and has been used for asthma therapy since the 1930s. Today, it is the most common drug administered in the United States for chronic asthma. As with the beta adrenergic agents, it relaxes bronchial smooth muscle and prevents mediator release, but probably acts through a different mechanism. Today, more is known about the dosing and metabolism of theophylline than almost any other drug. It is particularly popular because the timed-release tablets and capsules can be administered every 12 hours to control asthma, thereby avoiding the need for medications while at school.

We now know that sudden changes in theophylline dosage needs can occur. Most importantly, the body's ability to clear (**metabolize**) a prescribed dose may suddenly decrease, creating the risk of drug overdose. Factors that can alter the rate of metabolism include viral infections (especially influenza), certain other drugs such as erthromycin, alterations in diet, liver diseases such as hepatitis, and heart failure. Any patient who receives regular theophylline therapy should be aware of possible signs of drug overdosage and bring these to the attention of his or her parents and physician. Most commonly, theophylline toxicity results in headache, nausea, and vomiting. If severe, it can also cause convulsions. These symptoms can be reversed by decreasing the dosage. If theophylline is used regularly to treat childhood asthma, the dosage must be established by determining the amount of theophylline in the child's blood. These blood tests may need to be repeated periodically to assure that the child is receiving an adequate dose.

Cromolyn This drug is the mainstay of chronic asthma therapy in many countries. It has been available in the United States since 1976. Cromolyn protects against asthma by preventing the release of inflammatory mediators from mast cells. Beneficial effects are cumulative; after three weeks, it may diminish the frequency and severity of acute asthma attacks. It is delivered to the lungs as a fine powder that is dispersed during a deep inhalation with a spinhaler. It is an impressively safe preparation; a mild cough is the only common side effect. It appears to work better in those children whose provoking factors involve inhaled allergens, but is also effective in preventing exercise-induced asthma.

Steroids Steroids such as cortisone, hydrocortisone, and their derivatives are potent medications that have impressive therapeutic benefits for asthma. They act in a number of ways to decrease the inflammation about the airways and to improve responses to the other medications. When administered daily in high doses, they can also cause severe side effects. The common side effects of oral steroids in children include weight gain, decreased linear growth, decreased natural steroid production by the adrenal glands, high blood pressure, cataracts, and acne. The list of other possible side effects is lengthy. Because of these side effects, recent steroid research has focused on dosing tactics that minimize side effects and on the development of safer, topical (inhaled) steroid preparations.

Oral steroids may be lifesaving in severe asthma that requires treatment in a hospital. For severe acute attacks, they are given for a short time only (seven to ten days) and rarely cause side effects. Oral steroids may also be required, over a longer period of time, by a small number of asthmatic children whose asthma cannot be sufficiently controlled with the beta adrenergic agents, theophylline, or cromolyn. Side effects from long-term steroid administration can be minimized by giving the drug every other day rather than daily. Another way of reducing toxicity from steroids is to administer them by inhalation. The new inhaled steroids are active in the lungs but are poorly absorbed into the body. The major side effects are coughing, just after administration, and occasional topical fungal infections (thrush) within the mouth. The latter responds easily to treatment. During acute attacks, the inhaled steroids may aggravate bronchospasm, thus switching to oral steroids may be advised. These medications should never be stopped abruptly, unless done under the supervision of a physician. Unlike the beta adrenergic agents, theophylline, and cromolyn, steroids offer no protection for exercise-induced asthma.

Immunotherapy

Some children may do poorly despite environmental control and appropriate medications. If inhaled allergic factors are prominent, immunotherapy (allergy shots) may be used to decrease the specific sensitivity to these allergens. They are not a substitute for environmental control, but may help alleviate some of the asthma symptoms that occur upon exposure to allergens that cannot be effectively controlled.

Psychological Factors in Asthma

Severe asthma can cause emotional stress for a child and his or her family. These emotions can, in turn, intensify the frequency and severity of asthma symptoms. Both the disease and the emotional climate interrelate so that if one factor is changed, the other is also affected. The first step toward improving the emotional climate should be good medical care and the proper use of asthma medications. If a child does not improve with the usual suggested medical treatments, the illness may be playing a special role for the family. Some parents submerge themselves in concern for their child's illness to focus away from other painful sources of marital discord. Some children use their allergic symptoms to manipulate their family and school environment. Wheezing might be used as a means of avoiding school. Medications might be avoided to assure more constant parental attention. Both parents and teachers must make sure that this does not occur too often. Overprotection due to the asthma may retard the child's development of self-reliance.

Often children can benefit from an *asthma teaching program*. These organized sessions incorporate family and peer interactions to increase coping skills within the home. They promote understanding as well as self-reliance. Additional psychological approaches are also available. Family therapy, hypnosis, and behavior modification can provide an added dimension of care for children in whom emotions or family turmoil constantly provoke asthma symptoms. Rarely, a child with very severe asthma may require a residential treatment center either to control environmental provoking factors or to provide a healthier emotional climate.

PROGNOSIS

The prognosis of asthma in childhood is improving because of advancements in drug therapy and increased precision in identifying specific triggers. With age, many children will outgrow their need for daily medication, although they may still develop bronchospasm in response to potent stimuli such as methacholine or exercise. Some, unfortunately, will continue their symptoms into adulthood. Even for this group, new research developments hold great promise to allow a more normal life with minimal intrusion of asthma symptoms or medication side-effects.

EDUCATIONAL IMPLICATIONS

School attendance is a relative health indicator—children with asthma tend to miss more school than other children, particularly if their asthma is severe. In addition to the stress of their chronic illness, these children also have to cope with its impact on school performance and peer relations. Although the pattern of excessive absenteeism can be reversed with appropriate care, residual difficulties may still exist. Side effects of asthma medications, particularly the beta adrenergic agents and theophylline, may include tremor or altered attention span, which might compromise school performance. If exercise continues to activate asthma attacks, it will continue to handicap the child in physical education and sports activities. Here again, recognition of the problem and appropriate adjustment of medications are extremely important. Although many medications are now available as timed-release preparations, a few still require doses to be given at school, especially those medications used to prevent exercise-induced asthma. Accurate information about the correct dosage and reasonably expected side effects becomes essential.

SUMMARY

Asthma is the most common chronic lung disease in school-age children. It may affect one out of every ten children. Some will never realize that they have asthma, but will suffer persistent cough or diminished exercise performance. Others will develop obvious recurrent wheezing attacks leading to excessive school absenteeism, poor physical performance, peer ridicule, and loss of self-esteem. The degree to which this can be alleviated depends upon the cooperation between child, parents, teachers, and physician. With appropriate management, asthmatic children should be able to enjoy normal school and play activities, with a minimum intrusion of their disease or their medications.

REFERENCES

Bierman, C. W., & Pearlman, D. S. Asthma. In E. L. Kendig, Jr. & V. Chernick (Eds.), *Disorders of the respiratory tract in children* (4th ed.). Philadelphia: W. B. Saunders, 1983.

Pearlman, D. S., & Bierman, C. W. Asthma (bronchial asthma, reactive airways disorder). In C. W. Bierman & D. S. Pearlman (Eds.), *Allergic diseases of infancy, childhood and adolescence*. Philadelphia: W. B. Saunders, 1980.

Souhrada, J. F., & Buckley, J. M. Value and use of pulmonary function testing in the office. In C. W. Bierman & D. S. Pearlman (Eds.), *Allergic diseases of infancy, childhood and adolescence*. Philadelphia: W. B. Saunders, 1980.

James J. Corrigan, Jr., M.D., *is professor and chief of the section of pediatric hematology-oncology in the Department of Pediatrics at the College of Medicine, The University of Arizona, Tucson.* **Mary Lou Damiano, B.A., R.N.,** *is nurse coordinator of the Mountain States Regional Hemophilia Center in the Department of Pediatrics at the College of Medicine, The University of Arizona, Tucson.*

Although numerous diseases of the blood could be considered physical disabilities, only three of the most common disorders will be discussed here: hemophilia, sickle cell anemia, and thalassemia. Blood is composed of cells within a liquid called **plasma.** The plasma contains many important proteins including those necessary for normal clotting. When blood (or plasma) clots, some of the proteins are used in the clot and the resulting fluid, thinner than plasma, is called serum. There are various types of blood cells, each with a specific function. *Red cells,* the most nu-

CHAPTER 15

Blood Diseases

merous, contain hemoglobin and transport oxygen from the lungs to cells of the body and carbon dioxide wastes from the body to the lungs. The *white cells* protect the body against infection. The *platelet,* the third cell, is the smallest of the three types. Its function is to help control bleeding, but in a way different from the plasma proteins. All the blood cells are produced by the bone marrow. As they age, they are destroyed by specialized cells (**phagocytes**), especially in the spleen. The three specific blood disorders to be discussed in this chapter are inherited conditions that affect specific parts of the blood: thalassemia and sickle cell anemia affect only the red cells, hemophilia is due to deficiencies in certain plasma proteins.

HEMOPHILIA

Hemophilia, a disorder of blood **coagulation,** affects approximately 25,000 males in the United States, making it one of this country's most common hereditary diseases. Hemophilia is not a new disease. It was described as early as 200 B.C. and received notoriety because of its prevalence in the royal houses of England, Spain, Germany, and Russia. There is no cure for hemophilia, but recent developments have dramatically improved the quality and length of life of those afflicted with the disease.

Although hemophilia A (classical hemophilia) is the most common form, there are actually three types of hemophilia: A, B, and C. In each type of hemophilia, a specific protein necessary for blood coagulation is defective and does not function normally.

In humans, a complex mechanism exists to prevent excess bleeding following injury. Through a complex interaction of blood platelets and plasma proteins the blood forms a clot that seals off the injured **blood vessel.** When an injury occurs and a blood vessel is broken, three steps are taken to arrest bleeding. First, the vessel contracts in an attempt to cut itself off from the general circulation. Second, the platelets that are circulating in the blood form a small plug at the site of injury. Third, changes in the plasma proteins convert the liquid blood to a solid clot.

If an injury is small, the contraction of the vessel or the platelet plug may be all that is needed to stop bleeding, but when the injury is more extensive, all three mechanisms must be put into action to plug the wound. When a vessel is injured, a substance (collagen) within the vessel wall is exposed to the circulating platelets. Platelets adhere to collagen and then release a chemical that causes the shape of the platelets to change from smooth to spiny. These spines cause the platelets to aggregate or stick to each other until a platelet plug is formed over the wound.

If a stronger clot is needed to stop the bleeding, the third line of defense, the plasma proteins, are activated. These proteins or clotting factors circulate in the plasma in an inactive form. Each factor has a unique molecular structure and has been assigned a particular Roman numeral. When there is an injury, a chemical is released into the bloodstream by the injured tissue and by the platelets that causes the first clotting factor to become activated. Each factor in turn triggers the activation of the next in a specific sequence (often called a cascade) that results in the formation of a strong fibrous clot. When one factor is decreased or remains inactive, the entire chain of events halts, a clot is not formed, the wound is not sealed, and bleeding continues.

Once the clotting process proceeds normally and the injury is sealed, the clot itself begins to contract, drawing the edges of the wound together. The body cells soon replace the clot with new tissue and the injury is permanently mended. Because the body is constantly repairing small leaks and breaks in vessels, a safety mechanism is needed to prevent the random formation of blood clots. This is known as the fibrinolytic system. Within each clot, there is a substance that becomes active after the clot has completed its function as a plug. This substance slowly dissolves, or lyses, the fibrin clot and keeps the **hemostatic** mechanism in delicate balance.

Hemophilia is a disorder of coagulation—specifically, it is the production of a defective clotting factor. In hemophilia A, the defective protein is factor VIII. Eighty-five percent of all hemophiliacs have this type of hemophilia. In Hemophilia B, factor IX is defective. In Hemophilia C, a very rare disorder, factor XI is abnormal. If all the factor VIII or IX produced by the body does not function (i.e., if it remains in its inactive state during the sequence of activation), the hemophiliac has virtually no clotting ability and is classified as having severe hemophilia. The normal levels of factor VIII or IX are 0.5–1.5 units per milliliter of plasma. Depending upon what percent of the factor VIII becomes active, a person may be classified as a severe (<0.01), moderate (0.01–0.10), or mild (>0.10) hemophiliac.

The bleeding patterns in each classification vary. The severe hemophiliac will frequently bleed spontaneously, whereas the moderate hemophiliac has rare spontaneous hemorrhages but will bleed abnormally after minor trauma or surgery. The patient with mild hemophilia usually bleeds abnormally only after serious trauma or surgery. However, there is a wide range of variability within each classification and some moderately affected individuals will have more bleeding episodes than others who are classified as severe.

Etiology

How does a child get hemophilia? Hemophilia A and B are sex-linked recessive disorders (Jones, 1974). That is, the disease is transmitted genetically only through females and only to their sons. The gene for a defective factor VIII or IX molecule is carried on the X chromosome. Women carrying the defect have a 50 percent chance of passing it onto their sons and a 50 percent chance of passing the carrier status onto their daughters. Approximately 20 percent of hemophiliacs have no previous family history of unusual bleeding. Their hemophilia is believed to be caused by a spontaneous gene mutation. Hemophilia C, factor XI deficiency, is an autosomal dominant disorder.

It affects males or females and may be transmitted by either sex.

Characteristics

The hemophiliac does not bleed abnormally from small cuts and scratches (Hilgartner, 1976). The platelets act to seal these types of injuries and hemophiliacs have normal platelet function. The patient with hemophilia has most of his bleeding into joints (hemarthroses) and muscles. These hemorrhages are painful and temporarily limit the use of the joint or muscle. After the bleeding has been stopped, motion is gradually regained and pain is gone. However, after repeated bleeding episodes, the joint becomes permanently damaged and weakened and has a greater tendency to rebleed.

One of the most frequently affected joints is the knee because of its weight-bearing nature (Figure 15–1). A normal knee joint has a capsule enclosing the joint. The capsule is lined by the synovial membrane, which secretes a slippery fluid that keeps the joint lubricated and moving smoothly. The end of each leg bone is padded with a tough layer of cartilage. The **capillaries** in the synovial membrane break and bleed. If bleeding is allowed to continue, the entire joint space fills with blood. The knee then becomes inflamed: very swollen, hot, and extremely painful.

When the bleeding stops, certain enzymes are released into the joint space to clean up the clotted blood. Eventually these enzymes begin to digest cartilage and bone as well as blood, and the surface of the bones are no longer padded with cartilage. The bones become rough and irregular and the joint be-comes chronically stiff and inflamed, an arthritislike condition. This type of joint damage need not occur if each bleeding episode is treated very soon after the bleeding starts, before the joint has filled with blood.

Diagnosis

The first step in the diagnosis of hemophilia is a family history of bleeding. A child usually does not exhibit signs and symptoms of hemophilia until as a toddler he experiences his first few lumps and bumps. Some patients with mild hemophilia are not diagnosed until adolescence or early adulthood when they experience significant bleeding from surgery or a tooth extraction. Coagulation tests can verify that a clotting problem exists. A specially equipped coagulation laboratory can measure the activity of the different clotting factors in the patient's plasma.

Treatment

Within the last twenty years, great strides have been made in the treatment of hemophilia. With the advent of blood fractionation, whole blood from normal donors could be separated into its various components—red cells, white cells, platelets, and plasma or serum—thus allowing patients to receive only those portions of blood necessary for their particular problem. When a pack of fresh plasma is flash frozen, then slowly defrosted and spun in a centrifuge, a cloudy precipitate sinks to the bottom of the pack. This cloudy material, cryoprecipitate, is rich in factor VIII. When a hemophiliac who is deficient in factor VIII is bleeding, cryoprecipitate can be **infused** intrave-

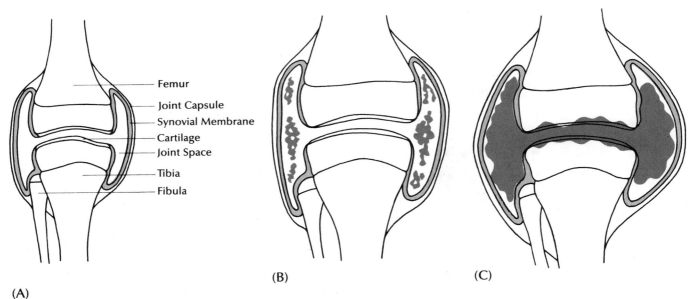

(B)

(C)

(A)

Figure 15–1   Hemarthrosis of the Knee
A: A normal knee

B: Early hemarthrosis (bleeding into the knee joint)
C: Acute hemarthrosis.

Femur
Joint Capsule
Synovial Membrane
Cartilage
Joint Space
Tibia
Fibula

nously, thereby supplying him with enough factor VIII to allow his hemostatic mechanism to go to completion, form a clot, and stop the hemorrhage.

More recently, factor VIII has been extracted from cryoprecipitate from large pools of donors, then freeze dried and bottled. Each vial is labeled with the exact number of factor VIII units contained inside. This factor VIII concentrate can then be reconstituted with sterile water and the desired number of units can be injected into the patient's vein. Through a slightly different procedure, factor IX is also extracted from plasma and freeze dried for use by patients with factor IX deficiency, Hemophilia B.

Most patients describe the feeling of early joint hemorrhage as a tingling or bubbling sensation in the joint. At this point, there is no pain or swelling. This is when the episode should be treated to prevent permanent damage. This is also one reason for the development of Home Treatment Programs. In a Home Treatment Program, the patient and his family undergo comprehensive training. They are taught about the disease and its clinical course and prognosis. They are also taught how to properly infuse the missing coagulation factor (Figure 15–2) and proper storage and reconstitution of clotting concentrates. Routine bleeding episodes can then be treated at home in the earliest stages—before the joint is blood-filled, swollen, and painful. Home treatment has done much to reduce the severe crippling often seen in older patients. It has also done much to normalize the patient's lifestyle, allowing him more responsibility for his own care and fewer trips to the hospital for treatment.

The administration of clotting factor also makes surgery and dental work safe for the hemophiliac. After an infusion of an appropriate amount of factor, the patient's blood will clot normally for the next eight to twelve hours and a surgical procedure or dental extraction can be done in relative safety. Infusions are then given every eight to twelve hours until healing is complete.

Most hemophiliacs receive much of their care through Hemophilia Centers, at which a special coagulation laboratory can accurately measure plasma levels of clotting factor. A Hemophilia Center also has a multidisciplinary staff experienced in all aspects of hemophilia care (Hilgartner, 1979). The staff usually includes pediatric and adult hematologists, orthopedic surgeons, physical therapists, social workers, dentists, an oral surgeon, a genetic counselor, and a nurse coordinator to coordinate inpatient and outpatient care. The center staff also maintains close contact with school personnel and offers financial and employment counseling to its patients.

Prognosis

Hemophilia affects so many aspects of a patient's life that optimal care can only be provided by a cooperative effort. The family, the school, and the health care team can ensure that hemophilia does not have a devastating effect on the child's physical, social, or intellectual development. Hemophilia cannot be cured, but it can be controlled with modern treatment methods and a comprehensive approach to care. The child with hemophilia can now look forward to a productive and nearly normal life.

Educational Implications

Education is of prime importance for the hemophiliac. Severely affected individuals will not be able to be employed in jobs that require strenuous physical activity without having increased bleeding into the joints and muscles. Therefore, they need to emphasize their intellectual skills. In the past, schooling was sadly neglected because frequent bleeding caused so much absence. Some children have spontaneous bleeding episodes as often as once a week. Home therapy has done much to improve school performance and reduce absences. A child who can be treated at home at the first sign of bleeding rarely must have a joint immobilized for several days. Most children will treat a bleeding episode immediately and then

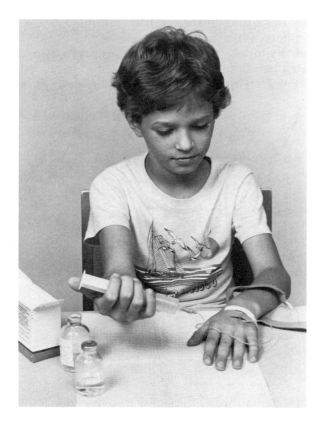

Figure 15–2   A Child Infuses Himself at Home

proceed to school. If the joint is treated early, it will not become swollen, stiff, and painful.

Frequently, the family, school, and Hemophilia Center staff need to work together to ensure an optimal education for the child (Damiano, Inman, & Corrigan, 1980). If absences are frequent, a conference may be in order to work out a solution to the child's problem. This should be done before the child falls behind in his work and becomes discouraged.

Physical activity is a necessary part of developing a strong, healthy body and plays an essential role in social development. Contact sports are not allowed, not only because of the great stress put on the muscles and joints, but because a blow to the head, neck, or abdomen can cause life-threatening bleeding in a hemophiliac. (Intracranial hemorrhage is the leading cause of death in the hemophiliac.) Muscles that are well exercised give the joints good support and are less likely to become strained by normal physical activity.

THALASSEMIA AND SICKLE CELL DISEASE

Thalassemia and sickle cell disease are inherited entities that produce anemia, but the mechanism causing the anemia is different. Thalassemia is due to inability to synthesize normal amounts of normal hemoglobin, whereas sickle cell is due to the synthesis of an abnormal hemoglobin (i.e., hemoglobin S) (Miller, Pearson, Baehner, & McMillan, 1978).

Red blood cells contain hemoglobin, a specific protein necessary for oxygen transport. These cells are produced by the bone marrow and the type of hemoglobin synthesized is under genetic control. In general, anemia occurs if the bone marrow (a) cannot produce red cells (and therefore hemoglobin), (b) can produce red cells but not enough hemoglobin (i.e., thalassemia), or (c) produces red cells with normal or abnormal types of hemoglobin (i.e., sickle cell), but the cells are prematurely lost and do not live their normal life span of 120 days. In the third example, hemorrhage can cause anemia because of loss of red cells through bleeding, or the red cells can be removed by the phagocytes faster than they are being produced. This latter mechanism is called hemolytic anemia.

In thalassemia, the red cells that are produced do not contain enough normal hemoglobin. In addition, those that are in the blood have a shortened survival time. Thus, anemia results because of defective production of red blood cells as well as excessive destruction of the cells. Sickle cell anemia, on the other hand, is predominately due to a shortened survival time. The production of sickle cells by the bone marrow is normal to increased. However, because of the

abnormal shape of the cell (see Figure 15–4), these red cells are prematurely removed from the circulation by phagocytes.

Etiology

Thalassemia and sickle cell anemia are inherited conditions (Wintrobe, 1980). Genetic information is found in chromosomes and the chromosomes are generally subgrouped into the sex and autosomal chromosomes. Thus, inherited traits are described as being autosomal or sex-linked depending on the chromosome in which the gene(s) for determining the trait is found. The hemoglobins are inherited in an autosomal manner. There are three hemoglobins in the normal individual: hemoglobin A, A_2, and F (for fetal). Each hemoglobin is composed of four small protein chains. Two of the four are the same for all hemoglobins (called alpha chains), and two are different (beta chains for A, gamma chains for F, and delta chains for A_2). The alpha, beta, gamma, and delta chains are dependent upon different genes for their production. We inherit genes for alpha, beta, gamma, and delta chains, one type from each of the two chromosomes. Thus, hemoglobin A has two alpha chains and two beta chains, A_2 has two alpha chains and two delta chains, and F has two alpha chains and two gamma chains.

In thalassemia, there is a defect in the production of these normal chains. The thalassemias are named according to which chains are affected. If the defect is in the production of normal beta chains, then it is called beta-thalassemia; alpha chains, alpha-thalassemia, and so forth. In the heterozygote (beta-thalassemia trait in Figure 15–3), i.e., when only one of the chromosomes is affected, only half of the chains are normally produced. Thus, a patient with heterozygous beta-thalassemia can produce normal amounts of alpha, gamma, and delta chains, but only half of the beta chains.

In the homozygous condition (beta-thalassemia major in Figure 15–3), no beta chains are produced. In beta-thalassemia, the bone marrow can produce red cells, but the cells will contain only a fraction of the normal amount of hemoglobin A. Because hemoglobin A is the major hemoglobin of the red cell (95 percent of the hemoglobin), anemia can result in the heterozygous condition, and severe anemia is a symptom of the homozygous state. The heterozygous condition is called thalassemia trait (thalassemia minor) and the homozygous state is called thalassemia major (Cooley's anemia).

In sickle cell anemia (see Figure 15–3), an abnormal hemoglobin, hemoglobin S, is produced. An abnormal autosomal gene is responsible for the alteration of the beta chains so that a specific abnormal

Normal A Hemoglobin   Sickle Hemoglobin

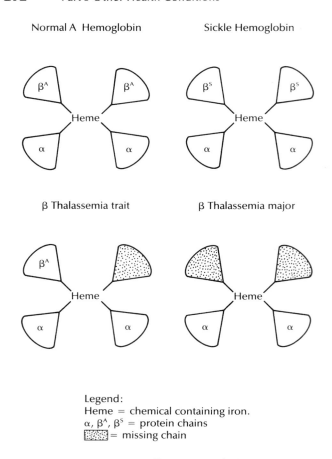

β Thalassemia trait   β Thalassemia major

Legend:
Heme = chemical containing iron.
α, β^A, β^S = protein chains
▓▓▓ = missing chain

Figure 15—3   A Small Protein Chain.

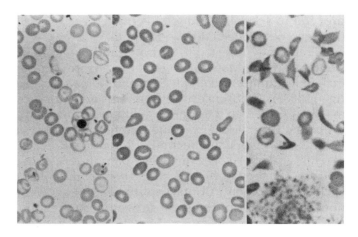

Figure 15—4   Red Blood Cells
In the left panel are cells in thalassemia, in the middle panel are normal cells, and sickle cells are shown on the right.

beta chain is synthesized that, when combined with normal alpha chains, produces hemoglobin S. In this condition, there is no impairment in the synthesis of hemoglobin protein chains. The problem is in the synthesis of an abnormal beta chain. In the heterozygous state, hemoglobins A, A$_2$, F, and S are found. In the homozygous condition, only S, A$_2$, and F are produced. The heterozygote is called sickle trait, and the homozygous condition is called sickle cell disease.

Characteristics

Thalassemia   Thalassemia (from the Greek word for the sea) was first described in 1925 and was thought to be rare and restricted to certain Mediterranean groups (Whipple & Bradford, 1936). Today, we know that the thalassemias occur throughout the world and are among the most common diseases inherited by human beings. They are most common in the Mediterranean region and in Southeast Asia. Furthermore, we know that thalassemia is not a single condition, but a heterogenous group of disorders that affect hemoglobin synthesis.

Common to all the thalassemias is a varying inability to produce normal hemoglobin. Thus, the red blood cells appear pale and small (called hypo-

chromic microcytic red blood cells) (Figure 15–4). In the heterozygous condition (thalassemia minor), such red cells are present but the child usually is not anemic and has no symptoms. However, in the homozygous state, severe anemia occurs. These children are pale, have growth impairments, and require frequent transfusions of normal red blood cells in order to maintain their well-being. Between these two extremes is a condition called thalassemia intermedia, which is either a mild form of thalassemia major or a severe manifestation of thalassemia minor. These children are anemic, but not as severely as those with thalassemia major and rarely require blood transfusions.

Sickle Cell Anemia   Normal red blood cells are round and flat (see Figure 15–4) and have an increased amount of hemoglobin toward their edges, leaving a slightly pale, depressed central area. They are very flexible and can be bent or twisted without damage. In sickle cell, the red cells contain the sickle hemoglobin. In the presence of adequate amounts of oxygen, the cells appear normal. However, a reduction in oxygen, as in venous blood, causes the abnormal hemoglobins to interact with each other so that the cell no longer maintains its disklike shape. It becomes an elongated cell with sharp ends (see Figure 15–4), rather like a sickle. Because sickled cells are odd in shape, they are recognized by the body as being not normal and removed at a fairly rapid rate. The rapid destruction causes anemia and jaundice, a yellow discoloration of the skin, eyes, and mucous membranes. Thalassemia and sickle cell disease both produce anemia, causing children to look pale, but sickle cell also produces jaundice, due to the accelerated destruction of the red cells.

Sickle hemoglobin has a distinctive racial distribution. Primarily it affects Blacks, although it is found in people from areas of the Mediterranean and Middle and Near East. In the United States, it has been estimated that the trait occurs in one out of ten Blacks, and that 1 out of 400 have anemia. Therefore, there are about 50,000 cases of sickle cell anemia in the United States.

Because sickled red cells are rigid, they do not pass through small blood vessels easily, and can block the blood flow. This phenomenon is called a vaso-occlusive episode. It is a serious complication of sickle cell anemia because it deprives the organs of oxygen and, therefore, causes cell death and extreme pain in certain areas of the body. For example, a vaso-occlusive episode within a bone will produce swelling, warmth, and pain in that area. Many times it can mimic arthritis. If the episode occurs in the intestines, then the child will complain of severe abdominal pain, which can be so severe that it could be mistaken for appendicitis, or other common pediatric problems. Vaso-occlusive episodes can affect other organs such as the brain, the spleen, the liver, the lungs, and so forth. If the episode involves the brain, it can cause a stroke with resulting weakness or paralysis of an arm or a leg (hemiplegia) and other types of motor disability. Infections are common in patients with sickle cell anemia and frequently cause death. In addition, these patients can die from heart or kidney failure.

Diagnosis

Thalassemia and sickle cell disease are diagnosed by a test called hemoglobin electrophoresis. As noted previously, patients with thalassemia will have anemia and their red blood cells will appear pale (hypochromic) and small (microcytic). Sickle cell patients will also have anemia, and the blood smear will show the specific type of abnormal cells, i.e., sickle cells. Through hemoglobin electrophoresis, one can determine if a patient has thalassemia or sickle cell disease.

In hemoglobin electrophoresis, the patient's hemoglobins are placed on paper or gels. In an electric current, the different hemoglobins migrate to the poles at different rates. By using appropriate standards, one can do an electrophoresis and determine what types of hemoglobins an individual has. Thus, in a normal patient, one would see hemoglobin A as the predominant type of hemoglobin and a little bit of A_2 and F. In the patient with heterozygote beta-thalassemia, there would be the presence of hemoglobin A, but increased amounts of A_2 or F. In sickle cell trait, there would be hemoglobin A, A_2, and F, but also S. However, in homozygous sickle cell, there would only be hemoglobin S with some A_2 and F.

The diagnosis of alpha-thalassemia is more difficult. These patients would have an inability to produce normal alpha chains. Therefore, all three normal hemoglobins, A, A_2, and F, would be reduced. However, on an electrophoresis, the test would show that these hemoglobins are present and would not clearly indicate that a thalassemia condition exists as it does with beta-thalassemia. In such situations, chemical chain analysis may be necessary. That is, there should be equal amounts of alpha chains for the beta, gamma, and delta chains. In patients with alpha-thalassemia, there would be fewer alpha chains for the number of beta, gamma, and delta chains present.

Treatment

Thalassemia   Patients with heterozygote alpha- and beta-thalassemia rarely require any treatment. Even though they may have a mild anemia, these children are asymptomatic and have normal growth and development without any disabilities. Children with thalassemia in the homozygous state, however, are severely anemic and require frequent transfusions of red blood cells in order to maintain a normal hemoglobin. This is necessary so that growth and development can be normal, and so the child can be maintained in some form of good health.

However, repeated transfusions are accompanied by complications, the most serious being iron overload. In this condition, the child receives iron through transfusions of red blood cells faster than the body can remove the iron. Thus, the iron builds up over a matter of years in various tissues. This condition is called hemosiderosis. In time, the iron will cause damage to vital organs such as the liver or the heart. This damage can result in heart disease later in life and contributes to the mortality seen in this group of children.

Sickle Cell Disease   Patients with sickle cell are also anemic but not as severely anemic as patients with homozygous thalassemia. Thus, patients with sickle cell do not receive transfusions of normal red blood cells because of anemia as a common practice. However, the other complications from the disease (e.g., the vaso-occlusive episodes) may require other types of therapy including transfusions. If episodes are severe, the child may have to be admitted to the hospital for therapy to alleviate the pain and, hopefully, to shorten the course of the crisis. Various approaches have been attempted to prevent these crises. At the present time, there is no uniformity of opinion as to what is the most beneficial. The same applies for the treatment of the crisis. Certain things such as fever, cold, infections, and operations appear to precipitate a crisis. Furthermore, anything that reduces the oxygen in the blood even slightly can precipitate a crisis. Therefore, activities such as climbing mountains or travel at high altitudes, flying in airplanes that do not have pressurized cabins, and holding one's breath for long periods of time should be restricted in these patients.

Prognosis

There are no cures for either thalassemia or sickle cell anemia. The prognosis for patients with thalassemia is poor but is somewhat better than it was ten years ago due to advances in the use of transfusions and attempts to remove iron from the body at the time transfusions are given. However, a lot of research is needed to improve the medical treatment of this particular condition and reduce its high mortality by adolescence.

The outlook has improved somewhat over the years for those with sickle cell disease, but there is still an unacceptable mortality rate from the complications of vaso-occlusive episodes. Survival to adult life is common in patients with sickle cell anemia. A normal life expectancy is seen in sickle trait.

EDUCATIONAL IMPLICATIONS

All children with anemia, no matter what the cause, will have short attention spans and certain difficulties with physical activity. Active participation in physical education may not be possible because these children tire easily and cannot keep up with their peers or engage in strenuous exercise. In addition, the child with sickle cell who has a crisis clearly is uncomfortable and may not be able to attend school for five–ten days per crisis. The child who does attend school during a crisis may not be able to perform adequately. If a crisis occurs in the central nervous system, then the child may develop a disability similar to that from a stroke. Neither thalassemia nor sickle cell directly affects intelligence or learning ability. An important aspect of the educational process is to provide vocational guidance for these children because they must take a sedentary occupation.

SUMMARY

Hemophilia, thalassemia, and sickle cell anemia are inherited blood diseases that have the propensity for causing physical disability but rarely impair intelligence. Hemophilia most commonly affects males, whereas thalassemia and sickle cell can affect either sex. Hemophilia is due to an inability of the blood to clot normally, thus these patients have a bleeding disorder. Common bleeding sites are the muscles and joints which can, in time, cause disability, especially in the legs. Treatment consists of replacing the miss-

ing coagulation factor at the earliest sign of a hemorrhage. Delay in treatment of a joint or muscle hemorrhage invariably will lead to a disabled limb. These patients have normal intelligence but, because of their condition, they may manifest behavior disorders or forms of physical disability, which must be appreciated by the educator. Current studies would suggest that, with modern day management, these patients should have a normal life-span and minimal disabilities.

Thalassemia and sickle cell anemia are different blood diseases that cause anemia. In thalassemia, this is due to the inability of the patient to synthesize normal amounts of hemoglobin. Sickle cell anemia is caused by the synthesis of an abnormal hemoglobin (sickle hemoglobin), which causes the red blood cell to assume an abnormal shape (elongated with pointed ends instead of round). Because of this, the cells are destroyed rapidly by the body. In addition, these sickle cells can aggregate and plug small blood vessels, which causes a vaso-occlusive crisis. Transfusion of normal red blood cells (which contain normal amounts and types of hemoglobin) temporarily correct the anemia of thalassemia and sickle cell anemia. There is no cure for either of these conditions. Thalassemia and sickle cell anemia patients fatigue easily because of the anemia and, therefore, cannot engage in strenuous exercise. Additionally, sickle cell patients may miss many days of school because of crises. An important aspect of the educational process is to provide vocational guidance for children with hemophilia, thalassemia, and sickle cell anemia because they must take a sedentary occupation.

REFERENCES

Damiano, M. L., Inman, M., & Corrigan, J. J. Hemophilia: The role of the school nurse. *Journal of School Health*, 1980, *50*(8), 451–454.

Hilgartner, M. W. *Hemophilia in children*. Littleton, Mass.: Publishing Sciences Group, Inc., 1976.

Hilgartner, M. W. *Comprehensive care of hemophilia*. Washington, D. C.: U.S. Department of Health, Education, and Welfare, 1979. (DHEW Publication No. (HSA) 79–5129)

Jones, P. *Living with hemophilia*. London: F. A. Davis, 1974.

Miller, D. R., Pearson, H. A., Baehner, R. L., & McMillan, C. W. *Smith's blood diseases of infancy and childhood* (4th ed.). St. Louis: C. V. Mosby, 1978.

Whipple, G. H., & Bradford, W. L. Mediterranean disease-thalassemia (erythroblastic anemia of Cooley): Associated pigment abnormalities simulating hemochromatosis. *Journal of Pediatrics*, 1936, *9*, 279–311.

Wintrobe, M. M. *Blood, pure and eloquent*. New York: McGraw-Hill, 1980.

Roger W. Yurt, M.D., Major, MC, is senior surgeon at the U.S. Army Institute of Surgical Research, Brooke Army Medical Center, Fort Sam Houston, Texas.
Basil A. Pruitt, Jr., M.D., Colonel, MC, is commander and director of the U.S. Army Institute of Surgical Research at Brooke Army Medical Center, Fort Sam Houston, Texas.

The potential impact of burn injury on child development and education must be considered not only in terms of the number of children injured, but also in relation to the long-term implications of these injuries. Burns are the second and third leading cause of injury in the young (one–four years) and older child, respectively (O'Neill, 1979). Of the approximately two million burn injuries each year, more than 35 percent are sustained by those under age seventeen (Artz, 1979) and an estimated 5 percent require hospitalization. The extent of injury is responsible for the duration of therapy and the child's chance of survival

CHAPTER 16

Burns

(Table 16–1). Age is an additional factor; the young and elderly are more likely to die from burns than the overall population.

Table 16–1   Burn Mortality Rate

	Percent of Body Burned					
	0–30	30–40	40–50	50–60	60–100	Total
Number of Patients	2,302	678	555	392	729	4,656
Percent Expired	3.3	18.6	32.1	49.0	84.9	25.6

Source: Institute of Surgical Research, 1964–1980.

The amount of illness (morbidity) due to childhood burns is difficult to represent in numbers. In a limited study, 75 percent of students with small burns were able to return to school with their classmates. However, a majority of these children required special tutoring both in the hospital and at home. The remaining patients had significant setbacks in spite of tutoring and reentered school behind their peer groups (Chang & Herzog, 1976). Students who sustain larger burns would be expected to have even higher morbidity and, consequently, greater disruption of their educational progress. The duration of a hospital stay generally equals the extent of burns as a percentage of the total body surface; that is, a day in the hospital for each percent of body surface lost.

ETIOLOGY

A majority of childhood burns occurs in the home. A younger child is more often scalded during a bath or from accidentally spilled hot liquids (Feller, 1980). Burns caused by contact with hot stoves and irons are usually small in area but may cause deep injury. The epidermis (outer layer of skin) of a young child is thin. This is partially responsible for the severity of injury sustained by exposure to hot materials. The older child is more like an adult in that most burns are from exposure to flames. Interest in development of fire resistant bed clothing for children during the middle 1970s testifies to the belief that burning clothing is a significant cause of burns in this group. One study suggested that regulating the flammability of childrens' sleepwear has decreased the incidence of burns attributed to this cause (McLoughlin, Clarke, Stahl, & Crawford, 1977). A few childhood burn injuries are caused by chemicals and electrical injury. Electrical injury often comes from contact with household electrical wiring, frequently when a child puts a wire in his mouth (Pruitt, 1979).

Inflicted burns account for 5–10 percent of injuries to battered children. Three-quarters of these patients sustain immersion burns; the rest are caused by splash or contact burns (Lenoski & Hunter, 1977). The distribution and magnitude of the burns, particularly when they are inconsistent with the history of the incident, should prompt investigation into the etiology of these wounds. Because contact injury results from direct conduction of heat to the tissue, the burn reproduces the shape of the hot object and the injury is usually uniform throughout. In contrast, accidental contact produces a burn that is more intense on one side.

CHARACTERISTICS

The characteristics of burn injuries to children fall into three general areas: complications, physical limitations, and psychological implications.

Complications

The skin is the largest organ in the human body and one of the most important. Immediately after injury, large amounts of body fluid shift to the burn wound where the fluid is either trapped or leaks to the outside. This fluid is effectively lost from the intravascular compartment (within the blood vessels). For this reason, patients with more than 25 percent of their body surface burned will go into shock if this fluid is not rapidly replaced. Even after this fluid is replaced, burn patients continue to lose large amounts of fluid through their wounds because the skin is no longer present to prevent evaporation. Furthermore, evaporation leads to heat loss. The patient with a large burn must be kept warm or his body temperature can drop to dangerously low levels causing the additional stress of cold.

Another major function of the skin is as a barrier to keep foreign materials and infections from getting into the body. Infection of burn wounds is most often caused by bacteria or fungi that are normally present on skin at all times. When the defensive barrier of skin is broken down, these organisms readily gain access to the tissue and blood. Unfortunately, the patient with larger burns also has a decreased ability to fight off the infecting organisms when they start to invade (this subject will be reviewed later).

The loss of skin function combined with the stress of the injury may affect virtually every organ of the body. With large burns, the kidneys, lungs, heart, liver, and brain may all be damaged due to the changes caused by tissue loss and damage. Except for superficial burns such as mild sunburn (first degree burn), all burns involve tissue loss. Partial thickness skin damage (second degree burn) will heal by regeneration of the superficial skin (the epidermis); whereas full thickness injury, commonly termed third degree burn, will not heal spontaneously. Small areas of full thickness injury heal by scar formation; however, skin **grafting** is necessary to restore the outer layer of skin in most cases of third degree injury.

Even with grafting, a certain amount of scar tissue will form. Although measures can be taken to limit the amount of scar formation, we as yet are unable to completely eliminate this problem. In some patients scarring is a major complication. Healing tissue tends to contract. If this occurs in areas where motion is important, function can be severely limited. Figure 16–1 shows how scarring can lead to contracture and loss of movement of joints. Figure 16–2 is an example of the effects of scarring on neck function and its "pulling" effect on other tissue, thus causing deformity to the mouth and eyelids. Patients with such deformities, if not controlled by vigorous physical

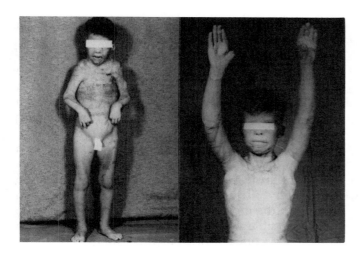

Figure 16—1 Patient With Scarring of Neck and Axillae Before (Left) and After (Right) Surgical Release

therapy, require multiple surgical procedures to regain function and appearance.

Healing is a dynamic process that requires at least a year before the tissue begins to stabilize. Although the skin will never be normal, this period is the time when healing or grafted skin is most susceptible to further damage from even minor trauma such as rubbing clothes and shoes. In addition, healing tissue commonly itches and further damage may be caused by scratching. When the injured area is large the itching can be especially severe.

Damage to the sensory organs is of utmost concern. Damage to the eyes from direct thermal injury is unusual; however, vision can be impaired due to damage to the **cornea.** Healing of the cornea requires the absence of infection. The eyes may be damaged from a full thickness burn on or about the eyelids, which leads to contracture of one or both lids and

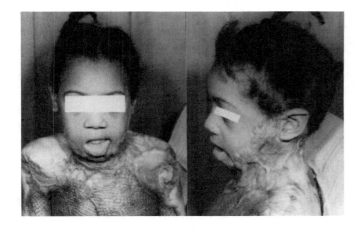

Figure 16—2 Severe Scar Formation on Neck and Lower Face After Full Thickness Burn

exposure of the eye. Subsequent drying or infection of the eye may lead to loss of visual **acuity.** Direct chemical injury to the eye frequently causes loss of vision. **Cataract** formation may be a long-term result of electrical injury and may not become apparent until twelve months or more after the injury.

Except for the external ear, direct injury to the auditory system is rare. Delayed appearance (often five–six weeks after injury) of an infection in the auricular (ear's) cartilage following deep burns can severely deform the external ear. Certain antibiotics required during burn therapy can cause a loss of hearing, which may be permanent. Disturbance in the sense of taste and smell sometimes occurs in severely burned patients as a result of zinc deficiency.

Permanent skin sensory deficits do not occur with partial thickness burns, but spotty areas of full thickness injury may lead to sensory deficits. When sensation does return after split thickness skin grafting (the type most commonly used in burn treatment), it follows the pattern of the recipient site, but the extent of reinnervation (nerve stimulation) is unpredictable. Pain perception is the first of the deficits to return, often occurring at approximately twelve months after grafting. The appreciation of touch and the ability to differentiate hot and cold often do not occur until later if at all (Moncrief, 1979). Delayed specialized grafting procedures may be performed in an attempt to enhance recovery of sensory deficits.

As mentioned previously, infection is a major complication of burn injury. Not only is infection a problem at the site of the burn, but also at sites distant to the injury. This increased susceptibility to infection is more frequent with larger burns and may lead to pneumonia or kidney and bladder infections. The increased chance of infection appears to persist until all the burned areas are covered with skin. In addition, damage caused by these infections may lead to later recurrent infection. Infection of the heart (endocarditis) may occur after burns, especially if intravascular cannulae (intravenous tubes) are required for physiologic monitoring. With regard to the lungs, inhalation damage caused by **noxious** fumes and chemical products of combustion may cause lung infection and even diminished lung function at a later date.

In the past, formation of stomach ulcers and bleeding was common in patients with large burns. More recently, the incidence of significant intestinal bleeding has been sharply decreased by the use of antacids and other prophylactic medication. Gastric surgery due to ulcers is rarely required in the burn patient.

The body's normal response to a major burn injury includes a dramatic increase in use of energy, often requiring a caloric intake of two to three times normal to maintain energy balance. Part of the increased energy is to bring about healing of the wounds. This process requires all organ systems to work harder; e.g., the heart may be called on to pump two to three times as much blood as normal. In order to meet these energy demands, diet supplements are required. Even then, weight loss is common. This requirement for additional calories, protein, vitamins, minerals, and trace metals persists at least until all wounds are healed. Proper nutrition is essential until normal weight is regained.

Physical Limitations

Because the recently damaged outer layer of skin and skin grafts do not regain normal function immediately, physical activity must be limited during the postburn period. The fragile skin must be protected from exposure to the sun, which necessitates wearing hats and clothes to shield these areas of the body. At the same time, clothes must be loose and allow freedom of movement so that injury will not recur. Participation in outdoor activity is necessarily limited to noncontact sports and games. Because most skin grafts do not contain sweat glands, students with large grafted areas will have a reduced tolerance for heat or strenuous exercise.

As a general rule, all areas that have been grafted or deeply burned are potential sites for the formation of thick scar tissue. In order to soften and maintain flexibility of this tissue, elastic garments must be worn constantly for the first year after healing has started. These garments further limit the child's activity. Figure 16–3 shows a child wearing one of these elastic garments. In cases where scar contractures have already formed, limitation of motion will persist until further surgical procedures are performed. Scar-

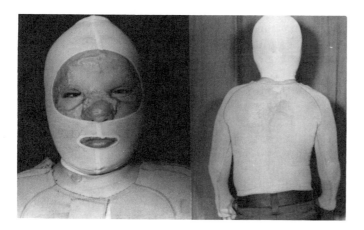

Figure 16–3 Patient Wearing Elastic Garments on Face, Head, Back, Chest, and Arms

ring on or about the face and neck may make speech difficult and allow drooling to occur.

In cases of severe injury, amputation of extremities may be required. This is particularly the case with fingers or toes that have been damaged or deformed. Such students require ongoing physical therapy. In addition, prostheses are difficult to fit when adjacent skin has been injured.

As previously outlined, visual, auditory, and skin sensory deficits may limit the student. Those patients who have sustained electrical injuries may develop neurologic deficits lasting from several days to two years after the incident. These deficits may be severe and irreversible. In addition, these patients may have sustained **fractures** during electrical shock.

Psychological Implications

In a follow-up study of 198 burned children (conducted two–five years after injury), as many as 80 percent have been reported emotionally disturbed as compared to 14 percent in a control group of uninjured children (Woodward, 1959). In addition, it was suggested that the emotional state of the mother following the burn directly correlated with the changes reported in the child. A substantial number of problems were attributed to the practice, then current in England, of restricting parental visits to children under five years of age to sleeping hours. Nevertheless, nearly 50 percent of older children, without such restrictions, were reported to have residual emotional problems. Although the objective causes of such disturbances are difficult to delineate, several major factors can be cited.

Guilt The circumstances that caused the burns and the parents' response may lead the child to feel responsible for the accident. Such cases are manifest by the child's unusual acceptance of the pain and fear associated with burn injury. The most dramatic example of such behavior is seen in children who have been abused and who believe that the suffering is punishment for past misdeeds (Long & Cope, 1961). Of equal importance is the guilt parents feel over their inability to alleviate the pain of the injury and the stress of separation on the child. The child senses these feelings in a parent. If siblings were involved in the incident, further repercussions may occur when questions of responsibility arise.

Pain and Confinement The reality of pain from every movement, exercise, dressing change, or injection may quickly alienate the child not only from the physicians and personnel who are caring for him, but also from the parents who are "allowing" it. Regression may occur in such circumstances, manifested by

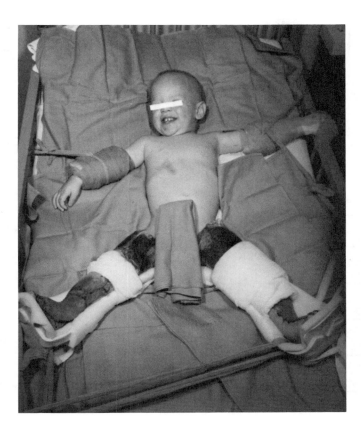

Figure 16—4   Restraints to Protect Skin Grafts on Patient's Legs. Splints on the legs prevent shearing of recently applied skin.

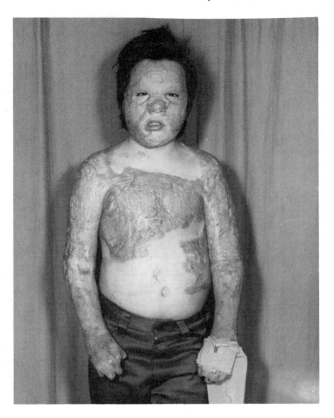

Figure 16—5   Disfigurement. This patient sustained deep burns of the face, chest, arms, and hands. Deep injury to the fingers led to amputation.

behavior more reminiscent of a young child (e.g., refusal to eat, thumb sucking).

Although narcotics, often in high doses, are administered for relief of pain, some discomfort persists. Complete obliteration of sensory input can lead to pulmonary and cardiac complications and the associated dulling of sensation impairs food intake. The repeating cycle of pain, "forced" exercise, and eating may lead to deepening depression and confusion in the child.

The child who responds with aggressive behavior is subjected to restraints to protect himself and his wounds (Figure 16–4), thus leading to further feelings of helplessness. Physical pain and the absence of parents and siblings further stress the patient. Failure to recognize the dynamics of the child's behavior can cause those taking care of him to reject the patient. The patient responds with further withdrawal or alienation, making care and emotional support ever more difficult.

Disfigurement   From early in the patient's hospitalization, the effects of scarring concern the parents. It is not until the acute phase is over that this be-

comes real to the child. Acceptance of deformity, particularly of the face and hands (Figure 16–5), is generated through support by parents, siblings, ward personnel, and other burned patients. The acceptance of a grotesque child on the part of both parents and teachers may be aided by psychiatric support.

As with adults (Hamburg, Hamburg, & de Goza, 1953), discharge from the hospital brings to the surface fears that the patient will not be accepted by others. Unsympathetic questioning and teasing by classmates can intensify feelings of rejection and lead to overcompensation by the patient, resulting in delinquency (Chang & Herzog, 1976). Alternatively, the disfigured burn patient may simply withdraw and severely limit any interaction with others. One way to deal with this problem is to have parents or a social worker visit the class before the child returns to explain both the nature of the injury and the child's appearance. This may ease the transition and reduce peers' morbid curiosity.

Morbidity and Mortality   While the question of survival is raised by parents immediately after their child's injury, the patient is frequently so distracted by the unfamiliar surroundings and his injury that it is not of immediate concern to him. Even after observation of the death of other patients, the young patient is most affected by the feelings generated by those close to him. A child senses fear and anxiety in his parents and those emotions are also transmitted to the child by physicians and ward personnel, who frequently react more strongly to an injured child than an injured adult. Later during their hospital stay, patients are faced with the possibility of physical limitations due to their injury. Questions of whether the patient will be able to run, use his hands, or play ball may only be answered after numerous operations and extensive physical therapy. The months of uncertainty are a continual stress to both the patient and his family.

Burn Estimate and Diagram
Age vs. Area

Area	Birth 1 yr.	1-4 yr.	5-9 yr.	10-14 yr.	15 yr.	Adult	2°	3°	Total	Donor Areas
Head	19	17	13	11	9	7				
Neck	2	2	2	2	2	2				
Ant. Trunk	13	13	13	13	13	13				
Post. Trunk	13	13	13	13	13	13				
R. Buttock	2½	2½	2½	2½	2½	2½				
L. Buttock	2½	2½	2½	2½	2½	2½				
Genitalia	1	1	1	1	1	1				
R.U. Arm	4	4	4	4	4	4				
L.U. Arm	4	4	4	4	4	4				
R.L. Arm	3	3	3	3	3	3				
L.L. Arm	3	3	3	3	3	3				
R. Hand	2½	2½	2½	2½	2½	2½				
L. Hand	2½	2½	2½	2½	2½	2½				
R. Thigh	5½	6½	8	8½	9	9½				
L. Thigh	5½	6½	8	8½	9	9½				
R. Leg	5	5	5½	6	6½	7				
L. Leg	5	5	5½	6	6½	7				
R. Foot	3½	3½	3½	3½	3½	3½				
L. Foot	3½	3½	3½	3½	3½	3½				

TOTAL

Age_____
Sex_____
Weight_____

Burn Diagram

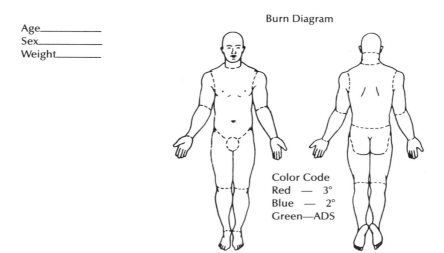

Color Code
Red — 3°
Blue — 2°
Green—ADS

Figure 16–6 Chart to Map and Calculate Percentage of Body Surface Burned. The distribution of body surface changes with age.

DIAGNOSIS

Accurate recording of the circumstances surrounding the incident, the past medical history, the extent of burn injury, and any associated injuries is necessary to organize an appropriate plan of therapy. The extent of burn injury is assessed by calculating the percentage of the total body surface that is burned and the depth of injury. Because the distribution of body surface area varies with age, calculation of percent of area burned is best done using a standard chart such as the one used at the Institute of Surgical Research (Figure 16–6).

The depth of tissue injury is classified as partial thickness (second degree) or full thickness (third degree). Partial thickness injury spares enough epidermis to allow healing without skin grafts. These burns are characterized by blistering (a pink color); sensation remains intact (Figure 16–7). Full thickness injury implies loss of all **dermis,** hair **follicles,** and sweat glands so that primary healing will not be spontaneous and grafts are necessary. These wounds lack sensation and are frequently leathery in appearance and to the touch (Figure 16–8). Even the most experienced physician cannot always accurately determine the depth of burns during the acute phase. In these cases, judgement may have to be reserved until the wound is assessed for healing, about two weeks after the injury. When full thickness injury completely surrounds an extremity, repeated assessment of blood flow is necessary because tissue pressure can rise high enough to block off blood flow to the limb.

High voltage electrical injuries are more difficult to assess because burns at the surface bear no rela-

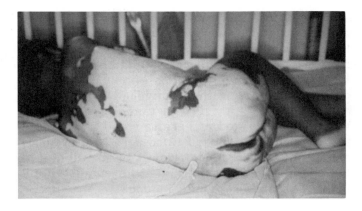

Figure 16–8   Full Thickness Burns of the Back and Buttocks

tionship to the amount of internal injury. Although there are usually deep entrance and exit burns, other areas may sustain flash or flame burns. Frequent evaluation of heart rhythm, neurologic status, muscle function and tone, and of the abdomen are necessary to detect additional injury. X rays of the spinal column and injured extremities are taken to identify coexisting fractures.

The position of the child when burned can be determined by the distribution of scald burns from the immersion; likewise, the authenticity of circumstances surrounding splash burns can be confirmed by accurately recording the distribution of the burn. All suspected cases of child abuse should have radiologic (X-ray) studies to determine the presence of old or new fractures of the skull and long bones.

A history of flame burns in a closed space signals the possibility of lung injury due to the inhalation of smoke or other noxious gases. Carbonaceous sputum (secretions from the lower respiratory tract) further suggests such injury. These injuries can be detected by lung scans, direct visualization of the airways, and tests of lung function.

TREATMENT

Treatment of patients with large burns requires a multidisciplinary approach and the skills of surgeons, nurses, physical and occupational therapists, dieticians, psychologists, social workers, and psychiatrists. It is not unusual for patients with extensive burns to require hospital care for 60–90 days or more. Treatment of burn-injured children can be divided into acute and chronic care.

Acute

Surface burns of less then 15 percent of the body surface area usually are treated on an outpatient ba-

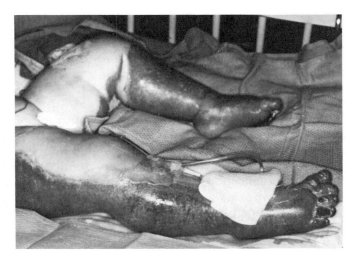

Figure 16–7   Partial and Full Thickness Burns on a Child's Legs. Differentiation between partial and full thickness injury during the acute phase may be difficult.

sis. The wounds are cleansed twice a day and a topical antibiotic cream, such as Silvadene, is applied. Patients with burns of greater extent or with burns on the face, hands, or **perineum** should be admitted to the hospital for treatment. As previously mentioned, patients with larger burns require fluid administration and close monitoring of their cardiovascular status. Wounds are cleaned as necessary and topical antibiotic creams are applied twice daily to prevent or control infection. Partial thickness burns will heal in two to three weeks if infection is prevented, but full thickness burns will require grafting.

Chronic

Grafting of full thickness burns begins as soon as the patient is stable (generally three–four days after injury). Patients with large areas of full thickness burn usually require multiple operative procedures for grafting. Burned limbs are placed in individually fitted splints to maintain position while healing occurs (Figure 16–9). Function of extremities is maintained through exercise under the direction of a physical therapist during and after hospitalization. The increased energy requirements of the burn patient are satisfied by supplemental feedings and tube feedings. If energy balance cannot be obtained by these methods then high caloric intravenous feedings may be used.

At the time of discharge from the hospital, patients and their families are instructed in continuing care, which includes the use of elastic garments, care of recently healed skin, and an outline of physical therapy. During follow-up appointments, the patients status and progress are evaluated by the surgeon and

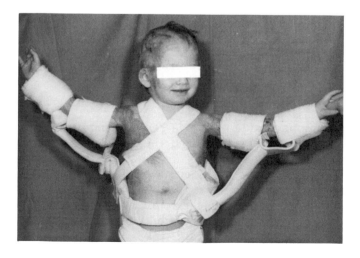

Figure 16–9   Splints to Maintain Adduction
Splints keep this child's arms away from his body after skin grafts to the arms, axillae, and chest.

physical therapist. **Ulceration** of healed skin may be treated with topical antibiotics (e.g., Silvadene) and measures taken to prevent further injury to the area. Discharge medication may include a lanolin cream to moisturize the skin and antihistamines to control itching. Neither pain medication nor systemic (internal) antibiotics are required at this time.

PROGNOSIS

Although numerous other methods have been advocated, the patient is best evaluated by considering the percent of total body surface burned, other associated injury, and age at injury. These continue to form the main method to initially assess the outcome for burned patients. There is a direct relationship between percent of body surface burned and mortality (shown in Table 16–1). However, no available method discriminates between those patients with a particular size injury who will or will not survive. Indeed, such lack of ability to prognosticate is a compelling reason for full medical support for even the most extensively burned patients.

For the majority of burn patients that survive the acute phase, the prognosis is good, assuming that continuing support is provided. As previously indicated, the duration of hospitalization for patients with burns covering 30 percent or more of the total body surface can be anticipated to approximate one day per percent of burn. Those patients who have survived severe burn injuries or have sustained complications such as neurologic injury will often require years of extensive physical therapy and psychological support. In each such case, the prognosis will depend on the anatomic distribution of the burn injury, extent of scarring and contractures, severity of associated injury, and the psychological response of the individual patient.

EDUCATIONAL IMPLICATIONS

Mental capacity seems little affected by burn injury per se, but may be impaired if the patient has experienced (a) prolonged shock from associated injuries, delayed or inadequate resuscitation, or septic (pus-forming) complications from infection, (b) severe or prolonged hypoxia (lack of sufficient oxygen) due to inhalation injury, obstruction of the airway, or severe pneumonia, (c) direct injury to the brain at the time of burn injury, or (d) brain injury from a central nervous system infection. These injuries to the brain may also produce epilepsy or loss of function of body parts. Any such residual effects must be taken into account in planning educational and physical rehabilitation.

In-Hospital

Because hospitalization for burn victims may be prolonged, ongoing tutoring is arranged to accompany the treatment program. The intensity of care, recurring and frequent episodes of discomfort associated with necessary care, and the occurrence of complications generally preclude even individual tutoring during the acute phase (until initial wound coverage). During this time, however, the social worker, surgeon, psychologist, physical therapist, parents, and teacher should develop plans to place the child in an organized educational program as soon as the burn wounds have healed or been grafted.

Evaluation of the home environment is essential considering the emotional problems that may exist. Particularly in cases of suspected child abuse, in-depth investigation of the home is made. The teacher should be aware of such evaluation as he or she may be the first to observe continuing abuse problems. The educational program should be tailored to the individual child's needs and capabilities and must take into account the child's physical and psychological injuries and their residual effects.

After Discharge

Depending on the extent of residual deficits, the student may continue to require in-home tutoring prior to and during integration into an educational program. Throughout this time and for a year or longer, the extensively burned patient will need to perform specialized exercises, many of which require professional assistance. An educational program will have to allow for therapy at the school or other facilities. The physical limitations resulting from the burn or subsequent complications should be recognized in planning for rehabilitation, but the patients must be encouraged and allowed to do as much as possible for themselves. Misguided helpfulness will only foster continued and increased unnecessary dependency. Six to twelve months after the injury patients with contractures or disfigurement become candidates for reconstructive surgery. The possibility of multiple hospitalizations and their timing has to be considered within the structure of continuing education.

Individualized nutritional programs may need to be provided for those who are underweight or malnourished. Often, supplemental feedings can be provided from the student's home. Requirements for medication should be minimal but can include vitamins and antihistamines to control itching. Because antihistamines may sedate some patients, the timing and the dosage of such medications may have to be manipulated in order to allow the student to participate in classwork. In addition to antihistamines, cooling baths or showers and moisturizing creams may be used to control itching.

Interaction between the burn-injured child and his peer group may be difficult because of the child's prolonged absence from school and his increased self-consciousness. Disfigurement, contractures, and special garments lead to questions and teasing. Furthermore, the patient may be restricted from joining the scheduled recreation and physical education activities. Recent burn victims are intolerant of heat and cold due to the impaired thermoregulatory (temperature control) capacity of healed and grafted burn wounds and graft donor sites. This means that they must avoid temperature extremes at school and they must avoid any strenuous or prolonged exercise that exceeds the patient's tolerance. Elastic garments necessary for scar control may further narrow the comfortable temperature range of the burn patient. As convalescence proceeds and the burn wounds and grafts mature during a twelve–eighteen month period, temperature and exercise tolerance improve, and the patient's environmental and exercise restrictions can be relaxed. The reintegration of these students among their peers is indeed a challenge for the parent, teacher, and burn team.

Emotional instability or behavioral problems, which may affect rehabilitation in all spheres, can result from the injury and its residual effects or reflect ongoing problems that predate the burn injury. The source of these problems should be sought and dealt with, as it would be with any other child. The child's attention span may be markedly short in early convalescence and scheduled teaching should take this into account. Teaching sessions can be lengthened as the immediacy of the injury experience recedes.

The effects of a burn injury on a child's education, as outlined above, are confirmed in a study by Woodward (1959). In this study, the teachers of 151 students who had sustained burns of more than 10 percent of body surface within the previous two–five years were asked to comment on the child's attendance, attainments, attitudes toward teachers and other children, and behavior in general and during recreation. Of these students, 68 percent were listed as having problems in one or more areas, and 51 percent were felt to have problems in two or more areas. Woodward concluded that the two basic problem areas were difficulty in personal relationships and inability to maintain satisfactory educational progress.

SUMMARY

The high incidence of burns during childhood, increases in survival of burn-injured children, and the frequent morbidity (illness) associated with burn injury indicates that increasing numbers of burn-injured children will require specialized education. The integration of these burn victims into educational programs is compromised by a multitude of acute and long-term complications. The amount of illness that follows these injuries is determined by the extent and distribution of damaged tissue. Although duration of hospitalization often correlates with the percentage of the body surface that is burned, the subsequent physical limitations, such as scar contractures, depend on the location of injury.

A significant number of patients experience psychological effects in addition to the residual physical effects of burn injury. During hospitalization, these patients face pain, disfigurement, separation from family, and guilt. Adjustment after discharge is a problem for most of them. The combined efforts of surgeons, psychiatrists, psychologists, social workers, nurses, dietitians, physical and occupational therapists, parents, and teachers are essential if the burn-injured child is to recover fully.

REFERENCES

Artz, C. P. Epidemiology: Causes and prognosis. In C. P. Artz, J. A. Moncrief, & B. A. Pruitt, Jr. (Eds.), *Burns: A team approach.* Philadelphia: W. B. Saunders, 1979.

Chang, F. C., & Herzog, B. Burn morbidity: A follow-up study of physical and psychological disability. *Annals of Surgery,* 1976, *18,* 34–37.

Feller, I. Prevention for one and two year olds. *NBIE Newsletter.* 1980, *1,* 1–2.

Hamburg, D. A., Hamburg, B., & deGoza, S. Adaptive problems and mechanisms in severely burned patients. *Psychiatry,* 1953, *16,* 1–20.

Lenoski, E. F., & Hunter, K. A. Specific patterns of inflicted burn injuries. *Journal of Trauma,* 1977, *17,* 842–846.

Long, R. T., & Cope, O. Emotional problems of burned children. *New England Journal of Medicine,* 1961, *264,* 1121–1127.

McLoughlin, E., Clarke, N., Stahl, K., & Crawford, J. D. One pediatric burn unit's experience with sleepwear-related injuries. *Pediatrics,* 1977, *60,* 405–409.

Moncrief, J. A. Grafting. In C. P. Artz, J. A. Moncrief, & B. A. Pruitt, Jr. (Eds.), *Burns: A team approach.* Philadelphia: W. B. Saunders, 1979.

O'Neill, Jr., J. A. Burns in children. In C. P. Artz, J. A. Moncrief, & B. A. Pruitt, Jr. (Eds.), *Burns: A team approach.* Philadelphia: W. B. Saunders, 1979.

Pruitt, Jr., B. A. The burn patient: I. Initial care. *Current Problems in Surgery,* 1979, *16,* 1–62.

Woodward, J. Emotional disturbances of burned children. *British Medical Journal,* 1959, *1,* 1009–1013.

John J. Hutter, Jr., M.D., is associate professor in the section of pediatric hematology-oncology of the Department of Pediatrics at the College of Medicine, The University of Arizona, Tucson. **Fran Z. Farrell, R.N., M.S.W.,** is nurse social worker in the section of pediatric hematology-oncology in the Department of Pediatrics at the College of Medicine, The University of Arizona, Tucson.

Cancer is an inclusive term, applied to a large variety of different **malignant** tumors. A malignant tumor results from excessive growth of abnormal cells that have the potential to spread to other parts of the body. The manner in which a particular cancer affects the body depends on the type of the malignant tumor. Certain cancers invade only surrounding local structures, whereas others spread to areas of the body distant from the primary tumor via the lymph system (to regional lymph nodes) or the blood system (to the bones, lungs, etc.). Because the term cancer is applied to many different types of malignant disorders,

Cancer in Children

it can show a variety of initial manifestations and patterns of spread to other parts of the body, each of which requires different forms of treatment.

Fortunately, cancer in children is relatively rare, approximately one case per 10,000 children under fifteen years of age each year. Children are most frequently affected by cancers in the leukemia-lymphoma group (Figure 17–1). Tumors of the nervous system and bone tumors are the next most frequent in the school-age child. The most common types of cancer in adults (breast cancer, lung cancer, and **gastrointestinal** cancer) rarely occur in children (Sutow, 1977).

The chance for long-term **remission** and survival of children with cancer has increased significantly over the last several decades. As more effective, but

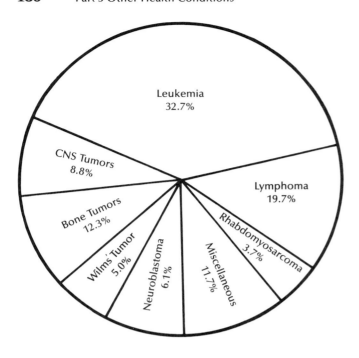

Figure 17–1 Frequency of Types of Cancer in Children

often intensive, treatment methods have been developed, childhood cancer often has been reduced from an acute to a chronic illness. Historically, the child's treatment began with removal of the tumor through surgery. Surgical treatment, however, is effective only when the cancer is limited to a portion of the body where complete removal of the tumor can be accomplished. The next mode of treatment for cancer to be developed was radiation (X-ray) therapy (Figure 17–2).

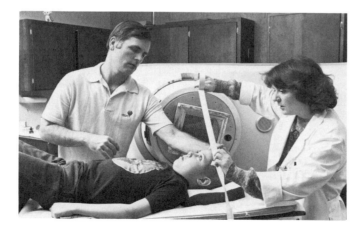

Figure 17–2 Radiation Therapy. A child with leukemia is having measurements made prior to the delivery of cranial radiation. The linear accelerator which will be used for radiation treatment is in the background.

X-ray therapy improved the outlook for children with certain types of cancer that could not be controlled by surgery alone (e.g., Hodgkin's lymphoma) but it still could only be applied to a limited portion of the body. The development of effective drug treatment (chemotherapy) has enabled the control of some cancers that are always spread throughout the body (e.g., leukemia). For many forms of cancer, the marked improvements in treatment have resulted from the combination of the use of surgery, radiation, and chemotherapy. The complexity of combined treatments has necessitated that a program be designed and instituted by a specialized children's cancer treatment center, although much of the actual ongoing treatment can be administered within the child's local community.

The ultimate goal in the treatment of a child with cancer is to both eradicate the cancer and to have the child live as normally as possible. Part of the return to normal living includes the return of a school-age child to school. Because childhood cancers are rare and usually unfamiliar to educators, the child's return to school requires open communication among the family, the specialized personnel at the pediatric oncology center, and the classroom teacher.

This chapter summarizes the etiology, characteristics, diagnosis, treatment, and prognosis of children with cancer. The educational implications of both the disease and its treatment are emphasized.

ETIOLOGY

The causes for most human cancers remain unknown. The development of cancer in an individual is most likely to evolve from a complex interplay of several factors including genetic constitution, infectious agents, and environmental exposure. Some types of cancer in children are hereditary, but only a minority of childhood cancers. An example of a hereditary type of cancer is **retinoblastoma**, a cancer of the eye. Affected individuals, particularly where both eyes are involved, produce offspring with a markedly increased probability for a similar type of cancer. Viruses have been demonstrated to cause cancer in many animals. Very specific viruses have produced leukemia in birds, rodents, and cats. It is still unclear what role, if any, viruses may play in the development of leukemia in people, and there is no indication that childhood cancer is contagious.

Environmental exposure has also been implicated in the development of certain human cancers, including leukemia. Exposure to large doses of radiation may lead to the development of leukemia, as evidenced by the increased incidence of leukemia in the survivors of the atomic bombings at Hiroshima and Nagasaki. Chemical agents have also been implicated in the development of some human leukemias, such as the leukemia that developed in some Turkish shoe workers who were exposed to benzene.

Despite the above associations, the exact cause for most types of cancer in an individual child usually remains unknown. When the cause is unknown, it is important to emphasize to families that (a) the disease did not result from anything that they did and (b) there is nothing known that could have been done to prevent the development of this rare disorder.

CHARACTERISTICS

The different types of cancer in children produce different symptoms and produce different physical abnormalities. This section will review some of the initial signs and symptoms of the more frequent types of cancer in the school-age child.

Acute Leukemia

Approximately one-third of all children with cancer have leukemia. The most frequent type of leukemia in children is acute lymphoblastic leukemia, which has its highest incidence in children aged four to seven years. Leukemia is a cancer of the blood cells, most often the white blood cells. There are three types of normal cells that circulate in the blood: *red blood cells,* which carry oxygen to the tissues; *white blood cells,* which fight infection; and *platelets,* which help the blood to clot after injury to small blood vessels. A child with active leukemia has decreased levels of normal red blood cells (anemia), decreased levels of platelets (thrombocytopenia), and decreased levels of normal white cells (increased risk of serious infection). This means that at the onset or during relapse of the disease, the child is usually moderately to severely anemic and, as a result, is pale and has decreased appetite and decreased activity. Fever, often due to infection, is frequently present. Because of the low platelet count, children with leukemia have an increased tendency to bruise very easily or to develop nosebleeds.

Many children with leukemia often have severe pain in their bones and joints, which is related to the involvement of the bones and bone marrow by the leukemic cells. These signs and symptoms improve as the disease is controlled and the child enters remission. Even in remission, however, there is increased risk for the development of certain serious infections.

Lymphoma

Lymphomas are cancers of the lymph nodes and lymph system. The lymph nodes and lymph drainage in the region of the face and neck are illustrated in

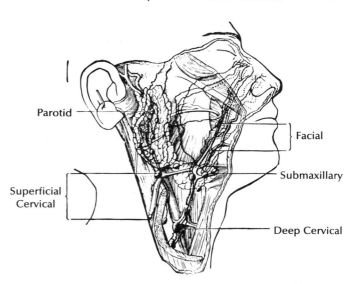

Figure 17–3 Lymph Drainage of the Face Into the Facial, Parotid, Submaxillary, and Cervical Lymph Nodes

Figure 17–3. Similar types of lymph drainage systems exist throughout the body. Lymphomas occur more frequently in older children and adolescents than in younger children. Lymphomas can be subdivided into two major groups: Hodgkin's disease and non-Hodgkin's lymphomas. Hodgkin's disease tends to remain localized to the lymph nodes system but occasionally involves the liver, lungs, and bone. Non-Hodgkin's lymphomas are more likely to involve other organ systems, such as the liver, lungs, skin, bone marrow, and central nervous system.

Central Nervous System Tumors

The majority of central nervous system tumors in children are brain tumors. The initial symptoms of brain tumors in children are most often severe headache and persistent vomiting, which often is most prominent early in the morning. Alterations in balance and other neurological signs may be present as well. Most brain tumors do not spread to areas of the body outside the nervous system.

Wilms's Tumor

Wilms's tumor is a malignant tumor of the kidney. Most often its initial manifestation is the development of a large mass in the abdomen. This tumor most commonly involves the preschool-age child but occasionally can develop in the young school-age child.

Rhabdomyosarcoma

Rhabdomyosarcoma is a malignant tumor that arises from skeletal muscle. It can occur anywhere in the body that skeletal muscle is present including the head and neck, genitourinary system, and extremities. Rhabdomyosarcoma of the genitourinary system is more common in the young infant and preschool child, whereas rhabdomyosarcoma of an arm or leg is more common in the school-age child and adolescent. The initial manifestation is likely to be a large mass, often painful, within the extremity. The lymph nodes may be enlarged due to the regional spread of rhabdomyosarcoma.

Bone Tumors

The two most common bone tumors in children are Ewing's sarcoma and osteogenic sarcoma. These tumors most often occur in preadolescents and adolescents. The usual initial manifestation in both sarcomas is an extremely painful swelling in and around an area of bone. In osteogenic sarcoma, the long bones of the leg and upper arm are the most commonly involved. Ewing's sarcoma can involve the bones of the pelvis and other parts of the skeleton in addition to the arms and legs.

DIAGNOSIS

The diagnosis of cancer usually requires the removal of all or part of the malignant tissue for a microscopic examination of the malignant cells. The patient's symptoms, physical findings, X rays, and other tests may strongly suggest the presence of a cancer. Exact diagnosis, however, requires that the microscopic appearance of the cells be assessed to determine the nature of the malignancy. This is usually accomplished when the tumor is surgically removed or through a biopsy. In certain instances, such as the presence of a tumor deep within the vital tissues of the brain, the diagnosis of cancer may have to be made without a biopsy. This latter example, however, is the exception rather than the rule. Whenever possible, biopsy of a suspected malignant tumor should be performed prior to the institution of treatment.

Acute Leukemia

In many cases of acute leukemia, the patient's symptoms and physical findings along with the presence of leukemia cells in the blood strongly suggest the possibility of this condition. Some cases of leukemia, however, do not have malignant cells that are easily identified in the blood. Blood cells are produced in the marrow cavity within the bones. In leukemia, the marrow is almost invariably affected by the cancer. Therefore, leukemia is diagnosed by examining bone marrow obtained by needle from the bone marrow cavity.

Lymphoma

Lymphoma is usually diagnosed by examination of a biopsy from an involved lymph node. In certain cases, the diagnosis can be established by examining other body tissues, such as bone marrow, which are affected by the lymphoma.

Central Nervous System Tumors

The physician who suspects a child of having a central nervous system tumor will often recommend a specialized radiographic study of the brain known as a Computerized Tomographic (CT or CAT) scan. This X ray will usually indicate that an abnormal mass is present within the substance of the brain. To establish that the mass is cancerous, however, surgical biopsy is usually required.

Wilms's Tumor

When a child has an abnormal mass in the abdomen, a specialized X ray of the genitourinary system (intravenous pyelogram or IVP) and an ultra-sound examination of the abdomen are usually obtained. Because Wilms's tumor is derived from the kidney, indications of this particular tumor will show up on the intravenous pyelogram. However, because benign conditions can also produce this type of renal mass, microscopic examination is required for an exact diagnosis.

Rhabdomyosarcoma

Rhabdomyosarcoma is diagnosed by a surgical biopsy of the tumor mass. As this particular type of cancer can be difficult to distinguish from other types of malignant cancers in older children, evaluation of the tumor material by an electron microscope is strongly recommended.

Bone Tumors

When a child has painful swelling around an area of bone, an X ray is usually taken. The X ray of a child with a bone tumor will demonstrate destruction of bone with invasion of the tumor into the soft tissues surrounding the bone (Figure 17–4). As infections and other benign conditions can also on occasion produce extensive destruction of bone, it is important to perform a biopsy for the exact diagnosis of a child with a bone tumor.

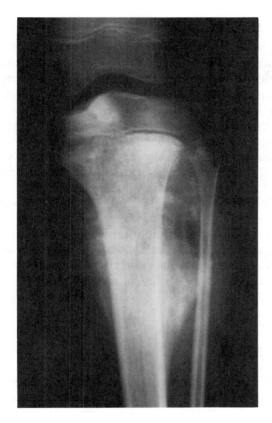

Figure 17—4   X Ray of a Bone Tumor

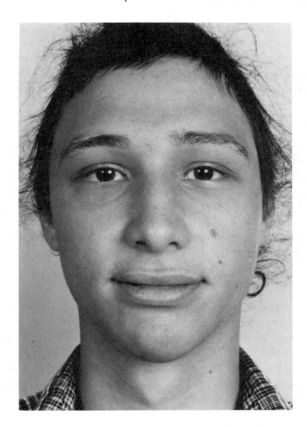

Figure 17—5   Hair Loss as a Result of Intensive Chemotherapy

TREATMENT

After the diagnosis of cancer has been established, further tests are often performed to determine the extent of the cancer throughout the body. The assessment of the extent of the cancer is often referred to as a determination of the *stage* of the tumor. This evaluation is very important, because the outlook differs with the stage of the cancer, and the stage of the cancer often determines the type of treatment to be administered.

Acute Leukemia

Leukemia is a cancer of the blood. As the blood goes everywhere in the body, acute leukemia is never localized. In some cases, leukemia can involve the nervous system. Because it is more difficult to administer adequate doses of chemotherapy to the nervous system, it is important to determine whether the nervous system is involved and to try to prevent it from developing in the nervous system during the course of treatment.

Children who are receiving intensive chemotherapy for leukemia or other forms of cancer often lose their hair as a result of the treatment (see Figure 17–5). This loss of hair may produce major adjustment problems upon a child's return to school. Because the treatment for leukemia can run several years, the child may have frequent absences from school. Certain forms of treatment also produce **nausea** and vomiting, which further may aggravate the problem of having to miss school.

Recently, it has been observed that children with leukemia who received radiation treatments to the brain during their preschool years sometimes have a higher incidence of learning disabilities during their school years. Generally, children with leukemia have normal intelligence and normal physical growth and development during and following their treatment. The learning disabilities that have been observed following radiation treatment may require specific remedial work. The school should be aware of this potential problem. Assessment of these children for consideration of special educational services is strongly recommended.

Children with leukemia who are undergoing treatment are usually able to maintain normal activities. However, they are more likely to experience complications from certain types of infection, particularly chickenpox and measles. If children with leukemia who are undergoing treatment are exposed to chickenpox and measles, their families should be told immediately so that appropriate measures can be taken to prevent the development of measles or chickenpox in the susceptible child with leukemia.

Lymphomas

Children with Hodgkin's disease in its early stages are often successfully treated with radiation alone. Children in the later stages of Hodgkin's disease often require chemotherapy or chemotherapy combined with radiation treatments. Because non-Hodgkin's lymphoma has a high tendency to spread outside the lymph node system, chemotherapy treatments are usually indicated.

Central Nervous System Tumors

There are several different types of brain tumors and the form of treatment varies with the particular type. Surgical removal of the tumor is usually performed. When the tumor is located in certain vital areas of the brain, however, it may not be possible to completely remove it by surgery. Some forms of tumors, particularly medulloblastoma, respond well to radiation treatment. Because most types of chemotherapy do not penetrate well into the brain substance, this treatment has not been as effective in brain tumors as in lymphomas. On occasion, children with brain tumors develop hydrocephaly, in which the flow of cerebral spinal fluid from the ventricles is blocked and consequently intracranial pressure increases. Because of this, it is sometimes necessary to insert a shunt from the ventricular system of the brain in order to alleviate the pressure.

Wilms's Tumor

Usually, the initial step in managing malignant renal tumors is to surgically remove the tumor and the involved kidney. In about one out of every twenty cases, however, the tumor involves both kidneys. In this situation, the more involved kidney is removed and an attempt is made to salvage as much function as possible in the lesser involved kidney. Wilms's tumor is fortunately very sensitive to radiation treatment and chemotherapy.

Rhabdomyosarcoma

The outlook for children with rhabdomyosarcoma has improved markedly by the combined use of surgery, radiation therapy, and chemotherapy. The exact combination to be used in a particular case varies with the location of the rhabdomyosarcoma and the stage of the disease.

Bone Tumors

Ewing's sarcoma is sensitive to radiation treatments and often can be managed by using a combination of radiation treatment and chemotherapy and may not require complete surgical removal. Osteogenic sarcoma does not respond as well to radiation and, therefore, complete surgical excision of the tumor is required. This often means that the extremity must be amputated although, more recently, attempts to salvage the limb despite removing the tumor and the bone have been performed in selected cases.

Because radiation therapy to the involved extremity can result in muscle atrophy, children with Ewing's sarcoma or rhabdomyosarcoma often need physical therapy as well. Children with osteogenic sarcoma, both amputees and those with limb salvage procedures, require physical rehabilitation programs too.

PROGNOSIS

The outlook and potential for survival for children with cancer has improved markedly over the past two decades. The prognosis in any given individual child, however, varies greatly with the type of cancer present and the stage of the disease.

Acute Leukemia

There are many different types of acute leukemia. Acute lymphoblastic leukemia is the most common type in children and makes up approximately 80 percent of childhood leukemia. However, even among children with acute lymphoblastic leukemia, there are several subgroups which have different prognoses and may require different treatments. With current treatments, children in the more favorable subgroup can expect a greater than 60 percent chance of long-term survival and a potential cure of their disease. Children in the more unfavorable subgroups of acute lymphoblastic leukemia or children with acute myelogenous or monoblastic leukemia have a much poorer prognosis.

Lymphomas

Children with localized Hodgkin's disease have an excellent prognosis with a potential greater than 90 percent cure rate. With the development of more effective chemotherapy regimens, the outlook also has improved for children with more advanced stage Hodgkin's disease and also for children with non-Hodgkin's lymphoma.

Central Nervous System Tumors

The prognosis for a child with a central nervous system tumor depends on the type of tumor as well as its location within the brain. Unfortunately, the tumor may involve an important area of brain function. In this situation, the child may have continued impairment of neurologic function, despite successful treatment and control of the tumor.

Wilms's Tumor

The prognosis for a child with Wilms's tumor depends on its appearance under the microscope (histological appearance). The majority of children with Wilms's tumor have favorable histologic appearance. For a child with favorable histologic appearance and localized disease the outlook is excellent, with a greater than 90 percent cure rate. However, for a child with an unfavorable histologic appearance the outlook is not as good, because of an increased tendency for this tumor to spread to the lungs, bone, and brain.

Rhabdomyosarcoma

The prognosis is excellent for children with localized disease and much more guarded for those in more advanced stages. With modern treatment, children with rhabdomyosarcoma can often be spared an amputation or other surgical procedure that would create a major deformity. For example, certain cases of rhabdomyosarcoma of a limb can be treated by surgical removal of the tumor along with radiation therapy and chemotherapy. As a result of this treatment, a functional limb can be preserved.

Bone Tumors

When Ewing's sarcoma is localized to an area of bone on the extremities, the prognosis is excellent; more than 60 percent of the children so affected have a favorable response to treatment. The outlook is slightly less favorable for those with Ewing's sarcoma of the pelvic bones.

The prognosis for children with osteogenic sarcoma depends on whether the tumor has spread to the lungs, the size of the tumor, and the age of the patient. In general, older adolescents tend to have a slightly better chance for survival than preadolescents who have osteogenic sarcoma.

EDUCATIONAL IMPLICATIONS

The diagnosis of cancer in a child evokes a multitude of feelings. For the teacher, these can include shock, disbelief, rage, and fear. These feelings are further compounded by the fears and anxiety of the child's family and the reactions of other children and their parents. Anger and a sense of loss is a normal reaction to the discovery that a child is experiencing a serious illness. It is a challenge for the teacher to learn to accept serious illness in a child who was previously healthy and able to pursue all kinds of school activities. There are a number of areas relative to loss with which the teacher must learn to cope:

1. Frequent absences due to both complications of the illness and the need for prolonged treatment;
2. A slowing down in the usual learning and growth patterns in the child;
3. Possible failure of normal academic advancement;
4. Changes in physical appearance;
5. Physical deterioration and decreased participation in extracurricular activities; and
6. Disability and the possibility of death.

In order for a child with cancer to have the opportunity to achieve and maintain a normal life, it is essential that the teacher be part of the team working with the child. As a first step, teachers may begin by exploring their own feelings as they find themselves in this difficult situation. These feelings and concerns can be shared with physicians, nurses, or social workers who are involved in treating the child.

Specific information that may be of value to the teacher in planning the child's return to school includes (a) the type of cancer and how long the child will be treated; (b) the type of treatment the child is receiving, when it is administered, and what the possible side effects of treatment are on behavior and appearance; (c) an idea of the schedule for treatments and tests that may require the student's absence from school; (d) an outline of any specific limitations on the student's activities, and (e) an idea of the child's understanding of the illness and what the parents would like the classmates to know.

A good understanding and communication with the child's family is crucial at this time. It is important for the teacher to have the parents' permission both to speak with the child and to share information with others in the school. This might be the time to get to know the family with respect to its constellation, how many members are included, and the mode of communication used within this family. Just how are feelings handled? What seem to be the predominant values, lifestyle, and philosophy of life for this particular family? How do they define quality and what is important for them at this time for their child? What are the external support systems and how does the teacher view the family member relationships? Recognize that parents are probably very eager to talk about their child at this time, but are still experiencing many feelings. Perhaps the greatest difficulty that parents may have is in dealing with the ambiguities of their child's prognosis. In order to eliminate a feeling of isolation, which is a problem children with cancer and their families face, it is important to institute early communication and maintain it on a regular basis while the child is absent from school.

Teachers may find it helpful to visit the child in the hospital and, if possible, bring with them each time cards and messages from the class. Notes, articles, paintings, and phone calls, if permissible, are readily accepted by the child. The important thing is to institute and maintain a vital link with the child during the absence from school. This might be the time that the teacher, in a conversation with the ill child, can begin to discern the information that the child would wish to share with classmates. It is important that peers be prepared with information regarding the side effects of treatment (such as hair loss) so that they may be supportive. Ultimately, the teacher wishes to provide an environment where the child will be understood, supported, and respected.

It is essential that the teacher recognize that cancer is merely one aspect of the child's life. For the most part, youngsters with cancer wish to maintain as normal a lifestyle as possible. They should not be overprotected. Rather, they should have the same limits on their behavior as their classmates. Overprotection and special treatment will result in resentment by peers and also can be devastating to the youngster with cancer.

The current attitude in most pediatric oncology centers favors complete honesty. Physicians urge parents to relate as much of the diagnosis as the child can understand (Cotter & Schwartz, 1978). Those children who are fully aware of their diagnosis and can therefore approach the topic openly with adults and other children tend to cope better with treatment. Some parents, however, just cannot bring themselves to deal with the disclosure of the illness. Thus, some children may not understand the truth regarding their illness. There is evidence in the literature indicating that the families and children who suffer most are those who attempt to protect themselves by not dealing with the diagnosis openly. In these instances, the teacher is placed in the unfortunate position of maintaining a pretense. Parents who avoid dealing with the implications of a serious illness commonly withdraw. In denying the facts, they subsequently close off communication with others concerning their feelings.

For some parents, the admission of fear is viewed as incompatible with a belief in a possible cure. They may make statements such as, "We're going to lick this and use positive thinking so we don't talk about anything unless it is positive." In an attempt to protect themselves and the child from the reality of the illness, the child may become isolated and withdrawn. The child may be unable to express his or her own concerns and fears. Too often, fears of the unknown are more alienating and frightening than those that are known. Children are perceptive and can sense when they are being shielded and overprotected. Their own fear may manifest itself in resentment, which may include morose and gloomy behavior. The frustrations of a teacher in these instances require the support of the health care team.

The subsequent support of the child and family requires the united effort of all who are caring for the child. Assuming that the diagnosis is going to be handled openly with the child, the teacher may find the following suggestions helpful:

1. Prepare the students (peers) by generally exploring their feelings about illness. Use these responses to discuss how they themselves might treat a friend who was ill, possibly with cancer.

2. Discuss the type of cancer and its treatment and the way that this disease and treatment may affect the child's behavior and appearance. Changes in appearance could promote teasing that can be a source of great distress for the ill child. Should teasing occur, the teacher might attempt to understand the teasers' motives, rather than reprimand them. This might provide an excellent opportunity for the teacher to uncover some of the unresolved feelings such as fear and anxiety with which the teasers may be attempting to cope. Reassure the students that the cancer is not contagious and that the cause of the cancer remains unknown.

3. This may provide an excellent opportunity for the ill child to educate his peers. The child and his peers may prepare a research report on the specific type of cancer and its treatment. Some students have invited the personnel from their treatment center or even someone from the American Cancer Society to make a presentation on cancer to the class.

A child frequently reacts to the diagnosis of cancer by feeling helpless, powerless, vulnerable, and perhaps fearful. Initially, there may be alternating anxiety, hostility, and withdrawal. For the most part, children want to maintain contact with their friends and want to continue to go to school. However, because the side effects of their treatment may make them seem "different," the teacher may note varied degrees of withdrawal. The child who has been absent for a long while may be reluctant to return to school for fear of not "fitting in." Ultimately, the solution to many of the problems that the child will encounter is communication—communication between parents and the teacher, the child and the teacher, the child and other children, and the teacher with the health care team.

Despite significant improvements that have been made in the treatment of cancer, some children ultimately die. The child's death may be preceded by a series of relapses. The issue becomes one of how to manage the child in the classroom during the terminal phase and how to deal with the other children. For many children, contact with school and peers is their main source of enjoyment at this time. This is a crucial time to help the child derive as much from life as is possible. In other words, the focus is on living fully even as one is dying. The teacher's task is to view the child as a living child rather than a dying child. This is acceptance of the terminal phase of life.

Children in this phase generally know they are dying and frequently have conversations with a confidant about their feelings and concerns. They seem to know intuitively with whom they can share their innermost feelings. In cooperation with the family, the teacher's flexibility at this time is crucial as measures are implemented to accommodate the child with every possible degree of comfort. It may be that the child can only attend school an hour a day. However, this hour may be the most rewarding of the child's day if he is cared for with genuine concern.

Children generally dislike pity and condescending behavior. They are quick to perceive it; thus, it is crucial that the teacher and classmates deal with their own feelings. At this time, the teacher may wish to invite to school a member of the health care team (e.g., a nurse or social worker) in order to discuss the feelings and concerns that the teacher and classmates are experiencing. Honest, straightforward discussion at this time offers the greatest support.

When the child dies, the teacher should be prepared to handle a myriad of feelings. The following suggestions may be helpful:

1. Examine your own feelings and fears. Recognize the need to grieve. A crucial source of support is the health care team who are also experiencing similar feelings.
2. Create an environment where classmates may share their feelings. Recognize that the expression of grief is unique and that the children's reactions will vary. It is not unusual to see classmates respond with indifference or aloofness. The feeling of loss may be too frightening for some of these youngsters. Respect each child's individual pace of dealing with loss. By sharing feelings openly with the students, the teacher gives them permission to express their own feelings. Students, however, should not be manipulated to accept certain feelings as better than others.
3. The ability to concentrate and follow through with schoolwork may diminish temporarily. The teacher needs to be particularly sensitive to the impact of death on each student. It is possible that feelings associated with a previous loss in a student's life are activated. Thus, the teacher is placed in a unique position of observing each student's behavior on a daily basis. If a student demonstrates a behavior change beyond a period of several weeks, the teacher may wish to speak with the student's parents.
4. It may be appropriate to read and discuss issues pertaining to death. The school librarian may be a valuable resource in helping the teacher to select appropriate reading material.
4. Attending the memorial service or funeral as a group may be a way of assisting the classmates in dealing with the finality of death. The teacher may extend the invitation to all in such a way that each student will feel able to choose or not choose to attend without fear of being judged. This, again, is a sensitive and delicate subject for the teacher.
6. Visit the parents a few weeks after child's death. The adults in the child's life comprise a significant network for the parents and siblings. In dealing with their grief, it is not uncommon for them to wish to speak of the child and look at pictures and other mementos.

SUMMARY

Cancer describes a wide variety of malignant diseases, each of which has different characteristics, treatment, and prognosis. Childhood cancers are rare, but the presence of cancer has a major impact on the affected child and family. The etiology of most childhood cancers remains unknown. Leukemia, lymphoma, central nervous system tumors, Wilms's tumor, rhabdomyosarcoma, and bone tumors are the most common types of cancer that affect the school-age child. In recent years, the prognosis for children with cancer has improved. This improved prognosis has been the result of a multidisciplinary approach to the child and improved diagnostic techniques as well as improved therapeutic techniques.

The issues confronting the teacher and other school personnel associated with the child who has cancer are indeed varied and challenging. Some forms of cancer in children require prolonged treatment over several years. The focus should remain on the individual needs of the child. The maintenance of school attendance, with its daily opportunities for peer contact and stimulating activities, constitutes the basis for a child's feeling of "normalcy". Every effort should be made to facilitate the child's participation at school. Flexibility on the part of the school personnel is crucial.

The teacher is a vital member of the "team" that includes the family and health care providers. They orchestrate their efforts to help the child maintain a high quality of life. Communication is the key to implementing a "normal" life.

Anyone who has ever had contact with a child who has cancer can attest to the fact that these youngsters have much to offer other people. Oftentimes, there is a sense of living with strength and fortitude that they seem to cultivate in their lives. In sharing the journey with them as they endure and cope with a life-threatening illness, they become our "teachers" in learning how to live with value and meaning.

REFERENCES

Cotter, J. M., & Schwartz, A. D. Psychological and social support of the patient and family. In A. J. Altman & A. D. Schwartz (Eds.), *Malignant diseases of infancy, childhood and adolescence.* Philadelphia: W. B. Saunders, 1978.

Sutow, W. W. General aspects of childhood cancer. In W. W. Sutow, T. J. Vietti, & D. J. Fernback (Eds.), *Clinical pediatric oncology* (2nd ed.). St. Louis: C. V. Mosby, 1977.

Robert J. Winter, M.D., *is associate professor in the Department of Pediatrics at the Northwestern University Medical School, Chicago, Illinois, and is associate in the division of endocrinology at the Children's Memorial Hospital, Chicago.*

Diabetes mellitus is a common, multisystem metabolic disease. It is often thought of as a silent or invisible disease because those who have diabetes show no obvious sign of the disease. Diabetes is classified into two forms depending on whether or not injections of insulin are essential to the preservation of life. The diabetes that commonly exists in children is of the insulin dependent variety; hence, insulin injections are required on a daily basis. In fact, insulin dependent diabetes is sometimes referred to as juvenile onset diabetes. Diabetes requires constant attention for proper management, an alertness that must continue 24 hours a day, seven days a week. An underlying theme of this chapter is the unique responsibility that this disease places upon a child in terms

Childhood Diabetes Mellitus

CHAPTER 18

of self-management, understanding, and psychological adaptation.

Insulin dependent diabetes affects 1 out of 600 school-aged children. For this reason, most educators are likely to confront the disease at one time or another. In 1976, a national commission under the auspices of Congress estimated that ten million Americans had some form of diabetes. Each year approximately five to eight billion dollars is spent in this country for the care of diabetics and their related problems. Clearly, it is a disease of striking magnitude.

The goal of therapy for the diabetic child is to make possible normal growth, development, school performance, and a sound sense of psychological well-being. These goals are attainable, but require considerable effort on the part of all involved. A less easily obtained goal, but certainly of equal importance, is to prevent the long-term complications of this disease, which will be discussed later.

Diabetes mellitus is a disease known from antiquity. The term, derived from the Greek, means excessive volumes of sweet urine. The insulin dependent form, common to children, invariably resulted in death during childhood prior to the discovery of insulin in 1921. This discovery by Banting and Best soon enabled afflicted individuals to survive, although their lifestyle had to accommodate multiple daily insulin injections. In more recent decades insulin preparations have been modified to permit a more normal lifestyle, but no way has been found to normalize the metabolic abnormality. As present and future research focuses on the development of more physiologic modes of therapy, the long-term prognosis for the diabetic should greatly improve. To date, no cure for diabetes has been developed.

ETIOLOGY

Important to the understanding of diabetes is its classification. In the past, little distinction was drawn between diabetics of any age or type. Diabetes was classified as juvenile onset or maturity onset, terms which were not sufficiently specific to describe either the age at onset or the presence of insulin dependency. These terms have since been replaced by insulin dependent diabetes (Type I) and noninsulin dependent diabetes (Type II). Although the vast majority of children with diabetes have Type I, these newer terms help avoid the confusion that often arose in the past.

The new terminology is based on the presence or absence of insulin dependency, which implies an insulin deficiency. Insulin is a hormone produced by the B cells of the Islets of Langerhans in the endocrine pancreas. The pancreas, which consists of both exocrine (digestive **enzymes**) and endocrine (hormone) cells, lies adjacent to the stomach and the spleen in the abdomen (Figure 18–1). Insulin is the primary hormone in the metabolism of food energy. The food we eat is converted, in large part, to glucose (sugar) through digestive and enzymatic processes. Indeed it is glucose, and only glucose, that serves as the energy source for most of the cells of the body. The glucose derived from consumed food circulates in the bloodstream, but it requires insulin to transport it across the cellular membrane, where it serves as fuel for cellular function. For example, muscular function cannot proceed unless glucose is present inside the cell. Glucose cannot be transported into each cell without insulin.

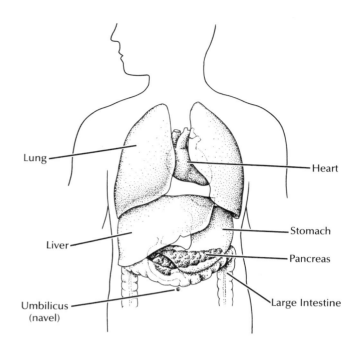

Figure 18–1   A Teaching Aid to Instruct Families of Diabetics. This aid illustrates the basic anatomical relationships of the pancreas.

Insulin's primary function is to make glucose available for use by the cells. As human beings do not eat continuously, insulin must be responsive to the needs of the body whether fed or fasting. After a meal, insulin is actively secreted by the pancreas to release the glucose from the food consumed. The utilization involves not only glucose transport for immediate energy needs, but storage of glucose in the liver and in the fat stores of the body for future needs. During the fasting state, such as overnight, very small quantities of insulin circulate through the body, but these quantities are tightly regulated to maintain a normal blood glucose level. At these low levels, insulin regulates the production of glucose from storage depots (the liver, fat, and muscle), a process called gluconeogenesis. The responsiveness of the pancreatic B cells to variations in blood glucose is extremely precise. As a result, the blood sugar remains in a reasonably narrow range. In normal young individuals, the postprandial (following a meal) blood sugar seldom exceeds 150 mg/dl (dl is a deciliter, one-tenth of a liter), and during fasting it is seldom lower than 60 mg/dl. During a normal routine of eating and sleeping, the average blood sugar over a 24-hour period in normal individuals is approximately 100 mg/dl.

This chapter will limit itself to insulin dependent diabetes as it commonly occurs in children. Diabetes is a condition of insulin deficiency; the B cells of the pancreatic islets no longer retain the ability to synthesize and secrete insulin. One is then left with an inability to transport glucose into the cells and, clearly, the cells cannot function without a source of energy. It is similar to an automobile with a broken fuel line; the gas tank is full, but the car cannot run. In contrast to the automobile, however, the human being has numerous compensatory mechanisms triggered as diabetes develops. As the ability of the pancreas to make insulin decreases, the blood glucose level rises. This stimulates the pancreas to increase insulin output, but it cannot respond. As the blood sugar rises, the body invokes its first protective mechanism via the kidney. The kidney responds to a level of blood sugar above its preset maximum and it releases glucose into the urine, which lowers the blood sugar level. In most people, the renal (kidney) threshold for glucose is approximately 175 mg/dl; as the blood sugar level goes above 175 mg/dl, glucose appears in the urine. The amount of glucose in the urine is proportional to the degree of blood sugar elevation. As the blood sugar gets higher (and it can get to 1000 mg/dl or higher), the kidney attempts to eliminate glucose quickly. To do this, the kidney must also remove water, otherwise, the urine would become quite thick, like maple syrup. This process is known as osmotic diuresis, in which an excessive amount of water is leached from the body to facilitate the excretion of some other substance, in this case glucose.

Loss of water from the body causes dehydration. This first becomes noticed as an excessive thirst, a normal reaction to dehydration. Two of the earliest symptoms of diabetes are polyuria (excessive urination) and polydipsia (excessive drinking). The third common early symptom of diabetes is polyphagia, or excessive eating. Polyphagia is also a direct consequence of insulin deficiency. On one hand, a tremendous number of calories (as glucose) are lost in the urine. A ten-year-old child might normally require 2,000 calories a day, but in an untreated diabetic child, perhaps 1,500 of these calories will be lost in the urine as **glucosuria.** Only 500 calories are now available in the blood. On the other hand, as glucose cannot be transported across the cell membrane, the cells are depleted of glucose and are literally starving. This stimulates the individual to eat more, in an attempt to compensate.

We are left at this point with an individual who is urinating excessively, and eating and drinking a great deal. Furthermore, this individual does not feel at all well, looks gaunt and haggard (due to loss of body mass from inadequate calorie utilization and water loss from dehydration), and may be irritable or behaving strangely (Table 18–1). But there is one additional problem that ultimately forces the undiagnosed diabetic to seek medical care. This relates to insulin deficiency as well, but to insulin's "other" function. In the fasting state, low concentrations of insulin in the

Table 18–1 Symptoms of Undiagnosed or Uncontrolled Diabetes

Usually Present
Polyuria   (Excessive Urination)
Polydipsia   (Excessive Thirst)
Polyphagia   (Excessive Hunger)

Sometimes Present
Weight Loss
Irritability
Fatigue
Infections, particularly skin
Diminished physical performance
Diminished school performance
Blurred vision

Late Sequelae
Deep, Rapid Breathing
"Fruity" Breath
Lethargy
Vomiting, Abdominal Pain
Unconsciousness
Shock
Death

bloodstream regulate the release of stored glucose from the body (gluconeogenesis) to prevent the blood sugar from falling to dangerously low levels. In untreated diabetes, there is virtually no insulin left. Therefore, the regulation of gluconeogenesis is defective. As a result, the body is fooled into thinking that there is not enough sugar around—and there really isn't *inside* the cell. Therefore, gluconeogenesis continues unrestrained and tremendous quantities of glucose are produced. On top of the already high blood sugar levels from failure of glucose transport, tremendous additional quantities of glucose are released into the blood by the liver, through the breakdown of muscle and fat. By-products of gluconeogenesis are ketones, which are quite acidic. With tremendous quantities of ketones being produced (ketosis) and with little or no ability to eliminate them, the acid-base (pH) status of the individual is altered. The process is called ketoacidosis and, combined with the **hyperglycemia** (high blood sugar) and dehydration, it creates a life-threatening medical emergency. This process is diagrammed in Figure 18–2.

It is evident that the early warning signs of impending diabetes (polyuria, polydipsia, and polyphagia) are important. If diabetes is suspected on the basis of these warning signs and symptoms, and the diagnosis confirmed prior to deterioration into ketoacidosis, a potentially disastrous medical emergency can be avoided. Therefore, it is important to

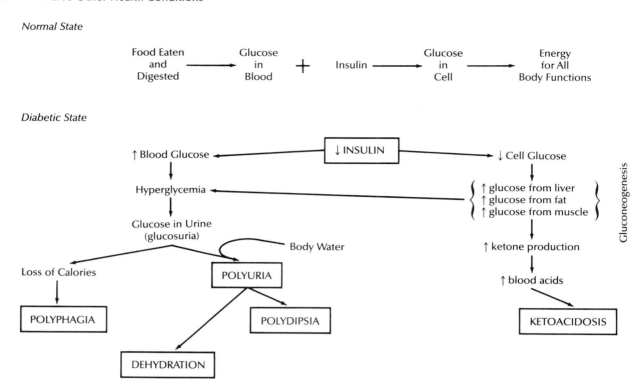

Figure 18–2   Pathophysiology of Insulin Dependent Diabetes

recognize early warning symptoms, when pupils require frequent trips to the lavatory and the water fountain.

What causes insulin deficiency? Although the precise etiology of diabetes is not yet clear, there is no doubt that it is an inherited disease. The precise mode of inheritance is not certain as yet, but the genetic trait probably must come from both sides of the family. One must have a genetic predisposition to develop diabetes, but not all individuals with such a predisposition manifest the clinical disease. Current evidence suggests that, in most people, the expression of the genetic predisposition is a result of two factors. On one hand, a rather nonspecific viral infection probably includes a mild infection of the pancreatic islets, an infection which does not destroy the islets outright but alters their structure somewhat. In response to this disruption of the pancreatic B cells, the genetically predisposed individual initiates an autoimmune response. The immune system of the body, normally present to protect the body from infection, foreign substances, etc., turns against itself. This is similar to what occurs when foreign tissue is rejected as in kidney and heart transplants. In an autoimmune process, the body's own tissue is literally rejected. In the case of diabetes, the pancreatic B cells are the target of this rejection. The end result is a total destruction of the insulin producing cells in the pancreas, thus causing insulin deficiency.

This hypothesis, for which there is a growing body of data, is diagrammed in Figure 18–3. One begins with the genetic predisposition, then the combination of infectious and autoimmune events precipitates the demise of the B cells. Presumably those individuals with a predisposition for diabetes, but without the clinical disease, have not been exposed

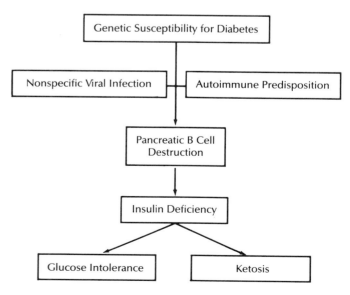

Figure 18–3   Presumed Etiology of Insulin Dependent (Type I) Diabetes

to an infectious or autoimmune stimulus sufficient to result in B cell destruction. The presumed necessity for these events to occur may explain the extremely variable age at onset of diabetes.

CHARACTERISTICS

The characteristics of insulin dependent diabetes at its onset have been covered, in large part, in the previous paragraphs. In addition to the classical symptoms, most children experience fatigue, **malaise**, poor school performance, weight loss, frequent infections particularly of the skin, and behavior changes (Table 18–1). The most common age of onset is during puberty, but the disease can begin early in infancy or not until adulthood. Most children are not overweight at the time of diagnosis. The symptoms may be recognized rather quickly (in several weeks) or may proceed for months before the diagnosis is confirmed. If the diagnosis is delayed and ketoacidosis ensues, deterioration is rather rapid and can proceed to frank **coma** and death. Diagnosis of diabetes is based on laboratory tests: urinary glucose, urinary ketones, and elevated blood sugar. Despite the fact that it is a common disease, early symptoms are similar to those seen in other illnesses. Frequently diabetes is not suspected initially, and can be missed for some time by both layman and professional alike.

Diabetes is really an invisible disease, most of the time. In the absence of complications, the diabetic youngster can and should maintain a lifestyle that will be nearly indistinguishable from that of his peers. There are exceptions to this: instances of insulin reactions, poorly controlled diabetes leading to ketoacidosis, and occasionally the psychosocial interactions between the diabetic and his family and friends. These will all be discussed later.

DIAGNOSIS

The diagnosis of symptomatic diabetes is confirmed by laboratory testing of blood and urine. Asymptomatic diabetes is extremely uncommon, but when suspected, can be proven or disproven by a glucose tolerance test. The suspected diabetic drinks a high glucose preparation while in a fasting state, followed by frequent monitoring of the blood and urine glucose levels. The test usually takes three–five hours.

Rarely, a type II (noninsulin dependent diabetes) diabetic pattern is found in childhood. These children may be overweight and tend to have a stronger family history of this form of diabetes. The children may not require insulin but be able to control the disease by diet and oral medication, especially if weight loss can

be achieved. Glucose tolerance testing is necessary in those relatively rare instances as well.

TREATMENT

Treatment of insulin dependent diabetes in childhood requires the coordinated effort of a health care team. At the very minimum, this includes a physician skilled in the care of diabetes, the child, and the family. Optimally, the health care team would also include a nurse or nurse educator, a social worker, a psychologist, a dietician/nutritionist, and school personnel including the teacher and school nurse. The involvement of each of these team members depends, in large part, on the needs of the individual. Nevertheless, the availability of such personnel and their familiarity with the individual's particular needs ensures that the diabetes can be managed as well and as inconspicuously as possible.

Treatment of insulin dependent diabetes involves several concerns: the use of insulin, diet, exercise, education, behavioral/psychological problems, and cost.

Insulin

The insulin deficient individual is dependent upon insulin injections for survival. Traditionally these have been administered once daily, in the morning, and usually consist of two types of insulin with different courses of action. The goal of this regimen is to "cover the day" with insulin that, to one degree or another, maintains reasonable blood levels of insulin during the portions of the day in which food is consumed. Some time between the ages of eight and twelve, children are generally taught to administer their own insulin injections (Figure 18–4). Initially, there is an almost universal reluctance to give and receive injections, both by the child and his parents. Nevertheless, with time, the injections are extremely well tolerated and become one of the least onerous tasks the diabetic is expected to do (Rifkin & Raskin, 1981).

The success of insulin therapy has been measured in numerous ways. On the home front, most insulin dependent diabetics monitor their urinary glucose four times each day (before each meal and at bedtime). The urine is tested for glucose, and simultaneously for ketones, by a variety of methods. A "second void (urination) technique" is used to get freshly made urine by voiding a second time, thirty minutes after the first void. The second voided urine most closely approximates the current blood sugar level. Daily urine testing can be bothersome, and compliance with it frequently is less than optimal (Fig-

Figure 18—4   Child With Diabetes Learning to Administer Her Own Insulin

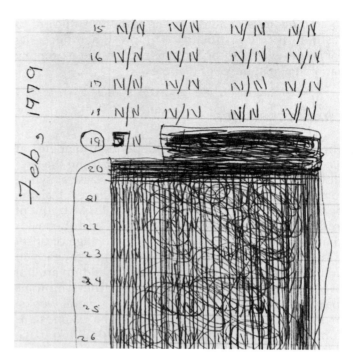

Figure 18—5   Urine Test Record. This urine test record was brought by a diabetic teenager to his clinic appointment. Not only is the record neatly filled in, suggesting that it was completed at one sitting rather than at the time of each test, but the record was initially completed to the end of the month, well beyond the day of his appointment (even to the 31st of February). Note that he attempted to "correct" this by scratching out those "prospective" testing results. This is an unusually obvious example of poor compliance.

ure 18–5). In general, the urine test should be sugar free as much as possible.

As the long-term complications of diabetes are found to be a direct result of the metabolic abnormality—the hyperglycemia itself—more aggressive attempts are being made to normalize blood sugar. To obtain sugar free urine simply implies that the blood glucose level is below the renal threshold, approximately 175 mg/dl. This may result in an average blood glucose over the 24-hour period of 175–225 mg/dl, considerably higher than the 100 mg/dl average for nondiabetic individuals. This comparison is graphically illustrated in Figure 18–6, where the unphysiologic pattern of blood insulin achieved with one daily injection of insulin is apparent. The difference between conventional diabetic therapy and normal metabolism may well contribute to the long-term complications, which will be discussed later. In response to these realities, and to the limitations of urine glucose testing, there have been recent attempts at home blood glucose monitoring. The diabetic tests his or her blood with a glucose sensitive testing stick, after pricking a finger to get the blood specimen. Relatively painless methods for finger pricking have been developed, and this methodology is gaining enthusiasm. If not used on a daily basis,

home glucose monitoring still may be extremely useful when there are problems with the diabetes, or for questions concerning control. As attempts are being made to tighten glucose control, insulin delivery methods are also changing. Instead of once-daily insulin injections, some individuals now are taking insulin several times per day, in an attempt to duplicate the physiological delivery of insulin of a normal person. Newer devices for insulin delivery that will be even more physiologic are being developed.

Diet

In a nondiabetic individual, insulin secretion is perfectly matched to dietary intake, as shown in Figure 18–6. As a result, the difference between a small snack and a large meal is not in the blood sugar obtained, but rather in the amount of insulin secreted to maintain normal blood glucose. In the diabetic individual, on normal insulin regimens, the amount of insulin should not change from one day to the next. As a result, the food consumed must be matched with the

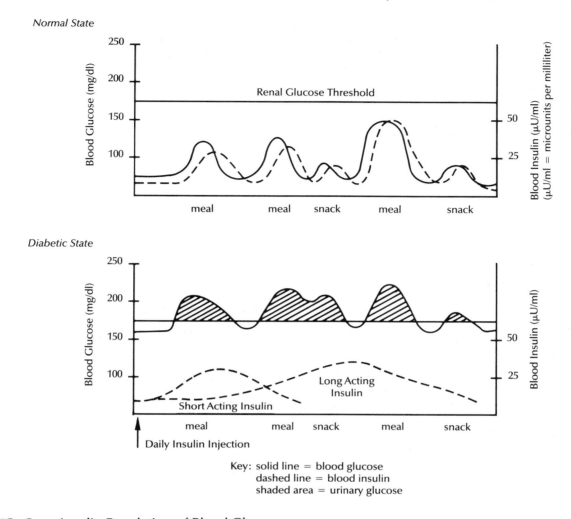

Normal State

Diabetic State

Key: solid line = blood glucose
dashed line = blood insulin
shaded area = urinary glucose

Figure 18–6   Insulin Regulation of Blood Glucose

insulin prescribed. When too much food is eaten blood glucose level elevates further. A diet that is consistent from day to day and reasonably well matched to the insulin delivery, is essential to the management of diabetes.

Dietary aspects of diabetes are, for most insulin dependent children, the most annoying part of the disease. Even the word diet implies some restriction or voluntary sacrifice, although generally this really isn't true. Because of the limitation in insulin delivery systems, the food consumed needs to follow certain guidelines.

1. The diet must be similar in composition from day to day, both as to the types of food consumed and their caloric content.
2. Concentrated carbohydrates, such as sweetened soft drinks, candy, etc., should be avoided, as they are readily absorbed and sufficient insulin is not available to metabolize them adequately.
3. A diabetic diet is nothing more than a good nutritious diet. It can be incorporated into the lifestyle

of the entire family so that the diabetic youngster does not feel segregated from the family during meals.

Despite the necessity for good dietary compliance, most children recognize quite readily that "going off their diet" will not result in disaster. Through trial and error they learn the boundaries of indiscretion, and seem, in the short term, to suffer no ill side effects. Because they feel well, there is little incentive to maintain strict dietary compliance, particularly for the teenager. When urine testing becomes simply a reminder that they are not sticking to their diet, that task becomes haphazard as well. These issues of compliance are the most difficult task the health care team must face.

Exercise

It is important for all diabetic youngsters, and everyone else, to exercise regularly. What is unique to the diabetic is the necessity to plan the exercise and to keep it reasonably consistent from day to day. Exercise that is excessive and occurs without proper planning can cause a sudden drop in blood sugar and an insulin reaction. The problem is not the exercise but the lack of adequate planning and precautions. The health care team can help the diabetic accommodate whatever athletic activity is desired. There are numerous examples of professional athletes who have diabetes. With appropriate planning, participation in virtually any sport is possible (Bierman & Toohey, 1977).

Education

The diabetic youngster and his family should be thoroughly educated about diabetes. The process takes a long time and cannot be accomplished successfully at the time of initial diagnosis. Indeed, the emotional response of the family may preclude education at that time. Therefore, the health care team must continue to reeducate the family throughout the duration of their contact. With this education, the day-to-day problems that emerge can be more successfully managed at home, independent of the health care team. Numerous books and articles are available and organizations such as the American Diabetes Association (ADA) conduct extensive patient education programs. In addition, the ADA publishes a magazine for diabetics called *Forecast,* which has become a superb instrument for ongoing education (Travis, 1978).

Behavioral/Psychological Problems

Diabetes places extraordinary demands on the growing child. In essence, one asks such a child to accept the reality of a lifelong, chronic illness, an acceptance that many adults cannot well achieve. Most of us, at one time or another, have had to acknowledge our limitations and disabilities. For a child to accept the reality of the disease without a distorted self-perception or sense of worth can be tenuous at best. In addition, the child must manage the mundane aspects of diabetes: urine testing, dietary compliance, etc. Furthermore, this is combined with the recognition that despite what one might do to control diabetes, one might become blind or die of renal failure as a young adult. Thus, the potential for psychological problems is great. It is imperative that the health care team, including school personnel, recognize this, and that appropriate referral for counseling be made when necessary.

Cost Considerations

Diabetes can be a very expensive disease to treat. The cost of medication, testing materials, doctor's bills, and hospitalization can become enormous. Insurance through private carriers can be difficult and expensive unless group insurance programs are available. In families with tight budgets, the percentage of the family budget needed for the diabetes can cause further polarization of the diabetic in the family.

PROGNOSIS

There is a twofold prognosis for the youngster with diabetes. In the short term, with reasonable control of the metabolic state, the diabetic can lead a very normal, active life. The threat of long-term complications such as blindness, kidney failure, and premature heart attacks, remains a cloud on the horizon (Rifkin & Raskin, 1981).

Short-Term Problems

The acute problems of diabetes reflect the difficulties in balancing insulin, food intake, and exercise. This can result in either hyperglycemia (high blood sugar) or hypoglycemia (low blood sugar). The most common problem is hypoglycemia, or an insulin reaction, in which the blood sugar falls to an inappropriately low level. In a nondiabetic, the glucose level seldom if ever falls below 60 mg/dl because the counterregulatory mechanisms of the body are designed to maintain normal blood glucose levels. These mechanisms are distorted in the insulin dependent individual making it possible for the blood sugar to fall to a much lower level. As this occurs, the individual exhibits certain symptoms and requires prompt therapy to raise the blood sugar. Symptoms of an insulin reaction include hunger, sweatiness, rapid heart rate, facial pallor, weakness, a feeling of anxiety, drowsiness, and if not treated, hypoglycemic coma (Table 18–2). On occasion, younger children can actually have seizures or convulsions. Irritability, behavior changes, or poor mental function can also occur. Insulin reactions occur most commonly before meals or during or after active exercise. Treatment is simple, giving the diabetic a readily available carbohydrate: five–ten sugar cubes, a 6–12 ounce glass of orange juice or sweetened soft drink, or a candy bar. Symptoms usually subside in 15–20 minutes, when the blood sugar level rises to normal. If the child is unable to swallow, nothing should be given by mouth and medical attention is needed at once. Diabetics should carry some form of sugar with them at all times in order to treat these problems promptly; hard candy is a popular method.

Many diabetics have occasional insulin reactions. This reflects, on one hand, the fact that they are maintaining reasonably normal blood sugar levels much of

Table 18–2   Characteristics of an Insulin Reaction

Symptoms: (vary from person to person)

Hunger	Weakness
Anxiety	Shakiness
Nervousness	Tremulousness
Perspiration	Headache
(cool, clammy,	Decreased
pale skin)	Mental
Rapid Heart Rate	Acuity
Nausea, Vomiting	Drowsiness
Irritability	Confusion
Mood Changes	Convulsions
	Coma (hypo-glycemic)

Associated Conditions: Most common before meals, during or after exercise

Most children can and should learn their own warning signs and treat them appropriately

All children should have some form of sugar immediately available at all times

Causes: insulin   food

Imbalance of ▽ results in an insulin reaction

exercise

Examples:
  Unusually strenuous exercise
  Delayed meal
  Need for insulin dose adjustment

Treatment: Oral sugar if child can swallow—prompt medical attention otherwise

the time. On the other hand, it reflects their active interaction with their environment; they are not letting their diabetes dictate every thought and action. As long as the reactions are infrequent, preceded by adequate warning symptoms, not severe, and do not involve seizures, they should be tolerated as well as possible.

The other metabolic complication that can occur is extreme hyperglycemia leading to ketoacidosis. It usually occurs insidiously, in contrast to the rapid development of symptoms in an insulin reaction. The treated diabetic is especially prone to hyperglycemia during a serious infection or period of stress, emotional or otherwise. It can result from a lax compliance to diet or monitoring, and certainly when insulin

is omitted. It is essential that the insulin dose be taken every day. When there are extenuating circumstances, such as illness or vomiting, a member of the health care team should be consulted immediately. The symptoms of hyperglycemia are identical to those outlined in Table 18–1. With adequate attention to the details of management and the availability of a responsive health care team, the incidence of ketoacidosis in treated diabetics should be quite low.

Overall growth and development should proceed normally in well-controlled diabetic youngsters. School performance, height and weight gain, and sexual maturation should not be grossly different from that of nondiabetic youngsters.

The stress of a chronic illness on the child and his family increases the potential for psychological problems in these children. A strong family structure, which is able to keep in perspective that this problem can be lived with successfully, decreases the potential for serious psychological problems. Unfortunately, an ideal family perspective is not always possible. The perspective of the family and the health care team must be very realistic. One must recognize the practical limitations of living with diabetes, and not place unusual or unattainable expectations on the child. It is unrealistic to demand that a teenager test his urine four times daily and never indulge in the food-related activities of his peers. It is preferable to tell the teenager that you understand that the urine tests will not always be done and that occasional dietary indiscretions will occur. The diabetic who feels that these transgressions can be discussed and acknowledged, rather than secretively hidden away, adapts much better psychosocially. Nevertheless, it is essential that behavioral scientists be part of the health care team, and that they are periodically involved in the care of the diabetic youngster.

Long-Term Problems

The long-term problems facing a diabetic have been previously mentioned in this chapter. The hyperglycemia of diabetes results in or contributes to long-term vascular complications affecting both the large and small blood vessels. This is probably a result of structural changes in the blood vessels caused by many years of abnormally high blood sugar levels. In the case of the microvascular (small vessel) disease, the blood vessels of the eye, the kidney, and the peripheral nerves seem to be most severely affected. This can result in blindness, kidney failure, and peripheral neuropathy. Peripheral neuropathy can result in gangrene, requiring amputation. The macrovascular (large vessel) disease affects the coronary arteries in the heart and the large blood vessels such as the aorta. The most severe consequences of this are heart attacks at an early age and peripheral vascular disease also requiring, at times, amputation.

The long-term complications are thought to be a result of long-standing hyperglycemia. After twenty years of diabetes, 75–90 percent of individuals will manifest some form of long-term complication. It may be mild in nature and slowly progressive. On the other hand, it may be severe and result in the complications listed above. Diabetes is the leading cause of new blindness in adults and is the cause of death from renal failure in roughly half of insulin dependent diabetics. The life expectancy of an individual with insulin dependent diabetes is reduced by approximately a third.

The specter of these complications is a significant factor in the psychological adaptation of the diabetic. These long-term complications provide a reasonable incentive for diabetics to maintain tight control of their blood sugar. Nevertheless, to most children, long-term complications are far away and the temptation of leading a normal life is near at hand. The immediate rewards are far greater than the long-term gains from being tightly regimented in one's routine. One can see the potential for conflict between the youngster and those around him, such as his family. Perhaps diabetes in the long term would be more adequately regulated if hyperglycemia were painful. It is not unusual to find insulin dependent diabetics with blood sugar levels in excess of 300 mg/dl. If hyperglycemia caused some noxious response in the body, the incentive for tighter metabolic control, leading hopefully to fewer long-term complications, would be much greater.

In the face of both the short-term requirements for management and the threat of long-term complications, it is not surprising that the diabetic is prone to certain misgivings about the future. This can affect interpersonal relationships revolving around marriage and family, career choice, and general lifestyle. In the past, there has been some job discrimination against diabetics. Although it is not as prevalent today, it can still occur. Diabetics are not, or should not be, excluded from career choices except where disqualified by any chronic medication, such as being a professional airline pilot. Most diabetics have very good work records. Nevertheless, the misperceptions of employers about diabetes and the poor track records of a minority of diabetics, who are lax in their own care, can result in job discrimination (Sims, 1980).

A tremendous amount of research is under way concerning all facets of diabetes, in an attempt to discover ways of preventing the long-term complications. The outlook from this research is a very bright one, particularly regarding the development of a more physiologic delivery of insulin, which will enable complete normalization of blood glucose.

EDUCATIONAL IMPLICATIONS

One of the greatest needs is the education of educators. Diabetes is still a mysterious disease to most school personnel, including most school nurses. As a result, there is a tremendous amount of anxiety and confusion surrounding the diabetic pupil. Fear of insulin reactions stems directly from not understanding what they are, what to do about them, and the basic physiological principles underlying them. Communication is often nonexistent or inadequate between school personnel and members of the health care team. Members of the health care team may be reluctant to take the time to educate school personnel adequately. The turnover in school personnel and the number of people involved are considered stumbling blocks in this regard. Nevertheless, it is often the student who suffers most. The child is sent home immediately when there is any disruption in the routine, be it an insulin reaction, a headache, or a skin rash. The family and health care team are expected to cope with the problem even though it might easily have been solved in school, and another school day is lost. This situation does not lend itself to an easy solution, but a lot of difficulty can be alleviated by adequate communication among the involved parties. In this regard, organizations such as the ADA are becoming more involved in educating school personnel through brochures, pamphlets, and educational programs specifically designed for teachers, educators, and school nurses.

The individual teacher who has a diabetic in the classroom must juggle numerous considerations. The primary goal is an uninterrupted education, achievable in most instances. Generally the metabolic requirements of the disease and the various daily routines expected of a diabetic, can be incorporated into the school program. This can be done without calling conspicuous attention to the disease, which will isolate the child as different. Insulin is generally given in the morning prior to leaving home, and perhaps later in the day after returning home from school. Urine testing is performed at home before breakfast, supper, and at bedtime. The lunchtime urine test is frequently omitted and, therefore, usually not a problem.

The diet should be modified as necessary for the school routine. Most diets consist of three meals, with afternoon and bedtime snacks. The afternoon snack is usually eaten after school, although this can be modified if the school session lasts until late in the day. Some children do require a midmorning snack, and this would require some modification at most schools. In virtually every instance, school lunch programs can be adapted into the child's diet by a nutritionist in the health care team. Occasional problems occur when lunch hours are unusually early or unusually late, and communication with the health care team may be necessary. Similarly, physical education classes held just prior to lunch may trigger insulin reactions and some modification may be necessary here as well. Modification may not involve a total change of class plan, just the addition of a small snack prior to the gym class to ward off any insulin reaction.

The child may miss time from school due to doctors' appointments or hospitalizations, which the teacher should understand. Children whose diabetes is not under good control may be urinating excessively, which can be disruptive to the class. In such instances, the teacher is certainly justified in pursuing this problem with the family and the health care team. Parents can, at times, have unrealistic expectations for school personnel, and the health care team may need to act as an intermediary in this regard. Lastly, there needs to be some education of the pupils in the classroom if the family and the diabetic both agree. Some families and youngsters are very open about the diabetes, others wish it to be a private problem with only close friends, school authorities, etc., in full knowledge of the details.

It is beyond the scope of this chapter to go into the behavioral and psychosocial problems associated with diabetes in any greater detail than has been done already. Under the best of circumstances, a child with diabetes should perform as well as any other youngster. Indeed, some of them are so embued with a sense of responsibility and the self-discipline required by their routine that they become model students. Nevertheless, given difficulties with metabolic control, a family that is not understanding and supportive, and the presence of intermittent or ongoing emotional stress, the ability of the diabetic to do well

can be severely compromised. Counseling does not afford any easy or quick solution, but may be essential to making any progress at all. If the counseling is conducted by school personnel, ongoing communication with the remaining members of the health care team is essential to success. The parents also need to perceive the interplay between the diabetes, school performance, and psychosocial adaptation.

SUMMARY

Diabetes is a lifelong disease that affects virtually every system in the body. It is a livable disease, but it can have serious long-term effects. The success with which it is managed depends on numerous variables, most of which depend on good, free-flowing communication among the individuals involved. It is imperative that the child's teachers feel a part of the health care team in this regard, as their involvement with the child is extensive. At best, the youngster with diabetes can be totally unobtrusive and his metabolic problem can be virtually invisible. At worst, the diabetic child can be inundated by problems that increase with severity, impinge upon the entire classroom, and create considerable difficulty for all involved. The usual circumstance is something in between; each diabetic presents a unique situation that requires individualized management.

REFERENCES

Bierman, J., & Toohey, B. *The diabetics sports and exercise book*. New York: Jove Publications, Inc., 1977.

Rifkin, H., & Raskin, P. (Eds.). *Diabetes mellitus* (Vol. 5). Bowie, Md.: Robert J. Brady Co., 1981.

Sims, D. *Diabetes—Reach for health and freedom*. St. Louis: C. V. Mosby, 1980.

Travis, L. B. *An instructional aid on juvenile diabetes mellitus* (5th ed.). Austin, Texas: South Texas Affiliate, American Diabetes Association, 1978.

John A. Mangos, M.D., *is professor and chairman of the Department of Pediatrics at the University of Texas, Health Science Center, San Antonio, Texas.*

Cystic fibrosis (CF) is one of the most common inherited disorders causing physical disability among children and young adults. It is a common cause of frequent lung problems and the major killer from lung damage in this age group. The disease was first described in 1936 by Dr. G. Fanconi in Switzerland and in 1938 by Dr. Dorothy Anderson, a pathologist, in America. Anderson established the relationship between destruction of the pancreas, the major digestive gland, and the development of chronic lung disease, which eventually caused the death of affected children. She named the disease *cystic fibrosis of the pancreas* because of the damage to the **ducts** of the pancreas, which consists of distention and extensive fibrosis (scarring). In most instances, the normal tissue of the pancreas is replaced by fatty and scar tissue. Anderson's term was a misnomer because

CHAPTER 19

Cystic Fibrosis

many organs other than the pancreas are affected by the disease. In fact, CF disorders to the lungs cause most of the health problems faced by the patient, including death. In Europe, physicians used the term *mucoviscidosis,* which is more descriptive of the abnormalities of body function (pathophysiology) in the disease. The mucus in a patient's body is viscous and this alters the function of many organs. This new name, however, did not catch on and the disease is presently known in America and internationally as cystic fibrosis.

CF is one of those "invisible" disabilities because, until the late changes due to lung damage, the only outward sign of the disease is frequent coughing spells. The Cystic Fibrosis Foundation conducts 128 centers for the specialized care of patients with CF.

The centers are also devoted to teaching and research in the disease. Many of these centers care for a variety of pulmonary and digestive disorders of children and young adults as well.

ETIOLOGY

In spite of the fact that CF has been recognized for almost 45 years, the specific functional abnormalities involved and their development and the basic biochemical defect have never been identified. CF is a hereditary disorder, transmitted by an autosomal recessive mode of inheritance (Figure 19–1). The birth of a child with this condition reveals that parents are heterozygotes (carriers) for the CF gene. An estimated 5 percent of white Americans are carriers, or one out of twenty. This makes the CF gene the most common abnormal gene among whites.

Considering the estimated frequency of the gene and the autosomal recessive nature of CF, the predicted frequency of birth of infants with CF would be 1 out of 1,600 live births (1/20 × 1/20 = 1/400, the statistical chance of a union between CF carriers; when such union occurs, the chances of having a

child with CF are one out of four; thus the expected frequency will be 1/400 × 1/4 = 1/1,600). Indeed, studies of the frequency of CF among whites in the United States have found the frequency to be between 1 in 1,500 and 1 in 2,000 live births. Among the other races, CF is less frequent: 1 in 17,000 live births among blacks, and 1 in 90,000 among Orientals.

One could describe the nature of CF as a generalized exocrinopathy, that is, a disease affecting the structure and function of the exocrine glands of patients. Exocrine glands produce fluids (sweat, saliva, pancreatic juice, respiratory tract mucus, etc.) that reach the outside of the body directly (sweat) or indirectly through a body cavity (saliva, pancreatic juice, respiratory mucus). Examination of these body fluids from patients with CF reveals two basic abnormalities: abnormal **electrolyte** composition and abnormal mucus.

The abnormal electrolyte composition is best exemplified by the increased salinity of the sweat of CF patients. The sweat of a one-year old infant with CF contains ten to twenty times more salt (NaCl) than the sweat of a child without CF. This difference in salt content has been used to develop a definitive diagnostic test for CF—the "sweat test". Other CF exocrine gland products exhibit more subtle changes in their electrolyte composition.

The mucus of CF patients, wherever in the body it is produced, has a cloudy appearance and abnormally viscous and sticky texture. The thick mucus obstructs ducts or other tubular passages of the body, causing tissue damage either from the obstruction alone or in combination with a secondary infection.

Many researchers have attempted to discover the pathophysiology of CF. Since its first description, more than 8,000 clinical and research articles have been published on this disease. Still, the basic defect of CF escapes detection; still, there are no tests to detect the carrier state in the general population; still, CF in the fetus cannot be detected through **amniocentesis** and **amniotic fluid** analysis; still, there is no direct therapy for this disease. This is most discouraging to the approximately 30,000 CF patients and their families in this country.

Why has it not been possible to discover the basic genetic defect of this disease? One of the basic problems with CF research has been the fact that, for many years, very little was known about the normal function of the target organs of CF, the exocrine glands. An entirely new body of information had to be developed in the area of exocrine gland physiology before beginning to understand the nature of CF. This is best exemplified by the search for an explanation for the increased salinity of the sweat in CF (Mangos, 1978). In 1952, di Sant'Agnese discovered that babies with CF had salty sweat. Immediately, the

The Genetics of Cystic Fibrosis

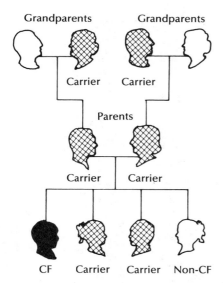

Figure 19–1   The Genetics of Cystic Fibrosis. One in twenty white Americans carry the gene for cystic fibrosis. The "carrier state" may be passed from generation to generation without causing CF. However, when two carriers mate, there is one chance in four in every pregnancy that the child will have CF, and one chance in two that the child will be another carrier.

question was asked: *"Why is the sweat salty?"* Because very little was known about sweat gland physiology, it took 21 years and some of the most difficult research before Mangos (1973) could say, *"Sweat in CF is salty because there is decreased conservation of salt in the duct of the sweat gland."* This led to the question: *"Why is sweat salt conservation decreased in CF?"* The answer has yet to be found. It is hoped that, with better scientific knowledge of the function of exocrine glands, future research efforts will move faster.

CHARACTERISTICS

As a rule, the prenatal period of CF children is uneventful and of normal duration. The disease may manifest itself immediately after birth as an intestinal obstruction, meconium ileus, which requires immediate surgery. About 15 percent of infants with CF have the obstruction, attributed to accumulation of sticky mucous material, the meconium, in the loops of the small bowel.

During the first year of life, untreated patients have (a) large, foul stools, (b) increased appetite but decreased weight gain, and (c) increased size of the abdomen due to **distention** of the intestines. The first signs of lung involvement may appear at any time after birth but, most frequently, they occur before the first birthday. A cough, noisy breathing, and wheezing are the cardinal symptoms. Repeated bouts of pneumonia may occur, particularly during any viral infection of the lungs. As the child progresses and after repeated bouts of pneumonia, the lungs become scarred, the bronchial tree becomes **dilated,** and the chest enlarges.

With advancing lung involvement and lung scarring, the ability decreases to exchange oxygen from air that is breathed in and replace it with carbon dioxide to be breathed out. Eventually, the right side of the heart, which sends blood into the lungs for oxygenation, enlarges and then fails, thus adding abnormal heart function to the already advanced abnormalities in lung function. The combination of abnormalities in the function of the lungs and heart develops a vicious cycle that handicaps the patient and eventually causes death.

At first, the lung infection is due to common pneumonia-causing organisms. After some time, *Staphylococcus aureus*, a drug resistant organism, invades the affected lungs, followed by **Pseudomonas aeruginosa** which, once established in the lungs, cannot be eliminated with present methods of therapy. Periodically, and most often after viral pulmonary infections, the *Pseudomonas aeruginosa* grows in the lungs and slowly destroys the lung tissue. In recent years, antibiotics have been combating this infection

and are used extensively for the therapy of CF patients. Other problems that CF patients have include: **cirrhosis** of the liver, duodenal ulcers, salt depletion from losses in the sweat during hot weather or fevers, diabetes mellitus, depressed growth, chronic sinus infections and nasal **polyps,** male sterility, and difficulties of conception in the female.

Children with CF have normal intelligence. Among 27 children with CF in the author's clinic, the median IQ was 124. Among 27 children without CF who matched these patients in age, sex, and socioeconomic status, the median IQ was 103. Thus, CF does not appear to cause any clinical disorders of the central nervous system. CF patients may have high intelligence test scores because of their increased conversational and communication skills, which evolve and progress very early because of their close and frequent contact with adults as a result of their illness.

The growth of patients with CF is usually slow because of depressed rates of linear growth and de-

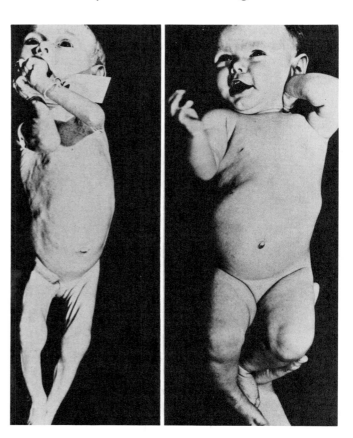

Figure 19—2 Baby With CF Before and After Initiation of Treatment. The first picture was taken at the time of diagnosis when the patient was five months of age. The second picture shows the same patient three months later.

Source: Cystic Fibrosis Foundation, Rockville, Md.

creased maturation of bones. Accordingly, most of these children are short and often appear emaciated (Figure 19–2). The buttocks are small, the extremities are thin, and the abdomen is often enlarged. Their sexual maturation may also be slow. Teenage girls often have late onset of menstruation and menstrual irregularities later in life. Teenage boys are short and often do not show signs of sexual maturation until their late teenage years.

Delays of sexual maturation are often bothersome to CF patients who want to be just like their peers. It was best expressed by a fifteen-year-old girl from the author's clinic who said, "What do you expect? I am a fifteen-year-old girl who has the body of a ten-year-old and can think and react emotionally as a twenty-year-old!" These young patients usually need counseling and emotional support during their teen years. Most of them eventually mature sexually and grow to a relatively normal height. In recent years, realization of the problems of these patients and the establishment of centers for comprehensive care have improved not only their life expectancy but also their psychoemotional outlook.

Pathogenesis

The multiple clinical features of CF can only be the result of a widespread disorder. Judging from other autosomal recessive disorders, one could assume that the basic biochemical defect of CF would be the absence or abnormal composition of a single protein. Because all available evidence suggests that CF is a disorder of the exocrine glands, one could assume that the basic biochemical defect must be involved in an important regulatory process that controls the function of the exocrine glands. Most of the observed pathological changes could be attributed, at least in their early stages, to obstruction of ducts or tubular organs of the body, leading to cell and tissue destruction and causing problems such as infection.

During **intrauterine** life, the viscous pancreatic juice of the fetus affected by CF obstructs the ducts

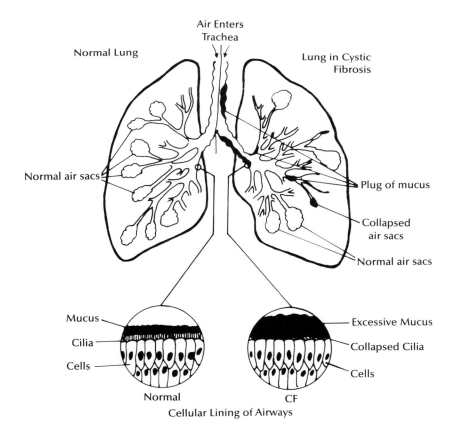

Figure 19–3 Pathological Lung Changes in CF. Plugging of the airways with mucus causes obstruction and collapse of the air sacs, where the exchange of gases (oxygen and carbon dioxide) between inspired air and blood takes place. The obstructed areas of the lungs become chronically infected, and scarring follows the healing of each bout of infection.

Normally, particles and bacteria on the inner surface of the airways are moved outward by the function of cilia, which push a layer of mucus continuously towards the outside of the lungs. In CF, the excess mucus causes the cilia to collapse and the further accumulation of mucus leads to infection.

of the pancreas and causes blockage and eventual death of all the cells that produce the digestive enzymes in this organ. The destroyed tissue is replaced by fibrous tissue (scar). By the time the baby is born, there is no identifiable pancreas in 90 percent of the cases. Precipitation of sticky mucous material in the small intestine may cause meconium ileus, as discussed above. Intestinal obstruction may occur later in life when sticky mucus and fecal material combine into gluey masses that can obstruct the bowel. The liver ducts also can become obstructed from thick bile mucus causing the beginning of liver cirrhosis. Similar changes may occur in the salivary glands, intestinal glands, and genital glands.

In the lungs, the earliest pathologic changes of CF are multiple obstructions of small bronchi by thick respiratory mucus. As shown in Figure 19–3, the lung is comprised of the bronchial tree and the alveolar sacs. The bronchial tree is lined by cells that have on their surface cilia, hairlike structures which beat rhythmically towards the outside world. On top of the cilia sits a layer of mucus produced by the bronchial glands. The mucus moves upward like an escalator belt, continuously propelled by the cilia that beat at the rate of 900–1,100 times per minute under normal circumstances.

Any particles, including microorganisms, that escape the upper airways during breathing eventually stick to the mucous blanket of the mucociliary transport mechanism, and begin the trek towards the upper end of the bronchial tree. From there, the collected mucus, containing particles and microorganisms, is either swallowed and digested in the stomach or expectorated. This protective mechanism probably becomes disrupted in CF and results in an accumulation of mucus along with the particles and microorganisms. These microorganisms are most likely responsible for the recurrent pneumonias of CF.

With every bout of lung infection it appears that the mucous glands are stimulated to secrete more of the abnormal mucus, resulting in more obstruction of the airways. The cycle of obstruction-infection-more obstruction-more infection is what eventually destroys the lungs of CF patients. Therapy aimed at interrupting this cycle, as described below, has improved the prognosis of patients with CF.

DIAGNOSIS

Once a physician suspects that a child may have CF, the diagnosis can be made on the basis of the past history, present physical condition, family history, and the "sweat test."

Past History

Prior to the examination, if the child has had clinical features of CF, such as meconium ileus, malabsorption of food due to pancreatic insufficiency, chronic cough and expectoration, **clubbing** of the fingers and toes, and delayed physical growth, this is presumptive evidence for CF.

Present Physical Condition

The evidence for presumptive diagnosis of CF is strengthened if the child has the physical signs described earlier in this chapter: enlarged abdomen, increased chest size, malnutrition, excess fat in the stools, absence of pancreatic enzymes, positive findings of lung infection, and changes seen on chest X rays.

Family History

If another sibling has had CF, the case for this diagnosis becomes even more convincing.

"Sweat Test"

If two of the above three criteria are positive or strongly suggestive, the physician is obliged to confirm the suspected diagnosis of CF with a "sweat test." This test is one of the most accurate tests in medicine if done appropriately by experienced personnel. It involves the stimulation of the sweat glands of a 5×5 cm area of the skin (usually the forearm) to secrete sweat (Figure 19–4). It is done by introducing a stimulatory drug into the skin by passing a light, painless, and harmless current through two skin electrodes.

Figure 19–4   The "Sweat Test". The "sweat test" is an easy, painless test that can reveal CF with almost total accuracy.

The area is cleansed and covered with a gauze and vapor barrier. Sweat is collected for 30 minutes and is then weighed and analyzed for salt content. If the salt content is over 60 milliequivalents per liter (mEq/L), this confirms the diagnosis of CF. Values of less than 50 mEq/L are negative for CF. Values between 50–60 mEq/L are questionable and the test is usually repeated.

The presence of two of the above criteria and a positive sweat test confirms the diagnosis of CF with almost total accuracy. There is actually no substitute for the sweat test, which is admittedly time-consuming. Many shortcuts for this test have been proposed, but none have the accuracy and acceptability of the standard test. There are about six other conditions that could give high salt content of the sweat, but they are so easily diagnosed and so different that confusion is improbable.

TREATMENT

According to those who care for CF patients, the prognosis depends on the treatment. To prevent frequent, incapacitating lung infections, the CF patient requires continuing, comprehensive and, most importantly, optimistic management of the disease. The greatest success in reducing the frequency of illness and early death of CF patients has occurred in those care centers that provide intensive management. The treatment of CF can be divided into three general areas: treatment of lung involvement; improved nutrition; other treatments.

There is no direct therapy against the basic defect of CF which would reverse the pathogenetic process; that is, CF has no cure. All forms of treatment are aimed at alleviating the symptoms of the disease. The separation of the treatments into areas is artificial because one organ or system always interrelates with the others. For example, a CF patient who is extremely malnourished has muscle weakness and cannot breathe or cough effectively. This worsens the lung infection that, in turn, disturbs the metabolism and makes the child lose more weight—and so on. At all times the treatment of CF patients must be comprehensive and must cover every possible angle of the disease.

Treatment of Lung Involvement

As described earlier in this chapter, the lungs of a CF patient are susceptible to obstruction and infection of the airways, which is followed by scarring and gradual destruction of the functioning lung tissue. Thus, the treatment is directed towards eliminating the obstruction and treating the infection through antibiotics and other chemotherapeutic agents, chest physical therapy, and inhalation of aerosols.

Antibiotics and Other Chemotherapeutic Agents These drugs are taken by mouth or by injection in the veins of patients. Antibiotics are given orally to suppress bacterial growth in the lungs when there are chronic pulmonary problems. This is done to keep patients from having acute lung infections that will require hospitalization and intravenous administration of antibiotics against the special microorganisms, *Staphylococcus aureus* and *Pseudomonas aeruginosa,* which usually occupy the lungs of the CF patients. *Pseudomonas aeruginosa* in particular requires effective antibiotics that can only be given intravenously and are needed in relatively high doses. The use of antibiotics by aerosol directly into the lungs has become less and less frequent in recent years.

Chest Physical Therapy This is a form of therapy given either by trained therapists or by the patient's own relatives. It involves percussion of the chest, vibration, and positioning during effective cough (Figure 19–5). This treatment has been shown to be effective in removing the infected secretion from the airways of the patients, thus decreasing the need for antibiotics.

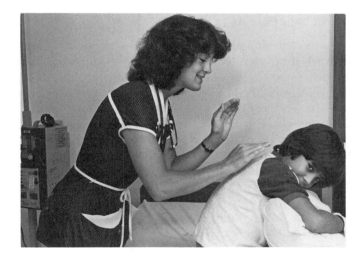

Figure 19–5 Chest Physical Therapy. The chest physical therapy involves pounding and vibration of the patient's chest in different positions. It can be done by a physical therapist, nurse, parent, or anyone else who has been trained.

Inhalation of Aerosols CF patients often inhale therapeutic agents in the form of aerosols, small nebulizers that vaporize medications in solution either mechanically or ultrasonically. The agents delivered into the lungs by this method include antibiotics (less common now), substances to liquify mucus (mucolytic agents), and substances to dilate the airways and facilitate elimination of the infected lung secretions. Effective use of inhalation therapy before chest physical therapy increases the effectiveness of the latter.

In previous years, mist tent therapy was popular. CF patients slept in tents filled with a water mist in the hope of adding water to the respiratory mucus during sleep, thus making it easier to expectorate. Although the idea was good, the therapy was abandoned when it was demonstrated that the water in the mist tents never entered the lungs of the patients.

Improved Nutrition

Special formulas that provide nutrients that do not require pancreatic enzymes for absorption have revolutionized the care of the CF infant. Good nutrition is now available to infants during this critical period of life. Various preparations of pancreatic enzymes, special nutritional supplements, better understanding of the metabolism of vitamins and trace elements in CF, availability of nutritional fluids for intravenous administration, and carefully planned diets have markedly improved the nutrition of older CF patients and, undoubtedly, have contributed to the improved prognosis.

Other Treatments

Surgery and anesthesia for the CF patient have improved dramatically as the pathophysiology of CF becomes better understood. Measures to prevent complications to the right heart, and when that isn't possible its treatment, have improved the care of the CF patient. The home use of oxygen, particularly liquid oxygen and oxygen-concentrators, has been most beneficial. Treatment of various complications has improved. Real advancement has been made in the psychoemotional support of patients, their families, and the society around them. Comprehensive psychoemotional care should be an integral part of any accepted treatment for CF patients.

PROGNOSIS

The prognosis for CF patients has shown a steady improvement over the past twenty years. The Cystic Fibrosis Foundation maintains a computer registry of patients who are cared for in CF centers around the country. Twenty years ago the life expectancy was one to three years. In 1980, the calculated life expectancy was 21.5 years. It is generally believed that this is the result of the comprehensive therapy used today.

EDUCATIONAL IMPLICATIONS

The presence of a CF child in a classroom always has some impact on the teacher and the class. The experience can be emotionally devastating or it can be positive. What happens will depend on the teacher's knowledge of CF and its implications and how this is communicated to the class. The CF child, whether in kindergarten or high school, may show no symptoms at all or may be handicapped in many ways. The presence of such a child in the class offers an excellent opportunity to improve acceptance and understanding of chronic disease by the entire class and to properly educate the class on the hereditary nature of CF.

Children with CF want to be like any one of their friends. They will do anything to avoid attracting attention to their disease. Often, CF patients cannot hide the fact that they are different. A chronic cough, having to take medications, frequent absences from school, overprotective parents, and the inability to compete physically differentiate them from their peers.

Chronic Cough

Chronic coughing often disturbs the class. In our society, a chronic cough has been associated with chronic lung infections such as tuberculosis, which often are contagious. Parents get alarmed when they hear about a child in the class with a chronic cough. The teacher has an excellent opportunity to educate both the students and their parents. The points of emphasis should be:
1. A cough is the best defense mechanism we have to keep our lungs clear;
2. Suppression of cough in someone with chronic lung disease may be very dangerous and even fatal (four to six CF children die every year because well-meaning physicians prescribed cough suppressants for them);
3. The cough of a CF patient is in no way contagious to other children; and
4. Coughing is as essential to a CF patient as breathing.

Multiple Medications

With the contemporary rejection of the drug culture in this country, it is important to emphasize the judicious use of drugs by explaining the need for them; for example, the use of capsules of pancreatic enzymes to replace missing pancreatic function and restore digestion to normal in CF patients. The use of antibiotics could be emphasized in order to explain how these drugs work selectively against pathogenic organisms without hurting the cells of the patient's body.

Absences from School

CF patients are often hospitalized for two to three weeks at a time or stay home to care for respiratory tract infections. The teacher should be familiar with these needs of the student and should be able to explain to the class adequately and informatively the reasons for the patient's absences from school.

Overprotective Parents

The parents of most CF children are well informed about their children's disease. Sometimes they become overly protective, embarrassing the child and annoying the teacher. The teacher should try to develop a kind and understanding attitude and prevent conflicts with the parents. In this respect, the teacher may need help from physicians and other health professionals involved in the care of the particular child.

Inability to Compete Physically

The desire to compete with peers and be the same as or better than them is part of human nature, particularly among children. Patients with advanced CF often cannot compete in physical education or competitive sports. Teachers find themselves in a very delicate position. They can lead a patient to inactivity, which would be most detrimental, or push a child toward competitiveness with the fear and danger of hurting the child. This is a case where consultation with the child's physician will help establish and maintain the parameters of the patient's physical capabilities and limitations. The child's competitiveness could be directed to the arena of intellectual competition, when this is apropos.

Other Concerns

A crisis occurs in any class in which a child dies. If the child is in the hospital for an extended period of time prior to death, the teacher has time to prepare the class for the coming death of their peer. This, however, is most difficult and risky, particularly because the child could recover and return to school. Usually, the crisis intervention is arranged by the teacher immediately after the death of the patient, preferably prior to the funeral. The teacher and the appropriate health professionals should meet with the class, discuss the issues surrounding the death of a chronically ill child, and answer any questions the students may have. This is a unique opportunity to do some of the finest classroom teaching and to positively influence the lives of students.

The socioeconomic impact of a chronic illness such as CF can be devastating. The annual expenses for a child with moderately severe CF have been estimated to be between $10,000–40,000. Very few families can take this kind of financial blow year after year. The teacher who senses that the family of a given patient is financially strained should notify the school counselors and alert them to the special problems of that family.

CF has a marked impact on the patient, the family, and the microcosm of the school. Appropriate knowledge of the nature of CF and kind handling of the adverse situations resulting from CF in school can bring about the harmony and positive attitude that are absolutely necessary. The teacher plays a key role in reaching these goals and in making the life of a CF child a little better and a little more enjoyable.

SUMMARY

CF is a hereditary disease affecting many school-age children that causes lung damage, difficulties in digestion of food, problems with growth and maturation, and other physical complications. CF shortens the life of affected children and may impair the quality of their existence. The presence of a CF child in a classroom creates interesting circumstances which, appropriately handled, may be beneficial to both students and teachers.

REFERENCES

Mangos, J. A. Microperfusion study of the sweat gland abnormality in cystic fibrosis. *Texas Reports of Biology and Medicine*, 1973, *31*, 651–663.

Mangos, J. A. Cystic fibrosis. In T. E. Andeoli, J. F. Hoffman, & D.E. Fanestil (Eds.), *The physiology of disorders of biomembranes.* New York: Plenum Press, 1978.

Michael W. Cohen, M.D., *is clinical associate in the Department of Pediatrics at the College of Medicine, The University of Arizona, Tucson, and medical director for the Arizona School for the Deaf and Blind, Tucson.*

Enuresis and encopresis are relatively frequent among schoolchildren. These symptoms may have considerable impact on a child's psychological and social adjustment, and thus affect academic performance. Understanding the physiological origins of these symptoms can often allow the educational professional to provide understanding and support to the child and his family.

ENURESIS

Enuresis is defined as involuntary discharge of urine, though it often refers to wetting during nighttime sleep (*nocturnal* enuresis). Daytime wetting is termed

CHAPTER 20

Enuresis and Encopresis

diurnal enuresis. The diagnosis of enuresis should be reserved for wetting beyond the age of five in girls and six in boys, reflecting the sex-related differences in development. Nocturnal enuresis exists in approximately 15 percent of one to five-year-olds, 7 percent of eight-year-olds, and 3 percent of twelve-year-olds. Lower socioeconomic groups, families with lower educational levels, and institutionalized people report a higher prevalence of enuresis. Males predominate at all ages within all enuretic populations, with the differential being greater in older children. Somewhat less than 10 percent of all enuretics also have daytime wetting. Diurnal enuresis occurs alone rather infrequently.

Primary enuresis exists when a child has never achieved consistent dryness. Primary enuresis is generally found in children with physical handicaps, cognitive deficits, neurological disorders, or developmental delays or immaturities. A child with *secondary* enuresis is generally one who was able to remain dry for at least three to six months and is commonly called a relapser or an onset enuretic. Among enuretic children, secondary enuresis generally increases with age, with over half of all enuretics being onset type by age twelve (Cohen, 1975).

Etiology

Enuresis is a symptom with multiple etiologies. For the vast majority of children with primary nocturnal enuresis, the symptom is due to a combination of a hereditary pattern of immaturity or developmental delay in neuromuscular bladder control and sleep pattern with long phases of especially deep sleep. The immature bladder has a lower functional capacity despite its anatomic normality. With relatively little urine, the bladder signals its fullness to the deeply sleeping brain. The brain doesn't perceive this stimuli and no inhibition of micturation (relaxation of the detrusor muscle and tightening of the urethral sphincter) occurs (Figure 20–1). The bladder empties involuntarily.

Organic etiologies primarily focus on the genitourinary and nervous systems. Obstructive lesions of the distal outflow tract, such as posterior urethral valves (Figure 20–2), have received particular attention as both a cause of urinary tract infections and as an independent cause of enuresis. A current urinary tract infection or a history of previous infections may be factors in causing enuresis. Nervous system dysfunction may be associated with enuresis, either through lumbosacral disorders that affect bladder innervation or control or as a reflection of cerebral disorders and global mental retardation. Myelomeningocele (See Chapter 11) is the prototype of vertebral abnormalities affecting voluntary bladder control. An isolated radiologic (X-ray) finding of spina bifida occulta (lack of closure of one or several vertebra) does not indicate a cause of enuresis. Depressed cognitive functioning is a common cause of enuresis among handicapped youngsters. A lack of comprehension of control mechanisms, inability to understand social expectations, or an inability to direct bladder inhibition may allow the symptoms in these children.

Medical conditions that lead to increased urinary volume may precipitate primary or secondary enuresis. Diabetes mellitus (Chapter 18), diabetes insipi-

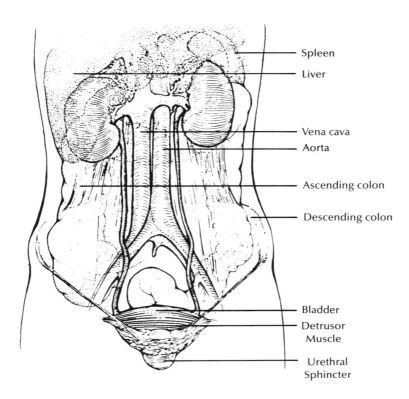

Spleen
Liver
Vena cava
Aorta
Ascending colon
Descending colon
Bladder
Detrusor Muscle
Urethral Sphincter

Figure 20–1   Anatomy of the Urinary Tract

Source: D. R. Smith. *General urology,* 10th ed. Los Altos, Calif.: Lange Medical Publication, 1981, page 3. Reprinted with permission.

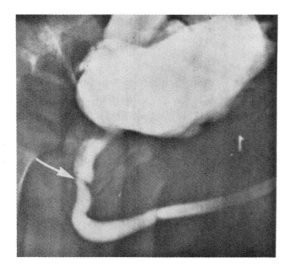

Figure 20–2 X Ray Demonstrates a Defect in the Opacified Urethra. The defect was due to a posterior urethral valve (*arrow*), which has caused obstructive dilation of the bladder, kidney, and ureter.

Source: J. G. Teplick & M. E. Haskin. *Roentgenologic diagnosis, vol. 2: A complement in radiology to the Beeson and McDermott textbook of medicine.* Philadelphia: W. B. Saunders Company, 1976, page 831. Reprinted with permission.

dus, inflammatory diseases of the kidneys (**nephritis**) (Chapter 24) or other causes of **proteinuria,** ingestion of **diuretic** drugs or chemicals, and psychogenic water intoxication are in this category. Sickle cell anemia (Chapter 15) causes an inability to concentrate urine and, therefore, increased urine volume and enuresis. Although no definite proof exists, some allergists feel that various food by-products, when present in the urine, may create an irritation or spasm of the bladder and enuresis.

Psychological functioning may relate to enuresis at two levels. The enuresis may be only one aspect of a child's general difficulty in behavioral adaptation, or it may be an isolated symptom in a child whose behavioral functioning is otherwise adequate. "Problem" children, as defined by behavioral questionnaires, interviews, and observations, make up a small percentage of an enuretic population. There is no justification in presuming **psychopathology** based on the mere presence of enuresis. As an isolated phenomenon, enuresis sometimes may be determined by poor or deficient learning of a habit pattern during toilet training. Resistance to initial training efforts, despite the nature of the techniques utilized, appears to be a critical factor.

Statistical estimates of the distribution of youngsters within these various diagnostic categories is

highly biased by the professional perspective of the evaluating clinician. Comparisons among studies within the medical literature are virtually impossible because of variations in diagnostic criteria and patient selection.

Characteristics

Developmental enuretics are usually free of any serious medical problem, have normal growth, and often demonstrate mild immaturities and delays in other areas of functioning. For example, there is a high incidence of enuresis among children with immature behavioral impulse control or attentional deficit disorders (MBD or ADD). These children demonstrate increase in daytime urinary frequency and urgency throughout their preschool years. They often have "accidents" while playing outside and are labelled as lazy. The family histories are often quite impressive. If one parent was enuretic, there is a 40 percent chance that any child in the family will be enuretic. If both parents shared the symptom, there is a 70 percent chance of it occurring in any of their children.

Urinary tract pathology may be asymptomatic except for the enuresis. Chronic infection may cause growth inadequacy, chronic malaise, or poor appetite. Neurologic pathology is often the focus of attention long before efforts are undertaken to evaluate or manage the enuresis. The characteristics of these children are defined by their neurological profile of strengths and weakness determined by the location and severity of their neurological lesion. The medical conditions leading to diuresis (excess production of urine) are defined by their typical features. Diabetes mellitus in children will often appear as secondary diurnal and nocturnal enuresis and a concomitant increase in fluid intake to compensate for water losses. Proteinuria can appear as excessive thirst and general body swelling.

Diagnosis

All children with enuresis should have a thorough medical assessment, including a medical history, physical and neurological examination, urinalysis, and screening test for infection. The physical examination should focus on the general health of the child and check for signs of various medical conditions. Neurologically, intactness of the lumbosacral innervation should be confirmed by testing genital, rectal, and lower extremity reflexes. Urinalysis will supply information regarding infection, the presence of sugar, protein, or blood, and the concentration ability of the kidneys. Radiologic studies with contrast media, (intravenous pyelogram or cystourethrogram, Figure 20–3), are indicated only when there is a strong suspicion of an obstructive abnormality. An EEG is not

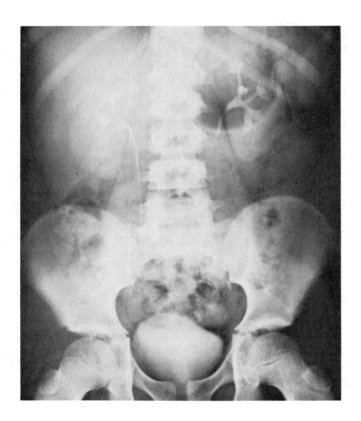

Figure 20–3   Normal Intravenous Pyelogram (IVP)

Source: Reproduced with permission from Silverman, F. N.: The Urinary Tract and Adrenal Glands, in Caffey, J., et al.: PEDIATRIC X-RAY DIAGNOSIS, 7th edition. Copyright © 1978 by Year Book Medical Publishers, Inc., Chicago.

indicated unless the history suggests the likelihood of a seizure disorder and associated urinary incontinence. Psychological and educational testing are selectively indicated in the appropriate circumstances. Observations of the youngster at home and at school may be helpful in understanding environmental and psychological factors that encourage or reinforce the wetting.

Treatment

The appropriate therapy relates to the diagnosis. For the child with developmental nocturnal enuresis, many modes of therapy have been utilized. An optimistic approach is warranted. The spontaneous remission rate is 15 percent per year in the remaining wetting population from ages five to fifteen. Reassurance may be the best therapy for younger children or for children developing transient secondary enuresis in response to environmental stress. Supportive counseling for the child and his parents may be nec-

essary to develop a level of comfort with the reassurance. As the child grows older, fear of exposure or embarrassment may limit his activities and thus deter his social or psychological development. At this point, a more specific mode of therapy may be indicated. Pharmacologic agents (specifically, the antidepressant drug, imipramine—Tofranil) have had widespread use in enuresis. The mechanism of action is either (a) as a direct anticholinergic effect by relaxing the bladder muscle or (b) directly on the central nervous system, increasing its sensitivity to bladder stimuli during sleep. The effectiveness of this and similar agents remains controversial and often relates more to the optimistic enthusiasm and experience of the prescribing physician. However, increasing concern regarding the thin margin of safety of this drug and the potential serious effect of overdose is beginning to reflect in alternate choices of therapy.

Enuresis conditioning instruments (Figure 20–4) involve a moisture-sensitive mattress device connected to an alarm that wakes the child when wetting starts. Classical Pavlovian conditioning is the therapeutic goal of these devices. Success rates in experienced hands are comparable to the drug approach. Relapses are common in both treatments. Bladder training therapy is based on the observation that many children with enuresis have a decreased bladder capacity. The goal of this training is to transform a functionally infantile bladder into one with adult volume and coordination by directing the child to inhibit his voiding for as long as possible once a day for several months. Although the safety of this technique has created considerable attraction, predictable benefit has not been defined. Hypnosis is growing in

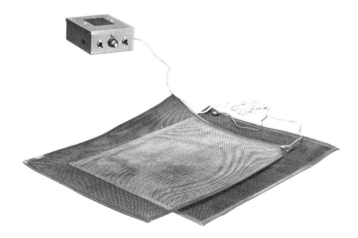

Figure 20–4   Moisture-Sensitive Bed-Buzzer Device

Source: Electronic Monitors, Inc. Reprinted by permission.

popularity as a treatment for nocturnal enuresis. During induced hypnotic trances, selective pleasurable memories are linked with the feeling of a dry bed, while expectations for dryness are encouraged. Limited experimental series have reported excellent results. Because none of these approaches to treatment of developmental enuresis has a unique superiority, the safety of the treatment and comfort or experience of the clinician usually guides the choice.

Urinary tract disease may require specific medical treatment (antibiotics) or surgery. Most neurological conditions are not amenable to definitive repair. A total lack of nerve supply may require continuous credeing (massage of the bladder) to allow for emptying. Conditioning techniques, as popularized by Azrin and Foxx (1971), have demonstrated significant gains in retarded individuals who were previously felt to be untrainable.

The various medical etiologies of enuresis require very specific treatments after diagnosis and evaluation. Psychotherapeutic, counseling, and behavior management programs may have a role when psychological factors are the primary factor or an associative or secondary concern in the enuretic child and his family.

Prognosis

For the developmental enuretic the prognosis is excellent. Although the success of the various therapeutic regimens remains controversial, the likelihood of spontaneous remission is excellent. Persistence of enuresis beyond maturation may occur if environmental variables have either conditioned the behavior or sustained the expectation of wetting. The prognosis for the medical, surgical, or neurological condition depends on the type, severity, and complications of the condition. Neurological conditions present a particularly frustrating, resistant enuretic profile because of the fixed deficits and the inability to remediate the situation. Psychological conditions will respond to therapy (a) to the extent that the child and family are motivated to actively participate in the process and (b) depending on the skills of the therapist.

Educational Implications

Because most children are dry during the day, the educational implications are based on the symptoms' indirect effect on their development, psychological adjustment, and social comfort. These parameters will be markedly affected by the reaction to the symptom within the household, the appropriateness of the medical assessment and therapy, and the child's skills in other areas of functioning. The risks to a child's developmental and adaptational profile can be minimized by a compassionate, informed approach that is realistic, encouraging, and empathetic.

Youngsters who wet during the daytime may suffer social embarrassment and exclusion depending on how prevalent the symptom is within a classroom. In a class of severely handicapped and low-functioning children, the symptom may represent the norm and go unnoticed. However, children in a mainstream classroom will react quite differently. This consequence should be considered prior to placement by attempting to achieve optimal functioning or by the development of coping techniques (e.g., frequent visits to the restroom) to avoid accidents.

ENCOPRESIS

Encopresis is a functional disorder in which a child, past the expected age for toilet training, regularly passes semiformed or formed stools in locations other than the toilet. This symptom is commonly associated with chronic stool retention for organic, psychological, or developmental reasons. *Primary* encopretics have been incontinent all their lives and have never been fully bowel trained. *Secondary* encopresis exists when the child has demonstrated full bowel control for a period of at least three–six months before onset of the symptom. The incidence of encopresis is approximately 2 percent of the pediatric population, with a trend toward increasing frequency. The symptom is seen five to six times more often in boys than in girls. Its onset is most common between the ages of three to eight, with the symptom rarely occurring during adolescence. About 30 percent of seven-year-old children with encopresis will also have enuresis (Davidson, Kugler, & Bauer, 1963).

Etiology

Chronic stool retention is the basic mechanism involved in the development of encopresis. Stool retention leads to dilation of the smooth muscle of the large bowel, resulting in a decreased ability to voluntarily control the act of defecation. Stool impaction will often create a mass within the large bowel blocking everything but water or liquid stool, which can leak around the mass. Semiformed or loose stools are then passed involuntarily, soiling the child's pants. Formed stool incontinence may also occur as segments of the impacted stool break off and move through the large dilated bowel, with no effective mechanism present to inhibit defecation.

Chronic stool retention has multiple etiologies. Rarely, congenital anatomic abnormalities cause chronic constipation and retention. Aganglionic megacolon (Hirschsprung's disease) is a disorder in which areas of the bowel have no nervous innervation and thus no functional activity. A physiologic obstruction results, leading to bowel dilatation. Innervation to the bowel may be inadequate because of spinal cord and vertebral disorders such as myelomeningocele. Anal **stenosis** and **atresia** create a similar structural obstruction with the same sequence of events. Anatomical obstruction can also occur subsequent to a surgical procedure. **Anal fissures, hemorrhoids,** or perianal rashes may cause pain on defecation and thus the child will retain stool involuntarily. Various chemical or hormonal imbalances may lead to stool retention: **hypothyroidism, hypocalcemia,** and lead intoxication. Pharmacologic agents may create or aggravate an existing retention problem. Phenothiazines (e.g., Thorazine or Mellaril) or codeine are typical offenders in this category.

Developmental disorders such as depressed cognitive function and impulse control disorders (ADD) are frequently etiologic factors. The impulse-ridden child may be difficult to toilet train because of inadequate attention devoted to learning bowel control. Inability or lack of desire to sit on the toilet long enough to evacuate the bowel can lead to gradual retention. Various experiences in a child's life may initiate a voluntary or unconscious stool withholding or retention pattern. Toilet training is usually attempted during the second or third year of a child's life. At this stage, most youngsters are quite assertive, negative, and relatively noncompliant. These characteristics may precipitate a rejecting posture towards training efforts and withholding. Painful defecation due to an intestinal infection, diarrhea, or a temporary bout of constipation may begin the retention cycle. The perception of inadequate or inappropriate toilet facilities, such as a big toilet for a toddler (fear of falling in), the lack of privacy in a school restroom, or an objectionable odor may initiate retention. Psychopathological or emotional stress factors also may occasionally create circumstances in which retention results.

Once the retention cycle persists for a significant period of time, physiologic changes (bowel dilatation) compromise the child's ability to control his bowel functioning. Because of soiling of pants and encopretic acts, adults may label the child as lazy, unmotivated, rebellious, or emotionally disturbed, and may have little understanding of the child's physiologic inability to comply with adult expectation. Patterns of behavior in terms of the child's relationship with others, his social participation, and general adaptation may be highly biased by his physiologic status. Emotional factors that are often implicated in the cause of the encopretic pattern usually result from an uncontrollable cycle.

Characteristics

Youngsters with encopresis face the challenge of embarrassment daily. Because they often have little or no bowel control, an "accident" can occur at any time and make them the target of harassment. They are often labelled as lazy, irresponsible, or rebellious and cast into the mold that those titles imply. Nicknames like "stinky" are easily attained but have little affection attached to them. Magical thinking may create unsuccessful coping mechanisms; for example, bizarre eating habits such as avoiding certain foods or eating times. Multiple activities presumed to precipitate soiling are actively avoided. Peer interaction is kept to a minimum, thus limiting the child's social development. At home, misguided, unsympathetic parents may punish, ridicule, or embarrass the child; siblings may be cruel in their exposure of the personal problem. In essence, an isolated symptom (encopresis) can have broad ramifications that affect the child's total adjustment, development, academic performance, and social comfort (Levine, 1975).

Diagnosis

Due to presumed psychological factors, this symptom often evades medical assessment for a surprisingly long period of time. The soiling is often misunderstood as diarrhea and is subject to inappropriate home cures. Once the stool retention pattern is recognized as a consequence of chronic constipation and as the cause of the soiling, the diagnostic protocol proceeds relatively rapidly.

Historical data should elucidate events precipitating the constipation in order to explain the sequence of events to a concerned family. However, this information usually does not alter the treatment. A developmental history will provide information concerning associated cognitive deficits and attentional disorders. Discussion of a general behavioral and functional profile will provide clues regarding the unusual child with psychopathology as the etiology of this symptom.

A physical examination is often deceptively normal because the ability to **palpate** impacted stool depends on the unique physical features of the child (e.g., obesity). If there is a doubt about stool retention, a plain X ray of the abdomen (Figure 20–5) will reveal retained stool and dilated bowel. A rectal-digital exam may reveal a dilated rectosigmoid area that may or may not contain impacted stool. True anatomical origins of the problem are rare, create symptoms from early in life, and are associated with chronic illness. Therefore, pursuit of these diagnoses is rarely indicated. Assessment of a metabolic or en-

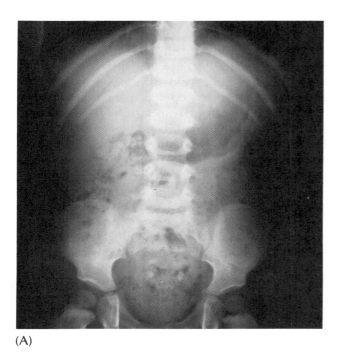

(A)

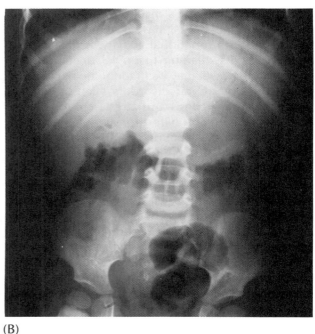

(B)

Figure 20–5   X Ray of an Impacted Bowel. A: X ray of the abdomen that shows impacted fecal material in the large bowel.

B: Repeat X ray done one week after bowel cleansing efforts. Note the significant decrease in the amount of fecal material.

docrinologic cause should be pursued if there are any associated signs of these disorders.

Treatment

The specific treatment regimen for encopresis will be determined by the particular diagnosis. There is always a basic need to provide an element of understanding and organization to what usually represents the chaotic effort to treat the symptom. When the child has stool retention and bowel dilatation and dysfunction, the goal of therapy is to maintain total evacuation of the bowel to allow for regained muscle tone in the bowel wall. As muscle tone is re-established, the bowel can be retrained to perform voluntary defecation. The bowel must be totally emptied at the initiation of therapy by use of mineral oil, stool softeners, dietary measures, or enemas. X rays are often required to ensure that the bowel has been evacuated. Total regular emptying must be maintained by scheduled bowel movements after each meal, with mineral oil, high roughage diet including whole grain products, stool softeners, or pharmacologic agents. This program usually takes three to six months, depending on the severity of the original problem. A gradual improvement in defecative ability is noted. Relapses are frequent because of loss of enthusiasm, lack of compliance, premature percep-

tion of cure, unavoidable interruption in the regimen, and a lack of adult concern as the situation grows less acute. Treatment failures frequently occur if total evacuation of the bowel has not initially been achieved.

Specific medical and anatomic causes should be treated surgically, pharmacologically, and nutritionally. Deficits in neurological innervation are particularly difficult to train. Conditioning management programs should be designed for the moderately and severely retarded youngsters. Attentional deficits should be treated primarily with bowel training incorporated into a total treatment program. Identified psychopathology should be treated by appropriate therapy.

Prognosis

With clinical perseverance, the prognosis for the child with stool retention and secondary encopresis is excellent. If treatment enthusiasm can be maintained and the resulting social and psychological issues can be overcome, frequent success can be expected. This optimism is probably inappropriate for the severely retarded because stool incontinence is common and training efforts are often resisted. Youngsters with attentional disorders have a good prognosis for controlled behavior and bowel retraining. Specific medical conditions are treatable with the likelihood of a positive result. Children with spinal cord and vertebral conditions are not likely to improve because of their limited physiologic abilities. The extent of success with therapeutic efforts for the emotionally disturbed child will dictate the probability of amelioration of the encopresis.

Educational Implications

The characteristics of encopretic children can present a challenge to the educational professional. The potential ramification of the symptom in terms of general adjustment and development often severely limit the child's functional profile and sense of adequacy. Teachers will often find themselves in the role of advocate for the child, encouraging families to seek medical attention and comply with treatment programs. Empathetic positive reinforcement for defecation schedules, dietary directions, and drug administration can be very helpful to the ambivalent or discouraged child. Peer response can be "guided" by a skilled teacher.

Because of the limited physiologic capabilities of physically handicapped children, teachers must be supplied with enough medical information to generate appropriate expectations. Many frustrating training hours can be avoided with this knowledge. School personnel can often assist in medical evaluation by supplying the clinician or parents with relevant classroom observations.

In a classroom where soiling or incontinence is common, hygiene and physical management problems are realistic. Bathroom facilities must be close and of adequate size to accommodate cleanup and changing procedures. Specific types of toilets may be needed, depending on the children's physical characteristics. Stool odors can be very persistent and require extensive cleaning efforts. Administrative cooperation is imperative in assuring the availability of these facilities and resources.

SUMMARY

Enuresis is a symptom of multiple etiologies with a wide range of severity and prognosis. Understanding the diagnostic mechanism involved in creation of the symptom for any child is essential to the development of a therapeutic approach. Collaboration between educational professionals and medical clinicians is imperative for the design of an optimal remediation program. For example, teachers must be aware of the intactness of nervous innervation of the bladder before they can begin a conditioning program to extinguish the symptom. Much frustration, disappointment, and wasted energy could be avoided if successful interprofessional communication were achieved.

Encopresis is usually the result of a relatively limited psychologic or physiologic sequence of events. Most families have limited insight into the dynamics involved and have chaotically attempted to deal with the problem. A sensitive, thorough, informative medical consultation can often clarify misconceptions, provide a successful treatment program, and generate optimism for a discouraged child and family. School personnel can play a critical role in the diagnostic and treatment process. For children with physiologic intactness, the prognosis is excellent for remediation of this potentially pervasive symptom.

REFERENCES

Azrin, N. H., & Foxx, R. M. A rapid method of toilet training the institutionalized retarded. *Journal of Applied Behavior Analysis*, 1971, *4*, 89–99.

Cohen, M. W. Enuresis. *Pediatric Clinics of North America*, 1975, *24*, 545–560.

Davidson, M., Kugler, M. M., & Bauer, C. H. Diagnosis and management of children with severe and protracted constipation and obstipation. *Journal of Pediatrics*, 1963, *62*, 261–275.

Levine, M. D. Children with encopresis: A descriptive analysis. *Pediatrics*, 1975, *56*, 412–416.

J. Timothy Bricker, M.D., is a fellow in Pediatric Cardiology at Texas Children's Hospital, Houston, Texas. Dan G. McNamara, M.D., is professor of pediatrics and chief of the Lillie Frank Abercrombie section at Baylor College of Medicine and Texas Children's Hospital, Houston, Texas.

Heart disorders are much less common in children than in adults. Nonetheless, they may cause health problems of great importance during childhood. Children with heart disorders may show no symptoms at all to total incapacitation. A large number of children with heart disorders have symptoms that can be managed with medical treatment. Some children with heart disorders require no treatment. Operations can correct or improve many heart defects. Physicians often use the terms disease, disorder, and malformation interchangeably in referring to abnormalities of the cardiovascular system. The degree of disability may be minimal in an individual to whom the term "heart disease" is applied.

CHAPTER 21

Heart Disorders

ETIOLOGY

Heart disease that is present at birth is termed congenital heart disease. The estimated occurrence of various congenital heart defects is presented in Table 21–1. These abnormalities are often not apparent at birth. Approximately 1 percent of children have congenital heart disease (Keith, 1978a). About a third of these children, if untreated, will die before reaching school age. Both environmental and hereditary factors have been implicated in certain instances of congenital heart disease. A number of environmental factors have been found to cause defects, which include congenital heart disorders: prenatal viral infections (such as rubella) (Rowe, 1978), **teratogenic** drugs (such as thalidomide) (Lenz & Knapp, 1962), excessive

Table 21–1   Estimated Occurrence of Various Cardiac Defects

Anomalous pulmonary venous connection	1 in 5,000 live births
Aortic valve stenosis	1 in 2,000 live births
Atrial septal defects	1 in 1,000 live births
Coarctation of the aorta	1 in 1,000 live births
Endocardial cushion defects	1 in 2,500 live births
Patent ductus arteriosus	1 in 830 live births
Pulmonary valve stenosis	1 in 1,000 live births
Tetralogy of Fallot	1 in 1,000 live births
Transposition of the great vessels	1 in 2,000 live births
Tricuspid valve atresia	1 in 5,000 live births
Truncus arteriosus	1 in 20,000 live births
Ventricular septal defects	1 in 400 live births

alcohol intake during pregnancy (Fanaroff, 1979), etc. There are examples of families with a high incidence of congenital heart disease in which hereditary factors play a prominent role (Nora, 1977). In some cases, heart disease is only a portion of a syndrome of malformations. Down's syndrome (trisomy 21) is a chromosomal defect which frequently has associated heart disease. In approximately 90 percent of those with congenital heart disease no environmental or hereditary causes can clearly be identified (Nora, 1977). It is normal for parents to express concern about the etiology of congenital cardiovascular disorders. It is important to reassure them that we know of nothing that could have caused or prevented the heart disease, when this is the case.

Acquired heart disease (due to an occurrence after birth) is less common in children than in adults. A number of different causes of acquired heart disease occur in children. Rheumatic heart disease following streptococcal throat infections is no longer common. Less than 1 percent of individuals will develop abnormalities of the immune system after streptococcal infections which result in inflammation of the heart (Keith, 1978a). Although rheumatic fever was the second leading cause of death from disease in childhood in the years before antibiotics, this cause of heart disease has diminished. The current incidence of rheumatic heart inflammation is approximately a tenth of 1 percent of all schoolchildren. About a fourth of these children with inflammation of the heart during an attack of rheumatic fever will have permanent heart disease. Infectious heart diseases occur in childhood. Pericarditis (inflammation of the membrane covering the heart) may be due to viral or bacterial infection (Pinsky, Jubilirer, & Nihill, 1981). Myocarditis (inflammation of heart muscle) is usually due to viral infection (Duff, 1981). Endocarditis (inflammation of the inner lining of the heart) is fre-

quently due to a bacterial infection (Harford, 1981). Neuromuscular disorders, nutritional deficiencies, tumors, diseases of metabolism, arthritic diseases, trauma, and endocrine gland disorders are all very rare causes of acquired heart disease in children (Whittemore & Caddell, 1977). High blood pressure and atherosclerotic coronary artery disease, the major types of acquired heart disease in adult life, probably have their origins in childhood (Carter & Lauer, 1977; Loggie, 1977).

CHARACTERISTICS

Normal circulation (Figure 21–1) requires the return of the blue, venous (low oxygen level) blood to the right atrium (right-sided receiving chamber). From the right atrium, blood flows through the tricuspid valve into the right ventricle (right-sided pumping chamber). The right ventricle pumps blood across the pulmonary valve into the pulmonary artery (the blood vessel leading to the lungs). As the venous blood passes through thin walled capillaries, close contact with oxygen in the **alveoli** of the lungs results in oxygen entering the dark venous blood. The blood becomes bright red when oxygenated. Red blood (now oxygenated) returns from the lungs through pulmonary veins to the left atrium (the left-sided receiving

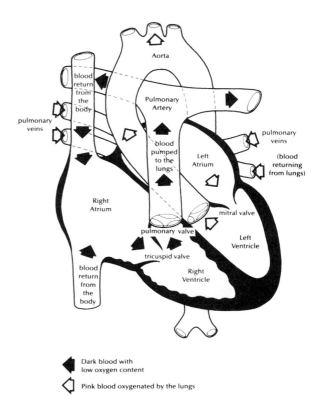

Figure 21–1   Normal Blood Flow

chamber). Blood passes across the mitral valve into the left ventricle, which is the left-sided pumping chamber. The left ventricle pumps blood across the aortic valve to the aorta, the largest artery of the body. Branches of the aorta are the blood vessels which supply the heart, the brain, the kidneys, and the rest of the body.

Heart disorders may be classified in many different ways. Disorders range from those that are benign and of no functional significance to those that cause no present symptoms but may deteriorate in the future to symptomatic defects, to defects that are life threatening. They may be classified as occurring on the left or the right side of the heart. Another classification of cardiovascular abnormalities refers to the pulmonary blood flow: excessive, normal, or diminished. Symptoms of excessive blood flow to the lungs include rapid breathing, shortness of breath, limited endurance, increased susceptibility to respiratory infections, and growth abnormalities. Not all children with excessive pulmonary blood flow have these problems. There are numerous other causes of these symptoms. Children with diminished blood flow to the lungs will have a smaller amount of blood than normal that becomes oxygenated. In these children the lips and nailbeds may appear blue (cyanosis). Bulbous swelling of the tips of the fingers and toes (clubbing) may develop in those with long-standing cyanosis (Figure 21–2). Congenital heart disease in which there is a diminished amount of oxygenated blood has been referred to as cyanotic congenital heart disease.

Congestive heart failure is a term that refers to the situation in which the pumping action of the heart is inadequate to meet the needs of the body. Congestive heart failure is a component of many types of congenital and acquired heart disease. Symptoms of congestive heart failure include rapid breathing, excessive sweating, poor appetite, and growth failure (Rudolph, 1974).

Chest pain, although a common symptom of heart disease in adults, is uncommon as a symptom of heart disease in children. Transient chest pain of no medical significance is common in healthy children and adolescents (Driscoll, Blicklith, & Gallen, 1976). Evaluation by a physician, however, is recommended.

Heart murmurs are common in childhood. Most children with heart murmurs do not have heart disease. Some characteristic murmurs, however, are indicative of specific cardiovascular abnormalities.

Patent Ductus Arteriosis

Patency of the ductus arteriosus (Figure 21–3) is an abnormality in which there is usually increased blood flow to the lung. The ductus arteriosus connects the aorta and the pulmonary artery during fetal life. Shortly after birth, the ductus constricts and closes this communication. Persistence of the ductus results in **shunting** of blood from the left-sided circulation (from the aorta) to the right-sided circulation (to the

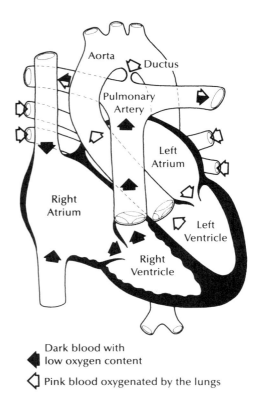

▶ Dark blood with low oxygen content

◁ Pink blood oxygenated by the lungs

Figure 21–3   Patent Ductus Arteriosus. Note the ductus, or connection between the aorta and the pulmonary artery.

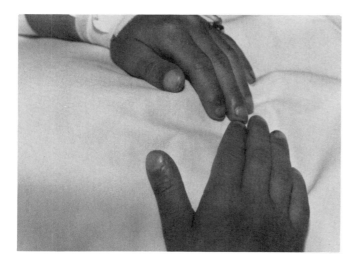

Figure 21–2   Clubbing of the Fingers

pulmonary artery). Persistent patency of the ductus arteriosus commonly is found in premature infants. This abnormality may exist as an isolated defect or as a feature of another cardiovascular defect.

Ventricular Septal Defect

Ventricular septal defect (Figure 21–4) refers to abnormal communications between the left- and right-sided ventricles. Blood flows from the high pressure left ventricle to the relatively low pressure right ventricle, which results in increased blood flow to the lungs. Small defects may have only minimally increased pulmonary blood flow and may be asymptomatic. Large defects may result in symptoms of excessive pulmonary blood flow and congestive heart failure (Mohrman, 1979).

Atrial Septal Defect

An atrial septal defect (Figure 21–5) is an abnormal communication between the left- and the right-sided atria. The result is an increase in the amount of blood which flows through the lungs due to blood shunted from the left to the right circulation across the atrial septal defect. Most often this type of defect is asymp-

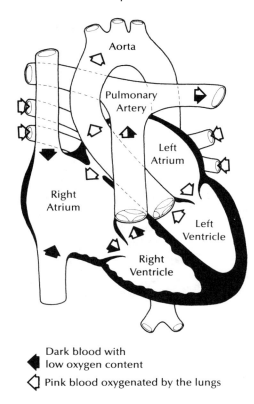

◀ Dark blood with low oxygen content

◁ Pink blood oxygenated by the lungs

Figure 21—5   Atrial Septal Defect. Note the opening in the wall between the right and left atria.

tomatic in childhood. Occasionally children may have symptoms of increased blood flow to the lungs and congestive heart failure. Atrial septal defects may exist in association with other congenital defects or as an isolated problem (Mohrman, 1979).

Tetralogy of Fallot

Tetralogy of Fallot (Figure 21–6) is a cardiovascular disease in which an inadequate flow of blood to the lungs results in a cyanotic individual. The name refers to the four aspects of this malformation described by a French physician, Dr. Fallot, in the 1800s. This is the most common cyanotic congenital defect. Blue (low oxygen) blood is shunted from the right heart to the left heart through a ventricular septal defect. A pulmonary stenosis (a narrowing of the pulmonary valve) obstructs the blood flow to the lungs and counteracts the pressure difference between the left and right ventricles. This results in an inadequate blood flow to the lungs and a flow of mixed blood (oxygenated and low oxygen) to the body. The condition may be exacerbated if the septal defect is high enough that the aorta communicates directly with the right ventricle. Blood also may be shunted between the left and right atria, but usually in small amounts.

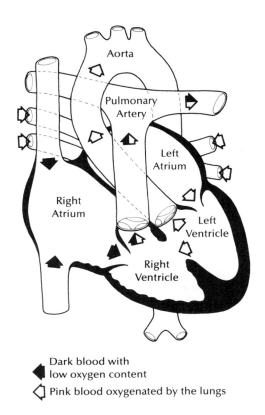

◀ Dark blood with low oxygen content

◁ Pink blood oxygenated by the lungs

Figure 21—4   Ventricular Septal Defect. Note the opening in the wall between the right and left ventricles.

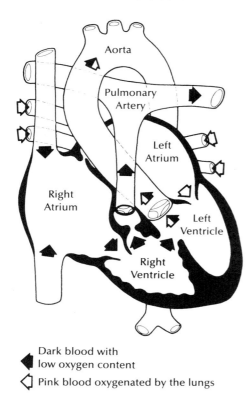

Dark blood with low oxygen content

Pink blood oxygenated by the lungs

Figure 21–6   Tetralogy of Fallot. Note these three aspects of the tetralogy of Fallot: (1) the opening between the right and left ventricles; (2) the stenosis, or narrowing, of the pulmonary valve and below the valve; and (3) the hypertrophy, or thickening, of the walls of the right ventricle below the pulmonary valve. The fourth aspect is cyanosis.

Transposition of the Great Arteries

Transposition of the great arteries (Figure 21–7) describes the defect in which the pulmonary artery and the aorta are attached to the wrong ventricles. Thus, blue blood from the body returns to the right-sided circulation and is pumped back to the body through an aorta that is attached to the right ventricle.

Other Cyanotic Defects

Other cyanotic defects exist. In tricuspid atresia (Figure 21–8) the tricuspid valve (between the right atrium and right ventricle) has never developed. Low oxygen blood from the body flows from the right atrium into the left atrium (through a defect in the wall) instead of to the right ventricle and then to the lungs. Truncus arteriosus (Figure 21–9) is a defect in which both the aorta and the pulmonary artery fuse into a single large artery. The arterial supply to the body and that to the lung come from a single mixed source. When the blood returning from the lungs enters the heart at a

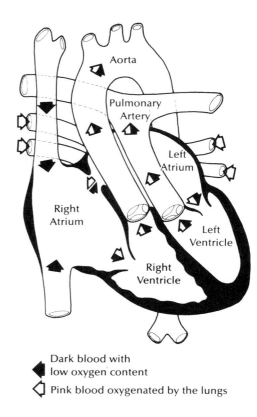

Dark blood with low oxygen content

Pink blood oxygenated by the lungs

Figure 21–7   Transposition of the Great Arteries. Note that the aorta connects with the right ventricle instead of the left ventricle, and the pulmonary artery connects with the left ventricle instead of the right ventricle.

location other than the left-sided atrium the defect is termed anomalous venous return (Figure 21–10). Numerous defects involve hearts with only one ventricle (Mohrman, 1979).

Aortic Stenosis

Stenosis refers to an obstruction of the blood flow. Often this is at a valve (e.g., mitral stenosis). Regurgitation, or insufficiency, of a valve describes what occurs when a valve is "leaky" and blood flows backward across that valve. Stenosis and regurgitation of the valves may be due to a congenital abnormality or to an acquired abnormality (such as that resulting from rheumatic heart disease).

Aortic stenosis (Figure 21–11) occurs when there is obstruction of blood flow out of the left ventricle, at the mitral valve. If the condition shows symptoms in a newborn, it heralds an extremely serious disorder. Many milder, often asymptomatic forms of the disorder are not discovered until later in infancy or in childhood. In coarctation of the aorta (Figure 21–12) the blood flow to the body from the left ventricle is also obstructed. In this disorder the obstruction is

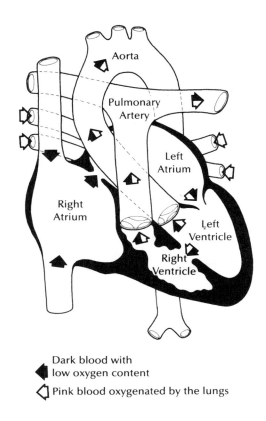

Dark blood with low oxygen content

Pink blood oxygenated by the lungs

Figure 21—8   Tricuspid Atresia. Note that there is no tricuspid valve between the right atrium and the right ventricle. Also there are openings in the walls between the right and left atria and between the left and right ventricles.

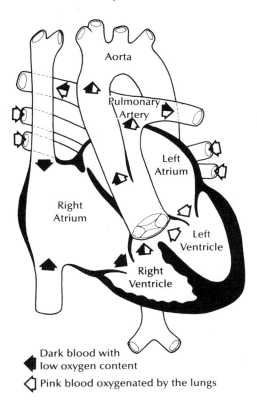

Dark blood with low oxygen content

Pink blood oxygenated by the lungs

Figure 21—9   Truncus Arteriosus. Note that the aorta and the pulmonary artery come together to form a single large artery that emanates from both ventricles and branches into the aorta and the pulmonary artery.

due to a narrowing of the aorta after it leaves the heart. This defect also ranges from mild and asymptomatic to extremely severe.

Pulmonary Stenosis

Pulmonary stenosis (Figure 21–13) refers to an obstruction of the blood flow from the right ventricle into the lungs in or around the pulmonary valve. This may occur with other defects (e.g., as a part of tetralogy of Fallot) or as an isolated problem. Generally, this is an asymptomatic disorder, although severe forms exist.

Other Disorders

A number of congenital and acquired disorders of heart muscle function exist. They may be due to toxins, hereditary disorders, or infectious illnesses. The symptoms are those of congestive heart failure and may include abnormalities in the heart rhythm, as would be found in disorders of heart muscle function.

Abnormalities of the cardiac rate and rhythm occur in childhood. These may be symptoms of a

congenital or acquired heart disease or simply irregularities in otherwise normal children. Heart block refers to abnormal electrical conduction, and has nothing to do with any blockage of blood flow. Many normal children will have extra or skipped heart beats. Some disorders in the rate and rhythm of the heart, however, can be life threatening and require appropriate investigation and treatment. Various forms of tachycardia (rapid heart rate) occur in childhood. Normal tachycardia occurs with fever or exercise. Inappropriate tachycardias may require further investigation and treatment (Gillette & Garson, 1981).

DIAGNOSIS

A detailed history and physical examination is the initial step in the evaluation of a child with suspected heart disease. The presence or absence of symptoms that may relate to the cardiovascular system is evaluated. Examination of the child's growth, breathing rate, heart rate, blood pressure, pulse, breath sounds, heart sounds and murmurs, size of abdomi-

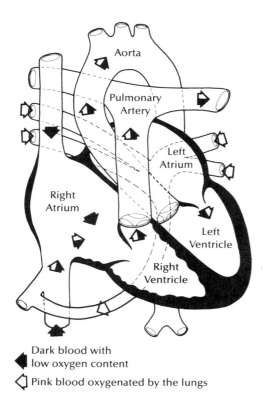

Dark blood with low oxygen content

Pink blood oxygenated by the lungs

Figure 21–10 Anomalous Pulmonary Venous Connection. Note that the pulmonary veins do not connect with the left atrium. Where these veins do connect is variable, but the result is less oxygenated blood supplied to the body.

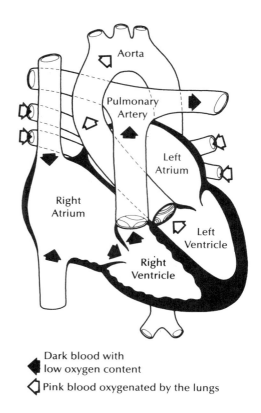

Dark blood with low oxygen content

Pink blood oxygenated by the lungs

Figure 21–11 Aortic Valve Stenosis. Note the stenosis, or narrowing, of the aortic valve.

nal organs, and presence or lack of blue coloration are among numerous aspects of a complete physical examination. As previously mentioned, most children with heart murmurs do not have heart disease. Often, a careful physical examination is adequate to ascertain that a particular heart murmur is a normal one.

Radiographic (X-ray) evaluation of the chest is used to ascertain the heart's size and shape and to judge whether blood flow to the lungs appears to be increased or decreased. Electrocardiographic (EKG or ECG) evaluation charts the electrical activity of the heart in order to assess the cardiac rhythm and can indicate possible enlargement of various chambers of the heart (Figure 21–14).

Echocardiographic techniques (Figure 21–15) for cardiac investigation are relatively new. High frequency sound waves are bounced off cardiac structures. The time required for those sound waves to return from various cardiac structures is related to the depth of those structures in the chest. This technique can be used to evaluate the heart in motion and can give information about cardiac dimensions and anat-

omy. It is a noninvasive test, which involves no pain or risk to the patient.

Nuclear techniques are occasionally used in the evaluation of children with heart disease. Radioactive isotopes, which are taken up by heart muscle, are used to obtain an image of the heart with radiation counters.

Exercise testing may be done to evaluate the degree of exercise tolerance, the changes in the cardiac rate and rhythm with exercise, exertional blood pressure changes, and the degree of EKG changes when the heart is working its hardest. This test is performed under controlled circumstances, under the observation of a physician.

Cardiac catheterization is the procedure for a definitive cardiovascular evaluation when a serious disorder is suspected. Small plastic tubes are advanced through blood vessels into the various chambers of the heart. The pressure and the oxygen concentration may be measured in various parts of the heart. This physiologic information is quite important in planning heart surgery. Injection of X-ray contrast dye with movie recording of the X ray (cineangiocardiography) can define the anatomy of the heart. Other diagnostic and therapeutic procedures in the catheterization laboratory are discovered almost daily.

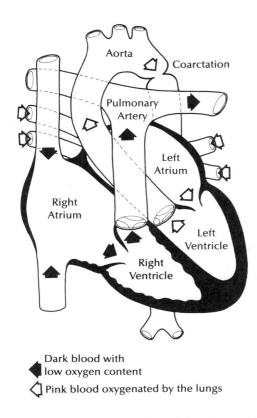

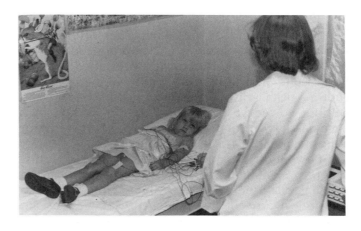

Figure 21–14 An Electrocardiograph Charts the Electrical Activity of This Girl's Heart

Dark blood with low oxygen content

Pink blood oxygenated by the lungs

Figure 21–12 Coarctation of the Aorta. Note the narrowing of the aorta after it leaves the heart.

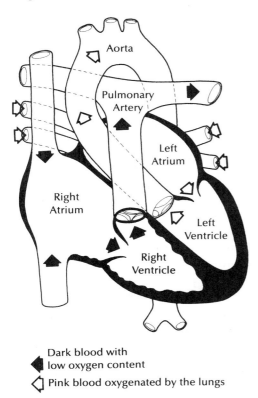

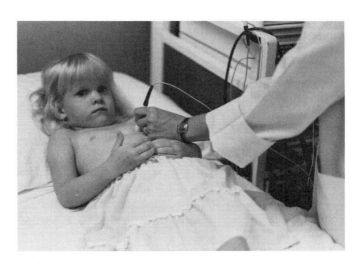

Figure 21–15 An Echocardiograph Is Completely Painless

Dark blood with low oxygen content

Pink blood oxygenated by the lungs

Figure 21–13 Pulmonary Valve Stenosis. Note the stenosis, or narrowing, of the pulmonary valve.

TREATMENT

Treatment for heart disease includes operative and nonoperative interventions. Nonoperative treatments include medications to increase the force of cardiac contraction (such as the digitalis preparations), medications to diminish the blood volume by increasing the amount of urine produced (diuretics), and medications to decrease the amount of work that the heart must do (vasodilators). Various medications for rhythm disturbances are also available.

Surgery may be performed to correct a heart defect or to improve the heart's function when correction is not possible. Corrective surgery may be performed on most children with congenital heart disease: transposition, tetralogy of Fallot, total anomalous pulmonary venous return, truncus arteriosus, etc. Palliative operations are those done for physiologic improvement of a cardiovascular disorder. Although normal circulation is not produced by this type of operation, considerable improvement in function results. Individuals with palliative operative procedures usually live a great many comfortable years without corrective heart surgery. Implantation of a pacemaker is one of the operations performed to treat abnormalities of cardiac rate or rhythm.

Prevention of acquired and congenital cardiac disorders is sometimes possible. Children with cardiovascular disorders require antibiotics during dental or surgical procedures to prevent infection of the inner structures of the heart. Other aspects of prevention of heart disease are listed in Table 21–2.

Table 21–2   Prevention of Cardiac Disorders in Children

Prevention of congenital defects
  Rubella immunization of the community and the individual.
  Regulations regarding drugs possibly unsafe to the unborn child.
  Optimal prenatal care.
  Abstaining from alcohol during pregnancy.
  Prevention of teenage pregnancy.
  Prevention of pregnancy late in life.
  Prevention of pregnancy in families at known high risk for congenital cardiac defects.
Prevention of rheumatic heart disease
  Prompt antibiotic therapy for streptococcal throat infections.
  Antibiotic prophylaxis for individuals with previous rheumatic fever.
Prevention of infectious endocarditis
  Antibiotic prophylaxis during dental and surgical procedures for individuals known to be at increased risk for endocarditis.
Prevention of atherosclerotic heart disease (adult coronary artery disease)
  Prevention of adolescent smoking.
  Prudent diet with limited animal fat intake.
  Blood fat screening in families at high risk.
Prevention of hypertensive cardiac disease
  Blood pressure screening in childhood.
  Prevention of obesity.
  Prudent salt intake.

PROGNOSIS

The prognosis for individuals with congenital heart disease is quite varied. At one end of the spectrum is the infant with a defect, such as underdevelopment of the left ventricle, that is incompatible with life for more than a few hours. At the other end of the spectrum is the elderly individual with an asymptomatic abnormality, such as two rather than three leaflets of the aortic valve, which is found unexpectedly at an autopsy. In the days before cardiac surgery, the prognosis was quite grim for most children with cyanotic congenital defects. Many individuals with corrections of congenital defects now are expected to have a near normal life span. Children who have had palliative operations often survive well into adulthood. The prognosis of cardiac defects must be determined individually for each patient. The severity of the defect, rather than simply the defect itself, influences prognosis. We convey optimism even in situations in which the prognosis seems to be grim. Advances in medical management and cardiovascular surgical techniques have developed rapidly and are continuing to do so.

The prognosis for children with acquired rheumatic heart disease depends upon the extent of valvular injury and the degree to which it is possible to prevent future episodes of rheumatic fever (Keith, 1978b). Children with heart disease are, in general, not likely to "drop dead." Unlike coronary disease in adults, chest pain in children usually doesn't indicate a serious disorder (Driscoll et al., 1976). Many young women with serious cardiovascular disease prefer to adopt rather than take the considerable risk of childbearing.

EDUCATIONAL IMPLICATIONS

Children with cardiac disease most often will have a normal intellect (Fyler, Silbert, & Rothman, 1976). Many children who grew up with cyanotic congenital heart disease or other severe cardiac abnormalities became successful professionals as adults (Taussig, Kallman, Naget, Baumgardener, Momberger, & Kirk, 1975). The presence of heart disease alone is not a reason to limit educational expectations (Neill & Haroutunian, 1977).

In some instances, heart disease is associated with the malformation of many organ systems. Down's syndrome is an example in which heart disease is a part of a constellation of abnormalities that include developmental delay (Smith & Wilson, 1973). Intellectual impairment in this situation would call for special educational planning.

Delayed gross motor development often is seen in infants with serious cardiovascular abnormalities. This simply may be due to a general debilitation from circulatory abnormality and development is not necessarily otherwise impaired. Prolonged severe malnutrition due to serious cardiovascular abnormalities may also inhibit or delay development.

The psychological implications of heart disease in a child may be considerable (Carr, 1976). Parents may transmit their anxiety about the child's heart problem to the child (Chapman & Goodall, 1980). In many families in which a child has heart disease, the normal developmental stresses of separation are amplified. As would be expected, school may represent a threat to such a family. Regression, school phobia, and behavioral disturbances may result and require expert intervention. The child with obvious cyanosis may be quite self-conscious about looking different. Chest scars from cardiac surgery, chest deformity from cardiac disease, and delayed growth may all be a source of embarrassment for the child or adolescent with heart disease. When it has been necessary to miss school, these children may feel even more isolated from their classmates.

School attendance is usually possible even for children with severe cardiac disorders. It is rare that homebound education is required for more than brief periods of time. However, school attendance may require special arrangements. Children with limited exercise tolerance may require additional time between classes, the use of elevators rather than stairs, and the scheduling of classes in rooms close together. Children with congestive heart failure who are taking diuretic therapy may require additional opportunities to use the restrooms. Excessively warm situations may be a problem for some children with heart disease.

Occasionally, these children are advised not to participate in physical education (Cumming, 1965). Physical conditioning would not be expected to improve cardiac performance in the majority of these children. Children with heart disease who are permitted to participate in physical education are not to be pushed beyond the point at which they feel tired. We are aware of situations in which individuals with heart disorders have dropped out prior to high school graduation because of inability of the educational system to take this into consideration. Many children are allowed full activity without restriction but are advised not to participate in competitive athletics (Cumming, 1965). Isometric exercises are generally more detrimental to cardiac performance than isotonic activities (Compton, Hill, & Sinclair, 1973; Lind, McNicol, & Donald, 1966). Emotional excitement is not detrimental for most children with heart disease. The enjoyment of physical activity without risk to the child requires communication with the physician.

There may be an increased number of school absences. Children with increased blood flow to the lungs may have more episodes of bronchitis and pneumonia than normal children. We occasionally recommend that such children stay home from school during major influenza outbreaks. Annual in- fluenza immunization may be recommended for children with symptomatic cardiac disease. The child with active rheumatic heart involvement will require an extended period of bedrest (Keith, 1978b) and homebound education. Understanding and communication permits continued educational progress in spite of such circumstances.

Career planning for a child with heart disease, depending upon the severity of the defect, need not be all that unique. In some instances, careers involving stressful manual labor will be unwise and occupations with exposure to low atmospheric oxygen tension may be inadvisable to some. Military careers are often not possible. Obtaining health and life insurance may be difficult for individuals with heart disease (Neill & Haroutunian, 1977).

SUMMARY

Cardiac diseases in childhood result in health problems of varying severity. In most circumstances, these physical disabilities do not preclude a comfortable, happy, productive life. Many individuals with heart disease benefit from operations to correct their defects or improve the physiologic function of their cardiovascular system. The prognosis for those with cardiac defects depends on the severity of the physiologic impairment and the degree to which surgery is feasible. The development of new surgical techniques and of medical advances, as well as the variability of cardiac malformations, means that the prognosis is a very individual matter and may improve with further discoveries. Participation in school is almost always possible. Educational goals and career planning for children with heart disease, as a group, do not differ greatly from those for children without heart disease.

REFERENCES

Carr, R. P. Psychological adaptation to cardiac surgery. In B. S. L. Kidd & R. D. Rowe (Eds.), *The child with congenital heart disease after surgery.* New York: Futura Publishing Company, 1976.

Carter, G. A., & Lauer, R. M. Atherosclerosis. In A. J. Moss, F. H. Adams, & G. C. Emmanouilides (Eds.), *Heart disease in infants, children, and adolescents.* Baltimore: Williams & Wilkins, 1977.

Chapman, J. A., & Goodall, J. Helping a child to live whilst dying. *Lancet,* 1980, 1, 753–756.

Compton, D., Hill, P. M., & Sinclair, J. E. Weight-lifters blackout. *Lancet,* 1973, 2, 1234–1237.

Cumming, G. R. The physician and physical education of the school child. *Pediatric Clinics of North America,* 1965, 12, 1015–1026.

Driscoll, D. J., Blicklith, L. B., & Gallen, W. J. Chest pain in children: A prospective study. *Pediatrics*, 1976, *57*, 648–653.

Duff, D. Viral and bacterial myocarditis. In R. D. Feigin & J. D. Cherry (Eds.), *Textbook of pediatric infectious disease*. Philadelphia: W. B. Saunders, 1981.

Fanaroff, A. A. Fetal alcohol syndrome. In W. E. Nelson, V. C. Vaughan, R. J. McKay, Jr., & R. E. Behrman (Eds.), *Textbook of pediatrics*. Philadelphia: W. B. Saunders, 1979.

Fyler, D. C., Silbert, A. R., & Rothman, K. J. Five year follow-up of infant cardiacs: Intelligence quotient. In B. S. L. Kidd & R. D. Rowe (Eds.), *The child with congenital heart disease after surgery*. New York: Futura Publishing Company, 1976.

Gillette, P. C., & Garson, Jr., A. *Pediatric cardiac dysrhythmias*. New York: Grune & Stratton, 1981.

Harford, C. G. Bacterial endocarditis. In R. D. Feigin & J. D. Cherry (Eds.), *Textbook of pediatric infectious disease*. Philadelphia: W. B. Saunders, 1981.

Keith, J. D. Prevalence, incidence, and epidemiology. In J. D. Keith, R. D. Rowe, & P. Vlad (Eds.), *Heart disease in infancy and childhood*. New York: Macmillan, 1978. (a)

Keith, J. D. Rheumatic fever and rheumatic heart disease. In J. D. Keith, R. D. Rowe, & P. Vlad (Eds.), *Heart disease in infancy and childhood*. New York: Macmillan, 1978. (b)

Lenz, W., & Knapp, K. Die thalidomid-embryopathie. *Deutsche Med. Wochenschrift*, 1962, *87*, 1232–1242.

Lind, A. R., McNicol, G. W., & Donald, K. W. Circulatory adjustments to sustained (static) muscular activity. In K. Evang & K. L. Anderson (Eds.), *Physical activity in health and disease*. Baltimore: Williams & Wilkins, 1966.

Loggie, J. H. M. Systemic hypertension. In A. J. Moss, F. H. Adams, & G. C. Emmanouilides (Eds.), *Heart disease in infants, children, and adolescents*. Baltimore: Williams & Wilkins, 1977.

Mohrman, M. E. Cardiovascular disorders. In K. B. Roberts (Ed.), *Manual of clinical problems in pediatrics*. Boston: Little, Brown and Company, 1979.

Neill, C. A., & Haroutunian, L. M. The adolescent and young adult with congenital heart disease. In A. J. Moss, F. H. Adams, & G. C. Emmanouilides (Eds.), *Heart disease in infants, children, and adolescents*. Baltimore: Williams & Wilkins, 1977.

Nora, J. J. Etiologic aspects of congenital heart disease. In A. J. Moss, F. H. Adams, & G. C. Emmanouilides (Eds.), *Heart disease in infants, children, and adolescents*. Baltimore: Williams & Wilkins, 1977.

Pinsky, W. W., Jubilirer, D. P., & Nihill, M. R. Infectious pericarditis. In R. D. Feigin & J. D. Cherry (Eds.), *Textbook of pediatric infectious disease*. Philadelphia: W. B. Saunders, 1981.

Rowe, R. D. Cardiovascular disease in the rubella syndrome. In J. D. Keith, R. D. Rowe, & P. Vlad (Eds.), *Heart disease in infancy and childhood*. New York: Macmillan, 1978.

Rudolph, A. J. Cardiac failure in children: A hemodynamic overview. In H. P. Brunwald (Ed.), *The myocardium: Failure and infarction*. New York: H. P. Publishing, 1974.

Smith, D., & Wilson, A. *The child with Down's syndrome*. Philadelphia: W. B. Saunders, 1973.

Taussig, H. B., Hallman, C. H., Naget, D., Baumgardener, R., Momberger, N., & Kirk, H. Longtime observations in the Blalock-Taussig operation. VII. Twenty to twenty-eight year follow-up on patients with tetralogy of Fallot. *Johns Hopkins Medical Journal*, 1975, *137*, 13–19.

Whittemore, R., & Caddell, J. L. Metabolic and nutritional diseases. In A. J. Moss, F. H. Adams, & G. C. Emmanouilides (Eds.), *Heart disease in infants, children, and adolescents*. Baltimore: Williams & Wilkins, 1977.

Allen C. Crocker, M.D., is associate professor in the Department of Pediatrics at the Harvard Medical School, Boston, and director of the Developmental Evaluation Clinic at The Children's Hospital Medical Center, Boston, Massachusetts.

This work was supported in part by the U.S. Department of Health and Human Services, Maternal and Child Health Service, Project #928, and Administration on Developmental Disabilities, Project #59-P-05163.

An inborn error of metabolism refers to a hereditary condition in which one's body lacks the ability to perform an essential chemical task. The term inborn refers to the inscrutable, constitutional nature of the variation, determined by the child's genetic makeup. The concept of an error of metabolism speaks to the fact that normal biochemical processes are altered, with varying degrees of significance.

The most basic characteristics of humans are determined by the actions of many thousands of genes.

CHAPTER 22

Inborn Errors of Metabolism

Genes, the fundamental units of inheritance, are arranged in rows on the 23 pairs of chromosomes found in every cell nucleus. In the simplest view, each gene controls the production of one chemical catalyst, an enzyme, which in turn expedites a special chemical reaction. Inborn errors of metabolism result when the function of a gene is deficient, hence the enzyme action is inadequate. Usually that gene abnormality must be doubly present, that is, inherited from both the mother and the father. The parents each carry a single aberrant gene which is paired with a normal gene, thus assuring their own functional integrity. This is called carrier status. During the mixture of genes which occurs at conception, a couple who are both carriers have one chance in four of producing the double gene combination in their offspring, who would have the inborn error of metabolism. This is recessive inheritance; rarely does one see the error in more than one generation, but on occasion more than one sibling may be affected.

In these biochemical diseases, there is often a marker, an abnormality in the blood or urine, that indicates the involved status. Particular abnormal genes are common in the human constitution; all people are thought to carry several dozen of them, but most remain silent because they have been inherited from only one parent and are balanced by a comparable normal gene from the other parent.

Inasmuch as there are vast numbers of biochemical processes involved in the human metabolism, there can be many hundreds of inborn errors of metabolism. Most are quite rare, because the number of carriers is relatively low and the chance of them mating is even lower. Sometimes, genetic diseases show an increased incidence in a specific ethnic group where a relatively stable gene stock has been maintained through the generations. These include, for example, Tay-Sachs disease in Ashkenazi Jews, sickle cell anemia in blacks, and Cooley's anemia in persons of Greek or Italian extraction.

The biological effects of the various inborn errors of metabolism can be classified by the type of molecule that is part of the chemical difficulty. Some are *large molecule diseases*, such as those involving the lipids and mucopolysaccharides. In these diseases, one sees extensive local structural effects in the lysosomes of the cells and cell membranes, which cause changes in the size and architecture of the skeleton, the liver and spleen, the white blood cells, and commonly, the brain. Children with these problems often have an unusual appearance (phenotype), mental retardation, and limited survival. In contrast, *small molecule diseases*, affecting metabolism of carbohydrates or amino acids, are more dynamic. These soluble materials circulate in the blood, affecting blood vessels, brain cells, and other health-related areas. Such children usually have a normal appearance, and developmental and survival issues are variable.

In the material that follows, basic principles are presented which relate to understanding the child who has an inborn error of metabolism. For this purpose, two prototypes have been selected: Hurler syndrome (a large molecule disorder) and PKU (a small molecule disease).

HURLER SYNDROME

Hurler syndrome is one of a cluster of hereditary disorders involving alterations in the metabolism of

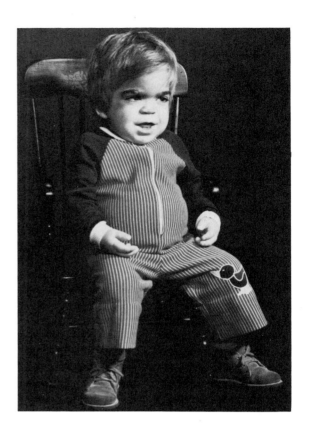

Figure 22–1   A Remarkable Boy with Hurler Syndrome, Who Later Died of Cardiac Failure

mucopolysaccharides, which are large structural polymers prominent in cartilage, connective tissue, the cornea, the heart, and brain cells. In the population as a whole, extremely few children are born with Hurler syndrome, but most special education collaboratives or pediatric nursing homes will eventually have one or more such children. The syndrome is named for Gertrud Hurler, who first described a brother and sister with this syndrome from Switzerland in 1919. As could be expected, earlier examples of such children have since been found in the literature. Boys and girls with Hurler syndrome have a remarkable appearance (Figure 22–1), many bodily handicaps, and do not survive childhood. They have characteristically evoked a conflicted response from educators. When a creative relationship has been achieved, a situation of vigorous mutual enthusiasm has generally resulted.

Etiology

Due to a deficiency in the enzyme, iduronidase, the person with Hurler syndrome is unable to process mucopolysaccharides (McKusick, Neufeld, & Kelly, 1978). Hurler syndrome is a homozygous (double gene) abnormality; therefore, both parents are carriers of a partial (single gene) iduronidase deficiency, which does not affect their personal health or development. In a marriage between two carriers, there is a 25 percent risk of bearing a child with Hurler syndrome in each pregnancy. The risk is not influenced by parental age, obstetrical issues, or the gender of the child. It is this critical enzymatic deficiency that produces all of the subsequent difficulties which the children will experience. Other mucopolysaccharidosis conditions include the Hunter's, Sanfilippo, Morquio, and Maroteaux-Lamy syndromes (based on the names of those who discovered or first described them), each with somewhat different enzyme abnormalities and clinical problems.

Characteristics

The child with Hurler syndrome is a wonderful individual, with serious special needs but with a warmth and charm that affect all those with whom he comes in contact. The child's appearance at birth is near normal, but the body and facial features gradually alter during the first year. The full picture, evident during the second year but even more enhanced later, includes a large head, with a full-appearing forehead, a broad nose, full lips, and a prominent tongue. All joints are restricted from full extension, so that the child stands with the hips, knees, and elbows partially flexed. The fingers do not open fully. There is usually a deformity of the spine, a kyphos (angle) in the midback. The abdomen is full because of an enlarged liver and spleen. Growth is accelerated in the first year, but arrests after two to three years, with final height not over 42 inches. The corneas develop a hazy appearance, but this does not critically restrict vision. Hearing handicaps are common, hernias are common at the navel or in the groin, the skin has increased hair, a chronic runny nose is characteristic, and seizures may occur in the later years. A variety of cardiac issues is present and progressive, involving the heart valves, the heart muscle, and the coronary arteries. Frequent respiratory infections can cause significant problems.

Psychomotor development begins normally but, as is usual in metabolic disorders, decelerates after a year or so of age. These children may walk independently by one to one and a half years of age, but do not gain good motor skills after that age. Talking begins late and will always be limited. Toilet training and other independence skills are almost never achieved. During the period from about one and a half to three years of age development reaches a plateau; very little new material is learned. After that, there is a slow reduction in previously mastered capabilities. Ambulation is gradually lost, so is language and cognition, as the universal changes in the neurones of the central nervous system progress. Survival is threatened both by the compelling brain disease and the increasing cardiac liability. Death commonly occurs in middle childhood.

Diagnosis

Hurler syndrome is usually suspected by the parents and pediatrician when they notice that the child's appearance is unusual, often at around a year of age. The diagnosis is tentatively confirmed by X rays showing changes in the bones, and increased mucopolysaccharide excretion in the urine. A definitive diagnosis requires enzyme studies on white blood cells or cultured cells from a skin biopsy. This same enzyme (iduronidase) analysis can be performed on cultured fetal cells after an amniocentesis, thus providing prenatal diagnosis (in subsequent pregnancies of the same couple). Whereas identification of the child with Hurler syndrome is always secured, diagnosis of involvement with some of the other, milder mucopolysaccharidosis syndromes may be more obscure and delayed.

Treatment

A great deal can be done to alleviate the symptoms of Hurler syndrome, but no specific (enzyme replacement) treatment is yet possible. Hernias can be repaired, adenoids removed for relief of nasal discharge, shunts inserted to relieve increased intracranial pressure, and seizures controlled with anticonvulsant medication. Infections need prompt and vigorous management. Cardiac drugs will assist temporarily if heart failure develops. Most of all, the family needs support in their guidance of this unique child: an understanding of the mechanism, attention to specific symptoms, genetic counseling, contact with other families, respite care, and encouragement for the siblings (Crocker & Cullinane, 1972). Most families who have been appropriately assisted in rearing their child come to feel a fulfillment and gratification that counteracts the tragic implications of the illness.

Prognosis

The inexorable nature of the toll taken by the inherent enzyme deficiency, especially the progression of the cardiac and central nervous system handicaps, can have only a single outcome. The entire child care team must work in a coordinated fashion, one day at a time, seizing on daily opportunities but not denying the fatal implications.

Educational Implications

The educator (in the early intervention, preschool, and early school years) is presented with a very special challenge. Acknowledgement and accommodation must be made to a unique situation: learning is limited at first, fading in the middle period, and negative in the final phase. There is much defense for an early stimulation program, begun as soon as the diagnosis is known, in the hope of building good initial skills. Stimulation is again the key in the preschool years, with the goal of holding existing capabilities by active interest and motivation. Adapted physical education can deal with the child's modest physical skills and the limited movement from joint stiffness. The child should be led but not pushed; the joint contractures will not yield to physical therapy, for example. Preacademic activities are of value, but advancement will be constrained. Use of sensory exercises is good, as is socialization training. Respiratory infections and other somatic (bodily) problems may restrict regularity of attendance, but attendance for the full school week should be sought. Recreational activities are usually very successful. Parental involvement is also important. In the last year or two of life, the child with Hurler syndrome may be much less attentive and may need more quiet times. The child's happy manner and other lovable qualities generally move the classroom or day activities program personnel to match the schedule to the tolerance of this unique student. To keep his world as large as practicable, and to retain the joy of life, will do much to redeem the shortness of the trip.

PHENYLKETONURIA (PKU)

PKU is an inborn error of metabolism in which a person is incapable of metabolizing an amino acid, phenylalanine, which is a small molecule. In contrast to Hurler syndrome, it is a nonfatal disorder and one in which medical intervention has a definitive effect on the developmental outcome (Levy, 1979). The condition was originally identified in 1934 by Fölling as a cause of serious mental retardation accompanied by unusual chemicals in the urine. The implications were completely revised as Bickel discovered in 1953 that early dietary treatment could prevent the retardation. In 1962, Guthrie found that routine blood testing could detect the disease in newborn infants, so that a proper diet could be begun at once. Although PKU is also a relatively rare disease (about 1 in 14,000 births in the United States), it has accrued a special importance as the prototype of genetic disorders in which the retardation is completely preventable by prompt dietary treatment. Some details of management are

still in debate, but the outlook is very positive. An understanding and cooperative attitude by educators is essential if young people with PKU are to make good adjustment and optimal progress.

Etiology

PKU is an expression of the homozygous (double gene) abnormality in the production of an enzyme, phenylalanine hydroxylase, which is involved in the normal conversion of the amino acid phenylalanine to tyrosine. As with Hurler syndrome, both parents must be carriers of the partial enzymatic deficiency and their health is not altered by this state. Again, this recessively transmitted condition has a 25 percent risk of occurrence with each pregnancy of a marriage between carriers. No external circumstances modify this theoretical probability. It is felt that all of the features of PKU can be accounted for by the effects of an elevated blood level of phenylalanine, although the exact fashion in which this acts on the brain to produce retardation is not known. In addition to the usual or classical PKU syndrome, there are also several atypical or variant conditions somewhat related to it. These will not be discussed here.

Characteristics

It is necessary to consider separately the treated and untreated picture of the child with PKU. Since the widespread introduction of newborn screening for PKU and early dietary management, beginning in 1963, one seldom sees the natural or untreated condition in a school-age child. Compulsory testing is enforced in virtually all states of the United States, and compliance is very high. The untreated PKU child has a serious developmental delay, reaching a stable and irreversible level of mental retardation, occasionally mild but usually severe. It had been noted that these children were characteristically blond (in contrast to their siblings), might be troubled with eczema, and that their urine had an unusual mousey odor.

On the other hand, the child who has been treated with the proper diet, begun early and followed carefully, has a normal appearance, growth, and general health. Intelligence is characteristically fully normal, but school progress may be hampered by mild impairment of perceptual motor functioning (i.e., performance IQ less than verbal IQ, visual and fine motor coordination problems) and, occasionally, language development. Behavioral or adjustment difficulties may result from the challenge of regular medical handling, the special diet, and the learning difficulties. With good guidance to the child and his family, and appropriate educational support, these issues are not serious. When one looks at the children attending a modern PKU clinic, one sees a splendid, attractive group of young people.

Diagnosis

In current times, the diagnosis of PKU is signaled by the identification of an abnormal "blood spot" (Figure 22–2) in the mass testing programs performed on all newborn babies while they are still in the maternity unit. This detection effort is viewed as a public health function which protects the rights of infants and families. When a concerning result is noted, the child is retested with more precise methods, using several **assays** to evaluate the blood phenylalanine level. Measurement of the specific enzyme involved is not possible in the blood; a biopsy of the liver would be required, but this is not necessary in classical PKU.

Clinics that see large numbers of children with mental retardation of unknown origin commonly retest their blood or urine for phenylalanine elevation. One very rarely encounters a "missed" child for whom some logistical complication prevented the usual newborn screening. At present, prenatal diagnosis of PKU is not possible.

Treatment

The central component of successful treatment of the child born with PKU is a strict diet that is nearly free of the amino acid, phenylalanine (Figure 22–3). This involves extensive restriction of protein-containing foods, such as milk, cheese, meat, fish, breads, and cereals. A specially prepared formula, in which phenylalanine has been eliminated, is supplied to the family. (The formula is usually paid for with public funds.) The diet is adjusted as the months proceed, based on the control of blood phenylalanine levels (measured on filter-paper blood "spots" that are mailed in, or more accurately on blood tests during clinic visits), with liberalization of dietary ingredients geared to the child's tolerance. Needless to say, this is a stressful concept for the family to accept, but the thoughtful attentions of a good nutritionist assist in the adjustment. Accommodation is usually achieved in the first weeks of life, with gratification felt by the family from the knowledge of the treatment goals. Various dietary cookbooks assist in maintaining an interesting intake, but social challenges begin as the child reaches the age where he is more often out of the household. Until recently, the diet was usually terminated in the three to six year age group because it was felt that brain maturation was then adequate to tolerate elevated blood phenylalanine levels. Now, most clinics are advising continuing the diet indefinitely, including during the school years, because early discontinuation may not be entirely safe (Waisbren, Schnell, & Levy, 1980).

The guidance of child and family in the management of PKU treatment is preferably carried out in an

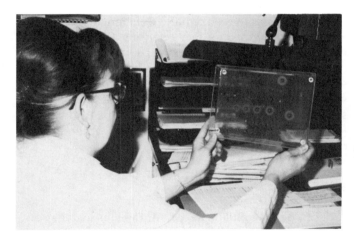

Figure 22–2   Mass Testing of All Infants for PKU. Inspection of a Guthrie Bacterial Inhibition Assay plate on which blood specimens from newborn infants have been placed. A positive result, indicating the presence of PKU, is seen in the upper right-hand corner. Other specimens are from normal infants, plus a row of standard control discs in the center of the plate.

Source: Dr. Harvey Levy, Massachusetts State Laboratory Institute.

Figure 22–3   The Principal Elements of a Diet for a Child With PKU. These include special formula materials (Lofenalac R or Phenyl-free R) and specified amounts of low-protein fruits, vegetables, and juices, such as those pictured. Low-protein grain products (Aprotein R, Dietetic Paygel R) may also be used.

Source: Rosanne Howard and Frances Rohr, Developmental Evaluation Clinic.

interdisciplinary setting in a medical center. These facilities exist in most major metropolitan areas. At the center the growing knowledge about the syndrome can be shared, psychological testing can be accomplished regularly, and group sessions can aid in personal reassurance. Late institution of dietary therapy may be required for the child whose diagnosis was missed in infancy. In these cases, the effects are beneficial but do not duplicate those achieved by treatment begun in the first weeks of life.

A new problem is emerging as significant numbers of young women with treated PKU are reaching the child-bearing age. It is known that maternal PKU involves a high degree of risk for the fetus, who would not in himself have PKU but would be adversely affected by the high blood phenylalanine level of the mother during pregnancy. Such babies are often born with microcephaly and may be retarded. It is hoped that dietary treatment in the mother before conception and in planned pregnancies will prevent this unfortunate outcome, but to date insufficient experience exists to be certain of this.

Prognosis

As mentioned, with ideal management the outlook for the child with PKU is excellent. However, ideal management is a large assignment. The child's parents must be diligent about maintaining the diet and attentive to clinical problems in general. Furthermore, the growing child is faced with dietary restrictions that can be significantly stressful. The disorder is not life threatening and treatment assures a positive outcome. Regrettably, the young woman with PKU has an extra burden as she anticipates her own adult life.

Educational Implications

Children with treated PKU will attend regular classes. As mentioned, many of them may need some assistance because of mild delays in learning. They may have some difficulty in spatial relationships, timed tests, and arithmetic (Koff, Boyle, & Pueschel, 1977). Verbal instructions may be easier for them, and occupational therapy may offer useful support. The children have difficulty concentrating, and have often been described as immature or hyperactive. An underlying cause may be a deficit in short-term memory. Like many other students, they will usually develop compensatory mechanisms as the years proceed.

Food during school hours can present a particular challenge. The older, well adjusted child will learn to cope with lunches brought from home or selective use of the school's cafeteria. Parties and other special occasions can be an added pressure, but some mild lapses are probably justified. The family, the child, the school, and the clinic can hopefully find a common philosophy for dealing with these matters (Henderson, Trahms, & Berlow, 1980).

Underlying the education of children with PKU is a need for resolution of basic feelings. The child is inherently stigmatized, yet looks normal and deserves to be considered as an intact person. A balance must be achieved between the tendency to blame all problems on the genetic disorder, whether justified or not, and the need to be sympathetic to a somewhat special situation. It seems fair to assume that if the adults around the child impart their belief in his basic normalcy and independence, he will work out the personal details successfully. For the child to declare that he has a food allergy is a useful defense. Discussion of PKU in biology or food science courses is an option on which the child deserves to be consulted, to determine how frankly he wishes to expose his own uniqueness. Counseling in these areas can be coordinated between the clinic and school.

SUMMARY

The area of the "inborn errors of metabolism" represents another instance wherein the clinician and the educator have common concerns regarding support to the child with special needs. These needs can be quite complex. In the circumstances of the two inherited diseases discussed here, Hurler syndrome and PKU, there are widely different biologic implications from the respective enzymatic deficiencies. The child with Hurler syndrome faces serious and progressive cerebral (and somatic) handicaps, and his educator must adapt to limited goals. The child with PKU should be assumed to have full opportunities for personal progress, but requires an empathetic support system. Current research is enlarging the understanding of the mechanisms of these and other genetic disorders.

REFERENCES

Crocker, A. C., & Cullinane, M. M. Families under stress: The diagnosis of Hurler's syndrome. *Postgraduate Medicine,* 1972, *51,* 223–229.

Henderson, R. A., Trahms, C. M., & Berlow, S. *PKU and the schools.* Washington, D.C.: U.S. Department of Health and Human Services, 1980. (DHHS Publication No. [HSA] 80-5233)

Koff, E., Boyle, P., & Pueschel, S. M. Perceptual-motor functioning in children with phenylketonuria. *American Journal of Diseases of Children,* 1977, *131,* 1084–1087.

Levy, H. L. Treatment of phenylketonuria. In C. B. Bartsocas & C. J. Papadatos (Eds.), *The management of genetic disorders.* New York: Alan R. Liss, Inc., 1979.

McKusick, V. A., Neufeld, E. F., & Kelly, T. E. The muco-polysaccharide storage diseases. In J. B. Stanbury, J. B. Wyngaarden, & D. S. Fredrickson (Eds.), *The metabolic basis of inherited disease.* New York: McGraw-Hill, 1978.

Waisbren, S. E., Schnell, R. R., & Levy, H. L. Diet termination in children with phenylketonuria: A review of psychological assessments used to determine outcome. *Journal of Inherited Metabolic Disorders,* 1980, *3,* 149–153.

Virgil Hanson, M.D., is professor in the Department of Pediatrics at the School of Medicine, University of Southern California, Los Angeles, and head of the Division of Rheumatology and Rehabilitation at Children's Hospital of Los Angeles.

This paper was supported in part by grants from the Southern California chapter of the Arthritis Foundation and the Bureau of Community Health Services, Office for Maternal and Child Health, U.S. Public Health Services, Department of Health and Human Resources, MCT Project 991.

Juvenile rheumatoid arthritis (JRA) is a form of chronic arthritis that occurs in children and is a major cause of crippling in the United States today. The fact that chronic arthritis occurs in children comes as a shock to most people. However, there are many syndromes associated with chronic arthritis that affect children and adolescents. Most of these have overlapping features. With rapidly advancing knowledge, the definiton and classification of these syndromes

CHAPTER 23

Juvenile Rheumatoid Arthritis

have become the subject of controversy. However, JRA is the most common and can serve well to illustrate the problems of classification and management for the group as a whole. Out of the ferment, some new names have been proposed for JRA and now appear with some regularity in medical writings: juvenile chronic polyarthritis, juvenile chronic arthritis, and juvenile arthritis. These terms have all been used as somewhat synonymous with JRA, although they are not equivalent.

JRA is characterized by chronic or chronically recurrent inflammation of the joints and, to a lesser extent, other tissues of the body. The nature of arthritis is such that the severity of the symptoms fluctuate widely from morning to afternoon, from day to day, week to week, or month to month. How then can one plan the educational program for a child with JRA, a disease that, especially in its early years, may be so variable in its effect on the child? The objectives of this chapter are to briefly describe the underlying disease process, its variable clinical manifestations, the general approach to treatment, and some of the problems that may be significant in school.

ETIOLOGY

Before delving deeply into etiology, it is worthwhile to review the structure and function of joints. The more than 500 joints in the body are divided into two major classes: diarthrodial and synarthrotic. *Diarthrodial* joints allow angular motion about a fulcrum of two or more opposing bone ends, separated from each other by joint space and surrounded by synovial lining. *Synarthrotic* joints have no joint space. The bone ends are joined by fibrous tissue and allow, at most, only a few degrees of motion. The diarthrodial joints are the more important in JRA.

The major anatomic elements of a diarthrodial joint are shown diagrammatically in Figure 23–1. Each element shown is important to the joint and is affected directly or indirectly by the arthritis. The joint space is exaggerated in the diagram. In fact, the cartilage surfaces are separated by only a very thin film

of joint fluid. Motion occurs by sliding of one cartilage surface over another. The cartilage layer is not calcified and is at most only a few millimeters thick, but provides the smooth resilient surface essential to joint function. The synovial lining (Figure 23–2), normally only one or two cells thick, encloses the joint space and secretes the joint fluid, which nourishes and lubricates the cartilage. Immediately below the synovial lining is a layer of loose connective tissue with a few small blood vessels and fibroblasts (cells that make collagen fibers). The capsule is composed of intertwined collagen fibers and is relatively thick to hold the joint together. Its function is supported by specialized fibrous ligaments composed of collagenous tissue that can stretch sufficiently to accommodate moderate twists and strains. The muscles and their tendons are outside the joint structure but provide the power for joint movement and hold the joint in any selected position.

Arthritis literally means inflammation of the joints. Although inflammation is an important part of the body's defense and healing mechanisms (Hanson, 1981), if it persists for too long, the process will result in further injury to the inflamed tissue. The inflammatory system is outlined, in a simplified form, in Figure 23–3. One should note that the processes of tissue repair are part of the system and are initiated early.

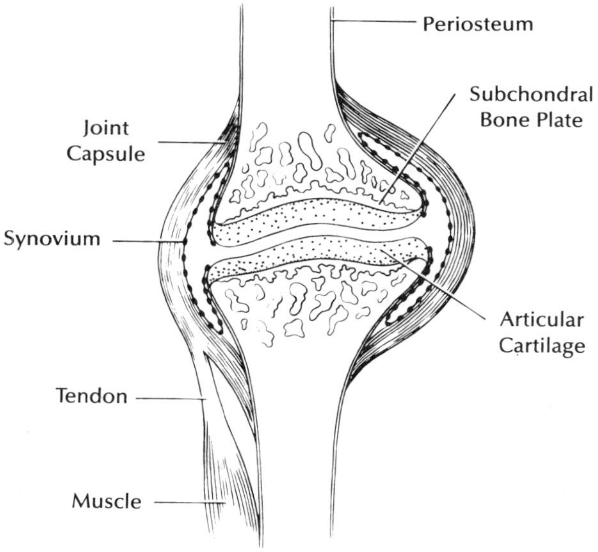

Figure 23–1 A Diarthrodial Joint. The single layer of cells lining the joint cavity is designated here as synovium which usually also includes the loose connective tissue (not shown) between the capsule and the lining cells.

Source: The Arthritis Foundation.

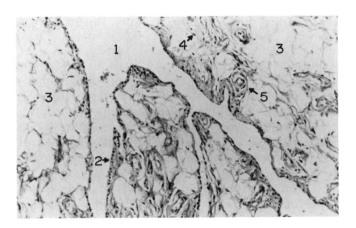

Figure 23–2 Synovial (Joint Lining) Magnified 100 Times. Around the cartilage margins the synovial tissue projects into the joint space in villous folds. The lining cells are flattened and most easily identified by their dark nuclei.
1: Joint space.
2: Lining cell.
3: Connective tissue.
4: Fibroblast.
5: Blood vessel.

Source: The Arthritis Foundation.

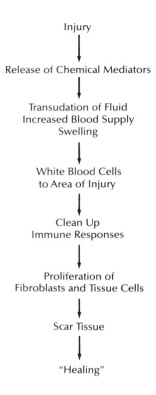

Injury

↓

Release of Chemical Mediators

↓

Transudation of Fluid
Increased Blood Supply
Swelling

↓

White Blood Cells
to Area of Injury

↓

Clean Up
Immune Responses

↓

Proliferation of
Fibroblasts and Tissue Cells

↓

Scar Tissue

↓

"Healing"

Figure 23–3 Tissue Injury, Inflammation, and Immunity. Tissue injury from any cause (trauma, chemicals, infection, or immune reaction) sets in motion the processes of inflammation. These vary in detail according to the cause of injury, but in general proceed through these steps. In the rheumatic diseases the healing steps are often prevented or delayed by frequent reactivation of the early phases by immune reactions.

In general, inflammation can be initiated by any tissue injury; the most common are probably minor infections or minor scratches from which recovery is rapid and complete. However, even the most sophisticated studies have failed to reveal evidence of infection in the inflamed joints or tissues of patients with JRA, nor can trauma be implicated as a primary cause.

Through extensive research, the immune mechanisms of the body have been identified as the major factors in sustaining rheumatoid inflammation. Thus the disease is, at least in part, autoimmune, that is, the body's own immune system is causing the injury. One or more parts of the body become the target of the immune response which can, in turn, trigger the inflammation mechanism before the tissue has been injured. The processes of inflammation are inextricably intertwined with those of immunity. Furthermore, once set in motion, each bodily defense system may activate others. To this date, no one has found the cause that initiates the autoimmune inflammation of JRA.

One effect of inflammation is swelling due to an outpouring of fluid from the capillaries into the joint space and the surrounding tissues. The blood supply is increased. If one could look inside the joint, the lining would appear red and thickened like a sore on the skin. With the fluid comes a vast army of white blood cells of all kinds, taking up positions in the tissue just below the lining and in the joint fluid (Figure 23–4). These components drive the symptoms of disease and the damage to the joint structures. Muscle function is profoundly affected by inflammation of joint tissue. In the early stages, this effect is the more significant factor limiting the child's capabilities because it results in morning stiffness, atrophy of muscles, and contractures.

The damage or actual breakdown of the various components of the joint generally takes a good deal longer. It is accomplished more slowly by the white blood cells that pour into the joint tissues and spaces. Some of their products amplify the inflammatory and immune responses, but many are enzymes that break down the structural elements of cartilage, bone, and

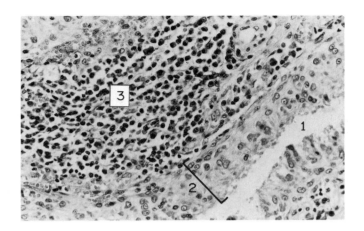

Figure 23—4 Inflamed Synovial Tissue Magnified About 400 Times. The joint space (1) is between two villous folds with a lining layer (2) now five to six cells thick. The tissue below the lining layer is crowded with white blood cells (3).

fibrous supporting structures. At the cellular and biochemical level, in general, there is an inhibitor for every activator. Thus the dissolution of joint tissue is slowed or even reversed for variable periods of time. These inhibitors and the early activation of tissue repair give rise to the widely fluctuating signs and symptoms in the early stages of JRA and, along with proper treatment, enable the majority of children to reach adult life with little or no disability. For many, however, the net effect of a continuing cycle of inflammation then inhibition and treatment, results in slowly accumulating damage to joint structures that ultimately exceed the body's capacity for repair. The consequence is long-lasting disability and deformity of moderate to severe degree.

Even though the initiating cause of JRA has not been identified, it is clear that susceptibility is not uniform for all children. JRA is not directly inherited, but those children who have certain inherited markers on the surfaces of their cells are significantly more likely to develop this disease. Girls are more frequently affected than boys in a ratio of 3:2, and JRA is more common among whites than other races. Almost any disease results from the interaction among an inciting agent or agents, the constitution of the host, and environmental factors. There is evidence that psychological and social (environmental) factors may influence the clinical expression of the disease and its ultimate outcome, although these factors are not directly causes. Among children between birth and age eighteen, 1 in 500 or 1,000 have some form of chronic arthritis; one-half to two-thirds of these children have JRA, but accurate prevalence figures are still not available.

CHARACTERISTICS

Children who develop JRA generally have enjoyed excellent health prior to the onset of their disease. The first symptoms are usually (a) pain and swelling in one or more joints, (b) stiffness with pain on motion when arising in the morning, and (c) in about 25 percent of the children, fever (temperature greater than 38 degrees C or 100 degrees F). The fever is an intermittent daily occurrence with temperatures rising from normal in the morning to abnormal in the afternoon or evening. When these daily temperatures rise to very high levels (103–105 degrees F), they indicate one of the subtypes of JRA. Here it is important to note that JRA begins with at least three different modes of onset, which delineate the major subtypes: pauciarticular, polyarticular, and systemic onset JRA.

Briefly, the *pauciarticular* onset is limited to those children with fewer than five joints affected during the first six months of disease. Ultimately, about a fourth of these children will develop arthritis in many more joints and resemble those with polyarticular onset. *Systemic* onset JRA is characterized by daily high temperature rises (103–105 degrees F) and frequently transient rash as well as other general signs. Generalized aches and pains are common and often severe in the beginning. The fever may recur for weeks or even many months before objective evidence of arthritis is detectable. The fevers eventually subside or are brought under medical control but the arthritis persists and progresses independently of the fever. In *polyarticular* onset JRA, many joints are involved in the first few months with a predilection for the small joints in the hands and fingers. The onset is usually less sudden than in the other two types. Early symptoms are pain and stiffness, particularly in the morning, and the gradual development of joint swelling.

Significant extraarticular complications are much more common in children with pauciarticular or systemic onset JRA than in those with polyarticular disease. About 10–20 percent of children with pauciarticular onset develop chronic iridocyclitis, an almost symptomless inflammation of the anterior chamber of the eye. Significant and sometimes severe impairment of vision in the affected eye or eyes is a potential consequence. Thus frequent ophthalmologic examinations are essential. Iridocyclitis also occurs in the other two subtypes of JRA, but only rarely. Pericarditis, inflammation of the pocket around the heart, is the most significant complication of the systemic group. Although it can be life threatening, pericarditis responds readily to treatment and does not result in permanent impairment of cardiac function.

Commonly, all detectable signs of disease completely disappear for months or occasionally even for years in the pauciarticular and systemic subtypes. Although not complications in themselves, these remissions and exacerbations serve to emphasize the variability of the disease and are significant in educational planning. Thus a child who seems to have recovered completely may be handicapped suddenly again by his arthritis.

Once the arthritis is established, the cardinal symptoms, signs, and limitations due to the arthritis are similar in all three subtypes of JRA. Morning stiffness is a characteristic early symptom and may last well into the school day. The child awakes to find the affected extremities stiff and difficult to move in any direction, and usually painful to move. With persistent attempts to stand, move, and walk about, the joints gradually loosen until normal or near normal motion is possible. The joints may loosen up within a few minutes or take many hours. They may stiffen again after prolonged periods of sitting (e.g., in a theater or classroom) and again require a few minutes before useful motion is restored to the affected joints.

In some joints, the loosening process is only partial. Full range of motion cannot be restored during the waking hours. The child must walk or work with one or more bent joints. In such cases, contractures (inability to straighten the joints completely) develop, particularly in the absence of appropriate treatment (Figure 23–5). These contractures are usually progressive so that the degree of flexion contracture may increase to the point where a function such as walking is impossible. The joint may also become frozen in its flexed position so that little or no motion is possible in any direction even though significant damage to the joint structures has not occurred. These findings reflect the profound effect of joint inflammation on muscle function previously noted.

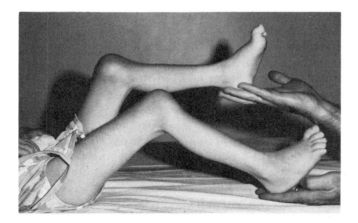

Figure 23–5   Typical Contractures of the Knees. This child has flexion contractures of the knees, which cannot be straightened past the position shown. The muscles are small and atrophic.

With or without conscious perception, the noxious stimuli arising from the inflamed joints activate complex sensory-motor reflex mechanisms, which act to limit joint motion. Physiologically, the mechanisms are set to favor positions of flexion. The tendency to flexion is reinforced by the fact that straightening the joint increases pressure within the capsule, thus increasing pain. The net effect is inhibition of the extensor muscles in favor of the stronger flexors, again encouraging a flexed position. Understanding these relationships is the key to understanding most of the problems that the child experiences during the school day.

DIAGNOSIS

The basic criteria for the diagnosis of JRA are (a) persistence of active arthritis in at least one joint for six weeks or longer, (b) onset before sixteen years of age, and (c) exclusion of other causes of chronic arthritis (Bernstein & Lehman, 1980). The first criterion separates JRA, a chronic long-lasting condition, from the many transient kinds of arthritis that affect children (e.g., rheumatic fever). With this in mind, it is apparent that the diagnosis of JRA can only be probable during the first six weeks. The second criterion defines juvenile by a specific age, based on the fact that most children will have completed most of the changes of puberty by age sixteen.

The third criterion, exclusion of other diseases that may cause arthritis, is important because JRA is a member of a family of diseases that share overlapping features. In the past, this group of diseases has been referred to variously, though inappropriately, as collagen-vascular diseases, collagen diseases, or connective tissue diseases. They are probably best termed immunoinflammatory diseases as they share the immunoinflammatory nature of JRA. A partial list of the immunoinflammatory diseases and other important conditions to be excluded is shown in Table 23–1.

The task of exclusion or differential diagnosis is not quite as formidable as the list might imply, however. Most diseases are recognized by a typical constellation of signs and symptoms. In JRA these include the arthritis, morning stiffness, a tendency to improve during the day, pattern of fever, **evanescent** rash, and other findings associated with the major subtypes previously described. Abnormal laboratory test results are common, but none is specific for JRA. In particular, the presence or absence of rheumatoid factor in the blood does not confirm or deny the diagnosis of JRA. Rheumatoid factor is an interesting substance. It is an antibody to the antibody that is strongly associated with severe rheumatoid arthritis

Table 23–1   Differential Diagnosis of Arthritis in Childhood

1. *Immunoinflammatory Diseases*
    a. Juvenile rheumatoid arthritis
    b. Rheumatic fever
    c. Systemic lupus erythematosus
    d. Henoch-Schonlein Purpura
    e. Systemic vasculitis
    f. Erythema nodosum
    g. Dermatomyositis
    h. Scleroderma
    i. Mixed connective tissue disease
    j. Ankylosing spondylitis
    k. Ulcerative colitis
    l. Regional enteritis
    m. Psoriasis
    n. Sarcoid
    o. Reiter's syndrome
    p. Stevens-Johnson syndrome
    q. Polyarteritis nodosa
    r. Kawazaki's disease
2. *Infection in Joints*
3. *Heritable Disorders*
4. *Neoplastic Diseases*
5. *Miscellaneous*

in adult life, but also is found in many other diseases. It is found in about a half of the children with polyarticular JRA, but rarely in the other subtypes.

The seemingly diverse clinical syndromes at onset of JRA are held together by a common histopathology (i.e., by the findings observed when the joint lining tissue is studied under the microscope; see Figure 23–4). Here one can see that the synovial lining cells have been stimulated to proliferate. The tissues just below the lining are filled with aggregates of lymphocytes and plasma cells, widely distributed macrophages, and here and there, collections of granulocytes; all of which are derived from the white blood cells circulating in the bloodstream. These microscopic findings, although not specific to JRA, suggest this diagnosis. A biopsy of synovial tissue is sometimes justified in doubtful cases. In the final analysis, the diagnosis of JRA is based upon clinical judgement of all the evidence obtained from the patient's history, physical examination, special examinations such as X rays, and laboratory tests.

TREATMENT

Many new remedies for adult and juvenile rheumatoid arthritis are reported each year in the news media. It is a reasonable hypothesis that their effectiveness is in inverse proportion to their number.

Most of the nostrums sold in the United States are harmless unless they divert the patient's and family's attention from the steps necessary to avert or minimize contractures and deformity. Some of the medications obtained from other countries, however, contain cortisonelike compounds or other potent medications that may be harmful when their administration is uncontrolled. Many books have been published that advocate various diets for the treatment of adult and juvenile rheumatoid arthritis. There is no evidence that either juvenile or adult rheumatoid arthritis is affected by diet, except adversely when the diets are deficient in essential nutrients. Another frequently advocated form of therapy is the administration of large doses of various vitamins. Very large doses of some vitamins are toxic to the body. Again, there is no evidence that large doses of even the safe vitamins in any way affect the course of chronic arthritis.

In contrast, carefully controlled studies of treatments designed to affect the systems of inflammation and immunity consistently show beneficial effects. These treatments are effective only as long as they are continued, however, and no cure has yet been found for juvenile or adult rheumatoid arthritis. Rather than cure, the goals of therapy are to bring the child to adult life capable of economic and social independence. Ninety percent of children with JRA can achieve these goals with a well-designed treatment program, which includes medication, physical and occupational therapy, orthopedic surgery when needed, counseling, and education.

The objectives of treatment are (a) to reduce inflammation in the joints, (b) to prevent contractures, weakness, and deformity through a program of physical management, (c) to correct contractures and deformities when they occur, and (d) to provide to the child the educational skills and motivation to cope with this disease (Hollister, 1981). The best results should come from informed health and education professionals who provide coordinated services. For this last purpose, an efficient and effective communication system needs to be designed.

Medication

The suppression of inflammation is important to reduce discomfort, improve motion, and enhance the effectiveness of the other therapies. Medications are usually required to accomplish this. The four principal classes of medications prescribed and a partial listing of the commonly used drugs in each class is shown in Table 23–2. The classes are listed in order of increasing toxicity and, therefore, decreasing frequency of use. The first drugs prescribed are those that have a prompt effect on the arthritis.

Table 23—2 Medical Treatment of Juvenile Rheumatoid Arthritis

Initial treatment:
 Aspirin
 Tolmetin
 Naproxen
 Fenoprofen*
 Ketoprofen*
 Sulindac*
Prescribed when above inadequate:
 Gold salts (injection)
 D-Penicillamine*
 Hydroxychloroquine*
Prescribed for severe complications, rarely for very severe arthritis:
 Cortisonelike compounds
Prescribed last for unresponsive destructive arthritis:
 Immunosuppressive drugs**

 *Drugs currently in controlled testing for effectiveness in JRA.
 **Use still considered experimental.

In the treatment of JRA aspirin is far more than simply a pain killer; it has very significant anti-inflammatory effects, especially when given regularly and in relatively large doses. Aspirin in these large doses is not always well tolerated by the children. In these cases, other drugs in this class may be prescribed, although only two are fully approved for use with children under fourteen years of age. These drugs must be taken regularly to achieve the best results.

When the fast-acting drugs are not adequate, the second class of slowly acting drugs are often added. The soluble salts of gold are the most commonly prescribed but they must be given by injection, usually weekly for the first few months and then every two to three weeks for years. Because of the potential toxicity to the bone marrow or kidneys, laboratory tests are required before each injection. However, treatment with gold salts will result in complete remission of all signs of the arthritis in some of the children who have severe disease and even allow for some healing of damaged cartilage surfaces. Again, the treatment is only effective while continued. Relapses are common within weeks to months after discontinuing the medication. The use of cortisonelike compounds and immunosuppressive drugs is limited to very severe or special cases.

Physical and Occupational Therapy

The program of physical management is equally important. It includes specific exercises and activities of daily living to be done each day to improve or maintain strength or range of motion. It also includes the application of special treatments for special problems (e.g., warm baths for morning stiffness, icebags on immobile joints, and cylinder casts with frequent changes to reduce contractures). The forces that favor contractures and shape the deformities of the future, however, are at work constantly, including during the school day. To be most effective, the physical therapy plan should include constant treatments to counter these forces, a program that requires cooperation by all members of the team.

During the day, a provision for frequent changes in position is important because prolonged sitting strongly reinforces the tendency to flexion contractures at the hips and knees. The opportunity to stand or move about at 20–30 minute intervals during the day helps to prevent the return of the stiffness of immobility, which is so prominent in the mornings. The opportunity to lie prone (on the belly) for 30 minutes or an hour two or three times daily is an effective way to combat hip flexion contractures. The opportunity to work in a standing position as well as in a sitting position is also very helpful. The use of wheelchairs should be avoided because of the constant sitting position. Light-weight plastic splints are often prescribed for daytime use, particularly on the wrists, for the same purpose (Figure 23–6). The physical management program is active therapy, but there is a limit to the tolerance of inflamed joints for motion. Brief periods of rest during the day are often helpful.

Orthopedic Surgery

A wide variety of procedures are available to the orthopedic surgeon to aid in treating arthritis and correcting deformity. Nonsurgical treatments include the application of specialized mechanical devices to prevent or reduce contractures, and braces and other orthotic devices to improve function. Surgical treatments include release of severely contractured tissues, repair or transfer of tendons, selective removal or fusion of bone, and total joint replacements (Figure 23–7). The ability to walk is of major importance in the habilitation of arthritic children. The development of total artificial hips and knees to replace these joints has been a major advance in the treatment of severe JRA. The replacements, however, must be deferred until the growth of the affected parts has been completed.

Counseling

The psychology of chronic physical illness is an important consideration in the treatment of JRA, but facile generalizations about this aspect of treatment should be considered suspect. A number of recent studies suggest that positive adaptation is more the rule than the exception and that, in fact, children with

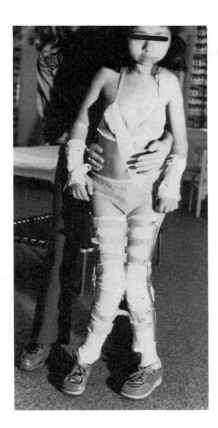

Figure 23—6   Plastic Wrist Splints. The wrist splints are made of strong light-weight plastic as are the molded shells forming the posterior part of the braces on the legs. The patient has had severe JRA for ten years.

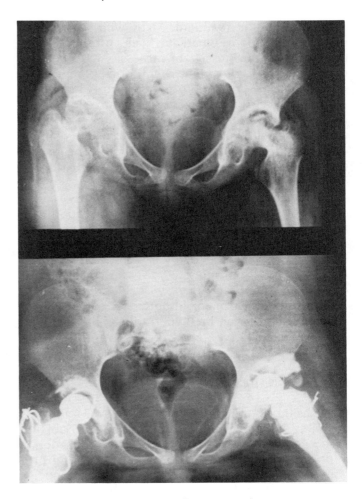

Figure 23—7   X Rays of a Hip Replacement. X rays of the hip joints just before and after total hip replacement. In the upper picture the head of the femur and the acetabulum (pelvic socket) are both grossly distorted due to the effects of JRA. In the lower picture the metal replacements of the femoral heads stand out sharply. The replaced acetabulum is made of a special plastic that does not show on X rays.

JRA are as emotionally healthy as their physically normal peers. Likewise, follow-up studies of young adults indicate that their educational, employment, and social achievements are comparable. Counseling and education for the family and for the child when old enough are important to prevent the development of unnecessary dependency and to secure the best cooperation with the treatment program. The presence of a child with chronic arthritis in the family does impose added strain on the family relationships and adds costs in terms of both time and money, which are a drain on the family's resources. The aid of the social worker is invaluable to help families deal with these problems. Pre-existing psychological problems within the child's home will be accentuated by these demands. Psychological or psychiatric treatment is important in some cases.

PROGNOSIS

Approximately 70 percent of children with JRA will reach high school graduation or age eighteen with minimal or no limitations of ordinary activities, pro-

viding they have received reasonably good care (Hanson, Kornreich, Bernstein, King, & Singsen, 1977). This limited statement of prognosis leaves many questions unanswered, particularly those of recovery, relapse, and the impact on adult life. The percentage of children who recover completely (i.e., they have no stigmata of JRA of any kind and no future recurrence) is unknown. Relapses after many years of apparent complete recovery are known to occur in adults in their thirties. In other cases, the apparently insignificant disease smoulders on with slowly progressive joint damage. For these reasons, the lifelong prognosis of JRA is not known.

Most patients who have continuing or recurrent JRA in adult life will continue to function well if they have appropriate treatment. Many with severe crippling disease adapt remarkably well and successfully manage jobs, businesses, or professional careers, as well as homes and families. Reproductive capacity is not impaired. Survival into middle age is essentially unimpaired, although the risk of death due to disease-related causes is somewhat greater in the systemic onset subtype (2 percent within ten years of onset) than in the other two subtypes. The risk of uncorrectable crippling is probably less than 10 percent during the first twenty years after onset.

One can summarize the prognosis for those children with JRA who have had reasonably good care and treatment as follows: The outlook is good for function but unknown for complete recovery. The risk of relapse after recovery is significant well into adult life. Slowly progressive disease may smoulder on in many patients for many years without a predictable endpoint. Of major importance, even severely affected patients can be helped to lead independent and productive lives.

EDUCATIONAL IMPLICATIONS

Quite aside from mandates of Public Law 94–142, it is desirable that children with JRA attend school full time whenever possible. The totality of education is important to their habilitation. Home teaching programs should be limited to periods of absolute necessity. Intellectual function is not impaired by the disease. The prevalence of mental retardation may be less than in the general population. Furthermore, the children's motivation to attend school is strong and they usually do not exploit their symptoms to avoid attendance.

The problems of the child with JRA in school grow out of the nature and characteristics of their disease as described: the waxing and waning inflammation, the rapidly varying symptoms, the reflex neuromuscular adaptations, and the damage to joint structures. Fever and fatigue are manifestations of inflammation that may present problems. The daily temperature rise of 2–3 degrees F in some children with JRA is often well tolerated. However, in the past, regulations in some school districts have excluded these children from attendance. Exceptions should be made for arthritic children because these mild fevers are not contagious and may recur daily for months and sometimes even years. A ready channel of communication between the rheumatology consultant and teacher or nurse can be helpful in resolving problems in connection with such fevers.

Another manifestation of extensive inflammation is early fatigue. In these cases, much of the body's energy stores are diverted to combat inflammation, with little left over for ordinary activities. If a mid-morning rest period is not possible, a shorter school day and reduced curriculum may be the best solution for such students and is preferable to home teaching programs. Within weeks or months the inflammation usually will be controlled with medication or will subside from natural causes. The patient will again be ready to assume a full academic load.

The neuromuscular adaptive mechanisms lead to problems of mobility. The persistence of morning stiffness into the school day may be prolonged by long bus rides to school or by the need to remain in the sitting position for prolonged periods in class. Movement when necessary often seems slow and painful, and the teacher may be confounded later in the day to see the student moving about or even running as if there were no arthritis. Here, understanding of the stiffness of immobility in JRA is helpful.

Loosening of the muscles and joints may require only a few minutes of active movement after a period of desk work, but the loosening period of five to fifteen minutes is often longer than the period normal children have for changing tasks or locations. In upper grades, where multiple classroom changes are usual, the student may be unable to reach the next class on time. However, the exercise in transit may have allowed for sufficient loosening so that no difficulty is evident on arrival in the next classroom. Some possible solutions to the problems of the stiffness of immobility may also help to reduce the tendency to contractures. The opportunity to work on a desklike surface while standing for fifteen to twenty minutes in the middle of any classroom hour would be of substantial benefit. This benefit would be increased by the opportunity to walk fifteen or twenty paces within any given classroom hour.

The complaint of pain in the joints is not a contraindication to school attendance or moderate activity except in extreme instances. Interestingly, complaints of pain are more frequent and of greater magnitude in adolescents (twelve years of age and older) than in grammar school or kindergarten pupils. They are also variable from day to day as well as from month to month. When pain is prominent, some reduction in required physical activities is indicated. The pain is most often noticed when changing positions. It frequently decreases, as does the stiffness of immobility, after a few minutes of motion.

Some modification of physical education activities is essential for most of the children with active arthritis. Many children with mild JRA can participate in regular physical education activities if minor modifications of the program or some degree of flexibility is acceptable. In general, tests of endurance or maximum performance as well as competitive running and jumping events should be avoided. If some flexibility is possible, the child's participation could be altered when the symptoms are increased. The child may continue to participate but as a scorekeeper, timekeeper, or umpire, rather than as an active competitor. Continued involvement in physical education is important to the child whenever his condition permits. Adaptive physical education programs are ideal, where available. In these programs, a group of activities graded for level of exercise stress can be prescribed.

The schoolchild with JRA might need casts, braces, splints, and various assistive devices. Temporary casts are sometimes used to help straighten joints. When applied to the lower extremities, these casts are usually adapted for walking, which is a desirable part of the treatment (Figure 23–8). The use of wheelchairs is to be avoided whenever possible as these strongly reinforce immobility and encourage hip and knee contractures, usually counteracting other efforts toward rehabilitation.

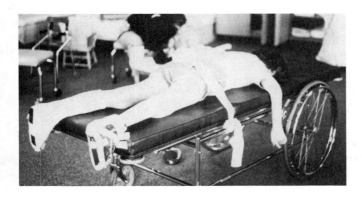

Figure 23—8 Temporary Casts on This Child's Feet Help Correct Contractures. Casts applied to the feet and ankles aid in correcting contractures. Walking plates are incorporated in the bottoms of the cast to facilitate walking. The patient is in prone position on a gurney cart to reduce hip flexion contractures.

SUMMARY

JRA is characterized by chronic inflammation in the joints and often other tissues of the body. This inflammation is sustained and enhanced by the patient's immune mechanisms and is, therefore, autoimmune in nature. However, the precipitating cause of the autoimmune reaction is unknown. The inflammation persists for many years and, in some cases, throughout life, but it varies in intensity, as do the resulting symptoms. Adaptive reflex neuromuscular mechanisms limit the motion of the joints and favor positions of flexion and flexion contractures. Long-lasting inflammation ultimately results in damage to the joint structures and deformity. Although there is no known cure for JRA, the children can be substantially helped with a comprehensive program of medications, physical and occupational therapy, and when indicated, surgery. With such a program, most children with JRA reach adult life with little or no disability. There is no significant intellectual impairment associated with the disease. Most of the problems that arise in school are related to the variable symptoms and limitations so characteristic of JRA. Understanding the nature of the disease and making minor adjustments in the classroom and physical education programs can be very helpful in the children's habilitation.

REFERENCES

Bernstein, B., & Lehman, T. J. A. Juvenile rheumatoid arthritis. In H. F. Conn & R. B. Conn, Jr. (Eds.), *Current diagnosis*. Philadelphia: W. B. Saunders, 1980.

Hanson, V. Systemic lupus erythematosus, dermatomyositis, scleroderma, and vasculitides in childhood. In W. Kelly, E. D. Harris, Jr., S. Ruddy, & C. B. Sledge (Eds.), *Textbook of rheumatology*. Philadelphia: W. B. Saunders, 1981.

Hanson, V., Kornreich, H., Bernstein, B., King, K. K., & Singsen, B. Prognosis of juvenile rheumatoid arthritis. *Arthritis and Rheumatism*, 1977, *20*, 279–284.

Hollister, J. R. Collagen vascular disease. In S. S. Gellis & B. M. Kagan (Eds.), *Current pediatric therapy*. Philadelphia: W. B. Saunders, 1981.

Eric H. Prosnitz, M.D., *is associate in the Department of Internal Medicine at the College of Medicine, The University of Arizona, Tucson, and medical director of the Artificial Kidney Center (Central), Dialysis Foundation of Southern Arizona, Tucson.*

The kidneys are a pair of organs lying behind the intestines at the level of the upper lumbar spine (Figure 24–1). Blood is supplied to each kidney by one or more arteries, which branch from the abdominal aorta. Blood that has been filtered by the kidney leaves via a vein that enters the vena cava. The ureter drains urine from the kidney to the bladder. Bladder urine is then excreted via the urethra.

The functioning units of the kidney are called nephrons (Figure 24–2). Each kidney has approximately one million nephrons. They are organized structurally to accomplish three major physiologic processes: filtration, reabsorption, and secretion (Brenner & Rector, 1981). Filtration takes place in the first part of the nephron, the glomerulus. Blood flows

CHAPTER

24

Kidney Disorders

into the glomerulus where water and solutes (substances dissolved in the water) move across a filter into the next part of the nephron, the proximal tubule. The filter prevents blood cells and blood proteins from leaving the bloodstream and entering the urine. However, water and many substances such as sodium, potassium, calcium, phosphorus, glucose, creatinine, and urea pass with relative ease through the filter. In fact, the volume of filtrate formed is very large, approximately 20 percent of the noncellular blood volume. If this volume of filtrate were simply excreted from the body as urine, the blood volume would rapidly diminish to levels unable to sustain life.

To prevent massive loss of body fluids into the urine, the filtrate flows through a long winding tubule that reabsorbs some water and solutes back into the

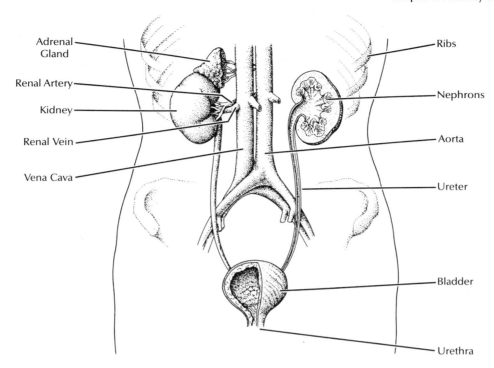

Figure 24—1   The Kidney

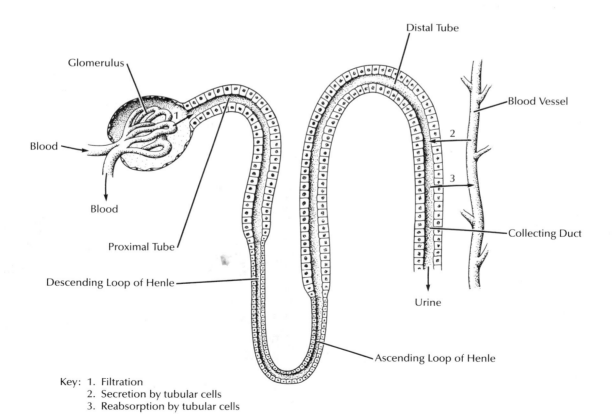

Key: 1. Filtration
     2. Secretion by tubular cells
     3. Reabsorption by tubular cells

Figure 24—2   The Nephron   2: Secretion by tubular cells
1: Filtration   3: Reabsorption by tubular cells

bloodstream. The tubule also acts to move substances from the bloodstream into the urine. This process is called secretion. The actions of the tubule are illustrated in Figure 24–2. The tubule is organized sequentially into a proximal tubule, the descending and ascending segments of the loop of Henle, the distal tubule, and the collecting duct. Each of these segments of the tubule are highly specialized to perform different types of reabsorption and secretion. Eventually, urine drains from the tubules into the ureter and to the bladder.

END STAGE KIDNEY DISEASE

Etiology

End stage kidney disease occurs when the glomeruli are no longer able to filter enough water and waste products from the bloodstream (Schrier, 1980). There are many causes of end stage kidney disease. The most common cause is glomerulonephritis, an inflammation of the glomeruli. (This disorder is discussed in detail later in this chapter.) Diabetes and hypertension are the next most common causes of end stage kidney failure. A less common cause is congenital abnormalities of the kidneys, particularly obstruction to the flow of urine and the presence of many **cysts** in the kidney. Urinary tract infections usually do not cause end stage kidney disease unless there is some other underlying problem. In the United States, there are approximately 50 people with end stage kidney disease in every million people.

Characteristics

Children with end stage kidney disease are short in stature and may appear younger if the underlying disease has been chronic. Anemia is very common and causes fatigue and shortness of breath. Because of disturbances in calcium and phosphorus metabolism, patients will often have bone pain and itching. Numbness, tingling, pain, and weakness in the arms and legs are also common. The patient usually has a poor appetite and may find meat particularly distasteful. Nausea and vomiting frequently occur. Water retention sometimes causes swelling of the face and extremities. Children are usually irritable and listless.

Diagnosis

The diagnosis of end stage kidney disease is made by measuring the levels of creatinine and urea in the blood. These levels are markedly elevated in end stage kidney disease. The cause of the kidney failure can be determined by examining urine under the microscope and by doing special X-ray studies of the kidneys and special blood tests.

Treatment

Initial treatment consists of special diets to control the amount of fluid, protein, and potassium that the patient ingests. Medications are also given to control blood pressure (which usually rises when the kidneys fail) and abnormalities in blood chemistries. Treatment with diet and medication is only a temporary measure. Eventually, dialysis or transplantation is required.

Two methods of dialysis are currently in use. These are hemodialysis and peritoneal dialysis. In hemodialysis, the patient's blood is cycled through a machine that has a synthetic filter. After the filter removes excess water and waste products, the blood is returned to the patient. Hemodialysis requires repetitive access to the patient's blood vessels. This access is established by connecting an artery and a vein through minor surgery in the patient's forearm or, less commonly, the upper arm or thigh (Figure 24–3). Hemodialysis is usually performed three times weekly with each dialysis treatment lasting three to four hours. This schedule can disrupt the patient's normal activities. It is sometimes feasible to train the child and a family member to perform the dialysis treatments at home at more convenient times. Also, dialysis is sometimes available after school or in the evening.

Peritoneal dialysis is performed by inserting a tube into the abdomen, filling the abdomen with a premixed solution, and then draining the solution from the abdomen. Removal of body wastes is accomplished by diffusion of these substances from abdominal blood vessels into the solution. This procedure takes six to eight hours but can be done at home by a family member as the child sleeps. Recently, con-

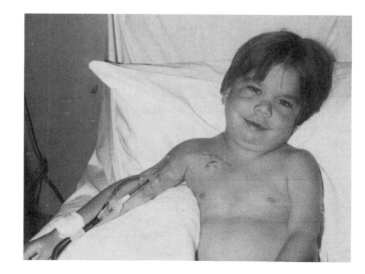

Figure 24–3 A Child Undergoing Hemodialysis

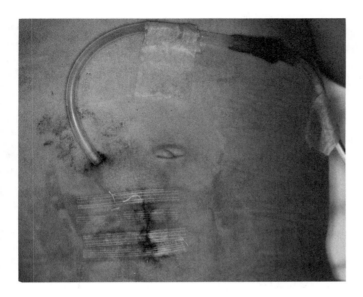

Figure 24—4 A Child Undergoing Chronic Ambulatory Peritoneal Dialysis (CAPD)

siderable success has been achieved with chronic ambulatory peritoneal dialysis (CAPD). With this technique, the abdominal tube is **sutured** into the abdominal wall and left in place indefinitely (Figure 24–4). The patient then can do self-dialysis throughout the day and night by attaching to the abdominal tube a small collapsible plastic bag filled with dialysis solution. The bag must be changed every eight hours. This takes about twenty minutes and can be done in any clean location where the patient can sit. CAPD allows the patient to go about daily activities with minimal disruption.

Although hemodialysis and peritoneal dialysis greatly improve the way the patient feels, they do not eliminate the adverse effects of end stage kidney disease. Most patients must remain on restricted diets and multiple medications. They may require periodic hospitalization. In addition, they must cope with physical and psychologic dependence on the dialysis machinery. Many physicians believe that kidney transplantation is preferable to hemodialysis or peritoneal dialysis for children. Donor kidneys may be obtained from cadavers or from living relatives. Kidneys from close relatives are less likely to be rejected, but still require that the transplant recipient receive long-term treatment with drugs that suppress the immune system and, unfortunately, make the patient more susceptible to infection.

Prognosis

It is not yet known whether dialysis can allow for a normal life span. However, many patients are doing well after ten or more years of dialysis. Most children

are treated by kidney transplantation. Approximately 80 percent of transplant recipients are alive ten years after the operation. Six years after the operation, approximately 70 percent of the transplanted kidneys still function. Successful transplantation results in excellent social and psychologic rehabilitation for most patients.

Educational Implications

The child with a well-functioning transplanted kidney usually is able to function intellectually and physically at the level of his or her peer group, although growth retardation may present psychological difficulties. The child being treated with dialysis will have more difficulties. Schooling may be interrupted by the dialysis procedure itself. Easy mental and physical fatigue may persist. Perhaps most importantly, the child will have to cope with a sense of chronic illness and dependency on persons and technology. Educators need to make sure that there are frequent communications between the child's teachers, nurses, dietitians, social workers, and physicians. Optimal care of the child requires continuing input by all of these professionals.

GLOMERULONEPHRITIS

Etiology

Glomerulonephritis is an inflammatory condition of the filtering units (glomeruli) of the kidney (see Figure 24–2). The inflammation may take one of many pathologic forms and may be caused by a wide variety of situations: viral and bacterial infections, drug reactions, systemic diseases such as rheumatoid arthritis, and primary inflammations of the kidney (Leaf & Cotran, 1976). Most types of glomerulonephritis occur when antigens and antibodies accumulate in the glomeruli. In many cases, we do not yet understand what causes these immune complexes to accumulate.

Characteristics

The exact characteristics of acute glomerulonephritis vary according to the underlying cause. Acute poststreptococcal glomerulonephritis is the classic example of childhood glomerulonephritis. The kidney disease occurs one to three weeks following a streptococcal bacterial infection of the throat or skin. As many as 50 percent of affected children will have no symptoms. The most common nonspecific symptoms are malaise and anorexia (loss of appetite). Other characteristics include fever and edema (swelling), which may be quite prominent around the eyes. The urine almost always contains blood and proteins and may turn the color of Coca-Cola. Moderate to severe **hypertension** frequently occurs.

Diagnosis

The diagnosis of glomerulonephritis is made by examining the urine under the microscope and measuring blood levels of creatinine and urea. Determining the type of glomerulonephritis requires a careful history, various specific blood tests and, often, a kidney biopsy (microscopic examination of tissues or cells removed from a living patient).

Treatment

Treatment depends entirely on the underlying cause of the glomerulonephritis and its severity. In many cases, no treatment is necessary. In other cases, multiple medications and even short-term dialysis are required.

Prognosis

As with treatment, prognosis is determined by the underlying cause. Poststreptococcal glomerulonephritis generally resolves within three weeks and only rarely results in significant long-term kidney damage. On the other hand, less common types of glomerulonephritis frequently lead to end stage kidney disease.

Educational Implications

Children who are found at the time of school physical exams to have protein or blood in their urine, edema, or elevated blood pressure should be referred promptly to a physician for a complete medical evaluation. Children with glomerulonephritis rarely have a contagious disease. However, children who come in close contact with streptococcal infections are very likely to become infected themselves. Teachers should be aware that classmates and family members should receive medical attention if any skin or throat infection is suspected. Prompt treatment with antibiotics may help prevent glomerulonephritis from occurring later.

NEPHROTIC SYNDROME

Etiology

The nephrotic syndrome is a manifestation of glomerulonephritis in which the glomerular damage allows excessive amounts of protein to leak into the urine and then be excreted from the body. Virtually any type of glomerulonephritis can cause the nephrotic syndrome. In children, the most common cause is termed minimal change disease or nil disease. These terms come from the microscopic appearance of the glomeruli. When kidney tissue is examined with an ordinary microscope, the glomeruli appear normal. However, examination of the tissue with a special electron microscope reveals characteristic changes in certain parts of the glomeruli.

Characteristics

Children with the nephrotic syndrome usually have mild to severe swelling of the extremities, face, and abdomen. Elevated blood pressure and increased susceptibility to infection are also common.

Diagnosis

Diagnosis of the nephrotic syndrome is made by measuring the amount of protein excreted in the urine over a 24-hour period. A kidney biopsy is required to determine the type of glomerular disease which is causing the syndrome.

Treatment

Treatment is determined by the results of the kidney biopsy. For children with minimal change disease, the standard treatment is *Prednisone*, an adrenal steroid taken as a pill. Sometimes additional medications such as *Cytoxan* or *Imuran* are used.

Prognosis

Prognosis depends on the type of glomerular damage. Minimal change disease generally responds very well to treatment. The amount of protein leakage and swelling of the body decreases. A cure or long-term remission is achieved in 80 percent of children. End stage kidney disease occurs in only 2 percent of cases. Prednisone, Cytoxan, and Imuran are very potent medications which have numerous side effects including suppression of the bone marrow, increased susceptibility to infection, loss of bone minerals which may lead to fractures, elevation of blood pressure, changes in mood, and a distinctive type of swelling of the face, abdomen, and upper back. The patient's prognosis is improved by using only the minimal dose of drugs needed to control the protein leakage.

Educational Implications

Children with the nephrotic syndrome generally perform normally and can participate in all activities provided that swelling is controlled. The child who is taking medication should be watched carefully for any signs of infection or pain in the hips or knees. Also, any cut or scrape, no matter how minor, must be cared for promptly and thoroughly because the medication will suppress the symptoms of an infection but not the infection itself. Some children can become depressed or euphoric while taking Prednisone, which may adversely affect their classroom performance.

HYPERTENSION

Etiology

Hypertension refers to an abnormally high blood pressure. Approximately 35 million persons in the United States have hypertension. In 90 percent of cases, no specific cause for the elevated blood pressure can be found and the hypertension is called essential hypertension. The remaining 10 percent of cases are almost always due to diseases that reduce kidney function, cause narrowing in the arteries that supply blood to the kidneys, cause excessive secretion of hormones by the adrenal glands, or cause narrowing of the major artery that takes blood from the heart (coarctation of the aorta).

Characteristics

Most patients with hypertension have no symptoms. Headaches, blurred vision, and recurrent nosebleeds are seen with hypertension but are not specific symptoms because they also occur with many other medical conditions.

If the hypertension is caused by excessive secretion of adrenalin and noradrenalin by the adrenal glands, about 50 percent of patients will have headaches, excessive sweating, and a rapid heartbeat. If the hypertension is caused by excessive secretion of aldosterone by the adrenal glands, the patient may urinate frequently and have weakness and muscle cramps. Coarctation of the aorta often can be detected by the presence of a weak pulse in one arm or in both legs.

Diagnosis

Blood pressure is measured with a device called a sphygmomanometer, which is wrapped around the upper arm and inflated (Figure 24–5). As the device is deflated, the examiner listens for heartbeats in the crook of the elbow. The point at which heartbeats are first heard is the *systolic* pressure. The point at which the heartbeat becomes muffled or disappears is the *diastolic* pressure. In adults, the upper limits of "nor-

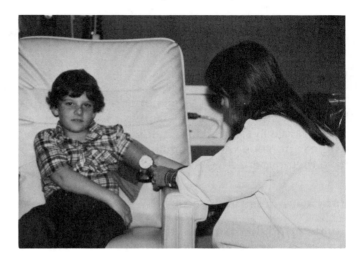

Figure 24–5   A Child Having His Blood Pressure Taken

mal" are defined as 140 mmHg systolic and 90 mmHg diastolic. Normal levels for children vary according to the child's age but are always less than 140 mmHg systolic and 90 mmHg diastolic. Charts that illustrate normal blood pressure values for boys and girls from infancy through adolescence are available from several sources including the American Heart Association.

If the blood pressure is elevated on routine examination, which should be performed each year, and on any follow-up examination by a physician, tests should be done to determine whether the hypertension is essential or caused by one of the disorders mentioned above. These tests include microscopic examination of the urine, blood tests to evaluate kidney function, measurement of adrenal hormones in the blood or urine, and special X-ray studies of the kidneys and adrenal glands. Not all of these tests need to be done for every patient.

Treatment

Treatment in most cases of essential hypertension consists of drug therapy and dietary reduction of salt intake. A wide variety of effective drugs exists for treatment of essential hypertension. The most commonly used drugs are diuretics, which increase salt and water excretion by the kidneys. The major side effect of diuretics is loss of body potassium into the urine, which may lead to muscle cramps, weakness, and disturbances of heart function. Children taking diuretics should have their blood levels of potassium measured periodically.

Treatment of hypertension caused by coarctation of the aorta, narrowing of the arteries leading to the kidneys, or diseases of the adrenal gland generally requires surgery.

Prognosis

The prognosis for the vast majority of patients with hypertension is excellent. Persons with essential hypertension may need to take medications indefinitely, whereas persons with secondary hypertension often have their hypertension cured by surgery.

Educational Implications

Children should have their blood pressure measured at yearly school examinations by a person trained in the use of a sphygmomanometer. Each school should have a chart that illustrates the normal levels of blood pressure in children so that students with hypertension can be referred for medical evaluation. Children with hypertension that is controlled by medication may participate in all activities including contact sports.

SUMMARY

The kidneys are extraordinarily complex organs that perform a large number of vital physiologic processes. This chapter has summarized the basic structure and function of the kidneys and described the important features of end stage kidney disease, glomerulonephritis, the nephrotic syndrome (which is a manifestation of glomerulonephritis), and hypertension. Physicians and educators who care for children with kidney disease should communicate frequently to minimize the physical and psychological problems which arise from these disorders and are often chronic in nature.

REFERENCES

Brenner, B. M., & Rector, F. C., Jr. (Eds). *The kidney* (2nd ed.). Philadelphia: W. B. Saunders, 1981.

Leaf, A., & Cotran, R. S. *Renal pathophysiology.* New York: Oxford University Press, 1976.

Schrier, R. W. (Ed.). *Renal and electrolyte disorders* (2nd ed.). Boston: Little, Brown and Company, 1980.

PART

4

The
Education Environment

Mary Kay Dykes, Ph.D., is professor in the Department of Special Education, University of Florida, Gainesville, Florida. **John Venn, Ph.D.,** is assistant professor in the Department of Special Education, University of North Florida, Jacksonville, Florida.

Knowing about etiology, prognosis, and terminology related to various conditions and diseases in children is often fascinating in itself. However, it is not an adequate base of knowledge for the educator who is responsible for comprehensive programming and evaluation. Educators as well as nurses, therapists, psychologists, social workers, and other specialists in the schools must be aware of (a) *what* to observe in the child who has physical handicaps, (b) *how* to observe it, (c) *when* to provide assistance, (d) *what* to do in case of emergency, and (e) *how* to adapt the environment, facilitate positive self-regard and social interaction, advocate for the child and family, and provide for optimal learning and the general well-being of the individual.

Using Health, Physical, and Medical Data in the Classroom

CHAPTER 25

At school, teachers most often are the professionals responsible for the child: for making sure that all information is gathered, known, and understood by the entire professional team before decisions are made. For the child who has a physical handicap, data concerning physical functioning will be especially important in planning both long- and short-term interventions. Therefore, educators and other professionals in the schools must understand not only the basic physiology and pathology related to the more frequently occurring conditions and diseases, but also should know what observations to make, what questions to ask for more information, and to whom these questions should be asked. They also need to know the resources for information and referral, and the procedures and vocabulary required for making referrals to professionals who do not usually work in schools.

Frequently, school personnel have no information or communication with those who provide health care services for a child. This is generally true for children who receive medical services through (a) state agencies (e.g., children's medical services or mental health, mental retardation, or developmental disabilities services); (b) federal programs (e.g., Champus for children eligible for military related health care); or (c) private sector physicians, clinics, and health maintenance organizations. The school nurse, social worker, or teacher may obtain relevant data from the child's physician or medical center after receiving written parental permission to do so. When a child with a physical handicap enters school, such a request should be made of the parents. Parents should be asked to cooperate in the exchange of information between the physician and school personnel and with any other health care specialists, such as therapists, who work with the child outside of school.

A persistent effort should be made to keep an ongoing exchange of information and to keep records up to date. Information to be exchanged between the school and medical center includes changes in medication, behavior, or attitude; potential scheduling of nonemergency surgery; parental needs, and so forth.

Medical information may take many forms: surgery reports, clinic notes, prescriptions for medication or equipment, adapted scheduling, or general developmental, diagnostic, or follow-through reports. At times, data reported to the school may not be brought to the teacher's attention. Therefore, teachers need to learn to request health information and to "track it down" once it enters the school system. It is useful to have a district plan that will keep information coming to the classroom teacher and to those who provide daily services for the child.

The remainder of this chapter will deal with several concerns that relate to using health, physical, and medical data in the classroom. Information will be presented about definitions and services, the roles of medical and health-related personnel, the learning characteristics of children with physical handicaps, social-emotional concerns that can influence learning and general development, adaptations in the educational environment, commonly used adaptive equipment, and strategies for classroom organization.

DEFINITION AND SERVICES

The need for services beyond those provided in a regular classroom causes a child to be labeled physically handicapped for *educational purposes*. A child

may have obvious or hidden physical problems that do not require additional services in the school. For example, a child with congenital amputation of one or both arms may function independently by using legs, feet, and toes instead of arms, hands, and fingers to write, dress, dial a telephone, drive, steer a tricycle, program a computer, and so on.

On the other hand, a child with no obvious physical handicap (e.g., cystic fibrosis or cancer) may require either continuous or intermittent additional services in order to stay in school and to profit from instruction. Such a child may require medication, therapy, positioning, a limited schedule, rest, or frequent testing of bodily functions.

Even when children appear to have approximately the same level of physical dysfunction, they may not require the same type or amount of help. One child may have greater intellectual potential, the other may have more tenacity or self-determination. One may have been taught to expect others to wait on him. The other may have been taught that "If you don't do it, it won't get done" or "Help comes to those who help themselves." The diagnosis, condition, and observable dysfunctions are not the only considerations in determining who will need additional help, what kind of help, and how much will be needed.

The children most frequently seen in school programs for those with physical handicaps have cerebral palsy (CP), spina bifida, or muscular dystrophy (MD). Some regions of the country have more children in need of special services due to rheumatic fever, Legg-Perthes, or polio. It may be that, in two adjoining school districts, one program primarily serves children with CP, whereas the other will have only one or two children with CP, but numerous children with spina bifida or MD.

In school programs, a diagnosis of mental retardation usually takes precedence over a diagnosis of physical handicap for purposes of placement into a special education program. Therefore, a child placed in a program for physically handicapped children is considered to have at least near normal intelligence and to be capable of obtaining the cognitive skills expected of his age group.

Programs for the multiply handicapped include children with cognitive, physical, behavioral, and sensory disabilities. For example, a severely involved athetoid CP child may have a hearing deficit that interferes with learning to communicate and to complete performance tasks. This child requires assessment and extensive intervention from numerous professionals in order to receive an appropriate education.

It is easy to understand how a child with multiple impairments could be incorrectly labeled mentally retarded. Even if a child is bright, he may be unable to show and tell what he knows through normal means (e.g., manipulation and speech). This problem has created some very unfortunate situations in the past. In some cases, very bright individuals with CP were institutionalized as retarded and not provided an education because they "obviously could never use it." The exemplary careers of individuals with severe CP such as Irish author and poet Christy Brown, attorney Curtis Brewer who founded Untapped Resources, Harold Yuker Provost of Hofstra University, and pediatrician Dr. Earl Carlson demonstrate that people with severely physically limiting conditions make major contributions to society. In addition, multiply handicapped individuals such as Helen Keller and Dr. Richard Kinney of the Hadley School for the Blind in Illinois have demonstrated that they can make significant contributions to society if they are provided the opportunity to receive an appropriate education. Obviously, not all or even most individuals with severely, physically, or multiply handicapping conditions will become university provosts or poet laureates. On the other hand, how many children in regular classrooms will achieve such a status?

ROLE OF MEDICAL AND HEALTH-RELATED PERSONNEL

A wide range and variety of medical and health-related personnel provide services to children who are physically or multiply handicapped. Educators and other professionals who work in schools need to know the roles of health care professionals, especially because these persons can help the school meet a child's educational needs. The treatment and education of a child with a physical impairment are often explained in terms of the personnel who provide services. At times, these persons may provide services in coordination with each other. However, each profession has its own domain and services and its own information-gathering and intervention system. Information gathered may or may not be made known to others. Unless all professionals share information and decisions for appropriate intervention, there is a strong possibility that optimal, comprehensive intervention and care will not be provided. The characteristics of uncoordinated intervention systems include fragmented service delivery, gaps in the service system, costly duplication of services, and parent frustration. To guard against such problems, the team approach that should be used to ensure (a) the child is provided a consistent, stable treatment and education program that enables maximum growth and (b) the parent has input into the decisions and is made aware of how the child is being taught and cared for.

To be effective team members, teachers and other educational personnel need to understand the roles and responsibilities of the various medical and health-related personnel. This knowledge is vital to ensure that the relevant medical aspects of each child's disability are incorporated into the day-to-day education. Additionally, this knowledge helps the teacher to make effective medical and health-related referrals. The teacher learns what information should be reported, how it should be reported, and to whom it should be reported.

If the teacher fails to detect a medical or health-related problem, it may never be identified because few others interact with the child as intensely for as long a period of time. One way in which an appropriate referral and intervention system can be started is by establishing an interdisciplinary team. The cooperation and participation of the child's parents as key team members are essential in carrying out the referral and intervention process. The role descriptions of many medical and health-related professionals have been included here so that, by referring to this information, educators and others can identify appropriate resources for referral and information. The professionals whose roles are described here are the *physician* (including the pediatrician, orthopedist, neurologist, and other specialists) and *health-related personnel* (including the occupational therapist, physical therapist, nurse, speech-language therapist, rehabilitation counselor, and social worker).

The Physician

The term physician refers to a number of professionals who are licensed medical doctors. The role of the physician consists of, but is not limited to, prescribing and providing treatment for the physical aspects of a child's growth and development. For the child who is physically handicapped, this may include prescriptions and referrals for physical therapy, occupational therapy, orthopedic treatment, and medications, plus recommendations for the extent and duration of various treatments. Although school personnel are most likely to come into contact with the pediatrician, contacts with other physicians is often necessary.

Pediatrician   The pediatrician is a physician who specializes in the treatment of infants, children, and adolescents. In most cases, the pediatrician is the primary physician for a physically handicapped child and is responsible for making referrals to other physicians and health-related personnel for specialized services. Directly, the pediatrician supervises immunizations, treats childhood illnesses, and provides instruction for parents in proper care. The pediatrician also conducts periodic physical examinations that isolate abnormalities in growth and development that may indicate disease or disability.

Orthopedist   The orthopedist (also called orthopod or orthopedic surgeon) is a physician who specializes in preventing and correcting impairments of the joints, bones, and muscles of the body. Diganosis of orthopedic impairments includes direct observation, X ray, and other internal structural examinations as well as evaluation of joint, muscle, and nerve functioning. Treatment of orthopedic impairments frequently involves surgical procedures, the use of braces, prosthetic devices such as artificial limbs, and the application of assistive devices called orthoses (e.g., adapted feeding equipment or splints). The orthopedist also prescribes occupational and physical therapy and frequently uses therapists as part of the clinical team for diagnosis and evaluation. The orthopedist treats children who have skeletal deformities (such as amputation, scoliosis, and osteogenesis imperfecta); muscle, joint, and bone defects associated with CP, spina bifida, or arthritis; and traumatic conditions such as fractures, dislocation, and spinal cord injury.

Neurologist   The neurologist or neurosurgeon is a specialist in the diagnosis and treatment of impairments to the nervous system. The neurologist may diagnose and treat a variety of handicapping conditions in children who have nervous system dysfunctions including convulsive disorders, hydrocephalus, spina bifida, CP and MD. Diagnosis and evaluation techniques used by neurologists include compiling a medical history, assessing motor function, evaluating spinal fluid, obtaining an electroencephalogram (EEG) and electromyogram (EMG). Neurological treatment may include surgical procedures involving nerve tissues or prescribing medications and therapy.

Other Specialists   Other specialists may evaluate and treat children with physically handicapping conditions when the need arises. The *dentist* provides for oral hygiene and for evaluation of oral functioning. The *geneticist* provides evaluation and counseling related to various inherited and genetic disorders. Diseases and disorders of the eye and the visual process are the specialty of the *ophthalmologist*. Mental illness and emotional disturbance are diagnosed and treated by the *psychiatrist*, who may prescribe various therapeutic treatments including medication, other invasive procedures, and counseling or other external therapy. The *urologist* deals with structural defects

and disorders of the urinary system. Children who are paralyzed, for example, those with spina bifida, often receive continued treatment from a urologist. The *otorhinolaryngologist* (ENT—ear, nose, throat) diagnoses and treats diseases, disorders, and conditions of the head and neck. The *radiologist* uses X rays and radioactive substances to diagnose and treat diseases of the human body. Finally, diseases and disorders of the heart are evaluated and treated by the *cardiologist*. In each field there are technicians and assistants who have specialized tasks in the delivery of health care services.

Health-Related Personnel

Occupational Therapist   The occupational therapist is concerned with the whole individual, including the child's physical, social, and vocational needs. The occupational therapy process may emphasize self-help skills, activities of daily living, prevocational skills, recreation skills, leisure-time skills, and fine motor skill development. Occupational therapy is medically prescribed to help an individual recover from an impairment.

In school, the occupational therapist functions as part of an interdisciplinary team that provides a coordinated program designed to fulfill the unique needs of each student. The occupational therapist works closely with the physical therapist, speech therapist, classroom teacher, physician, and the student's family. Therapy includes teaching various daily-living and motor-perceptual skills. In addition, the therapist provides instruction in the use of various assistive devices such as hand splints, adaptive typewriters, special eating utensils (Figure 25–1), and so forth.

Figure 25—1   Adaptive Devices

Physical Therapist The physical therapist is primarily concerned with the restoration of function in children who are physically handicapped. Physical therapy techniques include exercise for increasing strength, flexibility, coordination, and range of motion of the joints of the body; facilitating motor movement, particularly ambulation; and the use of physical agents such as heat, sound, energy, and cold to relieve pain and improve physical status. In educational settings, the therapist coordinates therapy with other team members including the occupational therapist, teachers, and the child's parents.

Nurse At school, the nurse is responsible for a number of medical and health-related matters. The nurse makes sure that all children have the necessary inoculations required for school attendance, identifies and reports infectious diseases, and coordinates health education programs. The nurse teaches school personnel about special considerations of a variety of conditions, such as convulsive disorders and cardiac defects. Another role is to oversee and administer medications prescribed by the child's physician. The nurse assists in developing plans for dealing with medical emergencies at school or on the bus. In addition, the nurse may serve as liaison and counselor for families who need assistance in identifying community health resources. In many school districts, the nurse is expected to initiate and receive referrals to or from other agencies. The nurse also may become the child's primary teacher in learning to care for special bodily needs (e.g., catheter maintenance) as well as for family life or sex education.

Speech-Language Therapist Speech-language therapists provide therapy to individuals who have disorders in speech, language, or communication skills. In the public schools, the speech-language therapist may provide therapy on either a resource or itinerant basis after children have been evaluated and enrolled in a speech or language program. Although articulation therapy accounts for a large percentage of the therapist's referrals and intervention, there are numerous other services the speech-language therapist may provide, such as therapy for language delay, voice disorders, difficulty in expressive language, and interference with motor production. The therapist may evaluate for and teach a nonoral method of communication, and also may provide training in use of an augmentative language or speech system. The therapist plays a role in identifying children who have hearing problems or physical problems with the oral system that may require corrective dental work. Supervising or conducting hearing screening evaluations of all children in certain grades each year as well as providing follow-up evaluations and referrals are all a part of the therapist's domain.

Rehabilitation Counselor The rehabilitation counselor is a specially trained health-related professional who provides vocational guidance and related services to disabled youth and adults. The role of the rehabilitation counselor includes assessing vocational aptitudes and interests, arranging for necessary medical treatment, arranging for work training and work experience, and providing various job placement and follow-up services. The rehabilitation counselor is responsible for having a complete knowledge of the existing jobs in the local area and of the entry-level skills necessary for those jobs. The counselor is responsible for being aware of the service agencies and institutions that provide prevocational, vocational, and medical rehabilitation services for those who are physically disabled. In most states, rehabilitation counselors are employed by the state vocational rehabilitation agency. In some school districts, a vocational counselor/placement specialist is employed. This individual may have training in rehabilitation counseling, special education, or vocational education. High-school-age students work with this specialist in securing and maintaining positions in the community in order to gain work experience while still in school.

Social Worker The social worker is an active participant in the evaluation, treatment, and education of children who are physically handicapped. The social worker is concerned with the sociological components of children's lives, particularly as related to the impact of disability, illness, and other problems. The social worker assists the child and the family through counseling and by identifying appropriate financial, social, and personal resources that may help in adjusting to severe or prolonged illness or disability in the family. The social worker may serve as the coordinator of all agency, school, and medical services received by the family.

LEARNING CHARACTERISTICS OF CHILDREN WHO ARE PHYSICALLY HANDICAPPED

Teachers should be aware that a variety of different learning characteristics are found in relation to the various physically handicapping conditions identified in children. At school, these learning characteristics may mean that the child requires a special individualized curriculum, specialized teaching methods, and often, special materials and equipment. Overall, the primary learning characteristic of physically handicapped students is that they learn like normal children; they have more in common with children who are not physically handicapped than their obvious differences. Indeed, most students who are physically impaired are educated in regular classes, follow the normal curriculum, and need no special education. These students may only need special equipment such as wheelchairs, typewriters, tape recorders, and other devices and aids to compensate for physical impairments.

However, a considerable number of students have severe physical impairments and associated handicaps that present a variety of atypical learning characteristics. Many of these students are educated in special education programs for part or all of their school day. These students often have related problems with vision, hearing, motor development, intellectual ability, and language and communication, which can interfere with normal learning.

Vision

Physically handicapped students may have one of three major types of visual problems: visual perception problems, partial sight, and blindness. Visual perception problems, the most common, are seen in approximately 30 percent of children who have CP and also in children with other physical disabilities. The problems of partial sight demand several specialized materials and equipment. Problems asssociated with blindness demand highly specialized changes in services. Therefore, we will not discuss this problem here.

The definition of blindness that is used in the education environment is that the child cannot use print as a learning modality. However, physicians and other professionals use a different definition of blindness—one based on acuity or legal standards. A person who is legally blind after best correction may still be able to read print. This child would be considered partially sighted, not blind, for purposes of education. Even though the child may require modification in visual presentation, print can still be used as a primary learning modality.

Students with physical handicaps may need glasses to compensate for acuity problems. However, many functional vision problems such as those of visual perception and depth perception do not involve acuity and are not corrected by lenses. A student may have 20/20 vision, but still not be able to read satisfactorily. In CP, for example, children often have visual problems, but not problems with acuity. Problems with the muscles that control eye movements are common. These include strabismus, nystagmus, and **amblyopia.** All of these muscle problems can result in visual difficulties.

The major visual perception problems associated with CP involve figure-ground, part-whole relationships, rotations, reversals, and categorization. *Figure-ground* refers to the ability to pick out the relevant details in a visual image. *Part-whole relationships* involve the ability to perceive a whole image when only seeing parts of that image. Children who *rotate* or *reverse* visual images may see words upside down or backwards. Visual memory skills may be adequately developed in children with CP, but *categorization* skills may be weak. Children with CP or other physical handicaps who have visual perceptual problems may be auditory learners primarily and may require special instruction in the optimal use of auditory and tactile learning. Poor depth perception is another visual problem sometimes seen in children who are physically handicapped. This problem may be especially evident when a child is walking downstairs or stepping off curbs.

The problem of partial sight is also seen in children with physical impairments. Children who are partially sighted may require large print books and may also need to learn how to use low vision aids such as handheld and illuminated magnifiers. Partially sighted students may benefit from the use of a high quality lamp attached to or placed on the desk. A child with partial sight should always be seated in a well-lighted place in the classroom, which is free from shadows and flickering light patterns.

Hearing

Children who are physically handicapped usually have normal hearing ability, although certain handicaps do affect hearing, even to the point of deafness. Hearing impairment is often associated with athetoid CP. It is also associated with osteogenesis imperfecta as the child matures. Children who are physically handicapped and deaf as well require special services for their deafness: sign language, interpreters, auditory training, speech therapy, training in speech reading, curriculum adjustments, and other special provisions.

Children with juvenile rheumatoid arthritis who are taking aspirin may have a high tone hearing loss that can interfere with understanding speech. This problem is a side effect of aspirin and disappears when the treatment is stopped.

In physically handicapped children, auditory perception problems are much more common than deafness. Auditory perception refers to the ability to receive and process sounds correctly. Children who have auditory perception difficulties may not be able to accurately identify specific sounds or sound combinations. They may have auditory memory deficits and may have difficulty discriminating between sounds. Identification and diagnosis of auditory perception problems and proper intervention can improve a child's auditory perception skills.

Auditory memory difficulties are one of the more common auditory perception problems. The child with memory problems may have difficulty remembering more than one direction at a time and may not always remember what was learned the day before. The child may appear to understand an idea or concept, but forget it very quickly. The child may be disorganized and have difficulty remembering where school supplies and personal belongings were left. Teaching methods for children with auditory memory problems include providing a structured, stable learning environment; using special techniques for teaching academic tasks; giving special instruction in listening to comments and following directions; and teaching children to compensate by learning through their senses of touch and vision.

Auditory decoding deficits are another problem seen in children who are physically handicapped. Children with auditory decoding problems have difficulty accurately perceiving sounds, parts of words, or parts of phrases. Auditory decoding problems may result from difficulties in sorting out and identifying the important sounds in a verbal message. For example, a child may understand only parts of a conversation. Listening to lectures and following verbal directions may be extremely difficult for children with this problem. Teaching methods for auditory decoding problems include making sure the child is paying attention when receiving auditory information, and teaching the child to compensate by learning through the visual sense.

Some children have difficulty completing sentences, completing verbally expressed ideas, answering questions, and drawing verbal conclusions based on abstract ideas. All of these problems are associated with deficits in auditory closure. Teaching methods for children with auditory closure deficits focus on compensation through other senses.

Motor Development

Motor development refers to movement involving the muscles of the body. Children who are physically handicapped present a wide range and variety of motor development problems. These include relatively minor problems such as restrictions or special concerns about participation in physical education activities by children who have diabetes, heart disease, or asthma. They also include temporary motor problems such as occur in Legg-Perthes disease and scoliosis, as well as degenerative conditions such as MD and cystic fibrosis. Finally, there are severe physically disabling conditions such as mixed CP, in which a child

is profoundly handicapped and has little or no voluntary control of motor movements.

Despite this wide range of motor problems, several characteristics that occur frequently in children who are physically handicapped need to be considered in meeting each child's unique needs. Many of these children are restricted in their ability to move easily within their environment, which restricts the quality and quantity of the child's experiences. These restrictions not only result in poor motor development but also may negatively affect the development of many skills: language, social, academic, intellectual, self-help, daily living, recreation, and leisure.

Some children who have severe motor impairments may retain primitive reflexes, which are normally integrated by approximately six months of age. These children are rarely ambulatory. The retention of primitive reflexes inhibits the development of higher level movement patterns needed for balance and locomotion.

As these children grow and develop, they may develop restricted range of motion, contractures, **adhesions,** and structural changes in the skeletal bones, which result in permanent deformities and prevent further motor development. Early intervention is critical to prevent permanent deformities. Physical therapy, surgery, medications, exercise, and adapted equipment are all used to treat these physical problems.

Some children who are physically handicapped may experience transitional motor problems. For example, children who are recovering from orthopedic surgery to relieve spasticity may be placed in casts for several weeks after surgery. Postoperative follow-up therapy is critical in obtaining maximum function and cosmetic improvement.

Fine motor development problems (i.e., problems in voluntary, controlled movement of the small muscles of the body) may cause children difficulties in completing performance activities, academic tasks, and various self-help and daily living skills. A variety of adaptive materials and equipment is used to help children compensate for their poor fine motor skills.

Intellectual Ability

Most students who are physically disabled have normal intellectual ability. In fact, many have superior intellectual ability. However, a substantial number of physically handicapped students are also mentally handicapped. Although the estimates vary, it has been thought that as many as 60 percent of all CP children may be mentally handicapped to some degree. As defined on standardized tests, the primary characteristic of mental impairment is that the child does not learn as quickly as other children of the same age.

Furthermore, the child's ultimate level of intellectual achievement as an adult may be lower than normal.

Language and Communication

Some language and communication problems are frequently seen in children who are physically handicapped: a general delay in language development, a variety of speech defects, and in severe cases of CP, extreme difficulty in coordinating the movement of the speech mechanism to produce even the simplest speech sounds. Children develop language from their experiences and interaction with the environment. There is a normal sequence and pattern for language development that children follow as they grow and develop. Children who are physically handicapped may be delayed in at least one area of language development due to their impairment directly or indirectly because of a lack of experiences.

Expressive language development may be delayed in children whose severe motor disability re-sults in speech difficulties. Other children may be delayed in both expressive and receptive language development due to motor disability that restricts mobility and thus reduces opportunities for interaction and experiential learning. Chronic illness, which restricts the range and variety of interactions and experiences in the environment, could also delay language development. Finally, additional disabilities associated with physical impairment (e.g., mental retardation or sensory deficits) may contribute to language delays.

A unique language characteristic frequently seen in children with spina bifida is the "cocktail party syndrome." This syndrome refers to a form of excessive verbalism in which the child is relatively high in vocabulary, verbal interaction, and social skills, but is weak in intellectual, memory, and academic skills. At first, these children may appear to be quite bright. Actually, they function at a low level in abstract and conceptual thinking.

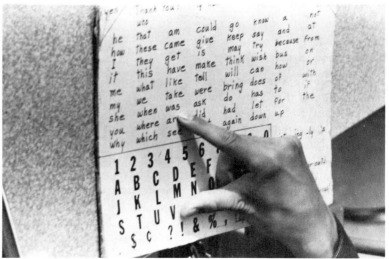

Figure 25–2   This Student Uses a Communication Board to Tell a Joke

Source: Reprinted with permission from J. L. Bigge, *Teaching individuals with physical and multiple disabilities,* 2nd ed. Columbus, Ohio: Charles E. Merrill, 1982, page 85.

Some children who are physically handicapped display normal language development but have speech problems. Speech defects are frequently associated with CP. The speech problems commonly observed include articulation disorders such as **omissions, substitutions,** and **distortions** and voice disorders in pitch, loudness, voice flexibility, and voice quality. Children with speech problems usually receive individual speech therapy as a part of their individual education program.

Some children have adequate receptive language but such a severe speech impairment that they are never likely to develop adequate speech. For these children, there are several alternative methods of expressive communication. A communication board is the most common of the "nonvocal" communication alternatives. Communication boards (Figure 25–2) include manual-boards that contain words, pictures, or symbols in which the child communicates by pointing or otherwise indicating a message. There are also a variety of electronic communication boards (Figure 25–3) that type or print a message or, in some cases, use synthetic speech to provide a voice output. Encoding techniques using eye movements have also been developed for children with the most severe physical handicaps who have little voluntary control of their movements. Some children who are nonvocal can use fingerspelling to communicate expressively.

Figure 25–3   Communication Board Atop a Display Printer, Both Manufactured by Zygo

Source: Reprinted with permission from J. L. Bigge, *Teaching individuals with physical and multiple disabilities,* 2nd ed. Columbus, Ohio: Charles E. Merrill, 1982, page 104.

SOCIAL-EMOTIONAL CONCERNS

Social-emotional development refers to the ability to adapt and adjust early to one's environment and to changes in that environment. It also refers to the development of self-concept and the ability to get along well with others. Physically handicapped children may have special problems in social-emotional development because of the nature of their physical disability or because of others' reactions to their disability. The families of children who are physically handicapped face special problems in social-emotional development.

Parents and others react to a child who is physically handicapped with denial, rejection, overprotection, or acceptance. Overprotection is perhaps most devastating to the child's social-emotional development. Overprotection is characterized by excessive sympathy and pity for the child and is manifested in a number of ways. The overprotective adult (a) may not let the child do things independently despite his capability, (b) may prohibit the child from participating in games and activities due to the handicap, even though he may be capable, (c) may make most decisions for the child, thereby denying the child opportunities to learn to solve problems and make decisions, and (d) may not permit the child to explore, get dirty, or take risks. A pattern of overprotection forces the child into extreme dependency. It inhibits the child's development of a positive self-concept and the ability to get along well with others. Parents, teachers, and others who offer the youngster acceptance rather than sympathy enhance the child's social-emotional development. An accepting attitude by teachers and aides sets the tone for acceptance and interaction among the students in the class.

Many physically handicapping conditions cause children to be nonambulatory. They may have to use assistive devices such as wheelchairs and other adaptive equipment to move about. Even with assistive devices, some children who are physically handicapped may not be able to move about independently, thus severely restricting mobility. Mobility is important for many reasons but it is particularly important for learning to get along with others and general social development because so many social contacts and opportunities for interaction depend on being mobile.

It is necessary for some children, especially young children, to spend considerable time in a hospital. The extent and duration of the hospitalization depend on the nature of the child's particular impairment or condition. A hospital is not a natural place for a child to stay. A child may feel fear, anger, insecurity, or abandonment, all of which cause considerable stress and pain in the hospital. Repeated hospitalizations may increase this stress and insecurity. During a hospital stay, feelings of loneliness, insecurity, low self-esteem, isolation, and rejection may grow. A child needs increased attention, support, and reassurance to successfully deal with these problems. The child's feelings and needs should be discussed before, during, and after hospitalization.

Several problems associated with adolescence deserve special attention. Perhaps most important, physical appearance is especially important to self-concept during this age period. The physique is frequently given a high value and is closely associated with self-concept and self-esteem. Friends from elementary school may suddenly become too busy with new friends and activities or become embarrassed to be seen with someone who looks different. Emotionally, adolescence overlaps both childhood and adulthood. It is a critical period for changes in self-concept and self-awareness, particularly in the areas of sexuality and sex-appropriate behavior. For all of these reasons, adolescents who are physically handicapped need counseling, guidance, support, friendship, and understanding to grow and mature into well-adjusted young adults.

Childen who are terminally ill experience unique social-emotional characteristics and special problems. Most chronic and terminal illnesses are not static, stable conditions. The child's situation is constantly changing. Even small changes in the medical condition or a move from the hospital to the home may alter the whole picture of adjustment and result in intense emotional reaction. Parents, educators, and other caregivers must be aware of even small changes so that special help in adjusting and coping can be made available. Methods of helping terminally ill individuals include open discussions of the problem and active listening to give the individual opportunities to express feelings, fears, anxieties, and hopes.

Another social-emotional adjustment problem is experienced when children must take medications that produce a negative behavioral side effect: lethargy, aggressiveness, hyperactivity, unpredictable behavior, depression, anxiety, or drowsiness. In school, teachers may need to know the possible side effects of specific medications. In addition, teachers have a unique opportunity to observe children over long periods of time and notice adverse reactions to medications and behavioral changes that could signal changes in medical status.

ADAPTATIONS IN THE EDUCATIONAL ENVIRONMENT

Once a child's needs, goals, and current levels of performance are known, the educator can facilitate the specific changes required to implement an appropriate educational program. These changes or adaptations may involve a wide variety of concerns: emergency and medical procedures, educational placement, medications and medical services, barrier-free design, transportation, the special physical needs of children, teaming and working with others, school management of children with physical handicaps, and physical inspection of children in the classroom.

Emergency and Medical Procedures

School districts that have an ongoing program for physically or multiply handicapped children may already have procedures for handling medical emergencies in the schools. If not, a policy should be developed. Also, there should be a specific written policy to be followed within each school. Procedures should be known by all teachers and given to the parents of each child. If parents know that their child's needs cannot be met by the given procedure, they must immediately let the teacher know what to do and what not to do.

A school policy should include the specific procedure to follow in case of a *seizure, severe bleeding, cardiac arrest, fainting,* or *choking*. If necessary, it can contain information on other specific procedures. Teachers should have, in writing, a copy of the approved school policy for handling a medical emergency: who to notify first, how to notify them, how to have the rest of the class supervised when meeting the emergency, and what to do to meet the needs of the individual.

It is a good idea to use an expanded medical record card form for children who are physically or multiply handicapped (Figure 25–4). Additional data about the nature of the condition or disease, medications, and emergency procedures should be included. All educators and therapists who work with the child should know the information on the card. If school personnel gather appropriate data but do not use them in their daily programming or do not know what to do when a child has a medical emergency, they have not met the child's needs.

Teachers who work with children who have physical or multiple handicaps are often required to know first aid and cardiopulmonary resuscitation (CPR). These programs are available through the Red Cross, YMCA, or scouting groups; and the certificate of knowledge should be kept current.

Educational Placement

Most children with identified physical handicaps are educated in the regular classroom and may never require special education or therapy services in school.

School Medical Emergency Card

Child's Name _____ Age _____

Person to contact in emergency _____

      Phone _____

Second person to contact _____

      Phone _____

Parent's/Guardian's Name _____

      Address _____

      Phone: Home _____ Work _____ Other _____

Physician's Name _____

      Address _____

      Phone _____

My initials appear before the correct instruction(s) below:

    In case of medical emergency:

    _____ 1. Please take   (Child's Name)   to   (Medical Facility) .
          The staff there has my permission to begin necessary
          medical treatment if it is needed in an emergency.

    _____ 2. Please take   (Child's Name)   to   (Medical Facility) .
          No medical treatment should be given until I give my
          permission.

    _____ 3. Please call Dr.   (Physician's Name) .

    _____ 4. The physician at the medical facility should treat the child.

School Medical Emergency Card
(Back of Card)

Eligibility for special medical funding (e.g., state, military, etc.): _____

_____

Medications currently being taken: (Name and Amount) _____

_____

Known reactions to medications (include date): _____

Blood type _____

Medical conditions (seizures, heart problems, etc.): _____

_____

Past medical history: _____

_____

_____

Child's Social Security number _____

_____   _____
Parent/Guardian Signature   Date

Figure 25—4   Expanded Medical Card

Only when a child's physical condition necessitates additional services or varied routines does the child enter the realm of special education. Usually, a child can be maintained in the regular classroom if consultation services are provided the teacher, therapy is provided the child, and rest periods are included in the school day. When a child's needs are so different from others that the youngster requires major changes in routine, position, equipment, or instructional procedures in order to develop cognitive, daily living, and social skills, then placement in a special education program becomes appropriate. This placement may be for part-day or full-day programs. Educational programs may be provided in a center, hospital, or home, whichever of these is the least restrictive environment for the child's physical condition. For most children, one of the above facilities is only a temporary arrangement. The child, upon stabilizing, healing, or regaining function, will return to the classroom.

The teacher is responsible for coordinating the services between the local school and the hospital or homebound teacher. Homebound programs should not be used to protect a child from society, placate parents, or keep the district from providing needed services to children who have never been in school. Students are homebound for a limited time and a specific purpose. For the most part, they are expected to return to school in the near future.

Medications and Medical Services in the Schools

As a general rule, the only health care procedure teachers may legally administer is to see that a typical playground wound is cleaned with soap and water. Depending on the state and local board policy, teachers may be accused of medical malpractice if they bandage a wound, help a student take any medication, take a temperature, apply a topical ointment or alcohol, or even cut a hangnail.

Even when a parent has sent a signed and dated note requesting that the teacher administer or oversee a child take medication, malpractice is an issue. Educators and other non-health-related professionals in schools should know local district policy on the administration of medications. If no written policy exists, then teachers, parents, and other professionals in the schools should make sure that one is developed and approved as soon as possible.

Barrier-Free Design

The child who uses a wheelchair or braces needs to be able to gain access to the cafeteria, bathroom, chemistry room, etc., just as all other students do. Numerous changes have been made to make environments more accessible and safe, many adaptations still need to be made. Although a new or remodeled facility may meet building inspection and state code requirements, yet (a) the doors may be too heavy for the child to open, even though the door handle has been modified, (b) bathroom stalls, though enlarged, may be inaccessible because there is no space to maneuver the wheelchair in order to enter the stall, (c) the ramps built to overcome the barrier of stairs may be so steep that the electric wheelchair cannot pull the grade or the ramp may start an inch above the ground, (d) the threshhold plate may be too tall for the child to push himself over even though the door has been widened, and so on. If a program for children with physical handicaps or a single child with a physical handicap is anticipated, a tour of the school by the children or child, as early as possible ahead of time, could identify needed changes in the physical environment.

Transportation

Although it may not seem to be all that important, transportation arrangements (or lack of them) often dictate who gets which services, where, and for how long. Transportation should facilitate educational programs, not dictate the services provided. This is a problem particularly in programs for low-incidence handicapped children: those who are autistic, deaf, blind, deaf-blind, or physically handicapped. Often, these children are bused for considerable distances in specially equipped buses. In some school districts, transportation officers have told administrators that a child's school day must end at noon or be otherwise limited because "We just can't make any other arrangements." The law requires that appropriate transportation services be provided to each child who has a handicap. A shortened day so that buses can run other places is *not* part of an appropriate education. Bus drivers need training in managing the child who has a handicap. Bus drivers who serve special populations should receive additional training in managing and understanding these children.

Special Physical Needs

Within a program for children with physical or multiple handicaps, the educator's role is changed. The teacher not only develops cognitive and social behaviors, but also makes sure that the child gains and uses the physical skills needed to process the information acquired.

Educators must know what and how the occupational, physical, and speech therapists are training the child in order to follow through with appropriate activities in the classroom. All too often, therapy occurs in isolation, without the teacher being involved.

Changes cannot be expected very quickly or perhaps at all if the only time the child "does it right" is during the few minutes of therapy each week. Positions, adaptive equipment, relaxation techniques, and so forth can be used with the child if taught to the teacher by the therapists so that a comprehensive and appropriate education can be provided.

Teaming and Working With Others

The more severely handicapped a child is, the more likely it is that many professionals and aides will work with the child during any school day. Therefore, educators must know how to work with other professionals, how to use the information others provide, how to gain needed services from other professionals, and how to instruct others to provide training for a child.

For these children, the classroom teacher's duties include consulting with professionals from health and social service fields and training and overseeing the work of aides. The teacher of physically or multiply handicapped children often facilitates communication between (a) health personnel, (b) teachers who have the child in their regular classrooms, and (c) parents.

A number of problems make it hard for professionals to work together. *Time* is a major problem. Both the lack of time for team meetings and the off-task discussions that waste what time there is create problems. *Jargon* or vocabulary is a problem. Each professional has been trained to describe or think using a specific set of constructs and words. Frequently, one team member will have to ask another to translate the terms just used. *Lack of personal or professional regard* and lack of regard for the value of teaming is a third problem area. Some team members may have biases against other professions represented on the team. This kind of attitude works against learning to work as a team or ever developing a team that will be of value to the student. On the other hand, when teaming works, mental health, job satisfaction, and performance are better. Parents, students, and educational personnel seem to respect and to nurture each other more for mutual benefit.

School Management of Children With Physical Handicaps

In addition to responsibilities for teaching academic and social skills, the teacher of children with physical or multiple handicaps also has to observe each child for changes in condition, illness, effects of medication, and general physical well-being. When questions about the child's physical problems or health arise, the teacher must make appropriate referrals. The referrals may be to the parents, the school nurse, a physician, a health agency, a therapist, or a social worker. A record of the referrals and when and to whom they are made should be kept.

The educator who is not used to observing a child's physical status requires a new awareness and a new orientation. When a child first enters the classroom, before the more traditional lessons begin, the teacher should automatically go through a health check of the child. This may be an informal, quick, visual inspection of the child, or it may be a more detailed inspection, especially with a severely handicapped child who lacks the verbal skills to communicate that he does not feel well, that his braces hurt, that the wheelchair lock is not working, and so forth.

The educator observes for signs that indicate emergency health needs, infection, skin breakdown, communicable diseases, cleanliness, and general physical status. In addition, daily observation includes checking the functioning of equipment and its general fit and usability.

Physical Inspection   In looking over the child for potential problems, the teacher should include the following checkpoints:
General:
Does he seem as peppy as usual? (energy level, smile, greeting, etc.)
Does he initiate contact as usual?
Does any physical feature attract your attention unusually?
Does his skin tone seem to be normal?
Are there sores, rashes, cuts, blisters, or callouses that you haven't seen before?
Does clothing seem to fit differently? (protrusions, swelling, etc.)
Does he hold his stomach or other body parts as though they hurt or are tender?
Equipment:
Does he require orthotics in order to function? (braces, crutches, glasses, hearing aids, wheelchair, splint, etc.)
Are any parts of the equipment missing?
Are sharp edges exposed or are cracks appearing in upholstery?
Are grips, tips, or heads of crutches worn?

When observing a child whose skin tone is different from that of the observer, special care must be taken to recognize the physical cues, which may vary. For example, a white teacher observing a black child should be aware that a rash will not appear as red or pink bumps, but may appear as darkened, black, or deep brown bumps.

Just as skin tone varies from pinks to yellows in white children, it also varies in children who are black, native American, Asian, or of other heritage. A teacher should check with a child's parents or with health care professionals of the same group to learn

Table 25—1   Physical Signs for Teacher Observation

	General	Whites	Blacks	Asians	Indians
Skin	hot, cold, clammy, bumpy, bumps, bruises, callouses, keloids, rashes, cuts, sores, swelling	abnormally red, blue, or yellow tints	gray or ashy		heightened red tone when flushed, rose color for rash
Mouth	coating on tongue, color & wetness of mucous membranes				
Gums	healthy pink tone		may normally have brown areas		
Eyes	clear, bright, crusty, red rimmed, lack of moisture, colored fluid	bloodshot	bloodshot may normally have brown spots on sclera	bloodshot	bloodshot
Nose	mucus visible, crusty, blood in mucus				
Lips	clear, pink to red tones	blue when cold	gray or ashy when cold		purple-blue when cold
Ears	discharge from canal, reddened		lobes may be reddened if fever is present		
Lymph Nodes	swollen or tender				
Hair	dull, matted, patchy, nits, flaky, crusty		many blacks do not produce much oil from the scalp, therefore may only shampoo once every week or two; may add oil for sheen		
Fingernails	clear, solid without imbedded corners or creases without nail		longitudinal brown streaks may appear normally		
Fingernail Beds or Base		when cold or cyanotic may become blue	when cold or cyanotic may become gray or ashy		purplish-blue when cold
Respiration	shallow, labored, noisy, cough with phlegm				
Other			heightened incidence of umbilical hernia		

the specific signs of variance of skin tone, appearance of bruises, callouses, **keloids,** rashes, as well as signs of respiratory distress, shock, and temperature change. Parts of the body that often can be read for signs of dysfunction are included in Table 25–1.

ADAPTIVE EQUIPMENT

Appropriate educational and medical interventions with children who are physically handicapped may involve the use of a diverse array of equipment. Individuals may require prostheses (aids designed to function as limbs), orthoses (aids for assistance), mobility devices such as wheelchairs, positioning aids, or academic aids in order to function in the classroom.

Prostheses

A prosthesis provides an artificial replacement for a missing body part (Figure 25–5). Present-day prostheses allow the individual to function in ways that were not possible. No single device or set of devices is best for everyone. A good prosthesis provides for optimal function, comfort, and **cosmesis**

based upon the individual's condition, vocation, and desires. The primary function of a prosthesis is to replace lost function, lost support, or both. To do this, the device must duplicate normal movements as much as possible and restrain residual or facilitative normal or adapted functioning as little as possible.

Teachers of children who use an artificial limb should be aware of the child's responses to the weight, function, and general comfort of the device. Children often do not want to wear a prosthesis. They may say that they can "do better" or "go faster" without it. In this instance, parents, teachers, and therapists should jointly discuss with the child how important it is for the child to wear the prosthesis. Will the child derive more long-term benefit from wearing the limb and becoming proficient in its use, or is there a more functional alternative for this child?

Orthoses

The primary *upper-extremity* orthoses are splints (Figure 25–6). A splint should help a child to attain desired actions. Using the device should help a child use his limb more efficiently. An orthosis may make hand use more functional, or it may make it possible for a child to complete certain tasks. At times, a splint may not be helpful for arm and hand functioning, especially for specific tasks. Therefore, the teacher needs to know from therapists or special educators what to expect of the child when he wears the splint, how the splint should be worn, for how long, etc.

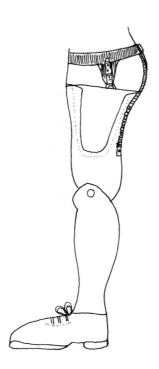

Figure 25–5   Long Leg Prosthesis

Source: Reprinted from J. Venn, L. Morganstern, & M. K. Dykes, Checklists for evaluating the fit and function of orthoses, prostheses, and wheelchairs in the classroom. *Teaching Exceptional Children,* 1979, *11*(2), page 51.

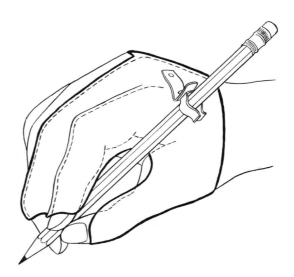

Figure 25–6   A Splint Provides Greater Control of Fine Hand Movements

Source: Reprinted with permission from J. L. Bigge, *Teaching individuals with physical and multiple disabilities,* 2nd ed. Columbus, Ohio: Charles E. Merrill, 1982, page 238.

The primary *lower-extremity* orthoses are braces, which come in three major forms: short leg braces, long leg braces, and hip-leg braces. Their main purposes are to support body weight, control involuntary movements, and prevent or correct deformities.

When the condition occurs at the ankle joint, an ankle-foot orthosis (AFO) (Figure 25–7) or short leg brace may be prescribed. When the bar extends past the knee joint, the brace is called a knee-ankle-foot orthosis (KAFO) or long leg brace (Figure 25–8). This device prevents buckling or **hyperextension** of the knee. When a long leg brace is used to control movements of the hip joint as well, a pelvic band is attached to the top of the upright bars. This is called a hip-knee-ankle-foot orthosis (HKAFO) or long leg brace with pelvic band (Figure 25–9).

Orthotists have begun to make some appliances of plastics instead of metal and leather. Currently, less expensive and easy-to-use plastics of various types are being used to meet many functional and structural demands. Plastic materials allow greater flexibility in design, easier adjustment, lower appliance weight, and improved cosmesis.

When observing a child in braces, the teacher should note the general functioning of the brace. Does the child call attention to himself because he squeaks or because he seems to be constantly adjusting something? The teacher should know enough about the brace to know how it should look when it is aligned and working properly. Often, the teacher is the first person to notice when a brace seems to be positioned incorrectly or when it needs repair.

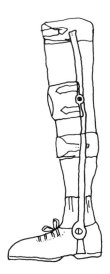

Figure 25–8   Knee-Ankle-Foot Orthosis (KAFO)

Source: Reprinted from J. Venn, L. Morganstern, & M. K. Dykes, Checklists for evaluating the fit and function of orthoses, prostheses, and wheelchairs in the classroom. *Teaching Exceptional Children*, 1979, *11*(2), page 51.

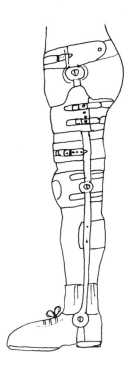

Figure   25–9   Hip-Knee-Ankle-Foot   Orthosis (HKAFO)

Source: Reprinted from J. Venn, L. Morganstern, & M. K. Dykes, Checklist for evaluating the fit and function of orthoses, prostheses, and wheelchairs in the classroom. *Teaching Exceptional Children*, 1979, *11*(2), page 51.

Figure 25–7   Ankle-Foot Orthosis (AFO)

Source: Reprinted from J. Venn, L. Morganstern, & M. K. Dykes, Checklists for evaluating the fit and function of orthoses, prostheses, and wheelchairs in the classroom. *Teaching Exceptional Children*, 1979, *11*(2), page 51.

Wheelchairs

A wheelchair (Figure 25–10) is prescribed by a physician for individuals who are unable to ambulate or for those for whom ambulation is unsteady, unsafe, or too strenuous. In some cases, a person may be ambulatory but unable to rise unassisted from sitting to standing. This person may also need to use a wheelchair.

The most commonly used type of wheelchair has four wheels and is made of metal and upholstery. The two back wheels are large and have a separate rim that can be grasped to propel the chair. The two small front wheels are casters that pivot freely. There are numerous special parts and features that may be included, depending on the individual's needs. A wheelchair is always fitted to the needs of the individual. There is no single standard wheelchair that will meet the needs of all nonambulatory pupils.

Recent developments include more lightweight, adaptive wheelchairs as well as motorized wheelchairs. Lightweight chairs are designed for children. Motorized wheelchairs of various designs may be prescribed for people who are unable to propel themselves independently. In schools, children who have MD or who have high-level spinal injuries are most often the ones who use motorized chairs.

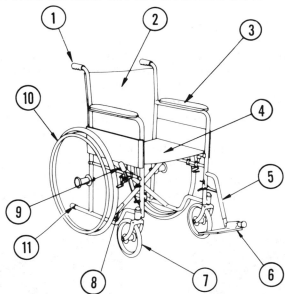

Figure 25–10   Wheelchair Terminology
1. Handgrips
2. Back Upholstery
3. Armrests
4. Seat Upholstery
5. Front Rigging
6. Footplate
7. Casters
8. Crossbraces
9. Wheel Locks
10. Wheel and Handrim
11. Tipping Lever

Source: Everest and Jennings.

In the classroom, a chair with removable desk arms should be used whenever possible. This affords the child the opportunity to pull up to tables and to participate in more activities. Removable leg rests and foot plates give the child access to a greater variety of environments and make it easier to transport the chair. Depending on the child's needs, the therapist should be able to modify the wheelchair without jeopardizing the child's need for support, balance, maintenance, or positioning.

At times, positioning cushions are added to the wheelchair. These should not be removed unless the therapist or physician gives permission. The teacher should be aware that rips in upholstery can tear the child's skin and serve as sources for bacterial growth and odor. Torn upholstery should be replaced as soon as possible. As the child grows, the wheelchair will need to be replaced or modified. The teacher should notify therapists and parents when the child seems to be top heavy in the chair, confined by a too-tight seat, or generally uncomfortable in the chair.

In the schools, several devices are taking the place of some wheelchairs. These include motorized golf carts, or scooterlike devices, as well as travel chairs and stressed strollers.

Positioning aids

Numerous pieces of equipment may be used to enhance physical development or positioning to allow greater participation in class. A prone board (Figure 25–11) is used to help align the child, provide a change of position, get the child upright against gravity, or help the child develop weight-bearing ability. A number of children may use the same prone board during the day; therefore, many adjustments in the board may be needed in order for each child to be properly positioned. Adjustments can be made by using bands or pads, or by adjusting the angle or height of the board. The amount of time that each child spends in each position will need to be determined on an individual basis. No child should be positioned on a prone board unless supervised by the physical or occupational therapist. No child should be left unattended on a prone board.

Therapists should be available, not only to evaluate which child needs which equipment, but also to demonstrate how the child should use the board or other pieces of equipment. This is true for barrel chairs and all other specialized furniture and equipment used by the child. If equipment is used incorrectly, it will not only work against the child but may also cause him to develop compensations, such as poor posture, which may lead to contractures or ultimately to deformities. This inhibits future gains.

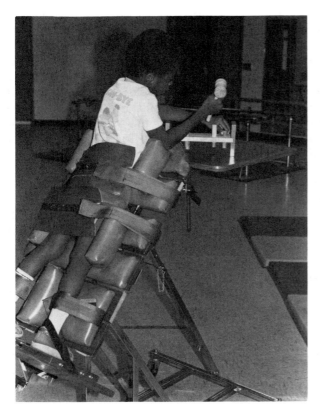

Figure 25—11   Prone Board

Academic Aids

There are a number of academic aids, including various materials, equipment, and adaptive devices, that can be extremely useful to students who are physi-cally handicapped. Academic aids can help students compensate for lack of coordination and restricted hand function. They can make it easier to understand and express ideas and concepts in class. Aids for physically handicapped students include very simple devices (such as pencils with built-up grasps), and complex machines (such as typewriters controlled by eyeblinks).

Typewriters   Typewriters (Figure 25–12) are used frequently and are considered the preferred method of written communication for students whose hand-writing is illegible or tediously slow. Adaptations for the typewriter include special typing tables that ac-commodate wheelchairs and other orthotic devices, typing sticks and mouth sticks, and various arm sup-ports. Keyboard guards (Figure 25–13) are frequently used. A keyboard guard is a metal or plastic plate that has holes punched to correspond to the keys of the typewriter. The guard is useful as a resting place for the hands. The user can apply pressure to the guard to help steady himself. Both IBM and Smith-Corona supply keyguards for their typewriters. Electronic memory storage systems, printers, scanners, and sorters are also available. These enable more ad-vanced use of the typewriter.

Other Writing Aids   For the student who is phys-ically handicapped but capable of writing by hand, a clipboard that holds papers and worksheets can help the student to write as precisely as possible. Pens and pencils can be adapted for individuals by building up the handles with foam, drilling a hole in a small rub-ber ball and pushing the writing utensil through the hole (Figure 25–14), or using rubber tubing. These adaptations increase the holding area and provide a better grip surface. Felt-tipped pens, primary pencils, and other markers may be used because they require less pressure to produce legible markings. More

Figure 25—12   Using a Mouth Stick to Type

Source: Reprinted with permission from N. G. Har-ing (Ed.), *Behavior of exceptional children,* 2nd ed. Columbus, Ohio: Charles E. Merrill, 1978, page 367.

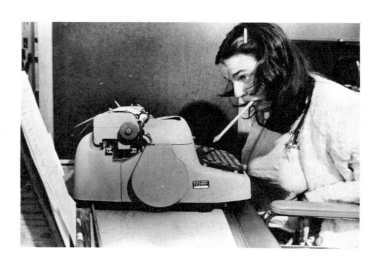

Figure 25–13 The Keyboard Guard Makes It Easier for Students to Type

Source: Reprinted with permission from N. G. Haring (Ed.), *Behavior of exceptional children,* 2nd ed. Columbus, Ohio: Charles E. Merrill, 1978, page 367.

complex writing aids such as a hand splint (see Figure 25–6) can be constructed by occupational therapists. Splints may be used to compensate for a poor or weak grasp or for reduced joint movement in the fingers or thumb. Positioning of the whole body is important in stabilizing a child for writing. A chair that allows the child's feet to rest solidly on the floor and a positioning dowel for the other hand may be as important as any built-up writing device to help the child learn to write efficiently.

General Aids for Assistance in Class Using typewriters or specialized writing aids and equipment is not practical in some academic situations. Often, carbonless notepaper can be used by a fellow student to record information for the student who is physically handicapped. At other times, a talking book may be useful. Talking books are cassette tape recorders or record players used for recording and playing information. Talking books are available as a free

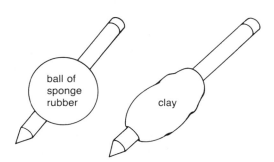

ball of sponge rubber

clay

Figure 25–14 Aids to Help a Child Grasp a Pencil

Source: Reprinted with permission from J. L. Bigge, *Teaching individuals with physical and multiple disabilities,* 2nd ed. Columbus, Ohio: Charles E. Merrill, 1982, page 234.

service for all blind and physically handicapped individuals who are unable to hold a book, turn a page, or take written notes. Talking books are useful for recording classroom lectures and other auditory information. In addition, a wide range and variety of stories, novels, textbooks, and magazines are available through talking books. Specialized talking books called compressed speech machines play back recorded speech at faster than normal speed with very little distortion. Compressed speech recorders can be useful when large amounts of information must be learned quickly. Talking book services are available free from the Library for the Blind and Physically Handicapped. Regional units of this national library are located in most large cities and provide services to a specific area.

Reading Aids Aids that assist in reading books and magazines include book holders and page turners. Book holders are available in several types. Some are fixed supports; others are adjustable to various angles. Book holders may be purchased from health supply stores or can be homemade. Page turners include rubber thimbles to provide friction, handheld devices with sticks, mouthpieces and headbands with rubber-tipped sticks, and electrically operated page turners, which can be purchased commercially.

CLASSROOM ORGANIZATION

Knowledge of everything that has been discussed thus far comes into play when the teacher attempts to organize and operate the classroom. The major concerns in classroom organization are (a) the importance of teaming and planning, (b) the problems that can develop or be prevented because of scheduling, and (c) the benefits that can be realized by effectively working with parents and families.

Teaming and Planning

A major difference in teaching children with physical handicaps is that they require a great deal more consulting, referring, planning, and adaptation of environments, equipment, and lessons. The classroom teacher must know which of the professionals in medicine, allied health, psychology, and social service are trained to provide what type of developmental data, services, and evaluations. The teacher must work closely with professionals in these areas in order to develop the comprehensive individualized education plan for the child. The teacher is responsible for making sure that (a) all services needed by the child are being provided and (b) all services provide for the general well-being of the child in the school.

Just as there are teachers who prefer not to teach children with physical handicaps, so are there professionals in each of the related fields who do not want to work with these children and who are not trained to do so. Therefore, teachers need to be aware of those professionals in the local community who are particularly interested in providing high quality services to children with handicaps and who are trained to do so.

A child's needs are not met if each professional simply identifies his own goals and objectives and staples these to the educator's objectives. This does not make for an appropriate program. Rather, therapists, teachers, and others together need to determine priority goals and objectives that all will work toward together. When an objective is agreed upon, one member of the team may determine the best way to teach the child that particular task. This procedure will train the other members so that everyone can work with the child in the same way. Each professional on the team is responsible not only for assessing, planning with the team, and training the child, but also for training the other professionals and aides and for conducting evaluations related to acquisition of certain skills or tasks. Plans for school-based services for children with physical handicaps should include objectives for acquiring academic skills as well as motor, language, self-help, social, and adult living skills. These plans should be implemented in a way that allows professionals to assist each other in all training.

Professionals work together to provide services for children with handicaps in four primary areas of interaction: diagnosis, planning, treatment, and evaluation. These are included in Table 25–2. In order to develop an appropriate comprehensive program for a child, an exchange of information among professionals is required. There are specific questions that each team member may expect others to answer. For example, Table 25–3 contains a list of questions that an

educator might ask of a physician. A similar list of questions may be developed for other interactions (between the speech-language therapist and physical therapist, school nurse and teacher, parent and psychologist, etc.).

Table 25–2   A Model for Comprehensive Intervention With Children Who Are Handicapped

Identification	*Compile an Educational, Medical, and Social History* Gather developmental or achievement data Gather medical and other records Conduct initial family interview
Diagnostic	*Conduct a Comprehensive Diagnostic Evaluation* Conduct an educational evaluation in all learning areas Refer for further medical or therapy evaluations if needed Conduct specialized evaluations as necessary
Planning	*Determine Priorities for Intervention* Conduct a team meeting with input from all For each learning area determine: strengths, weaknesses, gaps in development, splinter skills, and priorities for programming
	Develop an IEP Involve parents and all other team members Establish the goals, nature, and extent of the child's program including related services to be provided
Treatment / Programming	*Implement a Daily Plan* List daily objectives, activities, and person responsible for skill teaching and evaluation
Evaluation	*Record Child's Progress Systematically* *Reevaluate and Update Planning and Programming Components*

Table 25–3 Questions Educators May Need to Ask Physicians

1. *General*

   Is there any question that what the child sees, hears, or feels (e.g., pressure, heat) is not within the normal range?

   Have referrals been made for evaluations by medical specialists (orthopedist, urologist, etc.)?

   Has the child received all inoculations as are appropriate?

   Are dietary or activity restrictions or changes required by the child?

2. *Long Term*

   Will the condition or disease have impact on the child's abilities as an adult? What is the general prognosis?

   Will *what* the child does or *how* he does it need to be different from that expected of the normal child in school? If so, how? Are there signs I should look for concerning the child's functioning or change in ability or attitude?

   What type of information or input do you desire from the teacher relevant to the child's functioning?

   Are there indications or contraindications relevant to classroom or school activities, behaviors, or expectations that I should know? What are they?

3. *Immediate*

   Medications:

   If the child is on medication, are there potential effects or side effects that I should know about?

   Must the child take the medication while at school or is it possible for it to be administered at other times?

   If the medication must be administered at school, *put in writing* all instructions for (1) how it is to be given, (2) how much, (3) how often, (4) for how long, and (5) if the child requires assistance in administering it. (If no school nurse is available to assist the child, should the teacher assist in the administration of the medication?) This written prescription for administration and use of the medication must be on file at the school after it is made available to the teacher.

   Implications:

   Should I expect to see changes in behavior, cognitive ability, physical ability, etc., as a result of the condition or disease? What is the expected course of such changes (speed, intensity, plateauing, etc.)?

   Are there related services (e.g., physical therapy, counseling, etc.) that the child or family will need as a result of the condition or disease? Have you *requested in writing* that such services be provided or that evaluations for potential services in these areas are appropriate?

   From a health viewpoint, is there special equipment that the child will need in order to participate in school activities?

Scheduling

When establishing the daily program for a child with a physical handicap, which professional (the teacher, therapist, nurse, etc.) should decide when a particular service or training session will be held? At times, the issue of priority in scheduling has worked against the child by setting educator against therapist, therapist against therapist, etc.

Appropriate scheduling for each child should be done on a priority basis. If the most important skills to be developed for the child at this time are determined by the team to be language and the speech-language therapist is the agreed-upon team member to present the training to the child and to train the team members to use specific procedures, *then* the speech-language therapist should be given first priority in the daily scheduling of activities for the child. If reading or group social-skill development is the priority goal, then the teacher would be the first one to have input in determining the child's sequence of activities during the day.

All decisions, whether they concern medical, education, or quality of life issues, must be made ultimately by the family or with explicit input from the family or guardian of the individual. The individual who is old enough and capable of input also should be included in decision making. Each professional who provides services to children with handicaps should (a) consult with, (b) inform, (c) train and, above all, (d) listen to and support the parents or guardians of each child.

We, as professionals, should never lose sight of the concept that all children have the same needs for love, caring, and growth. We must see the child, not the handicap, as the basis for services rendered. We provide services to meet the needs of a child who has physical or multiple handicaps, not to a physically handicapped child. Our attitudes toward the child and the family or guardian are critical to the long-term effectiveness and worth of our interventions.

SUMMARY

In this chapter, several concerns related to using health, physical, and medical data in the classroom have been discussed. These concerns include definitions and services, the roles of various medical and health-related personnel, the learning characteristics of children who have physical handicaps, and the social-emotional concerns that can influence their learning and their lives. Adaptations needed in the educational environment, various adaptive equipment that is typically used in classrooms, and the major concerns in classroom organization were also discussed. In large part, the purpose has been to show that the information presented in the previous chapters of this book has implications for daily functioning in the classroom and, in the long term, for the lives of the children and their families. The reader who is interested in further information about physical functioning or educational programming for children who have physical or health impairments should consult the resources listed below.

FOR MORE INFORMATION

The references listed below will be useful as sources for additional information about physical functioning (i.e., the nature of physically handicapping conditions and health impairments) and educational programming.

Physical Functioning

Batshaw, M. L., & Perret, W. M. *Children with handicaps: A medical primer.* Baltimore: Paul H. Brookes, 1981.

Cruickshank, W. M. (Ed.). *Cerebral palsy: A developmental disability* (3rd ed.). Syracuse: Syracuse University Press, 1976.

Gyulay, J. *The dying child.* New York: McGraw-Hill, 1978.

Haslam, R. H., & Valletutti, P. J. (Eds.) *Medical problems in the classroom: The teacher's role in diagnosis and management.* Baltimore: University Park Press, 1975.

Jacob, S., & Francone, C. *Elements of anatomy and physiology.* Philadelphia: W. B. Saunders, 1976.

Mullins, J. B. *A teacher's guide to management of physically handicapped students.* Springfield, Ill.: Charles C Thomas, 1979.

Lemeshaw, S. *Handbook of clinical types in mental retardation.* Boston: Allyn & Bacon, 1982.

Peterson, R., & Cleveland, J. (Eds.). *Medical Problems in the classroom: An educator's guide.* Springfield, Ill.: Charles C. Thomas, 1976.

Rubin, B. A. Black skin. *Journal of School Health,* 1977, *47,* 365–367.

Educational Programming

Best, G. A. *Individuals with physical disabilities: An introduction for educators.* St. Louis: C. V. Mosby, 1978.

Bigge, J. (Ed.). *Teaching individuals with physical and multiple disabilities* (2nd ed.). Columbus, Ohio: Charles E. Merrill, 1982.

Calhoun, M. L., & Hawisher, M. F. *Teaching and learning strategies for physically handicapped students.* Baltimore: University Park Press, 1979.

Deloach, C., & Greer, B. *Adjustment to severe physical disability: A metamorphosis.* New York: McGraw-Hill, 1981.

Dykes, M. K. Teaching students with physical disabilities and health impairments. In M. Hardeman, M. W. Egan, & E. Landau (Eds.), *What will we do in the morning?* Dubuque, Iowa: William C. Brown, 1981.

Edgington, D. *The physically handicapped child in your classroom: A handbook for teachers.* Springfield, Ill.: Charles C Thomas, 1976.

French, R., & Jansma, P. *Special physical education.* Columbus, Ohio: Charles E. Merrill, 1982.

Hale, G. *Source book for the disabled.* New York: Bantam Books, 1979.

Kleinberg, S. *Education of the chronically ill child.* Rockville, Md.: Aspen Systems Corp., 1982.

Lindmann, J. E. *Psychological and behavioral aspects of physical disabilities.* New York: Plenum Books, 1981.

Love, H. D. *Teaching physically handicapped children: Methods and materials.* Springfield, Ill.: Charles C Thomas, 1978.

Silverman, F. H. *Communication for the speechless.* Englewood Cliffs, N.J.: Prentice-Hall, 1980.

Umbreit, J., & Cardullias, P. J. (Eds.). *Educating the severely physically handicapped* (Vols. 1–4). Reston, Va.: Division on the Physically Handicapped, The Council for Exceptional Children, 1980.

Wright, B. A. *Physical disability: A psychological approach.* New York: Harper & Row, 1960.

This section presents information about the major parent and professional organizations that are concerned with the various disorders discussed in Sections Two and Three. The organizations are described under two general headings: (a) orthopedic and neurological disorders, and (b) health conditions or impairments. Under each heading, the order of the organizations corresponds to the order in which each physical disability or health problem was discussed in the earlier chapters. This material is intended to serve as a resource for those who are interested in more information about the health care and education of physically disabled and health impaired children.

ORTHOPEDIC AND NEUROLOGICAL DISORDERS

Cerebral Palsy

American Academy for Cerebral Palsy and Developmental Medicine   P.O. Box 11083; 2405 Westwood Avenue; Richmond, Virginia, 23230.

Resources

AACPDM is a multidisciplinary scientific society devoted to (a) the study of cerebral palsy and related neurological handicapping disorders, and (b) professional education in developmental medicine. The academy was founded in 1948 to foster and stimulate professional education, research, and interest in the problems involved in understanding these disorders and in improving the care and rehabilitation of their victims. The academy actively supports both education and research. Educational activities include sponsorship of a national conference and several regional conferences each year. Research activities are supported through a program of small grants.

United Cerebral Palsy Association, Inc.   66 E. 34th Street; New York, New York, 10016.

UCP is a nationwide voluntary organization that targets services on the multiple handicaps of cerebral palsy. Its mission is (a) to involve in the mainstream of society individuals with cerebral palsy and their families and those with similar service needs by assuring their rights as citizens and their ability to receive services as needed, and (b) to prevent cerebral palsy and minimize its effects. To accomplish these ends, UCP provides community services for persons with disabilities and their families, serves as an advocate in helping disabled persons gain access to services, funds research and professional education related to disability, and conducts a nationwide program to educate the public about cerebral palsy and the means of preventing its occurrence. UCP has nearly 250 state and local affiliates, which serve designated geographic areas.

Curvatures of the Spine

The Scoliosis Association, Inc. 1 Penn Plaza; New York, New York, 10001.

TSA was founded by scoliosis patients and their families. Its goals include the education of the general public about scoliosis and other spinal deviations. The association has encouraged and sponsored scoliosis screening programs in schools throughout the country and has published a screening manual for school health personnel to use in these programs. The association also sponsors the formation of scoliosis "clubs," or chapters, throughout the country. These chapters are parent/patient support groups that afford the scoliosis patient and his or her family a meeting place every month with other families involved with scoliosis. The association publishes a quarterly newsletter, *Backtalk*.

Epilepsy

Epilepsy Foundation of America 1828 L Street, N.W.; Washington, D.C., 20036.

EFA is a national voluntary agency specifically dedicated to the welfare of people who have epilepsy. It is governed by an all-volunteer board of directors. EFA is committed to the prevention and control of epilepsy and to improving the lives of those who have it. The foundation works to achieve these goals through a broad range of programs in information and education, advocacy, support of research, and the delivery of needed services to people with epilepsy and their families. More than 100 local organizations throughout the country are affiliated with EFA.

Limb Deficiencies

National Amputation Foundation 12-45 105th Street; Whitestone, New York, 11357.

NAF was founded in 1919 by a group of veterans who suffered the loss of a limb during World War I. Originally, the foundation dedicated all of its efforts to helping veteran amputees. Since then, the foundation has expanded its facilities to include all amputees. NAF provides many services, including legal counsel, vocational guidance and placement, social activities, liaison with outside groups, psychological aid, and training in the use of prosthetic devices. Since 1961, the foundation has maintained a Prosthetic Centre for manufacturing and repairing prosthetic devices and to train people in the use of these devices. NAF publishes a monthly magazine, *The AMP*.

Muscular Dystrophy

Muscular Dystrophy Association 810 Seventh Avenue; New York, New York, 10019.

MDA is a national voluntary health agency that provides medical services to people with neuromuscular diseases. Diagnostic and treatment services are provided in more than 230 hospital-affiliated clinics. In addition to medical care, MDA, through its more than 200 chapters, also provides many other services: the provision of orthopedic aids, recreation at MDA summer and winter camps, and transportation assistance. All services are provided without charge. MDA supports nearly 800 research projects worldwide. These projects focus on 40 neuromuscular diseases (including the spinal muscular atrophies). In addition to medical services and research, MDA conducts educational programs for the public and for medical professionals.

Musculoskeletal Disorders

The American Brittle Bone Society 1256 Merrill Drive; West Chester, Pennsylvania, 19380.

ABBS is a national health organization that was founded in 1977 to help people who have osteogenesis imperfecta (OI) and their families. The society (a) provides information and support for families with OI, (b) promotes public and professional education about OI, and (c) encourages and funds research that will lead to improved treatment, carrier detection, and possibly for a cure for OI.

Spina Bifida

Spina Bifida Association of America 343 S. Dearborn, Suite 319; Chicago, Illinois, 60604.

SBA is a national voluntary association that includes many local chapters. The goals of the association are to promote research, treatment, training of personnel, and public awareness of the problems of spina bifida. SGA (a) offers consultation to parents, (b) develops educational materials for parents, lay people, and professionals, and (c) sponsors an annual national conference that includes seminars on scientific, social, medical, and educational programs. The association also publishes a bimonthly newsletter called *Pipeline*.

Spinal Cord Injury

National Spinal Cord Injury Foundation 369 Elliot Street; Newton Upper Falls, Massachusetts, 02164.

NSCIF is a voluntary health agency that was founded in 1948 by the Paralyzed Veterans of America. Its goals are to prevent spinal cord injuries, to develop systems of care, to promote basic research, and to improve the quality of life for persons who have a spinal cord injury. The foundation's membership includes individuals who have a spinal cord injury, their families, friends, and professionals. NSCIF has a national office, a research office, professional advisory committees, and 40 chapters throughout the United States.

HEALTH PROBLEMS

Asthma

American Lung Association 1740 Broadway; New York, New York, 10019.

ALA is a national voluntary organization that includes one or more affiliates in each state. The purpose of the association is to prevent and control lung disease. ALA's activities focus on pediatric lung disease programs, adult lung disease programs, environmental health, antismoking, community health, and professional education and training. Grants for research in lung disease are provided both by ALA and its state affiliates.

National Foundation for Asthma, Inc. P.O. Box 50304; Tucson, Arizona, 85705.

NFA was incorporated in 1949 to provide health services for peole whose asthma caused a financial hardship. The foundation is governed by a volunteer board of community leaders who are concerned with the special problems of asthma. NFA supplements the cost of patient services, which may include medical evaluation and treatment, physical therapy, breathing retraining, biofeedback, counseling, and X rays and lab work when required. The foundation also has a program of grants for continuing medical education and for research.

Blood Diseases

The National Hemophilia Foundation 25 W. 39th Street; New York, New York, 10018.

NHF has more than 50 chapters that help families of hemophiliacs confront the financial and other difficulties associated with the disease. The foundation fosters and maintains a directory of treatment centers. It also sponsors research projects, provides scholarships for hemophilic students, and encourages federal and state agencies to open up more sources of financial aid. Locally, chapters register hemophiliacs, counsel them and their families about treatment facilities and interested physicians, and direct them to bureaus that offer assistance. For school personnel, NHA chapters provide literature and arrange medical consultation or other informed guidance about a hemophilic child and his family.

Cancer

American Cancer Society, Inc. 777 Third Avenue; New York, New York, 10017.

ACS is a voluntary organization dedicated to the control and eradication of cancer. The society includes 58 incorporated chartered divisions throughout the United States. Programs of research, education, and service to the cancer patient are sponsored by ACS. The society's long-range objective is to eliminate cancer entirely as a disease. The immediate goal is to save more lives and to diminish suffering from cancer to the fullest extent possible. The immediate goal is accomplished largely through (a) education of the public to the dangers of cancer and the possibilities of cure, (b) education of the medical profession about the latest advances in diagnosis and treatment of cancer, and (c) direct service to the cancer patient and his or her family.

Childhood Diabetes Mellitis

American Diabetes Association 2 Park Avenue; New York, New York, 10016.

ADA is a national voluntary organization that combats the problem of diabetes through research, patient education, professional education, and public education and detection. Research activities include supporting research that aims to learn more about the nature and causes of diabetes and its care and treatment. Patient education activities include keeping those who have diabetes fully informed of the need for proper management of the disease. As part of this effort, ADA publishes a bimonthly magazine, *Diabetes Forecast*. Professional education activities include keeping physicians and other health personnel abreast of the latest developments to assure continuing improvement in treatment. This involves publishing two ADA journals—*Diabetes* and *Diabetes Care*. Public education and detection activities include increasing public understanding and awareness of diabetes, and discovering unknown diabetics and alerting them to the need for proper treatment.

Cystic Fibrosis

Cystic Fibrosis Foundation   6000 Executive Boulevard, Suite 309; Rockville, Maryland, 20852.

CFF was incorporated in 1955 as the National Cystic Fibrosis Research Foundation. The organization was started by parents and families of children with cystic fibrosis, but now includes many professionals and lay people. Currently, there are 72 state and local chapters. The foundation's purpose is to find the means for the prevention, control, and effective treatment of cystic fibrosis. CFF pursues this objective through programs in research, care, and education at nearly 130 cystic fibrosis centers affiliated with hospitals and university clinics. One of the foundation's major activities is maintaining a national registry of patients who have been seen in the cystic fibrosis centers.

Heart Disorders

American Heart Association   7320 Greenville Avenue; Dallas, Texas, 75231.

AHA is a national voluntary organization that is dedicated solely to the reduction of early death and disability from heart disease and stroke. The association supports research, directs fund raising, and develops community programs and materials for use by patients, health professionals, and the general public. AHA comprises 55 affiliates throughout the country which are further divided into components at the community level. Community service programs are directed specifically at seven key areas: high blood pressure, emergency cardiac care, cardiac rehabilitation and exercise, stroke, heart health education in the young, smoking control, and nutrition.

Juvenile Rheumatoid Arthritis

The Arthritis Foundation   3400 Peachtree Road, N.E.; Atlanta, Georgia, 30326.

AF is a voluntary health agency that has many local chapters throughout the country. The foundation's purpose is to seek the cause, prevention, and cure of arthritis. This is done through support of research, patient and community services, public health information and education, and professional education and training.

Kidney Disorders

National Kidney Foundation, Inc.   2 Park Avenue; New York, New York, 10016.

NKF is a voluntary health agency that has many affiliates in communities throughout the country. The foundation's purpose is to seek the total answer to diseases of the kidney: prevention, treatment, and cure. NKF's activities include support of research, patient services, a nationwide organ donor program, professional education, and public information.

acetabulum A cup-shaped depression on the external surface of the innominate bone (hip bone) in which the head of the femur fits.

acuity Sharpness; clearness; distinctness.

adhesion A uniting of two surfaces or parts, especially the union of the opposing surfaces of a wound.

allergen A substance that stimulates an altered cellular response in the animal or human body, thereby resulting in manifestations of allergy.

ambient Surrounding; present, for example, in the atmosphere.

amblyopia Dimness of vision; a partial loss of sight occurring as a result of nonuse that prevents accurate focusing on the retina.

ambulatory Able to walk about.

amniocentesis Aspiration (drawing out) of amniotic fluid.

amniotic fluid A liquid, secreted by the amniotic membrane, that surrounds the fetus and protects it from injury.

Glossary

amputation The cutting off of a limb or part of a limb.

anal fissures A crack or slit in the mucous membrane of the anus that is very painful and difficult to heal.

aneurysm Circumscribed dilation of an artery or a blood-containing tumor that connects directly with the lumen (space in the interior) of an artery.

anomaly Anything unusual, irregular, or contrary to the general rule.

anoxia Lack of oxygen in organs and tissues.

antibody A modified protein in the blood serum or plasma of an animal, usually formed in response to doses of antigen (material that stimulates an immune response).

arthritis Inflammation of a joint.

arteriogram   An X-ray picture of an artery after injection of a contrast medium into it.

assays   Tests of purity.

ataxia   Loss of the power of muscular coordination.

atherosclerosis   One type of hardening of the arteries through deposits or degenerative accumulation of materials in the inner coat of a blood vessel.

athetosis   A condition in which there is a constant succession of slow, writhing, involuntary movements of flexion, extension, pronation, and supination of the fingers and hands, and sometimes of the toes and feet.

atresia   Closure of a normal opening, passage, or cavity.

atria   The upper chambers of each half of the heart that receive blood and transmit it to the ventricle on the same side.

automatisms   Nonreflex acts performed without conscious volition; conscious or unconscious, but involuntary, performance of certain acts that are often purposeless and sometimes foolish or harmful.

axial skeleton   That portion of the skeleton situated in the central part of the body, in the head and trunk as distinguished from the extremities.

Babinski reflex   Extension instead of normal flexion of the great toe, sometimes with plantar flexion of the other toes, following stroking of the sole; usually associated with organic disease of the pyramidal tracts.

benign   The mild character of an illness or the nonmalignant character of a neoplasm (tumor).

biopsy   Gross and microscopic examination of tissues or cells removed from a living patient, for the purpose of diagnosis or prognosis of disease, or to confirm normal conditions.

blood vessel   A tube (artery, capillary, vein, or sinus) that conveys blood.

brainstem   The midbrain; the pons and medulla oblongata.

bronchitis   Inflammation of the mucous membrane of the bronchial tubes.

bronchospasm   Spasmodic narrowing of the lumen (interior space) of a bronchus (a subdivision of the trachea that conveys air to and from the lungs).

capillary   One of the microscopic blood vessels.

cardiopulmonary   Relating to the heart and lungs.

cataract   A loss of transparency in the crystalline lens of the eye, or of its capsule.

cerebellum   The posterior brain mass that lies above the pons and medulla and beneath the posterior portion of the cerebrum (the principal portion of the brain).

chemotherapy   Treatment of disease by means of chemical substances or drugs.

choreiform syndrome   A term commonly used by medical personnel to refer to a learning disability.

circulatory system   The system of the body responsible for ensuring continuous circulation of the blood, fluid, and other elements of the blood system.

cirrhosis   A disease of the liver. The liver becomes inflamed and degenerates, leading to reduced circulation of blood and bile.

clubbing   Broadening or thickening of the ends of fingers.

coagulation   Clotting; the process of change from a liquid state to that of a soft jellylike solid.

collagen fibers   The white fibers of the skin, tendon, and other connective tissue.

coma   A state of profound unconsciousness from which one cannot be roused.

contracture   A permanent muscular contraction (shortening or increase in tension; shrinkage or reduction in size).

cornea   A transparent membrane that forms a portion of the outer coat of the eyeball.

cosmesis   A regard in therapeutics, especially in surgical operations, for the appearance of the patient; an operation which will improve the looks, or avoidance of one that will disfigure in any way.

cyst   An abnormal sac containing gas, fluid, or a semisolid material.

deciduous teeth   The primary or "baby" teeth.

dentin   The ivory forming the mass of the tooth.

dermatomyositis   A condition characterized by muscle weakness and nonspecific, eczemalike skin eruptions; the muscles are tender and, owing to weakness, the patient is unable to perform normal tasks.

dermis   The deeper or connective tissue layer of the skin.

digestive system   The system of the body primarily concerned with the ingestion, transport, and digestion of food and with the elimination of waste materials.

dilated   Enlarged.

dislocation   Displacement of an organ or body part; specifically, a disturbance or disarrangement of the normal relation of the bones entering into the formation of a joint.

distension   The act or state of being distended or stretched.

distortion   Improper production of a sound, often resulting from the tongue being positioned improperly when speaking.

diuretic   An agent that increases the amount of urine produced relative to the amount of liquid ingested.

duct   A tubular structure giving exit to the secretion of a gland, or conducting any fluid.

dyskinesia Difficulty in performing voluntary movements.

dystonia A state of abnormal tone in any of the tissues.

electrolyte Any compound which, in solution, conducts a current of electricity and is decomposed by it (e.g., sodium, potassium, chloride).

electromyogram A graphic representation of the electrical currents generated in an active muscle.

emphysema A swelling of the lungs due to presence of trapped air or dilation (enlargement) of the pulmonary alveoli or sacs, usually as a result of chronic inflammation.

encephalitis Inflammation of the brain.

endocrine The internal secretion of a gland; denoting a gland that furnishes an internal secretion.

endocrine system The system of ductless glands that is responsible for the secretion of hormones.

evanescent Of short duration; gradually disappearing.

extension The position of a limb that is extended (straightened).

facioscapulohumeral muscular dystrophy A form of progressive muscular dystrophy that affects the face, the scapula (shoulder blades), and the upper arms; onset is usually in early adolescence.

febrile Relating to fever.

femoral head The upper end of the femur or thigh bone.

femur The thigh bone.

flexion The position of a limb or other body part that is flexed (bent); bending of a joint.

flexor A muscle that has the action of flexing (bending or contracting) a joint.

follicle A more or less spherical mass of cells sometimes containing a cavity.

fracture A break, especially a breaking in a bone or cartilage.

gastrointestinal Relating to both the stomach and intestine.

glucosuria The excretion of sugar (glucose) in the urine.

grafting A procedure in which something is inserted into something else to make it an integral part of the latter; specifically, a bit of epidermis, strip of skin, piece of bone, tooth, etc., inserted to supply a defect.

heart murmur A sound, either soft or loud and harsh, produced within the heart and heard by using a stethoscope.

hemorrhoids Dilated veins causing painful swelling in the anus.

hemostatic Arresting the flow of blood within the vessels.

hormone A chemical substance that is formed in one organ or part of the body and carried in the blood to another organ or part which it stimulates to functional activity.

hydrocephalus A condition, usually congenital, marked by excessive accumulation of fluid in the cerebral ventricles, dilating these cavities, thinning the brain, and causing a separation of the cranial bones.

hyperextension Extension of a limb beyond the normal limit.

hypertension High arterial blood pressure.

hypocalcemia Abnormally low levels of calcium in the circulating blood.

hypothyroidism Diminished production of thyroid hormone leading to thyroid insufficiency.

hypotonia A condition in which there is reduced tension or a loss of muscle tone; as a consequence, the muscles may be stretched beyond their normal limits.

hypoxia Decreased amount of oxygen in organs and tissues.

hypsarrhythmia An abnormal and characteristically chaotic brain wave pattern commonly found in patients with infantile spasms.

idiopathic Of unknown cause.

incontinent Unable to prevent the discharge of any of the excretions, especially of urine or feces.

infuse To introduce a fluid other than blood (e.g., saline solution) into a vein.

integument The enveloping membrane of the body or covering of any body or part; the skin.

intracranial Within the skull.

intracranial hemorrhage Bleeding within the skull.

intrauterine Within the uterus.

keloid A firm, movable nodule that develops in the skin, usually after a traumatic injury or a burn.

kyphosis A posterior curvature of the spine when viewed from the side; humpback; hunchback.

ligament A band or sheet of fibrous tissue that connects two or more bones, cartilages, or other structures, or serves as support for muscles or fascia (the tissues that envelop the muscles).

limb-girdle muscular dystrophy A form of muscular dystrophy that initially affects the proximal muscles of the pelvic and shoulder girdles; the rate of progression varies from quite slow to fairly rapid; onset is usually between the first and third decade of life.

lordosis An anterior curvature of the spine when viewed from the side; swayback.

malaise A feeling of general discomfort or uneasiness; an out-of-sorts feeling.

malignant Resistant to treatment; occurring in severe form and frequently fatal; in the case of a tumor, having uncontrollable growth or recurrence after removal, or both.

medial Toward or closest to the midline, middle, or center.

meningitis Inflammation of the membranes of the brain or spinal cord.

metabolize To produce chemical changes whereby the function of nutrition is effected.

microscopy Investigation of minute objects by means of a microscope.

minimal cerebral palsy A term sometimes used by medical personnel to refer to a learning disability.

mucosa Mucous membrane.

mucus The clear viscid secretion of the mucous membranes.

musculoskeletal system The systems involving the muscles and skeleton of the body.

mutation A change in the character of a gene that is perpetuated in subsequent divisions of the cell in which it occurs.

myelogram An X-ray picture of the spinal cord after injecting a contrast medium into it.

myocardial infarction Obstruction of an area of the heart as a result of occlusion (closing) of a coronary artery; a type of heart attack.

myoneural junction A point at which muscle tissue and nerve tissue meet.

myopathy Any abnormal condition or disease of the muscular tissues.

nausea Sickness at the stomach; an inclination to vomit.

nephritis Inflammation of the kidneys.

neural tube The tubular structure formed from the neural plate by the closure of the neural folds; the brain develops from its cephalic (head) portion and the spinal cord from its more caudal (tail) portions.

neurogenic Originating in, starting from, or caused by the nervous system.

neuropathy Any disease of the nervous system.

noxious Injurious.

nystagmus Rhythmical oscillation of the eyeballs, either horizontal, rotary, or vertical.

omission The act of leaving out a sound when speaking.

orthopedic A branch of surgery that deals with the treatment of chronic diseases of the joints and spine, and with the correction of deformities.

orthotic An orthopedic appliance.

osteochondrodystrophy A deforming defect of skeletal growth resulting in dwarfism, including a short neck and trunk, usually kyphosis, moderate shorting of the extremities, and limitations in movement at the hip joint.

palpate To examine by feeling and pressing with the palms of the hands and the fingers.

paroxysmal Relating to or occurring in sharp spasms or convulsions.

pathology Disease process; essential nature, causes, and development of abnormal conditions.

pathophysiology Derangement of function seen in disease; alteration in function as distinguished from structural defects.

pelvis The massive cup-shaped ring of bone, with its ligaments, at the lower end of the trunk.

perinatal Occurring, or pertaining to, before, during, or after the time of birth, although time designations before and after birth are arbitrary.

perineum The area between the thighs extending from the coccyx to the pubis and lying below the pelvic diaphragm.

periosteum The thick fibrous membrane covering the entire surface of a bone except its articular cartilage.

phagocyte A cell possessing the property of ingesting bacteria, foreign particles, and other cells.

phlegm Mucus.

plasma The fluid portion of the circulating blood, distinguished from the serum obtained after coagulation.

polyps A general term used to describe any mass of tissue that bulges outward, upward, or downward from the normal surface level. Polyps may be areas of inflammation, malformations, or new growth.

posterior Behind or after.

postnatal Occurring after birth.

postural reactions The response of a muscle or other living tissue related to or affected by posture.

prenatal Before birth.

prehension Grasping; taking hold of.

prosthesis The replacement of a lost body part by an artificial one.

proteinuria The excretion of any protein in the urine.

pseudomonas aeruginosa A type of bacteria sometimes found in intestinal dejecta (fecal matter), sinuses, and suppurating (pus-forming) wounds.

psychopathology Emotional disturbance.

pulmonary Relating to the lungs.

reflex A reaction; an involuntary movement or exercise of function in a part, excited in response to a stimulus applied to the periphery and transmitted to the nervous centers in the brain or spinal cord.

remission A lessening in severity; a temporary abatement of the symptoms of a disease.

respiratory system All of the air passages from the nose to the pulmonary alveoli (the air cells of the lungs where gas exchange is thought to occur).

retinoblastoma A tumor of the retina. The tumor is composed of cells that originate before birth. The disorder often affects both eyes, usually before the fourth year, and exhibits a familial tendency.

rigidity   A condition in which there is resistance to passive movement throughout the entire range of motion; the resistance can be constant (lead-pipe type) or intermittent (cogwheel type).

sclera   The white portion of the eyeball.

scoliosis   Lateral curvature of the spine. There are usually at least two curves in the scoliotic spine; the main or original curve, and a compensatory curve in the other direction.

shunting   A term applied to the passage of blood or body fluid through other than the usual channel.

skull   The bony framework of the head that consists of 22 bones: 14 of the face and 8 of the brain case.

spasticity   A state of increased muscular tone with exaggeration of the reflexes.

spina bifida   A limited defect in the spinal column involving an absence of the vertebral arches through which the spinal membranes, with or without spinal cord tissue, protrude.

stenosis   A narrowing of any opening. Usually associated with the narrowing of one of the cardiac valves.

sternum   The breastbone.

strabismus   A constant lack of parallelism of the visual axes of the eyes; crossed eyes, walleyes, squinting.

Strauss syndrome   A syndrome in which children show unique patterns of learning disabilities that require special training and are probably due to brain injury.

substitution   Substituting one sound for another.

suture   The surgical uniting of two surfaces by means of stitches.

teratogenic   Disturbed growth processes resulting in the development of malformations of any part of the anatomy.

toxemia   A clinical syndrome caused by toxic substances in the blood.

toxoplasmosis   Any of a group of conditions caused by *Toxoplasma gondii,* which are small, cresentic, intercellular organisms that are presumed to be protozoan parasites.

traction   Pulling; a procedure used to set or straighten bones.

trauma   A wound; an injury inflicted, usually more or less suddenly, by some physical agent.

tremor   A condition involving rhythmic, regular oscillations of the extremities or trunk.

ulceration   The formation of an ulcer (lesion on the surface of the skin or mucous membrane).

urogenital system   The system of the body primarily concerned with the production and secretion of urine and with human reproduction.

vascular lesion   A wound, injury, or pathologic change involving the blood vessels.

vertebral column   The spine or backbone; the structure of vertebrae that extends from the cranium to the coccygeal bone, providing support and forming a flexible bony case for the spinal cord.

Abducens nerve, 25
Absence attack, *see* Petit mal seizure
Academic aids, 276–277
    mouth stick, 139, 144, 276
    reading aids, 277
    talking books, 277
    typewriters, 276
    writing aids, 273, 276–277
Accessory nerve, 25
Acetabulum, 86
Acetylcholine, 6, 18
Achondroplasia, 115
Acoustic nerve, 25
ACTH, for epilepsy, 79, 83
Acute appendicitis, 10
Acute glomerulonephritis, 253, 254
Acute leukemia, *see* Leukemia
Acute lymphoblastic leukemia, 190
Acute myelogenous leukemia, 190
Acute poststreptococcal
    glomerulonephritis, 253, 254
Acute transverse myelitis, spinal cord
    injury caused by, 134
Adaptations to the educational
    environment, *see* Educational
    implications
Adolescent muscular dystrophy, *see*
    Fascioscapulohumeral muscular
    dystrophy
Adrenal cortex, 12
Adrenal glands, 11–12

American Academy for Cerebral Palsy
    and Developmental Medicine,
    281
American Brittle Bone Society, The, 282
American Cancer Society, Inc., 283
American Diabetes Association, 283
American Heart Association, 284
American Lung Association, 283
Amniocentesis, 207
    for spina bifida, 122–123
Amniotic fluid, 207
Amputations, 93–94
    see also Limb deficiencies
Anal atresia, stool retention and, 219
Anal fissures, stool retention and, 219
Anal stenosis, stool retention and, 219
Anatomy
    blood system, 13–15
    circulatory system, 8–9
    digestive system, 9–11
    endocrine system, 11–12
    heart, 8–9
    musculoskeletal system, 3–7
    respiratory system, 7–8
    skin (integumentary system), 12–13
    urogenital system, 12
    see also Neuroanatomy
Anemia, 15
    end stage kidney disease and, 252
    sickle cell, 167, 171–172, 172–173,
        173–174, 216
    thalassemia, 167, 171, 172, 173, 174

Aortic stenosis, 223, 226–227, 228, 229
Aphasic seizure, 80
Appendix, 10
Arnold-Chiari malformation, in spina
    bifida, 118, 119
Arrector pili muscles, 13
Arrested hydrocephalus, 120, 124
Arteriogram, for spinal cord injury, 137
Arthritis, 4
    see also Juvenile rheumatoid
        arthritis
Arthritis Foundation, The, 284
Arthrogryposis multiplex congenita,
    109–111, 113, 115, 147
Articulation therapy, 263
Artificial hand, 97
Artificial limbs, *see* Prostheses
Ascending colon, 10
Aspirin, for juvenile rheumatoid
    arthritis, 246, 264
Asthma, 8, 159–160
    American Lung Association, 283
    characteristics, 161–162
    diagnosis, 162–163
    educational implications, 166, 265
    etiology, 160–161
    exercise-induced, 163–164
    incidence, 159–160
    mast cell in, 161, 162
    National Foundation for Asthma,
        Inc., 283

INDEX

Adrenalin, 11–12
    see also Epinephrine
Adrenal medulla, 11–12
Adult muscular dystrophy, *see* Limb-
    girdle muscular dystrophy
Adult rheumatoid arthritis, 245
    see also Juvenile rheumatoid
        arthritis
Aganglionic megacolon, stool
    retention and, 218–219
Agonists, muscles as, 6
Akinetic seizure, 79, 83
Albuterol, asthma and, 164
Allergens, asthma and, 160
Alpha feto-protein (AFP), spina bifida
    and, 122–123
Alveolar sacs, 8
Alveoli, 223
Amblyopia, cerebral palsy and, 264
Ambulation, *see* Walking

Aneurysms, epilepsy caused by, 76
Ankle-foot orthoses, 274
Anomalous pulmonary venous
    connection, 223, 228
Anomaly of the vertebrae, congenital
    spinal deformity due to, 61
Antagonists, muscles as, 6
Antibiotics
    cystic fibrosis and, 211
    heart disease requiring for dental or
        surgical procedure, 230
Antibodies, asthma and, 161
Anticonvulsant medications, for
    epilepsy, 78, 79, 81–83, 84
    see also specific medications
Antidepressant drugs, enuresis and,
    217
Antihistamines, burns and, 182, 183
Aorta, 8
    coarctation of the, 223, 255

prognosis, 160, 166
psychological factors in, 165–166
treatment, 163–166
    environmental control, 163
    immunotherapy, 165
    medications, 164–165, 166
Asthma teaching program, 166
Asymmetric tonic neck reflex (ATNR),
    33, 34
    cerebral palsy and, 46, 48
Ataxia, 21, 42, 49
Atherosclerosis, 9, 223, 230
Athetoid cerebral palsy, 42, 47–48, 52,
    264
Atrial septal defects, 223, 225
Atrium (atria), 8
Attentional deficit disorders, *see*
    Minimal brain dysfunction
Auditory deficiencies, *see* Hearing loss
Aura, in psychomotor seizures, 79

Autoimmune disease, 242
  see also Juvenile rheumatoid
    arthritis
Automatisms, cerebral palsy and, 46,
  48
Autonomic dysreflexia, in spinal cord
  injury, 140
Autonomic nervous system, see
  Nervous system
Avoiding reaction, cerebral palsy and,
  48
Axial skeleton, 5
Axon, 17, 18

Babinski reflex, 52
Back, see Spinal cord injury; Spinal
  deformities
Barrel chairs, 275
Barrier-free design, in schools, 270
Basal ganglia, 21
  cerebral palsy and, 42, 48
Battered child, see Child abuse
Bed wetting, see Enuresis
Benzedrine, cerebral palsy and, 55
Beta adrenergic agents, asthma and,
  164, 166
Biochemical diseases, see Inborn
  errors of metabolism
Birth trauma, spinal cord injury and,
  133–134
Bite reflex, cerebral palsy and, 50
Bladder, 12
  burns and, 177
  neurogenic, 136
    spina bifida and, 121, 127–128, 215
    spinal cord injury and, 136, 137,
      140
    spinal muscular atrophy, 153
  urologist, 262
  see also Enuresis
Blindness, 264
  insulin dependent diabetes and, 202,
    203, 204
  see also Vision
Blood, 13–15
  cells, 4, 5
    platelets, 167, 187
    red, 14–15, 167, 187
    white, 14–15, 167, 187
  circulation, 223–224
  hemophilia, 167, 168–171
  leukemia, 15, 185, 186–187, 188, 189–
    190
  see also Anemia
Blood pressure, 12, 255
  sphygmomanometer for, 256
  see also Hypertension
Blood sugar, 196, 197
  hyperglycemia, 202, 203, 204
  hypoglycemia, 202–203, 204, 205
  see also Insulin dependent diabetes
Bone
  formation of, 111
  osteogenesis imperfecta, 111–116,
    264
  skeletal system, 3–6
  trauma to, 4
  tumors of, see Cancer
Bowel control
  encopresis, 10, 218–220
  spina bifida and, 121–122, 128, 215
  spinal cord injury and, 136, 137, 140
Braces, 96, 273–274
  ankle-foot, 274

arthrogryposis and, 110
congenital dislocation of the hip
  and, 89
hip-knee-ankle-foot, 274
juvenile rheumatoid arthritis and,
  246
knee-ankle-foot, 274
Legg-Perthes disease and, 88
lower extremity, 274
mild spinal muscular atrophy and,
  151–152
muscular dystrophy and, 106–107
osteogenesis imperfecta and, 115
spina bifida and, 125–126
spinal cord injury and, 138–139, 142
spinal deformities and, 66–67
upper extremity, 273
Brain, 17, 18–21
  cerebral palsy and, 42, 43, 48, 53
  spinal cord injury and, 133, 134
  tumors of, 21–22, 187, 190
Brainstem, 17, 21–23, 25, 27, 33
Breastbone, see Sternum
Brittle bone disease, see Osteogenesis
  imperfecta
Broca's area, 26, 27
Bronchioles, 8
Bronchitis, 8, 160
Bronchospasm, asthma and, 163
Bronchus(i), 7–8
Bulbous end organs, 13
Burns, 13, 175
  battered child and, 176, 178, 181, 183
  complications, 176–178
  diagnosis, 181
  educational implications, 182–183
  electrical, 178, 181
  etiology, 176
  full thickness, 176, 177, 181, 182
  healing in, 176–177
  infection and, 176, 177, 182
  mental capacity, 182
  morbidity, 175, 176, 179–180
  mortality rate, 175, 179–180, 182
  partial thickness, 181
  physical limitations, 178
  prognosis, 182
  psychological implications, 178–180,
    183
  of sensory organs, 177, 178
  thermoregulation and, 175, 183
  treatment, 181–182
    grafting, 176–177, 178, 179, 183
    nutrition, 178, 182, 183

Calcarine fissure, 20
Cancer, 185–186
  American Cancer Society, Inc., 283
  bone tumors, 185, 188, 189, 190, 191
    Ewing's sarcoma, 188, 190, 191
    osteogenic sarcoma, 188, 190, 191
  central nervous system tumors, 185,
    187, 188, 190, 191
  characteristics, 187–188
  death from, 193
  diagnosis, 188, 191, 192
  educational implications, 189, 191–
    193
  etiology, 186–187
  family and, 191–192, 193
  incidence, 185–186
  leukemia, 15, 185, 186–187, 188, 189–
    190

lymphoma, 185, 186, 187, 190
  Hodgkin's, 186, 187, 190
  non-Hodgkin's, 187, 190
remission in, 185–186
retinoblastoma, 186
rhabdomyosarcoma, 187–188, 190,
  191
treatment, 186, 189–191
  chemotherapy, 186, 189, 190
  radiation, 186, 189, 190
  surgery, 186, 190
Wilms's tumor, 187, 188, 190, 191
Capillaries, 169
CAPP terminal device, 96, 97
Cardiac catheterization, for heart
  disease, 228
Cardiac defects, see Heart disorders
Cardiac muscle, 6
Cardiac sphincter, 10
Cardiologist, 262
Career planning
  cerebral palsy and, 56
  heart disease and, 231
  hemophilia and, 170
  insulin dependent diabetes and, 204
  rehabilitation counselor for, 263
  sickle cell anemia and, 174
  spinal muscular atrophy and, 155
  thalassemia and, 174
Cartilage, 4
Catheterization
  cardiac, 228
  intermittent, 128, 140
  in spina bifida, 128
  in spinal cord injury, 140
Cauda equina, 22
Cecum, 10
Central cord lesion, 135, 136
Central nervous system, See Nervous
  system
Cerebellum, 21
  cerebral palsy and, 42
Cerebral hemisphere of brain, 18–21
Cerebral palsy, 41–42, 57
  American Academy for Cerebral
    Palsy and Developmental
    Medicine, 281
  associated problems, 41, 50–51
    hearing loss, 48, 50, 55
    opthalmological, 44, 50, 55, 264
    of oropharyngeal area, 50–51
    seizures, 51, 55
    tactile-kinesthetic sensory loss, 50
  ataxia, 42, 49
  brain involvement with, 42, 43
  changing physical findings in, 50
  diagnosis, 51–52
  dyskinesia, 47
    athetosis in, 42, 47–48, 52, 264
    dystonia in, 48
    hypotonia in, 48–49
    rigidity in, 48, 52
    tremor in, 49
    vision in, 44, 50, 55, 264
  educational implications, 55, 56–57,
    260
  etiology, 42
  frequency, 41–42
  mixed types of, 50
  prognosis, 56
  spasticity, 43
    diagnosing, 52
    spastic diplegia, 44, 45
    spastic hemiplegia, 44, 50

Cerebral palsy *(continued)*
    spastic paraplegia, 44
    spastic quadriplegia, 44–47, 48, 50
    treatment, 53, 54–55
  spinal deformities with, 61, 63
  treatment, 52–56
    communication, 55, 56, 267
    contractures and deformities, 54–55
    feeding, 54
    inhibitory and facilitory methodology and, 35
    medications, 55–56
    motor function, 52–54
    personality development, 56
    postural reactions, 35
    sensory function, 55
    surgery, 54–55
    tonic labyrinthine reflex, 35
  United Cerebral Palsy Association, Inc., 281–282
Cerebrospinal fluid (CSF), 18, 21, 119
Cervical lordosis, 60
Cervical vertebrae, 5
Charcot-Marie-Tooth disease, 61
Chemical chain analysis, thalassemia and, 173
Chemotherapy
  cancer and, 186, 189
  cystic fibrosis and, 211, 212–213
  see also Medications
Chest physical therapy, cystic fibrosis and, 211
Chickenpox, leukemia and, 189–190
Child abuse
  burns and, 176, 178, 181, 183
  osteogenesis imperfecta differentiated from, 113
Childhood diabetes mellitus, *see* Insulin dependent diabetes
Childhood muscular dystrophy, *see* Duchenne muscular dystrophy
Chilomicrons, 13–14
Choreiform syndrome, 37
Choreoathetosis, cerebral palsy and, 48
Chronic ambulatory peritoneal dialysis (CAPD), 253
Circulatory system, 8–9
Cirrhosis of the liver, cystic fibrosis and, 208, 210
Clean intermittent catheterization (IC), in spina bifida, 128
Clonopin, for epilepsy, 78, 79, 83
Clubbing fingers and toes
  cystic fibrosis and, 210
  heart disorders and, 224
Club feet, in spina bifida, 127
Coagulation, 168
  hemophilia and, 167, 168–171
Coarctation of the aorta, 223, 255
Coccygeal bones, 5
Cochlea, 26
Cochlear nerve, 26
Cocktail party syndrome, in spina bifida, 266
Collagen, 53
Collagen diseases, 244, 245
  see also Juvenile rheumatoid arthritis
Collagen fibers, 241
  osteogenesis imperfecta and, 111
Colon, 10
Coma, diabetic, 199

Comes to sit, as normal gross motor milestone, 31
Common bile duct, 10
Common iliac arteries, 8
Communication boards, 266, 267
Communication, *see* Language and communication problems
Compensated hydrocephalus, 120, 124
Complex-partial seizure, *see* Psychomotor seizure
Computerized tomographic (CT or CAT) scan, for central nervous system tumor, 188
Congenital dislocation of the hip, 88–90, 109
Congenital heart disorders, 222–223, 224, 230
Congenital limb deficiencies, 93
  see also Limb deficiencies
Congenital scoliosis, congenital spinal deformity due to, 61
Congestive heart failure, 9, 224, 231
Connective tissue diseases, 244, 245
  see also Juvenile rheumatoid arthritis
Contractures, 265
  in arthrogryposis, 109
  in burns, 176–177, 178
  in cerebral palsy, 43, 54–55
  in juvenile rheumatoid arthritis, 244, 245, 246, 249
  in spinal cord injuries, 138–139
  in spinal muscular atrophy, 151, 152, 155
Convulsions, *see* Epilepsy; Seizures
Cooley's anemia, 171
  see also Thalassemia
Cornea, 177
Cortex, cerebral palsy and, 42, 48
Cortisonelike compounds, for juvenile rheumatoid arthritis, 246
Coxa plana, *see* Legg-Perthes disease
Cranial nerves, 21, 24–25, 25
Crawling, as normal gross motor milestone, 31
Creatine phosphokinase (CPK) test, for Duchenne muscular dystrophy, 102, 104
Creeping, as normal gross motor milestone, 31
Cretinism, 11
Cromolyn, asthma and, 165
Cross-eye, *see* Strabismus
Cruising, as normal gross motor milestone, 31
Cryoprecipitate, hemophilia and, 169–170
Cursive seizure, 80
Curvatures of the spine, *see* Spinal deformities
Cyanosis, 224, 226, 230
  in grand mal seizure, 77
Cyanotic congenital heart disease, 224, 230
Cyanotic defects, 223, 226, 227, 228
Cystic fibrosis (CF), 8, 206–207
  characteristics, 208–209
  chronic cough in, 212
  cost of, 213
  Cystic Fibrosis Foundation, 284
  death and, 213
  educational implications, 212–213
  etiology, 207–208
  growth and, 208–209

  heart and, 208
  life expectancy of, 212
  lungs in, 208, 209, 210, 211, 212
  pathogenesis, 209–210
  prognosis, 212
  sexuality and, 208, 209
  sweat test for, 207, 210–211
  treatment, 211–212, 213
Cystic Fibrosis Foundation, 284
Cysts, in the kidney, 252
Cytomegalic inclusion disease, cerebral palsy caused by, 42
Cytoxan, nephrotic syndrome and, 254

Death
  cancer and, 193
  cystic fibrosis and, 213
Deciduous teeth, 112
Deep tender reflexes (DTR), cerebral palsy and, 52
Defecation, *see* Bowel control
Dendrites, 17
Dental defects, *see* Teeth
Dentin, in teeth, 113
Dentinogenesis imperfecta, 112
Dentist, 262
Depakane, for epilepsy, 78, 79, 82
Depth perception, in physically handicapped, 264
Dermatomyositis, 104
Dermis, 13
Derotative righting reaction, 36
Descending colon, 10
Dexedrine, cerebral palsy and, 55
Diabetes mellitus, 11, 12
  end stage kidney failure and, 252
  noninsulin dependent, 199
  see also Insulin dependent diabetes
Dialysis, *see* Kidneys
Diaphragm, 8
Diarthrodial joints, 241
Diastolic pressure, 255
Diastometamyelia, 61
Diet
  end stage kidney failure and, 252, 253
  epilepsy and, 83
  hypertension and, 255
  insulin dependent diabetes and, 200–201, 204–205
  muscular dystrophy and, 107
  phenylketonuria and, 236, 237, 238
  see also Nutrition
Digestive system, 9–11
Digitalis, for heart disease, 229
Dilantin
  cerebral palsy and, 55
  epilepsy and, 78, 82
Dimaox, for epilepsy, 78
Diplegia, 43
  spastic, 44, 45
Distention of the intestines, 208
Diuretic drugs
  enuresis and, 216
  heart disease and, 229
  hypertension and, 255
Diurnal enuresis, 28, 214, 218
  see also Enuresis
Doman-Delacato system, for cerebral palsy, 53
Dopamine, 18
Double hemiplegia, 43
Down's syndrome, heart disease and, 223, 230

D-Penicillamine, for juvenile rheumatoid arthritis, 246
Drugs, see Chemotherapy; Medications
Duchenne muscular dystrophy, 61, 100, 101–102, 104
see also Muscular dystrophy
Duodenal ulcers, cystic fibrosis and, 208
Duodenum, 10, 11, 208
Dwyer system of anterior instrumentation, 68, 69
Dysgraphia, 7
Dyskinesia, see Cerebral palsy
Dystonia, cerebral palsy and, 48

Ear, 25–26
see also Hearing loss
Echocardiogram (ECG), 228, 229
Eczema, 13
Educational implications
of arthrogryposis, 111
of asthma, 166
barrier-free design, 270
of burns, 182–183
of cancer, 191–193
of cerebral palsy, 55, 56–57, 260
classroom organization, 277–279
of congenitally dislocated hip, 90
emergency and medical procedures, 268, 269
of encopresis, 221
of end stage kidney disease, 253
of enuresis, 218
of epilepsy, 82, 84
follow through on therapy in classroom, 270–271
of glomerulonephritis, 254
of heart disease, 230–231
of hemophilia, 170–171
homebound programs, 270
for burns, 183
for congenitally dislocated hip, 90
for hemophilia, 170–171
for juvenile rheumatoid arthritis, 248
for rheumatic heart, 231
of Hurler syndrome, 236
of hypertension, 256
informational needs, 259–260
of insulin dependent diabetes, 204–205
interdisciplinary team approach, 70, 261–263, 271, 278–279
for cerebral palsy, 57
for diabetes, 204, 205
health-related personnel, 262–263
medical personnel, 261–262
for spinal deformity, 70
of juvenile rheumatoid arthritis, 248–249
of kidney disorders, 253, 254–255, 256
learning characteristics of physically handicapped, 263–264
hearing, 264–265
intellectual ability, 265
language and communication, 266–267
motor development, 265
vision, 264
of Legg-Perthes disease, 88
of limb deficiencies, 98–99

mainstreaming
enuresis and, 218
osteogenesis imperfecta and, 116
spinal cord injured child and, 145
medications in school, 270
of muscular dystrophy, 106–107, 260
of nephrotic syndrome, 254–255
observation of physically handicapped child, 271–273
of osteogenesis imperfecta, 116
of phenylketonuria, 238
scheduling, 279
of sickle cell anemia, 174
of slipped capital femoral epiphysis, 91
social-emotional concerns, 267–268,
see also Psychological implications
special education, 260–261, 264, 268, 270
of spina bifida, 122, 130, 260
of spinal cord injury, 140, 143–146
of spinal deformity, 69–70
of spinal muscular atrophy, 155
of thalassemia, 174
transportation, 270
see also Mental retardation; Physical education
Education for All Handicapped Children Act (Public Law 94–142), 30, 37
Elastic garments, burns requiring, 178, 183
Electrical burn, 181
Electrical shock, 178
Electrocardiogram (EKG), 228, 229
Electroencephalogram (EEG), 81
Electrolytes
cystis fibrosis and, 207
kidneys and, 12
skin and, 13
Electromyogram (EMG), 151, 152
Emphysema, 160
Encephalitis, cerebral palsy caused by, 42
Encopresis, 10, 218–221
Endocardial cushion defects, 223
Endocarditis, 223, 230
Endocrine system, 11–12
epiphyseal slippage due to abnormality in, 90
End stage kidney disease, 252–253, 254
Enuresis, 214–218
diurnal, 28, 214, 218
nocturnal, 214, 215, 217, 218
primary, 214–215
secondary, 215
Enzymes, 196
see also Inborn errors of metabolism
Epidermis, 13
Epiglottis, 7
Epilepsy, 74–75, 76, 84–85
aphasic seizure, 80
burns and, 182
cursive seizure, 80
diagnosis, 80–81
educational implications, 84
electroencephalogram for, 83
Epilepsy Foundation of America, 282
etiology, 75–76
febrile seizures, 76–77
focal seizure, 19, 79, 82, 84
gelastic seizure, 80

grand mal, 75, 77, 79, 82, 83
status epilepticus, 78
idiopathic, 76, 80, 83
Jacksonian seizure, 79
laughing seizure, 80
music-induced seizure, 80
petit mal triad, 77
akinetic seizures, 79, 83
infantile myoclonic seizures, 78–79, 82, 83
petit mal seizure, 77–78, 82, 83, 84
photic-stimulated seizure, 80, 83, 84
prognosis, 83–84
psychomotor seizures, 75, 78, 79, 82
reading, 80, 84
salaam seizures, 79, 83
startle-induced seizures, 80
status epilepticus, 78, 80, 82
temporal lobe seizures, 82, 84
trauma-induced seizures, 83, 84
treatment
anticonvulsant medications, 78, 79, 81–83, 84
history of, 74–75
tuberous sclerosis and, 80
withdrawal seizure, 82
Epilepsy Foundation of America, 282
Epinephrine, asthma and, 164
see also Adrenalin
Epineurium, 24
Epiphysis, 4
Esophagus, 10
Essential hypertension, 255, 256
Eustachian tube, 26
Evanescent rash, in juvenile rheumatoid arthritis, 244
Ewing's sarcoma, 188, 190, 191
Exercise-induced asthma, 163–164
Exercise testing, for heart disease, 228
Exocrine glands, cystic fibrosis and, 207, 208, 209–210
Expanded medical card, 268, 269
External powered terminal device, 97
Extraocular movement, muscle system of, 6
Eye, 6
burns and, 177
iridocyclitis, 243, 244
retinoblastoma, 186
sclera, 111, 112
see also Vision
Eye-hand coordination, 33

Facial nerve, 25
Facioscapulohumeral muscular dystrophy, 100, 101
Factor VIII, for hemophilia, 169–170
Family, 267
asthma and, 165, 166
burns and, 178, 190
cancer and, 191–192, 193
cystic fibrosis and, 213
enuresis and, 217
Hurler syndrome and, 236
insulin dependent diabetes and, 205
overprotection by, 267
spinal cord injured child and, 143
spinal muscular atrophy and, 162, 154
team working with, 271
see also Child abuse
Farsightedness, 50
Fascia, 53

Febrile seizures, 76–77
Femoral head, 86
Femur, epiphyseal slippage and, 91
Fenoprofen, for juvenile rheumatoid arthritis, 246
Fibroblasts, 241
Figure-ground relationships, cerebral palsy and, 264
Fine motor development, 30, 32–33, 265
Finger-to-nose test, ataxia identified with, 49
Flat bones, 4
Flexor muscle tone, 29, 30, 33
Flexor spasm, see Salaam seizure
Flight or fight reflex, 11–12
Fluid balance
    burns and, 176, 182
    limb deficiencies and, 95
Focal seizure, 19, 79, 82, 84
Foramen magnum, 22
Free nerve endings, 13
Frontal lobe, 18–19
Full thickness burn, 176, 177, 181, 182

Gag reflex, cerebral palsy and, 50
Gallbladder, 11
Ganglions, 23
Gastrointestinal cancer, 185
Gastrointestinal reflux, 10
Gelastic seizure, 80
Genes, 233
Genetic disorders, see Asthma; Congenital dislocation of the hip; Cystic fibrosis; Duchenne muscular dystrophy; Hemophilia; Hurler syndrome; Insulin dependent diabetes; Osteogenesis imperfecta; Phenylketonuria; Sickle cell anemia; Spina bifida; Spinal muscular atrophy; Thalassemia
Geneticist, 262
Glial cells, 18
Glomerulonephritis, 252, 253–254
Glomerulus, 250
    see also Kidney
Glossopharyngeal nerve, 25
Gluconeogenesis, 196, 197
Glucose, 196, 197
    insulin regulation of, 199–200, 201
    urine tested for, 199
    see also Insulin dependent diabetes
Glucose tolerance test, 199
Glucosuria, 197
Gold salts, for juvenile rheumatoid arthritis, 246
Goosebumps, 13
Gower's sign, 100, 104, 105
Grafting, in burns, 176, 177, 178, 179, 183
Grand mal seizure, 77, 78, 79, 82, 83
Grasping
    in arthrogryposis, 110
    upper-limb prosthesis for, 96–97
Grasp reflex, 32, 33
Gray matter, 18, 27
Gross motor development, 30–32
Gunshot wounds, spinal cord injury caused by, 133, 134
Guthrie bacterial inhibition assay, for phenylketonuria, 236, 237

Hair loss, chemotherapy and, 189
Hand muscles, 6–7
Handplay, beginning, 33
Hand splint, 273, 277
Harrington rod instrumentation system, 68
Health-related personnel, as team members, 262–263
Hearing loss, 264–265
    cerebral palsy and, 48, 50, 55, 264
    juvenile rheumatoid arthritis and, 264
    osteogenesis imperfecta and, 112, 264
    see also Ear
Heart, 8–9
    burns and, 177, 178
    cystic fibrosis and, 208, 209
    muscle, 6
Heart attack, see Myocardial infarction
Heart block, 227
Heartburn, 10
Heart disorders, 222
    acquired, 223
    American Heart Association, 284
    anomalous pulmonary venous connection, 223, 228
    aortic stenosis, 223, 226–227, 228, 229
    atherosclerotic coronary artery disease, 223, 230
    atrial septal defect, 223, 225
    characteristics, 223–224
    coarctation of the aorta, 223, 255
    congenital, 222–223, 224, 230
    congestive heart failure, 9, 224, 231
    cyanotic congenital heart disease, 224, 231
    cyanotic defects, 223, 226, 227, 228
    dental procedures and, 230
    diagnosis, 227–228, 229
    Down's syndrome and, 223, 230
    educational implications, 230–231, 265
    endocardial cushion defects, 223
    endocarditis, 223, 230
    etiology, 222–223
    heart block, 227
    heart murmur, 224, 228
    myocardial infarction, 9, 202, 204
    myocarditis, 223
    patent ductus arteriosis, 223, 224–225
    pericarditis, 223, 243
    prognosis, 230
    psychological implications of, 231
    pulmonary stenosis, 233, 227, 229
    rheumatic, 223, 230
    rhythm anomalies, 227
    surgical procedures and, 230
    tachycardia, 227
    tetralogy of Fallot, 223, 225, 226
    transposition of the great arteries, 223, 226
    treatment, 229–230
    tricuspid atresia, 223, 226, 227
    truncus ateriosus, 223, 226, 227
    ventricular septal defect, 223, 225
    see also Hypertension
Heart murmurs, 224, 228
Heel-toe walking, ataxia identified with, 49
Hemarthrosis, 169
Hematocrit, 15

Hemiplegia, 43
    spastic, 44, 50
Hemodialysis, 252, 253
Hemoglobin, 14, 15
Hemoglobin electrophoresis, 173
Hemophilia, 167, 168–171
    National Hemophilia Foundation, 283
Hemophilia A, 168
Hemophilia B, 168, 170
Hemophilia C, 168–169
Hemophilia Center, 170, 171
Hemorrhoids, 219
Hemosiderosis, 173
Hepatitis, 11
Hereditary disorders, see Genetic disorders
Hiatal hernia, 10
High blood pressure, see Hypertension
Higher-limb deficiencies, 98
High regard, in early walking, 31
Hip, 45, 86
    dislocation
        cerebral palsy and, 45, 46
        congenital, 88–90, 109
        spina bifida and, 126, 127
    Legg-Perthes disease, 86–88
    replacement, 246, 247
    slipped capital femoral epiphysis, 90–91
Hip-knee-ankle-foot orthosis (HKAFO), 274
Hirschsprung's disease, 218–219
Hodgkins's lymphoma, 186, 190
Homebound programs, see Educational implications
Hormones, 11–12, 90
Hospital
    burn victims requiring teaching in, 183
    reaction to stay in, 267–268
Hunter's syndrome, 235
Hurler syndrome, 234–236
Hydrocephalus, 19, 22
    arrested (compensated), 120, 124
    brain tumors and, 190
    in spina bifida, 119–120, 122, 123–124, 129
Hydroxychloroquine, for juvenile rheumatoid arthritis, 246
Hyperglycemia, 197, 198, 200, 202, 203–204
Hypertension, 223, 230, 255–256
    end stage kidney failure and, 252
    essential, 255, 256
    glomerulonephritis and, 254
    secondary, 256
Hypertonic, 36
Hypnosis, for enuresis, 217–218
Hypocalcemia, stool retention and, 219
Hypoglossal nerve, 25
Hypoglycemia, 202–203, 204, 205
Hypothalamus, 11
Hypothyroidism, stool retention and, 219
Hypotonia, 30, 36
    cerebral palsy and, 48–49
Hypoxia, cerebral palsy caused by, 42
Hypsarrhythmia, 79

Idiopathic epilepsy, 76, 80, 83
Idiopathic scoliosis, 60–61, 62, 64–65, 69

Iduronidase, Hurler syndrome and, 234–236
Ileum, 10
Imipramine, enuresis and, 217
Immunization process, lymph nodes and, 9
Immunoinflammatory diseases, 244, 245
see also Juvenile rheumatoid arthritis
Immunosuppressive drugs, for juvenile rheumatoid arthritis, 246
Immunotherapy, asthma and, 165
Imuran, nephrotic syndrome and, 254
Inborn errors of metabolism, 233–234
large molecule disease, 234
Hurler syndrome, 234–236
small molecule diseases, 234
phenylketonuria, 234, 236–238
Incontinence, see Bladder; Bowel control
Infantile myoclonic seizures, 78–79, 82, 83
Infantile spinal muscular atrophy, 147, 148
Inferior vena cava, 8
Inflammation of the joints, 241–243
see also Juvenile rheumatoid arthritis
Infusion, for hemophilia, 169–170
Inhalation therapy, cystic fibrosis and, 212
Inherited disorders, see Genetic disorders
Inhibitory and facilitory methodology, 35
Inner ear, 26
Insulin, 12, 196–197
as therapy for diabetes, 199–200, 201, 204
see also Insulin dependent diabetes
Insulin dependent diabetes, 195–196
American Diabetes Association, 283–284
characteristics, 197, 199
cystic fibrosis and, 208
diagnosis, 199
educational implications, 204–205, 265
enuresis and, 215–216
etiology, 196–199
heart attacks and, 202, 204
hyperglycemia and, 202, 203, 204
hypoglycemia and, 202–203, 204, 205
incidence, 195
pathophysiology of, 197, 198
prognosis, 202–204
symptoms, 197–198
treatment, 195–196, 199
behavioral/psychological problems, 202, 203, 204, 205
cost considerations, 202
diet, 200–201, 204–205
education, 202
exercise, 201–202
insulin, 199–200, 201, 204
vascular disease and, 203–204
Insulin reaction, see Hypoglycemia
Integumentary system, see Skin
Intellectual ability
in physically handicapped child, 265
predicting, 33
see also Mental retardation

Interdisciplinary team, see Educational implications
Intermediate spinal muscular atrophy, 149, 150, 151, 153–154
Intermittent catheterization (IC)
in spina bifida, 128
in spinal cord injury, 140
Internal fixation devices, for spinal deformities, 68, 69, 70
Intracranial brain tumor, 22
Intracranial hemorrhage
cerebral palsy caused by, 42
in hemophilia, 171
Intraspinal tumors, 61
Intravenous pyelogram (IVP), enuresis and, 216, 217
Iridocyclitis, pauciarticular onset juvenile rheumatoid arthritis and, 243, 244
Iron, thalassemia and, 173
Islands of Langerhans, 12
see also Insulin dependent diabetes; Pancreas
Isoproterenol, asthma and, 164

Jack-knife spasm, 79
Jacksonian seizure, 79
Jaundice, 11
Jejunum, 10
Jobs, see Career planning
Joints, 241
inflammation of, 241–243, see also Juvenile rheumatoid arthritis
Juvenile onset diabetes, see Insulin dependent diabetes
Juvenile rheumatoid arthritis (JRA), 240–241
The Arthritis Foundation, 284
characteristics, 243–244, 264
diagnosis, 244–245
educational implications, 248–249
etiology, 241–243
incidence, 243
iridocyclitis and, 243
pauciarticular onset, 243, 244
pericarditis and, 243
polyarticular onset, 243, 245
prognosis, 247–248
systemic onset, 243, 244, 248
treatment, 245–247
medication, 245–246, 264
orthopedic surgery, 246, 247
physical and occupational therapy, 246
psychological implications, 246–247

Ketoacidosis, 197, 198, 199, 203
Ketogenic diet, for epilepsy, 83
Ketones, 197
urine tested for, 199
Ketoprofen, for juvenile rheumatoid arthritis, 246
Ketosis, 197
Keyboard guard, 276, 277
Kidneys, 12, 250–252
burns and, 177
dialysis, 253
end stage kidney disease and, 252–253
glomerulonephritis and, 254
hemodialysis, 252, 253
peritoneal, 252–253

disorders
cysts, 252
end stage kidney disease, 252–253, 254
glomerulonephritis, 252, 253–254
hypertension, 254, 255–256
nephrotic syndrome, 254–255
Wilms's tumor, 187, 188, 190, 191
glucose and, 197
insulin dependent diabetes and, 202, 203
National Kidney Foundation, Inc., 284
spina bifida and, 121, 122, 127–128
spinal cord injury and, 140
transplantation, 253
Knee, 169
hemarthrosis of the, 169
hyperextension of, 274
Knee-ankle-foot orthosis (KAFO), 274
Kugelberg-Welander disease, see Mild, spinal muscular atrophy
Kyphosis, see Spinal deformities

Labyrinth, 26
Lamellated corpuscles, 13
Landau reaction, 36
Language and communication problems, 25, 266–267
cerebral palsy and, 46, 48, 50–51, 55, 56, 266
communication boards for, 266, 267
speech-language therapist, 263
spina bifida and, 266
Lanolin cream, burns and, 182, 183
Large intestine, 10
Large molecule diseases, 234
Hurler syndrome and, 234–236
Larynx, 7
Lateral protective extension, 36
Laughing seizure, 80
Lead intoxication, stool retention and, 219
Learning disabilities
leukemia and, 189
motor improvements and, 36–37
phenylketonuria and, 236, 237, 238
spina bifida and, 122, 129
Legg-Perthes disease, 86–88, 265
Leukemia, 15, 185, 186–187, 188, 189–190
Leukopenia, 15
Ligaments, femoral head and, 88
Limb deficiencies, 93–99
acquired, 92, 93–94
congenital, 93
National Amputation Foundation, 282
prostheses for, 94–95, 96–98
Limb-girdle muscular dystrophy, 100, 101
see also Muscular dystrophy
Limbic system, 19, 20
Lipid colloid particles, 13–14
Liver, 10, 10–11
cystic fibrosis and, 208, 210
Long bones, 4, 5
Long leg prosthesis, 273
Lordosis, see Spinal deformities
Lower-extremity orthoses, 274
Lower-limb prostheses, 98, 99
Lumbar lordosis, 60
Lumbar vertebrae, 5

Lungs, 7–8, 159
 alveoli of, 223
 bronchitis, 8, 160
 burns and, 177
 function, 160, 162–163
 pneumonia, 78, 177
 pulmonary stenosis, 223, 227, 229
 see also Asthma; Cystic fibrosis;
  Respiration; Respiratory
  infections
Luque rods, 68, 70
Lymphatic system, 9
 lymphoma, *see* Cancer
 nodes, 187
Lymphoma, *see* Cancer

Mainstreaming, *see* Educational
  implications
Malignant tumor, 185
 see also Cancer
Malleus, 26
Maroteaux-Lamy syndrome, 235
Marrow, of bones, 4
Mast cell, in asthma, 161, 162
Measles, leukemia and, 189–190
Mebaral, for epilepsy, 82
Meconium ileus, in cystic fibrosis, 208
Medical emergencies, handling, 268,
  269
Medical personnel, as team members,
  261–262
Medical record card, expanded, 268
Medications
 cancer chemotherapy, 186, 189
 for cerebral palsy, 55–56
 for cystic fibrosis, 211, 212–213
 for end stage kidney disease, 252,
  253
 for enuresis, 217, 218
 for epilepsy, 78, 84
 for glomerulonephritis, 254
 for heart disease, 229
 for hypertension, 255
 for juvenile rheumatoid arthritis,
  245–246, 264
 for nephrotic syndrome, 254, 255
 in the schools, 263, 270
 social-emotional adjustment
  problem with, 268
 for stool retention, 219
 teratogenic, 222
 see also specific medications
Medulla oblongata, 21, 22, 25
Medulloblastoma, 190
Melanin, 13
Membranous bones, 4
Meningitis, cerebral palsy caused
  by, 42
Meningocele, 61, 117, 118
Mental retardation, 265–266
 cerebral palsy and, 48, 50
 Hurler syndrome and, 234–236
 hypotonia and, 48
 incorrect labeling of handicapped
  as, 260–261
 motor development abnormality
  and, 37
 phenylketonuria and, 236, 237, 238
 problem-solving in, 33
 special education program for, 260
 spina bifida and, 119–121, 122
 spinal muscular atrophy and, 155
Metabolism, 165
 see also Inborn errors of metabolism

Metaproterenol, asthma and, 164
Microscopy, 15
Midbrain, 21, 25
Middle ear, 26
Mild, as degree of severity, 43
Mild spinal muscular atrophy, 146, 147,
  149, 150–151, 152, 153–154
Minimal brain dysfunction (MBD)
 encopresis and, 219, 220
 enuresis and, 216
Minimal cerebral palsy, 37
Minimal change disease, 254
Mist tent therapy, cystic fibrosis and,
  212
Moderate, as degree of severity, 43
Monoblastic leukemia, 190
Mononucleosis, 9, 15
Monoplegia, 43
Moro reflex, 27, 33–34
Morquio syndrome, 235
Motility, 30
Motor development, 29–30
 abnormalities of, 36–37
 in cerebral palsy, 51–52
 deviance and, 36, 37
 dissociation and, 37
 fine, 30, 32–33
 gross, 30–32
 motor delay and, 36, 37
 in physically handicapped child, 265
 postural reaction, 30, 33, 35–36
 spina bifida and, 120–121, 124–126
 spinal deformity and, 61
 teacher and, 37
 see also Primitive reflexes
Motor deviancy, 36, 37
Mouthstick, 139, 144, 276
Mucopolysaccharides, Hurler
  syndrome and, 234–236
Mucopolysaccharidosis syndromes,
  234–236
Mucosa, 77
Mucoviscodosis, 206
 see also Cystic fibrosis
Mucus, *see* Cystic fibrosis
Muscular dystrophy (MD), 100–107
 Duchenne's, 61, 100, 101–102, 104
 educational implications, 260
 facioscapulohumeral, 100, 101
 limb-girdle, 100, 101
 Muscular Dystrophy Association, 282
 pseudohypertrophic, 101, 102, 103
 spinal deformities in, 61, 63
 swallowing defects in, 7
Muscular Dystrophy Association, 282
Musculoskeletal system, 3–7
 achondroplasia, 115
 The American Brittle Bone Society,
  282
 arthrogryposis multiplex congenita,
  109–111
 osteogenesis imperfecta, 111–116
 see also Muscular dystrophy
Music-induced seizure, 80
Myasthenia gravis, 6, 61
Myelin, 18, 27
Myelodysplasia, 61, 118
 kyphosis causing, 62
 see also Spina bifida
Myelogram, for spinal cord injury, 137
Myelomeningocele, 61, 117, 118, 122,
  129
 enuresis and, 215

spina bifida and, *see* Spinal
  deformities
 spinal deformities in, 63
Myocardial infarction, 9
 insulin dependent diabetes and, 202,
  204
Myocarditis, 223
Myoclonic seizures, 78–79, 82, 83
Myology, 6
 see also Muscles
Myoneural junction, 6
Myopathic arthrogryposis multiplex
  congenita, 109
Myopathic disease, 61, 109
Mysoline, for epilepsy, 78, 82
Myxedema, 11

Naproxen, for juvenile rheumatoid
  arthritis, 246
Nasal polyps, cystic fibrosis and, 208
National Amputation Foundation, 282
National Foundation for Asthma, Inc.,
  283
National Hemophilia Foundation, 283
National Kidney Foundation, Inc., 284
National Spinal Cord Injury
  Foundation, 283
Nearsightedness, 50
Nephritis, enuresis and, 216
Nephrons, 250, 251
 see also Kidney
Nephrotic syndrome, 254–255
Nerve endings, in the skin, 13
Nerve plexus, 24
Nervous system, 16–17, 75
 autonomic, 17, 23–24
  parasympathetic, 17, 23–24
  sympathetic, 17, 23–24
 central, 17, *see also* under Spinal
  cord
  brain, 17, 18–21
  brain stem, 17, 21–23, 25
  tumors of, 185, 187, 188, 190, 191
 cranial nerves, 24–25
 hearing system, 25–26, *see also*
  Hearing loss
 historical study of, 16
 monitoring the, 81
 neurodevelopment of, 27
 neurologist, 262
 neuron, 17–18
 peripheral, 17, 22
 for speech, 27, *see also* Language
  and communication problems
 visual system, 25, *see also* Vision
Neural spinal dysraphism, spinal
  deformity associated with, 61
 see also Meningocele; Spina bifida
Neural tube, 118
 deficit, *see* Spina bifida
Neurodevelopment, 27
Neurofibromatosis, spinal deformity
  associated with, 61
Neurogenic bladder, *see* Bladder
Neurologist, as team member, 262
Neuromonitoring, 81
Neuromuscular junction disease, 61
Neuromuscular scoliosis, 61–62, 65, 66,
  67, 68, 69–70
Neuron, 17–18, 75
Neuronal diseases, 61
 see also Spinal muscular atrophy
Neuropathic arthrogryposis multiplex
  congenita, 109

Neuropathy, fetal, 109
Neurotransmitter, 18
Nil disease, 254
Nocturnal enuresis, 214, 215, 217, 218
    see also Enuresis
Non-Hodgkin's lymphomas, 187, 190
Noninsulin dependent diabetes, 196,
    199
Noradrenaline, 18
Noxious fumes, burns and, 177
Nuclear techniques, for heart disease,
    228
Nucleus pulpous, 5
Nurse, school, 263
Nutrition
    burns and, 178, 182, 183
    cystic fibrosis and, 212
    spinal cord injury and, 138
    spinal muscular atrophy and, 154
    see also Diet
Nystagmus, 41
    ataxia and, 49
    cerebral palsy and, 264

Observation, as treatment for spinal
    curvatures, 65–66
Occipital lobe, 19, 20
Occupational therapist, 262
    Registered, 96
Occupational therapy, 262
    for juvenile rheumatoid arthritis,
        246, 247
    for limb deficiencies, 99
    for spinal muscular atrophy, 153, 154
    therapist, 96, 262
Occupations, see Career planning
Ocular motor nerve, 25
Olfactory nerve, 24
Omissions, as articulation disorder,
    267
Ophthalmologist, as team member, 262
    see also Vision
Optic nerve, 24
Organ of Corti, 26
Orthopedist, as team member, 262
Orthoses, see Braces
Osmotic diuresis, 197
Osteochondrodystrophies, spinal
    deformities due to, 60
Osteogenesis imperfecta, 111–116, 264
    congenita, 112–113, 114, 115–116
    tarda, 113
Osteogenic sarcoma, 190, 191
Osteoporosis, in spinal muscular
    atrophy, 154
Otorhinolaryngologist, as team
    member, 262
Oval corpuscles, 13

Pancreas, 10–11, 196, 197, 198
    Islands of Langerhans, 12
    see also Cystic fibrosis; Insulin
        dependent diabetes
Parachute reaction, 46
Paraldehyde, for epilepsy, 82
Paralysis, in spina bifida, 119, 120, 124,
    125, 126
    see also Spinal cord injury
Paraplegia, 43
    life expectancy, 143
    spastic, 44
    with spinal cord injury, 143, 144, 145
Parasympathetic nervous systems, 17,
    23–24

Parathyroid glands, 12
Parents, see Family
Parietal lobe, 18, 19–20
Paroxysmal disorder, 78
Partial sight, 264
    see also Vision
Partial thickness burns, 181
Part-whole relationships, with cerebral
    palsy, 264
Pathophysiology, 78
Patterning, for cerebral palsy, 53
Pauciarticular onset juvenile
    rheumatoid arthritis, 243, 244
Pediatrician, as team member, 261–262
Pelvic obliquity, 63, 64
Pelvis, 5, 6
    spinal deformity and, 63, 64
Pericarditis, 223
    pauciarticular onset juvenile
        rheumatoid arthritis and, 243,
        244
Perineum, 182
Perineurium, 24
Periosteum, 4
Peripheral nervous system, 17, 22
Peripheral neuropathy, 61
    in insulin dependent diabetes, 203
Peristalsis, 10
Peritoneal dialysis, 252–253
Perspiration, see Sweat
Petit mal seizure, 77–78, 82, 83, 84
Petit mal triad, see Epilepsy
Phagocytes, 167
Phenobarbitol
    cerebral palsy and, 55
    epilepsy and, 78, 82
Phenothiazines, stool retention and,
    219
Phenylalanine, phenylketonuria diet
    and, 237
Phlegm, 141
Phocomelia, 94
Photic-stimulated seizure, 80, 83
Physical education, 265
    arthrogryposis and, 110
    asthma and, 163, 166, 265
    cystic fibrosis and, 213
    heart disease and, 231, 265
    hemophilia and, 171
    Hurler syndrome and, 236
    insulin dependent diabetes and, 205,
        265
    juvenile rheumatoid arthritis and,
        248–249
    muscular dystrophy and, 107
    osteogenesis imperfecta and, 116
    sickle cell anemia and, 174
    slipped capital femoral epiphysis
        and, 91
    spina bifida and, 130
    spinal cord injury and, 144–145
    spinal muscular atrophy and, 155
    thalassemia and, 174
    wheelchair sports
        arthrogryposis and, 110
        spina bifida and, 130
        spinal cord injury and, 145
Physical therapist, as team member,
    263
Physical therapy, 263, 265
    for juvenile rheumatoid arthritis,
        246, 247
    for limb deficiencies, 99
    for muscular dystrophy, 106

Physician
    questions of educators for, 279
    as team member, 261–262
Pineal body, 12
Pituitary gland, 11, 20
PKU, see Phenylketonuria
Plasma, 167
Platelet, 167, 187
PL 94–142, see Education for All
    Handicapped Children Act
Pneumonia, 7, 8
    burns and, 177
Poliomyelitis, spinal deformity
    associated with, 61
Polyarticular onset juvenile
    rheumatoid arthritis, 243, 244,
    245
Polydipsia, insulin dependent diabetes
    and, 197
Polyphagia, insulin dependent
    diabetes and, 197
Polyuria, insulin dependent diabetes
    and, 197
Pons, 21, 25
Positioning aids, 275, 276
Positive support reflex (PS), 33, 34
Posterior protective extension, 36
Postictal depression, 77
Poststreptococcal glomerulonephritis,
    253, 254
Postural reactions, 30, 33, 35–36
Prednisone, nephrotic syndrome and,
    254, 255
Prehension, in arthrogryposis, 110
    see also Grasping
Pressure sores, in spinal cord injury,
    139–140
Primary encopresis, 218
Primary enuresis, 214–215
Primitive reflexes, 27, 29, 30, 33–35
    assymetric tonic neck reflex, 33, 34
    Babinski reflex, 52
    cerebral palsy and, 46, 49
    grasp, 32, 33
    Moro reflex, 27, 33–34
    positive support reflex, 33, 34
    tone manifested by, 36
    tonic labyrinthine reflex, 33, 34–35
Primitive reflex profile, 33
Problem-solving skills, 33
Progressive muscular dystrophy, see
    Duchenne muscular dystrophy
Prone board, 275, 276
Prostate gland, 12
Prostheses, 273
    for limb deficiencies, 94–95, 96–98
    long leg, 273
    prosthetists, 96
Protective extension, 36
Prosthetists, 96
Proteins, 14
Proteinuria, enuresis and, 216
Proximal femoral focal deficiency
    (PFFD), 94
Pseudohypertrophic muscular
    dystrophy, 101, 102, 103
Pseudomonas aeruginosa, cystic
    fibrosis and, 208, 211
Psoriasis, 13
Psychiatrist, as team member, 262
Psychological implications
    adolescence and, 268
    of asthma, 165–166
    of burns, 178–180, 183

Psychological implications *(continued)*
of heart disease, 231
of insulin dependent diabetes, 202, 203, 204, 205
of juvenile rheumatoid arthritis, 246–247
medications causing, 268
terminal illness and, 268
see also Encopresis; Enuresis
Psychomotor seizure, 78, 79, 82
Pulmonary function test, asthma and, 162–163
Pulmonary stenosis, 223, 227, 229
Pyelonephritis, spina bifida and, 121
Pyramidal tract, cerebral palsy and, 42

Quadriplegia, 43
spastic, 44–47, 48, 50
with spinal cord injury, 139, 143, 144, 145

Radiation therapy, cancer and, 186
Radiologist, as team member, 262
Reading aids, 277
Reading epilepsy, 80
Rectum, 10
Red blood cells, 14–15, 167, 187
see also Anemia
Reflex activity
with motor impairments, 265
with spinal cord injury, 136
see also Primitive reflexes
Reflex postural adjustment, for cerebral palsy, 53
Registered Occupational Therapists (OTRs), 96
Rehabilitation counselor, as team member, 263
Remission, cancer and, 185–186
Respiration, 7–8
in spinal cord injury, 136, 141–142
see also Lungs
Respiratory infections
in spinal cord injury, 141–142
in spinal muscular atrophy, 153–154
Reticular activating system, 21
Retinoblastoma, 186
Reversals, with cerebral palsy, 264
Rhabdomyosarcoma, 187–188, 190, 191
Rheumatic heart disease, 223, 230, 231
Rheumatoid factor, 244–245
Rheumatoid inflammation, *see* Juvenile rheumatoid arthritis
Rhomberg test, ataxia identified with, 49
Rigidity, cerebral palsy and, 48, 52
Ritalin, cerebral palsy and, 55
Rolling over, as normal gross motor milestone, 31
Rooting reflex, cerebral palsy and, 50
Rotations, with cerebral palsy, 264
Rubella herpes, cerebral palsy caused by, 42
Running, as normal gross motor milestone, 31

Sacral vertebrae, 5
Salaam seizure, 79, 83, *see also* Infantile myoclonic seizures
Sanfilippo syndrome, 235
Scar tissue, burns and, 176–177, 178, 183
School, *see* Educational implications
School nurse, 263

Sclera, 111
in osteogenesis imperfecta, 112
Scoliosis, *see* Spinal deformities
Scoliosis Association, Inc., The, 282
Seal limb, 94
Sebaceous glands, 13
Secondary encopresis, 218
Secondary enuresis, 215
Secondary hypertension, 256
Segmental roll reaction, 36
Seizures
cerebral palsy and, 47, 50, 55
spastic hemiplegia and, 44
spina bifida and, 119
see also Epilepsy
Seizure threshhold, 76, 84
Sensation
cerebral palsy and, 53, 55
spina bifida and, 121, 126–127, 128
spinal cord injury and, 136, 137, 139–140, 144
Sensory end organs, 13
Sensory integration approach, for cerebral palsy, 53
Septal defect, 223, 225
Severe, as degree of severity, 43
Severe infantile spinal muscular atrophy, 147, 148, 149, 150, 154
Sexuality
cystic fibrosis and, 208, 209
spina bifida and, 122, 128–129
spinal cord injury and, 141
Shunts
hydrocephalus and, 123–124, 129
patent ductus arteriosis and, 224–225
Sickle cell anemia, 167, 171–172, 172–173, 173–174, 216
Sickle trait, 172
Sigmoid colon, 10
Sitting
delays in, 32
as normal gross motor milestone, 31
Skeletal system, 3–6, 7
axial, 5
Skin, 12–13, 176
see also Burns
Skull, 5
Slipped capital femoral epiphysis, 90–91
Slipped disc, 5
Small molecule diseases, 234
phenylketonuria, 234, 236–238
Smooth muscles, 6
Social-emotional concerns, 267–268
see also Psychological implications
Social worker, as team member, 263
Soma, 17
Spastic diplegia, 44, 45
Spastic hemiplegia, 44, 50
Spasticity, 19
see also Cerebral palsy
Spastic paraplegia, 44
Spastic quadriplegia, 44–47, 48, 50
Special education, 260–261, 264, 268, 270
Special school
spinal cord injury and, 144
spinal muscular atrophy and, 155
Speech, 7
nervous system and, 27
see also Language and communication problems
Speech-language therapist, as team member, 263

Sphygmomanometer, 255, 256
Spina bifida, 5–6, 117–118, 131
characteristics, 119–122
hydrocephalus, 119–120, 122, 123–124, 129
language impairment, 266
learning problems, 122, 129
motor development problems, 120–121, 124–126
orthopedic problems, 120, 124–126
paralysis, 119, 120, 124, 125, 126
sensation impairments, 121, 126–127, 128
sexuality and, 122, 128–129
urinary and bowel problems, 121–122, 128, 215
diagnosis, 122–123
educational implications, 130, 260
etiology, 118–119
incidence, 119
occulta, 61, 117, 118
prognosis, 129–130
Spina Bifida Association of America, 282–283
treatment, 123
of hydrocephalus, 123–124
of learning problems, 129
of motor development problems, 124–126
of orthopedic problems, 124–126
of sensory impairment, 126–127, 128
of sexual problems, 128–129
of urinary and bowel problems, 127–128
Spina Bifida Association of America, 282–283
Spinal cord, 17, 22, 132, 133, 134, 135
congenital defects of, 117–118, *see also* Spina bifida
vertebral column of, 5
see also Spinal muscular atrophy
Spinal cord injury, 132–133
autonomic dysreflexia in, 140
bowel control and, 136, 137, 140
central cord lesion, 135, 136
characteristics, 134–137
diagnosis, 137–138
educational implications, 140, 143–146
etiology, 133–134
incidence, 133, 134
level of, 135, 137
National Spinal Cord Injury Foundation, 283
neurogenic bladder in, 136, 137, 140
in newborn, 137–138
paraplegia and, 143, 144–145
prognosis, 143
quadriplegia and, 139, 143, 144, 145
reflex activity with, 136
respiratory infections in, 136–137, 141–142
sensation in, 136, 137, 139–140, 144
sexuality and, 141
treatment, 138–143
contracture prevention, 138–139
nutrition, 138
pressure sores in, 139–140
psychological, 142–143
of quadriplegia, 139
rehabilitation, 138–139
respirator, 141–142

Spinal cord injury *(continued)*
  vascular supply and, 135–136
  vertebral column in, 142
Spinal deformities
  combined forms of, 64
  diagnosis, 64–65
  educational implications, 69–70
  kyphosis, 59
    cerebral palsy and, 45–46
    characteristics, 62–63
    thoracic, 60
  lordosis, 59
    cerebral palsy and, 46
    cervical, 60
    characteristics, 63, 64
    lumbar, 60
    muscular dystrophy and, 103
  multiple, 64
  prognosis, 69, 71, 72
  scoliosis, 59, 60, 265
    arthrogryposis with, 109
    cerebral palsy and, 46, 54
    characteristics, 62
    congenital, 61
    idiopathic, 60–61, 62, 64–65, 69
    neuromuscular, 61–62, 63, 66, 67,
      68, 69–70
    prognosis, 69
    The Scoliosis Association, Inc., 232
    spina bifida and, 120
    spinal cord injury and, 142
    in spinal muscular atrophy,
      152–153
    treatment, 59–60, 63, 64
  in spina bifida, 125–126
  treatment, 65
    observation, 65–66
    orthotics, 66–67
    surgery, 67–68, 69, 70
Spinal muscular atrophy, 61, 147–148,
  149
  adolescence and, 154–155
  characteristics, 148, 149, 150–151
  diagnosis, 151
  educational implications, 155
  etiology, 150
  incontinence in, 153
  intermediate, 149, 150, 151, 153–154
  mild, 146, 149, 150–151, 152, 153–154
  occupational therapy in, 153, 154
  prognosis, 154–155
  respiratory function in, 153–154
  scoliosis prevention in, 152–153
  severe infantile, 147, 148, 149, 150,
    154
  treatment, 151–154
Spinocerebellar degenerative disease,
  spinal deformity associated
  with, 61
Splints, 273
  in juvenile rheumatoid arthritis, 247
  see also Braces
Split hook, 96–97
Standing, as normal gross motor
  milestone, 31
Stapes, 26
Staphylococcus aureus, cystic fibrosis
  and, 211
Startle-induced seizure, 80
Status epilepticus, 78, 80, 82
Stenosis, 226
  aortic, 223, 226–227, 228, 229
  pulmonary, 223, 227, 229
Sternum, 4, 5

Steroids, 12
  asthma and, 165
Stomach, 10
Stool retention, encopresis and,
  218–219, 220
  see also Bowel control
Strabismus, 41, 50
  cerebral palsy and, 55, 264
  spina bifida and, 119
Strauss syndrome, 37
Strep throat, 9
Striated muscles, 6
Substitutions, as articulation disorder,
  267
Sugar, *see* Blood sugar
Suctioning, spinal cord injury and, 141,
  142
Sulcus of Rolando, 19
Sulindac, for juvenile rheumatoid
  arthritis, 246
Superior vena cava, 8
Swallowing mechanism, 7, 9–10
Sweat, cystic fibrosis and, 207
Sweat test, cystic fibrosis and, 207,
  210–211
Symmetrical tonic neck reflex, cerebral
  palsy and, 46, 48
Sympathetic nervous system, 23–24
Synapse, 17, 23
Synaptic cleft, 17
Synaptic transmission, 18
Synarthrotic joints, 241
Synkinesis, 27
Synovial tissue, 241
  inflamed, 242, 243
Synovitis, 87
Systemic onset juvenile rheumatoid
  arthritis, 243, 244, 248
Systolic pressure, 255

Tachycardia, 227
Tactile-kinesthetic sensory loss, with
  cerebral palsy, 50
Talking books, 277
Teacher, *see* Educational implications
Team approach, *see* Educational
  implications
Teeth
  deciduous, 112
  dentinogenesis imperfecta, 112
  dentist, 262
  heart disorders and, 230
  osteogenesis imperfecta and, 112,
    113
Tegretol
  cerebral palsy and, 55
  epilepsy and, 78, 82
Temperature control, *see*
  Thermoregulation
Temporal lobe, 18, 19
Temporal lobe epilepsy, 82, 84
Teratogenic drugs, 222
Terbutaline, asthma and, 164
Terminal device, as prosthesis, 96–97
Terminal illnesses, 268
  see also Death
Testicle, 12
Tetralogy of Fallot, 223, 225, 226
Tetraplegia, *see* Quadriplegia
Thalassemia, 167, 171, 172, 173, 174
Thalassemia major, 171
Thalassemia trait, 171
Thalidomide, limb deficiencies caused
  by, 93, 94

Theophylline, asthma and, 164–165,
  166
Thermoregulation
  burns and, 175, 183
  limb deficiencies and, 95
Thoracic kyphosis, 60
Thoracic vertebrae, 5
Thoraco-lumbar brace, for spinal
  deformities, 66, 67
Thorazine, cerebral palsy and, 55
Thymus, 12
Thyroid gland, 11
Tolmetin, for juvenile rheumatoid
  arthritis, 246
Tonic-clonic seizure, 77
Tonic labyrinthine reflex (TL), 33, 34–35
Tonic neck reflexes, cerebral palsy
  and, 49
Toxemia, cerebral palsy caused by, 42
Toxoplasmosis, cerebral palsy caused
  by, 42
Trachea, 7
Tracheotomy, spinal cord injury and,
  140
Transplantation, kidney, 253
Transportation to/from school, 270
Transposition of the great arteries, 223,
  226
Transverse colon, 10
Trauma
  epiphyseal slippage and, 91
  spinal deformity and, 61
Trauma-induced seizures, 83, 84
Tricuspid valve atresia, 223, 226, 227
Tridione, for epilepsy, 82
Trigeminal nerve, 25
Tripod sitting, 30–31, 36
Trochlear nerve, 25
Truncus arteriosus, 223, 226, 227
Tuberous sclerosis, epilepsy and, 80
Tumor
  malignant, 185, *see also* Cancer
  spinal cord injury caused by, 134
Type I diabetes, *see* Insulin dependent
  diabetes
Type II diabetes, 199
Typewriters, 276

Ulceration, burns and, 182
United Cerebral Palsy Association,
  Inc., 281–282
Upper-extremity orthoses, 273
Upper-limb prostheses, 96–97, 98
Ureter, 12
Urethra, 12
  enuresis and, 215, 216
Urine, testing for diabetes, 199–200
  see also Bladder; Kidney
Urogenital system, 12
  see also Bladder; Kidney
Urologist, as team member, 262

Vagus nerve, 25
Valium
  cerebral palsy and, 55
  epilepsy and, 78, 82
Vascular disease, insulin dependent
  diabetes and, 203–204
Vasodilators, for heart disease, 229
Ventricular septal defects, 223, 225
Ventricular system, 21
Vertebral column, 5
  see also Spina bifida; Spinal cord
  injuries; Spinal deformities

Visceral muscles, 6
Vision, 25, 264
  burns and, 177
  cerebral palsy and, 44, 50, 55, 264
  farsightedness, 50
  insulin dependent diabetes and, 202,
      203, 204
  juvenile rheumatoid arthritis and,
      243, 244
  nearsightedness, 50
  opthalmologist, 262
  optic nerve, 24
  spina bifida and, 121
  see also Blindness; Nystagmus;
      Strabismus

Vocal cords, 7
Vocations, *see* Career planning
Voluntary grasp, 32, 33
Voluntary muscles, 6

Walking
  ataxia identified with, 49
  cerebral palsy and, 54, 56
  delays in, 32
  lower-limb prostheses for, 98
  as normal gross motor milestone, 31
Werdnig-Hoffmann disease, *see* Severe
      infantile spinal muscular atrophy
Wernicke's area for speech, 26, 27
Wheelchairs, 275

wheelchair sports, *see* Physical
      education
White blood cells, 14, 15, 167, 187
  thymus and, 12
White matter of brain, 18
Wilms's tumor, 187, 188, 190, 191
Withdrawal seizures, 82
Worster-Landau-Draught-Gascon
      syndrome, *see* Aphasic seizure
Writing aids, 273, 276–277

X-ray therapy, cancer and, 186

Zarontin, for epilepsy, 78, 82